ALSO BY ELIZABETH BISHOP

North & South (1946)

A Cold Spring (1955)

The Diary of "Helena Morley" (translation) (1957)

Brazil (with the editors of *Life*) (prose) (1962)

Questions of Travel (1965)

The Ballad of the Burglar of Babylon (1968)

The Complete Poems (1969)

An Anthology of Twentieth-Century Brazilian Poetry
(edited with Emanuel Brasil) (1972)

Geography III (1976)

The Complete Poems, 1927–1979 (1983)

The Collected Prose (edited by Robert Giroux) (1984)

One Art: Letters (edited by Robert Giroux) (1994)

Exchanging Hats: Paintings (edited by William Benton) (1996)

Edgar Allan Poe & The Juke-Box:
Uncollected Poems, Drafts, and Fragments (edited by Alice Quinn) (2006)

Elizabeth Bishop: Poems, Prose, and Letters
(selected by Robert Giroux and Lloyd Schwartz) (2008)

Words in Air: The Complete Correspondence Between
Elizabeth Bishop and Robert Lowell
(edited by Thomas Travisano with Saskia Hamilton) (2008)

Elizabeth Bishop and The New Yorker
(edited by Joelle Biele) (2011)

Poems (2011)

PROSE

PROSE

ELIZABETH BISHOP

EDITED BY LLOYD SCHWARTZ

FARRAR, STRAUS AND GIROUX   NEW YORK

Farrar, Straus and Giroux
18 West 18th Street, New York 10011

Copyright © 2011 by the Alice H. Methfessel Trust
Editor's Note and compilation copyright © 2011 by Lloyd Schwartz
All rights reserved
Distributed in Canada by D&M Publishers, Inc.
Printed in the United States of America
First edition, 2011

Published simultaneously in hardcover (as part of a two-volume boxed set with
Elizabeth Bishop's *Poems*) and in paperback

Grateful acknowledgment is made for permission to reprint portions of the Life World
Library volume "Brazil" by Elizabeth Bishop, copyright © 1962, 1967 by Time-Life
Books, Inc. Reprinted by permission of Direct Holdings Americas Inc.

All facsimiles appear by permission of Special Collections, Vassar College Libraries,
and the Alice H. Methfessel Trust.

Library of Congress Cataloging-in-Publication Data
Bishop, Elizabeth, 1911–1979.
   [Prose works. Selections]
   Prose / Elizabeth Bishop ; edited by Lloyd Schwartz.
     p. cm.
   Includes bibliographical references and index.
   ISBN 978-0-374-12557-8 (cloth : alk. paper)
   I. Schwartz, Lloyd, 1941–   II. Title.

PS3503.I785A6 2011
808.88'8—dc22

2010051292

Paperback ISBN: 978-0-374-53273-4
Boxed Set ISBN: 978-0-374-12558-5

Designed by Jonathan D. Lippincott

www.fsgbooks.com

1 3 5 7 9 10 8 6 4 2

Contents

Editor's Note

Although Elizabeth Bishop's admirers have discovered since her death that she attempted to write—and occasionally completed—many more poems than the hundred or so she published during her lifetime, she was nevertheless always a vastly more prolific prose writer than poet. She produced short stories and memoirs, memorials and tributes, book reviews and blurbs. And since she spent much of her life traveling, she also wrote translations, travel essays, a volume on the history and culture of Brazil (where she lived for nearly two decades), and thousands of letters. Like her poems, these all capture her astonishing eye (and ear) for detail and her unmistakable speaking voice: thoughtful, droll, wryly—sometimes scathingly—ironic, loving. From her high school days, she thought deeply about the nature of prose. She admired the way seventeenth-century essayists conveyed "the mind in action," and that familiar and crucial element of her poems is also present—and began to surface even earlier—in her prose, where her language and imagery often anticipate her poems.

Parallel to the way Bishop's poems are formally traditional and yet also experimental, in her prose she often deliberately blurs the distinction between fiction and memoir. In such pieces as "In the Village," "Gwendolyn," "The Country Mouse," "The U.S.A. School of Writing," and "Memories of Uncle Neddy," she treats what are clearly autobiographical narratives as if they were fiction. Other stories, some bordering on the surrealistic, are more obviously "made up," while such pieces as "Gregorio Valdes, 1879–1939" and her extended remembrance of her mentor and friend Marianne Moore, "Efforts of Affection," land more firmly on the memoir end of this polarity. She never actually completed the Moore piece to her fullest satisfaction, though she included it in a table of contents for a possible volume of prose (see facsimile on page 2). Bishop herself had difficulty characterizing her prose pieces by genre, wondering whether she should call the book "IN THE VILLAGE & OTHER STORIES" or "IN THE VILLAGE: STORIES & ESSAYS?" (question mark hers). Unfortunately, her plan cannot be carried out because several of the items she listed are either lost or incomplete. The present volume includes almost all of her mature published prose works, and the most significant pieces that remained unpublished while she was alive.

While the majority of her poems appeared in *The New Yorker*, both her fiction and nonfiction are more fugitive, never having had a regular venue. (In 1970, remembering her own earlier inquiry, *The New Yorker* engaged her to replace Louise Bogan as its poetry critic; but she never completed a review.) Bishop distrusted literary criticism, and her most resonant literary utterance is not part of a seriously worked-out essay but a statement she makes in passing in a note she wrote for a talk in Rio, beginning with a sentence that reveals her own ambivalence about the value of poetry: "Writing poetry is an unnatural act." She goes on to list the qualities she most admired in poems: *"Accuracy, Spontaneity, Mystery"*—qualities that surely describe her own work. Brett Millier, her biographer, reports that she considered her finest page of prose the ultimately unpublished statement she wrote for the catalog of an exhibition by artist Wesley Wehr—another indirect self-portrait, reflecting her own artistic humility and her predilection for small (as with Klee and Webern) but hardly "small-scale" works of art.

Bishop's criticism could be witty (she calls e.e. cummings "the famous man of little letters"), knowingly sympathetic (about William Jay Smith's almost successful translations of Laforgue), quirky (her deep affection for a Walter de la Mare anthology of poems "for the Young of All Ages"), or tough, as in "The Riddle of Emily Dickinson" (published here for the first time), a review she submitted to *The New Republic* attacking a biography of Catherine Scott Anthon—whom the author claims Dickinson was in love with—for the reductive assertion that there is only one explanation for poetic genius.

During the 1950s and '60s, the period during which she was writing the poems for her book *Questions of Travel*, Bishop also wrote her most important travel pieces. For *The New York Times Magazine*, she published a colorful and amusing article on Rio. A more ambitious travel essay about her visit with Aldous Huxley and his wife to the as yet unfinished Brasilia and to an endangered Indian tribe was rejected by *The New Yorker*, and she never succeeded in publishing it elsewhere. She was offered her largest advance ($10,000) to provide the text for the Life World Library *Brazil*, but famously disliked how the editors changed what she wrote ("The Editors of LIFE" are actually credited as co-authors), especially in the book's later chapters. Her original final chapter, completely different from the published chapter, deals with what the United States and Brazil have in common, and in it she praises Brazil's more effective way of dealing with issues of race. So here, for the first time, is the closest we can come to Bishop's original version, taken mainly from her own typescript at Vassar. (Since the surviving draft of her opening chapter, though very close to what was published, is too chaotic to reproduce directly, and the draft of her fifth chapter is missing, these chapters are reprinted here with the handwritten corrections she wrote in the margins of her personal copy of the published book, which is now in the collection of Harvard's Houghton Library.)

Bishop was always reluctant to discuss either personal matters or her work. But when the poet Anne Stevenson undertook the very first monograph on Bishop (for Twayne Publishers), the questions in her letters elicited from Bishop some of her most eloquent and forthright thoughts about her writing and her life. Included here is the first publication of extensive selections from their correspondence.

The one major Bishop prose work that is too long to reprint here in its entirety is her book-length translation of the Brazilian classic *Minha Vida de Menina*—the actual diary of a young girl who lived in the small mining town of Diamantina in the 1890s (published in this country as *The Diary of "Helena Morley"*). It is represented here by both Bishop's substantial introductory essay and the excerpts she published independently, before the appearance of the book, in *Harper's Bazaar*. Bishop captures the authentic voice of the exuberant and mischievous young girl with a mind of her own, just as in her other major prose translation, her uncanny English version of three short fables by the Brazilian fiction writer Clarice Lispector, she captures that author's more sophisticated and unsettling world view.

Elizabeth Bishop began writing poems and stories when she was still a child, but one might say that her "career" began with the stories, reviews, and personal essays that appeared in her high school magazine, the Walnut Hill School's *The Blue Pencil* (which is still active). In the appendix here of her early prose are some prescient examples of Bishop's most profound later concerns. The essay "A Mouse and Mice" includes her first explicit reference to a theme—Virgil's "sunt lacrimae rerum" and its image of life's inherent tears—that will play a central role in one of the most touching of her early stories, "The Last Animal," and in such major poems as "The Man-Moth" and "Sestina." The main character in "The Thumb," a kind of surrealistic Jamesian horror story, prefigures the disturbing narrator in her celebrated story "In Prison." Her meditation "on being alone" inaugurates a comparable theme that will become a central issue over the entire course of her life. Perhaps her most sophisticated and imaginative discussions of literature turn up among the essays she published as a Vassar undergraduate, including two breathtaking metaphors—images of a shooting gallery and of migrating birds in flight—for the complexities of a writer's sense of timing.

After her death, Bishop's remaining papers were acquired by Vassar, which now holds the major collection of her unpublished work. The unpublished pieces that appeared in Robert Giroux's 1984 edition of Bishop's *Collected Prose* are reprinted here as he edited them. Additional unpublished work is taken from manuscripts and typescripts in the Vassar College Libraries for Special Collections (numerous unfinished drafts with memorable passages require a volume of their own). The Anne Stevenson correspondence, which is printed with the kind cooperation of Ms. Stevenson, comes from the Modern Literature Collection at Washington University. All the works Bishop herself published are here reprinted from their original sources. Each section of this book is arranged, as nearly as possible, in chronological order.

The editor is profoundly grateful to the following individuals and institutions: Jonathan Galassi, president of Farrar, Straus and Giroux, who commissioned, supported, and inspired a good deal of the thought that went into this volume, and his invaluable and ceaselessly helpful assistant, Jesse Coleman; Frank Bidart, Elizabeth Bishop's close friend, most astute reader, and literary executor; the late Alice Methfessel; Anne Stevenson; Alice Quinn; Candace MacMahon, Bishop's bibliographer; the American Bishop scholars Joelle Biele, Gary Fountain, Laura Menides, Brett Millier, George Monteiro, Barbara Page, Thomas Travisano (a tireless resource of information and material), and Saskia Hamilton (who generously spent countless hours helping with this enterprise); the Brazilian Bishop scholars Regina Przybycien, Maria Lúcia Milléo Martins, Carmen Oliveira, and Bishop's Brazilian translator, the poet Paulo Henriques Britto; the Vassar College Libraries for Special Collections: Ron D. Patkus, associate director, and Dean M. Rogers, Special Collections assistant; Modern Literature Collection/Manuscripts, Washington University: John Hodges, curator; the staff of Harvard University's Houghton Library; the Library of America, Geoffrey O'Brien, editor in chief; and above all, my most generous, dependable, and indispensable sounding board, David Stang.

—L.S.

STORIES AND MEMOIRS

: Stories & Essays ?

IN THE VILLAGE & OTHER STORIES   (???)

with Sts — & intro.

Early Stories

1. The Baptism
2. The Sea & its Shore
   In Prison
3. The Hanging of the Mouse & (??)
4.
5. The Housekeeper

~~IN THE VILL~~

In the Village

6. Gwendolyn
7. In the Village
8. Uncle ~~Edward~~ *Neddy*
9. ~~Primer Class~~   (another 2?)

number

Later

  The ~~Golden Glasses~~ or Lulu & his Wife, *n The Golden Glass*
10. Going to the Boutiquim
  -another Brazilian one ?
~~Mexico, 1943 (?) (autobiographical...)~~
~~Marianne Moore?~~

Personal ~~Stories~~

12. Mexico, 1943   *Gregorio Valley* —
11. The Merced's Home (K.W.)
  ~~Mexico, 1943~~

13. *Marianne Moore*

The Baptism

It was November. They bent in the twilight like sea-plants, around their little dark centre-table hung with a cloth like a seaweed-covered rock. It seemed as if a draught might sway them all, perceptibly. Lucy, the youngest, who still did things for her sisters, rose to get the shawls and light the lamp. She sighed. How would they get through the winter?

"We have our friends!"

Yes, that was true and a consolation. They had several friends. They had old Mrs. Peppard and young Mrs. Gillespie and old Mrs. Captain Green and little Mrs. Kent. One of them was bound to drop in almost every afternoon.

When the weather was fine they themselves could make a call, although they preferred to stay at home. They were more in command of conversation when they sat close together around their own table. Antiphonally, they spoke to their friends of the snowstorm, of health, of church activities. They had the church, of course.

When the snow grew too deep—it grew all winter, as the grain grew all summer, and finally wilted away unharvested in April—old Mr. Jonson, who had the post-office now, would bring the newspaper on his way home.

They would manage, but winter was longer every year. Lucy thought of carrying wood in from the wood-shed and scratching her forearms on the bark. Emma thought of hanging out the washing, which was frozen before you got it on to the line. The sheets particularly—it was like fighting with monster icy seagulls. Flora thought only of the difficulties of getting up and dressing at six o'clock every morning.

They would keep two stoves going: the kitchen range and an airtight in the sitting-room. The circulatory system of their small house was this: in the ceiling over the kitchen stove there was an opening set with a metal grille. It yielded up some heat to the room where Lucy and Emma slept. The pipe from the sitting-room stove went up through Flora's room, but it wasn't so warm, of course.

They baked bread once a week. In the other bedroom there were ropes and ropes of dried apples. They ate apple-sauce and apple-pie and apple-dumpling, and a kind of cake paved with slices of apple. At every meal they drank a great deal of tea and ate many slices of bread. Sometimes they bought half a pound of store cheese, sometimes a piece of pork.

Emma knitted shawls, wash-cloths, bed-socks, an affectionate spider-web around Flora and Lucy. Flora did fancy work and made enough Christmas presents for them to give all around: to each other and to friends. Lucy was of no use at all with her fingers. She was supposed to read aloud while the others worked.

They had gone through a lot of old travel books that had belonged to their father. One was called *Wonders of the World*; one was a book about Palestine and Jerusalem. Although they could all sit calmly while Lucy read about the tree that gave milk like a cow, the Eskimos who lived in the dark, the automaton chess-player, etc., Lucy grew excited over accounts of the Sea of Galilee, and the engraving of the Garden of Gethsemane as it looks to-day brought tears to her eyes. She exclaimed "Oh dear!" over pictures of "An Olive Grove," with Arabs squatting about in it; and "Heavens!" at the real, rock-vaulted Stable, the engraved rocks like big black thumb-prints.

They had also read: (1) *David Copperfield*, twice; (2) *The Deer-Slayer*; (3) *Samantha at the World's Fair*; (4) *The Autocrat of the Breakfast Table*.

Also two or three books from the Sunday School library which none of them liked. Because of the source, however, they listened as politely as to the minister's sermons. Lucy's voice even took on a little of his intonation, so that it seemed to take forever to get through them.

They were Presbyterians. The village was divided into two camps, armed with Bibles: Baptists and Presbyterians. The sisters had friends on both sides.

Prayer-meeting was Friday night. There was Sunday School and Church on Sunday, and Ladies' Aid every other week at different friends' houses. Emma taught the smallest children in Sunday School. Lucy and Flora preferred not to teach but to attend the class for adults held by the minister himself.

Now each was arranging the shawl over her shoulders, and just as Lucy lit the lamp old Mrs. Peppard came to call. She opened the back door without knocking, and said, "Anybody home?" This was the thing to do. She wore a very old mud-brown coat with large black frogs down the front and a black, cloth-covered hat with a velvet flower on it.

Her news was that her sister's baby had died the day before, although they had done everything. She and Emma, Flora and Lucy discussed infant damnation at some length.

Then they discussed the care of begonias, and Mrs. Peppard took home a slip of theirs. Flora had always had great luck with house-plants.

Lucy grew quite agitated after Mrs. Peppard had gone, and could not eat her bread and butter, only drank three cups of tea.

Of course, as Emma had expected because of the tea, Lucy couldn't sleep that night. Once she nudged Emma and woke her.

"Emma, I'm thinking of that poor child."

"Stop thinking. Go to sleep."

"Don't you think we ought to pray for it?"

It was the middle of the night or she couldn't have said that. Emma pretended to be asleep. In fact, she was asleep, but not so much that she couldn't feel Lucy getting out of bed. The next day she mentioned this to Flora, who only said "Tsch—Tsch." Later on they both referred to this as the "beginning," and Emma was sorry she'd gone back to sleep.

In prayer-meeting one Friday the minister called for new members, and asked some of those who had joined the church lately to speak. Art Tinkham stood up. He talked of God's goodness to him for a long time, and said that now he felt happy all the time. He had felt so happy when he was doing his fall ploughing that he had kept singing, and at the end of every furrow he'd said a Bible verse.

After a while the minister called on Lucy to give a prayer. She did it, quite a long one, but at last her voice began to tremble. She could scarcely say the Amen, and sat down very quickly. Afterwards her sisters said it had been a very pretty prayer, but she couldn't remember a word of it.

Emma and Lucy liked the dreamy hymns best, with vague references in them to gardens, glassy seas, high hills, etc. Flora liked militant hymns; almost her favourite was "A Mighty Fortress."

Lucy's was: "Sometimes a light surprises the Christian while he sings." Emma's: "There is a green hill far away without a city wall."

Lucy was not yet a church member. Emma and Flora were, but Lucy had been too young to join when they had. She sometimes asked her sisters if she were good enough.

"You are too good for us, Lucy."

"That's not what I mean," Lucy said.

At night she felt that Emma's prayers were over all too quickly. Her own sometimes lasted almost an hour, and even then did not seem quite long enough. She felt very guilty about something. She worried about this so much that one day she almost convinced Flora that she must have been guilty of the gravest misdemeanour as a young girl. But it was not so.

It got to be Christmas-time. The snow was up to the window-sills, practically over, as if they inhabited a sinking ship. Lucy's feeling of guilt grew heavier and heavier. She talked constantly about whether she should join the church or not.

At Christmas an elderly missionary, Miss Gillespie, young Mr. Gillespie's aunt, came home from India on furlough. The Ladies' Aid had special meetings for her. At them this tall, dark-brown, moustached woman of sixty-four talked, almost shouted, for hours about her life work. Photographs were handed around. They represented gentle-faced boys and young men, dressed in pure white loin-cloths and earrings. Next, the same boys and young men were shown, in soiled striped trousers and shirts worn with the tails outside. There were a few photographs of women, blurred as they raised a hand to hide their faces, or backed away from the camera's Christian eye.

Emma and Flora disliked Miss Gillespie. Flora even said she was "bossy." But Lucy liked her very much and went to see her several times. Then for three weeks she talked about nothing but going as a missionary. She went through all the travel books again.

Flora and Emma did not really think she would ever go, but the thought of living without her sometimes horrified one or the other of them. At the end of the third week she stopped speaking of it and, in fact, became very untalkative.

Lucy was growing thinner. The skin of her forehead seemed stretched too tightly, and although she had never had a temper in her life, Flora and Emma could see that it was sometimes an effort for her not to speak crossly to them.

She moved very slowly. At supper she would eat half a slice of bread and put the other half back in the bread dish.

Flora, who was bolder to say things than Emma, said: "She makes me feel that I'm not as good as she is."

Once when Lucy went out to get wood from the woodshed she didn't come back for fifteen minutes. Emma, suddenly realising how long it had been, ran outside. Lucy, with no coat or shawl, stood holding on to the side of the house. She was staring at the blinding dazzle the sun made on the ice-glaze over the next field. She seemed to be humming a little, and the glaring strip made her half shut her eyes. Emma had to take hold of her hand before she would pay any attention. Speaking wasn't enough.

It was the night of the day after this that the strange things began to happen.

Lucy kept a diary. It was written in pencil in a book that said "Jumbo Scribbler" in red letters on a tan cover. It was really a record of spiritual progress.

"*January 3rd.* This morning was clear again so Flora did some of the wash and we hung it in the garden, although it was hard to with the wind. For dinner we had a nice stew with the rest of the lamb and the carrots Mr. Jonson brought in. I say a nice stew, but I could not touch a bite. The Lord seems very far away. I kept asking the girls about my joining but they did not help me at all."

Here Lucy copied out three Bible verses. Sometimes for several days the diary was made up of nothing but such quotations.

"*January 16th.* It was eighteen below zero last night. We had to get father's old buffalo robe from the spare-room. I didn't like the smell, but Emma didn't mind it. When the lamp was out I prayed for a long time, and a little while after I got into bed I felt that face moving towards me again. I can't make it out, but it is very large and close to mine. It seemed to be moving its lips. Is it reproachful?"

Four days after this Lucy began crying in the afternoon and cried almost all evening. Emma finally cried a little, too. Flora shook her by the shoulder, but left Lucy alone.

Emma wished that she and Flora slept together instead of she and Lucy, so that they could talk about Lucy together privately.

Flora said: "What has she ever done wrong, Emma? Why should she weep about her soul?"

Emma said: "She's always been as good as gold."

"*January 20th.* At last, at last, I know my own mind," she began, "or rather I have given it up completely. Now I am going to join the church as soon as I can. But I am going to join the *Baptist* church, and I must not tell Flora and Emma beforehand. I cannot eat, I am so happy. Last night at four o'clock a terrible wind began to blow. I thought all the trees were breaking, I could hear the branches crashing against the house. I thought the chimney would come down. The house shook, and I thought about the House founded on the Rock. I was terribly frightened. Emma did not wake up. It went on for hours in the dark and I prayed that we would all be safely delivered. Then there was a lull. It was very black and my heart pounded so I thought I was dying. I couldn't think of a prayer. Then suddenly a low voice began to talk right over the head of the bed. I couldn't make out the words, they weren't exactly words I knew, but I seemed to understand them. What a load dropped from my mind! Then I was so happy I woke Emma and said: 'Emma, Emma, Christ is here. He was here just now, in this room. Get up and pray with me.' Emma got out of bed and knelt, then she said the floor was cold and wanted to pull the rug over under our knees. I said: 'No, Emma. Why do we need rugs when we have all Christ's love to warm our hearts?' She did not demur after that, and I prayed a long time, for Flora, too. When we got back in bed I told Emma about the voice I had heard."

The next day Lucy called on the Baptist minister and told him she had decided to join his church. He was very severe, older than the Presbyterian minister, and Lucy felt at once that he was a much better man.

But a problem came up that she had not considered. She now believed ardently in the use of total immersion as practised by the Baptists, according to their conception of the methods of John the Baptist. She could not join without that, and the river, of course, was frozen over. She would have to wait until the ice went out.

She could scarcely bear it. In her eagerness to be baptised and her disappointment she forgot she had intended not to tell her sisters of her change of faith. They did not seem to mind so much, but when she asked them, they would not consider changing with her.

She was so over-excited they made her go to bed at five o'clock. Emma wrapped up a hot stove-lid to put at her feet.

"*January 25th.* I felt very badly last night and cried a great deal. I thought how mother always used to give me the best of everything because I was the smallest, and I took it not thinking of my sisters. Emma said 'For mercy's sake, Lucy, stop crying.' I explained to her, and she became much softened. She got up and lit the lamp. The lamplight on her face made me cry afresh. She went and woke Flora, who put on her grey wrapper and came in and sat in the rocking-chair. She wanted to make me something, but I said No. The lamp began to smoke. The smoke went right up to the ceiling and smelt very strong and sweet, like rose-geranium. I began to cry and laugh at the same time. Flora and Emma were talking together, but other people seemed to be talking, too, and the voice at the head of the bed."

A few days later Lucy became very sad. She could neither pray nor do anything around the house. She sat by the window all day long.

In the afternoon she pointed at the road which went off towards the mountains between rows of trees, and said: "Flora, what does it matter where the road goes?"

Emma and Flora were taking apart Emma's blue silk dress and making a blouse. A moth crawled on the window-pane. Emma said: "Get the swatter, Lucy."

Lucy got up, then sat down and said again: "What does it matter?"

She got out the scribbler and wrote in it from memory all the stanzas of "Return, O heavenly Dove, return."

After supper she seemed more cheerful. They were sitting in the kitchen evenings now, because it was warmer. There was no light but one lamp, so the room was quite dark, making the red circles around the stove-lids show.

Lucy suddenly stood up.

"Emma, Emma, Flora. I see God."

She motioned towards the stove.

God, God sat on the kitchen stove and glowed, burned, filling all the kitchen with a delicious heat and a scent of grease and sweetness.

Lucy was more conscious of his body than his face. His beautiful glowing bulk was rayed like a sunflower. It lit up Flora's and Emma's faces on either side of the stove. The stove could not burn him.

"His feet are in hell," she remarked to her sisters.

After that Lucy was happy for a long time and everything seemed almost the way it had been the winter before, except for Lucy going to the Baptist church and prayer-meeting by herself.

She spoke often of joining. It had happened once or twice that when people had wanted to join the church in the winter a hole had been broken in the ice to make a font. Lucy begged the minister that this might be done for her, but he felt that it was unnecessary in her case.

One had been a farmer, converted from drinking and abusing his wife. He had chopped the ice open himself. One a young man, also a reformed drunkard, since dead.

Flora said: "Oh Lucy, wait till the ice goes out."

"Yes," Lucy said in bitterness, "and until my soul is eternally lost."

She prayed for an early spring.

On the nineteenth of March Flora woke up and heard the annually familiar sound, a dim roaring edged with noises of breaking glass.

"Thank goodness," she thought. "Now, maybe, Lucy won't even want to be baptized."

Everyone had heard the cracking start, off in the hills, and was at the bridge. Lucy, Emma, and Flora went too. The ice buckled up in shining walls fifteen or twenty feet high, fit for heavenly palaces, then moved slowly downstream.

Once in a while a space of dark brown water appeared. This upset Lucy, who had thought of the water she would be baptized in as crystal-clear, or pale blue.

The baptism took place on the twenty-fourth. It was like all the others, and the village was even used to such early ones, although they were usually those of fervent young men.

A few buggies were on the bank, those of the choir, who stood around in coats and hats, holding one hymn-book among three or four people. Most of the witnesses stood on the bridge, staring down. One boy or young man, of course, always dared to spit over the railing.

The water was muddy, very high, with spots of yellow foam. The sky was solid grey cloud, finely folded, over and over. Flora saw the icy roots of a tree reaching into the river, and the snow-banks yellow like the foam.

The minister's robe, which he wore only on such occasions, billowed until the water pulled it all down. He held a clean, folded handkerchief to put over Lucy's mouth at the right minute. She wore a robe, too, that made her look taller and thinner.

The choir sang "I am coming, Lord, coming now to Thee," which they always dragged, and "Shall we gather at the river where bright angel feet have trod?" After the baptism they were to sing something joyful and faster, but the sisters did not remain to hear it.

Lucy went under without a movement, and Flora and Emma thought she'd never come up.

Flora held Emma's heavy coat all ready to put around her. Rather unconventionally, Emma sat in the buggy, borrowed from Mrs. Captain Green, so as to drive off home as soon as Lucy reached the bank. She held the reins and had to keep herself from taking up the whip in her other hand.

Finally it was over. They put the dripping Lucy in the middle. Her hair had fallen down. Thank goodness they didn't live far from the river!

The next day she had a bad head-cold. Emma and Flora nursed her for a week and then the cold settled in her chest. She wouldn't take to bed. The most they could get her to do was to lie on the couch in the kitchen.

One afternoon they thought she had a high fever. Late in the day God came again, into the kitchen. Lucy went towards the stove, screaming.

Emma and Flora pulled her back, but not before she had burned her right hand badly.

That night they got the doctor, but the next night after Lucy died, calling their names as she did so.

The day she was buried was the first pleasant day in April, and the village turned out very well, in spite of the fact that the roads were deep with mud. Jed Leighton gave a beautiful plant he had had sent from the city, a mass of white blooms. Everyone else had cut all their geraniums, red, white and pink.

1937

The Sea and Its Shore

Once, on one of our large public beaches, a man was appointed to keep the sand free from papers. For this purpose he was given a stick, or staff, with a long, polished wire nail set in the end.

Since he worked only at night, when the beach was deserted, he was also given a lantern to carry.

The rest of his equipment consisted of a big wire basket to burn the papers in, a box of matches for setting fire to them, and a house.

This house was very interesting. It was of wood, with a pitched roof, about 4 by 4 by 6 feet, set on pegs stuck in the sand. There was no window, no door set in the door-frame, and nothing at all inside. There was not even a broom, so that occasionally our friend would get down on his knees and with his hands brush out the sand he had tracked in.

When the wind along the beach became too strong or too cold, or when he was tired, or when he wanted to read, he sat in the house. He either let his legs hang over the door-sill, or doubled them up under him inside.

As a house, it was more like an idea of a "house," than a real one. It could have stood at either end of a scale of ideas of houses. It could have been a child's perfect play-house, or an adult's ideal house—since everything that makes most houses nuisances had been done away with.

It was a shelter, but not for living in, for thinking in. It was, to the ordinary house, what the ceremonial thinking-cap is to the ordinary hat.

Of course, according to the laws of nature, a beach should be able to keep itself clean, as cats do. We have all observed:

> "The moving waters at their priestlike task
> Of pure ablution round earth's human shore."

But the tempo of modern life is too rapid. Our presses turn out too much paper covered with print, which somehow makes its way to our seas and their shores, for nature to take care of herself.

So Mr. Boomer, Edwin Boomer, might almost have been said to have joined the "priesthood."

Every night he walked back and forth for a distance of over a mile, in the dark, with his lantern and his stick, and a potato sack on his back to put the papers in—a picturesque sight, in some ways like a Rembrandt.

Edwin Boomer lived the most literary life possible. No poet, novelist, or critic, even one who bends over his desk for eight hours a day, could imagine the intensity of his concentration on the life of letters.

His head, in the small cloud of light made by his lantern, was constantly bent forward, while his eyes searched the sand, or studied the pages and fragments of paper that he found.

He read constantly. His shoulders were rounded, and he had been forced to start wearing glasses shortly after undertaking his duties.

Papers that did not look interesting at first glance he threw into his bag; those he wanted to study he stuffed into his pockets. Later he smoothed them out on the floor of the house.

Because of such necessity for discrimination, he had grown to be an excellent judge.

Sometimes he transfixed one worthless or unprinted paper after another on the nail, until it was full from what might be called the hilt to the point. Then it resembled one of those pieces of office equipment that used to be seen on the desks of careless business men and doctors. Sometimes he would put a match to this file of papers and walk along with it upraised like a torch, as if they were his paid bills, or like one of those fiery meat dishes called kebabs, served in Russian or Syrian restaurants.

Besides reading and such possibilities of fitful illumination, papers, particularly newspapers, had other uses. He could put them under his coat in the winter, to help keep out the cold wind from the sea. In the same season he could spread several layers of them over the floor of the house, for the same reason. Somewhere in his extensive reading he had learned that the ink used in printing newspapers makes them valuable for destroying odours; but he could think of no use to himself in that.

He was acquainted with all qualities of paper in all stages of soddenness and dryness. Wet newspaper became only slightly translucent. It stuck to his foot or hand, and rather than tearing, it slowly separated in shreds in a way he found rather sickening.

If really sea-soaked, it could be made into balls or other shapes. Once or twice when drunk (Boomer usually came to work that way several times a week), he had attempted a little rough modelling. But as soon as the busts and animals he made had dried out, he burned them, too.

Newspaper turned yellow quickly, even after a day's exposure. Sometimes he found one of the day before yesterday that had been dropped carelessly, half folded, half crumpled. Holding it up to the lantern he noticed, even before the wars and murders, effects of yellowed corners on white pages, and outer pages contrasting with inner ones. Very old papers became almost the colour of the sand.

On nights that Boomer was most drunk, the sea was of gasoline, terribly dangerous. He glanced at it fearfully over his shoulder between every sentence he read, and built his fire far back on the beach. It was brilliant, oily, and explosive. He was foolish enough then to think that it might ignite and destroy his only means of making a living.

On windy nights it was harder to clean up the beach, and at such times Boomer was more like a hunter than a collector.

But the flight of the papers was an interesting thing to watch. He had made many careful comparisons between them and the birds that occasionally flew within range of the lantern.

A bird, of course, inspired by a brain, by long tradition, by a desire that could often be understood to reach some place or obtain some thing, flew in a line, or a series of curves that were part of a line. One could tell the difference between its methodical flights to obtain something and its flights for show.

But the papers had no discernible goal, no brain, no feeling of race or group. They soared up, fell down, could not decide, hesitated, subsided, flew straight to their doom in the sea, or turned over in mid-air to collapse on the sand without another motion.

If any manner was their favourite, it seemed to be an oblique one, slipping sidewise.

They made more subtle use of air-currents and yielded to them more whimsically than the often pig-headed birds. They were not proud of their tricks, either, but seemed unconscious of the bravery, the ignorance, they displayed, and of Boomer, waiting to catch them on the sharpened nail.

The fold in the middle of large news sheets acted as a kind of spine, but the wings were not co-ordinated. Tabloids flew slightly better than full-sized sheets. Small rumpled scraps were most fantastic.

Some nights the air seemed full of them. To Boomer's drunken vision the letters appeared to fly from the pages. He raised his lantern and staff and ran waving his arms, headlines and sentences streaming around him, like a man shooing a flock of pigeons.

When he pinned them through with the nail, he thought of the Ancient Mariner and the Albatross, for, of course, he had run across that threatening poem many times.

He accomplished most on windless nights, when he might have several hours of early morning left for himself. He arranged himself cross-legged in the house and hung the lantern on a nail he had driven at the right height. The splintery walls glistened and the tiny place became quite warm.

His studies could be divided into three groups, and he himself classified them mentally in this way.

First, and most numerous: everything that seemed to be about himself, his occupation in life, and any instructions or warnings that referred to it.

Second: the stories about other people that caught his fancy, whose careers he followed from day to day in newspapers and fragments of books and letters; and whose further adventures he was always watching out for.

Third: the items he could not understand at all, that bewildered him completely but at the same time interested him so much that he saved them to read. These he tried, almost frantically, to fit into first one, then the other, of the two categories.

We give a few examples from each of the groups.

From the first: "The Exercitant will benefit all the more, the more he secludes himself from all friends and acquaintances and from all earthly solicitude, for example, by moving from the house in which he dwelt, and taking another house or room, that there he may abide in all possible privacy . . . (obliterated) he comes to use his natural faculties more freely in diligently searching for that he so much desires."

That certainly was plain enough.

This was the type of warning that worried him: "The habit of perusing periodical works may properly be added to Averrhoe's catalogue of ANTI-MNEMONICS, or weakeners of the memory. Also 'eating of unripe fruit; gazing on the clouds and on movable things suspended in the air (that would apply); riding among a multitude of camels; frequent laughter (no); listening to a series of jests and anecdotes; the habit of reading tombstones in churchyards, etc.'" (And these last might.)

From the second category: "She slept about two hours and returned to her place in the hole, carrying with her an American flag, which she placed beside her. Her husband has brought her meals out to her and she announced that she intends to sit in the hole until the Public Social Service Company abandons the idea of setting a pole there."

Boomer wondered about this lady for two nights. On the third he found this, which seemed, to his way of looking at things, to clarify the situation a little further. It was part of a page from a book, whereas the first item was a bit of newspaper.

"Her ladyship's assumption was that she kept, at every moment of her life, every advantage—it made her beautifully soft, very nearly generous; so she didn't distinguish the little protuberant eyes of smaller social insects, often endowed with such range, from . . ."

It might be two nights more, or two weeks, however, before he would find the next step in this particular sequence.

Among the third group, of things that fascinated but puzzled, Boomer saved such odds and ends as this: (a small, untorn slip of pink paper).

"JOKE SPECS WITH SHIFTING EYES. Put on the spectacles and place the mouthpiece in the mouth. Blow in air intermittently; the eyes and eye-brows will then be raised and lowered. The movement can be effected quickly or slowly according to what joke effect it is desired to obtain. If the ear pieces are too short in case of a large head bend the curved portion behind the ear. Celluloid is inflammable! Consequently do not bring your spectacles near a naked flame!!"

This would seem properly to belong to the set of warnings referring to himself. But if he was able to heed the last warning, there was much in the earlier instructions that he could not understand.

And this, written in pencil on letter-paper, blurred but readable:

"I wasn't feeling well over my teeth, and I had three large ones taken out, for they made me nervous and sick sometime, and this is the reason I couldn't send in my lesson although I am thinking of being able to write like all the Authors, for I believe that is more in my mind than any other kind of work, for I am concentrating on the lessons, frequently, many times.

"Mr. Margolies, I am thinking of how those Authors write such long stories of 60,000 or 100,000 words in those magazines, and where do they get their imagination and the material.

"I would be very pleased to write such stories as those Writers."

Although Boomer had no such childish desire, he felt that the question posed was one having something to do with his own way of life; it might almost be addressed to him as well as to the unknown Mr. Margolies. But what was the answer? The more papers he picked up and the more he read, the less he felt he understood. In a sense he depended on "their imagination," and was even its slave, but at the same time he thought of it as a kind of disease.

We shall give one more of our friend's self-riddles. It was this, in muddy type on very old, brown paper: (he made no distinction between the bewilderments of prose and those of poetry).

"Much as a one-eyed room, hung all with night,
    Only that side, which adverse to the eye
Gives but one narrow passage to the light,
    Is spread with some white shining tapestry,
An hundred shapes that through the flit airs stray,
Rush boldly in, crowding that narrow way;
And on that bright-faced wall obscurely dancing play."

That sounded like something he had experienced. First his house seemed to him to be the "one-eyed room, hung all with night," and then it was his whole life at night on the shore. First the papers blowing in the air, then what was printed on them, were the "hundred shapes."

Should we explain that by the time he was ready to start reading Boomer was usually not very drunk? The alcohol had worn off. He still felt isolated and self-important, but unnaturally wide-awake.

But what did these things mean?

Either because of the insect-armies of type so constantly besieging his eyes, or because it was really so, the world, the whole world he saw, came before many years to seem printed, too.

Boomer held up the lantern and watched a sandpiper rushing distractedly this way and that.

It looked, to his strained eyesight, like a point of punctuation against the "rounded, rolling waves." It left fine prints with its feet. Its feathers were speckled; and especially on the narrow hems of the wings appeared marks that looked as if they might be letters, if only he could get close enough to read them.

Sometimes the people who frequented the beach in the day time, whom he never saw, felt inclined to write in the sand. Boomer, on his part, thought that erasing these writings was probably included in his duties, too. Lowering the lantern, he carefully scuffed out "Francis Xavier School," "Lillian," "What the Hell."

The sand itself, if he picked some of it up and held it close to one eye, looked a little like printed paper, ground up or chewed.

But the best part of the long studious nights was when he had cleared up the allotted area and was ready to set fire to the paper jammed in the wire basket.

His forehead already felt hot, from drink or from reading so much, but he stood as near as he could to the feverish heat of the burning paper, and noticed eagerly each detail of the incineration.

The flame walked up a stretch of paper evenly, not hurriedly, and after a second the black paper turned under or over. It fell twisting into shapes that sometimes resembled beautiful wrought-iron work, but afterwards they dropped apart at a breath.

Large flakes of blackened paper, still sparkling red at the edges, flew into the sky. While his eyes could follow them he had never seen such clever, quivering manœuvres.

Then there were left frail sheets of ashes, as white as the original paper, and soft to the touch, or a bundle of grey feathers like a guinea-hen's.

•

But the point was that everything had to be burned at last. All, all had to be burned, even bewildering scraps that he had carried with him for weeks or months. Burning paper was his occupation, by which he made his living, but over and above that, he could not allow his pockets to become too full, or his house to become littered.

Although he enjoyed the fire, Edwin Boomer did not enjoy its inevitability. Let us leave him in his house, at four one morning, his reading selected, the conflagration all over, the lantern shining clearly. It is an extremely picturesque scene, in some ways like a Rembrandt, but in many ways not.

1937

In Prison

I can scarcely wait for the day of my imprisonment. It is then that my life, my real life, will begin. As Nathaniel Hawthorne says in *The Intelligence-Office*, "I want my place, my own place, my true place in the world, my proper sphere, my thing which Nature intended me to perform . . . and which I have vainly sought all my life-time." But I am not that nostalgic about it, nor have I searched in vain "all my life-time." I have known for many years in what direction lie my talents and my "proper sphere," and I have always eagerly desired to enter it. Once that day has arrived and the formalities are over, I shall know exactly how to set about those duties "Nature intended me to perform."

The reader, or my friends, particularly those who happen to be familiar with my way of life, may protest that for me any actual imprisonment is unnecessary, since I already live, in relationship to society, very much as if I were in a prison. This I cannot deny, but I must simply point out the philosophic difference that exists between Choice and Necessity. I may live now as if I were in prison, or I might even go and take lodgings near, or in, a prison and follow the prison routine faithfully in every detail—and still I should be a "minister without portfolio." The hotel-existence I now lead might be compared in many respects to prison-life, I believe: there are the corridors, the cellular rooms, the large, unrelated group of people with the different purposes in being there that animate every one of them; but it still displays great differences. And of course in any hotel, even the barest, it is impossible to overlook the facts of "decoration," the turkey carpets, brass fire-extinguishers, transom-hooks, etc.,—it is ridiculous to try to imagine oneself in prison in such surroundings! For example: the room I now occupy is papered with a not unattractive wall-paper, the pattern of which consists of silver stripes about an inch and a half wide running up and down, the same distance from each other. They are placed over, that is they appear to be inside of, a free design of flowering vines which runs all over the wall against a faded brown background. Now at night, when the lamp is turned on, these silver stripes catch the light and glisten and seem to stand out a little, or rather, in a little, from the vines and flowers, apparently shutting them off from me. I could almost imagine myself, if it would do any good, in a large silver bird-cage! But that is parody, a fantasy on my real hopes and ambitions.

One must be *in*; that is the primary condition. And yet I have known of isolated villages, or island towns, in our Southern states, where the prisoners are not really imprisoned at all! They are dressed in a distinctive uniform, usually the familiar picturesque suit of horizontal black and white stripes with a rimless cap of the same material, and sometimes, but not always, a leg iron. Then they are deliberately set at large every morning to work at assigned tasks in the town, or to pick up such odd jobs for themselves as they can. I myself have seen them, pumping water, cleaning streets, even helping housewives wash the windows or shake the carpets. One of the most effective scenes that I have ever seen, for color-contrast, was a group of these libertine convicts, in their black and white stripes, spraying, or otherwise tending to, a large clump of tropical shrubbery on the lawn of a public building. There were several varieties of bushes and plants in the arrangement, each of which had either brilliantly colored or conspicuously marked leaves. One bush, I remember, had long, knife-like leaves, twisting as they grew into loose spirals, the upper side of the leaf magenta, the under an ochre yellow. Another had large, flat, glossy leaves, dark green, on which were scrawled magnificent arabesques in lines of chalk-yellow. These designs, contrasting with the bold stripes of the prison uniform, made an extraordinary, if somewhat florid, picture.

But the prisoners, if such they could be called,—there must have hung over their lives the perpetual irksomeness of all half-measures, of "not knowing where one is at." They had one rule: to report back to the jail, as "headquarters," at nine o'clock, in order to be locked up for the night; and I was given to understand that it was a fairly frequent occurrence for one or two, who arrived a few minutes too late, to be locked out for the night!— when they would sometimes return to their homes, if they came from the same district, or else drop down and sleep on the very steps of the jail they were supposed to be secured in. But this short-sighted and shiftless conception of the meaning of prison could never satisfy me; I could never consent to submit to such terms of imprisonment,—no, never!

Perhaps my ideas on the subject may appear too exacting. It may seem ridiculous to you for me to be laying down the terms of my own imprisonment in this manner. But let me say that I have given this subject most of my thought and attention for several years, and I believe that I am speaking not entirely from selfish motives. Books about imprisonment I like perhaps the best of all literature, and I have read a great many; although of course one is often disappointed in them in spite of the subject-matter.

Take *The Enormous Room*. How I envied the author of that book! But there was something artificial about it, something that puzzled me considerably until I realized that it was due to the fact that the author had had an inner conviction of his eventual release all during the period of his imprisonment,—a flaw, or rather an airbubble, that was bound by its own nature to reach the surface and break. The same reason may account for the perpetual presence of the sense of humor that angered me so much. I believe that I like humor as well as the next person, as they say, but it has always seemed a great pity to me that so many intelligent people now believe that everything that can happen to them must be funny. This belief first undermines conversation and letter-writing and makes them monotonous, and then penetrates deeper, to corrupt our powers of observation and comprehension—or so I believe.

The Count of Mount Cristo I once enjoyed very much, although now I doubt that I should be able to read it through, with its exposure of "an injustice," its romantic tunnel-digging, treasure-hunting, etc. However, since I feel that I may well be very much in its debt, and I do not wish to omit or slight any influence, even a childish one, I set the title down here. *The Ballad of Reading Gaol* was another of the writings on this subject which I never could abide,—it seemed to me to bring in material that although perhaps of great human interest, had nothing whatever to do with the subject at hand. "That little tent of blue, Which prisoners call the sky," strikes me as absolute nonsense. I believe that even a key-hole of sky would be enough, in its blind, blue endlessness, to give someone, even someone who had never seen it before, an adequate idea of the sky; and as for calling it the "sky,"— we all call it the sky, do we not; I see nothing pathetic whatever about that, as I am evidently supposed to. Rather give me Dostoyevsky's *House of the Dead, or Prison Life in Siberia*. Even if there seems to have been some ambiguity about the status of prisoners there, at least one is in the hands of an authority who realizes the limitations and possibilities of his subject. As for the frequently published best-sellers by warders, executioners, turn-keys, etc., I have never read any of them, being determined to uphold my own point of view, and not wanting to introduce any elements of self-consciousness into my future behaviour that I could possibly avoid.

I should like a cell about twelve or fifteen feet long, by six feet wide. The door would be at one end, the window, placed rather high, at the other, and the iron bed along the side,—I see it on the left, but of course it could perfectly well be on the right. I might or might not have a small table, or shelf, let down by ropes from the wall just under the window, and by it a chair. I should like the ceiling to be fairly high. The walls I have in mind are interestingly stained, peeled, or otherwise disfigured; gray or whitewashed, blueish, yellowish, even green—but I only hope they are of no other color. The prospect of unpainted boards with their possibilities of various grains can some-times please me, or stone in slabs or irregular shapes. I run the awful risk of a red brick cell; however, whitewashed or painted bricks might be quite agreeable, particularly if they had not been given a fresh coat for some time and here and there the paint had fallen off, revealing, in an irregular but bevelled frame (made by previous coats), the regularity of the brick-work beneath.

About the view from the window: I once went to see a room in the *Asylum of the Mausoleum* where the painter V——— had been confined for a year, and what chiefly impressed me about this room, and gave rise to my own thoughts on the subject, was the view. My travelling companion and I reached the Asylum in the late afternoon and were admitted to the grounds by a nun, but a family, living in a small house of their own, seemed to be in charge. At our calls they rushed out, four of them, eating their dinner and talking to us at the same time with their mouths full. They stood in a row, and at the end of it their little black and white kitten was busy scratching in the dirt. It was "an animated scene." The daughter, age eight, and a younger brother, each carrying and eating half a long loaf of bread, were to show us around. We first went through several long, dark, cellar-like halls, painted yellow, with the low blue doors of the cells along one side. The floors were of stone; the paint was peeling everywhere, but the general effect was rather solemnly pretty. The room we had come to see was on the ground floor. It might have been very sad if it had not been for the two little chil-dren who rushed back and forth, chewing their bites of white bread and trying to outdo each other in telling us what everything was. But I am wan-dering from my subject, which was the view from the window of this room: It opened directly onto the kitchen-garden of the institution and beyond it stretched the open fields. A row of cypresses stood at the right. It was rapidly growing dark (and even as we stood there it grew too dark to find our way out if it had not been for the children) but I can still see as clearly as in a photograph the beautiful completeness of the view from that win-dow: the shaven fields, the black cypress, and the group of swallows posed dipping in the gray sky,—only the fields have retained their faded color.

As a view it may well have been ideal, but one must take all sorts of things into consideration and consoling and inspirational as that scene may have been, I do not feel that what is suited to an asylum is necessarily suited to a prison. That is, because I expect to go to prison in full possession of my "faculties,"—in fact it is not until I am securely installed there that I expect fully to realize them,—I feel that something a little less rustic, a little harsher, might be of more use to me personally. But it is a difficult question, and one that is probably best decided, as of course it must be, by chance alone.

What I should like best of all, I might as well confess, would be a view of a court-yard paved with stone. I have a fondness for stone court-yards that amounts almost to a passion. If I were not to be imprisoned I should at least attempt to make that part of my dream a reality; I should want to live in a farm house such as I have seen in foreign countries, a farm-house with an absolutely bare stone platform attached to it, the stones laid in a simple pattern of squares or diamonds. Another pattern I admire is interlocking cobble-stone fans, with a border of larger stones set around the edge. But from my cell window I should prefer, say, a lozenge design, outlined by long stones, the interior of the lozenges made of cobbles, and the pattern narrowing away from my window towards the distant wall of the prison-yard. The rest of my scenery would be the responsibility of the weather alone, although I should rather face the east than the west since I much prefer sunrises to sunsets. Then, too, it is by looking towards the east that one obtains the most theatrical effects from a sunset, in my opinion. I refer to that fifteen minutes or half an hour of heavy gold in which any object can be made to look magically significant. If the reader can tell me of anything more beautiful than a stone court-yard lit obliquely in this way so that the shallowly rounded stones each cast a small shadow but the general surface is thickly sanded with gold, and a pole casts a long, long shadow and a limp wire an unearthly one,—I beg him to tell me what it is.

I understand that most prisons are now supplied with libraries and that the prisoners are expected to read the *Everyman's Library* and other books of educational tendencies. I hope I am not being too reactionary when I say that my one desire is to be given one very dull book to read, the duller the better. A book, moreover, on a subject completely foreign to me; perhaps the second volume, if the first would familiarize me too well with the terms and purpose of the work. Then I shall be able to experience with a free conscience the pleasure, perverse, I suppose, of interpreting it not at all according to its intent. Because I share with Valery's *M. Teste* the "knowledge that our thoughts are reflected back to us, too much so, through expressions made by others"; and I have resigned myself, or do I speak too frankly, to deriving what information and joy I can from this—lamentable but irremediable—state of affairs. From my detached rock-like book I shall be able to draw vast generalizations, abstractions of the grandest, most illuminating sort, like allegories or poems, and by posing fragments of it against the surroundings and conversations of my prison, I shall be able to form my own examples of surrealist art!—something I should never know how to do outside, where the sources are so bewildering. Perhaps it will be a book on the cure of a disease, or an industrial technique,—but no, even to try to imagine the subject would be to spoil the sensation of wave-like freshness I hope to receive when it is first placed in my hands.

Writing on the Wall: I have formulated very definite ideas on this important aspect of prison life, and have already composed sentences and paragraphs (which I cannot give here) I hope to be able to inscribe on the walls of my cell. First, however, even before looking into the book mentioned above, I shall read very carefully (or try to read, since they may be partly obliterated, or in a foreign language) the inscriptions already there. Then I shall adapt my own compositions, in order that they may not conflict with those written by the prisoner before me. The voice of a new inmate will be noticeable, but there will be no contradictions or criticisms of what has already been laid down, rather a "commentary." I have thought of attempting a short, but immortal, poem, but I am afraid that is beyond me; I may rise to the occasion, however, once I am confronted with that stained, smeared, scribbled-on wall and feel the stub of pencil or rusty nail between my fingers. Perhaps I shall arrange my "works" in a series of neat inscriptions in a clear, Roman print; perhaps I shall write them diagonally, across a corner, or at the base of a wall and half on the floor, in an almost illegible scrawl. They will be brief, suggestive, anguished, but full of the lights of revelation. And no small part of the joy these writings will give me will be to think of the person coming after me,—the legacy of thoughts I shall leave him, like an old bundle tossed carelessly into a corner!

Once I dreamed that I was in Hell. It was a low, Netherlands-like country, all the marsh-grass a crude artificial green, lit by brilliant but almost horizontal sunlight. I was dressed in an unbecoming costume of gray cotton: trousers of an awkward length and a shirt hanging outside them, and my hair cut close. I suffered constantly from extreme dizziness, because the horizon (and this was how I knew I was in Hell) was at an angle of forty-five degrees. Although this useless tale may not seem to have much connection with my theme, I include it simply to illustrate the manner in which I expect my vision of the outside world to be miraculously changed when I first hear my cell door locked behind me, and I step to the window to take my first look out.

I shall manage to look just a little different in my uniform from the rest of the prisoners. I shall leave the top button of the shirt undone, or roll the long sleeves half-way between wrist and elbow,—something just a little casual, a little Byronic. On the other hand, if that is already the general tone in the prison, I shall affect a severe, mechanical neatness. My carriage and facial expression will be influenced by the same motive. There is, however, no insincerity in any of this; it is my conception of my role in prison life. It is entirely a different thing from being a "rebel" outside the prison; it is to be unconventional, rebellious perhaps, but in shades and shadows.

By means of these beginnings, these slight differences, and the appeal (do not think I am boasting here, or overestimating the power of details, because I have seen it work over and over again) of my carefully subdued, reserved manner, I shall attract to myself one intimate friend, whom I shall influence deeply. This friend, already an important member of the prison society, will be of great assistance to me in establishing myself as an authority, recognized but unofficial, on the conduct of prison life. It will take years before I become an *influence*, and possibly,—and this is what I dare to hope for, to find the prison in such a period of its evolution that it will be unavoidable to be thought of as an *evil influence*. . . . Perhaps they will laugh at me, as they laughed at the Vicar of Wakefield; but of course, just at first, I should like nothing better!

Many years ago I discovered that I could "succeed" in one place, but not in all places, and never, never could I succeed "at large." In the world, for example, I am very much under the influence of dress, absurd as that may be. But in a place where all dress alike I have the gift of being able to develop a "style" of my own, something that is even admired and imitated by others. The longer my sentence, although I constantly find myself thinking of it as a life-sentence, the more slowly shall I go about establishing myself, and the more certain are my chances of success. Ridiculous as it sounds, and is, I am looking forward to directing the prison dramatic association, or being on the base-ball team!

But in the same way that I was led to protest against the ambiguity of the position of those prisoners who were in and out of prison at the same time (I have even seen their wives washing their striped trousers and hanging them on the line!) I should bitterly object to any change or break in my way of life. If, for example, I should become ill and have to go to the prison infirmary, or if shortly after my arrival I should be moved to a different cell,—either of these accidents would seriously upset me, and I should have to begin my work all over again.

Quite naturally under these circumstances I have often thought of joining our Army or Navy. I have stood on the side-walk an hour at a time, studying the posters of the recruiting-offices: the oval portrait of a soldier or sailor surrounded by scenes representing his "life." But the sailor, I understand, may be shifted from ship to ship without so much as a by-your-leave; and then too, I believe that there is something fundamentally uncongenial about the view of the sea to a person of my mentality. In the blithe photographs surrounding the gallant head of the soldier I have glimpsed him "at work" building roads, peeling potatoes, etc. Aside from the remote possibilities of active service, those pictures alone would be enough to deter me from entering his ranks.

You may say,—people have said to me—you would have been happy in the more flourishing days of the religious order, and that, I imagine, is close to the truth. But even there I hesitate, and the difference between Choice and Necessity jumps up again to confound me. "Freedom is knowledge of necessity"; I believe nothing as ardently as I do that. And I assure you that to act in this way is the only logical step for me to take. I mean, of course, to be acted *upon* in this way is the only logical step for me to take.

1938

Gregorio Valdes, 1879–1939

The first painting I saw by Gregorio Valdes was in the window of a barber-shop on Duval Street, the main street of Key West. The shop is in a block of cheap liquor stores, shoe-shine parlors and pool-rooms, all under a long wooden awning shading the sidewalk. The picture leaned against a cardboard advertisement for Eagle Whiskey, among other window decorations of red and green crepe-paper rosettes and streamers left over from Christmas and the announcement of an operetta at the Cuban school,—all covered with dust and fly-spots and littered with termites' wings.

It was a view, a real View, of a straight road diminishing to a point through green fields, and a row of straight Royal Palms on either side, so carefully painted that one could count seven trees in each row. In the middle of the road was the tiny figure of a man on a donkey, and far away on the right the white speck of a thatched Cuban cabin that seemed to have the same mysterious properties of perspective as the little dog in Rousseau's *The Cariole of M. Juniot*. The sky was blue at the top, then white, then beautiful blush pink, the pink of a hot, mosquito-filled tropical evening. As I went back and forth in front of the barber-shop on my way to the restaurant, this picture charmed me, and at last I went in and bought it for three dollars. My landlady had been trained to do "oils" at the Convent.—The house was filled with copies of *The Roman Girl at the Well*, *Horses in a Thunderstorm*, etc.—She was disgusted and said she would paint the same picture for me, "for fifteen cents."

The barber told me I could see more Valdes pictures in the window of a little cigar factory on Duval Street, one of the few left in Key West. There were six or seven pictures: an ugly *Last Supper* in blue and yellow, a *Guardian Angel* pushing two children along a path at the edge of a cliff, a study of flowers,—all copies, and also copies of local postcards. I liked one picture of a homestead in Cuba in the same green fields, with two of the favorite Royal Palms and a banana tree, a chair on the porch, a woman, a donkey, a big white flower, and a Pan-American airplane in the blue sky. A friend bought this one, and then I decided to call on Gregorio.

He lived at 1221 Duval Street, as it said on all his pictures, but he had a "studio" around the corner in a decayed, unrentable little house. There was a palette nailed to one of the posts of the verandah with *G. Valdes, Sign Painter* on it. Inside there were three rooms with holes in the floors and weeds growing up through the holes. Gregorio had covered two sections of the walls with postcards and pictures from the newspapers. One section was animals: baby animals in zoos and wild animals in Africa. The other section was mostly reproductions of Madonnas and other religious subjects from the rotogravures. In one room there was a small plaster Virgin with some half-melted yellow wax roses in a tumbler in front of her. He also had an old cot there, and a row of plants in tin cans. One of these was Sweet Basil which I was invited to smell every time I came to call.

Gregorio was very small, thin and sickly, with a childish face and tired brown eyes,—in fact he looked a little like the *Self Portrait* of El Greco. He spoke very little English but was so polite that if I took someone with me who spoke Spanish he would almost ignore the Spanish and always answer in English, anyway, which made explanations and even compliments very difficult. He had been born in Key West, but his wife was from Cuba, and Spanish was the household language, as it is in most Key West Cuban families.

I commissioned him to paint a large picture of the house I was living in. When I came to take him to see it he was dressed in new clothes: a new straw hat, a new striped shirt, buttoned up but without a necktie, his old trousers, but a pair of new black and white Cuban shoes, elaborately Gothic in design, and with such pointed toes that they must have been very uncomfortable. I gave him an enlarged photograph of the house to paint from and also asked to have more flowers put in, a monkey that lived next door, a parrot, and a certain type of palm tree, called the Traveller's Palm. There is only one of these in Key West, so Gregorio went and made a careful drawing of it to go by. He showed me the drawing later, with the measurements and colors written in along the side, and apologized because the tree really had seven branches on one side and six on the other, but in the painting he had given both sides seven to make it more symmetrical. He put in flowers in profusion, and the parrot, on the perch on the verandah, and painted the monkey, larger than life-size, climbing the trunk of the palm tree.

When he delivered this picture there was no one at home, so he left it on the verandah leaning against the wall. As I came home that evening I saw it there from a long way off down the street,—a fair sized copy of the house, in green and white, leaning against its green and white prototype. In the gray twilight they seemed to blur together and I had the feeling that if I came closer I would be able to see another miniature copy of the house leaning on the porch of the painted house, and so on,—like the Old Dutch

Cleanser advertisements. A few days later when I had hung the picture I asked Gregorio to a vernissage party, and in spite of language difficulties we all had a very nice time. We drank sherry, and from time to time Gregorio would announce, "more wine".

He had never seemed very well, but this winter when I returned to Key West he seemed much more delicate than before. After Christmas I found him at work in his studio only once. He had several commissions for pictures and was very happy. He had changed the little palette that said *Sign Painter* for a much larger one saying *Artist Painter*. But the next time I went to see him he was at the house at Duval Street, and one of his daughters told me he was "seek" and in bed. Gregorio came out as she said it, however, pulling on his trousers and apologizing for not having any new pictures to show, but he looked very ill.

His house was a real Cuban house, very bare, very clean, with a bicycle standing in the narrow front hall. The living room had a doorway draped with green chenille Christmas fringe, and six straight chairs around a little table in the middle bearing a bunch of artificial flowers. The bareness of a Cuban house, and the apparent remoteness of every object in it from every other object, gives one the same sensation as the bareness and remoteness of Gregorio's best pictures. The only decorations I remember seeing in the house were the crochet- and embroidery-work being done by one of the daughters, which was always on the table in the living room, and a few photographs,—of Gregorio when he had played the trombone in a band as a young man, a wedding party, etc., and a marriage certificate, hanging on the walls. Also in the hall there was a wonderful clock. The case was a plaster statue, painted bronze, of President Roosevelt manipulating a ship's wheel. On the face there was a picture of a barkeeper shaking cocktails, and the little tin shaker actually shook up and down with the ticking of the clock. I think this must have been won at one of the Bingo tents that are opened at Key West every winter.

Gregorio grew steadily worse during the spring. His own doctor happened to be in Cuba and he refused to have any other come to see him. His daughters said that when they begged him to have a doctor he told them that if one came he would "throw him away".

A friend and I went to see him about the first of May. It was the first time he had failed to get up to see us and we realized that he was dangerously sick. The family took us to a little room next to the kitchen, about six feet wide, where he lay on a low cot-bed. The room was only large enough to hold the bed, a wardrobe, a little stand and a slop-jar, and the rented house was in such a bad state of repair that light came up through the big holes in the floor. Gregorio, terribly emaciated, lay in bed wearing a blue shirt; his head was on a flat pillow, and just above him a little holy picture was tacked to the wall. He looked like one of those Mexican retablo paintings of miraculous cures, only in his case we were afraid no miraculous cure was possible.

That day we bought one of the few pictures he had on hand,—a still life of Key West fruits such as a cocoanut, a mango, sapodillos, a watermelon, and a sugar apple, all stiffly arranged against a blue background. In this picture the paint had cracked slightly, and examining it I discovered one eccentricity of Gregorio's painting. The blue background extended all the way to the table top and where the paint had cracked the blue showed through the fruit. Apparently he had felt that since the wall was back of the fruit he should paint it there, before he could go on and paint the fruit in front of it.

The next day we discovered in the Sunday *New York Times* that he had a group of fifteen paintings on exhibition at the Artists' Gallery in New York. We cut out the notice and took it to his house, but he was so sick he could only lie in bed holding out his thin arms and saying "Excuse, excuse". We were relieved, however, when the family told us that he had at last consented to have another doctor come to see him.

On the evening of the ninth of May we were extremely shocked when a Cuban friend we met on the street told us that "Gregorio died at five o'clock". We drove to the house right away. Several people were standing on the verandah in the dark, talking in low voices. One young man came up and said to us, "The old man die at five o'clock". He did not mean to be disrespectful but his English was poor and he said "old man" instead of "father".

The funeral took place the next afternoon. Only relatives and close friends attend the service of a Cuban funeral and only men go to the cemetery, so there were a great many cars drawn up in front of the house filled with the waiting men. Very quickly the coffin was carried out, covered with the pale, loose Rock Roses that the Valdes grow for sale in their back yard. Afterwards we were invited in, "to see the children".

Gregorio was so small and had such a detached manner that it was always surprising to think of him as a patriarch. He had five daughters and two sons: Jennie, Gregorio, Florencio, Anna Louisa, Carmela, Adela and Estella. Two of the daughters are married and he had three grandchildren, two boys and a girl.

I had been afraid that when I brought him the clipping from the *Times* he had been too sick to understand it, but the youngest daughter told me that he had looked at it a great deal and had kept telling them all that he was "going to get the first prize for painting in New York".

She told me several other anecdotes about her father,—how when the battleships came into Key West harbor during the war he had made a large scale model of one of them, exact in every detail, and had used it as an ice-cream cart, to peddle Cuban ices through the streets. It attracted the attention of a tourist from the north and he bought it, "for eighty dollars". She said that when the carnivals came to town he would sit up all night by the light of an oil lamp, making little pin-wheels to sell. He used to spend many nights at his studio, too, when he wanted to finish a sign or a picture, getting a little sleep on the cot there.

He had learned to paint when he and his wife were "sweethearts," she said, from an old man they call a name that sounds like "Musi",—no one knows how to spell it or remembers his real name. This old man lived in a house belonging to the Valdes, but he was too poor to pay rent and so he gave Gregorio painting lessons instead.

Gregorio had worked in the cigar factories, been a sign painter, an ice-cream peddler, and for a short time a photographer, in the effort to support his large family. He made several trips to Cuba and twenty years ago worked for a while in the cigar factories in Tampa, returning to Key West because his wife liked it better. While in Tampa he painted signs as well, and also the sides of delivery wagons. There are some of his signs in Key West,—a large one for the *Sociedad de Cuba* and one for a grocery store, especially, have certain of the qualities of his pictures. Just down the street from his house, opposite the *Sociedad de Cuba*, there used to be a little café for the workers in a near-by cigar factory, the Forget-Me-Not Café, *Café no me Olvidades*. Ten years ago or so Gregorio painted a picture of it on the wall of the café itself, with the blue sky, the telephone pole and wires, and the name, all very exact. Mr. Rafael Rodriguez, the former owner who showed it to us, seemed to feel rather badly because since the cigar factory and the café have both disappeared, the color of the doors and window frames has been changed from blue to orange, making Gregorio's picture no longer as perfect as it was.

This story is told by Mr. Edwin Denby in his article on Valdes for the Artists' Gallery exhibition: "When he was a young man he lived with an uncle. One day when that uncle was at work, Valdes took down the towel rack that hung next to the wash-basin and put up instead a painting of the rack with the towel on it. When the uncle came back at five, he went to the basin, bent over and washed his face hard; and still bent over he reached up for the towel. But he couldn't get hold. With the water streaming into his eyes, he squinted up at it, saw it and clawed at it, but the towel wouldn't come off the wall. 'Me laugh plenty, plenty,' Valdes said. . . ."

This classical ideal of verisimilitude did not always succeed so well, fortunately. Gregorio was not a great painter at all, and although he certainly belongs to the class of painters we call "primitive", sometimes he was not even a good "primitive". His pictures are of uneven quality. They are almost all copies of photographs or of reproductions of other pictures. Usually when he copied from such reproductions he succeeded in nothing more than the worst sort of "calendar" painting, and again when he copied, particularly from a photograph, and particularly from a photograph of something he knew and liked, such as palm trees, he managed to make just the right changes in perspective and coloring to give it a peculiar and captivating freshness, flatness, and remoteness. But Gregorio himself did not see any difference between what we think of as his good pictures and his poor pictures, and his painting a good one or a bad one seems to have been entirely a matter of luck.

There are some people whom we envy not because they are rich or handsome or successful, although they may be any or all of these, but because everything they are and do seems to be all of a piece, so that even if they wanted to they could not be or do otherwise. A particular feature of their characters may stand out as more praiseworthy in itself than others— that is almost beside the point. Ancient heroes often have to do penance for and expiate crimes they have committed all unwittingly, and in the same way it seems that some people receive certain "gifts" merely by remaining unwittingly in an undemocratic state of grace. It is a supposition that leaves painting like Gregorio's a partial mystery. But surely anything that is impossible for others to achieve by effort, that is dangerous to imitate, and yet, like natural virtue, must be both admired and imitated, always remains mysterious.

Anyway, who could fail to enjoy and admire those secretive palm trees in their pink skies, the Traveller's Palm, like "the fan-filamented antenna of a certain gigantic moth . . ." or the picture of the church in Cuba copied from a liquor advertisement and labelled with so literal a translation from the Spanish, "Church of St. Mary' Rosario 300 Years Constructed in Cuba."

1939

Mercedes Hospital

One day in the summer of 1940 the following notice appears in the Key West *Citizen*:

JOSÉ CHACÓN DIED TODAY
José Chacón, 84, died three o'clock this afternoon in the Mercedes Hospital. Funeral services will be held 5:30 p.m. tomorrow from the chapel of the Pritchard Funeral Home, Rev. G. Perez of the Latin Methodist Church officiating.

  The deceased leaves but one survivor, a nephew, José Chacón.

Directly underneath appears this poem:

FRIEND?
How often have you called
 Someone a friend
And thought he would be
 Everything it meant?

While you were on top of the world,
 With money in your hands,
They flocked around everywhere,
 Even at your command.

Now that you are old and gray,
 Your friends look the other way
When you meet them on the street;
 Never a "Hello" when you meet.

You go home to your little room
 And sit silent in the gloom,

Thinking of the once bright day,
   But now you are old and all alone.

But one comes to you every day
   As on your bed you must lay.
He stops and takes you by the hand,
   And the look on his face, you understand.

That smile on his face tells a lot
   As he sits by your bed and watches the clock
Ticking the hours softly by.
   With a tear in his eye, he says goodbye.

That was a Friend to the End.

I find this brief account of the death of an old man in what is really just the poorhouse, the Casa del Pobre, very touching. And of course the poem is touching too, but it naturally does not occur to me to connect them. Then I remember I am acquainted with a man named José Chacón who must be the nephew, but who certainly could never have written anything like it. He is a fat, talkative Cuban who runs a little open-air café, *La Estrella*. There are always several men sitting around the place, drinking coffee and playing dominoes, but the real money is made in the back room, where poker games and *bolito* drawings are held. José lives over the shop with his wife and several children; he is quite rich. Why he has let his uncle die in the Mercedes Hospital, I can't imagine.

I meet him on the street a few days later. José always speaks as though he were furiously angry, but it is just a rather common mannerism. I ask him what his uncle has died of, and he bursts out, as though the old man had been his bitterest enemy, that he died of drink, drink, drink. He demonstrates: he reels, emptying a bottle down his throat, and clutching at monsters in the air. He tells me a long story of how his uncle once hit a man with a bottle and had been taken to jail. I ask him why his uncle hasn't lived with him, and he says he couldn't live with anybody. He was a cigar maker for forty years; then he retired and pursued his real career of drinking. I ask if his uncle was a large or powerful man. "Yes, big and strong!" And again José expresses his opinion that it is drink that killed him.

It is a very hot day. The sky is thick bright blue, the same color as the painted lower halves of the windows of the Mercedes Hospital, as seen from the inside, where I am waiting for Miss Mamie Harris to appear. Miss Mamie has the local reputation of a saint. She is a nurse who has lived and worked at the Mercedes Hospital ever since it was opened. The parlor is hot and dark, as I examine the photographs of the hospital's founder.

The Mercedes Hospital was given to the town of Key West thirty years ago by Mr. Perro, the richest of the local cigar-factory owners. (Mr. Perro's favorite amusement was chess, and the high parapet of his former factory was adorned at intervals with knights cut from gray stones, as well as horse heads resting on little crenellated towers looking to all points of the compass. The inside covers of his cigar boxes had the same knights surrounded by gilt sunrays.) An enlarged photograph of Mr. Perro, yellow and indistinct, hangs in the parlor of the hospital, together with the original of his cigar-box decoration, done in watercolors.

On the walls there are also two or three mottoes, cross-stitched in wool on perforated cardboard; a crucifix; and a large lithograph, extremely yellow, of the life of the patriot Martí, with the major incidents of his life arranged in an oval; at the top, Martí in a toga is ascending into heaven. Besides the wall decorations, there are a few chairs, a Poor Box nailed to the wall for donations, and an old rolltop desk stuffed with forgotten papers. Mr. Perro left the hospital all these things, plus one hundred and thirty dollars a month forever and ever, and the name of his wife, Mercedes.

The hospital was originally his home. Being so rich, Mr. Perro had wanted to build his house in the Spanish style, like those of well-to-do businessmen in Cuba, but not wanting to go to the expense of importing stone, he had it built of wood. For that reason it looks a little strange—a high, square building with long Gothic windows, correctly built around a courtyard, but covered with clapboard and decorated here and there with quite American fretsaw work. The upstairs rooms rest on the thin wooden pillars around the patio, which is a dim, damp, battered square of cement with a drain in the middle. There is a well, but nothing at all picturesque—a square hole in the cement, with a galvanized bucket and a length of wet rope resting beside it. It is said that after Mr. Perro got his Spanish patio, he was uncertain as to what to do with it, so he stabled two horses there for several years.

The rooms, eight on each floor, are high and dark. The walls of horizontal boards were once painted in fearful shades of solid green, blue, or red, with moldings of contrasting fearful shades and gilt, but now they are as worn and faded as the painted walls of ancient tombs. Those of the parlor are different shades of blue, the dining room (at least I suppose it is a dining room, since there is a round table in the middle with four chairs pushed under it) different shades of brick and rose. One of the inmates' rooms suggests that it has been spinach-green, another ocher. But all these col-

ors, once so rich and bright, are scarcely there at all. They look as if they
had been soaked off by a long stay underwater. The whole hospital has the
air of having been submerged: the damp cement, the bare floors worn away
to the ridges of the grain, and the pillars and the patio so "sucked" by termites that they look like elongated sponges.

After a while I hear the staircase creaking, and then Miss Mamie comes in.
She is wearing a soiled white nurse's uniform, with a narrow white leather
belt dangling around her waist, white cotton stockings, and soiled long
white shoes. Her gray hair is cut very short, her face is full of indecipher-
able lines, and many of her teeth are missing. She always stands very close to
me with one hand on her hip and the other usually on my shoulder, smiling,
but watching my face closely like a doubtful child.

"My, how you keep plump," she says and gives me a leer and a pinch.
"I wish I could."

We talk for a while about the weather, about how she would like to get
out for a drive some evening soon but doesn't think she'll be able to, how
she has been there for thirty years, and how the "Collector" is in Cuba on a
little visit to her relatives, leaving her with more work to do than usual. The
"Collector" is a very old lady, supposedly the superintendent of the hospital,
who goes slowly around town from door to door, with a black imitation-
leather market bag over her arm, begging money to add to the one hundred
and thirty dollars a month.

After the "little talk," we take a tour around the ground floor to see the
"patients." There are only four today, and three of them are permanent
residents. First comes Mr. "Tommy" Cummers. Mr. Tommy has lived at the
Mercedes Hospital for fourteen years, and his cousin Mr. "Sonny" Cummers has lived there for three. Miss Mamie always uses the Mister, and although they are both over seventy they are called "Sonny" and "Tommy."
(It must be the idea of the helplessness it implies that makes the southern
use of childish names so sad. I hear old men speaking of "my daddy," and
another man I know, aged sixty, was found dead drunk under the counter
at the fish market, just two days after he had left his house, saying, "Mama,
I'm going to be a good boy from now on.")

Mr. Tommy is singing hymns as we step across the patio to his room. His
feet and ankles are paralyzed; he sits in an armchair beside the door with a
sheet over his knees, and sings hymns, out of time and out of tune, in a
loud rough voice all day long. He keeps a large Bible and two hymnbooks
beside him and is rather inclined to boast that he reads nothing else. He
sings the hymns partly to spite Mr. Sonny, who is sitting in the next room
just behind the folding doors and who, before he came to Mercedes Hos-

pital, was not able to lead as sheltered and virtuous a life as Mr. Tommy has for the last fourteen years.

While we are there, the housekeeper comes in. She is a plump little Cuban lady with little gold earrings shaking in her ears. She brings three cigars in a paper bag for Mr. Tommy, who takes a dime out of his breast pocket and pays her for them. As soon as we leave, he starts singing again, and while we call on Mr. Sonny, he is almost bellowing.

Mr. Sonny is dying of dropsy; we merely say good afternoon. He sits at the far end of one of the long side rooms, all alone, on a straight chair with his feet on a little footstool. His swollen body is wrapped in a gray blanket and his head is done up in a sort of turban of white. He bows to us indifferently; his thin pointed face is dark brown. He looks so exactly like an eighteenth-century poet that although Miss Mamie is chattering away to me about his desperate condition, I can't pay much attention to her. I'm expecting to hear him declaim from the shadows:

Cease, fond Nature, cease thy strife.

In another large room lies a tubercular Negro named Milton, here for the third time. Miss Mamie says, "We don't exactly take them, they have a place. But he is so sick and we have so few patients." She pulls me past the door, but I see a large black man with long thin legs stretched out on an iron cot under the mosquito bar. The walls of this room are ashes-of-roses. There are six beds but only Milton's is made up. It is on the sunny side of the building, it is hot, it smells strongly of disinfectant, and the long black legs look strange, seen through the ethereal cascade of mosquito netting.

Then we go into the sunlight, across a short gangplank, into a little square building.

"Our little crazy house," says Miss Mamie affectionately. "You haven't seen Antoñica, have you? Well, she isn't crazy any more. I'm going to take her back inside as soon as the doctor comes around again at the end of the week, but I have to keep her here awhile. She's only been here three weeks."

Sitting close to the window in an old-fashioned high-back rocking chair is a tiny creature in a long ragged flannel nightgown with a ruffle around the neck. The sun falls directly on her face; the hot wind blows in on her straight from the embers of the huge red Poinciana tree outside the window.

"She can't hear nothing and she can't see nothing," says Miss Mamie, "she's just like a little baby. I do everything for her just like a little baby."

She unclasps a hand from the arm of the rocking chair and holds it. It holds hers tightly, and Antoñica raises her face to Miss Mamie's and begins in Spanish in a loud harsh voice. I try to make out what she is saying, but Miss Mamie says it doesn't make any sense.

"She's terrible fond of me," she says. The old woman's hair has been cut so that it is about an inch long. Miss Mamie keeps rubbing her hand over the small skull, rather roughly, I think. But yes, it is true—Antoñica does appear to be fond of her. She snatches Miss Mamie's hand to her cheek, and jabbers louder than ever.

"She outlived all her folks, she ain't got anyone left, she's way over ninety," says Miss Mamie in a sort of coarse singsong, rubbing the old woman's white head and rocking her back and forth. "Terrible fond of me. I feed her just like a baby, just like a baby."

Antoñica's wool-white hair glistens in the sun. The ruff, the unnatural motion, her feet curled up off the floor, and her clutching hands make her look like a rare and delicate specimen of Chinese monkey. But her eyes, which are bright milky blue, like the flames of a gas burner when they have just been turned off and are about to sink back into the black pipes, give her an apocryphal appearance.

Perhaps she is an angel, speaking with "tongues."

Miss Mamie and I go back to the parlor and stand and talk some more. I know that some people consider her a saint. Probably they are right. She is capable of arousing the same feelings that the saints do: profoundest admiration and suspicion. Thirty dollars a month wages, thirty years of unselfish labor, "managing" on one hundred and thirty dollars a month for "everything" are all incredible feats—unless one does believe she is a saint.

There are other proofs of Miss Mamie's unusual character. There is her indifference to personal cleanliness (although she keeps her patients very clean). There is her solitariness: she rarely, if ever, leaves the hospital. There is her appearance: her face, her hands, and those long ascetic feet are all in her favor. Above all, there is her inquisitiveness and talkativeness and that childlike expression in her eyes when she takes hold of my shoulders and peers into my face and asks question after question—just as St. Anthony might have rushed out of his cell, and seized a traveler by the elbow and naïvely but determinedly asked him for news of the world. In fact, all the saints must have been insistent buttonholers, like Miss Mamie.

I suddenly remember José Chacón. Seeing Miss Mamie now, as sitting patiently at the mouth of her cavern on the edge of an endless desert, I wonder if the old man had been the wild "lion of the desert," coming to her roaring, with thorns in his paws? I ask about him.

"Oh, José. He was here lots of times, seven or eight times."

"He was a very big man, wasn't he?"

"José? Oh no, he wasn't big at all. I could lift him myself. He'd come here for a while, then he'd get better and go home again. He had a bad heart." If she knew about his alcoholism, she says nothing about it.

"How did he die?"

"He died so quick. The day he died, he seemed pretty good. I thought he was going to go home the next day, he seemed so good. I had his bed out in the front room by the window to get the air. Then I went to push it back into his room; he didn't weigh much. He was talking to me and, all of a sudden just as we got there, going through his door"—Miss Mamie cracked her finger—"it was his heart. Just stopped like that." Bump, the bed went over the threshold and José Chacón died.

Of course Miss Mamie could not have been the "Friend to the End" in the poem. If she read it in the paper, she wouldn't understand its sentiments, of which she certainly would have disapproved wholeheartedly, especially its self-praise. I could not conceive of such a poem being written or read there in Mercedes Hospital. Among Miss Mamie's saintly qualities, tenderness is lacking. In fact, it is the absence of tenderness that is the consoling thing about her.

It is time for me to leave, and after a little conversation about the "Collector" and about finances, I put ten dollars into Miss Mamie's hands, "for the Poor Box," and say goodbye. As I leave, I begin to think, Why didn't I put the money in the Poor Box myself? I know perfectly well that she won't do it.

It is a foolish as well as an unkind thought, because naturally Miss Mamie would have the key to the Poor Box; probably she wears it around her neck on a string. I realize my doubt is another proof of Miss Mamie's saintliness, and therefore of her ability to arouse suspicion. I've always thought the reason we suspect saints is the ambiguous nature of all good deeds, the impossibility of ever knowing why they are being performed. But that reasoning fails to explain Miss Mamie. She does away with the feeling that possibly she may be a saint for the wrong reason, by convincing one that she is being a saint for no ulterior reason at all.

There is no reason for or against her robbing the Poor Box, no more than there are reasons for or against her staying at the Mercedes Hospital, or being kind or cruel to the patients. St. Simeon Stylites probably thought he knew exactly what he was doing at the top of his pillar and rejoiced in it. Miss Mamie hasn't any idea that what she is doing where she is needs explaining. She has managed to transfer the same feeling to her patients— giving them security from hopelessness. Simplicity of heart, never the vulgarity of putting two and two together.

I go out, and the palm branches move slowly like prehistoric caryatids. The Mercedes Hospital seems so remote and far away now, like the bed of a dried-up lake. Out of the corner of my eye I catch a glimpse of the salty glitter at its bottom, a slight mica-like residuum, the faintest trace of joyousness.

1941

The Farmer's Children

Once, on a large farm ten miles from the nearest town, lived a hard-working farmer with his wife, their three little girls, and his children by a former marriage, two boys aged eleven and twelve. The first wife had been the daughter of a minister, a plain and simple woman who had named her sons Cato and Emerson; while the stepmother, being romantic and overgenerous, to her own children at least, had given them the names of Lea Leola, Rosina, and Gracie Bell. There was also the usual assortment of horses, cows, and poultry, and a hired man named Judd.

The farm had belonged to the children's father's grandfather, and although pieces of it had been sold from time to time, it was still very large, actually too large. The original farmhouse had been a mile away from the present one, on the "old" road. It had been struck by lightning and burned down ten years before, and Emerson's and Cato's grandparents, who had lived in it, had moved in with their son and his first wife for the year or two they had lived on after the fire. The old home had been long and low, and an enormous willow tree, which had miraculously escaped the fire and still grew, had shaded one corner of the roof. The new home stood beside the macadamized "new" road and was high and boxlike, painted yellow with a roof of glittering tin.

Besides the willow tree, the principal barn at the old home had also escaped the fire and it was still used for storing hay and as a shed in which were kept most of the farm implements. Because farm implements are so valuable, always costing more than the farmer can afford, and because the barn was so far from the house and could easily have been broken into, the hired man slept there every night, in a pile of hay.

Most of these facts later appeared in the newspapers. It also appeared that since Judd had come to be the hired man, three months ago, he and the children's father had formed the habit of taking overnight trips to town. They went on "business," something to do with selling another strip of land, but probably mostly to drink; and while they were away Emerson and Cato would take Judd's place in the old barn and watch over the reaper, the tedder, the hay-rake, the manure-spreader, the harrow, et cetera—all the weird and expensive machinery of jaws and teeth and arms and claws, of direct and reflex actions and odd gestures, apparently so intelligent, but, in this case, so completely helpless because it was still dragged by horses.

It was December and frightfully cold. The full moon was just coming up and the tin roof of the farmhouse and patches of the macadam road caught her light, while the farmyard was still almost in darkness. The children had been put outdoors by their mother, who was in a fit of temper because they got in her way while she was preparing supper. Bundled up in mackinaws, with icy hands, they played at raft and shipwreck. There was a pile of planks in a corner of the yard, with which their father had long been planning to repair some outhouse or other, and on it Lea Leola and Rosina sat stolidly, saved, while Cato, with a clothes-pole, stood up and steered. Still on the sinking ship, a chicken coop across the yard, stood the baby, Gracie Bell, holding out her arms and looking apprehensively around her, just about to cry. But Emerson was swimming to her rescue. He walked slowly, placing his heel against his toes at every step, and swinging both arms round and round like windmills.

"Be brave, Gracie Bell! I'm almost there!" he cried. He gasped loudly. "My strength is almost exhausted, but I'll save you!"

Cato was calling out, over and over, "Now the ship is sinking inch by inch! Now the ship is sinking inch by inch!"

Small and silvery, their voices echoed in the cold countryside. The moon freed herself from the last field and looked evenly across at the imaginary ocean tragedy taking place so far inland. Emerson lifted Gracie Bell in his arms. She clutched him tightly around the neck and burst into loud sobs, but he turned firmly back, treading water with tiny up-and-down steps. Gracie Bell shrieked and he repeated, "I'll save you, Gracie Bell. I'll save you, Gracie Bell," but did not change his pace.

The mother and stepmother suddenly opened the back door.

"Emerson!" she screamed. "Put that child down! Didn't I tell you the next time you made that child cry I'd beat you until you couldn't holler? Didn't I?"

"Oh Ma, we was just . . ."

"What's the matter with you kids, anyway? Fight and scrap, fight and scrap, and yowl, yowl, yowl, from morning to night. And you two boys, you're too big," and so on. The ugly words poured out and the children stood about the yard like stage-struck actors. But as their father said, "her bark was worse than her bite," and in a few minutes, as if silenced by the moon's bland reserve, she stopped and said in a slightly lower voice, "All right, you kids. What are you standing there waiting for? Come inside the house and get your supper."

The kitchen was hot, and the smell of fried potatoes and the warm yellow light of the oil lamp on the table gave an illusion of peacefulness. The two boys sat on one side, the two older girls on the other, and Gracie Bell on her mother's lap at the end. The father and Judd had gone to town, one reason why the mother had been unusually bad-tempered all afternoon. They ate in silence, except for the mother's endearments to Gracie Bell, whom she was helping to drink tea and condensed milk out of a white cup. They ate the fried potatoes with pieces of pork in them, slice after slice of white "store" bread and dishes of "preserves," and drank syrupy hot tea and milk. The oilcloth on the table was light molasses-colored, sprinkled with small yellow poppies; it glistened pleasantly, and the "preserves" glowed, dark red blobs surrounded by transparent ruby.

"Tonight's the night for the crumbs," Cato was thinking, and from time to time he managed to slide four slices of bread under the edge of the oilcloth and then up under his sweater. His thoughts sounded loud and ominous to him and he looked cautiously at his sisters to see if they had noticed anything, but their pale, rather flat faces looked blankly back. Anyway, it was the night for crumbs and what else could he possibly do?

The other two times he and Emerson had spent the night in the old barn he had used bits of torn-up newspaper because he hadn't been able to find the white pebbles anywhere. He and his brother had walked home, still half-asleep, in the gray-blue light just before sunrise, and he had been delighted to find the sprinkles of speckled paper here and there all along the way. He had dropped it out of his pocket a little at a time, scarcely daring to look back, and it had worked. But he had longed for the endless full moon of the tale, and the pebbles that would have shone "like silver coins." Emerson knew nothing of his plan—his system, rather—but it had worked without his help and in spite of all discrepancies.

The mother set Gracie Bell down and started to transfer dishes from the table to the sink.

"I suppose you boys forgot you've got to get over to the barn sometime tonight," she said ironically.

Emerson protested a little.

"Now you just put on your things and get started before it gets any later. Maybe sometime your pa will get them doors fixed or maybe he'll get a new barn. Go along, now." She lifted the teakettle off the stove.

Cato couldn't find his knitted gloves. He thought they were on the shelf in the corner with the schoolbags. He looked methodically for them everywhere and then at last he became aware of Lea Leola's malicious smile.

"Ma! Lea Leola's got my gloves. She's hid them on me!"

"Lea Leola! Have you got his gloves?" Her mother advanced on her. "Make her give them to me!"

Lea Leola said, "I ain't even seen his old gloves," and started to weep.

"Now Cato, see what you've done! Shut up, Lea Leola, for God's sake, and you boys hurry up and get out of here. I've had enough trouble for one day."

At the door Emerson said, "It's cold, Ma."

"Well, Judd's got his blankets over there. Go on, go along and shut that door. You're letting the cold in."

Outside it was almost as bright as day. The macadam road looked very gray and rang under their feet, that immediately grew numb with cold. The cold stuck quickly to the little hairs in their nostrils, that felt painfully stuffed with icy straws. But if they tried to warm their noses against the clumsy lapels of their mackinaws, the freezing moisture felt even worse, and they gave it up and merely pointed out their breath to each other as it whitened and then vanished. The moon was behind them. Cato looked over his shoulder and saw how the tin roof of the farmhouse shone, bluish, and how, above it, the stars looked blue, too, blue or yellow, and very small; you could hardly see most of them.

Emerson was talking quietly, enlarging on his favorite theme: how he could obtain a certain bicycle he had seen a while ago in the window of the hardware store in town. He went on and on but Cato didn't pay very much attention, first because he knew quite well already almost everything Emerson was saying or could say about the bicycle, and second because he was busy crumbing the four slices of bread which he had worked around into his pants pockets, two slices in each. It seemed to turn into lumps instead of crumbs and it was hard to pull off the little bits with his nails and flick them into the road from time to time from under the skirt of his mackinaw.

Emerson made no distinction between honest and dishonest methods of getting the bicycle. Sometimes he would discuss plans for deceiving the owner of the hardware store, who would somehow be maneuvered into sending it to him by mistake, and sometimes it was to be his reward for a deed of heroism. Sometimes he spoke of a glass-cutter. He had seen his father use one of these fascinating instruments. If he had one he could cut a large hole in the plate glass window of the hardware store in the night. And then he spoke of working next summer as a hired man. He would work for the farmer who had the farm next to theirs; he saw himself performing prodigious feats of haying and milking.

"But Old Man Blackader only pays big boys four dollars a week," said Cato, sensibly, "and he wouldn't pay you that much."

"Well . . ."

Emerson swore and spat toward the side of the road, and they went on while the moon rose steadily higher and higher.

A humming noise ran along the telephone wires over their heads. They thought it might possibly be caused by all the people talking over them at the same time but it didn't actually sound like voices. The glass conductors that bore the wires shone pale green, and the poles were bleached silver by the moonlight, and from each one came a strange roaring, deeper than the hum of the wires. It sounded like a swarm of bees. They put their ears to the deep black cracks. Cato tried to peer into one and almost thought he could see the mass of black and iridescent bees inside.

"But they'd all be frozen—solid," Emerson said.

"No they wouldn't. They sleep all winter."

Emerson wanted to climb a pole. Cato said, "You might get a shock."

He helped him, however, and boosted up his thin haunches in both hands. But Emerson could just barely touch the lowest spike and wasn't strong enough to pull himself up.

At last they came to where their path turned off the road, and went through a cornfield where the stalks still stood, motionless in the cold. Cato dropped quite a few crumbs to mark the turning. On the cornstalks the long, colorless leaves hung in tatters like streamers of old crepe paper, like the remains of booths that had stood along the midway of a county fair. The stalks were higher than their heads, like trees. Double lines of wire, with glinting barbs, were strung along both sides of the wheel tracks.

Emerson and Cato fought all day almost every day, but rarely at night. Now they were arguing amicably about how cold it was.

"It might snow even," Cato said.

"No," said Emerson, "it's too cold to snow."

"But when it gets awful cold it snows," said Cato.

"But when it gets real cold, awful cold like this, it can't snow."

"Why can't it?"

"Because it's too cold. Anyway, there isn't any up there."

They looked. Yes, except for the large white moon, the sky was as empty as could be.

Cato tried not to drop his crumbs in the dry turf between the wagon tracks, where they would not show. In the ruts he could see them a little, small and grayish. Of course there were no birds. But he couldn't seem to think it through—whether his plan was good for anything or not.

Back home in the yellow farmhouse the stepmother was getting ready for bed. She went to find an extra quilt to put over Lea Leola, Rosina, and

Gracie Bell, sleeping in one bed in the next room. She spread it out and tucked it in without disturbing them. Then, in spite of the cold, she stood for a moment looking down uneasily at its pattern of large, branching hexagons, blanched, almost colorless, in the moonlight. That had always been such a pretty quilt! Her mother had made it. What was the name of that pattern? What was it it reminded her of? Out from the forms of a lost childish game, from between the pages of a lost schoolbook, the image fell upon her brain: a snowflake.

"Where is that damned old barn?" Emerson asked, and spat again.

It was a relief to get to it and to see the familiar willow tree and to tug at one side of the dragging barn door with hands that had no feeling left in them. At first it seemed dark inside but soon the moon lit it all quite well. At the left were the disused stalls for the cows and horses, the various machines stood down the middle and at the right, and the hay now hung vaguely overhead on each side. But it was too cold to smell the hay.

Where were Judd's blankets? They couldn't find them anywhere. After looking in all the stalls and on the wooden pegs that held the harness, Emerson dropped down on a pile of hay in front of the harrow, by the door.

Cato said, "Maybe it would be better up in the mow." He put his bare hands on a rung of the ladder.

Emerson said, "I'm too cold to climb the ladder," and giggled.

So Cato sat down in the pile of hay on the floor, too, and they started heaping it over their legs and bodies. It felt queer; it had no weight or substance in their hands. It was lighter than feathers and wouldn't seem to settle down over them; it just prickled a little.

Emerson said he was tired and, turning on his side, he swore a few more times, almost cautiously. Cato swore, too, and lay on his back, close to his brother.

The harrow was near his head and its flat, sharp-edged disks gleamed at him coldly. Just beyond it he could make out the hay-rake. Its row of long, curved prongs caught the moonlight too, and from where he lay, almost on a level with them, the prongs made a steely, formal wave that came straight toward him over the floor boards. And around him in darkness and light were all the other machines: the manure-spreader made a huge shadow; the reaper lifted a strong forearm lined with saw teeth, like that of a gigantic grasshopper; and the tedder's sharp little forks were suspended in one of the bright patches, some up, some down, as if it had just that minute stopped a cataleptic kicking.

Up over their heads, between the mows, every crack and hole in the old roof showed, and little flecks, like icy chips of moon, fell on them, on the clutter of implements and on the gray hay. Once in a while one of the shingles would crack, or one of the brittle twigs of the willow tree would snap sharply.

Cato thought with pleasure of the trail of crumbs he had left all the way from the house to here. "And there aren't any birds," he thought almost gleefully. He and Emerson would start home again as they had the previous times, just before sunrise, and he would see the crumbs leading straight back the way they had come, white and steadfast in the early light.

Then he began to think of his father and Judd, off in town. He pictured his father in a bright, electrically-lit little restaurant, with blue walls, where it was very hot, eating a plate of dark red kidney beans. He had been there once and that was what he had been given to eat. For a while he thought, with disfavor, of his stepmother and stepsisters, and then his thoughts returned to his father; he loved him dearly.

Emerson muttered something about "that old Judd," and burrowed deeper into the hay. Their teeth were chattering. Cato tried to get his hands between his thighs, to warm them, but the hay got in the way. It felt like hoarfrost. It scratched and then melted against the skin of his numb hands. It gave him the same sensation as when he ate the acid grape jelly his stepmother made each fall and little sticks, little stiff crystal sticks, like ice, would prick and dissolve, also in the dark, against the roof of his mouth.

Through the half-open door the cornstalks in the cornfield stood suspiciously straight and still. What went on among those leaf-hung stalks? Shouldn't they have been cut down, anyway? There stood the corn and there stood, or squatted, the machines. He turned his head to look at them. All that corn should be reaped. The reaper held out its arm stiffly. The hayrack looked like the set coil of a big trap.

It hurt to move his feet. His feet felt just like a horse's hooves, as if he had horseshoes on them. He touched one and yes, it was true, it felt just like a big horseshoe.

The harnesses were hanging on their pegs above him. Their little bits of metal glittered pale blue and yellow like the little tiny stars. If the harnesses should fall down on him he would have to be a horse and it would be so cold out in the field pulling the heavy harrow. The harnesses were heavy, too; he had tried the collars a few times and they were very heavy. It would take two horses; he would have to wake up Emerson, although Emerson was hard to wake when he got to sleep.

The disks of the harrow looked like the side—those shields hung over the side—of a Viking ship. The harrow was a ship that was going to go up to the moon with the shields all clanging on her sides; he must get up into the seat and steer. That queer seat of perforated iron that looked uncomfortable and yet when one got into it, gave one such a feeling of power and ease. . . .

But how could it be going to the moon when the moon was coming right down on the hill? No, moons; there was a whole row of them. No, those must be the disks of the harrow. No, the moon had split into a sheaf of moons, slipping off each other sideways, off and off and off and off.

He turned to Emerson and called his name, but Emerson only moaned in his sleep. So he fitted his knees into the hollows at the back of his brother's and hugged him tightly around the waist.

At noon the next day their father found them in this position.

The story was in all the newspapers, on the front page of local ones, dwindling as it traveled over the countryside to short paragraphs on middle pages when it got as far as each coast. The farmer grieved wildly for a year; for some reason, one expression he gave to his feelings was to fire Judd.

1948

The Housekeeper

My neighbor, old Mrs. Sennett, adjusted the slide of the stereoscope to her eyes, looked at the card with admiration, and then read out loud to me, slowly, " 'Church in Marselaze, France.' " Then, "Paris." "Paris," I decided, must be an addition of her own. She handed the stereoscope over to me. I moved the card a little farther away and examined the church and the small figures of a man and woman in front of it. The woman was dressed in a long skirt, a tiny white shirtwaist, and a dotlike sailor hat, and, though standing at the foot of the church steps, through the stereoscope she and the man appeared to be at least fifty feet from the church.

"That's beautiful," I said, and handed the machine back to Mrs. Sennett. We had exhausted all the funny cards, like the one that showed a lady kissing the postman while her husband, leaning out of a window, was about to hit the postman on the head. Now we were reduced to things like the church and "King of the Belgians' Conservatory," in which all the flowers had been painted red by hand.

Outside, the rain continued to run down the screened windows of Mrs. Sennett's little Cape Cod cottage, filling the squares with cross-stitch effects that came and went. The long weeds and grass that composed the front yard dripped against the blurred background of the bay, where the water was almost the color of the grass. Mrs. Sennett's five charges were vigorously playing house in the dining room. (In the wintertime, Mrs. Sennett was housekeeper for a Mr. Curley, in Boston, and during the summers the Curley children boarded with her on the Cape.)

My expression must have changed. "Are those children making too much noise?" Mrs. Sennett demanded, a sort of wave going over her that might mark the beginning of her getting up out of her chair. I shook my head no, and gave her a little push on the shoulder to keep her seated. Mrs. Sennett was almost stone-deaf and had been for a long time, but she could read lips. You could talk to her without making any sound yourself, if you wanted to, and she more than kept up her side of the conversation in a loud, rusty voice that dropped weirdly every now and then into a whisper. She adored talking.

Finally, we had looked at all the pictures and she put the little green trunk containing the stereoscope and the cards back on the under shelf of the table.

"You wouldn't think to look at me that I was of Spanish origin, would you?" she asked.

I assured her with my hands and eyebrows that I wouldn't, expressing, I hoped, a polite amount of doubt, and eagerness to learn if she really were or not.

"Oh, yes," she said. "My mother was of pure Spanish blood. Do you know what my first name is?"

I shook my head.

"Carmen. That's Spanish. I was named after my mother."

I said "*Pret*-ty" as hard as I could. Mrs. Sennett was pleased and, looking down modestly, flicked a speck of dust off her large bosom. "Were you born in Spain, Mrs. Sennett?" I asked.

"No, not exactly. My father was on a ship and he brought my mother back to England with him. I was born there. Where were you born?"

I told her in Worcester.

"Isn't that funny? The children's uncle is the boxing commissioner there. Mr. Curley, their father's brother."

I nodded my knowledge of Mr. Curley.

"But you'd never think to look at me that I'm half Spanish, would you?"

Indeed, to look at Mrs. Sennett made me think more of eighteenth-century England and its literary figures. Her hair must have been sadly thin, because she always wore, indoors and out, either a hat or a sort of turban, and sometimes she wore both. Today the turban was of black silk with a white design here and there. Because of the rainy weather she also wore a white silk handkerchief around her throat; it gave the appearance of a poetically slovenly stock. Mrs. Sennett's face was large and seemed, like the stereoscope cards, to be at two distances at the same time, as if fragments of a mask had been laid over a background face. The fragments were white, while the face around them was darker and the wrinkles looser. The rims of her eyes were dark; she looked very ill.

"They're Catholic, you know," she told me in her most grating whisper, lest she should offend the ears of the children in the dining room. "I'm not, but their father doesn't mind. He had eleven housekeepers inside two and a half years, after their mother died when Xavier was born, and now I've been with them almost five years. I was the only one who could stand the noise and of course it doesn't bother me any since I can't even hear it. Some Catholics would never trust their children to a Protestant, but their father's a broadminded man. The children worry, though. I get them dressed up and off to Mass every Sunday and they're always tormenting me to come with them. Two Sundays ago, when they came back, Xavier was crying and crying. I kept asking him, 'What's the matter with you, Savey?,' but I couldn't get anything out of him and finally Theresa said, 'He's crying because Francis told him you'd have to go to Hell when you died.' "

Xavier had come to the door and was listening to the story. He was the youngest of the children. First came the twins Francis and John, and after them, Mary and Theresa. They were all fair, pretty children. Mrs. Sennett dressed the boys in overalls and before starting off with them for the cottage every summer she had their heads shaved, so she wouldn't have to bother about haircuts.

Seeing Xavier now, she said, "You bad, noisy children!" He came over and leaned against her chair, and she scrubbed her large hands over his bristly head. Then she told him that she had company, and he went back to the dining room, where Theresa was now reading old funny papers out loud to all of them.

Mrs. Sennett and I continued talking. We told each other that we loved the bay, and we extended our affection to the ocean, too. She said she really didn't think she'd stay with the children another winter. Their father wanted her to, but it was too much for her. She wanted to stay right here in the cottage.

The afternoon was getting along, and I finally left because I knew that at four o'clock Mrs. Sennett's "sit down" was over and she started to get supper. At six o'clock, from my nearby cottage, I saw Theresa coming through the rain with a shawl over her head. She was bringing me a six-inch-square piece of spice-cake, still hot from the oven and kept warm between two soup plates.

A few days later I learned from the twins, who brought over gifts of firewood and blackberries, that their father was coming the next morning, bringing their aunt and her husband and their cousin, also named Theresa, for a visit. Mrs. Sennett had promised to take them all on a picnic at the pond some pleasant day. They were going to cook outdoors and go swimming in fresh water, and they were going to take along cakes of Ivory soap, so that they could have baths at the same time. The men would walk to the pond, and a friend of Mrs. Sennett's in the village had promised to drive the rest of them there in his car. Mrs. Sennett rarely moved beyond her house and yard, and I could imagine what an undertaking the guests and the picnic would be for her.

I saw the guests arrive the next day, walking from the station with their bags, and I saw Mr. Curley, a tall, still young-looking man, greet Mrs. Sennett with a kiss. Then I saw no more of them for two days; I had a guest myself, and we were driving around the Cape most of the time. On the fourth day, Xavier arrived with a note, folded over and over. It was from Mrs. Sennett, written in blue ink, in a large, serene, ornamented hand, on linen-finish paper:

My Dear Neighbor,
    My Friend has disappointed me about the car. Tomorrow is the last day Mr. Curley has and the Children all wanted the Picnic so much. The Men can walk to the Pond but it is too far for the Children. I see your Friend has a car and I hate to ask this but could you possibly drive us to the Pond tomorrow morning? It is an awful load but I hate to have them miss the Picnic. We can all walk back if we just get there.
        Very Sincerely Yours,
        Carmen Sennett

The next morning my guest and I put them all in the car. Everybody seemed to be sitting on Mrs. Sennett. They were in beautifully high spirits. Mrs. Sennett was quite hoarse from asking the aunt if the children were making too much noise and, if she said they were, telling them to stop.

We brought them back that evening—the women and children, at least. Xavier carried an empty gin bottle that Mrs. Sennett said his father had given him. She leaned over to the front seat and shouted in my ear, *"He likes his liquor. But he's a good man."* The children's hair shone with cleanliness and John told me that they had left soapsuds all over the pond.

After the picnic, Mrs. Sennett's presents to me were numberless and I had to return empty dishes by the children several times a day. It was almost time for them to go back to school in South Boston. Mrs. Sennett insisted that she was not going; their father was coming down again to get them and she was just going to stay. He would have to get another housekeeper. She, Mrs. Sennett, was just going to stay right here and look at the bay all winter, and maybe her sister from Somerville would come to visit. She said this over and over to me, loudly, and her turbans and kerchiefs grew more and more distrait.

One evening, Mary came to call on me and we sat on an old table in the back yard to watch the sunset.

"Papa came today," she said, "and we've got to go back day after tomorrow."

"Is Mrs. Sennett going to stay here?"

"She said at supper she was. She said this time she really was, because she'd said that last year and came back, but now she means it."

I said, "Oh dear," scarcely knowing which side I was on.

"It was awful at supper. I cried and cried."

"Did Theresa cry?"

"Oh, we all cried. Papa cried, too. We always do."

"But don't you think Mrs. Sennett needs a rest?"

"Yes, but I think she'll come, though. Papa told her he'd cry every single night at supper if she didn't, and then we all *did*."

The next day I heard from Xavier that Mrs. Sennett was going back with them just to "help settle." She came over the following morning to say goodbye, supported by all five children. She was wearing her travelling hat of black satin and black straw, with sequins. High and sombre, above her ravaged face, it had quite a Spanish-grandee air.

"This isn't really goodbye," she said. "I'll be back as soon as I get these bad, noisy children off my hands."

But the children hung onto her skirt and tugged at her sleeves, shaking their heads frantically, silently saying "*No! No! No!*" to her with their puckered-up mouths.

1948

Gwendolyn

My aunt Mary was eighteen years old and away in "the States," in Boston, training to be a nurse. In the bottom bureau drawer in her room, well wrapped in soft pink tissue paper, lay her best doll. That winter, I had been sick with bronchitis for a long time, and my grandmother finally produced it for me to play with, to my amazement and delight, because I had never even known of its existence before. It was a girl doll, but my grandmother had forgotten her name.

She had a large wardrobe, which my Aunt Mary had made, packed in a toy steamer trunk of green tin embossed with all the proper boards, locks, and nailheads. The clothes were wonderful garments, beautifully sewn, looking old-fashioned even to me. There were long drawers trimmed with tiny lace, and a corset cover, and a corset with little bones. These were exciting, but best of all was the skating costume. There was a red velvet coat, and a turban and muff of some sort of moth-eaten brown fur, and, to make it almost unbearably thrilling, there was a pair of laced white glacé-kid boots, which had scalloped tops and a pair of too small, dull-edged, but very shiny skates loosely attached to their soles by my Aunt Mary with stitches of coarse white thread.

The looseness of the skates didn't bother me. It went very well with the doll's personality, which in turn was well suited to the role of companion to an invalid. She had lain in her drawer so long that the elastic in her joints had become weakened; when you held her up, her head fell gently to one side, and her outstretched hand would rest on yours for a moment and then slip wearily off. She made the family of dolls I usually played with seem rugged and childish: the Campbell Kid doll, with a childlike scar on her forehead where she had fallen against the fender; the two crudely felt-dressed Indians, Hiawatha and Nokomis; and the stocky "baby doll," always holding out his arms to be picked up.

My grandmother was very nice to me when I was sick. During this same illness, she had already given me her button basket to play with, and her scrap bag, and the crazy quilt was put over my bed in the afternoons. The button basket was large and squashed and must have weighed ten pounds, filled with everything from the metal snaps for men's overalls to a set of large cut-steel buttons with deer heads with green glass eyes on them. The scrap bag was interesting because in it I could find pieces of my grandmother's house dresses that she was wearing right then, and pieces of my grandfather's Sunday shirts. But the crazy quilt was the best entertainment. My grand-mother had made it long before, when such quilts had been a fad in the little Nova Scotian village where we lived. She had collected small, irregularly shaped pieces of silk or velvet of all colors and got all her lady and gentleman friends to write their names on them in pencil—their names, and sometimes a date or word or two as well. Then she had gone over the writing in chain stitch with silks of different colors, and then put the whole thing together on maroon flannel, with feather-stitching joining the pieces. I could read well enough to make out the names of people I knew, and then my grandmother would sometimes tell me that that particular piece of silk came from Mrs. So-and-So's "going-away" dress, forty years ago, or that that was from a necktie of one of her brothers, since dead and buried in London, or that that was from India, brought back by another brother, who was a missionary.

When it grew dark—and this, of course, was very early—she would take me out of bed, wrap me in a blanket, and, holding me on her knees, rock me vigorously in the rocking chair. I think she enjoyed this exercise as much as I did, because she would sing me hymns, in her rather affectedly lugubrious voice, which suddenly thinned out to half its ordinary volume on the higher notes. She sang me "There is a green hill far away," "Will there be any stars in my crown?," and "In the sweet bye-and-bye." Then there were more specifically children's hymns, such as:

> Little children, little children,
> Who love their Redeemer,
> Are the jewels, precious jewels,
> Bright gems for his crown. . . .

And then, perhaps because we were Baptists—nice watery ones—all the saints casting down their crowns (in what kind of a tantrum?) "around the glassy sea;" "Shall we gather at the river?;" and her favorite, "Happy day, happy day, when Jesus washed my sins away."

This is preliminary. The story of Gwendolyn did not begin until the follow-ing summer, when I was in my usual summer state of good health and had forgotten about the bronchitis, the realistic cat-and-kitten family in my chest, and the doctor's cold stethoscope.

Gwendolyn Appletree was the youngest child and only daughter of a large, widely spaced family that lived away out, four or five miles, on a lonely farm among the fir trees. She was a year or so older than I—that is, about eight—and her five or six brothers, I suppose in their teens, seemed like grown men to me. But Gwendolyn and I, although we didn't see each other very often, were friends, and to me she stood for everything that the slightly repellent but fascinating words "little girl" should mean. In the first place, her beautiful name. Its dactyl trisyllables could have gone on forever as far as I was concerned. And then, although older, she was as small as I was, and blond, and pink and white, exactly like a blossoming apple tree. And she was "delicate," which, in spite of the bronchitis, I was not. She had diabetes. I had been told this much and had some vague idea that it was because of "too much sugar," and that in itself made Gwendolyn even more attractive, as if she would prove to be solid candy if you bit her, and her pure-tinted complexion would taste exactly like the icing-sugar Easter eggs or birthday-candle holders, held to be inedible, except that I knew better.

I don't know what the treatment for diabetes was at that time—whether, for example, Gwendolyn was given insulin or not, but I rather think not. My grandparents, however, often spoke disapprovingly of the way her parents would not obey the doctor's orders and gave her whatever she wanted to eat, including two pieces of cake for tea, and of how, if they weren't more sensible, they would never keep her. Every once in a while, she would have a mysterious attack of some sort, "convulsions" or a "coma," but a day or two later I would see her driving with her father to the store right next door to our house, looking the same as ever and waving to me. Occasionally, she would be brought to spend the day or afternoon with me while her parents drove down the shore to visit relatives.

These were wonderful occasions. She would arrive carrying a doll or some other toy; her mother would bring a cake or a jar of preserves for my grandmother. Then I would have the opportunity of showing her all my possessions all over again. Quite often, what she brought was a set of small blocks that exactly fitted in a shallow cardboard box. These blocks were squares cut diagonally across, in clear reds, yellows, and blues, and we arranged them snugly together in geometric designs. Then, if we were careful, the whole thing could be lifted up and turned over, revealing a similar brilliant design in different colors on the other side. These designs were completely satisfying in their forthrightness, like the Union Jack. We played quietly together and did not quarrel.

Before her mother and father drove off in their buggy, Gwendolyn was embraced over and over, her face was washed one last time, her stockings were pulled up, her nose was wiped, she was hoisted up and down and swung around and around by her father and given some white pills by her mother. This sometimes went on so long that my grandfather would leave abruptly for the barn and my grandmother would busy herself at the sink and start singing a hymn under her breath, but it was nothing to the scenes of tenderness when they returned a few hours later. Then her parents almost ate her up, alternately, as if she really were made of sugar, as I half suspected. I watched these exciting scenes with envy until Mr. and Mrs. Appletree drove away, with Gwendolyn standing between them in her white dress, her pale-gold hair blowing, still being kissed from either side. Although I received many demonstrations of affection from my grandparents, they were nothing like this. My grandmother was disgusted. "They'll kiss that child to death if they're not careful," she said. "Oh, lallygagging, lallygagging!" said my grandfather, going on about his business.

I remember clearly three episodes of that summer in which Gwendolyn played the role of beautiful heroine—the role that grew and grew until finally it had grown far beyond the slight but convincing talents she had for acting it.

Once, my grandparents and I went to a church picnic. As I said, we were Baptists, but most of the village, including the Appletrees, were Presbyterians. However, on social occasions I think the two sects sometimes joined forces, or else we were broadminded enough to go to a Presbyterian picnic— I'm not sure. Anyway, the three of us, dressed in our second-best, took a huge picnic supper and drove behind Nimble II to the picnic grounds beside the river. It was a beautiful spot; there were large spruce and pine trees right to the edge of the clear brown water and mossy terra-cotta-colored rocks; the ground was slippery with brown pine needles. Pans of beans and biscuits and scalloped potatoes were set out on long tables, and all our varieties of pickles and relishes (chowchows and piccalillis), conserves and preserves, cakes and pies, parkins and hermits—all glistening and gleaming in the late sunshine—and water for tea was being brought to the boil over two fires. My grandmother settled herself on a log to talk to her friends, and I went wading in the river with mine. My cousin Billy was there, and Seth Hill, and the little McNeil twins, but Gwendolyn was missing. Later, I joined my family for supper, or as all Nova Scotians call their suppers, "tea." My grandmother spoke to one of the Appletree boys, filling his plate beside us, and asked him where his father and mother were, and how Gwendolyn was.

"Pretty poorly," he answered, with an imitative elderly-man shake of his head. "Ma thought we'd lost her yesterday morning. I drove down and got the doctor. She's resting better today, though."

We went on drinking our tea and eating in silence, and after a while my grandfather started talking about something else. But just before we finished, when it was beginning to get gray, and a sweet, dank, fresh-water smell had suddenly started to come up off the river, a horse and buggy turned rapidly in to the picnic grounds and pulled up beside us. In it were Mr. and Mrs. Appletree, and Gwendolyn—standing between them, as usual—wearing one of her white dresses, with a little black-and-white checked coat over it. A great fuss was made over them and her, and my grandfather lifted her down and held her on his knee, sitting on one of the rough benches beside the picnic tables. I leaned against him, but Gwendolyn wouldn't speak to me; she just smiled as if very pleased with everything. She looked prettier and more delicate than ever, and her cheeks were bright pink. Her mother made her a cup of weak tea, and I could see my grandmother's look as the sugar went into it. Gwendolyn had wanted to come so badly, her mother said, so they thought they'd bring her just for a little while.

Some time after this, Gwendolyn was brought to visit me again, but this time she was to spend the whole day and night and part of the next day. I was very excited, and consulted with my grandmother endlessly as to how we should pass the time—if I could jump with her in the barn or take her swimming in the river. No, both those sports were too strenuous for Gwendolyn, but we could play at filling bottles with colored water (made from the paints in my paintbox), my favorite game at the moment, and in the afternoon we could have a dolls' tea party.

Everything went off very well. After dinner, Gwendolyn went and lay on the sofa in the parlor, and my grandmother put a shawl over her. I wanted to pretend to play the piano to her, but I was made to stop and go outside by myself. After a while, Gwendolyn joined me in the flower garden and we had the tea party. After that, I showed her how to trap bumblebees in the foxgloves, but that was also put a stop to by my grandmother as too strenuous and dangerous. Our play was not without a touch of rustic corruption, either. I can't remember what happened, if anything, but I do remember being ordered out of the whitewashed privy in the barn after we had locked ourselves in and climbed on the seats and hung out the little window, with its beautiful view of the elm-studded "interval" in back of us. It was just getting dark; my grandmother was very stern with me and said we must never lock ourselves in there, but she was objectionably kind to Gwendolyn, who looked more angelic than ever.

After tea, we sat at the table with the oil lamp hanging over it for a while, playing with the wonderful blocks, and then it was bedtime. Gwendolyn was going to sleep in my bed with me. I was so overwrought with the novelty of this that it took me a long time to get ready for bed, but Gwendolyn was ready in a jiffy and lay on the far side of the bed with her eyes shut, trying to make me think she was asleep, with the lamplight shining on her blond, blond hair. I asked her if she didn't say her prayers before she got into bed and she said no, her mother let her say them in bed, "because I'm going to die."

At least, that was what I thought she said. I couldn't quite believe I had really heard her say it and I certainly couldn't ask her if she had said it. My heart pounding, I brushed my teeth with the icy well water, and spat in the china pot. Then I got down on my knees and said my own prayers, half aloud, completely mechanically, while the pounding went on and on. I couldn't seem to make myself get into my side of the bed, so I went around and picked up Gwendolyn's clothes. She had thrown them on the floor. I put them over the back of a chair—the blue-and-white striped dress, the waist, the long brown stockings. Her drawers had lace around the legs, but they were very dirty. This fact shocked me so deeply that I recovered my voice and started asking her more questions.

"I'm asleep," said Gwendolyn, without opening her eyes.

But after my grandmother had turned out the lamp, Gwendolyn began to talk to me again. We told each other which colors we liked best together, and I remember the feeling of profound originality I experienced when I insisted, although it had just occurred to me, that I had always liked black and brown together best. I saw them floating in little patches of velvet, like the crazy quilt, or smooth little rectangles of enamel, like the paint-sample cards I was always begging for at the general store.

Two days after this visit, Gwendolyn did die. One of her brothers came in to tell my grandmother—and I was there in the kitchen when he told her—with more of the elderly-man headshakes and some sad and ancient phrases. My grandmother wept and wiped her eyes with her apron, answering him with phrases equally sad and ancient. The funeral was to be two days later, but I was not going to be allowed to go.

My grandfather went, but not my grandmother. I wasn't even supposed to know what was taking place, but since the Presbyterian church was right across the village green from our house, and I could hear the buggies driving up over the gravel, and then the bell beginning to ring, I knew quite well, and my heart began to pound again, apparently as loudly as the bell was ringing. I was sent out to play in the yard at the far side of the house, away from the church. But through one of the kitchen windows—the kitchen was an ell that had windows on both sides—I could see my curious grandmother drawing up her rocking chair, as she did every Sunday morning, just behind a window on the other side of the ell, to watch the Presbyterians going to church. This was the unacknowledged practice of the Baptists who lived within sight of the church, and later, when they met at their own afternoon service, they would innocently say to each other things like "They had a good turnout this morning" and "Is Mrs. Peppard still laid up? I missed her this morning."

But today it was quite different, and when I peeked in at my grandmother at one side of the ell, she was crying and crying between her own peeks at the mourners out the other side. She had a handkerchief already very wet, and was rocking gently.

It was too much for me. I sneaked back into the house by the side door and into the shut-up parlor, where I could look across at the church, too. There were long lace curtains at the window and the foxgloves and bees were just outside, but I had a perfectly clear, although lace-patterned, view of everything. The church was quite large—a Gothic structure made of white clapboards, with non-flying buttresses, and a tall wooden steeple— and I was as familiar with it as I was with my grandmother. I used to play hide-and-seek among the buttresses with my friends. The buggy sheds, now all filled, were at the back, and around the large grass plot were white wooden pillars with double chains slung slackly between them, on which my cousin Billy, who lived right next door to the church, and I liked to clamber and swing.

At last, everyone seemed to have gone inside, and an inner door shut. No, two men in black stood talking together in the open outside doorway. The bell suddenly stopped ringing and the two men vanished, and I was afraid of being in the parlor alone, but couldn't leave now. Hours seemed to go by. There was some singing, but I didn't recognize the hymns, either because I was too nervous or because, as they sometimes did, the Presbyterians sang hymns unfamiliar to me.

I had seen many funerals like this before, of course, and I loved to go with my grandfather when he went to the graveyard with a scythe and a sickle to cut the grass on our family's graves. The graveyard belonging to the village was surely one of the prettiest in the world. It was on the bank of the river, two miles below us, but where the bank was high. It lay small and green and white, with its firs and cedars and gravestones balancing against the dreaming lavender-red Bay of Fundy. The headstones were mostly rather thin, coarse white marble slabs, frequently leaning slightly, but there was a scattering of small urns and obelisks and broken columns. A few plots were lightly chained in, like the Presbyterian church, or fenced in with wood or iron, like little gardens, and wild rosebushes grew in the grass. Blueberries grew there, too, but I didn't eat them, because I felt I "never knew," as people said, but once when I went there, my grandmother had given me a teacup without a handle and requested me to bring her back some teaberries, which "grew good" on the graves, and I had.

And so I used to play while my grandfather, wearing a straw hat, scythed away, and talked to me haphazardly about the people lying there. I was, of course, particularly interested in the children's graves, their names, what ages they had died at—whether they were older than I or younger. The favorite memorial for small children was a low rectangle of the same coarse white marble as the larger stones, but with a little lamb recumbent on top. I adored these lambs, and counted them and caressed them and sat on them. Some were almost covered by dry, bright-gold lichen, some with green and gold and gray mixed together, some were almost lost among the long grass and roses and blueberries and teaberries.

But now, suddenly, as I watched through the window, something happened at the church across the way. Something that could not possibly have happened, so that I must, in reality, have seen something like it and imagined the rest; or my concentration on the one thing was so intense that I could see nothing else.

The two men in black appeared again, carrying Gwendolyn's small white coffin between them. Then—this was the impossibility—they put it down just outside the church door, one end on the grass and the other lifted up a little, to lean at a slight angle against the wall. Then they disappeared inside again. For a minute, I stared straight through my lace curtain at Gwendolyn's coffin, with Gwendolyn shut invisibly inside it forever, there, completely alone on the grass by the church door.

Then I ran howling to the back door, out among the startled white hens, with my grandmother, still weeping, after me.

If I care to, I can bring back the exact sensation of that moment today, but then, it is also one of those that from time to time are terrifyingly thrust upon us. I was familiar with it and recognized it; I had already experienced it once, shortly before the bronchitis attack of the previous winter. One evening, we were all sitting around the table with the lamp hanging above it; my grandfather was dozing in the Morris chair, my grandmother was crocheting, and my Aunt Mary, who had not yet gone away to Boston, was reading *Maclean's Magazine*. I was drawing pictures when suddenly I remembered something, a present that had been given to me months before and that I had forgotten all about. It was a strawberry basket half filled with new marbles—clay ones, in the usual mottled shades of red, brown, purple, and green. However, in among them were several of a sort I had never seen before: fine, unglazed, cream-colored clay, with purple and pink lines around them. One or two of the larger ones of this sort even had little sprigs of flowers on them. But the most beautiful of all, I thought, was a really big one, probably an inch and a half in diameter, of a roughly shiny glazed pink, like crockery. It moved me almost to tears to look at it; it "went right through me."

Anyway, I started thinking about these marbles—wondering where they had been all this time, where I had put them, if they had got lost— until at last it became unbearable and I had to go and find them. I went out to the kitchen in the dark and groped around on the floor of a cupboard where I kept some of my belongings. I felt the edges of riffled old books and sharp mechanical toys, and then, at the back, I did feel the strawberry basket. I dragged it out and carried it into the sitting room.

My relatives paid no attention. I stared into the basket and took out a few of the marbles. But what could have happened? They were covered with dirt and dust, nails were lying mixed in with them, bits of string, cobwebs, old horse chestnuts blue with mildew, their polish gone. The big pink marble was there, but I hardly recognized it, all covered with dirt. (Later, when my grandmother washed it off, it was as good as new, of course.) The broad lamp flame started to blur; my aunt's fair hair started to blur; I put my head down on top of the marbles and cried aloud. My grandfather woke up with a jerk and said, "Heavens, what ails the child now?" Everyone tried to comfort me—for what, they had no idea.

A month or so after the funeral—it was still summer—my grandparents went away for the day to visit Cousin Sophy, "over the mountain." I was sup- posed to stay with another aunt, the mother of my cousin Billy, and to play with him while they were gone. But we soon left his yard and wandered back to mine, which was larger and more interesting, and where we felt the additional charm of being all alone and unwatched. Various diversions, quarrels, and reconciliations made up the long, sunny afternoon. We sucked water from jelly glasses through chive straws until we reeked of them, and fought for the possession of insects in matchboxes. To tease me, Billy deliberately stepped on one of the boxes and crushed its inhabitant flat. When we had made up after this violence, we sat and talked for a while, desultorily, about death in general, and going to Heaven, but we were growing a little bored and reckless, and finally I did something really bad: I went in the house and upstairs to my Aunt Mary's bedroom and brought down the tissue-paper-wrapped, retired doll. Billy had never seen her before and was as impressed with her as I had been.

We handled her carefully. We took off her hat and shoes and stockings, and examined every stitch of her underclothes. Then we played vaguely at "operating" on her stomach, but we were rather too much in awe of her for that to be a success. Then we had the idea of adorning her with flowers. There was a clump of Johnny-jump-ups that I thought belonged to me; we picked them and made a wreath for the nameless doll. We laid her out in the garden path and outlined her body with Johnny-jump-ups and babies'-breath and put a pink cosmos in one limp hand. She looked perfectly beautiful. The game was more exciting than "operation." I don't know which one of us said it first, but one of us did, with wild joy—that it was Gwendolyn's funeral, and that the doll's real name, all this time, was Gwendolyn.

But then my grandparents drove into the yard and found us, and my grandmother was furious that I had dared to touch Aunt Mary's doll. Billy was sent straight home and I don't remember now what awful thing happened to me.

1953

In the Village

A scream, the echo of a scream, hangs over that Nova Scotian village. No one hears it; it hangs there forever, a slight stain in those pure blue skies, skies that travellers compare to those of Switzerland, too dark, too blue, so that they seem to keep on darkening a little more around the horizon—or is it around the rims of the eyes?—the color of the cloud of bloom on the elm trees, the violet on the fields of oats; something darkening over the woods and waters as well as the sky. The scream hangs like that, unheard, in memory—in the past, in the present, and those years between. It was not even loud to begin with, perhaps. It just came there to live, forever—not loud, just alive forever. Its pitch would be the pitch of my village. Flick the lightning rod on top of the church steeple with your fingernail and you will hear it.

She stood in the large front bedroom with sloping walls on either side, papered in wide white and dim-gold stripes. Later, it was she who gave the scream.

The village dressmaker was fitting a new dress. It was her first in almost two years and she had decided to come out of black, so the dress was purple. She was very thin. She wasn't at all sure whether she was going to like the dress or not and she kept lifting the folds of the skirt, still unpinned and dragging on the floor around her, in her thin white hands, and looking down at the cloth.

"Is it a good shade for me? Is it too bright? I don't know. I haven't worn colors for so long now. . . . How long? Should it be black? Do you think I should keep on wearing black?"

Drummers sometimes came around selling gilded red or green books, unlovely books, filled with bright new illustrations of the Bible stories. The people in the pictures wore clothes like the purple dress, or like the way it looked then.

It was a hot summer afternoon. Her mother and her two sisters were there. The older sister had brought her home, from Boston, not long before, and was staying on, to help. Because in Boston she had not got any better, in months and months—or had it been a year? In spite of the doctors, in spite of the frightening expenses, she had not got any better.

First, she had come home, with her child. Then she had gone away again, alone, and left the child. Then she had come home. Then she had gone away again, with her sister; and now she was home again.

Unaccustomed to having her back, the child stood now in the doorway, watching. The dressmaker was crawling around and around on her knees eating pins as Nebuchadnezzar had crawled eating grass. The wallpaper glinted and the elm trees outside hung heavy and green, and the straw matting smelled like the ghost of hay.

Clang.

Clang.

Oh, beautiful sounds, from the blacksmith's shop at the end of the garden! Its gray roof, with patches of moss, could be seen above the lilac bushes. Nate was there—Nate, wearing a long black leather apron over his trousers and bare chest, sweating hard, a black leather cap on top of dry, thick, black-and-gray curls, a black sooty face; iron filings, whiskers, and gold teeth, all together, and a smell of red-hot metal and horses' hoofs.

Clang.

The pure note: pure and angelic.

The dress was all wrong. She screamed.

The child vanishes.

Later they sit, the mother and the three sisters, in the shade on the back porch, sipping sour, diluted ruby: raspberry vinegar. The dressmaker refuses to join them and leaves, holding the dress to her heart. The child is visiting the blacksmith.

In the blacksmith's shop things hang up in the shadows and shadows hang up in the things, and there are black and glistening piles of dust in each corner. A tub of night-black water stands by the forge. The horseshoes sail through the dark like bloody little moons and follow each other like bloody little moons to drown in the black water, hissing, protesting.

Outside, along the matted eaves, painstakingly, sweetly, wasps go over and over a honeysuckle vine.

Inside, the bellows creak. Nate does wonders with both hands; with one hand. The attendant horse stamps his foot and nods his head as if agreeing to a peace treaty.

Nod.

And nod.

A Newfoundland dog looks up at him and they almost touch noses, but not quite, because at the last moment the horse decides against it and turns away.

Outside in the grass lie scattered big, pale granite discs, like millstones, for making wheel rims on. This afternoon they are too hot to touch.

Now it is settling down, the scream.

Now the dressmaker is at home, basting, but in tears. It is the most beautiful material she has worked on in years. It has been sent to the woman from Boston, a present from her mother-in-law, and heaven knows how much it cost.

Before my older aunt had brought her back, I had watched my grand-mother and younger aunt unpacking her clothes, her "things." In trunks and barrels and boxes they had finally come, from Boston, where she and I had once lived. So many things in the village came from Boston, and even I had once come from there. But I remembered only being here, with my grandmother.

The clothes were black, or white, or black-and-white.

"Here's a mourning hat," says my grandmother, holding up something large, sheer, and black, with large black roses on it; at least I guess they are roses, even if black.

"There's that mourning coat she got the first winter," says my aunt.

But always I think they are saying "morning." Why, in the morning, did one put on black? How early in the morning did one begin? Before the sun came up?

"Oh, here are some house dresses!"

They are nicer. Clean and starched, stiffly folded. One with black polka dots. One of fine black-and-white stripes with black grosgrain bows. A third with a black velvet bow and on the bow a pin of pearls in a little wreath.

"Look. She forgot to take it off."

A white hat. A white embroidered parasol. Black shoes with buckles glistening like the dust in the blacksmith's shop. A silver mesh bag. A silver calling-card case on a little chain. Another bag of silver mesh, gathered to a tight, round neck of strips of silver that will open out, like the hatrack in the front hall. A silver-framed photograph, quickly turned over. Handkerchiefs with narrow black hems—"morning handkerchiefs." In bright sunlight, over breakfast tables, they flutter.

A bottle of perfume has leaked and made awful brown stains.

Oh, marvellous scent, from somewhere else! It doesn't smell like that here; but there, somewhere, it does, still.

A big bundle of postcards. The curdled elastic around them breaks. I gather them together on the floor.

Some people wrote with pale-blue ink, and some with brown, and some with black, but mostly blue. The stamps have been torn off many of them.

Some are plain, or photographs, but some have lines of metallic crystals on them—how beautiful!—silver, gold, red, and green, or all four mixed together, crumbling off, sticking in the lines on my palms. All the cards like this I spread on the floor to study. The crystals outline the buildings on the cards in a way buildings never are outlined but should be—if there were a way of making the crystals stick. But probably not; they would fall to the ground, never to be seen again. Some cards, instead of lines around the buildings, have words written in their skies with the same stuff, crumbling, dazzling and crumbling, raining down a little on little people who sometimes stand about below: pictures of Pentecost? What are the messages? I cannot tell, but they are falling on those specks of hands, on the hats, on the toes of their shoes, in their paths—wherever it is they are.

Postcards come from another world, the world of the grandparents who send things, the world of sad brown perfume, and morning. (The gray postcards of the village for sale in the village store are so unilluminating that they scarcely count. After all, one steps outside and immediately sees the same thing: the village, where we live, full size, and in color.)

Two barrels of china. White with a gold band. Broken bits. A thick white teacup with a small red-and-blue butterfly on it, painfully desirable. A teacup with little pale-blue windows in it.

"See the grains of rice?" says my grandmother, showing me the cup against the light.

Could you poke the grains out? No, it seems they aren't really there any more. They were put there just for a while and then they left something or other behind. What odd things people do with grains of rice, so innocent and small! My aunt says that she has heard they write the Lord's Prayer on them. And make them make those little pale-blue lights.

More broken china. My grandmother says it breaks her heart. "Why couldn't they have got it packed better? Heaven knows what it cost."

"Where'll we put it all? The china closet isn't nearly big enough."

"It'll just have to stay in the barrels."

"Mother, you might as well use it."

"*No,*" says my grandmother.

"Where's the silver, Mother?"

"In the vault in Boston."

Vault. Awful word. I run the tip of my finger over the rough, jewelled lines on the postcards, over and over. They hold things up to each other and exclaim, and talk, and exclaim, over and over.

"There's that cake basket."

"Mrs. Miles . . ."

"Mrs. Miles' spongecake . . ."

"She was very fond of her."

Another photograph—"Oh, that *Negro* girl! That friend."

"She went to be a medical missionary. She had a letter from her, last winter. From Africa."

"They were great friends."

They show me the picture. She, too, is black-and-white, with glasses on a chain. A morning friend.

And the smell, the wonderful smell of the dark-brown stains. Is it roses? A tablecloth.

"She did beautiful work," says my grandmother.

"But look—it isn't finished."

Two pale, smooth wooden hoops are pressed together in the linen. There is a case of little ivory embroidery tools.

I abscond with a little ivory stick with a sharp point. To keep it forever I bury it under the bleeding heart by the crab-apple tree, but it is never found again.

Nate sings and pumps the bellows with one hand. I try to help, but he really does it all, from behind me, and laughs when the coals blow red and wild.

"Make me a ring! Make me a ring, Nate!"

Instantly it is made; it is mine.

It is too big and still hot, and blue and shiny. The horseshoe nail has a flat oblong head, pressing hot against my knuckle.

Two men stand watching, chewing or spitting tobacco, matches, horse-shoe nails—anything, apparently, but with such presence; they are perfectly at home. The horse is the real guest, however. His harness hangs loose like a man's suspenders; they say pleasant things to him; one of his legs is doubled up in an improbable, affectedly polite way, and the bottom of his hoof is laid bare, but he doesn't seem to mind. Manure piles up behind him, suddenly, neatly. He, too, is very much at home. He is enormous. His rump is like a brown, glossy globe of the whole brown world. His ears are secret entrances to the underworld. His nose is supposed to feel like velvet and does, with ink spots under milk all over its pink. Clear bright-green bits of stiffened froth, like glass, are stuck around his mouth. He wears medals on his chest, too, and one on his forehead, and simpler decorations—red and blue celluloid rings overlapping each other on leather straps. On each temple is a clear glass bulge, like an eyeball, but in them are the heads of two other little horses (his dreams?), brightly colored, real and raised, un-touchable, alas, against backgrounds of silver blue. His trophies hang around him, and the cloud of his odor is a chariot in itself.

At the end, all four feet are brushed with tar, and shine, and he expresses his satisfaction, rolling it from his nostrils like noisy smoke, as he backs into the shafts of his wagon.

The purple dress is to be fitted again this afternoon but I take a note to Miss Gurley to say the fitting will have to be postponed. Miss Gurley seems upset.

"Oh dear. And how is—" And she breaks off.

Her house is littered with scraps of cloth and tissue-paper patterns, yellow, pinked, with holes in the shapes of A, B, C, and D in them, and numbers; and threads everywhere like a fine vegetation. She has a bosom full of needles with threads ready to pull out and make nests with. She sleeps in her thimble. A gray kitten once lay on the treadle of her sewing machine, where she rocked it as she sewed, like a baby in a cradle, but it got hanged on the belt. Or did she make that up? But another gray-and-white one lies now by the arm of the machine, in imminent danger of being sewn into a turban. There is a table covered with laces and braids, embroidery silks, and cards of buttons of all colors—big ones for winter coats, small pearls, little glass ones delicious to suck.

She has made the very dress I have on, "for twenty-five cents." My grandmother said my other grandmother would certainly be surprised at that.

The purple stuff lies on a table; long white threads hang all about it. Oh, look away before it moves by itself, or makes a sound; before it echoes, echoes, what it has heard!

Mysteriously enough, poor Miss Gurley—I know she is poor—gives me a five-cent piece. She leans over and drops it in the pocket of the red-and-white dress that she has made herself. It is very tiny, very shiny. King George's beard is like a little silver flame. Because they look like herring- or maybe salmon-scales, five-cent pieces are called "fish-scales." One heard of people's rings being found inside fish, or their long-lost jackknives. What if one could scrape a salmon and find a little picture of King George on every scale?

I put my five-cent piece in my mouth for greater safety on the way home, and swallow it. Months later, as far as I know, it is still in me, transmuting all its precious metal into my growing teeth and hair.

Back home, I am not allowed to go upstairs. I hear my aunts running back and forth and something like a tin washbasin falls bump in the carpeted upstairs hall.

My grandmother is sitting in the kitchen stirring potato mash for tomorrow's bread and crying into it. She gives me a spoonful and it tastes wonderful but wrong. In it I think I taste my grandmother's tears; then I kiss her and taste them on her cheek.

She says it is time for her to get fixed up, and I say I want to help her brush her hair. So I do, standing swaying on the lower rung of the back of her rocking chair.

The rocking chair has been painted and repainted so many times that it is as smooth as cream—blue, white, and gray all showing through. My grandmother's hair is silver and in it she keeps a great many celluloid combs, at the back and sides, streaked gray and silver to match. The one at the back has longer teeth than the others and a row of sunken silver dots across the top, beneath a row of little balls. I pretend to play a tune on it; then I pretend to play a tune on each of the others before we stick them in, so my grandmother's hair is full of music. She laughs. I am so pleased with myself that I do not feel obliged to mention the five-cent piece. I drink a rusty, icy drink out of the biggest dipper; still, nothing much happens.

We are waiting for a scream. But it is not screamed again, and the red sun sets in silence.

Every morning I take the cow to the pasture we rent from Mr. Chisolm. She, Nelly, could probably go by herself just as well, but I like marching through the village with a big stick, directing her.

This morning it is brilliant and cool. My grandmother and I are alone again in the kitchen. We are talking. She says it is cool enough to keep the oven going, to bake the bread, to roast a leg of lamb.

"Will you remember to go down to the brook? Take Nelly around by the brook and pick me a big bunch of mint. I thought I'd make some mint sauce."

"For the leg of lamb?"

"You finish your porridge."

"I think I've had enough now . . ."

"Hurry up and finish that porridge."

There is talking on the stairs.

"No, now wait," my grandmother says to me. "Wait a minute."

My two aunts come into the kitchen. She is with them, wearing the white cotton dress with black polka dots and the flat black velvet bow at the neck. She comes and feeds me the rest of the porridge herself, smiling at me.

"Stand up now and let's see how tall you are," she tells me.

"Almost to your elbow," they say. "See how much she's grown."

"Almost."

"It's her hair."

Hands are on my head, pushing me down; I slide out from under them.

Nelly is waiting for me in the yard, holding her nose just under in the watering trough. My stick waits against the door frame, clad in bark.

Nelly looks up at me, drooling glass strings. She starts off around the corner of the house without a flicker of expression.

Switch. Switch. How annoying she is!

But she is a Jersey and we think she is very pretty. "From in front," my aunts sometimes add.

She stops to snatch at the long, untrimmed grass around the gatepost.

"Nelly!"

Whack! I hit her hipbone.

On she goes without even looking around. Flop, flop, down over the dirt sidewalk into the road, across the village green in front of the Presbyterian church. The grass is gray with dew; the church is dazzling. It is high-shouldered and secretive; it leans backwards a little.

Ahead, the road is lined with dark, thin old elms; grass grows long and blue in the ditches. Behind the elms the meadows run along, peacefully, greenly.

We pass Mrs. Peppard's house. We pass Mrs. McNeil's house. We pass Mrs. Geddes's house. We pass Hills' store.

The store is high, and a faded gray-blue, with tall windows, built on a long, high stoop of gray-blue cement with an iron hitching rail along it. Today, in one window there are big cardboard easels, shaped like houses—complete houses and houses with the roofs lifted off to show glimpses of the rooms inside, all in different colors—with cans of paint in pyramids in the middle. But they are an old story. In the other window is something new: shoes, single shoes, summer shoes, each sitting on top of its own box with its mate beneath it, inside, in the dark. Surprisingly, some of them appear to be exactly the colors and texture of pink and blue blackboard chalks, but I can't stop to examine them now. In one door, great overalls hang high in the air on hangers. Miss Ruth Hill looks out the other door and waves. We pass Mrs. Captain Mahon's house.

Nelly tenses and starts walking faster, making over to the right. Every morning and evening we go through this. We are approaching Miss Spencer's house. Miss Spencer is the milliner the way Miss Gurley is the dressmaker. She has a very small white house with the doorstep right on the sidewalk. One front window has lace curtains with a pale-yellow window shade pulled all the way down, inside them; the other one has a shelf across it on which are displayed four summer hats. Out of the corner of my eye I can see that there is a yellow chip straw with little wads of flamingo-colored feathers around the crown, but again there is no time to examine anything.

On each side of Miss Spencer's door is a large old lilac bush. Every time we go by Nelly determines to brush off all her flies on these bushes—brush them off forever, in one fell swoop. Then Miss Spencer is apt to come to the door and stand there, shaking with anger, between the two bushes still shaking from Nelly's careening passage, and yell at me, sometimes waving a hat in my direction as well.

Nelly leaning to the right, breaks into a cow trot. I run up with my stick. *Whack!*

"Nelly!"

Whack!

Just this once she gives in and we rush safely by.

Then begins a long, pleasant stretch beneath the elms. The Presbyterian manse has a black iron fence with openwork four-sided pillars, like tall, thin bird cages, bird cages for storks. Dr. Gillespie, the minister, appears just as we come along, and rides slowly toward us on his bicycle.

"Good day." He even tips his hat.

"Good day."

He wears the most interesting hat in the village: a man's regular stiff straw sailor, only it is black. Is there a possibility that he paints it at home, with something like stove polish? Because once I had seen one of my aunts painting a straw-colored hat navy blue.

Nelly, oblivious, makes cow flops. Smack. Smack. Smack. Smack.

It is fascinating. I cannot take my eyes off her. Then I step around them: fine dark-green and lacy and watery at the edges.

We pass the McLeans', whom I know very well. Mr. McLean is just coming out of his new barn with the tin hip roof and with him is Jock, their old shepherd dog, long-haired, black and white and yellow. He runs up barking deep, cracked, soft barks in the quiet morning. I hesitate.

Mr. McLean bellows, "Jock! You! Come back here! Are you trying to frighten her?"

To me he says, "He's twice as old as you are."

Finally I pat the big round warm head.

We talk a little. I ask the exact number of Jock's years but Mr. McLean has forgotten.

"He hasn't hardly a tooth in his head and he's got rheumatism. I hope we'll get him through next winter. He still wants to go to the woods with me and it's hard for him in the snow. We'll be lost without him."

Mr. McLean speaks to me behind one hand, not to hurt Jock's feelings: "*Deaf as a post.*"

Like anybody deaf, Jock puts his head to one side.

"He used to be the best dog at finding cows for miles around. People used to come from away down the shore to borrow him to find their cows

for them. And he'd always find them. The first year we had to leave him
behind when we went up to the mountain to get the cows I thought it
would kill him. Well, when his teeth started going he couldn't do much with
the cows any more. Effie used to say, 'I don't know how we'd run the farm
without him.'"

Loaded down with too much black and yellow and white fur, Jock smiles,
showing how few teeth he has. He has yellow caterpillars for eyebrows.

Nelly has gone on ahead. She is almost up the hill to Chisolm's when I
catch up with her. We turn in to their steep, long drive, through a steep, bare
yard crowded with unhappy apple trees. From the top, though, from the
Chisolms' back yard, one always stops to look at the view.

There are the tops of all the elm trees in the village and there, beyond
them, the long green marshes, so fresh, so salt. Then the Minas Basin,
with the tide halfway in or out, the wet red mud glazed with sky blue until it
meets the creeping lavender-red water. In the middle of the view, like one
hand of a clock pointing straight up, is the steeple of the Presbyterian church.
We are in the "Maritimes" but all that means is that we live by the sea.

Mrs. Chisolm's pale frantic face is watching me out the kitchen window
as she washes the breakfast dishes. We wave, but I hurry by because she
may come out and ask questions. But her questions are not as bad perhaps
as those of her husband, Mr. Chisolm, who wears a beard. One evening he
had met me in the pasture and asked me how my soul was. Then he held
me firmly by both hands while he said a prayer, with his head bowed, Nelly
right beside us chewing her cud all the time. I had felt a soul, heavy in my
chest, all the way home.

I let Nelly through the set of bars to the pasture where the brook is, to
get the mint. We both take drinks and I pick a big bunch of mint, eating a
little, scratchy and powerful. Nelly looks over her shoulder and comes back
to try it, thinking, as cows do, it might be something especially for her. Her
face is close to mine and I hold her by one horn to admire her eyes again.
Her nose is blue and as shiny as something in the rain. At such close quarters my feelings for her are mixed. She gives my bare arm a lick, scratchy
and powerful, too, almost upsetting me into the brook; then she goes off
to join a black-and-white friend she has here, mooing to her to wait until
she catches up.

For a while I entertain the idea of not going home today at all, of staying safely here in the pasture all day, playing in the brook and climbing on
the squishy, moss-covered hummocks in the swampy part. But an immense,
sibilant, glistening loneliness suddenly faces me, and the cows are moving
off to the shade of the fir trees, their bells chiming softly, individually.

On the way home there are the four hats in Miss Spencer's window to
study, and the summer shoes in Hills'. There is the same shoe in white, in

black patent leather, and in the chalky, sugary, unearthly pinks and blues. It has straps that button around the ankle and above, four of them, about an inch wide and an inch apart, reaching away up.

In those unlovely gilded red and green books, filled with illustrations of the Bible stories, the Roman centurions wear them, too, or something very like them.

Surely they are my size. Surely, this summer, pink or blue, my grandmother will buy me a pair!

Miss Ruth Hill gives me a Moirs' chocolate out of the glass case. She talks to me: "How is she? We've always been friends. We played together from the time we were babies. We sat together in school. Right from primer class on. After she went away, she always wrote to me—even after she got sick the first time."

Then she tells a funny story about when they were little.

That afternoon, Miss Gurley comes and we go upstairs to watch the purple dress being fitted again. My grandmother holds me against her knees. My younger aunt is helping Miss Gurley, handing her the scissors when she asks. Miss Gurley is cheerful and talkative today.

The dress is smaller now; there are narrow, even folds down the skirt; the sleeves fit tightly, with little wrinkles over the thin white hands. Everyone is very pleased with it; everyone talks and laughs.

"There. You see? It's so becoming."

"I've never seen you in anything more becoming."

"And it's so nice to see you in color for a change."

And the purple is real, like a flower against the gold-and-white wallpaper.

On the bureau is a present that has just come, from an uncle in Boston whom I do not remember. It is a gleaming little bundle of flat, triangular satin pillows—sachets, tied together with a white satin ribbon, with an imitation rosebud on top of the bow. Each is a different faint color; if you take them apart, each has a different faint scent. But tied together the way they came, they make one confused, powdery one.

The mirror has been lifted off the bureau and put on the floor against the wall.

She walks slowly up and down and looks at the skirt in it.

"I think that's about right," says Miss Gurley, down on her knees and looking into the mirror, too, but as if the skirt were miles and miles away.

But, twitching the purple skirt with her thin white hands, she says desperately, "I don't know what they're wearing any more. I have no *idea!*" It turns to a sort of wail.

"Now, now," soothes Miss Gurley. "I do think that's about right. Don't you?" She appeals to my grandmother and me.

Light, musical, constant sounds are coming from Nate's shop. It sounds as though he were making a wheel rim.

She sees me in the mirror and turns on me: "Stop sucking your thumb!"

Then in a moment she turns to me again and demands, "Do you know what I want?"

"No."

"I want some humbugs. I'm dying for some humbugs. I don't think I've had any humbugs for years and years and years. If I give you some pennies, will you go to Mealy's and buy me a bag?"

To be sent on an errand! Everything is all right.

Humbugs are a kind of candy, although not a kind I am particularly fond of. They are brown, like brook water, but hard, and shaped like little twisted pillows. They last a long time, but lack the spit-producing brilliance of cherry or strawberry.

Mealy runs a little shop where she sells candy and bananas and oranges and all kinds of things she crochets. At Christmas, she sells toys, but only at Christmas. Her real name is Amelia. She also takes care of the telephone switchboard for the village, in her dining room.

Somebody finds a black pocketbook in the bureau. She counts out five big pennies into my hand, in a column, then one more.

"That one's for you. So you won't eat up all my humbugs on the way home."

Further instructions:

"Don't run all the way."

"Don't stop on the bridge."

I do run, by Nate's shop, glimpsing him inside, pumping away with one hand. We wave. The beautiful, big Newfoundland dog is there again and comes out, bounding along with me a ways.

I do not stop on the bridge but slow down long enough to find out the years on the pennies. King George is much bigger than on a five-cent piece, brown as an Indian in copper, but he wears the same clothes; on a penny, one can make out the little ermine trimmings on his coat.

Mealy has a bell that rings when you go in so that she'll hear you if she's at the switchboard. The shop is a step down, dark, with a counter along one side. The ceiling is low and the floor has settled well over to the counter side. Mealy is broad and fat and it looks as though she and the counter and the showcase, stuffed dimly with things every which way, were settling down together out of sight.

Five pennies buys a great many humbugs. I must not take too long to decide what I want for myself. I must get back quickly, quickly, while Miss

Gurley is there and everyone is upstairs and the dress is still on. Without taking time to think, quickly I point at the brightest thing. It is a ball, glistening solidly with crystals of pink and yellow sugar, hung, impractically, on an elastic, like a real elastic ball. I know I don't even care for the inside of it, which is soft, but I wind most of the elastic around my arm, to keep the ball off the ground, at least, and start hopefully back.

But one night, in the middle of the night, there is a fire. The church bell wakes me up. It is in the room with me; red flames are burning the wallpaper beside the bed. I suppose I shriek.

The door opens. My younger aunt comes in. There is a lamp lit in the hall and everyone is talking at once.

"Don't cry!" my aunt almost shouts at me. "It's just a fire. Way up the road. It isn't going to hurt you. Don't *cry!*"

"Will! Will!" My grandmother is calling my grandfather. "Do you have to go?"

"No, don't go, Dad!"

"It looks like McLean's place." My grandfather sounds muffled.

"Oh, not their new barn!" My grandmother.

"You can't tell from here." He must have his head out the window.

"*She's* calling for you, Mother." My older aunt. "I'll go."

"No. *I'll* go." My younger aunt.

"Light that other lamp, girl."

My older aunt comes to my door. "It's way off. It's nowhere near us. The men will take care of it. Now you go to sleep." But she leaves my door open.

"Leave her door open," calls my grandmother just then. "Oh, why do they have to ring the bell like that? It's enough to terrify anybody. Will, be *careful.*"

Sitting up in bed, I see my grandfather starting down the stairs, tucking his nightshirt into his trousers as he goes.

"Don't make so much noise!" My older aunt and my grandmother seem to be quarreling.

"Noise! I can't hear myself think, with that bell!"

"I bet Spurgeon's ringing it!" They both laugh.

"It must have been heat lightning," says my grandmother, now apparently in her bedroom, as if it were all over.

"*She's* all right, Mother." My younger aunt comes back. "I don't think she's scared. You can't see the glare so much on that side of the house."

Then my younger aunt comes into my room and gets in bed with me. She says to go to sleep, it's way up the road. The men have to go; my grandfather has gone. It's probably somebody's barn full of hay, from heat lightning. It's been such a hot summer there's been a lot of it. The church bell stops and her voice is suddenly loud in my ear over my shoulder. The last echo of the bell lasts for a long time.

Wagons rattle by.

"Now they're going down to the river to fill the barrels," my aunt is murmuring against my back.

The red flame dies down on the wall, then flares again.

Wagons rattle by in the dark. Men are swearing at the horses.

"Now they're coming back with the water. Go to sleep."

More wagons; men's voices. I suppose I go to sleep.

I wake up and it is the same night, the night of the fire. My aunt is getting out of bed, hurrying away. It is still dark and silent now, after the fire. No, not silent; my grandmother is crying somewhere, not in her room. It is getting gray. I hear one wagon, rumbling far off, perhaps crossing the bridge.

But now I am caught in a skein of voices, my aunts' and my grandmother's, saying the same things over and over, sometimes loudly, sometimes in whispers:

"Hurry. For heaven's sake, *shut the door!*"

"Sh!"

"Oh, we can't go on like this, we . . ."

"It's too dangerous. Remember that . . ."

"Sh! Don't let her . . ."

A door slams.

A door opens. The voices begin again.

I am struggling to free myself.

Wait. Wait. No one is going to scream.

Slowly, slowly it gets daylight. A different red reddens the wallpaper. Now the house is silent. I get up and dress by myself and go downstairs. My grandfather is in the kitchen alone, drinking his tea. He has made the oatmeal himself, too. He gives me some and tells me about the fire very cheerfully.

It had not been the McLeans' new barn after all, but someone else's barn, off the road. All the hay was lost but they had managed somehow to save part of the barn.

But neither of us is really listening to what he is saying; we are listening for sounds from upstairs. But everything is quiet.

On the way home from taking Nelly to the pasture I go to see where the barn was. There are people still standing around, some of them the men who got up in the night to go to the river. Everyone seems quite cheerful there, too, but the smell of burned hay is awful, sickening.

•

Now the front bedroom is empty. My older aunt has gone back to Boston and my other aunt is making plans to go there after a while, too.

There has been a new pig. He was very cute to begin with, and skidded across the kitchen linoleum while everyone laughed. He grew and grew. Perhaps it is all the same summer, because it is unusually hot and something unusual for a pig happens to him; he gets sunburned. He really gets sunburned, bright pink, but the strangest thing of all, the curled-up end of his tail gets so sunburned it is brown and scorched. My grandmother trims it with the scissors and it doesn't hurt him.

Sometime later this pig is butchered. My grandmother, my aunt, and I shut ourselves in the parlor. My aunt plays a piece on the piano called "Out in the Fields." She plays it and plays it; then she switches to Mendelssohn's "War March of the Priests."

The front room is empty. Nobody sleeps there. Clothes are hung there.

Every week my grandmother sends off a package. In it she puts cake and fruit, a jar of preserves, Moirs' chocolates.

Monday afternoon every week.

Fruit, cake, Jordan almonds, a handkerchief with a tatted edge.

Fruit. Cake. Wild-strawberry jam. A New Testament.

A little bottle of scent from Hills' store, with a purple silk tassel fastened to the stopper.

Fruit. Cake. "Selections from Tennyson."

A calendar, with a quotation from Longfellow for every day.

Fruit. Cake. Moirs' chocolates.

I watch her pack them in the pantry. Sometimes she sends me to the store to get things at the last minute.

The address of the sanitarium is in my grandmother's handwriting, in purple indelible pencil, on smoothed-out wrapping paper. It will never come off.

I take the package to the post office. Going by Nate's, I walk far out in the road and hold the package on the side away from him.

He calls to me. "Come here! I want to show you something."

But I pretend I don't hear him. But at any other time I still go there just the same.

The post office is very small. It sits on the side of the road like a package once delivered by the post office. The government has painted its clapboards tan, with a red trim. The earth in front of it is worn hard. Its face is scarred and scribbled on, carved with initials. In the evening, when the Canadian Pacific mail is due, a row of big boys leans against it, but in the daytime there is nothing to be afraid of. There is no one in front, and inside it is empty. There is no one except the postmaster, Mr. Johnson, to look at my grandmother's purple handwriting.

The post office tilts a little, like Mealy's shop, and inside it looks as chewed as a horse's manger. Mr. Johnson looks out through the little window in the middle of the bank of glass-fronted boxes, like an animal looking out over its manger. But he is dignified by the thick, bevelled-edged glass boxes with their solemn, upright gold-and-black-shaded numbers.

Ours is 21. Although there is nothing in it, Mr. Johnson automatically cocks his eye at it from behind when he sees me.

21.

"Well, well. Here we are again. Good day, good day," he says.

"Good day, Mr. Johnson."

I have to go outside again to hand him the package through the ordinary window, into his part of the post office, because it is too big for the little official one. He is very old, and nice. He has two fingers missing on his right hand where they were caught in a threshing machine. He wears a navy-blue cap with a black leather visor, like a ship's officer, and a shirt with feathery brown stripes, and a big gold collar button.

"Let me see. Let me see. Let me see. Hm," he says to himself, weighing the package on the scales, jiggling the bar with the two remaining fingers and thumb.

"Yes. Yes. Your grandmother is very faithful."

Every Monday afternoon I go past the blacksmith's shop with the package under my arm, hiding the address of the sanitarium with my arm and my other hand.

Going over the bridge, I stop and stare down into the river. All the little trout that have been too smart to get caught—for how long now?—are there, rushing in flank movements, foolish assaults and retreats, against and away from the old sunken fender of Malcolm McNeil's Ford. It has lain there for ages and is supposed to be a disgrace to us all. So are the tin cans that glint there, brown and gold.

From above, the trout look as transparent as the water, but if one did catch one, it would be opaque enough, with a little slick moon-white belly with a pair of tiny, pleated, rose-pink fins on it. The leaning willows soak their narrow yellowed leaves.

Clang.

Clang.

Nate is shaping a horseshoe.

Oh, beautiful pure sound!

It turns everything else to silence.

But still, once in a while, the river gives an unexpected gurgle. *"Slp,"* it says, out of glassy-ridged brown knots sliding along the surface.

Clang.

And everything except the river holds its breath.

Now there is no scream. Once there was one and it settled slowly down to earth one hot summer afternoon; or did it float up, into that dark, too dark, blue sky? But surely it has gone away, forever.

Clang.

It sounds like a bell buoy out at sea.

It is the elements speaking: earth, air, fire, water.

All those other things—clothes, crumbling postcards, broken china; things damaged and lost, sickened or destroyed; even the frail almost-lost scream—are they too frail for us to hear their voices long, too mortal?

Nate!

Oh, beautiful sound, strike again!

1953

Primer Class

Every time I see long columns of numbers, handwritten in a certain way, a strange sensation or shudder, partly aesthetic, partly painful, goes through my diaphragm. It is like seeing the dorsal fin of a large fish suddenly cut through the surface of the water—not a frightening fish like a shark, more like a sailfish. The numbers have to be only up to but under a hundred, rather large and clumsily written, and the columns squeezed together, with long vertical lines between them, drawn by hand, long and crooked. They are usually in pencil, these numbers that affect me so, but I've seen them in blue crayon or blurred ink, and they produce the same effect. One morning our newspaper delivery man, an old Italian named Tony, whom I'd seen over and over again, threw back the pages of his limp, black, oilcloth-covered account book to my page, and there, up and down, at right angles to the pages' blue lines, he had kept track of my newspapers in pencil, in columns of ones and ones, twos and threes. My diaphragm contracted and froze. Or Faustina, the old black lottery-ticket seller, and *her* limp school note-book with a penciled-off half-inch column waveringly drawn for each customer. Or my glimpse of a barkeeper's apparently homemade, home-stitched pad, as he consulted long thin numbers referring to heaven knows what (how many drinks each of his customers had had?), and then put the pad away again, under the bar.

The real name of this sensation is memory. It is a memory I do not even have to try to remember, or reconstruct; it is always right there, clear and complete. The mysterious numbers, the columns, that impressed me so much—a mystery I never solved when I went to Primer Class in Nova Scotia!

Primer Class was a sort of Canadian equivalent of kindergarten; it was the year you went to school before you went to "First Grade." But we didn't sit about sociably and build things, or crayon, or play, or quarrel. We sat one behind the other in a line of small, bolted-down desks and chairs, in the same room with grades one, two, three, and four. We were at the left, facing the teacher, and I think there were seven or eight of us. We were taught reading and writing and arithmetic, or enough of them to prepare us for the "First Grade"; also, how to behave in school. This meant to sit up straight, not to scrape your feet on the floor, never to whisper, to raise your hand when you had to go out, and to stand up when you were asked a question. We used slates; only the real grades could buy scribblers, beautiful, fat writing pads, with colored pictures of horses and kittens on the covers, and pale tan paper with blue lines. They could also go up front to sharpen their pencils into the wastebasket.

I was five. My grandmother had already taught me to write on a slate my name and my family's names and the names of the dog and the two cats. Earlier she had taught me my letters, and at first I could not get past the letter *g*, which for some time I felt was far enough to go. *My* alphabet made a satisfying short song, and I didn't want to spoil it. Then a visitor called on my grandmother and asked me if I knew my letters. I said I did and, accenting the rhythm, gave him my version. He teased me so about stopping at *g* that I was finally convinced one must go on with the other nineteen letters. Once past *g*, it was plain sailing. By the time school started, I could read almost all my primer, printed in both handwriting and type, and I loved every word. First, as a frontispiece, it had the flag in full color, with "One Flag, One King, One Crown" under it. I colored in the black-and-white illustrations that looked old-fashioned, even to me, using mostly red and green crayons. On the end pages I had tried to copy the round cancellation marks from old envelopes: "Brooklyn, N.Y. Sept. 1914," "Halifax, Aug. 1916," and so on, but they had not turned out well, a set of lopsided crumbling wheels.

The summer before school began was the summer of numbers, chiefly number eight. I learned their shapes from the kitchen calendar and the clock in the sitting room, though I couldn't yet tell time. Four and five were hard enough, but I think I was in love with eight. One began writing it just to the right of the top, and drew an S downwards. This wasn't too difficult, but the hardest part was to hit the bottom line (ruled on the slate by my grandmother) and come up again, against the grain, that is, against the desire of one's painfully cramped fingers, and at the same time not make it a straight line, but a sort of upside down and backwards S, and all this in *curves*. Eights also made the worst noise on the slate. My grandmother would send me outside to practice, sitting on the back steps. The skreeking was slow and awful.

The slate pencils came two for a penny, with thin white paper, diagonally striped in pale blue or red, glued around them except for an inch left bare at one end. I loved the slate and the pencils almost as much as the primer. What I liked best about the slate was washing it off at the kitchen sink, or in the watering trough, and then watching it dry. It dried like clouds, and then the very last wet streak would grow tinier and tinier, and thinner and thinner; then suddenly it was gone and the slate was pale gray again and dry, dry, dry.

I had an aunt, Mary, eleven or twelve years older than me, who was in the last, or next-to-last, year of the same school. She was very pretty. She wore white middy blouses with red or blue silk ties, and her brown hair in a braid down her back. In the mornings I always got up earlier than Aunt Mary and ate my porridge at the kitchen table, wishing that she would hurry and get up too. We ate porridge from bowls, with a cup of cream at the side. You took a spoonful of porridge, dipped it into the cream, then ate it; this was to keep the porridge hot. We also had cups of tea, with cream and sugar; mine was called "cambric tea." All during breakfast I listened for the school bell, and wished my aunt would hurry up; she rarely appeared before the bell started ringing, over on the other side of the river that divided the village in two. Then she would arrive in the kitchen braiding her hair, and say, "That's just the *first* bell!" while I was dying to be out the door and off. But first I had to pat Betsy, our little dog, and then kiss Grandmother goodbye. (My grandfather would have been up and out for hours already.)

My grandmother had a glass eye, blue, almost like her other one, and this made her especially vulnerable and precious to me. My father was dead and my mother was away in a sanatorium. Until I was teased out of it, I used to ask Grandmother, when I said goodbye, to promise me not to die before I came home. A year earlier I had privately asked other relatives if they thought my grandmother could go to heaven with a glass eye. (Years later I found out that one of my aunts had asked the same question when she'd been my age.) Betsy was also included in this deep but intermittent concern with the hereafter; I was told that of course she'd go to heaven, she was such a good little dog, and not to worry. Wasn't our minister awfully fond of her, and hadn't she even surprised us by trotting right into church one summer Sunday, when the doors were open?

Although I don't remember having been told it was a serious offense, I was very afraid of being late, so most mornings I left Mary at her breakfast and ran out the back door, around the house, past the blacksmith's shop, and was well across the iron bridge before she caught up with me. Sometimes I had almost reached the school when the second bell, the one that meant to come in immediately from the schoolyard, would be clanging away in the cupola. The school was high, bare and white-clapboarded, dark-red-roofed, and the four-sided cupola had white louvers. Two white outhouses were set farther back, but visible, on either side. I carried my slate, a rag to wash it with, and a small medicine bottle filled with water. Everyone was supposed to bring a bottle of water and a clean rag; spitting on the slates and wiping them off with the hand was a crime. Only the bad boys did it, and if she caught them the teacher hit them on the top of the head with her pointer. I don't imagine that wet slate, by itself, had a smell; perhaps slate pencils do; sour, wet rags do, of course, and perhaps that is what I remember. Miss Morash would pick one up at arm's length and order the owner to take it outside at once, saying *Phaaagh*, or something like that.

That was our teacher's name, Georgie Morash. To me she seemed very tall and stout, straight up and down, with a white starched shirtwaist, a dark straight skirt, and a tight, wide belt that she often pushed down, in front, with both hands. Everything, back and front, looked smooth and hard; maybe it was corsets. But close to, what I mostly remember about Miss Morash, and mostly looked at, were her very white shoes, Oxford shoes, surprisingly white, white like flour, and large, with neatly tied white laces. On my first day at school my Aunt Mary had taken me into the room for the lower grades and presented me to Miss Morash. She bent way over, spoke to me kindly, even patted my head and, although told to look up, I could not take my eyes from those silent, independent-looking, powdery-white shoes.

Miss Morash almost always carried her pointer. As she walked up and down the aisles, looking over shoulders at the scribblers or slates, rapping heads, or occasionally boxing an ear, she talked steadily, in a loud, clear voice. This voice had a certain fame in the village. At dinner my grandfather would quote what he said he had heard Miss Morash saying to us (or even to me) as he drove by that morning, even though the schoolhouse was set well back from the road. Sometimes when my grandmother would tell me to stop shouting, or to speak more softly, she would add, "That Georgie!" I don't remember anything Miss Morash ever said. Once when the Primer Class was gathered in a semicircle before one of the blackboards, while she showed us (sweepingly) how to write the capital *C*, and I was considering, rather, the blue sky beyond the windows, I too received a painful rap on the head with the pointer.

There was another little girl in the Primer Class, besides me, and one awful day she wet her pants, right in the front seat, and was sent home. There were two little Micmac Indian boys, Jimmy and Johnny Crow, who had dark little faces and shiny black hair and eyes, just alike. They both wore shirts of blue cotton, some days patterned with little white sprigs, on others with little white anchors. I couldn't take my eyes off these shirts or the boys' dark bare feet. Almost everyone went barefoot to school, but I had to wear brown sandals with buckles, against my will. When I went home the first day and was asked who was in Primer Class with me, I replied, "Manure MacLaughlin," as his name had sounded to me. I was familiar with manure—there was a great pile of it beside the barn—but of course his real name was Muir, and everyone laughed. Muir wore a navy-blue cap, with a red-and-yellow maple leaf embroidered above the visor.

There was a poor boy, named Roustain, the dirtiest and raggediest of us all, who was really too big for Primer Class and had to walk a long way to school, when he came at all. I heard thrilling stories about him and his brother, how their father whipped them all the time, *horsewhipped* them. We were still horse-and-buggy-minded (though there were a few automobiles in the village), and one of the darkest, most sinister symbols in our imaginations was the horsewhip. It *looked* sinister: long, black, flexible at a point after the handle, sometimes even with lead in it, tasseled. It made a swish *whissh*ing sound and sometimes figured in nightmares. There was even a song about the Roustains:

> I'm a Roustain from the mountain,
> I'm a Roustain, don't you see,
> I'm a Roustain from the mountain,
> You can smell the fir on me.

Not only did their father whip them, but their mother didn't take care of them at all. There were no real beds in their house and no food, except for a big barrel of molasses, which often swarmed with flies. They'd dip pieces of bread in the molasses, when they had bread, and that was all they had for dinner.

The schoolroom windows, those autumn days, seemed very high and bright. On one window ledge, on the Primer Class side, there were beans sprouting up in jars of water. Their presence in school puzzled me, since at home I'd already grown "horse bean" to an amazing height and size in my own garden (eighteen inches square), as well as some radishes and small, crooked carrots. Beyond, above the sprouting beans, the big autumn clouds went grandly by, silver and dazzling in the deep blue. I would keep turning my head to follow them, until Miss Morash came along and gave it a small push back in the right direction. I loved to hear the other grades read aloud, unless they hesitated too much on words or phrases you could guess ahead. Their stories were better, and longer, than those in my primer. I already knew by heart "The Gingerbread Boy" and "Henny Penny," in my primer, and had turned against them. I was much more interested when the third grade read about Bruce watching the spider spin his web. Every morning school began with the Lord's Prayer, sitting down, then we stood up and sang "O maple leaf, our emblem dear." Then sometimes—and not very well, because it was so much harder—we sang "God save our gracious king," but usually stopped with the first verse.

Only the third and fourth grades studied geography. On their side of the room, over the blackboard, were two rolled-up maps, one of Canada and one of the whole world. When they had a geography lesson, Miss Morash pulled down one or both of these maps, like window shades. They were on cloth, very limp, with a shiny surface, and in pale colors—tan, pink, yellow, and green—surrounded by the blue that was the ocean. The light coming in from their windows, falling on the glazed, crackly surface, made it hard for me to see them properly from where I sat. On the world map, all of Canada was pink; on the Canadian, the provinces were different colors. I was so taken with the pull-down maps that I wanted to snap them up, and pull them down again, and touch all the countries and provinces with my own hands. Only dimly did I hear the pupils' recitations of capital cities and islands and bays. But I got the general impression that Canada was the same size as the world, which somehow or other fitted into it, or the other way around, and that in the world and Canada the sun was always shining and everything was dry and glittering. At the same time, I knew perfectly well that this was not true.

One morning Aunt Mary was even later than usual at breakfast, and for some reason I decided to wait for her to finish her porridge. Before we got to the bridge the second bell—the bell that really meant it—started ringing. I was terrified because up to this time I had never actually been late, so I began to run as fast as I possibly could. I could hear my aunt behind, laughing at me. Because her legs were longer than mine, she caught up to me, rushed into the schoolyard and up the steps ahead of me. I ran into the classroom and threw myself, howling, against Miss Morash's upright form. The class had their hands folded on the desks, heads bowed, and had reached "Thy kingdom come." I clutched the teacher's long, stiff skirt and sobbed. Behind me, my awful aunt was still *laughing*. Miss Morash stopped everyone in mid-prayer, and propelled us all three out into the cloakroom, holding me tightly by the shoulder. There, surrounded by all the japanned hooks, which held only two or three caps, we were private, though loud giggles and whispering reached us from the schoolroom. First Miss Morash in stern tones told Mary she was *very* late for the class she attended overhead, and ordered her to go upstairs at once. Then she tried to calm me. She said in a very kindly way, not at all in her usual penetrating voice, that being only a few minutes late wasn't really worth tears, that everything was quite all right, and I must go into the classroom now and join in the usual morning songs. She wiped off my face with a folded white handkerchief she kept tucked in her belt, patted my head, and even kissed me two or three times. I was overcome by all this, almost to the point of crying all over again, but keeping my eyes fixed firmly on her two large, impersonal, flour-white shoes, I managed not to give way. I had to face my snickering classmates, and I found I could. And that was that, although I was cross with Aunt Mary for a long time because it was all her fault.

For me this was the most dramatic incident of Primer Class, and I was never late again. My initial experiences of formal education were on the whole pleasurable. Reading and writing caused me no suffering. I found the first easier, but the second was enjoyable—I mean *artistically* enjoyable—and I came to admire my own handwriting in pencil, when I got to that stage, perhaps as a youthful Chinese student might admire his own brushstrokes. It was wonderful to see that the letters each had different expressions, and that the same letter had different expressions at different times. Sometimes the two capitals of my name looked miserable, slumped down and sulky, but at others they turned fat and cheerful, almost with roses in their cheeks. I also had the "First Grade" to look forward to, as well as geography, the maps, and longer and much better stories. The one subject that baffled me was arithmetic. I knew all the numbers of course, and liked to write them—I finally mastered the eight—but when I watched the older grades at arithmetic class, in front of the blackboard with their columns of figures, it was utterly incomprehensible. Those mysterious numbers!

c. 1960

The Country Mouse

"My grandfather's clock was too tall for the shelf . . ." I knew that song very well, having been sung it many times by my other grandfather. But this grandfather himself seemed too tall—at any rate, too tall for this train we were on, the old Boston and Maine, gritting, grinding, occasionally shrieking, bearing us west and south, from Halifax to Boston, through a black, seemingly endless night. This grandfather snapped on the overhead light again.

He had taken off his boots. They stood on the floor, to the left. His coat and vest and necktie were hanging up on a hanger to the right, jiggling. He had kept his other clothes on, just unfastening his braces. He had been trying to sleep in the upper berth of our "drawing room." Now he descended, god-like and swearing, swept Grandma out of the way, and wedged himself into the lower berth. His thick silver hair and short silver beard glittered, and so did the whites of his eyes, rolled up as if in agony. (He was walleyed. At least, one eye turned the wrong way, which made him endlessly interesting to me. The walleye seemed only right and natural, because my grandmother on the other side in Canada had a glass eye.) His shoulders were up at an odd angle, a little frosted lamp shining over one of them.

This grandma, jiggling too, stood by helplessly, watching him writhe and grunt. She wore a long purple dressing gown and her curly white hair was partly pulled back into a small pigtail.

"Sarah! Get in the other way around!" She turned off the overhead light once more, and obeyed.

From where I lay, across the room, stretching my tiny bones on what they had called a "sofa," I peered at them in dumb wonder as they reclined, head-to-foot, in their dramatically lit, mysterious, dark-green-curtained niche. I can look back on them now, many years and train trips later, and clearly see them looking like a Bernini fountain, or a Cellini saltcellar: a powerful but aging Poseidon with a small, elderly, curly Nereid. But that night I was dazed, almost scandalized. I had never seen either of them *en déshabillé* before, not even in bed. In fact, I scarcely knew them.

The little light blinked out. We were off again (not that we had ever stopped, of course) through the night: *unk-etty, unk-etty, unk-etty,* doubtless still going through some black hairy forest I had watched out the window before the porter had made the beds. I felt as if I were being kidnapped, even if I wasn't. My sofa smelled of coal dust and tobacco, and its stiff green velour pricked right through the sheet. The train went into a long curve and tried to bend its stiff joints; my sofa tried to throw me off. The walls creaked. *Ee-eee-eee* went our whistle, miles ahead, and I held on for dear life. It was awful, but almost a relief, to hear from time to time, above the other noises, my grandfather growling savagely to himself in the pitch dark.

In the morning I was sick, and Grandma rushed me into the strange, solid tin (as I thought) bathroom just in time. I threw up, yellow, into something I referred to—probably thinking of the farm accoutrements I was more familiar with than bathrooms—as a "hopper." Grandpa, who was brushing his white hair with *two* brushes, like a trick, laughed loudly, displaying his many gold teeth. Grandma produced soda crackers from somewhere for me to chew. I got better. We went on with our complicated, embarrassing dressing and the porter arrived to do *his* tricks with our beds.

Yesterday's white socks were very dirty. "And she only has one pair, John," said Grandma. More embarrassment. Grandpa stopped buffeting his head. I soon learned that he had a way of suggesting an immediate and practical solution to almost any problem, after just a moment's thought, like (one gathers) the Duke of Wellington. "Turn them inside out," he commanded. This was done, but then white threads hung at my heels. However, they would be concealed, more or less, my grandparents agreed, by my black patent-leather slippers. Putting his watch in his vest pocket, Grandpa finally left us to get his breakfast. Grandma and I sat opposite each other on the two green seats, nibbling soda crackers for ours, and studying each other in the strong dust-filled sunlight.

Outside there were more woods, but no longer firs, and among the greens there were some yellows because it was September. We clanked over several bridges above little blue brooks. There were some birches. Three crows flew wildly off, sideways, cawing silently. I was beginning to enjoy this trip, a little.

Grandma was dressed in gray silk, with her hat on and her veil pushed up. She was very neat and tight and fitted. The neck of the dress was filled in with fine white net, and a small structure of the net stretched on little bones, around her neck, like a miniature fish weir. On the left of her bosom was a small round gold case that held a fine gold chain to her pince-nez coiled up tight, on a spring. One could pull it out and it would snap back— not that anyone was allowed to do this, but one was aware of it. She had blue eyes and a small, rather snub, nose, and the curling white hair was parted in the middle. She was very pretty, in a doll-like way, and she had already told me that she wore a size 3 shoe. The strongest exclamation I had heard her use was "Pshaw," and occasionally, "Drat."

Yes, I was beginning to enjoy myself a little, if only Grandma hadn't had such a confusing way of talking. It was almost as if we were playing house. She would speak of "grandma" and "little girls" and "fathers" and "being good"—things I had never before considered in the abstract, or rarely in the third person. In particular, there seemed to be much, much more to being a "little girl" than I had realized: the prospect was beginning to depress me. And now she said, "Where's your doll? Where's *Drusilla?*"

Oh dear. I had dolls, back home in Nova Scotia; I was even quite fond of one or two of them. But Grandma had found them all in no condition to go traveling in Pullmans. She had bought me the best our country store could provide, and made her a checked dress herself. And when I had been reluctant to name her, she had even given her that unappealing name. The doll (I couldn't say that name) was totally uninteresting, with embossed yellow-brown hair that smelled like stale biscuits, bright blue eyes, and pink cheeks, and I could scarcely conceal my real feelings about her. But that seemed to be one of Grandma's ideas: a "little girl" should carry a doll when she went traveling. I meekly dug out the horror from under a pillow and held her on my knee until we got to Boston.

It was 1917. When the chauffeur, Ronald, met us at North Station in his dark uniform, black leather puttees, and cap with a black visor, I thought at first he was a new kind of soldier. But he was too old to be a soldier; he was married and had four grown children. (Later we were to become good friends and I would ride in front with him in the Cadillac limousine, and he would tell me about his son in the army and, inevitably, how much his back ached.) Now Grandma and I were immediately driven to Stern's to buy me some decent clothes. Everything we bought was brown: a brown tweed coat, a brown beaver hat with streamers, two pairs of brown laced boots, long brown stockings. I hated them all but tactfully said nothing. Then we met Grandpa at the Touraine for lunch and I ate creamed chicken and was given an ice cream like nothing I had ever seen on earth—*meringue glacée*, it must have been.

After lunch we drove to Worcester. I think I must have fallen asleep, but I do remember arriving at a driveway lined with huge maple trees. To my slight resentment (after all, hadn't I been singing "O maple leaf, our emblem dear" for years?), they were pointed out and named to me. The front of the house looked fairly familiar, very much the same kind of white clapboards and green shutters that I was accustomed to, only this house was on a much larger scale, twice as large, with two windows for each of the Nova Scotia ones and a higher roof. As we drove up and around it, wings stuck out here and there; at one side was a quite incongruous curved porch, and at the other a glass-enclosed box on another porch, the "conservatory." Grandma and I went into the house through this.

I had been brought back unconsulted and against my wishes to the house my father had been born in, to be saved from a life of poverty and provincialism, bare feet, suet puddings, unsanitary school slates, perhaps even from the inverted *r*'s of my mother's family. With this surprising extra set of grandparents, until a few weeks ago no more than names, a new life was about to begin. It was a day that seemed to include months in it, or even years, a whole unknown past I was made to feel I should have known about, and a strange, unpredictable future.

The house was gloomy, there was no denying it, and everyone seemed nervous and unsettled. There was something ominous, threatening, lowering in the air. My father had been the oldest of eight children. All of them were dead, except for three—Aunt Marian, who was married and lived in Providence; Aunt Jenny, unmarried and the next-to-oldest after my father; and Uncle Neddy, the youngest. The latter two and my grandparents made up the family, though Aunt Jenny and Uncle Neddy were away a good deal of the nine months I lived there.

The old white house had long ago been a farmhouse out in the country. The city had crept out and past it; now there were houses all around and a trolley line went past the front lawn with its white picket fence. There was no doubt but what the neighborhood, compared to the old days, was deteriorating. The Catholics had been trying to buy the house for years; they wanted to build a church there. All the time I was there the subject was under debate—to sell or not to sell. However, there were still fifteen acres of land, an old apple orchard behind the house, and tall chestnut trees up on the hill. The life my grandparents still led was partly country, partly city. There were hens and two cows, and a large barn also up on the hill. They had their own cottage cheese and sometimes butter. There was a large vegetable garden, the greater part of which was planted in celery and asparagus. There were a Bartlett pear tree, a crab-apple tree, a dark green "summer house" with old robins' nests in it, and two tremendous horse-chestnut trees and under them two wonderful swings with broad seats and thick ropes. The trees had been cared for and cemented and propped up, very old and spreading. We could easily climb into many of them and hang on by bars rather than branches. They were preserved at all costs, like Grandpa's teeth.

There were also a weeping birch, a large bed of cannas, lilacs along one fence, lilies of the valley under them, and violets. Back of the house the lawn was graded in a long green wave, but a spring kept coming up there and in the next season the grading was soiled again at great expense. The house, Grandma said, was "a hundred and fifty years old." There were awful rats in the attic and they could be heard fighting and scuttling at night. The cats were ugly, orange and white; they lived in the barn and ran away from me—not like my black Nanny in Nova Scotia.

Later that same day I met Aunt Jenny for the first time, although she kept insisting she had known me before as a baby. She didn't seem particularly glad to see me. She was very tall, as so many people in the "States" seemed to be. She suggested that I walk up to the barn with her to get her car. As she turned to go and I saw her edgewise, I was amazed how tall and flat, like a paper doll, she looked. I tagged along slightly behind her. She had on a long jumper-like blue jersey garment, around whose middle was a wonderful chatelaine belt, all little chains, boxes, and medals that clinked as she moved her long legs. I wanted to examine it or ask her about it, but didn't dare. We walked out through the conservatory and, farther up the driveway, up a small hill. The barn was on two levels: on the ground floor there were three cows; on the upper floor, which opened on the other side onto the hillside, there was a large garage. On its big swinging doors were nailed rows and rows of old license plates because all the family had been early motoring enthusiasts. In fact, Uncle Neddy had driven in one of the first auto races from Boston to New York.

In the barn stood the limousine we had recently arrived in, and a blue, rather high, lady-like car, Aunt Jenny's Buick. She opened the screw top on the tank at the back and measured the gasoline with a yardstick. This was all fascinating, but what had caught my eye was a carriage sitting at the back of the garage, under the noses of the two cars. "Yes," said Aunt Jenny, "that's your grandma's carriage. It hasn't been used for many years now." It was dark green. I climbed inside by the two little steps. There were black lamps on either side; inside was dark brown leather, musty-smelling. It made the most beautiful little house imaginable. I wanted to stay in it forever, but Aunt Jenny had finished her checking up and invited me to ride down as far as the house with her, so I had to go.

She had also been an early driver, but always a very bad one. Uncle Neddy later pointed out the exact spot where "Jenny tipped Papa over." It was when she had her first car, a Ford, and had offered to show Grandpa how she could drive, and within two minutes of his getting into it, she had rounded the canna bed too fast and tipped over. They had landed inelegantly among the red and yellow cannas, squashing them flat. Grandpa had never driven with her again.

In the household there was a cook, a maid named Agnes, a gardener named Ed, and his son. A laundress came in once a week. Except for Ronald the chauffeur, they were all Swedish and spoke Swedish among themselves.

I became very fond of Agnes, perhaps because Grandma fought with her constantly. When Agnes would polish the beautiful mahogany dining-room table, Grandma kept after her: "*With* the grain, Agnes, *with* the grain." Ed, the gardener, in blue denim overalls and jacket, also fought regularly with Grandma, I don't know what about—once, I think, about the correct way of banking celery. Anyway, every so often he would lay down his rake or hoe or stop milking a cow, and announce that he was through. His young son would immediately take over where Ed had left off. This had been going on for thirty years. The next morning at seven o'clock, Ed would be back on the job again. He had been the driver for Grandma's horse-drawn carriage, but had refused flatly to learn to drive a car. One day the cook left dramatically, by the front door, out into a snowstorm. For four days Grandma cooked for us, very badly, and Grandpa had dinner at the hotel. Then another cook arrived, a very nice one this time, Swedish, fat, and cheerful. She and my dear Agnes hit it off immediately. Even dour Ed joined in the kitchen coffee parties. She made wonderful hard yellow coffee cakes, braided and frosted.

There was a dog, a Boston bull terrier nominally belonging to Aunt Jenny, and oddly named Beppo. At first I was afraid of him, but he immediately adopted me, perhaps as being on the same terms in the house as himself, and we became very attached. He was a clever dog; he wore a wide collar with brass studs, which was taken off every night before he went to bed. Every morning at eight o'clock he would come to my door with the collar in his mouth, and bang it against the door, meaning for us to get up and dressed and start the day together. Like most Boston terriers he had a delicate stomach; he vomited frequently. He jumped nervously at imaginary dangers, and barked another high hysterical bark. His hyperthyroid eyes glistened, and begged for sympathy and understanding. When he was "bad," he was punished by being put in a large closet off the sewing room and left there, out of things, for half an hour. Once when I was playing with him, he disappeared and would not answer my calls. Finally he was found, seated gloomily by himself in the closet, facing the wall. He was punishing *himself*. We later found a smallish puddle of vomit in the conservatory. No one had ever before punished him for his attacks of gastritis, naturally; it was all his own idea, his peculiar Bostonian sense of guilt.

Next door—that is, just across the maple-lined driveway—stood another large white house in the sort of "bungalow" style of the early part of the century. Grandpa had built it for Aunt Marian when she married, but she had moved away for good and it was now rented to a family named Barton. Mr. Barton was a banker, wore a derby, and drove about in a shiny black car. They had a very young chauffeur, Richard, who wore a dashing greenish uniform—again, not a soldier's. (I heard he was not fighting in Flanders because of some ailment whose nature I could not learn, eavesdrop though I tried.)

The day after our arrival, Grandma took me to call on the Bartons to meet Emma, who was to be my playmate. The mother was out and I met Emma's grandmother, an old old lady who sat in a wheelchair all day, knitting for the soldier boys. She had knitted ninety-two helmets and over two hundred "wristers," and let me try on one of each. She was deaf and had a sort of black box beside her to hear with. Emma's grandmother was much older than either of mine, who were old enough. Her daughter was a Christian Scientist, but apparently she permitted her old mother to be lame and deaf if she wanted to.

Emma appeared. She was five and a half, a year younger than me. She was a very pretty child. I immediately felt the aura of wealth surrounding her, like a young Scott Fitzgerald. Her hair was in a "Dutch cut" (so was mine), but hers was sleek and smooth and black. It even had blue highlights in it, but I suspect someone may have pointed that out to me. Her eyes were gray and her skin very white. She was a little plump, and was wearing a beautiful pair of "rompers," made of some spongy kind of crepe, deep rose red. She always wore rompers of the same material but in different colors, with a white ruff at the neck. I think I thought they were possibly a Christian Science costume.

Emma's grandmother said, "Aren't you going to show your new friend your playroom and your toys?" Emma looked put out. She said, ungraciously, "I've just put everything in *apple-pie order.*" It was the first time I had heard that expression and it baffled me. However, her grandmother finally persuaded her to show off her possessions and we went upstairs together, to a small white-walled room at the head of the stairs, with shelves around the walls and a bay window with a window seat in it. Outside a shop, I had never seen so many toys in my life; the display of dolls was overpowering. What I liked best was a milk can that wound up, played a little tune and, with his long ears first, up came a white woolly rabbit, who looked around him and sank down again. Emma was allowed to read the funny papers, which I was not. Now it seems to me that "Mutt and Jeff" and "Buster Brown and His Dog Tige" were rather highbrow fare for a little girl.

Naturally, Emma and I became very close friends. Often her mother came over to argue with Grandpa about Christian Science in the evenings. She was tall, with blue eyes and black hair like her daughter, and very high coloring. She got nowhere with Grandpa of course, who never even went to church, but he loved to argue with her and would pretend to give in on certain points just to be able to point his cigar at her and demolish her logic.

All this I understood, like Beppo, by tone of voice rather than by words, but I listened and listened while pretending to play cards and to read the *Literary Digest* myself.

Outside their house the Bartons had a catalpa tree. I don't know why this tree, or perhaps its name, fascinated me. I rather disliked its big hanging pale green leaves and those long beans, but every day Emma or I would say, "After lunch we'll meet under the catalpa tree." Once we had a fight, I don't remember what about. I pulled her shiny black hair, and she screamed. Agnes came running from our house and Emma's mother's maid from theirs, and they pulled us apart and we were not allowed to play together for three days.

At school the teacher's name was actually Miss Woodhead. She had bright red hair and was very pretty. We loved her so much we didn't even make fun of her name. We sat in alternate rows of boys and girls, and began every morning by singing "Good morning to you, good morning to you," bowing to either side. At my left sat a beautiful boy named Royal Something. His name made him doubly attractive to me, stuffed as I was with the English royal family, although I realized he wasn't really royal. He had dark eyes and shiny dark brown hair cut rather long. At the end of the day we helped each other on with our coats and once, when he helped me buckle my arctics, as I looked at his long shiny hair, neat starched collar, and red necktie, I felt a wonderful, powerful thrill go through my stomach.

I did stay on at school through Thanksgiving, I suppose, because there was the business of the Pilgrim Fathers. Miss Woodhead made a model of "The Landing of the Pilgrims" on a large tabletop. The Rock was the only real thing. Miss Woodhead made the ocean in a spectacular way: she took large sheets of bright blue paper, crumpled them up, and stretched them out over the table. Then, with the blackboard chalk, she made glaring whitecaps of all the points: an ocean grew right before our eyes. There were some little ships, some doll people, and we also helped make log cabins. (Twenty years later I learned the Pilgrim Fathers had no log cabins when they landed.) But I felt closely related to them all: *"Land where my father died / Land of the pilgrims' pride"*—for a long time I took the first line personally. Miss Woodhead asked us to bring anything we had at home to contribute to Plymouth and Thanksgiving, and in my conceit I said (to the wonder and admiration of the class, I hoped) that we had some real little trees, just the right size, with snow on them. So I contributed four trees from the toy village my grandparents let me play with, and from then on the village was half deforested when set up at home.

•

Whenever I could, I explored the house like a cat. It was an old colonial pre-Revolutionary house, but wings had been added and porches built on with no regard for period style. The front room was rarely used. Once in a while Grandma entertained a friend there in the afternoon. Yet it was my favorite. This was before the days when people were conscious of preserving the character of old houses. Perhaps because this room was so little used, it had been preserved by accident. The antique furniture was upholstered in gray blue, the walls were papered, and it all went together. There were even some paintings I now realize were primitives, in gold frames on the walls, done by an ancestress. It was a quiet room, and I could sit on the carpet there undisturbed and think. On both porches the floors were set with thick green panes of glass, frosted over and scratched, I suppose to give light to the cellar underneath. To me they were as beautiful as slabs of jade or malachite. Grandma's sitting room on the front, with a fireplace and bay windows onto the lawn, was called the "sewing room," but I never saw Grandma sew. In the dining room I studied each and every plate and cup on display in two glass cases, and the silver on the sideboard.

In the wing at the back, the largest room had once held a billiard table when the sons were alive; now it was used as a living room, but it was always referred to as the "billiard room." It had layers and layers of curtains, the innermost of brickish red velvet. The Oriental carpet was a slightly lighter red. In the middle there was a large square table with a lamp on it, and layers of magazines were laid out on the front. There were some black leather sofas and armchairs. At the back was an enormous rubber plant in a gigantic brass pot; Grandma was quite proud of it. There was an upright piano, a fireplace with magnificent brass fenders and fire tongs, and high on the mantel was a tiny pair of top boots that had belonged to my father.

In the evenings Grandpa sat in the billiard room in a leather chair, smoking cigars and reading the newspapers. He smoked thirteen or fourteen cigars a day and the room reeked of them. Occasionally, to my delight, he varied the cigars by smoking a long church-warden pipe. There was a rack of pipes on the wall at his side, and a plaster plaque of Dante's head. I sat under the big table, and pretended it was a ship, wheezing slightly. One of the table's large bulging legs became a sturdy mast. (I had once been taken aboard a docked sailing vessel, to my intense delight.) Grandma read the *Literary Digest* under the red lamp; then she played solitaire.

In the library there were some bookcases filled with dark leatherbound books, but I was the only one who ever used it. After two months or so of my sojourn, I got up my courage and slid open the glass doors. The carpet was a deep rich blue. There was a mahogany desk in the middle of the room, with a brass desk set and a paperweight in the form of three lifelike bronze cigars. It was heavy, but I picked it up many times and found it smelled of metal, not cigars.

I frequently had indirect questions aimed at me, like "Wouldn't some little girl like to take piano lessons?" So Miss Darling arrived. I was supposed to practice fifteen minutes at a time. The staves were enormous and I wrote notes in them as large as watermelons. I couldn't touch the pedals, of course. But how I loved the sound of the wide yellow piano keys!

The War was on. In school at recess we were marched into the central hall, class by class, to the music of an upright piano, a clumping march that has haunted me all my life and I have never yet placed. There we pledged allegiance to the flag and sang war songs: "Joan of Arc, they are ca-alllll-ing you." I hated the songs, and most of all I hated saluting the flag. I would have refused if I had dared. In my Canadian schooling the year before, we had started every day with "God Save the King" and "The Maple Leaf Forever." Now I felt like a traitor. I wanted us to win the War, of course, but I didn't want to be an American. When I went home to lunch, I said so. Grandma was horrified; she almost wept. Shortly after, I was presented with a white card with an American flag in color at the top. All the stanzas of "Oh, say, can you see" were printed on it in dark blue letters. Every day I sat at Grandma's feet and attempted to recite this endless poem. We didn't sing because she couldn't stay in tune, she said. Most of the words made no sense at all. "*Between his loved home and the war's desolation*" made me think of my dead father, and conjured up strange pictures in my mind.

Aunt Jenny gave a "War Party" to raise money for some organization, perhaps the Red Cross. I was allowed to help set the table. All I remember were the red, white, and blue bonbons and the red, white, and blue flowers. Mrs. Barton's mother continued to knit helmets and wristers and Grandma decided that I, too, should learn to knit. On a pair of needles that seemed awfully long I began to knit and purl some small squares to make an afghan, but I hated it. I cherish the memory of the colors, half bright pink and half pea-green, but knitting I thought almost as bad as the "numbers" game. It reached such a point that I would actually drop stitches when Grandma left the room, and so most of the afghan was finally knitted by her. She decided I wasn't any good with my hands. I have never knitted since.

There were the war cartoons, several big books of them: German helmets and cut-off hands haunted us. Aunt Jenny spoke of such things and was shushed. Because of the "Belgians," I ate my mashed potatoes. We were hoarders; in the closet under the front stairs were four barrels of sugar, which hardened like rock. In the kitchen one evening the cook hammered it with a rolling pin with all her might, redder than ever. There was something conspiratorial about the scene, which I associated with Aunt Jenny. Since she was rarely at home, I got the idea that her "War Work" was some kind of full-time profession. In Nova Scotia the soldiers, some of whom I actually knew, wore beautiful tam-o'-shanters with thistles and other insignia on them. When they got dressed up, they wore kilts and sporrans. One of them had come courting my young aunt in this superb costume, carrying a swagger stick, and let me examine him all over. The Johnny-get-your-gun type of soldier in Worcester seemed very drab to me. I missed black Nanny and the little gray cat, Tippy, named after the song. I liked "Tipperary" and "The long, long trail" and "Every nice girl loves a sailor" much better than the Worcester songs. I particularly hated "Joan of Arc, they are ca-alllll-ing you."

They talked about high prices at the table; I heard that eggs were five cents apiece. And the price of clothes! I rarely spoke, but this time I felt I had something to contribute. I said, "The last time my aunt in Nova Scotia bought a pair of shoes, they cost three dollars." Everyone laughed. I lost my courage about making conversation at the dinner table and I have never regained it.

Sunday morning there was always oyster stew and muffins. Afterwards Grandma and Uncle Neddy would argue; it seemed a Sunday-morning ritual. They always argued until it was time for Grandma to put on her high black satin hat and be driven to the Pilgrim Congregational Church. I was frightened; I thought they were really fighting and were about to come to blows. They would walk up and down together, round and round the billiard room, even out and around the house. Grandpa meanwhile would be reading the Sunday-morning papers, but would chip in a loud comment once in a while: "I told you that stock was no good, Ned. You're throwing your money away." "Jenny has no brains; never had. That woman is a damn fool." Sometimes he'd snort: "Why don't you two do your fighting someplace else? I swear I'll go down to the hotel." Finally I realized the sessions always ended with Uncle Neddy kissing Grandma, looking pleased with himself, and helping her into her black coat.

The dressmaker came. Her name, oddly, was Miss Cotton. Grandma was fond of her and she ate her lunch on a tray, while the fat orange canary shrieked overhead. She made me four hideous dresses, too long, too dark, and with decorations made from leftovers of Grandma's dresses. (Forty-three years later I can scarcely bear to think of those dresses.) Even Grandpa said, "Aren't that child's skirts too long?" Blue serge, large pockets, everything outlined with a silver braid that had a thread of red running through it.

Then Grandma decided I should have long hair and braids, like "nice little girls." Emma had short hair, but that didn't seem to count in my favor.

Grandpa once asked me to get his eyeglasses from his bedroom, which I had never been in. It was mostly white and gold, surprisingly feminine for him. The carpet was gold-colored, the bed was fanciful, brass and white, and the furniture was gold and white too. There was a high chest of drawers, a white bedspread, muslin curtains, a set of black leatherbound books near the bed, photographs of Grandma and my aunts and uncles at various ages, and two large black bottles (of whiskey, I realized years later). There were also medicine bottles and the "machines." There were two of them in black boxes, with electric batteries attached to things like stethoscopes—some sort of vibrator or massager perhaps. What he did with them I could not imagine. The boxes were open and looked dangerous. I reached gingerly over one to get his eyeglasses, and saw myself in the long mirror: my ugly serge dress, my too long hair, my gloomy and frightened expression.

Then I became ill. First came eczema, and then asthma. At nights Beppo and I scratched together, I in my bed and he outside my door. Roll and scratch, scratch and roll. No one realized that the thick carpets, the weeping birch, the milk toast, and Beppo were all innocently adding to my disorders. By then I was so sick that I had my breakfast in bed. Sometimes, around ten o'clock, I would get out of bed from boredom and go downstairs to watch Uncle Neddy having his breakfast. His hair was parted in the middle, his face was shiny and lightly freckled, his shirt was dazzling white, and his cuff-links glittered. I loved and hated him at the same time. He'd say things like, "At your age I'd be out and up the hill picking up all the nuts," and "What *you* need, young lady . . ." I wanted to be on good terms with everyone, but he would insist on making jokes I couldn't understand, and talking about spankings and other horrors.

One night something marvelous did happen. I was asleep when Grandma came in and said, "Grandpa wants you to come downstairs and see the present he's brought you from Providence." The lights in the kitchen were very bright. On the white enameled table, dazed and blinking, stood three little hens—no, two little hens and one rooster. They were Golden Bantams, for me. When one hen pecked at some cornmeal on the enamel table, and made miniature but hen-like sounds, I could have cried with pleasure. Where to put them for the night? The problem was solved by using one of the "set tubs" in the laundry off the kitchen. But hens and roosters have to perch, and Grandma found a bleached stick that the laundress used for stirring her wash. It was stuck into one stone tub and the three tiny fowl immediately and obligingly hopped on and clung to it. They were reddish, speckled, with tiny doll-like red combs; the rooster had long tail feathers. They were *mine*, and they were to live in a special henhouse Ed would fix in the morning. I could scarcely bear to leave my little poultry.

One night I was taken to the window in the upstairs front hall to see the ice on the trees, lit by the street lamp at the end of our drive. All the maple trees were bent by the weight of the ice. Branches had cracked off, the telephone wires were covered with ice, and so was the row of thin elms that grew along the street—a great pale blaze of ice filling the vision completely, seeming to circle and circle if one squinted a bit. My grandfather, wearing his nightshirt and red dressing gown, held me up to the window. "Squint your eyes, Grandpa," I said, "tight!" and he did. It was one of the few unselfconscious moments of that whole dismal time.

Then Agnes left. She was going back to Sweden to get married. I wept and clung to her skirts and large suitcase when she kissed me goodbye. After that, things went from bad to worse. First came constipation, then eczema again, and finally asthma. I felt myself aging, even dying. I was *bored* and lonely with Grandma, my silent grandpa, the dinners alone, bored with Emma and Beppo, all of them. At night I lay blinking my flashlight off and on, and crying. As Louise Bogan has so well put it:

> At midnight tears
> Run into your ears.

Three great truths came home to me during this stretch of my life, all hard to describe and equally important. Emma and I were sitting under the chestnut trees, making conversation in the way both children and adults do. She asked me about my parents. I said my father was dead; I didn't ever remember seeing him. What about my mother? I thought for a moment and then I said in a *sentimental* voice: "She went away and left me . . . She died, too." Emma was impressed and sympathetic, and I loathed myself. It was the first time I had lied deliberately and consciously, and the first time I was aware of falsity and the great power of sentimentality—although I didn't know the word. My mother was not dead. She was in a sanatorium, in another prolonged "nervous breakdown." I didn't know then, and still don't, whether it was from shame I lied, or from a hideous craving for sympathy, playing up my sad romantic plight. But the feeling of self-distaste, whatever it came from, was only too real. I jumped up, to get away from my monstrous self that I could not keep from lying.

I learned a second lesson when Grandma insisted I bring another little girl home from school to play with. I picked out an inoffensive small blonde whose name and features I can't remember. It was a winter afternoon and the lights were already lit in the kitchen. We were sitting on the dining-room floor, looking at magazines, and I felt bored bored bored. The cook was starting dinner, talking to Agnes, who was still with us. Light showed around the swinging kitchen door, and my ostensible playmate asked, "Who lives in that part of the house?" Social consciousness had struck its first blow: I realized this pallid nameless child lived in a poorer world than I (at this moment, at least, for I had never felt at all secure about my status), and that she thought we were in an apartment house. Fairly quickly, I think, I said tactfully, "Oh, a *family* . . ." and since the servants were all speaking Swedish, this was safe enough.

After New Year's, Aunt Jenny had to go to the dentist, and asked me to go with her. She left me in the waiting room, and gave me a copy of the *National Geographic* to look at. It was still getting dark early, and the room had grown very dark. There was a big yellow lamp in one corner, a table with magazines, and an overhead chandelier of sorts. There were others waiting, two men and a plump middle-aged lady, all bundled up. I looked at the magazine cover—I could read most of the words—shiny, glazed, yellow and white. The black letters said: FEBRUARY 1918. A feeling of absolute and utter desolation came over me. I felt . . . *myself*. In a few days it would be my seventh birthday. I felt *I, I, I,* and looked at the three strangers in panic. I was *one* of them too, inside my scabby body and wheezing lungs. "You're in for it now," something said. How had I got tricked into such a false position? I would be like that woman opposite who smiled at me so falsely every once in a while. The awful sensation passed, then it came back again. "You are you," something said. "How strange you are, inside looking out. You are not Beppo, or the chestnut tree, or Emma, you are *you* and you are going to be *you* forever." It was like coasting downhill, this thought, only much worse, and it quickly smashed into a tree. *Why* was I a human being?

1961

The U.S.A. School of Writing

When I was graduated from Vassar in 1934, during the Great Depression, jobs were still hard to find and very badly paid. Perhaps for those very reasons it seemed incumbent on me and many of my classmates to find them, whether we had to or not. The spirit of the times and, of course, of my college class was radical; we were puritanically pink. Perhaps there seemed to be something virtuous in working for much less a year than our educations had been costing our families. It was a combination of this motive, real need for a little more money than I had, idle curiosity, and, I'm afraid, pure masochism that led me to answer an advertisement in the Sunday *Times* and take a job. It was with a correspondence school, the U.S.A. School of Writing.

First I had an interview at the school with its head, or president, as he described himself, Mr. Black. His opening remark was that the U.S.A. School of Writing stood for "The United States of America School of Writing," and my pleasure in that explanation trapped me immediately. But I can see now that I was just made to order for Mr. Black, and he must have been mentally rubbing his hands and licking his chops over me all during our little talk. I couldn't type—properly, that is; I wanted to smoke while I worked, which was against the fire laws; and I had had no experience at anything at all. But I was from Vassar and I had had a story and three poems published in magazines. I hadn't the faintest idea of my own strength; he would have taken me, probably, even if I had asked for twenty-five dollars a week instead of the fifteen dollars he was offering, but of course such an idea never occurred to me. No doubt he was already plotting how my high-class education and my career in print could be incorporated into his newest circulars.

However, there was a slight catch to that. For a while, at least, I would have to fulfill my duties at the school under the name of Fred G. Margolies, which had been the name, not of my predecessor, but of the one before the one before that. It developed that some of Mr. Margolies's students were still taking the course and had to receive their corrected lessons signed by him, and I would have to be Mr. Margolies until they had all graduated.

Then I could turn into myself again, and steer new students. I felt I'd probably like to keep on being Mr. Margolies, if I could. He had had something published, too, although I never succeeded in delving deep enough into the history of the school to find out what it was. And he or they must have been good letter writers, or even fuller of idle curiosity than I was, or just very kindhearted men, to judge by the tone of the letters I received in our name. In fact, for a long time afterwards I used to feel that the neurotically "kind" facet of my personality *was* Mr. Margolies.

The school was on the fourth floor, the top floor, of an old tumble-down building near Columbus Circle. There was no elevator. I had accepted—although "accept" cannot be the right word—the job in the late fall, and it seems to me now that it was always either raining or snowing when I emerged mornings from the subway into Columbus Circle, and that I was always wearing a black wool dress, a trench coat, and galoshes, and carrying an umbrella. In the dark hallway there were three flights of steps, which sagged and smelled of things like hot iron, cigars, rubber boots, or peach pits—the last gasps of whatever industries were dying behind the lettered doors.

The U.S.A. School consisted of four rooms: a tiny lobby where one girl sat alone, typing—typing exactly what her colleagues were typing in the big room behind her, I discovered, but I suppose she was placed there to stave off any unexpected pupils who might decide to come to the school in person. The lobby had a few photos on the wall: pictures of Sinclair Lewis and other non-graduates. Then came the big room, lit grayly by several soot-and-snow-laden skylights, lights going all the time, with six to a dozen girls. Their number varied daily, and they sat at very old-model typewriters, typing the school's "lessons." At the other end of this room, overlooking the street, were two more tiny rooms, one of which was Mr. Black's office and the other Mr. Margolies and Mr. Hearn's office.

Mr. Hearn was a tall, very heavy, handsome woman, about thirty years old, named Rachel, with black horn-rimmed glasses, and a black mole on one cheek. Rachel and I were somewhat cramped in our quarters. She smoked furiously all the time, and I smoked moderately, and we were not allowed to keep our door open because of the poor transient typists, who were not allowed to smoke and might see us and go on strike, or report us to the nearest fire station. What with the rain and fog and snow outside and the smoke inside, we lived in a suffocating, woolly gray isolation, as if in a cocoon. It smelled like a day coach at the end of a long train trip. We worked back to back, but we had swivel chairs and spent quite a bit of our time swung around to each other, with our knees almost bumping, the two cigarettes under each other's nose, talking.

At first she was horrid to me. Again in my innocence I didn't realize it was, of course, because of my Vassar stigmata and my literary career, but her manner soon improved and we even got to like each other, moderately. Rachel did most of the talking. She had a great deal to say; she wanted to correct all the mistakes in my education and, as so many people did in those days, she wanted to get me to join the Party. In order to avoid making the trip to headquarters with her, to get my "card," something we could have done easily during any lunch hour, once I'd put an end to my nonsense and made the decision, I told her I was an anarchist. But it didn't help much. In spite of my principles, I found myself cornered into defending Berkman's attempt to assassinate Andrew Carnegie's partner, Henry Frick, and after that, I spent evenings at the Forty-second Street Library taking out books under "*An*," in desperate attempts to shut Rachel up. For a while I was in touch with an anarchist organization (they are hard to locate, I found) in New Jersey, and received pamphlets from them, and invitations to meetings, every day in my mail.

Sometimes we went out to lunch together at a mammoth Stewart's Cafeteria. I liked cafeterias well enough, but they afflict one with indecision: what to eat, what table to sit at, what chair at the table, whether to remove the food from the tray or eat it on the tray, where to put the tray, whether to take off one's coat or keep it on, whether to abandon everything to one's fellow diners, and go for the forgotten glass of water, or to lug it all along. But Rachel swept me ahead of her, like a leaf from the enchanter fleeing, toward the sandwich counter. The variety of sandwiches that could be made to order like lightning was staggering, and she always ate three: lox and cream cheese on a bun, corned beef and pickle relish on rye, pastrami and mustard on something-or-other. She *shouted* her order. It didn't matter much, I found, after a few days of trying to state my three terms loudly and clearly; the sandwiches all tasted alike. I began settling for large, quite unreal baked apples and coffee. Rachel, with her three sandwiches and three cups of black coffee simultaneously, and I would seat ourselves in our wet raincoats and galoshes, our lunches overlapping between us, and she would harangue me about literature.

She never attempted politics at lunch, I don't know why. She had read a lot and had what I, the English major, condescendingly considered rather pathetic taste. She liked big books, with lots of ego and emotion in them, and Whitman was her favorite poet. She liked the translations of Merezh-kovski, all of Thomas Wolfe that had then appeared, all of Theodore Dreiser, the Studs Lonigan series of James Farrell, and best of all she liked Vardis Fisher. She almost knew by heart his entire works to date. A feeling of nightmare comes over me as I remember those luncheons: the food; the wet, gritty floor under my hot feet; the wet, feeding, roaring crowd of people beneath the neon lights; and Rachel's inexorable shout across the table, telling me every detail of Vardis Fisher's endless and harrowing autobiography. She may have worked in some details from her own, I'm not sure; I made up my mind then never to read the books, which she offered to loan me, and I never have. I remember her quoting the line and a half from "Modern Love" from which Fisher had taken three titles in a row: "*In tragic life, God wot, / No villain need be! Passions spin the plot . . .*" and my wondering dazedly in all the hubbub why he had neglected the possibilities of "God wot," or if he'd still get around to it. I had recently come from a line analysis of *The Waste Land*, and this bit of literary collage failed to impress me.

"Realism" and only "realism" impressed *her*. But if I tried to imply, in my old classroom manner, that there was "realism" and "realism," or ask her what she *meant* by "realism," she would glare at me savagely, her eyes glittering under Stewart's lighting fixtures, and silently stretch her large mouth over the bulging tiers of a sandwich. Her mole moved up and down as she chewed. At first I was afraid of those slap-like glares, but I grew used to them. And when one day, back in our office, she asked me to read one of her sentences to see if the grammar was right, I knew that she had begun to like me in spite of my bourgeois decadence and an ignorance of reality that took refuge in the childishness of anarchism. I also knew she had already sensed something fishy about my alleged political views.

Overbearing, dishonest, unattractive, proud of being "tough," touchy, insensitive, yet capable of being kind or amused when anything penetrated, Rachel was something new to me. She had one rare trait that kept me interested: she never spoke of herself at all. Her salary was twenty-five dollars a week. Her clothes were shabby, even for Stewart's in those days, and dirty as well. The only thing I learned about her was that she had a sister in a state tuberculosis sanatorium whom she went to see once a month, but whom she didn't particularly like; the reason seemed to be because she was sick, and therefore "no good." Rachel herself had tremendous strength and I soon realized that she inspired fear, almost physical fear, in everyone at the so-called school, including President Black. I also soon realized that she was the entire brains of the place, and afterwards I even suspected that in her power and duplicity perhaps it was she who really owned it, and was using Mr. Black as a front. Probably not, but I never knew the truth about anything that went on there.

Her cigarettes were stolen for her somewhere by a "man" she knew—how, or who the man was, I never discovered. From time to time other objects appeared—a new bag, a fountain pen, a lighter—from the same source or perhaps a different "man," but she never spoke of love or romance, except Vardis Fisher's. She should have hated me; my constant gentle acquiescence or hesitant corrections must have been hard to take; but I don't think she did. I think we felt sorry for each other. I think she felt that I was one of the doomed, enjoying my little grasshopper existence, my "sense of humor," my "culture," while I could, and that perhaps at some not very future date, when the chips were down, she might even put in a good word for me if she felt like it. I think that later she may well have become a great business success—probably a shady business, like the writing school, but on a much larger scale. She seemed drawn toward the dark and crooked, as if, since she believed that people were forced into being underhanded by economic circumstances in the first place, it would have been dishonest of her not to be dishonest. "Property is theft" was one of her favorite sayings.

Poor Rachel! I often disliked her; she gave me a *frisson*, and yet at the same time I liked her, and I certainly couldn't help listening to every word she said. For several weeks she was my own private Columbus Circle orator. Her lack of a "past," of any definable setting at all, the impression she gave of power and of something biding its time, even if it was false or silly, fascinated me. Talking with her was like holding a snapshot negative up to the light and wondering how its murks and transparencies were actually going to develop.

The course we offered on "How to Write" was advertised in the cheapest farm magazines, movie and Western magazines. It was one of those "You, too, can earn money by your pen" advertisements, glowingly but carefully worded. We could instruct anyone, no matter what his or her education, in any branch of the writing art, from newspaper reporting to advertising, to the novel, and every student would receive the personal attention and expert advice of successful, money-making authors like Mr. Hearn and Mr. Margolies. There were eight lessons, and the complete course, payable in advance, cost forty dollars. At the time I worked there, the school had only about a hundred and fifty "students" going, but there had been a period, just before, when it had had many, many more, and more were expected again, I gathered, as soon as the courses had been "revised." There had been a big upheaval in the recent past, entailing the loss of most of the student body, and for some reason, everything, all the circulars, contract blanks, and "lessons," had to be revised immediately and printed all over again. That was why, off and on, so many typists were employed.

All these revisions, including the eight new lessons, were being done by Rachel. She sat with the school's former "literature" cut into narrow strips, and clipped together in piles around her. There were also stacks of circulars from rival correspondence schools, and a few odd textbooks on composition and short-story writing, from which she lifted the most dogmatic sentences, or even whole paragraphs. When she did work, she worked extremely rapidly. It sounded like two or three typewriters instead of one, and the nervous typists kept running in from the big skylighted room and back again with the new material like relay racers. But she talked to me a great deal of the time, or stared gloomily out the window at the falling snow. Once she said, "Why don't you write a pretty poem about *that*?" Once or twice, smelling strongly of whiskey, she buried herself sulkily in a new proletarian novel for an entire afternoon.

We scarcely saw Mr. Black at all. He received a good many callers in his office, men who looked just like him, and he served them the George Washington instant coffee he made on a Sterno stove, which smelled unpleasantly through the partition into our room. Once in a while he would bring us both coffee, in ten-cent-store cups of milky green glass with very rough edges you could cut yourself on. He would ask, "And how's the Vassar girl?" and look over my shoulder at the letter I was slowly producing on the typewriter with three or four fingers, and say, "Fine! Fine! You're doing fine! They'll love it! They'll love it!" and give my shoulder an objectionable squeeze. Sometimes he would say to Rachel, "Take a look at this. Save it; put the carbon in your file. We'll use it again." Rachel would give a loud groan.

It was here, in this noisome place, in spite of all I had read and been taught and thought I knew about it before, that the mysterious, awful power of writing first dawned on me. Or, since "writing" means so many different things, the power of the printed word, or even that capitalized Word whose significance had previously escaped me but then made itself suddenly, if sporadically, plain.

Our advertisements specified that when an applicant wrote in inquiring about the course, he was to send a sample of his writing, a "story" of any sort, any length, for our "analysis," and a five-dollar money order. We sent him the "analysis" and told him whether or not he really did have the right stuff in him to make a successful writer. All applicants, unless analphabetic, did. Then he was supposed to complete the first lesson, I think it was either "Straight Reporting" or "Descriptive Writing," within a month and send it back to us with the remaining thirty-five dollars. We "analyzed" that and sent it back along with lesson number two, and he was launched on the course.

I forget all the lessons now, but "Advertising" was fitted in somewhere. The students were required to write advertisements for grapefruit, bread, and liquor. Why the emphasis on food and drink, I don't know, unless that too was a sign of the times. Also included were a short story and a "True Confession" lesson. Almost all the students had the two genres hopelessly confused. Their original "samples" were apt to fall into the True Confession form, too. This sample, expanded or cut, censored or livened up, and the first letter to Mr. Margolies that accompanied it constituted the most interesting assignment for all concerned. My job was to write an analysis of each lesson in five hundred words, if I could, and as many of them a day as I possibly could, using a collection of previous lessons and analyses as models. I also had to write a short personal reply to the inevitable letter that arrived with each lesson. I was to encourage the student if he was feeling hopeless, and discourage him firmly if he showed any signs of wanting his money back.

Henry James once said that he who would aspire to be a writer must inscribe on his banner the one word "Loneliness." In the case of my students, their need was not to ward off society, but to get into it. Their problem was that on their banners "Loneliness" had been inscribed despite them, and so they aspired to be writers. Without exception the letters I received were from people suffering from terrible loneliness in all its better-known forms, and in some I had never even dreamed of. Writing, especially writing to Mr. Margolies, was a way of being less alone. To be printed, and to be "famous," would be an instant shortcut to identity, and an escape from solitude, because then other people would know one as admirers, friends, lovers, suitors, etc.

In the forms they filled out, they gave their ages and occupations. There were a good many cowboys and ranch hands. One of them printed his lessons, not with the printing taught for a while in fashionable schools, although it resembled it, but with the printing of a child concentrating on being neat and careful. There was a sheepherder, a real shepherd, who even *said* he was lonely, "in my line of work." Writing cheered him up because "sheep aren't much company for a man (ha-ha)." There were the wives of ranchers as well. There were several sailors, a Negro cook, a petty officer on a submarine, and a real lighthouse keeper. There were a good many "domestics," some of whom said they were "colored," and several students writing from addresses in the Deep South told me, as if they had to, that they were Negroes.

Of all the letters and lessons I read during my stay at the U.S.A. School, only one set showed any slight sign of "promise" whatever. They were the work of a "lady cattle-rancher and poultry farmer," an "old maid," she wrote, living at an R.F.D. address somewhere in Kansas. The stories she sent in, regardless of the nature of the assignment, were real stories. The other students' heartbreaking attempts were always incoherent, abrupt, curtailed. Hers bounced along exuberantly, like a good talker, and were almost interesting, with a lot of local color and detail. They were filled with roosters, snakes, foxes, and hawks, and they had dramatic and possibly true plots woven around sick and dying cows, mortgages, stepmothers, babies, wicked blizzards, and tornadoes. They were also ten times longer than anyone else's stories. After I gave up my job, I used to look into farm magazines, like *The Country Gentleman*, on the newsstands, hoping that she might have made publication at last, but I never saw her name again.

Most of my pathetic applicants seemed never to have read anything in their lives, except perhaps a single, memorable story of the "True Confession" type. The discrepancy between the odd, colorless, disjointed little pages they sent me and what they saw in print just didn't occur to them. Or perhaps they thought Mr. Margolies would wave his magic wand and the little heaps of melancholy word-bones, like chicken bones or fish bones, would put on flesh and vitality and be transformed into gripping, compelling, thrilling, full-length stories and novels. There were doubtless other, deeper reasons for their taking the "course," sending in all their "lessons," and paying that outrageous forty dollars. But I could never quite believe that most of my students really thought that they too could one day write, or even that they would really have to work to do so. It was more like applying for application blanks for a lottery. After all, they might win the prize just as well as the next person, and everyone knows those things aren't always run honestly.

There seemed to be one thing common to all their "primitive" writing, as I suppose it might be called, in contrast to primitive painting: its slipshodiness and haste. Where primitive painters will spend months or years, if necessary, putting in every blade of grass and building up brick walls in low relief, the primitive writer seems in a hurry to get it over with. Another thing was the almost complete lack of detail. The primitive painter loves detail and lingers over it and emphasizes it at the expense of the picture as a whole. But if the writers put them in, the details are often impossibly or wildly inappropriate, sometimes revealing a great deal about the writer without furthering the matter in hand at all. Perhaps it all demonstrates the professional writer's frequent complaint that painting is more fun than writing. Perhaps the ranchers' wives who sent in miserable little outlines for stories with no conversation and no descriptions of people or places wouldn't hesitate to spend long afternoons lovingly decorating birthday cakes in different-color icings. But the subject matter was similarly banal in both the paintings and the writing. There was also the same tendency in both primitive painting and writing to make it all right, or of real value to the world, by tacking on a grand, if ill-fitting, "moral," or allegorical interpretation. My students seemed to be saying: "Our experiences are real and true and from them we have drawn these unique, these noble conclusions. Since our sentiments are so noble, who could have the heart to deny us our right to Fame?"

What could I possibly find to say to them? From what they wrote me it was obvious they could hardly wait to receive my next analysis. Perhaps they hoped, each time, that Mr. Margolies would tell them he had found a magazine to publish their last lesson and was enclosing the check. All of them were eager, if not hardworking, or felt they had to pretend to be. One man wrote: "I slept on a hair all night, waiting to hear from you." They apologized for their slowness, for their spelling, for their pens or pencils (they were asked to use ink but quite a few didn't). One boy excused his poor handwriting by saying, "This is being written on the subway," and it may have been true. Some referred to the lessons as their "homework," and addressed Mr. Margolies as "Dear Teacher." One woman decorated her lessons with Christmas seals. To my surprise, there were two or three male students who wrote man-to-man obscenities, or retold well-worn dirty jokes.

I took to copying out parts of their letters and stories to take home with me. A Kansas City janitor wanted to learn to write in order to publish "a book about how to teach children to be good radicals, of the George Washington Type or the Jesus Christ Type." One woman revealed that her aged mother approved of her learning how to write to such an extent that she had given her the forty dollars and "*her own name* to write under." The daughter's name was Emma, the mother's was Katerina. Would I please address her as Katerina in the future?

Next to my "lady cattle-rancher and poultry farmer" I grew fondest of a Mr. Jimmy O'Shea of Fall River, aged seventy, occupation "retired." His was the nearest approach to a classical primitive style. His stories were fairly long, and like Gertrude Stein, he wrote in large handwriting on small pieces of paper. He had developed a style that enabled him to make exactly a page of every sentence. Each sentence—it usually began with *Also* or *Yes*—opened at the top left-hand and finished with an outsize dimple of a period in the lower right. Goodness shone through his blue-lined pages as if they had been little paper lanterns. He characterized everything that appeared in his simple tales with three, four, or even five adjectives and then repeated them, like Homer, every time the noun appeared. It was Mr. O'Shea who wrote me a letter which expressed the common feeling of time passing and wasted, of wonder and envy, and partly sincere ambition: "I wasn't feeling well over my teeth, and I had three large ones taken out, for they made me nervous and sick sometime, and this is the reason I couldn't send in my lesson. I am thinking of being able to write like all the Authors, for I believe that is more in my mind than any other kind of work. Mr. Margolies, I am thinking of how those Authors write such long stories of 60,000 or 100,000 words in those Magazines, and where do they get their imagination and the material to work upon? I know there is a big field in this art."

I stood the school for as long as I could, which wasn't very long, and the same week that I received this letter from Mr. O'Shea, I resigned. Mr. Black begged me to stay, I was just getting going, I was turning out more and more analyses every day, and he offered me two dollars and a half more a week.

Rachel seemed sorry to see me go, too. We went out for a last lunch together, to a different cafeteria, one that had a bar, and, going Dutch, had a twenty-cent Manhattan each before lunch. When I was cleaning out my desk, she gave me a present, a strange paperbound book she had just finished reading, written by a Chinese, almost in the style of some of our students. It was all about his experiences as an agricultural slave in the United States and on the sugarcane plantations of Cuba. It may have been true, but it was not "realism" because he used odd, Oriental imagery.

About two years later I met Rachel in Times Square one night on my way to the theater. She looked just the same, perhaps a little heavier and perhaps a little less shabby. I asked her if she still worked for the U.S.A. School of Writing and how Mr. Black was. Mr. Black, she announced casually, was in jail, for a second or third offense, for misuse of the mails. The U.S.A. School of Writing had been raided by the police shortly after I left, and all our work, and all my poor students' accumulation of lessons and earnest, confiding letters, had been confiscated. She said, "I didn't tell you while you were there, but that's why we were doing that revising. The U.S.A. School was a new name; up until a month before you came, it was something else. Black paid a big fine that time, and we were starting all over again."

I asked her what she was doing now, but she didn't tell me. I was dressed to go to the theater, and she looked me up and down contemptuously, I felt, but tolerantly, as if she were thinking, Some anarchist! Then Mr. Hearn and Mr. Margolies shook hands and parted forever.

1966

A Trip to Vigia

The shy poet, so soiled, so poor, so polite, insisted on taking us in his own car. A friend would go along as *mechanista*. The car was on its last legs; it had broken down twice just getting us around Belém the day before. But what could we do? I couldn't very well flaunt my dollars in his face and hire a better one.

He arrived at our hotel at nine (he had said eight) with José Augusto, one of his little boys, aged eleven, fair, and also very shy. Ruy, the poet, was dark, quiet, and softly heavy, his waxy face spattered with fine black moles like shot. His other children, four or five of them, were at home with "fever." They were sick all the time we were in Belém. This José Augusto scarcely spoke, but in the course of the long day his expression became by degrees more animated, more childlike. By midafternoon he grew restless, even active; he slept all the way back from the expedition in his father's arms.

Ruy was nervous. He kept telling us we probably wouldn't like the famous church at Vigia; it would be too "baroque" for us. Each time he said this, our imaginations added more belfries and a slightly wilder wave of carved stone. M. and I got into the back seat that slanted downwards so that our bottoms felt as if they were gently grazing the road. The *mechanista*, José Augusto, and Ruy were in front. Most of the time they kept their heads bent as if in prayer. Perhaps they were praying to the tired heart of the car to keep on beating just a little longer, until the expedition was safely over.

We had met Ruy just two days before. That morning I asked M. to let me know when the mystic moment arrived and she'd shift gears from addressing him as "Dr. Ruy" to "you." This use of the *você* or second person is always a delicate problem and I wanted to see how M., who has the nicest Brazilian manners, would solve it. Since Ruy was a poet and therefore could be considered sensitive, and since we found him very sympathetic, I felt it would be happening very soon.

Outside Belém we crossed a dead-looking railroad yard with old red freight cars scattered about in it, the end of the line. We passed under a fretwork arch, decorated with a long and faded banner and with cut bamboos turned sere brown. It had been set up to celebrate the opening of the new highway to Brasília. Just beyond it, the paved road stopped for good. However, the very thought of this new road to the capital had cheered up all of Belém considerably. Even the resigned Ruy spoke about the future optimistically.

Vigia was about a hundred kilometers away. We went off toward it on another narrower road to the left that went up and down, up and down, in low wavy hills, mostly through bushes. Because of the two daily rains (it was the rainy season), there was little dust. Slowly, slowly we rose and fell over the gravel. The silent *mechanista* was like a mother teaching the car to walk. But after a while it stopped.

He got out and lifted the hood. M. talked gaily of this and that. After fifteen minutes or so, the car started again: up a slight grade; down faster; up. The day was getting hot. The car was getting hot. But still it seemed as if we had just left Belém. We passed fields of pepper, big leafy pillars. It is grown on poles, like string beans, and is called Pimenta da Rainha, Queen's Pepper, because it originally belonged to the crown. They say that the whole history of Portugal since the fourteenth century is the history of pepper. It had recently become a big crop in the north. Ruy complained about it, saying it was already overplanted, the way any successful crop always is in Brazil, and the price was dropping. On the left, where an unseen stream ran, were occasional plantations of jute, a bright and tender green.

More pepper. A mud-and-wattle house or two. An oxcart: mild, lovely *zebus* with high humps and long hanging ears, blue-gray, a well-matched team. Skinny horses scrambled off into the bushes, or stood pat while we edged around them. A dismal mud-and-wattle church, half-painted bright blue: IGREJA BATISTA. Then a little bridge with half the planks missing. The *mechanista* got out and squatted to study it from the far side, before taking us over.

Fine and blue, the morning rain arrived. The gravel darkened and spurted away slowly on either side. We plowed dreamily along. Ruy was talking about T. S. Eliot. He read English, some, but spoke not a word. I tried a story about Ezra Pound. It was very well received but, I felt, not understood. I undertook some more literary anecdotes. Smiling politely, Ruy waited for every joke until the faithful M. had helped me put them into Portuguese. Often they proved to be untranslatable. The car stopped.

This time the *mechanista* took much longer. M. talked ever more gaily. Suddenly the rain came down hard, great white lashings. The bushes crouched and the gravel danced. M. nudged me, whispered *"Now,"* and in her next sentence to Ruy used a noticeable *você*; the mystic moment was past. The *mechanista* got back in, his clothes several shades darker with wet, and said we would stop at the next village for repairs.

•

The rains stopped and the sun came out. Certain varieties of glazed tropical leaves reflected the light like nickel, or white enamel, but as the car passed they returned to their actual gray-green. It was confusing, and trying to the eyes. Palm trees, more pepper and jute, more bushes. Here and there a great jungle tree had been left standing, and black specks were busy high around the tops; each tree held a whole community of birds. At least two hundred feet high, a Brazil nut tree blossomed; one could tell only by a smell like that of a thousand lilacs.

Three teams of *zebus*, loaded with jute. A small shower, like an afterthought right through the sunshine. We were driving north-northeast, skirting the great bay of Marajó, but we might as well have been in the middle of Africa or the Yucatan. (It *looked* a bit like the Yucatan.) More wretched little houses, with pigs, and naked children shining from the rain. The "village" was a crossroads, with a combined drink-shop and grocery store, a botequim, beside a spreading flamboyant tree. It took a moment to realize the car had really stopped; we stopped talking, and got out.

The store had been raided, sacked. Oh, that was its normal state. It was quite large, no color inside or cloud-color perhaps, with holes in the floor, holes in the walls, holes in the roof. A barrel of kerosene stood in a dark stain. There were a coil of blue cotton rope, a few mattock heads, and a bundle of yellow-white handles, fresh cut from hard *ipé* wood. Lined up on the shelves were many, many bottles of *cachaça*, all alike: Esperança, Hope, Hope, Hope. There was a counter where you could drink, if you wanted. A bunch of red-striped lamp wicks hung beside a bunch of rusty frying pans. A glass case offered brown toffees leaking through their papers, and old, old, old sweet buns. Some very large ants were making hay there while the sun shone. Our eyes negotiated the advertisements for Orange Crush and Guaraná on the cloud-colored walls, and we had seen everything. That was all.

The shopkeeper had gone off with our *mechanista*, so Ruy helped us to warm Orange Crush and over our protests put the money for it on the counter. "No cheese?" he inquired, poking about in back, as if he were in the habit of eating quantities of cheese with an Orange Crush every morning. He asked if we'd like a toffee, and urged us to take another *crooshy*. Then he said, "Let's go see the manioc factory."

This was right behind the botequim. It was an open-air affair of three thatched roofs on posts, one a round toadstool. A dozen women and girls sat on the ground, ripping the black skins off the long roots with knives. We were the funniest things they had seen in years. They tried not to laugh in our faces, but we "slayed" them. M. talked to them, but this did not increase their self-control. *Zebus* stood looking on, chewing their cuds. A motor, with belts slanting up under the thatch, chugged away, grinding up the raw manioc. The place smelled of *zebu*, gasoline, and people. Everyone talked, but it was murky and peaceful.

The greatest attraction was the revolving metal floor, a big disk, for drying out the flour. It was heated underneath by a charcoal fire and the area was partly railed off, like a small rink, so one could lean over and watch. The coarse white flour went slowly round and round, pushed back and forth in drifts by two men with long wooden hoes. The flour got whiter and whiter, but they were careful not to let it brown. In the north, people usually eat it white; in the south, they prefer it roasted to a pale tan.

We almost forgot we were on our way to Vigia. Then the *mechanista* collected us; in we got, out again, in again, and finally off. The motor now sounded languid and half sick but uncomplaining, like the poet himself.

Another ten kilometers and we came to a small house on the left, set among fruit and banana trees growing directly from the bare, swept earth. A wash was strung on the barbed-wire fence. Several skinny dogs appeared and a very fat young woman came out, carrying a baby, with two little boys tagging along behind. We all shook hands, even the baby boys. Her husband, a friend of Ruy's, was away but she invited us in—"for lunch," said the poor woman. We quickly explained we had brought our lunch with us. Ruy did the honors. "Ah! the water here is a *delicia*, isn't it, Dona Sebastiana? It's the best water, the only water, from here to Vigia. People come for miles to get water here. Wait till you try it."

Pegged to the side of the house was a fresh snake skin, a monster over ten feet long the husband had shot two days before. Dona Sebastiana brought out three glass jars, and a large tin can full of fat she'd rendered from the snake. She said it was the best remedy in the world for a great variety of ailments, including tuberculosis and "sore legs." Then she hurried in to make the coffee.

There were several small rooms in her house, and they were almost bare. There was no glass in the windows, and only the front room had a floor. It also had the *oratorio*, a yellowed print of Our Lady of Nazareth, with red paper roses in front of it, and that other light of the world, the sewing machine, a hand-run *Sin-ger*.

In the kitchen Dona Sebastiana was fanning hard, with a plaited palm leaf held in both hands, a charcoal fire in a clay trough. We admired a hanging lamp of tin, homemade, cleverly constructed to stay upright. It was the only thing to admire. "Oh," she said, "my girl friend left that to me when she died. We went to school together." There was almost nothing in her kitchen except a black pot or two. The only signs of food were some overripe cucumbers on the windowsill. How had she managed to be so fat? The upside-down *cafezinho* cups were modestly hidden under a fringed napkin, with a little boy pushing a wheelbarrow embroidered in red out-line. Dona Sebastiana had no white sugar, and she apologized for the cake of brown she scraped for us herself. We drank it down, the hot, bad, sad coffee, and went out back to see her river.

It really was a beautiful river. It was four yards across, dark, clear, run-ning rapidly, with white cascades and deep pools edged with backed-up foam, and its banks were a dream of the tropics. It splashed, it sang, it glit-tered over white pebbles. Little did it reck that it had almost reached the vast muddy bay, the mouth of the Amazon. It made up for a lot, and Dona Sebastiana was proud of it. José Augusto and the little boys went wading. The thin dogs stood in the water, and gulped at it, then looked back at us over their shoulders from *their* river.

It was one o'clock by now and we were starving. The hotel had given us a lunch, a good-sized roast hen, fresh rolls, butter, oranges, a hunk of de-sirable white cheese. But no one would eat a bite. They *never* ate lunch—what an idea! I made a chicken sandwich and offered it to José Augusto. He looked shocked and frightened, and moved closer to his father's knee. Finally M. and I miserably gobbled up some lunch by ourselves. The *mech-anista* soaked his feet, and rolled and smoked corn-husk cigarettes. Ruy let José Augusto accept one orange; Dona Sebastiana let her little boys accept two oranges. Then we shook hands all around, and back in our car we crawled away.

After a while, we got there. But first, from far off, we could see the pinna-cled tops of two square towers, dazzling white against the dark rainclouds. The church looked like a sacred bull, a great white zebu. The road was level now, the landscape low and flat; we were near the coast. The church towers could be seen a long way off, rising very high above the tops of the tall green-black mango trees around them.

The plaza was dark red, laid out with cement benches and lampposts stuck with round globes, like artificial pearls. Smack in the middle was a blue-and-white bandstand. It was hideous, but because it was so small it didn't spoil the effect at all—rather as if these absurd offerings had been laid out on the ground in front of the great, indifferent, sacred white zebu. The dark green mango trees were dwarfed by the church. On either side the little old houses were tile-covered, with Gothic blue-and-white, or yellow-and-white, tile-covered *azulejos*.

Ruy watched us. But we liked the church very much and said so. He looked greatly relieved. The church danced in the light. I climbed on a stone wall, the remains of another abandoned house, to get a photograph of the whole thing, if possible, but there was nothing high enough to take it all in. It started to rain. I got a picture, jumped down—a dozen people had gathered to watch me, all looking scandalized—tripped, and tore my petticoat, which fell down below my skirt. The rain poured.

The others were all inside the church. It was mostly blue and white—bare, cold, huge, echoing. Little children followed us and ran shouting up and down; Ruy's little boy joined in. We went out on the second-story galleries, beneath the row of huge whitewashed pillars. You could see a pattern of tile roofs and mango trees through the rain tapestry, red-brown, down to the river, where the masts of ships and boats showed. A battered blue truck ground along below, and the driver came in, too—another friend of Ruy's.

The sacristan, an old fisherman, appeared. There was little enough to be seen in the sacristy. He went to a cupboard, with the little children pressing close around him and me, crying, "Show her Father! Show her Father!" and he handed me—a bone. A skull. The children reached up for it. He patted the skull and said yes, that was Father So-and-So, a saint if ever there was one, a really holy man. Never went anywhere, thought of nothing but prayer, meditated and prayed seven hours a day. I thought he was speaking of some forgotten saint of the seventeenth century who had never been properly recognized. No, Father had died two years before. I kept trying to hand the skull back. He was too busy telling me about the final illness, his *agonia*, his death. It was the most wonderful thing in Vigia. The sacristan put the skull back in the corner of the bare cupboard. It was so dark in the sacristy we could scarcely see.

We went out. Huge thunderclouds rolled back and forth, the river was higher, the tide had turned. All the lights went on in the forsaken plaza, although it was not dark. The pearly, silent, huge church of Vigia had made us all feel somehow guilty at abandoning it once again. The town's little white houses were turning mauve. In the high, high skies, shafts of long golden beams fell through the thunderclouds. Nature was providing all the baroque grandeur the place lacked. We started back to Belém, and it soon began to get really dark.

The car didn't stop all the way home, except once on purpose for gasoline. The trip seemed to take forever and we all fell silent. The little boy fell sound asleep. There wasn't even a light for miles, and never a car; we met two trucks and overtook two. Our eyes fastened on the slightest light or movement—an oil lamp, like an ancient Greek lamp, on a bicycle; a few people on foot carrying umbrellas.

Then lights. We were coming to Belém. Lights on the mud walls and their political posters and endless slogans, with all the *N*'s and *S*'s written backwards. Tall narrow doorways, the murky light of an oil lamp, warm, yellow and black. A man carrying a lantern—oh, he's leading a cow and a calf. Goats. Look out, a zebu! We almost hit him, a high bony gray wall across the road. He lowered his horns sharply and snorted softly.

Suddenly we are in Belém. Huge black mango trees. Cars bumping over the cobblestones, bumpety-bump. How very, very bright this dim city can look! We ache in the dark. The church at Vigia, huge, white, alone on our consciences, has become a ghost story.

The hotel at last. It is almost nine o'clock. We invite Ruy in for a drink, at least. He comes, but will take only another *cafezinho*. The dingy café looks brilliant. The young literary men are there, with their rolled umbrellas, moving hands and black neckties, their hair slicked back. They all greet Ruy. Half asleep, we swallow the coffee and, behind our backs, Ruy pays for it.

1967

Efforts of Affection: A Memoir
of Marianne Moore

In the first edition of Marianne Moore's *Collected Poems* of 1951 there is a poem originally called "Efforts and Affection." In my copy of this book, Marianne crossed out the "and" and wrote "of" above it. I liked this change very much, and so I am giving the title "Efforts of Affection" to the whole piece.

I first met Marianne Moore in the spring of 1934 when I was a senior at Vassar College, through Miss Fanny Borden, the college librarian. A school friend and the friend's mother, both better read and more sophisticated in their literary tastes than I was, had told me about Marianne Moore's poetry several years earlier. I had already read every poem of Miss Moore's I could find, in back copies of *The Dial*, "little magazines," and anthologies in the college library. I hadn't known poetry could be like that; I took to it immediately, but although I knew there was a volume of hers called *Observations*, it was not in the library and I had never seen it.

Because Miss Borden seems like such an appropriate person to have introduced me to Marianne Moore, I want to say a little about her. She was the niece of the Fall River Lizzie Borden, and at college the rumor was that Lizzie Borden's lurid career had had a permanently subduing effect on Miss Fanny Borden's personality. She was extremely shy and reserved and spoke in such a soft voice it was hard to hear her at all. She was tall and thin; she always dressed in browns and grays, old-fashioned, muted, and distinguished-looking. She also rode a chainless bicycle. I remember watching her ride slowly up to the library, seated very high and straight on this curiosity, which somehow seemed more lady-like than a bicycle with a chain, and park it in the rack. (We didn't padlock bicycles then.) Once, after she had gone inside, I examined the bicycle, which was indeed chainless, to see if I could figure out how it worked. I couldn't. Contact with the librarian was rare; once in a long while, in search of a book, one would be sent into Miss Borden's office, shadowy and cave-like, with books piled everywhere. She weighed down the papers on her desk with smooth, round stones, quite big stones, brought from the seashore, and once when my roommate admired one of these, Miss Borden said in her almost inaudible voice, "Do you like it? You may *have* it," and handed it over, gray, round, and very heavy.

One day I was sent in to Miss Borden's office about a book, I no longer remember what. We continued talking a little, and I finally got up my courage to ask her why there was no copy of *Observations* by that wonderful poet Marianne Moore in the Vassar library. She looked ever so gently taken aback and inquired, "Do you *like* Marianne Moore's poems?" I said I certainly did, the few I'd been able to find. Miss Borden then said calmly, "I've known her since she was a little girl," and followed that with the question that was possibly to influence the whole course of my life: "Would you like to meet her?" I was painfully—no, excruciatingly—shy and I had run away many times rather than face being introduced to adults of much less distinction than Marianne Moore, but I immediately said, "Yes." Miss Borden said that she would write to Miss Moore, who lived in Brooklyn, and also that she would be glad to lend me *her* copy of *Observations.*

Miss Borden's copy of *Observations* was an eye-opener in more ways than one. Poems like "An Octopus," about a glacier, or "Peter," about a cat, or "Marriage," about marriage, struck me, as they still do, as miracles of language and construction. Why had no one ever written about things in this clear and dazzling way before? But at the same time I was astonished to discover that Miss Borden (whom I now knew to be an old family friend of the Moores) obviously didn't share my liking for these poems. Tucked in the back of the book were quite a few reviews that had appeared when *Observations* was published, in 1924, and most of these were highly unfavorable, some simply obtuse. There was even a parody Moore poem by Franklin P. Adams. Even more revealing, Miss Borden hadn't seen fit to place a copy of her friend's book in the college library. (Later that year I found a copy for myself, on a secondhand-book table at Macy's.)

The day came when Miss Borden told me that she had heard from Miss Moore and that Miss Moore was willing to meet me in New York, on a Saturday afternoon. Years later I discovered that Marianne had agreed to do this with reluctance; in the past, it seems, dear Miss Borden had sent several Vassar girls to meet Miss Moore and sometimes her mother as well, and every one had somehow failed to please. This probably accounted for the conditions laid down for our first rendezvous: I was to find Miss Moore seated on the bench at the right of the door leading to the reading room of the New York Public Library. They might have been even more strict. I learned later that if Miss Moore really expected *not* to like would-be acquaintances, she arranged to meet them at the Information Booth in Grand Central Station—no place to sit down, and, if necessary, an instant getaway was possible. In the meantime, I had been told a little more about her by Miss Borden, who described her as a child, a strange and appealing little creature with bright red hair—playful, and, as might have been expected, fond of calling her family and friends by the names of animals.

I was very frightened, but I put on my new spring suit and took the train to New York. I had never seen a picture of Miss Moore; all I knew was that she had red hair and usually wore a wide-brimmed hat. I expected the hair to be bright red and for her to be tall and intimidating. I was right on time, even a bit early, but she was there before me (no matter how early one arrived, Marianne was always there first) and, I saw at once, not very tall and not in the least intimidating. She was forty-seven, an age that seemed old to me then, and her hair was mixed with white to a faint rust pink, and her rust-pink eyebrows were frosted with white. The large flat black hat was as I'd expected it to be. She wore a blue tweed suit that day and, as she usually did then, a man's "polo shirt," as they were called, with a black bow at the neck. The effect was quaint, vaguely Bryn Mawr 1909, but stylish at the same time. I sat down and she began to talk.

It seems to me that Marianne talked to me steadily for the next thirty-five years, but of course that is nonsensical. I was living far from New York many of those years and saw her at long intervals. She must have been one of the world's greatest talkers: entertaining, enlightening, fascinating, and memorable; her talk, like her poetry, was quite different from anyone else's in the world. I don't know what she talked about at that first meeting; I wish I had kept a diary. Happily ignorant of the poor Vassar girls before me who hadn't passed muster, I began to feel less nervous and even spoke some myself. I had what may have been an inspiration, I don't know—at any rate, I attribute my great good fortune in having known Marianne as a friend in part to it. Ringling Bros. and Barnum & Bailey Circus was making its spring visit to New York and I asked Miss Moore (we called each other "Miss" for over two years) if she would care to go to the circus with me the Saturday after next. I didn't know that she *always* went to the circus, wouldn't have missed it for anything, and when she accepted, I went back to Poughkeepsie in the grimy day coach extremely happy.

The Circus

I got to Madison Square Garden very early—we had settled on the hour because we wanted to see the animals before the show began—but Marianne was there ahead of me. She was loaded down: two blue cloth bags, one on each arm, and two huge brown paper bags, full of something. I was given one of these. They contained, she told me, stale brown bread for the elephants, because stale brown bread was one of the things they liked best to eat. (I later suspected that they might like stale white bread just as much but that Marianne had been thinking of their health.) As we went in and down to the lower level, where we could hear (and smell) the animals, she told me her preliminary plan for the circus. Her brother, Warner, had given her an elephant-hair bracelet, of which she was very fond, two or three strands of black hairs held together with gold clasps. One of the elephant hairs had fallen out and been lost. As I probably knew, elephant hairs grow only on the tops of the heads of very young elephants. In her bag, Marianne had a pair of strong nail scissors. I was to divert the adult elephants with the bread, and, if we were lucky, the guards wouldn't observe her at the end of the line where the babies were, and she could take out her scissors and snip a few hairs from a baby's head, to repair her bracelet.

She was quite right; the elephants adored stale brown bread and started trumpeting and pushing up against each other to get it. I stayed at one end of the line, putting slices of bread into the trunks of the older elephants, and Miss Moore went rapidly down to the other end, where the babies were. The large elephants were making such a to-do that a keeper did come up my way, and out of the corner of my eye I saw Miss Moore leaning forward over the rope on tiptoe, scissors in hand. Elephant hairs are tough; I thought she would never finish her hair-cutting. But she did, and triumphantly we handed out the rest of the bread and set off to see the other animals. She opened her bag and showed me three or four coarse, grayish hairs in a piece of Kleenex.

I hate seeing animals in cages, especially small cages, and especially circus animals, but I think that Marianne, while probably feeling the same way, was so passionately interested in them, and knew so much about them, that she could put aside any pain or outrage for the time being. That day I remember that one handsomely patterned snake, writhing about in a glass-walled cage, seemed to raise his head on purpose to look at us. "See, he knows me!" said Miss Moore. "He remembers me from last year." This was a joke, I decided, but perhaps not altogether a joke. Then we went upstairs and the six-ring affair began. The blue bags held our refreshments: thermos jugs of orange juice, hard-boiled eggs (the yolks only), and more brown bread, but fresh this time, and buttered. I also remember of this first visit to the circus (there were to be others) that in front of us sat a father with three young children, two boys and a girl. A big circus goes on for a long time and the children began to grow restless. Marianne leaned over with the abruptness that characterized all her movements and said to the father that if the little girl wanted to go to the bathroom, she'd be glad to take her.

260 Cumberland Street

After graduating from Vassar I lived for a year in New York City; I returned to live there from time to time for thirty years or so, but it was during this first year that I got to know Miss Moore and her mother and became familiar with their small apartment in Brooklyn. It was in the fourth floor front of an ugly yellow brick building with a light granite stoop and a big white glass globe on a pillar at either side of the door. (Marianne told taxi drivers to stop at the apartment with the "two mothballs" in front.) The elevator was small and slow. After I had buzzed, I used to try to get up in it to the fourth floor before Marianne could get down in it to take me up personally, but I rarely managed to. A very narrow hall, made narrower by waist-high bookcases along one side, and with doors to two tiny bedrooms opening off it, led back to the living room. On the end of the bookcase nearest the front door sat the famous bowl of nickels for subway fare (nickels for years, then dimes, then nickels *and* dimes, and finally quarters). Every visitor was made to accept one of these upon leaving; it was absolutely *de rigueur.* After one or two attempts at refusing, I always simply helped myself to a nickel as I left, and eventually I was rewarded for this by Marianne's saying to a friend who was protesting, "Elizabeth is an *aristocrat*; she *takes* the money." (I should like to mention here the peculiar way Marianne had of pronouncing my Christian name. She came down very hard on the second syllable, E*liz*abeth. I liked this, especially as an exclamation, when she was pretending to be shocked by something I had said.)

The small living room and dining room were crowded with furniture that had obviously come from an older, larger home, and there were many pictures on the walls, a mixture of the old and the new, family possessions and presents from friends (these generally depicted birds or animals). One painting of trees and a stream had suffered an accident to its rather blurry tree passage, and Marianne herself had restored this—I felt, unkindly, not too successfully—with what she said was "Prussian blue." She was modestly vain of her manual skills. A set of carpenter's tools hung by the kitchen door, and Marianne had put up some of the bookshelves herself. In one doorway a trapeze on chains was looped up to the lintel. I never saw this in use, but it was Marianne's, and she said that when she exercised on it and her brother was there, he always said, "The ape is rattling her chains again." A chest stood in the bay window of the living room with a bronze head of Marianne on it by Lachaise. The chest was also always piled high with new books. When I first knew Marianne she did quite a bit of reviewing and later sold the review copies on West Fourth Street.

I was always seated in the same armchair, and an ashtray was placed on a little table beside me, but I tried to smoke no more than one or two cigarettes a visit, or none at all. I felt that Mrs. Moore disapproved. Once, as I was leaving and waiting for the slow elevator, I noticed a deep burn in the railing of the staircase and commented on it. Mrs. Moore gave a melancholy sigh and said, "*Ezra* did that. He came to call on Marianne and left his cigar burning out here because he knew I *don't like cigars* . . ." Many years later, in St. Elizabeths Hospital, I repeated this to Ezra Pound. He laughed loudly and said, "I haven't smoked a cigar since I was eighteen!" Beside the ashtray and even a new package of Lucky Strikes, I was sometimes given a glass of Dubonnet. I had a suspicion that I was possibly the only guest who drank this Dubonnet, because it looked very much like the same bottle, at the level it had been on my last visit, for many months. But usually we had tea and occasionally I was invited for dinner. Mrs. Moore was a very good cook.

Mrs. Moore was in her seventies when I first knew her, very serious—solemn, rather—although capable of irony, and very devout. Her face was pale and somewhat heavy, her eyes large and a pale gray, and her dark hair had almost no white in it. Her manner toward Marianne was that of a kindly, self-controlled parent who felt that she had to take a firm line, that her daughter might be given to flightiness or—an equal sin, in her eyes—mistakes in grammar. She had taught English at a girls' school and her sentences were Johnsonian in weight and balance. She spoke more slowly than I have ever heard anyone speak in my life. One example of her conversational style has stayed with me for over forty years. Marianne was in the kitchen making tea and I was alone with Mrs. Moore. I said that I had just seen a new poem of Marianne's, "Nine Nectarines & Other Porcelain," and admired it very much. Mrs. Moore replied, "Yes. I am so *glad* that Marianne has *decided* to give the inhabitants of the *zoo* . . . a *rest*." Waiting for the conclusion of her longer statements, I grew rather nervous; nevertheless, I found her extreme precision enviable and thought I could detect echoes of Marianne's own style in it: the use of double or triple negatives, the lighter and wittier ironies—Mrs. Moore had provided a sort of ground bass for them.

She wrote me one or two beautifully composed little notes on the subject of religion, and I know my failure to respond made her sad. At each of my leave-takings she followed me to the hall, where, beside "Ezra's" imagined cigar burn, she held my hands and said a short prayer. She said grace before dinner, and once, a little maliciously, I think, Marianne asked *me* to say grace. Mercifully, a childhood grace popped into my mind. After dinner Marianne wrote it down.

Of course Mrs. Moore and her daughter were what some people might call "prudish"; it would be kinder to say "over-fastidious." This applied to Mrs. Moore more than to Marianne; Marianne, increasingly so with age, was capable of calling a spade a spade, or at least calling it by its archaic name. I remember her worrying about the fate of a mutual friend whose sexual tastes had always seemed quite obvious to me: "What are we going to do about X . . . ? Why, sometimes I think he may even be in the clutches of a *sodomite* . . . !" One could almost smell the brimstone. But several novels of the thirties and forties, including Mary McCarthy's *The Company She Keeps*, were taken down to the cellar and burned in the furnace. I published a very bad short story a year or two after I first knew the Moores and I was reprimanded by both of them for having used the word "spit." (Two or three years later I was scolded for having used "water closet" in a poem, but by then I had turned obstinate.) Marianne once gave me her practical rules for the use of indecent language. She said, "Ordinarily, I would never use the word *rump*. But I can perfectly well say to Mother, 'Mother, there's a thread on your *rump*,' because *she* knows that I'm referring to Cowper's pet hare, 'Old Tiney,' who liked to play on the carpet and 'swing his rump around!'"

I was shown many old photographs and snapshots and, once, a set of postcards of their trip to England and Paris—at that time the only European traveling Marianne had done. The postcards were mostly of Oxford, and there was a handwritten menu, including the wines, of the luncheon George Saintsbury had given for her. I was also privileged to look into the notebooks, illustrated with Marianne's delicate sketches.

Besides exercising on the trapeze, Marianne was very fond of tennis. I never saw her play, but from the way she talked about it, it seemed as if she enjoyed the rules and conventions of the game as much as the sport. She engaged a young black boy to play with her, sometimes in Prospect Park and sometimes on the roof of the apartment house. He was finally dismissed because of his lack of tennis manners; his worst offense seemed to be that instead of "Serve!" he *would* say "Okay!"

The bathroom in the apartment was small, long, and narrow, and as if I were still a child, I was advised to go there when Marianne thought it would be a good idea. (Also in subway stations: "I'll hold your bag and gloves, Elizabeth.") In their bathroom was an object I liked, an old-fashioned shoeshine box with an iron footrest. On one visit this had just been repainted by Marianne, with black enamel, and so had a cast-iron horse, laid out on a piece of newspaper on its side, running, with a streaming mane. It looked as if it might have originally been attached to a toy fire engine. I asked about this little horse, and Mrs. Moore told me that when Marianne was two and a half years old she had taken her to visit an aunt; the horse had had to go along too. Mrs. Moore had gone into the guest room and discovered that Marianne had taken a length of lace, perhaps a lace collar, from the bureau and dressed the horse up in it. "Marianne!" she had said—one could imagine the awful solemnity of the moment—"You wouldn't take Auntie Bee's lace to put on your horse, would you?" But the infant Marianne, the intrepid artist, replied, "Pretty looks, Ma! Pretty looks!"

Mrs. Moore's sense of honesty, or honor, like her respect for the proprieties, was staggering. Marianne occasionally teased her mother about it, even in front of me. One story was about the time Mrs. Moore had decided that five empty milk bottles must be returned to the grocery store, and thence to the dairy. They were not STORE BOTTLES, as bottles then said right in the glass, nor the kind that were to be put out on the doorstep, but they all came from the same dairy. The grocer looked at them and pushed them back on the counter toward Mrs. Moore, saying, "You don't have to return these bottles, ma'am; just throw them away." Mrs. Moore pushed the bottles back again and told him quietly, "It *says* BORDEN on the bottles; they belong to the dairy." The grocer: "I know it does, ma'am, but it doesn't say STORE BOTTLES or RETURN. Just throw them away." Mrs. Moore spoke more slowly and more quietly, "But they don't belong to me. They are *their bottles.*" "I know, ma'am, but they really don't want them back." The poor man had underestimated Mrs. Moore. She stood firm, clarifying for him yet again the only honorable line of action to be pursued in regard to the five bottles. Finally the grocer took them all in his arms and, saying weakly, "My *God,* ma'am!" carried them into the back of the store.

Clothes were of course an endless source of interest to Marianne, increasingly especially so as she grew older. As she has written herself (in a piece for *The Christian Science Monitor*), her clothes were almost always hand-me-downs, sometimes very elegant ones from richer friends. These would be let out or, most frequently, let down (Marianne preferred clothes on the loose side, like the four-sizes-too-large "polo shirts"). The hats would be stripped of decorations, and ribbons changed so all was black or navy blue, and somehow perhaps *flattened.* There was the Holbein/Erasmus-type hat, and later the rather famous tricorne, but in the first years I knew her, only the large, flat, low-crowned hats of felt or summer straw.

Once when I arrived at the Brooklyn apartment, Marianne and her mother were occupied with the old-fashioned bit of sewing called "making over." They were making a pair of drawers that Marianne had worn at Bryn Mawr in 1908 into a petticoat or slip. The drawers were a beautiful garment, fine white batiste, with very full legs that must have come to below the knee, edged with lace and set with rows of "insertion." These I didn't see again in their metamorphosed state, but I did see and was sometimes consulted about other such projects. Several times over the years Marianne asked me abruptly, "E*l*izabeth, what do you have on under your dress? How much underwear do *you* wear?" I would enumerate my two or perhaps three undergarments, and Marianne would say, "Well, I know that I [or, Mother and I] wear many too many." And sometimes when I arrived on a cold winter evening dressed in a conventional way, I would be greeted by "E*liza*beth, silk stockings!" as if I were reckless or prone to suicide. My own clothes were subject to her careful consideration. The first time I ever met a publisher, I reported the next day by telephone and Marianne's first question was "What did you *wear*, Elizabeth?"

Marianne's hair was always done up in a braid around the crown of her head, a style dating from around 1900, I think, and never changed. Her skin was fair, translucent, although faded when I knew her. Her face paled and flushed so quickly she reminded me of Rima in W. H. Hudson's *Green Mansions*. Her eyes were bright, not "bright" as we often say about eyes when we really mean alert; they were that too, but also shiny bright and, like those of a small animal, often looked at one sidewise—quickly, at the conclusion of a sentence that had turned out unusually well, just to see if it had taken effect. Her face was small and pointed, but not really triangular because it was a little lopsided, with a delicately pugnacious-looking jaw. When one day I told her she looked like Mickey Rooney, then a very young actor (and she did), she seemed quite pleased.

She said her poem "Spenser's Ireland" was not about *loving* Ireland, as people seemed to think, but about *disapproving* of it. Yet she liked being of Irish descent; her great-great-grandfather had run away from a house in Merrion Square, Dublin (once, I went to look at it from the outside), and I remember her delight when the book in which the poem appeared was bound in Irish green.

She had a way of laughing at what she or someone else had just said if she meant to show outrage or mock disapproval—an *oh-ho* kind of sound, rough, that went with a backwards and sidewise toss of the head toward the left shoulder. She accepted compliments with this laugh too, without words; it disparaged and made light of them, and implied that she and her audience were both far above such absurdities. I believe she was the only person I have ever known who "bridled" at praise, while turning pink with pleasure. These gestures of her head were more pronounced in the presence of gentlemen because Marianne was innately flirtatious.

The Moore *chinoiserie* of manners made giving presents complicated. All of her friends seemed to share the desire of giving her presents, and it must sometimes have been, as she would have said, a "burden." One never knew what would succeed, but one learned that if a gift did not succeed it would be given back, unobtrusively, but somehow or other, a year or two later. My most successful gift was a pair of gloves. I don't know why they made such a hit, but they did; they weren't actually worn for a long time, but they appear in a few of her photographs, held in one hand. Marianne brought them to the photographer wrapped in the original tissue paper.

Another very successful gift was a paper nautilus, which became the subject of her poem "The Paper Nautilus":

> . . . its wasp-nest flaws
> of white on white, and close-
>
> laid Ionic chiton-folds
> like the lines in the mane of
> a Parthenon horse . . .

Fruit or flowers were acclaimed and examined but never, I felt, really welcomed. But a very unbeautiful bracelet from Morocco, alternate round beads of amber and black ambergris on a soiled string, was very well received. I was flattered to see this worn at a poetry reading, and afterwards learned that, as it was too loose for Marianne's wrist, Mother had carefully sewn it onto the edge of her sleeve. But another friend's attempt to give her a good gramophone was a disaster, a drama that went on for months. Eventually (it was portable but very heavy) it was carried back by Marianne to the shop in New York.

She liked to show her collection of jewelry, which had a few beautiful and valuable pieces. I once gave her a modest brooch of the semi-precious stones of Brazil, red and green tourmalines and amethysts; this she seemed to like so much that I gave her a matching bracelet. A few years later I wrote her from Brazil asking what I could bring her on my return to New York, and she wrote back, "I like *jewels.*"

Knowing her fondness for snakes, I got for her when I was in Florida a beautiful specimen of the deadly coral snake with inch-wide rose-red and black stripes separated by narrow white stripes, a bright new snake coiled in liquid in a squat glass bottle. This bottle sat on her hall bookcase, at the other end from the bowl of nickels, for many years. The colors gradually faded, and the formaldehyde grew cloudy, and finally I said I thought she could dispense with the coral snake. A mutual friend told me that Marianne was relieved; she had always hated it. Perhaps it had only been brought out for my visits.

Marianne once told me a story on herself about her aversion to reds. Her physician in Brooklyn for some years was a Turkish woman, Dr. Laf Loofy, whom she often quoted as a great authority on health. Dr. Loofy had prescribed for Marianne a large bottle of red pills, but before taking one, Marianne would wash it thoroughly until all the shiny red coating had disappeared. Something, perhaps digestive symptoms, made her confess this to Dr. Loofy, who was incredulous, then appalled. She explained that medical genius and

years of research, expressly for Marianne's benefit, had gone into develop-
ing the red enamel-like coating that she had deliberately washed away. Marianne was completely stoical about herself; once, at a New York doctor's
office, she proved to have a temperature of 104 degrees. The doctor wanted
to call a cab for her for the long trip back to Brooklyn, but Marianne
would have none of it. She insisted on returning by subway, and did.

Despite what I assumed to be her aversion to reds, she once showed
me a round, light tan, rather pig-like piece of luggage, bought especially for
her first trip to give readings on the West Coast, saying, "You will think this
too *showy*, Elizabeth." The long zipper on the top could be locked with a
bright red padlock. I said no, I thought it a very nice bag. "Of course,"
Marianne said, "the red padlock is the very best thing about it."

One winter Mrs. Moore was sick for a long time with a severe case of
shingles. She was just recovering from this long illness when she also had
to go to the dentist, whose office was in Manhattan. A friend who had a car
and I went to Brooklyn to take Marianne and her mother to the city. Mrs.
Moore was still feeling poorly. She was wearing a round flat fur cap, a very
1890-ish hat, mink, I think, or possibly sable, and since she couldn't bear
to put her hair up yet, the remarkably un-gray hair hung down in a heavy
pigtail. The dentist's office was high up in a tall office building. There were
a good many passengers in the elevator and an elevator boy; we shot upwards. What I remember most is that at the proper floor, as the passengers
stared, Marianne and her mother both bowed to the elevator boy pleasantly and thanked him, Mrs. Moore the more profusely, for the ride. He
was unaccustomed to such civility, but he was very pleased and tried hard
not to push his handle or close the doors as quickly as on the other floors.
Elevator men, subway changemakers, ticket takers, taxi drivers—all were
treated to these formalities, and, as a rule, they were pleasantly surprised
and seemed to respond in kind.

A very well known and polished writer, who had known Marianne since
he was a young man and felt great admiration for her, was never invited to
Cumberland Street although his friends were. Once, I asked innocently
why I never saw him there and Marianne gave me her serious, severe look
and said, "He *contradicted* Mother."

The atmosphere of 260 Cumberland Street was of course "old-fashioned,"
but even more, otherworldly—as if one were living in a diving bell from a
different world, let down through the crass atmosphere of the twentieth
century. Leaving the diving bell with one's nickel, during the walk to the
subway and the forty-five-minute ride back to Manhattan, one was apt to
have a slight case of mental or moral bends—so many things to be remembered; stories, phrases, the unaccustomed deference, the exquisitely pro-

longed etiquette—these were hard to reconcile with the New Lots Avenue express and the awful, jolting ride facing a row of indifferent faces. Yet I never left Cumberland Street without feeling happier: uplifted, even inspired, determined to be good, to work harder, not to worry about what other people thought, never to try to publish anything until I thought I'd done my best with it, no matter how many years it took—or never to publish at all.

To change the image from air to water: somehow, under all the subaqueous pressure at 260 Cumberland Street—admonitions, reserves, principles, simple stoicism—Marianne rose triumphant, or rather her voice did, in a lively, unceasing jet of shining bubbles. I had "taken" chemistry at preparatory school; I also could imagine that in this water, or heavy water glass, I saw forming the elaborate, logical structures that became her poems.

Writing and a Few Writers

On the floor of the kitchen at 260 Cumberland Street I once saw a bushel basket, the kind used for apples or tomatoes, filled to overflowing with crumpled papers, some typed, some covered with Marianne's handwriting. This basketful of papers held the discarded drafts of one review, not a long review, of a new book of poems by Wallace Stevens. When it was published I found the review very beautiful, as I still do. Nevertheless, Marianne chose to omit it from her collected essays; it didn't come up to her standards.

If she was willing to put in so much hard work on a review running to two or two and a half pages, one can imagine the work that went into a poem such as "The Jerboa," or "He 'Digesteth Harde Yron'" (about the ostrich), with their elaborate rhyme schemes and syllable-counting meters. When not at the desk, she used a clipboard with the poem under construction on it, carrying it about the apartment, "even when I'm dusting or washing the dishes, Elizabeth."

Her use of "light" rhymes has been written about by critics. On principle, she said, she disapproved of rhyme. Nevertheless, when she read poems to me, or recited them, she obviously enjoyed rhymes very much, and would glance up over her reading glasses and exclaim that *that* was "gusto"—her favorite word of praise. With great gusto of her own, she read:

> Strong is the lion—like a coal
> His eye-ball—like a bastion's mole
> His chest against the foes:

> Strong, the gier-eagle on his sail,
> Strong against tide, th'enormous whale
> Emerges as he goes.

She admired Ogden Nash and liked to quote his poem about the baby panda for the sake of its rhyme:

> I love the Baby Giant Panda;
> I'd welcome one to my veranda.

Once, I found her consulting a large rhyming dictionary and she said, yes, it was "indispensable"; and I myself was congratulated on having rhymed "antennae" with "many."

Besides "gusto" she admired the "courageous attack," and for this reason she said she thought it a good idea to start off a poem with a spondee.

In *Observations* she seems undecided between free verse and her own strict stanza forms with their variations on "light" rhyme. Although she still professed to despise it, rhyme then seemed to win out for some years. However, by the time *Collected Poems* was published, in 1951, she had already begun a ruthless cutting of some of her most beautiful poems, and what suffered chiefly from this ruthlessness were those very rhymes and stanza forms she had so painstakingly elaborated in the years just before.

A conflict between traditional rhymes and meters came during the seven years (1946–53) Marianne worked on translating La Fontaine's *Fables*. For my own amusement, I had already made up a completely unscientific theory that Marianne was possessed of a unique, involuntary sense of rhythm, therefore of meter, quite unlike anyone else's. She looked like no one else; she talked like no one else; her poems showed a mind not much like anyone else's; and her notions of meter and rhyme were unlike all the conventional notions—so why not believe that the old English meters that still seem natural to most of us (or *seemed* to, at any rate) were not natural to her at all? That Marianne from birth, physically, had been set going to a different rhythm? Or was the explanation simply that she had a more sensitive ear than most of us, and since she had started writing at a time when poetry was undergoing drastic changes, she had been free to make the most of it and experiment as she saw fit?

When I happened to be in New York during those seven years, I was usually shown the fable she was working on (or she'd read it on the phone) and would be asked to provide a rhyme, or to tell her if I thought the meter was right. Many other people must have had the same experience. These were strange requests, coming from someone who had made contemporary poets self-conscious about their crudities, afraid to rhyme "bone" with "stone," or to go *umpty-umpty-um*. Marianne was doing her best, one saw, to go *umpty-umpty-um* when she sensed that La Fontaine had gone that way, but it seemed to be almost—I use the word again—physically impossible for her to do so. If I'd suggest, say, that "flatter" rhymed with "matter," this to my embarrassment was hailed as a stroke of genius; or if I'd say, "If you leave out 'and' or 'the' [or put it in], it will go *umpty-umpty-um*," Marianne would exclaim, "E*li*zabeth, thank you, you have saved my life!" Although I too am mentioned in the introduction, I contributed next to nothing to the La Fontaine—a few rhymes and metrically smoothed-out or slicked-up lines. But they made me realize more than I ever had the rarity of true originality, and also the sort of alienation it might involve.

Her scrupulous and strict honesty could be carried to extremes of Protestant, Presbyterian, Scotch-Irish literalness that amazed me. We went together to see an exceptionally beautiful film, a documentary in color about Africa, with herds of gazelles and giraffes moving across the plains, and we loved it. Then a herd of elephants appeared, close up and clear, and the narrator commented on their feet and tread. I whispered to Marianne that they looked as if their feet were being lifted up off the ground by invisible threads. The next day she phoned and quoted my remark about the elephants' walk, and suddenly came out with, "Elizabeth, I'll give you ten dollars for that." There was often no telling how serious she was. I said something like "For heaven's sake, Marianne, please take it," but I don't believe it ever made an appearance in a poem. I confess to one very slight grudge: she *did* use a phrase of mine once without a note. This may be childish of me, but I want to reclaim it. I had been asked by a friend to bring her three glass buoy-balls in nets, sometimes called "witch balls," from Cape Cod. When I arrived at the old hotel where I lived, a very old porter took them with my bag, and as I watched him precede me down the corridor, I said to myself, "The bellboy with the buoy-balls." I liked the sound of this so much that in my vanity I repeated the phrase to Marianne a day or so later. You will find "The sea- / side burden should not embarrass / the bell-boy with the buoy-ball / endeavoring to pass / hotel patronesses" in the fifth stanza of "Four Quartz Crystal Clocks." It was so thoroughly out of character for her to do this that I have never understood it. I am sometimes appalled to think how much I may have unconsciously stolen from her. Perhaps we are all magpies.

> The deepest feeling always shows
> itself in silence;
> not in silence, but restraint.

These lines from her early poem "Silence" are simply another one of Marianne's convictions. Like Auden, whom she admired, she believed that graceful behavior—and writing, as well—demands a certain reticence. She told me, "Ezra says all dedications are *dowdy*," but it was surely more than to avoid dowdiness that caused her to write this postscript in *Selected Poems* (1935): "Dedications imply giving, and we do not care to make a gift of what is insufficient; but in my immediate family there is one 'who thinks in a particular way' and I should like to add that where there is an effect of thought or pith in these pages, the thinking and often the actual phrases are hers." This postscript was obviously meant for Mrs. Moore, and after her mother's death in 1947, Marianne became more outspoken about dedications; however, when she wrote an acrostic on the name of one of her oldest and closest friends, it too was semi-concealed, by being written upside down.

The first time I heard Marianne read poetry in public was at a joint reading with William Carlos Williams in Brooklyn. I am afraid I was a little late. There was a very small audience, mostly in the front rows, and I made my way as self-effacingly as I could down the steep red-carpeted steps of the aisle. As I approached the lower rows, she spotted me out of the corner of her eye and interrupted herself in the middle of a poem to bow and say, "Good evening!" She and Dr. Williams shared the rather small high stage and took turns reading. There were two high-backed chairs, far apart, and each poet sat down between readings. The decor seemed to be late-Victorian Gothic; I remember a good deal of red plush, dark wood, and Gothic points, knobs, and incised lines. Marianne, wearing a hat and a blue dress, looked quite small and seemed nervous. I had the impression that Williams, who was not nervous in the slightest, was generously trying to put her at her ease. As they changed places at the lectern, he would whisper to her and smile. I have no recollection of anything that was read, except for a sea-monster poem of Williams's, during which he gave some loud and realistic roars.

She seldom expressed opinions of other writers, and the few I remember were, to say the least, ambiguous or ambivalent. She developed the strategy of damning with faint praise to an almost supersonic degree. One writer whom I rather disliked, and I suspect she did too, was praised several times for her "beautifully laundered shirtwaist." One day when I was meeting her in New York, she said she had just run into Djuna Barnes again, after many years, on the steps of the Public Library. I was curious and asked her what Djuna Barnes was "like." There was rather a long pause before Marianne said, thoughtfully, "Well . . . she looked very smart, and her shoes were *beautifully* polished."

I do not remember her ever referring to Emily Dickinson, but on one occasion, when we were walking in Brooklyn on our way to a favored tea shop, I noticed we were on a street associated with the *Brooklyn Eagle,* and I said fatuously, "Marianne, isn't it odd to think of you and Walt Whitman walking this same street over and over?" She exclaimed in her mock-ferocious tone, "E*liz*abeth, don't speak to me about that man!" So I never did again. Another time, when she had been talking about her days on *The Dial,* I asked how she had liked Hart Crane when he had come into her office there. Her response was equally unexpected. "Oh, I *liked* Hart! I always liked him very much—he was so *erudite.*" And although she admired Edmund Wilson very much and could speak with even more conviction of *his* erudition, she once asked me if I had read his early novel *I Thought of Daisy,* and when I said no, she almost extracted a promise from me that I would *never* read it. She was devoted to W. H. Auden, and the very cat he had patted in the Brooklyn tearoom was produced for me to admire and pat too.

Lately I have seen several references critical of her poetry by feminist writers, one of whom described her as a "poet who controlled panic by presenting it as whimsy." Whimsy is sometimes there, of course, and so is humor (a gift these critics sadly seem to lack). Surely there is an element of mortal panic and fear underlying all works of art? Even so, one wonders how much of Marianne's poetry the feminist critics have read. Have they really read "Marriage," a poem that says everything they are saying and everything Virginia Woolf has said? It is a poem which transforms a justified sense of injury into a work of art:

> This institution . . .
> I wonder what Adam and Eve
> think of it by this time . . .
> Unhelpful Hymen!
> a kind of overgrown cupid
> reduced to insignificance
> by the mechanical advertising
> parading as involuntary comment,
> by that experiment of Adam's
> with ways out but no way in—
> the ritual of marriage . . .

Do they know that Marianne Moore was a feminist in her day? Or that she paraded with the suffragettes, led by Inez Milholland on her white horse, down Fifth Avenue? Once, Marianne told me, she "climbed a lamppost" in a demonstration for votes for women. What she did up there, what speech she delivered, if any, I don't know, but climb she did in long skirt and petticoats and a large hat. Perhaps it was pride or vanity that kept her from complaints, and that put her sense of injustice through the prisms dissected by "those various scalpels" into poetry. She was not too proud for occasional complaints; she was humorously angry, but nevertheless angry, when her publisher twice postponed her book in order to bring out two young male poets, both now almost unheard of. Now that everything can be said, and done, have we anyone who can compare with Marianne Moore, who was at her best when she made up her own rules and when they were strictest—the reverse of "freedom"?

Soon after I met Marianne in 1934—although I concealed it for what seemed to me quite a long time—somehow or other it came out that I was trying to write poetry. For five or six years I occasionally sent her my poems. She would rarely say or write very much about them except that she liked such and such a phrase or, oddly, the alliteration, which I thought I tended to overdo. When I asked her what the poems she had written at Bryn Mawr were like, she said, "*Just* like Swinburne, Elizabeth." Sometimes she suggested that I change a word or line, and sometimes I accepted her suggestions, but never did she even hint that such and such a line might have been influenced by or even unconsciously stolen from a poem of her own, as later on I could sometimes see that they were. Her notes to me were often signed "Your Dorothy Dix."

It was because of Marianne that in 1935 my poems first appeared in a book, an anthology called *Trial Balances*. Each of the poets in this anthology had an older mentor, who wrote a short preface or introduction to the poems, and Marianne, hearing of this project, had offered to be mine. I was much too shy to dream of asking her. I had two or three feeble pastiches of late seventeenth-century poetry called "Valentines," in one of which I had rhymed "even the English sparrows in the dust" with "lust." She did not like those English sparrows very much and said so ("Miss Bishop's sparrows are not revolting, merely disaffecting"), but her sponsorship brought about this first appearance in a book.

One long poem, the most ambitious I had up to then attempted, apparently stirred both her and her mother to an immediate flurry of criticism. She telephoned the day after I had mailed it to her, and said that she and her mother had sat up late rewriting it for me. (This is the poem in which the expression "water closet" was censored.) Their version of it arrived in the next mail. I had had an English teacher at Vassar whom I liked very much, named Miss Rose Peebles, and for some reason this name fascinated Marianne. The revised poem had been typed out on very thin paper and folded into a small square, sealed with a gold star sticker and signed on the outside "Lovingly, Rose Peebles." My version had rhymed throughout, in rather strict stanzas, but Marianne and her mother's version broke up the stanzas irregularly. Some lines rhymed and some didn't; a few other colloquialisms besides "water closet" had been removed and a Bible reference or two corrected. I obstinately held on to my stanzas and rhymes, but I did make use of a few of the proffered new words. I am sorry to say I can't now remember which they were, and won't know unless this fascinating communication should turn up again.

Marianne in 1940 gave me a copy of the newly published *Last Poems and Two Plays*, by William Butler Yeats, and though I dislike some of the emphasis on lechery in the poems, and so did she, I wrote her that I admired "The Circus Animals' Desertion" and the now famous lines "I must lie down where all the ladders start, / In the foul rag-and-bone shop of the heart." She replied:

> I would be "much disappointed in you" if you *could* feel about Yeats as some of his acolytes seem to feel. An "effect," an exhaustively great sensibility (with insensibility?) and genius for word-sounds and sentences. But after all, what is this enviable apparatus for? if not to change our mortal psycho-structure. It makes me think of the Malay princes—the *horde* of eunuchs and entertainers and "bearers" of this and that; then suddenly the umbrella over the prince lowered, because a greater prince was passing. As you will suspect from my treachery to W. B. Yeats, I've been to a lecture on Java by Burton Holmes, and one on Malay . . .

One day she abruptly asked me, "Do you like the *nude*, Elizabeth?" I said yes I did on the whole. Marianne: "Well, so do I, Elizabeth, but *in moderation*," and she immediately pressed on me a copy of Sir Kenneth Clark's new book, *The Nude*, which had just been sent to her.

Some Expeditions

This was a story told me by Mrs. Moore, of an outing that had taken place the summer before I met them. There had been a dreadful heat wave, and Marianne had been feeling "overburdened" (the word *burden* was an important one in the Brooklyn vocabulary) and "overtaxed." Her mother decided that Marianne "should take a course in the larger mammals" and said, "Marianne, I am going to take you to Coney Island to see Sheba," an unusually large and docile elephant then on view at a boardwalk sideshow. Coney Island is a long subway ride even from Brooklyn, but in spite of the heat and the crowds, the two ladies went. Sheba performed her acts majestically, and slowly played catch with her keeper with a shiny white ball. I asked about the elephant's appearance, and Marianne said, "She was very simply dressed. She was lightly powdered a matte rose all over, and wore ankle bracelets, large copper hollow balls, on her front legs. Her headdress consisted of three white ostrich plumes." Marianne was fond of roller coasters; a fearless rider, she preferred to sit in the front seat. Her mother told me how she waited below while the cars clicked agonizingly to the heights, and plunged horribly down. Marianne's long red braid had come undone and blew backwards, and with it went all her cherished amber-colored "real tortoiseshell" hairpins, which fortunately landed in the laps of two sailors in the car behind her. At the end of the ride, they handed them to her "very politely."

Two friends of Marianne's, two elderly Boston ladies, shared an exquisitely neat white clapboard house in northern Maine. I once spent a day there, and they teased Marianne about her habit of secreting food. She laughed, blushed, and tossed her head, and did not seem to mind when one of them told of going into Marianne's room for a book only to discover two boiled potatoes lying on the dresser. Some years later the older lady phoned Marianne from Boston and told her she was dying of cancer. She was perfectly stoical about it, and said she was in a hospital and knew she could not last very long. She asked Marianne to come and stay near her until she died, and Marianne went. At the hospital, she told Marianne that while she would be grateful to her if she came to see her every day, she knew that Marianne couldn't possibly spend all her time with her, so she had arranged for her to take driving lessons. Marianne, who must have been nearly seventy at the time, agreed that this was a good idea; she had always wanted to learn to drive, and she did, with a lesson at the driving school every day and a visit to the hospital. A day or so after her friend died, Marianne passed her driving test. She said she had a little trouble with the lights in Copley Square and confessed she thought the "policeman" giving her the test had been a little overlenient. I said I hoped she hadn't driven too fast, and she replied, "A steady forty-five, Elizabeth!" On her return she proudly showed her driving license to her brother, Warner, and he, sounding no doubt very much as her mother used to sound, said, "There must be some mistake. This must be sent back *immediately*."

Marianne was intensely interested in the techniques of things—how camellias are grown; how the quartz prisms work in crystal clocks; how the pangolin can close up his ear, nose, and eye apertures and walk on the outside edges of his hands "and save the claws / for digging"; how to drive a car; how the best pitchers throw a baseball; how to make a figurehead for her nephew's sailboat. The exact way in which anything was done, or made, or functioned, was poetry to her.

She even learned to tango. Before she acquired a television set of her own, she was in the habit of going down to the basement apartment at 260

Cumberland Street to watch the baseball games with the janitor and his wife, who had a set. During one of the games there was a commercial that advertised a Brooklyn dancing school. Any viewer who telephoned in was guaranteed a private tango lesson at a Brooklyn academy. Marianne announced that she had always liked the tango, and hurried to the fourth floor to put in her call, and got an appointment. The young dancers, male and female, may have been a little surprised, but soon they were competing with each other to dance with her. She was given a whole short course of lessons. I asked about the tango itself, and she allowed that they had felt perhaps it was a little too strenuous and had taught her a "modified" version of it. She had also learned several other steps and dances in more current use, and insisted everyone had enjoyed himself and herself thoroughly.

In the late winter or early spring of 1963, when I was in New York, one evening around eight I emerged from a Lexington Avenue subway station on my way to a poetry reading at the YMHA. Suddenly I realized that Marianne was walking ahead of me over half a block away, alone, hurrying along with a bag of books and papers. She reached the YMHA before I did, but she was not present at the function I was attending; I wondered what she could be up to. Later she informed me that she was attending the YMHA Poetry Workshop, conducted that term by Louise Bogan. She said she was learning a great deal, things she had never known before; Miss Bogan was another of the people she considered "erudite." Shortly afterwards I met Miss Bogan at a party and asked her about the workshop and her famous student. Poor Miss Bogan! I am sure Marianne never dreamed what suffering she was causing her. It seemed that Marianne took notes constantly, asked many questions, and entered into discussions with enthusiasm. But the other students were timid and often nonplused, and so was Miss Bogan, besides feeling that she was sailing under false colors and never knowing what technical question she might be expected to answer next.

I attended very few literary events at which Marianne was present, but I did go with her to the party for Edith and Osbert Sitwell given at the Gotham Book Mart. I hadn't intended to go to this at all; in fact, I really didn't want to, but Marianne, who was something of an Anglophile, was firm. "We must be *polite* to the Sitwells," she said.

The party was given by *Life* magazine and was rather awful. The photographers behaved as photographers do: strewing wires under our feet, calling to each other over our heads, and generally pushing us around. It took some time to separate the poets, who were the subjects of the picture, from the non-poets, and this was done in a way that made me think of livestock being herded into cattle cars. Non-poets and some real poets felt insulted; then the photographer announced that Miss Moore's hat was "too big." She refused to remove it. Auden was one of the few who seemed to be enjoying himself. He got into the picture by climbing on a ladder, where he sat making loud, cheerful comments over our heads. Finally the picture was taken with a sort of semicircular swoop of the camera. Marianne consented to let a friend and me take her to dinner and afterwards back to Brooklyn in a cab. I had on a small velvet cap and Marianne said, "I wish I had worn a *minimal* hat, like yours." The taxi fare to Brooklyn at that time was something over five dollars, not counting the tip. That evening my friend was paying for dinner and the cab. Between comments on the Sitwell party, Marianne exclaimed at intervals, "Mr. W———, this is *highway robbery*!"

She told me about another, more elegant literary party she had been to in a "penthouse," to celebrate the publication of a deluxe edition of a book, I think by Wallace Stevens. The chairs were upholstered in "lemon-colored velvet," there was a Matisse drawing she didn't altogether like, and she had taken a glass of champagne and regretted it all evening; it had made her face burn. I asked for further details. She became scornful: "Well, we signed our names several times, and after *that* thrill was over, I came home."

Sometimes we went to movies together, to *Kon-Tiki* twice, I recall. I never attempted to lure her to any dramatic or "artistic" films. Since Dr. and Mrs. Sibley Watson were her dearest friends, she must have seen his early experimental films, such as *Lot in Sodom*. I heard the sad story of two young men, however, who when they discovered that she had never seen Eisenstein's *Potemkin* insisted on taking her. There was a short before *Potemkin*, a Walt Disney film; this was when the Disney films still had charm and humor. After the movies they went to tea and Marianne talked at length and in detail about the ingenuity of the Disney film, and nothing more. Finally they asked her what she had thought of *Potemkin*. Her opinion was brief but conclusive: "Life," she said, "is not like that."

Twice we went together to the Saturday-morning lectures for children at the Museum of Natural History—once, to see Meshie, the three-year-old chimpanzee, who came onstage pedaling her tricycle and offered us bites of her banana. And once to see a young couple I had known in Mexico show their collection of pets, including Aguilla, the bald-headed American eagle they had trained to hunt like a falcon, who had ridden all the way to Mexico and back perched on a broomstick in their car. There were more lovable pets as well: Marianne held the kinkajou in her arms, an affectionate animal that clutched on to one tightly with his tail. In a homemade movie the couple also showed us, the young man himself was shown in his library taking a book from the shelf. As he did so, he unselfconsciously blew the dust off the top of its pages. Marianne gave one of her laughs. She loved that; it was an example of the "spontaneity" that she admired as much as she admired "gusto."

The next-to-last outing I went on with Marianne was in the summer of 1968. This was long after her mother's death, when she had moved from Brooklyn and was living at 35 West Ninth Street in Manhattan. I was staying nearby in the Village, and one day she telephoned and asked me if I would come over and walk with her to the election polls; she wanted to vote. It was the first time, I think, she had ever actually asked me for assistance. It was a very hot day. She was ready and waiting, with her hat on. It was the usual shape, of navy-blue straw, and she wore a blue-and-white-checked seersucker suit and blue sneakers. She had become a bit unsteady and was supposed to use a cane, which was leaning against the door frame. She hated it, and I don't think I ever saw her use it. The voting booths were quite near, in the basement of a public school off Sixth Avenue; there were a good many people there, sitting around, mostly women, talking. Marianne made quite a stir; they seemed to know who she was and came up to talk to her and to ask me about her while she voted. They were Greenwich Village mothers, with intellectual or bluestocking types among them. I thought to myself that Marianne's was probably the only Republican vote cast there that day.

It was the originality and freshness of Marianne's diction, in the most casual conversation, as well as her polysyllabic virtuosity, that impressed many people. She once said of a well-known poet, "That man is freckled like a trout with impropriety." A friend has told me of attending a party for writers and artists at which she introduced a painter to Marianne by saying, "Miss Moore has the most interesting vocabulary of anyone I know." Marianne showed signs of pleasure at this, and within a minute offhandedly but accurately used in a sentence a word I no longer remember that means an addiction, in animals, to licking the luminous numbers off the dials of clocks and watches. At the same party this friend introduced the then comparatively young art critic Clement Greenberg; to her surprise and no doubt to Mr. Greenberg's, Marianne seemed to be familiar with his writing and said, on shaking hands, "Oh, the *fearless* Mr. Greenberg."

There was something about her good friend T. S. Eliot that seemed to amuse Marianne. On Eliot's first visit to Brooklyn after his marriage to Valerie, his young wife asked them to pose together for her for a snapshot. Valerie said, "Tom, put your arm around Marianne." I asked if he had. Marianne gave that short deprecatory laugh and said, "Yes, he did, but very *gingerly*." Toward the last, Marianne entrusted her Eliot letters for safekeeping with Robert Giroux, who told me that with each letter of the poet's she had preserved the envelope in which it had come. One envelope bore Marianne's Brooklyn address in Eliot's handwriting, but no return address or other identification. Within, there was a sheet of yellow pad paper on which was drawn a large heart pierced by an arrow, with the words "from an anonymous and grateful admirer."

Last Years

The dictionary defines a memoir as "a record of events based on the writer's personal experience or knowledge." Almost everything I have recorded was observed or heard firsthand, mostly before 1951–1952, the year—as Randall Jarrell put it—when "she won the Triple Crown" (National Book Award, Bollingen and Pulitzer Prizes) and became really famous. She was now Marianne Moore, the beloved "character" of Brooklyn and Manhattan; the baseball fan; the friend of many showier celebrities; the faithful admirer of Presidents Hoover and Eisenhower and Mayor Lindsay; the recipient of sixteen honorary degrees (she once modeled her favorite academic hoods for me); the reader of poetry all over the country, in settings very unlike the Brooklyn auditorium where in the thirties I heard her read with William Carlos Williams. She enjoyed every bit of the attention she received, although it too could be a "burden." After those long years of modest living and incredibly hard work, she had—until the helplessness at the very last—thank heavens, an unusually fortunate old age.

She once remarked, after a visit to her brother and his family, that the state of being married and having children had one enormous advantage: "One never has to worry about whether one is doing the right thing or not. There isn't time. One is always having to go to market or drive the children somewhere. There isn't time to wonder, 'Is this *right* or isn't it?' "

Of course she did wonder, and constantly. But, as in the notes to her poems, Marianne never gave away the whole show. The volubility, the wit, the self-deprecating laugh, never really clarified those quick decisions of hers—or decisive intuitions, rather—as to good and bad, right and wrong; and her meticulous system of ethics could be baffling. One of the very few occasions on which we came close to having a falling out was when, in the forties, I told her I had been seeing a psychoanalyst. She disapproved quite violently and said that psychoanalysts taught that "Evil is not *evil.* But we know it *is.*" I hadn't noticed that my analyst, a doctor of almost saintly character, did this, but I didn't attempt to refute it, and we didn't speak of it again. We never talked about Presbyterianism, or religion in general, nor did I ever dare more than tease her a little when she occasionally said she believed there was something *in* astrology.

Ninety years or so ago, Gerard Manley Hopkins wrote a letter to Robert Bridges about the ideal of the "gentleman," or the "artist" versus the "gentleman." Today his ideas may sound impossibly Victorian, but I find this letter still applicable and very moving: "As a fact poets and men of art are, I am sorry to say, by no means necessarily or commonly gentlemen. For gentlemen do not pander to lust or other basenesses nor . . . give themselves airs and affectations, nor do other things to be found in modern works . . . If an artist or thinker feels that were he to become in those ways ever so great, he would still be essentially lower than a gentleman that was no artist and no thinker. And yet to be a gentleman is but on the brim of morals and rather a thing of manners than morals properly. Then how much more must art and philosophy and manners and breeding and everything else in the world be below the least degree of true virtue. This is that chastity of mind which seems to lie at the very heart and be the parent of all good, the seeing at once what is best, and holding to that, and not allowing anything else whatever to be even heard pleading to the contrary . . . I agree then, and vehemently, that a gentleman . . . is in the position to despise the poet, were he Dante or Shakespeare, and the painter, were he Angelo or Apelles, for anything that showed him *not* to be a gentleman. He is in a position to do it, but if he is a gentleman perhaps this is what he will not do." The word "gentleman" makes us uncomfortable now, and its feminine counterparts, whether "lady" or "gentlewoman," embarrass us even more. But I am sure that Marianne would have "vehemently agreed" with Hopkins's strictures: to be a poet was not the be-all, end-all of existence.

I find it impossible to draw conclusions or even to summarize. When I try to, I become foolishly bemused: I have a sort of subliminal glimpse of the capital letter *M* multiplying. I am turning the pages of an illuminated manuscript and seeing that initial letter again and again: Marianne's monogram; mother; manners; morals; and I catch myself murmuring, "Manners and morals; manners *as* morals? Or it is morals *as* manners?" Since like Alice, "in a dreamy sort of way," I can't answer either question, it doesn't much matter which way I put it; it *seems* to be making sense.

c. 1969

To the Botequim & Back

I go out to the botequim to buy some cigarettes and a Merenda, a soft drink similar to Orange Crooshy, and in the twenty minutes or so the expedition takes me I see "the following," as they say here. (The slight pretentiousness in speech of semi-literacy. Workmen love to say, "I want to say *the following*," colon, then say it. Or, "Now I shall say *the following*," after which they do.)

It is a beautiful bright morning, big soft clouds moving rather rapidly high up, making large patches of opaque blue on the green hills and rocky peaks. The third of February; summer has come. Everything has grown amazingly in a week or so. Two kinds of morning glory adorn the standing walls of a ruined house—a pale lavender kind and a bright purple, pink-centered kind, hundreds of gaudy flowers stretching open to the sun as wide as they possibly can. All along the way the stone walls are flourishing after the January rains with mosses, maidenhair ferns, and a tiny yellow flower. I look down at a garden inside another ruin, an attempt at beauty and formality about ten feet square: there are a square border and two diagonals, with a rosebush in the middle covered with small red roses. Everything straggly and untidy, unpruned, long shoots on the bushes swaying in the breeze. Two Monarch butterflies are flickering, with hundreds of bees getting at the blossoms. Two hummingbirds sucking at the morning glories—one the little brilliant iridescent kind, the other the big long-bodied hummingbird, gray, with white edges to its tail. A tree (almost) of orange-yellow dahlias; white roses; a common variety, yellow-white, untidy; lavender flowers in profusion, onions mixed up with them all along the border, and a little kale. Where a cascade passes under the street, and comes out below, there is a rank growth of "lily of the valley," a wild water plant with lush long leaves and big tired white blossoms that drag in the water. Every once in a while I catch their scent, overstrong and oversweet.

Palmyra had asked to leave work early this morning to go to have her throat blessed. Father Antonio was holding a Throat Blessing at the church at 6 a.m. (It's the feast of St. Blasius, the patron saint of throats.) Aurea had had a sore throat; Palmyra didn't, so apparently she was taking precautions.

I asked her how the blessing had gone. There had been "many folks"; the priest had blessed them all in general, then at the railing he had come up close to each one, with his arms crossed and candles burning on either side of him, murmuring a blessing.

The botequim is a little shop or "grocery store," where I buy a liter of milk every morning—that is, if it hasn't already turned sour. The bottles are usually left standing on the sidewalk, in a frame, all morning or all day, until they are sold. This store is owned by João Pica Pau, John Woodpecker. But, on the way, there is something new today. A "poolroom" has just opened, and there are five or six men and boys blocking the narrow sidewalk in front of the two open doors. It is a snooker table, I suppose, but so small it looks like a toy one, brand-new, with bright green felt. Two boys are playing, almost on the sidewalk.

Just before I get to João Pica Pau's, which is next to the barbershop, I meet three boys of twelve or so, brothers by their looks, all about the same size, mulattoes, with dark gray eyes. The two outside boys are helping the middle one, who is very thin, wasted, pale, wearing boots on his bare feet. He is languid and limp; his ragged shirt and blue trousers are very clean. He drags his feet and bends and sways like a broken stalk. His head turns toward me and he seems to have only one eye, a sunken hole for the other one—or is it an eye? I can't bear to look. His brother suddenly puts an arm under his knees and picks him up and takes him into the barber's. The barbershop is barely big enough for the chair, the barber, a fly-specked mirror, and an enormous atomizer. (At other times I've gone by, a child has been playing with the atomizer, spraying a rich synthetic scent out the door at his friends.) I glance in now and there are *two* people in the barber chair, the one-eyed boy sitting on his brother's lap, while the barber cuts his long frizzy hair. Everyone is silent as the brother holds him in a tight embrace. The boy cocks his one eye helplessly at the mirror.

Constant coming and going on the sidewalk, hot in the sun. A large black lady holds an apricot-colored umbrella, sheer and shiny, high over her head to give as much shade as possible to herself, the baby in her arms, and two little ones trailing behind. One of the local "characters" comes toward me, a miserable and shuffling old woman. She is broad and sagging; everything sags—breasts and stomach. She carries a black umbrella as a sunshade. Her shoes don't match; one is an old tennis shoe, almost falling off, the other an old black slipper. Her hair is wild and white; her crazy little eyes glitter at me. Two little girls follow, giggling. I give them a look.

I reach the botequim, but I find it closed. João Pica Pau has set up shop in the small cloth store next door. He has moved shop to the extent of pushing his milk bottles along the sidewalk a few feet, and setting up his glass case, which is filled with a wild variety of cheap cigarettes. I also see his pair of red scales, a huge knife, and a mess of small salamis in a basket, sitting on top of bolts of yard goods. He seems to be handling the sale of cloth as well. Ropes of garlic and a box of half-ripe tomatoes are all he has to offer fresh this morning. I drink a Pepsi-Cola, small size, while he wraps up the others for me. I also buy a pack of razor blades and some cheap candies. He spills the candies out all over the dirty counter for me to make my selection.

He tells me and anyone else interested—there are several men and boys in the shop, as usual, one already quite drunk at the far end drinking straight *cachaça* and another eating a small loaf of bread, all just staring and listening—about the awful fight last night. One man had a machete, another had a pocket knife, the third had a stick, and they were all drunk. He got them separated and closed his doors. "I hate fights, don't you?" he asks me. I say I do. "Someone might get killed," he says. He wanted three policemen to come and hit them with their rubber truncheons—he demonstrates—and that would have put a stop to the fighting, but he had no telephone, as the men well knew. But he wasn't afraid of them, or only of the one with the machete. Yes, too much killing goes on, it is easy to kill someone. He ends his little sermon by saying, "It is stupid, it is great nonsense to kill a man. Imagine, the police would catch him, he'd spend a year in jail, and lose his job, and confound his life completely." Everyone nods in agreement. The *cachaça* drinker, in a thick voice, asks for another. I take my purchases and leave the botequim.

Home again. No, the dishonest antique dealer hails me from his pale blue house hung with fake-antique lanterns and with a front yard full of old tables and cupboards. "Do you want an antique cupboard? I have three or four nice ones." He comes running across the road, wagging his fat hands like a baby. He's obviously making money. Three years ago he was just a day laborer and knew nothing of antiques. Now he has customers all over the state and sends things to dealers in Rio and Saõ Paulo. "I want to show you a house. I want the senhora to see it because she has such *good taste.*" I stopped speaking to him for two years because of a dirty trick he played on me over the most beautiful statue of St. Sebastian I have ever seen. I've started speaking again; it's useless to try to make him understand ethics. His fat wife smiles and waves her hands at me like a baby too.

At home I find a flyer, thrown in the yard—an invitation from the Ouro Prêto Department of Tourism inviting the people of the town and visitors

to witness the monumental parade of the Carnival Clubs in Tooth-puller Square on the 7th, 8th, 9th and 10th of the month of February.

The following clubs will parade: Zé Pereira of the Lacaios [footmen], Conjunto Brito Filho, Clube Recreative XV de Novembere, Escola de Samba Morro de Sant'ana, Bloco Estrela Dalva, Zé Pereira Infantil, and Escola do Bairro do Padre Faria.

On the 10th there will be a great competition for the prize for the best of the Carnival of 1970, and the great parade of Allegorical Cars [floats].

About a mile above the city, up a winding steep dirt road, you reach a high plateau. On the way you pass two small chapels in the distance, Our Lady of the Safe Delivery and Santa Ana. Up through Burnt Hill, past steep fields full of ruins. After two hundred years, a few ruins have turned back into houses again: one very small one, just four standing walls with openings for a door and window, now has a roof of tarpaulin, weighted with stones. It is hard to see how anyone lives in it, but a few hens scratch around the door and there's some washing spread out over the tops of the nearest weeds.

The tiniest house of all, mud brick, wattles showing through, stands against a magnificent view, overlooking a drop of a thousand feet or so, one end of the house merging into a small and very old bus body. The windows and door of the bus are all faded green, with a black rounded roof. Whether the house is an extension of the bus, or the bus the "new wing" of the house, is a hideous little riddle against a majestic backdrop. But someone lives there! It is a magnificent sight to the east, seemingly all the way to the coast, miles and miles and miles of blue hills, the nearer ones topped by crazy spars of gray stone, and one tall cross slanting slightly to the north.

On the left you can see where a small mill stood and fell down. There used to be a strange old iron mill wheel there, but some time ago the boys who came to make a very arty movie of the town stole it. (The boys then lived below me; I smelled their pot every evening and one, the youngest, stayed home alone and sniffed ether, almost etherizing me, in the bedroom above his, every night.)

The fields are filled with wild flowers. At first you see only tall ones, all nameless, yellow and purple, fuzzy seed-heads, red pods, and white ones too. Then you realize the ground is carpeted with flowers, short, shorter ones, moss-height ones. I pick dozens of wild flowers, little bright orange-and-yellow ones on a dry fine little bush, brilliant like orchids; lovely tall single white-yellow ones, each on its own thin green stock; hanging magenta bells. Before you can get these home, they have shut up tight forever.

This is the field of the Waterfall of the Little Swallows, and this is where the stream disappears, like the sacred river Alph in Coleridge's dream. It fans out over the red stone, narrows and rises in cold gray ridges, disappears underground, and then shows up again farther off, dashing downwards now through more beautiful rocks. It then takes off downwards for the Underworld. You can hang over the rocks and see it far below. It keeps descending, disappears into a cavern, and is never seen again. It talks as it goes, but the words are lost . . .

1970

Memories of Uncle Neddy

It's raining in Rio de Janeiro, raining, raining, raining. This morning the papers said it is the rainiest rainy season in seventy-six years. It is also hot and sticky. The sea—I'm writing in a penthouse apartment, eleven floors up, facing southeast over the sea—the sea is blurred with rain, almost hidden by the mixture of rain and fog, that rarity here. Just close enough inshore to be visible, an empty-looking freighter lunges heavily south. The mosaic sidewalks are streaming; the beach is dark, wet, beaten smooth; the tide line is marked by strands of dark seaweed, another rarity. And how it rains! It is seeping in under the french doors and around the window frames. Every so often a weak breeze seeps in, too, and with it a whiff of decay: something or other spoiled, fruit or meat. Or perhaps it's a whiff of mildew from my own old books and old papers, even from the shirt I have on, since in this weather even clothes mildew quickly. If the rain keeps up much longer the radio will stop working again and the hi-fi will rust beyond repair. At flood tide the sea may cross the avenue and start rising slowly up the base of the apartment building, as it's been known to do.

And Uncle Neddy, that is, my Uncle Edward, is *here*. Into this wildly foreign and, to him, exotic setting, Uncle Neddy has just come back, from the framer's. He leans slightly, silently backwards against the damp-stained pale-yellow wall, looking quite cheerfully into the eyes of whoever happens to look at him—including the cat's, who investigated him just now. Only of course it isn't really Uncle Neddy, not as he was, or not as I knew him. This is "little Edward," before he became an uncle, before he became a lover, husband, father or grandfather, a tinsmith, a drunkard, or a famous fly-fisherman—any of the various things he turned out to be.

Except for the fact that they give me asthma, I am very fond of molds and mildews. I love the dry-looking, gray-green dust, like bloom on fruit, to begin with, that suddenly appears here on the soles of shoes in the closet, on the backs of all the black books, or the darkest ones, in the bookcase.

And I love the black shadow, like the finest soot, that suddenly shows up, slyly, on white bread, or white walls. The molds on food go wild in just a day or two, and in a hot, wet spell like this, a tiny jungle, green, chartreuse, and magenta, may start up in a corner of the bathroom. That gray-green bloom, or that shadow of fine soot, is just enough to serve as a hint of morbidity, attractive morbidity—although perhaps mortality is a better word. The gray-green suggests life, the sooty shadow—although living, too—death and dying. And now that Uncle Neddy has turned up again, the latter, the black, has suddenly become associated with him. Because, after all these years, I realize only now that he represented "the devil" for me, not a violent, active Devil, but a gentle black one, a devil of weakness, acquiescence tentatively black, like the sooty mildew. He died, or his final incarnation died, aged seventy-six, some years ago, and two or three years before that I saw him for the last time. I don't know how he held out so long. He looked already quite dead then, dead and covered with shadow, like the mold, as if his years of life had finally determined to obscure him. (He had looked, too, then, like a dried-out wick, in the smoke-blackened chimney of an oil lamp.)

But here he is again now, young and clean, about twelve years old, with nothing between us but a glaze of old-fashioned varnishing. His widow, Aunt Hat, sent him to me, shipped him thousands of miles from Nova Scotia, along with one of his younger sisters, my mother, in one big crate. Why on earth did Aunt Hat send me the portrait of her late husband? My mother's might have been expected, but Uncle Neddy's came as a complete surprise; and now I can't stop thinking about him. His married life was long-drawn-out and awful; that was common knowledge. Can his presence here be Aunt Hat's revenge? Her last word in their fifty-odd-year battle? And an incredible last straw for him? Or is he here now because he was one of a pair and Aunt Hat was a fiend for order? Because she couldn't bear to break up a set of anything? He looks perfectly calm, polite—quite a pleasant child, in fact—almost as if he were glad to be here, away from it all.

(The frames these ancestor-children arrived in were a foot wide, painted and repainted with glittery, gritty gilt paint. They were meant to hang against dark wallpaper in a hair-cloth-and-mahogany northern parlor and brighten it up. I have taken the liberty of changing them to narrow, carefully dulled, gold ones, "modern." Now the portraits are reduced to the scale suitable for hanging in apartments.)

Uncle Neddy stands on an imaginary dark red carpet, against a dun-colored wall. His right arm rests on the back of a small chair. This chair is a holy wonder; it must have been the painter's "property" chair—at least I never saw anything like it in my grandmother's house. It consists of two hard-looking maroon-colored pads, both hung with thick, foot-long, maroon fringes; the lower one makes the seat, the upper one, floating in the airless air, and on which Uncle Neddy's arm rests, the back. Uncle Neddy wears a black suit, velveteen, I think; the jacket has pockets and is gathered to a yoke. He has a narrow white collar and white cuffs and a double black bow of what appears to be grosgrain ribbon is tied under the jacket collar. Perhaps his face is more oblivious than calm. Its not actually belonging to the suit or the chair gives it an extraneous look. It could almost have drifted in from another place, or another year, and settled into the painting. Plump (he was never in the slightest plump, that I can remember), his hair parted neatly on the left, his cheeks as pink as a girl's, or a doll's. He looks rather more like his sisters than like Uncle Neddy—the later versions of him, certainly. His tight trousers come to just below the knee and I can make out three ornamental buttons on each side. His weight rests on the left leg; his right leg is crossed in front of it and the toe of his right boot barely touches the other boot and the red carpet. The boots are very small, buttoned. In spite of his peaceful expression, they probably hurt him. I remember his telling me about the copper-toed boots he wore as a child, but these have no copper toes and must be his "good" boots. His body looks neatly stuffed. His eyes are a bright hazel and in the left one—right, to me—the painter has carefully placed a highlight of dry white paint, like a crumb. He never looked so clean and glossy, so peaceful and godly, so presentable, again— or certainly not as I remember him.

But of course he did have a streak of godliness somewhere, or else of a hypocrisy so common then, so unrecognized, that it fooled everyone including himself. How often did my grandmother tell me that as a small boy my Uncle Neddy had read the Bible, Old and New Testaments, straight through three times? Even as a child, I never quite believed this, but she was so utterly convinced that perhaps it really was true. It was the thing for children to do. Little Edward had also been a great text-memorizer and hymn-singer, and this much I did believe because when I knew him he often quoted texts, and not the well-known ones that everybody quoted, either; and he sang in the church choir. He also said grace before meals. Rather, he read grace. His memory for texts apparently didn't go that far. He had a little black book, printed in black on yellowish paper, with "artistic" red initial letters at the top and middle of each page, that gave two graces for every day in the year. This he held just under the edge of the table, and with his head down read the grace for that day and meal to his family, in a small, muffled voice. The little book was so worn with use that the pages were loose. Occasionally a few would fall out onto the floor and have to be retrieved when grace was over, while my little cousin Billy (Uncle Neddy's youngest child, a year or two younger than I was) and I, if I happened to be present, rolled our eyes at each other and giggled. My grandparents rather disapproved of their son for using a book. After all, my grandfather thriftily said the same grace every time, year in, year out, at all our regular meals. "Oh Lord," it began, "we have reasons to thank Thee"—but this sounded like "raisins," to me. (But then, at this time I also confused "as we forgive our debtors" with "taters," a word I'd heard used humorously for "potatoes.") However, if we had company to dinner or "tea," my grandfather was perfectly capable of producing a longer, more grateful one, or even making up one of his own to suit the occasion.

Until age or drink had spoiled it, Uncle Neddy had a very nice baritone voice, and Sundays when he was well enough to go to church he appeared in the back row of the choir. On those days he wore a navy blue suit and a hard collar, a dark blue satin tie with a red stripe, and a stickpin with a small, dead diamond in it, much like the white highlight in his left eye that I am contemplating right now.

But I want to try to be chronological about this little boy who doesn't look much like a little boy. His semidisembodied head seems too big for his body; and his body seems older, far less alive, than the round, healthy, painted face which is so very much in the present it seems to be taking an interest in it, even here, so very far away from where it saw such a very different world for so long.

The first dramatic episode of his life that I know about was when his foot got scalded. He told me the story more than once, usually as a warning to keep away from something hot. It concerned his boots, not these in the painting but his first pair of copper-toed boots, real little boots, no buttons or laces. Out of curiosity, he stood too near someone who was dipping boiling water out of the big boiler on the back of the kitchen stove and somehow a dipperful fell straight into a boot top. The boot was pulled off immediately, and then his sock. "And the skin came with it," Uncle Neddy always said, proud and morbid, while an icicle suddenly probed the bottom of my stomach. The family doctor came, and for a long time poor Uncle Neddy couldn't walk. His mother and sisters—he was the only son, the second child—all said he had been a very stoical boy; on that occasion he had only given one scream. Later on, he had performed prodigies of stoicism in respect to the Nova Scotian winter cold. He couldn't endure being bundled up and would run out of the house and all the way to school, with the thermometer at ten, or twenty, below, without his overcoat. He would condescend to wear mittens and a muffler, but no more, and his ears had been frostbitten over and over again, and once one was frozen.

After these feats of endurance, his life, except for the Bible reading, is unknown to me for a long time. No—it was Uncle Neddy who dug all the wax off the face of my mother's big wax doll from France, with his fingernails, and chewed it like chewing gum. The delicacy of the doll's complexion depended on this wax; without it, she was red-faced and common. Uncle

Neddy and my mother were playing upstairs; when my mother protested, he pushed her downstairs. Then when she pretended to faint and lay there at the foot of the stairs with her eyes shut, in great remorse he ran and got a quart dipper full of icy well water and threw it over her, crying out that he had killed his little sister.

And although she has been dead for over forty years, his little sister is here now, too, beside him. *Her* imaginary carpet is laid out geometrically in dark red, green, and blue, or is it supposed to be tiles? and her wall is darker than his. She leans on a fairly normal round table, draped in a long red tablecloth, and her left leg is crossed over her right one. She must be about nine. She wears a small bustle and a gold brooch, but her black hair is cut short all over, with a fringe over her eyes, and she looks almost more like a boy than he does.

The paintings are unsigned and undated, probably the work of an itinerant portrait painter. Perhaps he worked from tin-types, because in the family album the little girl's dress appears again. Or did she have only the one dress, for dress-up? In the painting it is dark blue, white-sprigged, with the bustle and other additions purple, and two white frills making a sort of "bertha." (In the tintype the French wax doll appears, too, seated on her lap, big and stiff, her feet sticking out in small white boots beneath her petticoats, showing fat legs in striped stockings. She stares composedly at the camera under a raffish blond wig, in need of combing. The tintype man has tinted the cheeks of both the doll and my mother a clear pink. Of course, this must have been before the doll had lost her waxen complexion under Uncle Neddy's fingernails.)

Or perhaps the painter did the faces—clearer and brighter than the rest of the pictures, and in Uncle Neddy's case slightly out of proportion, surely—from "life," the clothes from tintypes, and the rest from his imagination. He may have arrived in the village with his canvases already filled in, the unrecognizable carpets, the round table and improbable chair, ready and waiting to be stood on and leaned on. Did Uncle Neddy insist, "I want to be painted with the chair"? Did the two children fight, more than seventy years ago, over which one would have which background?

Well, Uncle Neddy grew up; he skated a great deal, winters (without bundling up), went through all the grades of the village school, and very early (I heard much later) began to fall in love and to—alas for Neddy—"chase women." I even heard, overheard, rather, that there had been prolonged family worry about a "widow." He must have begun drinking about this time, too, although that was never mentioned until years later when he became, on occasion, a public disgrace. It was hard to know what to do with him; he showed all the classical symptoms of being "wild." In vain family prayers morning and night, the childhood Bible-reading, choir practice, Sunday School ("Sabbath School" my grandfather called it), church itself, Friday prayer meetings, and the annual revivals at which Uncle Neddy went forward and repented of all. At one of these, Uncle Neddy even took the "pledge," the temperance pledge that he could still recite to me years later, although he had broken it heaven only knew how many times by then:

> Trusting in help from heaven above
> We pledge ourselves to works of love,
> Resolving that we will not make
> Or sell or buy or give or take
> Rum, Brandy, Whiskey, Cordials fine,
> Gin, Cider, Porter, Ale or Wine.
> Tobacco, too, we will not use
> And trust that we may always choose
> A place among the wise and good
> And speak and act as Christians should.

This was called the "Pledge of the Iron Age Band of Hope." The "Band of Hope" was an inspirational society for younger members of the church, but why "Iron Age"? Uncle Neddy didn't know and I never found out. It became vaguely associated in my mind with his profession. Because, after all these moral incentives, Uncle Neddy inevitably, immediately, began to show signs of being "wild" all over again and finally he was apprenticed to a tinsmith, to learn a trade—tinsmithing and installing and repairing wood-burning furnaces. And then, still very young, he married Aunt Hat. I got the impression later (I was a little pitcher with big ears) that perhaps he "had" to marry her, but I may be doing him an injustice.

Redheaded, rawboned, green-eyed, handsome, Aunt Hat came from Galway Mines, a sort of ghost town twenty miles off, where iron mining and smelting were still carried on in a reduced and primitive way. It had once been more flourishing, but I remember boarded-up houses, boarded-up stores with rotting wooden sidewalks in front of them, and the many deep black or dark red holes that disfigured the hills. Also a mountainous slag heap, dead, gray, and glistening. Long before I was born, one of these slag heaps, built up for years, I don't know why, right beside or on the river that farther downstream ran through our village, had given way and there had been a flood. I heard this story many times because my grandparents' house was on the lower side of the village, near the river, and it had been flooded. A warning had been given, but in the excitement of rescuing the older children, the clock, the cow and horse, my grandmother forgot the latest baby (later my aunt), and my grandfather had dashed back into the house to find her floating peacefully in her wooden cradle, bobbing over the kitchen floor. (But after this the poor baby had erysipelas.)

If Uncle Neddy was a "devil," a feeble, smokey-black one, Aunt Hat was a red, real one—redheaded, freckled, red-knuckled, strong, all fierce fire and flame. There *was* something of the Old Nick about her. They complemented each other; they were devils together. Rumor had it that the only other redhead for miles around was the parish priest at Galway Mines—the only Catholic community in the county. True or not, the village gossips drew their strictly Protestant and cruel conclusions.

My own recollections begin now, things I saw or heard: Uncle Neddy is a tinsmith, a married man, the father of three living and one or two dead children. He has a big shop across the green from my grandparents' house, in the only part of my grandfather's former tannery not torn down. (The local tanning trade had come to an end before I was born, when chemicals replaced tanbark.) From the entrance, with double doors, the shop starts out fairly bright; a large section is devoted to "store" galvanized pails and enameled pots and pans, two or three or more black kitchen ranges with nickel trimmings, farming implements, and fishing rods—the last because fishing was Uncle Neddy's passion. But the farther in one goes the darker and more gloomy it becomes; the floor is covered with acrid-smelling, glinting, black dust and the workbench stretching across the far end is black, with glints of silver. Night descends as one walks back, then daylight grows as one reaches the dirty windows above the workbench. This night sky of Uncle Neddy's is hung with the things he makes himself: milk pails, their bottoms shining like moons; flashing tin mugs in different sizes; watering pots like comets, in among big dull lengths of stove pipe with wrinkled blue joints like elephants' legs dangling overhead.

When he was at work, Uncle Neddy always wore a black leather cap, or perhaps it was so shiny with wear it looked like leather, and black, black overalls. He chewed tobacco. The plugs of chewing tobacco had a little red tin apple pressed into one corner; these he took off and gave to me. He loved children and was very good with them. When he kissed me, he smelled violently of "Apple" chewing tobacco and his sooty chin was very scratchy—perhaps he shaved only on Sundays. Frequently he smelled of something else violent, too, and I remember a black or dark brown bottle, unlabeled, kept in the murk under the workbench, being lifted out for a hasty swig.

The shop was full of fascinating things to look at, but surely most of their charm lay in the fact that, besides being brand-new, they were all out of place. Who would expect to see comfortable-looking kitchen stoves, with names like "Magee Ideal" and "Magic Home" on their oven doors, standing leaning sidewise, in a shop? Stone cold, too, with empty, brand-new teakettles hanging from the rafters over them and the stove-lid lifters hanging up in a bunch, like dried herbs? Or pots and pans, enameled brown or a marbleized blue-and-white, sitting on the floor? Or dozens of tin mugs, the kind we used every day of our lives and that Uncle Neddy actually made, hanging over-head, brilliantly new and clean, not dull and brown, the way they got at home? And kitchen pumps, sticky red or green, and the taller, thinner variety of pump for the barnyard, lying on the floor? Besides all these things there were fascinating black machines attached to the workbench and worked by hand. One was for rolling the blue-black sheet iron into stovepipes; one made turned-over edges on strips of tin so that they wouldn't cut the fingers, and there were others of more mysterious functions, all black and sinister. There were blowtorches and a sort of miniature forge, little anvils, heavy shears in all sizes, wooden mallets, boxes of stubby, gray-blue, flat-headed rivets and, best of all, solder. It came in thick silver rods, with a trade name stamped along them. What I liked best was to watch Uncle Neddy heat the end of a rod to the melting point and dribble it quickly to join a wide ribbon of tin and make a mug, sometimes a child-size mug, then solder on a strip already folded under on both sides in the folding machine for the handle. When they were cold, drops of solder that fell to the dirty floor could be picked up, pure silver, cool and heavy, and saved. Under the bench were piles of bright scraps of tin with sharp edges, curved shapes, triangles, pieces with holes in them, as if they'd been cut from paper, and prettiest of all, thin tin shavings, curled up tight, like springs. Occasionally, Uncle Neddy would let me help him hold a stick of solder and dribble it around the bottom of a pail. This was thrilling, but oh, to be able to write one's name with it, in silver letters! As he worked, bent over, clipping, hammering, soldering, he chewed tobacco and spat long black spits under the bench. He was like a black snail, a rather quick but cautious snail, leaving a silvery, shiny trail of solder.

Probably the paying part of his business was installing furnaces, but that didn't interest Billy and me, although Billy was sometimes allowed to go along. They went off, with a helper, down the shore, to places like Lower Economy, the red wagon loaded with furnace parts and stovepipes, pulled by Nimble, our horse.

While Uncle Neddy worked away, chewing and spitting and drinking, with an occasional customer to talk to (there were two kitchen chairs in the front of the shop where men sometimes sat and talked, about fishing, mostly), or with a child or two to keep him company, his wife was cleaning house. Scrub, scrub and polish, polish, she went, all day long, in the house, next door but up higher, on a grass-covered slope. The house was shingled, painted bright red, the only red house in the village, and although it seemed big enough for Uncle Neddy's family, it was never quite finished; another verandah, a spare room, were always in the process of being added on, or shingled, but never quite completed, or painted. A narrow verandah led from the street to a side door, the only one used, and chickweed grew profusely underneath it, down the slope. My grandmother would send me across the street to pick some for her canaries and Aunt Hat would come out, lean over, and ask me crossly what I was doing, or just bang a dust mop on the railing, over my head. Her sharp-jawed, freckled face and green eyes behind gold-rimmed glasses peered over at me, upside down. She had her good days and her bad days, as my grandmother said, but mostly they seemed to be bad and on those she did everything more vigorously and violently. Sometimes she would order me home, where I meant to go, anyway, and with my innocent handful of chickweed, I ran.

Her three living children—there were two girls, older than Billy and I—all had beautiful curly hair. The girls were old enough to comb their own hair, but when Billy's curls were being made, really made, for Sunday School, his shrieks could be heard all the way across the green to our house. Then Billy would arrive to go to Sunday School with me, his face smeared with tears, the beautiful red-brown curls in perfect tubes, with drops of water (Aunt Hat wet the curls and turned them over her finger with a hard brush) falling from the end of each onto the white, ruffled collar of his Sunday blouse. Mondays, Aunt Hat energetically scrubbed the family's clothes, summers, down below, out back. On good days she occasionally burst quite loudly into song as she scrubbed and rinsed:

> Oh, the moon shines tonight on pretty Red Wing,
> The breeze is sighing,
> The night bird's crying.
> Oh, far beneath the sky her warrior's sleeping
> While Red Wing's weeping
> Her heart awa-a-y . . .

This song is still associated in my mind not with a disconsolate Indian maiden and red wings but with a red house, red hair, strong yellow laundry soap, and galvanized scrubbing boards (also sold in Uncle Neddy's shop; I forgot them). On other weekdays, Aunt Hat, as I have said, cleaned house: it was probably the cleanest house in the county. The kitchen linoleum dazzled; the straw matting in the upstairs bedrooms looked like new and so did the hooked rugs; the "cosy corner" in the parlor, with a red upholstered seat and frilled red pillows standing on their corners, was never disarranged; every china ornament on the mantelpiece over the airtight stove was in the same place and dustless, and Aunt Hat always seemed to have a broom or a long-handled brush in her hand, ready to take a swipe either at her household effects or at any child, dog, or cat that came her way. Her temper, like her features, seemed constantly at a high temperature, but on bad days it rose many degrees and she "took it out," as the village said behind her back, in cleaning house. They also said she was "a great hand at housework" or "a demon for housework," sometimes, "She's a Tartar, that one!" It was also remarked on that in a village where every sunny window was filled with houseplants and the ladies constantly exchanged "slips" of this and that desirable one, Aunt Hat had "no luck" with plants; in fact, nothing would grow for her at all.

Yes, she was a Tartar; it came out in her very freckles. She sunburned easily. When we went on a picnic, one hour in the northern sun and the vee of her neck was flaming. Uncle Neddy would say, almost as if he were proud of it, "Hat's neck looks as if I'd taken a flat iron to it!" Wearing a straw hat and a gray cardigan instead of his black work clothes, even in the sunlight he still looked dark. But instead of being like a dark snail, he was a thin, dark salamander, enjoying, for a moment, his wife's fieriness.

His married life was miserable, we all knew that. My girl cousins whispered to me about the horrible, endless fights that went on, nights, under the low, slanting ceiling of their parents' bedroom, papered all over with small, pained-looking rosebuds, like pursed mouths. When things got too bad he would come to see "Mother" and they would shut themselves in the front parlor, or even in the pantry, standing up, for a talk. At our house, my grandmother was the one who did all the complaining; my grandfather never complained. When she said things about her daughter-in-law that he felt were too harsh, he merely murmured, "Yes, temper . . . temper . . . too bad," or maybe it was "too sad." (To Billy and me, when we quarreled, he said, "Birds in their little nests agree," a quotation I have never been able to place and even then didn't altogether agree with, from my observation of birds in their little nests.) There were days and weeks when these visits from a bedeviled-looking Uncle Neddy occurred often; dramas of which I knew nothing were going on; once in a while I made out that they concerned money, "deeds," or "papers." When Uncle Neddy had finally gone back to his shop, my grandmother would collapse into her kitchen rocking chair and announce: "*She* makes the balls and he fires them . . ." Then she would start rocking, groaning and rocking, wiping her eyes with the edge of her apron, uttering from time to time the mysterious remark that was a sort of chorus in our lives: "Nobody knows . . . *nobody knows* . . ." I often wondered what my grandmother knew that none of the rest of us knew and if she alone knew it, or if it was a total mystery that really nobody knew except perhaps God. I even asked her, "*What* do you know, Gammie, that we don't know? Why don't you tell us? Tell me!" She only laughed, dabbing at her tears. She laughed as easily as she cried, and one very often turned into the other (a trait her children and grandchildren inherited). Then, "Go on with you!" she said. "Scat!"

From the rocking chair by the window, she had a good view of all the green, the people on their way to the general store just around the corner, or on Sundays, to the tall white Presbyterian church opposite, and, diagonally to the right, of Uncle Neddy's shop and the red house. She disapproved of the way Aunt Hat fed her family. Often, around time for "tea," Billy or one of the girls could be seen running across to the store, and a few minutes later running back with a loaf of bread or something in a paper bag. My grandmother was furious: "Store bread! Store bread! Nothing but store bread!" Or, "More canned things, I'll bet! More *soda crackers...*" I knew from direct observation that when he was far too big for the family high chair, Billy was squeezed into it and given what was called "pap" for *his* "tea." This was a soup plate full of the soda crackers, swimming in milk, limp and adhesive, with a lot of sugar to make them go down. The "pap" would be topped off by two pieces of marble cake, or parkins, for dessert. Aunt Hat did bake those, if not bread, and her parkins were good, but, as if out of spite, hard enough to break the teeth.

Sometimes I inadvertently brought on my grandmother's tears myself, by repeating things Billy told me. Perhaps he, too, was firing the balls made on the other side of the green, or pebbles, suited to the verbal slingshot of his tender years. "Is it true that Nimble (the one horse—later there were two horses, the second unfortunately named Maud, the name, straight from Tennyson, of one of my aunts)—is it true that Nimble belongs to Uncle Neddy? Billy says he does. And that Nelly and Martha Washington do, too?" (The cow and her calf; I had named the calf myself.)

My grandmother grew indignant. "I *gave* your Uncle Edward that horse on his tenth wedding anniversary! Not only that, but he sold him back to me two years afterwards and he still keeps saying I haven't finished paying him yet! When I have! And he uses that horse all the time, much more than we do!"

"Oh pshaw, mother," said my grandfather. "That's an old story now."

"Oh yes," said my grandmother. "Nimble, and the buffalo robe, and the dinner service, and *pew rent*—they're all old stories now. *You'd* never remember anything. But *I* won't forget. *I* won't forget." And she set the rocking chair rocking as if it were, as it probably was, a memory machine.

I have a few more memories of Uncle Neddy at this period in his life when the tinsmith business was still going on, and the furnace business, flourishing or not, I don't know, but before the obvious decline had set in and before I went away to Boston and saw him at less and less frequent intervals. One memory, brief but poignant, like a childhood nightmare that haunts one for years, or all one's life, the details are so clear and so awful, is of a certain Christmas. Or maybe it was a Christmas Eve, because it takes place after the lamps were lit—but of course it grew dark very early in the winter. There was a large Christmas tree, smelling overpoweringly of fir, in the parlor. It was rather sparsely decorated with colored paper chains, strings of tinsel and popcorn, and a very few glass balls or other shiny ornaments: a country-fied, home-made tree, chopped down and brought fresh from the snow-covered "commons." But there were a few little silver and gold baskets, full of candies, woven from strips of metal by "the blind children," and clips holding twisted wax candles that after many warnings were finally lit. One of my aunts played "Holy Night" on the piano and the candles flickered in time to our singing.

This was all very nice, but still I remember it as "the Black Christmas." My other grandparents, in the States, had sent a large box of presents. It contained woolen caps and mufflers for Billy and me, and I didn't like them at all. His set was dark blue but mine was *gray* and I hated it at sight. There were also mittens and socks, and some of these were red or blue, and the high black rubber boots I'd wanted, but my pair was much too big. Laid out under the tree, even by flickering candlelight, everything looked shapeless and sad, and I wanted to cry. And then Santa Claus came in, an ordinary brown potato sack over his shoulder, with the other presents sagging in it. He was terrifying. He couldn't have been dressed in black, but that was my impression, and I did start to cry. He had artificial snow sprinkled on his shoulders, and a pointed red cap, but the beard! It wasn't white and woolly at all, it was made of rope, a mass of frayed-out rope. This dreadful figure cavorted around the room, making jokes in a loud, deep, false voice. The face that showed above the rope beard looked, to me, like a Negro's. I shrieked. Then this Santa from the depths of a coal mine put down his sack that could have been filled with coal, and hugged and kissed me. Through my sobs, I recognized, by touch and smell and his suddenly everyday voice, that it was only Uncle Neddy.

This Christmas, so like a nightmare, affected me so that shortly afterward I had a real nightmare about Uncle Neddy, or at least about his shop. In it, I crossed the road and was about to go into the shop when the door was blocked by a huge horse, coming out. The horse filled the doorway, towering high over me and showing all her big yellow teeth in a grin. She whinnied, shrill and deafening; I felt the hot wind coming out of her big nostrils; it almost blew me backward. I had the presence of mind to say to the horse, "You are a nightmare!" and of course she was, and so I woke up. But awake, I still felt uncomfortable for a long time about Uncle Neddy's possibly having been inside, his escape cut off by that fearful animal.

I said that Uncle Neddy was a great fisherman; it was the thing he did best of all, perhaps the only thing he did perfectly. (For all I know, his tin-ware, beautiful and shiny as it was, may have been badly made.) He could catch trout where no one else could and sometimes he would go off before daybreak and arrive at our house at seven o'clock with a string of rose-speckled trout for his mother's breakfast. He could cast into the narrowest brooks and impossibly difficult spots and bring out trout after trout. He tied beautiful flies, for himself and friends, and later for customers by mail.

> Our uncle, innocent of books,
> Was rich in lore of fields and brooks . . .

Whittier wrote of his, and it was true of mine.

But he was not altogether innocent of books. There had been all that childhood Bible-reading that had left the supply of texts from which he still quoted. And also, in his parlor, on a shelf above the "cosy corner" and in a small bookcase, there was an oddly assorted collection of books. I wasn't familiar with them the way I was, with the outsides, at least, of every single book on the shelves in the upstairs hall at my grandmother's (*Inglesby's Legends*; *Home Medicine*; *Emerson's Essays*; and so on), but this was only be-cause of Aunt Hat. Every time I managed to be alone in the parlor with Uncle Neddy's books, she soon found me and shooed me off home. But I did get to look at them, or some of them, usually the same ones over and over. It was obvious that Uncle Neddy had been strongly affected by the sinking of the *Titanic*; in his modest library there were three different books about this catastrophe, and in the dining room, facing his place at the table, hung a chromograph of the ship going down: the iceberg, the rising steam, peo-ple struggling in the water, everything, in full color. When I was left alone in the parlor, an ear cocked for Aunt Hat, I could scarcely wait to take out the *Titanic* books—one very big and heavy, red, with gilt trimmings—and look at the terrifying pictures one more time. There were also *The Tower of London*; a book about Queen Victoria's Diamond Jubilee; *Advice to Young Men* ("Avoid lonely walks . . ."); and several of a religious nature. Also some little fat books about a character named "Dolly Dimples" that looked nice, and were pleasant to hold, but proved boring to read. But the *Titanic* books with their pictures, some of them actual photographs, were the best.

The other chief attraction in Uncle Neddy's parlor was an Edison pho-nograph, very old, that still worked. It had a flaring, brown-and-gold horn and played thick black cylinders. My girl cousins were allowed to play it. I remember only two out of the box of cylinders: a brief Sousa march that could have marched people about fifty yards, and "Cohen on the Telephone," which I loved. I knew that it was supposed to be funny, and laughed, although I hadn't any idea who or what a Cohen was or what I was laughing at, and I doubt that Uncle Neddy entirely understood it, either.

I suppose that Uncle Neddy's situation in life, his fortune and prospects, could never have been considered happy, even in his small world, but I was very young, and except for an occasional overheard, or eavesdropped-on remark and those private conversations in the parlor or pantry that always upset my grandmother, nothing untoward came to my knowledge, consciously that is, for years. Then even I began to hear more about Uncle Neddy's drinking, and the shop began its long deterioration. There was no place to buy liquor in the village; the nearest government liquor store was in a town fifteen miles away. At first this meant a daylong drive behind Nimble or Maud; sometimes an overnight stay at the house of a relative, niece or cousin, of my grandfather's. Probably when Uncle Neddy went to town he brought back a supply of rum, the usual drink, heavy, dark, and strong. All I knew of alcohol at that time was the homemade wines the ladies sometimes served each other, or the hot toddy my grandfather sometimes made himself on freezing winter nights. But finally phrases like "not himself," "taken too much," "three seas over," sank into my consciousness and I looked at my poor uncle with new eyes, expectantly. There was one occasion when he had to be taken away from the home funeral of Mrs. Captain McDonald, an old woman everyone was very fond of. What at first passed for Uncle Neddy's natural if demonstrative grief had got "out of hand." My grandmother moaned about this; in fact, she moaned so loudly in her bedroom across the hall from mine that I could hear almost every word. "He'll disgrace us all; you'll see. I've *never* . . . There's *never* been a drunkard in *my* family . . . *None* of my brothers . . ." This time my grandfather remained quite silent.

Then Uncle Neddy bought a model-T Ford. There were very few cars in the village then; the family who had driven the coach to the railroad station, four miles off, for years and years, had been the first to acquire one, and there were only two or three more. Uncle Neddy got his Ford somehow, and the younger daughter, fifteen or so, with long curls just like Mary Pickford's, drove it hell-for-leather, expertly. Perhaps she drove her father the fifteen miles to town, in no time, to buy rum—anyway, he got it, and when he didn't have it, there was another unbelievable overheard remark, that he drank *vanilla.*

Meanwhile, the shop was changing. First, there were many more things for sale and less and less work seemed to be done at the old black-and-silver glinting workbench. There were many household effects that came ready-made: can openers, meat grinders, mixing spoons, gray-mottled enamel "sets" of saucepans. There were more fishing rods and then gorgeous barbed fish lures, displayed on cardboard stands. The stoves were now all, or almost all, white enamel, and there were white enamel kitchen sinks, and faucets, and electric water pumps. The chewing tobacco with the little tin apple in the corner was still on sale, but next to it one day there were chocolate bars: Moirs and Cadbury's, with nuts, without nuts, or in little sections with a different cream in each. These were magnetic, of course, but they cost five cents, or ten cents, and Billy and I had rarely had more than a penny to buy anything in our lives. Uncle Neddy was as kind to us, to any children, as always. He would take a whole ten-cent bar, divide it into its little squares, and share it out. A punchboard appeared, two or three of them. For ten cents one could punch out a little rolled-up paper with a number on it and, with luck, the number would win a whole big box of chocolates or a tin of biscuits. It was still a fascinating place to go, but not nearly as fascinating as when Uncle Neddy had been making tin mugs and soldering.

Then I went away to live in the States and came back just for the summers. Perhaps two or three years went by, I'm not sure, but one summer a gasoline pump appeared in front of the shop. Cars stopped to be filled up; not very often, but there were more of them, although the road was still dirt and gravel, "crowned" in the middle. Billy and I competed with each other as to which one had seen the most and the biggest trucks. If a truck stopped for gasoline, we rushed to examine it: red or blue paint, decorated with white lines or gold lines, with arrowheads, what load it was carrying, and where it was going. Sometimes Uncle Neddy poured water into its radiator from one of his own watering cans while it stood steaming and trembling. Another summer, and the road had been covered with tar. The red house still had an unpainted wing, its "new" shingles already gray. Another summer the Governor General drove through and stopped to make a speech in front of Uncle Neddy's shop. Another little girl, not me, curtsied and presented a large bouquet of flowers to his wife, Lady Bing.

Although there are more, these are all the memories I want to keep on remembering—I couldn't forget them if I tried, probably—and remembering clearly, as if they had just happened or were still happening. My grandfather dies. My grandmother goes to live with a daughter in Quebec. I go away to school, then to college. I come back at longer and longer intervals to Uncle Neddy's village. Once I go fishing with him and he deplores my casting, but, as always, very gently. He grows older—older, thinner, bent, and more unshaven, the sooty bristles mixed with silver. His voice grows weaker, too, and higher pitched. He has stomach ulcers. He is operated on, but won't stop, can't stop drinking—or so I am told. It has taken the form of periodic bouts and an aunt tells me (I'm old enough to be confided in) that "Everyone knows" and that "It will kill him." However, when he dies it is of something quite different.

The last time I saw him he was very weak and very bent. The eyes of the man who used to lean down to hug and kiss me were now on a level with mine. When I kissed him, the smell was only half the same: rum—he no longer chewed tobacco. I knew, and he said it, that he was "not long for this world." Aunt Hat had aged, too. The red hair had faded to pink, but her jaw, her freckles, and her disposition were exactly the same. She no longer shooed me out of the house. Now she expressed her feelings by pretending not to see the presents from the States, clamping her jaw tight, and swatting at flies. Some days she refused to speak; others, she spoke—disparagingly, of whatever subject came up. The filling station was owned and manned by others.

I don't believe that Uncle Neddy ever went anywhere in his life except possibly two or three times as far as Boston after his daughters had moved there and married, and I'm not sure of that. And now he is here, on the other side of the Equator, with his little sister, looking like the good boy in an Horatio Alger story: poor, neat, healthy, polite, and by some lucky accident—preventing a banker from having his pocket picked, or catching a runaway horse—about to start out being a "success" in life, and perhaps taking his little sister along with him. He is overdressed for this climate and his cheeks are so pink he must be sweating in his velveteen suit.

I am going to hang them here side by side, above the antique (Brazilian antique) chest of drawers. In spite of the heat and dampness, they look calmly on and on, at the invisible Tropic of Capricorn, at the extravagant rain still blotting out the southern ocean. I must watch out for the mildew that inevitably forms on old canvases in the rainy season, and wipe them off often. It will be the gray or pale-green variety that appears overnight on dark surfaces, like breath on a mirror. Uncle Neddy will continue to exchange his direct, bright-hazel, child's looks, now, with those of strangers—dark-eyed Latins he never knew, who never would have understood him, whom he would have thought of, if he had ever thought of them at all, as "foreigners." How late, Uncle Neddy, how late to have started on your travels!

1977

BRAZIL

Chapter 1. Paradoxes and Ironies.

The glaring paradox that illustrates the general contradictoriness of Brazil: the population explosion versus the high infant mortality rates. Wide variety of paradoxes great and small: Vast sources of wealth: appalling poverty; luxury: asceticism; snobbery: "familiarity"; pride: national inferiority complex; vitality: "laziness;" And the alterations of corrupt & extravagant regiimes with occasional puritanical reform regimes

Chapter 2. The Land of Dye-Wood.

The appeal to the imagination of the legendary Brazil. Early discoverers and accounts. The Indians. The extravagant flora / physical beauty of the country, its exotic flora and fauna, and some naturalists. The Portugese and the first two centuries. First slaves.

Chapter 3. The Only Western Empire.

Arrival of Dom João I; Dom Pedro I and independence from Portugal. The 40-year reign of Dom Pedro II , "the nation's schoolmaster." Republican ideas at work. Emancipation of the slaves: Abdication. Problems of the new republic, some still unsolved.

Chapter 4. Three Capitals, and other places.

Bahia until   . Rio de Janeiro until 1960. Brasilia. City life and small town life, old and modern. The "moving on" spirit, and the "hollow frontier." São Paulo.

Chapter 5. Vegetable, Mineral, and Animal.

Sugar, heyday and decline. Coffee, the "one crop." Gold, jewels, ores; untouched mineral wealth. Cattle-raising in the south. Difficulties of transportation. The types: Bahiano and fazendeira Cangaceiro, Grimpeiro, and Gaúcho.

Chapter 6. The Unselfconscious Arts.

Carnival. Folk art and festivals: Bumba meu Boi, Reizados, Maritimas, Iemanja, etc. the church. Sao João, São Pedro and Sao Jorge. Devlopment of the samba. Poplular songs, HUMOR.

Chapter 7. The Selfconscious Arts.

Contemporary Brazilian archtecture most important. Foreign influences in the past and preent. A few landmarks of Brazilian writing. Journalism. The importance of "poets" in Latin America. Serious music. Portinari, and some younger artists; work in black & white. Difficulties.

Chapter 8. Individiuals and Groups.

Race relations. Negros, Indians, Portugese; immigrants. General Rondon and Villas Boas. Women. Santos Dumont. Sports and changing society - futebol.

Chapter 9. The New Republic.

The legacy, good and bad, of 30 years of Vargas. Communicatons, migrating workers, crowded cities, illiteracy and sanitaion, etc. Elections. Power, irrigation,

Chapter 10. A New

K and the inflation. Problems presentd by Brasilia. The "opposition" in power. at last. The new State of Guanabara. Quadros - (São Paulo) again the "schoolmaster of the nation"?

Chapter 1

Recently in Rio de Janeiro one of those "human interest" dramas took place, the same small drama that takes place every so often in New York or London or Rome: a newborn baby was kidnaped from a maternity hospital. Her name was Maria da Conceição, or Mary of the Conception, but the newspapers immediately abbreviated this, Brazilian fashion, to Conceiçãozinha, or "Little Conception."

Conceiçãozinha made the headlines for a week, and while she did it is safe to say that the country's current inflation, the soaring cost of living, the shifts of power in the government—perhaps even the soccer scores—took second place for most readers.

The hospital staff was questioned. A feebleminded woman wandering in the neighborhood was detained. The police poked into culverts and clumps of weeds and around the *favelas*, Rio's notorious hillside slums. Somehow the kidnaping was kept from the baby's mother, but the young government-worker father was photographed at his desk, in postures of despair. Then, after three days, Conceiçãozinha was found, safe and sound. One of the hospital nurses, who had lost a child of her own by miscarriage shortly before, had stolen her.

So far it all could have happened in New York, London, or Rome. But now the story becomes Brazilian. The white nurse's mulatto lover, owner of a small grocery store, had promised her a house to live in if she had a child, and he had already given her the equivalent of fifty dollars for the baby's layette. So the nurse—determined, she told reporters, "to have a decent place to live in" with "home atmosphere," and also because she really wanted a baby—concealed her miscarriage and told her lover that the baby would be born on such and such a day. Until then she boarded Conceiçãozinha with her laundress, an old woman living in a *favela* shack. The nurse was arrested as she took them food. The baby was fat and well. The laundress, who could not read, knew nothing of the hubbub in the papers and protested her complete innocence. When the father was told the good news he sobbed and said, "This is the strongest emotion I have ever felt in my life." He was photographed embracing the police. Conceiçãozinha was taken back to the hospital, where "the doctors were shouting and the nurses weeping." Three or four hundred people had gathered outside. The swaddled baby was held up to a window, but the crowd screamed, "Show her little face!" So it was shown "to applause and cheers."

The next day the drama continued on a lower plane but in even more Brazilian style. The two sets of in-laws quarrelled as to which one would have the honor of harboring the child and her real mother first. One grand-mother denied that the chief of police had been asked to be Conceição-zinha's godfather, because "that is always a *family* affair." And the poor father was faced with fulfilling his *promessas*. If the baby was found alive, he had promised (1) to pay for four Masses; (2) to stop smoking for a year; (3) to give two yard-high wax candles, as well as a life-size wax model of a baby, to the Church of Our Lady of the Penha; and (4) to climb the steps of the same church on his knees, carrying a lighted candle. This 18th-century church perches on top of a weirdly shaped *penha*, or rock, that sticks up out of the plain just north of the city. It is a favorite church for pilgrimages and for the fulfilling of *promessas*. The steps up to it number 365.

The story of Conceiçãozinha contains a surprising amount of information about Brazilian life, manners, and character. Much of it, of course, is what one might expect to find in any Latin American country. Brazilians love children. They are highly emotional and not ashamed of it. Family feeling is very strong. They are Roman Catholics, at least in outward behavior. They are franker than Anglo-Saxons about extramarital love, and they are tolerant of miscegenation. Also—as one would expect in a very poor and in many ways backward country—many people are illiterate; there are feebleminded people at large who in other countries might be in institu-tions; and hospitals may not always be run with streamlined efficiency. So far it is all fairly predictable.

But there is more to it than that. The story immediately brings to mind one of Brazil's worst, and certainly most shocking, problems: that of infant mortality. Why all this sentimental, almost hysterical, concern over one small baby, when the infant mortality rate in Brazil is still one of the high-est in the world? The details of Conceiçãozinha's story are worth examin-ing not only for the interesting light they throw on that contradictory thing, the Brazilian character, but also because the tragic, unresolved problem they present is almost a paradigm of a good many other Brazilian problems, big and small.

First there is the obvious devotion to children. As in other Latin countries, babies are everywhere. Everyone seems to know how to talk to infants or dandle them, and unself-consciously. It is said that two kinds of small business never fail in Brazil, infants' wear shops and toy shops. The poorest workman will spend a disproportionate amount of his salary for a christening dress (or for milk if he happens to know it is vital to his child's health). Parents love to dress up their offspring; the children's costume balls are an important part of Carnival every year throughout the country.

In Catholic Brazil there is no divorce and no legalized birth control, and large families are the rule. Sometimes families run to twenty or more, and five or six children seems to be average. Brazil is a very young country; more than 52 per cent of the population is under nineteen years old. Early marriage is normal, and a baby within a year is taken for granted. Children are almost always wanted—the first three or four at least—and adored.

And yet the infant mortality rate stays appallingly high. In the poorest and most backward regions of the great northeast bulge and the Amazon basin, it is as high as 50 per cent during the first year of life, sometimes even higher. The cities of Recife and Rio, with their large *favelas*, are two of the worst offenders. During the three days when Conceiçãozinha was hidden in the washerwoman's shack, and survived, it is a safe guess that more than sixty babies died in Rio.

Most of this tragic waste of life is due to malnutrition. But often the malnutrition is due not so much to actual lack of food as to ignorance, a vicious circle in which poverty creates ignorance which then creates more poverty. In Rio, for example, there are many worthy free clinics. But fine doctors have been known to resign after working in them for years; they can no longer endure seeing the same children brought in time after time, sicker, weaker, and finally dying because the parents are too ignorant, or too superstitious, to follow simple instructions.

The masses of poor people in the big cities, and the poor and not-so-poor of the "backlands," love their children and kill them with kindness by the thousands. The wrong foods, spoiled foods, worm medicines, sleeping syrups—all exact a terrible toll on the "little angels," in paper-covered, gilt-trimmed coffins, blue for boys and pink for girls.

Nevertheless, the population of Brazil is increasing rapidly. Life expectancy has gone up considerably in the last few decades. The indomitable and apparently increasing vitality of Brazil shines through the grimmest death toll statistics. It is like the banana tree that grows everywhere in the country. Cut it back to a stump above ground, and in a matter of hours it sends up a new shoot and starts unfolding new green leaves.

•

Indeed, the banana tree is a fairly good symbol for the country itself and for what has happened and is still happening to it. Brazil struck all the early explorers as a "natural paradise," a "garden," and at its best moments it still gives that impression—a garden neglected, abused, and still mostly uncultivated, but growing vigorously nevertheless. Great resources have been squandered, but even greater ones are still there, waiting. Barring some worldwide disaster, material prosperity seems bound to arrive. But it is the mismanagement and waste of both human and material wealth along the way that shocks the foreigner as well as the educated, sensitive Brazilian. To give only one example of this: because of inadequate roads, poor transportation, and lack of refrigeration, some 40 per cent of all food produced spoils before it reaches the big markets.

Exploding birth rate and infant mortality, great wealth and degrading poverty—these are the two big paradoxes. But along with them come many smaller ones repeating the pattern, overlapping and interacting: passionate and touching patriotism combined with constant self-criticism and denigration; luxury and idleness (or admiration of them) combined with bursts of energy; extravagance and pride, with sobriety and humility. The same contrasts even appear in Brazilian history, periods of waste and corruption alternating with periods of reform and housecleaning.

Brazil is very big and very diverse. Brazilians vary widely from one region to another. A man may be a "Carioca" (from Rio—the name probably comes from an Indian expression meaning "white man's home"), a "Paulista" (from São Paulo), a "Mineiro" (from the State of Minas Gerais) or a "Bahiano" (from the State of Bahia), and he is proud of the peculiarities of his own region.

But not only does he vary geographically, he varies historically. Men from two, three or more eras of European history live simultaneously in Brazil today. The coastal cities, from Belém at the mouth of the Amazon River to Pôrto Alegre in the south, are filled with 20th-century men with 20th-century problems on their minds: getting on in the world and rising in it socially, how to pay for schools and doctors and clothes. Then in the surrounding countryside is a rural or semirural population who lead lives at least half a century behind the times, old-fashioned both agriculturally and socially. And for the people of the fishing villages, for those living on the banks of the great rivers, for cowboys and miners—all the backlands people—time seems to have stopped in the 17th century. Then, if one ventures even a little farther on, one enters the really timeless, prehistoric world of the Indians.

•

And yet there is one factor that unites Brazil more closely than some European countries which are only as big as a single Brazilian state: its language. Brazil is the largest Portuguese-speaking country in the world. Its Portuguese differs from that spoken in Portugal at least as much as American English differs from English English. But throughout Brazil the language is amazingly uniform, and Brazilians have no difficulty understanding each other.

It is a rather heavy and solemn tongue, with some of its grammatical forms actually dating back to the Latin of the Roman Republic. The tendency in Brazil is to be careless about grammatical niceties, at least in speaking, and to lighten the language with constant diminutives (as Maria da Conceição became Conceiçãozinha). In fact the Portuguese regard Brazilian Portuguese as "effeminate"—charming when women speak it, but no language for men.

Not only the constant use of diminutives but also the forms of address help create an atmosphere of familiarity, of affection and intimacy. Brazilian nomenclature is almost as complicated as Russian and is often compared to it, but in general women are addressed by "Dona" followed by the Christian name or pet name, and men by "Doutor" if they have a university degree or, if they have not, by a softened form of Senhor, "Seu," again followed by the Christian name.

Brazilians are very quick, both emotionally and physically. Like the heroes of Homer, men can show their emotions without disgrace. Their superb *futebal* (soccer football) players hug and kiss each other when they score goals, and weep dramatically when they fail to. Brazilians are also quick to show sympathy. One of the first and most useful words a foreigner picks up is *coitado* (poor thing!).

Part of the same emotionalism in social life is the custom of the *abraço*, or embrace. Brazilians shake hands a great deal, and men simultaneously embrace each other with their free arms. Women often embrace, too, and kiss rapidly on both cheeks: *left! right!* Under strong feeling the *abraço* becomes a real embrace.

A rich man will shake hands with and embrace a poor man and also give him money, try to find him a job, and pay his wife's doctor bills, because they grew up on the same *fazenda*, or country estate, made their first communions together, and perhaps are even "brothers of creation," a system of partial adoption that dates from slavery days. Servants are still often called *criados*, a term which originally meant they had been raised in the family. Even today one occasionally sees an elegant old lady out walking, leaning on the arm of a little dressed-up Negro girl, or taking tea or orangeade with her in a tearoom; the little girl is her "daughter of creation" whom she is bringing up.

In such relationships there is complete ease of manner on both sides. Sometimes Brazilians seem to confuse familiarity with democracy, although the attitude seems rather to be a holdover from slavery days, or feudalism, or even from the Roman Empire, when every rich man had his set of poor relations and parasites. Nevertheless, a sense of natural responsibility underlies the relationship and certainly contributes something toward the more difficult and somewhat broader conception of what democracy generally means today.

Home and family are very important in Brazil. But because there is no divorce, strange situations arise: second and third "marriages," unrecognized legally but socially accepted, in which there are oddly mixed sets of children. These situations merely give the Brazilians a chance to exercise their unique talent for kindly tolerance. In fact, in the spirit of mollification the courts more than two decades ago ruled that henceforth no one could be legally termed illegitimate.

There is a story about Rio de Janeiro and its beloved, decrepit *bondes* or open trolley cars. A *bonde* was careening along, overcrowded as usual, with men hanging to the sides like a swarm of bees. It barely stopped for a tall, gangling man to get off; and as he jumped from the step he fell, landing in a humiliating heap. His fellow passengers laughed. He pulled himself together, got up, and with great dignity shouted after them: "Everyone descends from the *bonde* in the way he wants to."

That is the perfect statement of the Brazilian belief in tolerance and forebearance: everyone should be allowed to descend from the *bonde* in his or her own way.

The greatest tolerance is naturally extended to love, because in Brazil that is always the most important emotion. Love is the constant element in almost every news story, street scene, or familiar conversation. If lunch is an hour or so late because the cook has been dawdling with the pretty delivery boy, her mistress will scold her, even lose her temper (for Brazilian tempers are quick, too), but there will be sympathy underneath and the cook's excuses will be frank, half humorous, possibly even indecent from the Anglo-Saxon point of view. "First things first" is the motto. Opposed to the constant preoccupation with love is the lack of sentimentality about marriage arrangements. There may be surface emotionalism, but there is Latin logic and matter-of-factness underneath.

A Brazilian woman shopping in New York was puzzled by the tag on a madras shirt she had bought for her husband: "Guaranteed to fade." In a country as rich as the United States, why would anyone want to wear faded clothes? Why do the Americans like to wear faded blue jeans? Surely that is false romanticism and just one more example of the childishness of the Anglo-Saxon as compared to the more adult Latin? Values are realistic in Brazil. Outside of fashionable circles, the poor are thin and the rich are fat, and fat is a sign of beauty, as it has been since the ancients.

Brazilians are in many ways quick, but they can also be woefully slow. The same mistress who scolds her cook for flirting will complain about the meals always being late. Yet if anyone asks naively, "But why not have lunch at one o'clock every day?" she will reply, "Oh, well—this isn't a factory."

Among the first settlers in Brazil were the big "captains," impoverished Portuguese noblemen and younger sons seeking quick fortunes, who were used to having feudal henchmen and slaves around them. They and the Portuguese of low rank who were also early on the scene soon established a tradition of having Indian and Negro slaves. One result is that to this day physical labor is looked down upon. Of all his inherited attitudes this one is the hardest for the Brazilian, free of so many other prejudices, to overcome. The upper-class Brazilian who visits the bustling North American continent cannot understand why there is so much eagerness for work. A rich boy mowing the lawn? More romanticism! A lifetime government job, white-collar work, or preferably no work at all, is the poor man's dream. A shabby, sickly bill collector, who can barely support his wife and six children, but who proudly carries a brief case and wears two fountain pens in his pocket, will tremble with rage if his position in society is misunderstood: "I?—Everyone knows I have never worked with my hands in my life!"

But along with admiration for a life of ease and luxury goes a strange indifference to physical comfort. Even in cold weather—and it can get quite cold south of São Paulo or in the higher regions of the interior—there is no heating of any kind. People simply put on more clothes. In the small towns in June or July, the coldest months, one often sees a pleasant, old-fashioned Brazilian scene: the large family, grandparents, parents, babies, visiting godparents, and a few odd cousins and fiancés, wearing sweaters or perhaps bathrobes over their clothes, all sitting around the dining-room table under a hanging lamp. Everyone is doing exactly what he wants: reading the paper, playing cards or chess, or relentlessly arguing over the other people's heads. Elsewhere, even the *granfinos*, the elegant, cosmopolitan-rich set of the upper-class, who have adopted the "English weekend" and spend it in Petrópolis or other resorts, present somewhat the same air of camping out in the winter. In freezing rooms, the ladies with mink coats over their slacks and rugs over their knees, the gentlemen wearing mufflers, they watch after-dinner movies, the latest chic diversion. Perhaps they will sip Scotch, again to be chic, but more likely *cafezinhos*, the boiling hot and very sweet little cups of coffee. The poor, meanwhile, drink the same *cafezinhos*, pile all their clothes on top of them and go to bed early.

Brazilians are a remarkably sober people. Two or three *cafezinhos* provide enough fuel for them to talk and argue on all night long. The late 19th-century sailor-author Captain Joshua Slocum (*Sailing Alone Around the World*) was, in his earlier days, in command of a ship on the South American coast. He speaks more than once of "my sober Brazilian sailors" who, unlike the sailors of other nationalities, always turned up again after a night in port—with no hang-overs.

Perhaps because Brazilians are usually as indifferent to cooking as they are to physical comfort, the staple diet is rice, dried meat, and black beans, cooked with a great deal of lard and garlic and served with a dish of manioc flour, to be sprinkled over the beans. However, there are many dishes of great refinement that use twenty or thirty ingredients, and wonderful desserts with even more wonderful names like Maiden's Drool, Bride's Pillow, and Blessed Mothers (small cakes).

The conversation in the caffeine-enlivened evenings will alternate between politics, real estate deals (a favorite pastime of all classes), and family reminiscences. Proud of their Latin logic, Brazilians are also a little proud of their reputation for "craziness." Family traits are cherished; such and such a family will be famous for its bad temper or for its obstinacy or for its green eyes—because looks, too, are very important. A good family nose will be traced down right to the last-born infant. This preoccupation with good looks may come from the knowledge that many of the oldest families have some Negro blood. Since everyone also wants to be as *claro*, or white, as possible, this is another of those contradictions that seem to bother no one.

Criticizing the country, running down the government and talking about the "national stupidity" with fearful and apocryphal examples are also favorite pastimes. It is sometimes hard to tell whether the speakers are really angry or merely excited, tolerant or unaware of any need for tolerance, naive or extremely sophisticated. Brazilians are mercurial: recently during Carnival a Negro dancing along the sidewalk with his wife suddenly ran into his two mistresses. There was a small riot and some hair-pulling, but an hour later all four were observed gaily dancing the samba together and holding hands. When the wife was asked why she put up with it, she answered helplessly but rather proudly, "He talked me into it. He's such a pretty talker!"

More taciturn peoples are likely to be suspicious of talkative ones and to think they are wasting their energy. One frequently meets among intellectuals a sort of Brazilian Hamlet-type, incapable of serious work or action, who seems to be covering up a deep anxiety with words, words, words, a pretended madness, a deliberately fanciful humor that is not frivolity although it resembles it. The earthy humor of the poor, the brutal cartoons in newspapers and magazines, the street boys who laugh at cripples or ugly women—this is directly in line with the humor of the Romans; but the humor of the intellectual is very different, wry, gentle, and a little wild.

They poke fun at their usually bloodless revolutions: "No one fought in that revolution—it was the rainy season." Like the Portuguese form of bullfighting in which there is no killing, Brazilian revolutions or *golpes* (coups) sometimes seem to be little more than political and rhetorical maneuvering. A man's speeches, his moral and physical courage, are admired, but actual violence is going too far. Duels are still fought in Argentina, but they are out of style in Brazil. Brazil has not fought a major war for almost a century. It has rarely wanted more land, already having more than it knows what to do with.

Jokes tell even more. There is an old favorite, perhaps not even Brazilian originally, about a man walking down the street with a friend. He is grossly insulted by a stranger, and says nothing. The friend tries to rouse his fighting instincts, "Didn't you hear what he called you? Are you going to take that? Are you a man, or aren't you?" The man replies, "Yes, I'm a man. But not *fanatically*." This is the true Brazilian temper.

Chapter 2

At least as early as the 9th century a land called "Brasil" was already a legend in Europe. It was wherever *bresilium* came from, a wood obtained in trade with the Far East, much in demand for dyeing cloth red. (Perhaps all the red woolens the peasants wear in the paintings of Brueghel were dyed with "brasil" wood?) The Medici Atlas of 1351 shows an island labelled "Brazil," and this imaginary island keeps re-appearing for several centuries, sometimes in one part of the world, sometimes in another, even after the present Brazil had been discovered. Columbus found the dyewood tree in the West Indies, but in his eagerness for gold he simply ignored it. But the first ships sent back from the continent of South America were loaded with brasil-wood, and "Brazil," or "Brasil," became the common name for the new country. (The spelling varies and sometimes the number; it was also called "The Brazils.")

In one of the parks of Rio de Janeiro stands a fine, flamboyant example of Latin-American park-sculpture, a much-bigger-than-life-size man dressed in a costume-pageant costume with wide sleeves, fringes, and skirts, and holding onto a ton or so of undulated bronze banner. One side of the huge pedestal says "1900" and the other "1500" and it was set up to commemorate the 400th anniversary of the discovery of Brazil by Pedro Alvares Cabral—according to some authorities. As the city has grown, this statue has been shunted from one place to another, and in somewhat the same way historians have shuffled the problem of whether Cabral really did discover Brazil or not. But most of them now agree that he did, in 1500, shortly after Easter. He was supposedly on his way to India in command of a fleet of thirteen tiny ships; if so, he was off his course by some [...] thousand miles to the west. Since the best astronomers, navigators, and mathematicians of the day were all employed at the court of King Manoel I of Portugal, it scarcely seems as though Cabral's extended side-trip could have been accidental. Probably the Portugese were really trying to get ahead of the Spaniards, who were very busy exploring the lands further north.

Two years after Columbus's first voyage, Portugal and Spain, then in the full flush of their age of discoveries, had grandly divided all the non-Christian world, known and as yet unknown, between them. The Treaty of Tordesillas, sanctioned by the pope, gave all lands east of a line drawn 370 miles west of the Cape Verde Islands to Portugal, and all lands west of it to Spain. The exact positon of this line was always vague, and the rivalry between the two countries was so strong that even after the treaty they tried to conceal their various voyages and discoveries from each other. (And thus made things harder for the historians.) But Portugal believed, or pretended to believe, that Brazil was within her rightful territories.

On Cabral's flagship there was a nobleman-merchant, Pero Vaz de Caminha, signed on as a scribe. The wonderfully vivid letter he wrote to King Manoel, describing Brazil and the Indians, or the little he saw of them, has been called "the first page of Brazilian history" and also, with equal justice, "the first page of Brazilian literature." After a brief account of the voyage west, Caminha calmly announces: "On this day at the vesper hours we caught sight of land, that is first of a large mountain, very high and round, and of other lower lands to the south of it, and flatland with great groves of trees. To this high mountain the captain gave the name of *Monte Passoal* ["pertaining to Easter"], and to the land, *Terra da Vera Cruz.*"

The mountain, in the present State of Bahia, still bears the same name. The King changed Vera Cruz to Santa Cruz, the official name until the middle of the century, when, over ecclesiastical protests, it became Brazil. But on the first maps it is either "Brazil" or the "Land of Parrots." Along with dye-wood, macaws were sent back to Europe, and their brilliant colors, large size, and loud shrieks obviously made a deep impression. (In 1531 a French ship took back three thousand leopard-skins, three hundred monkeys, and "six hundred parrots that already knew a few words of French.") On a *mapus mundi* published the year after Cabral's voyage the coastline of Brazil is not much more than a guess, but Caminha's "groves of trees" are there, lined up as formally as in a Portugese garden, and under them sits a group of giant macaws, to give explorers some idea of what to expect.

Even if not very original in the 16th century, the first name of *Vera Cruz* must have seemed appropriate. Cabral was a Knight of the Order of Christ and the fleet's sails and banners bore its red cross. The men landed to celebrate Easter Sunday with Mass, and set up a large cross. And for weeks they had all been watching the brilliant stars of the Southern Cross overhead; the fleet's astronomer also wrote to the King, just about this useful constellation. Ever since, Brazil has felt itself to be uniquely "The Land of the Southern Cross." It is on the flag; the nation's highest award is the Order of the Southern Cross; the present unit of money, the *cruzeiro*, is named for it,—and so are thousands of bars, restaurants, bus-lines, business firms, and manufactures. And with the frequent Brazilian abruptness of transition between the spiritual and the material, the 1,000 *cruzeiro* note, the highest denomination of money, shows a portrait of Cabral on one side and an engraving of that first Easter Mass on the other.

(In exactly the same way, the biggest church in Rio de Janeiro, Our Lady of Candelaria, where all official religious services took place until the change of capital in 1960, sits in a square completely surrounded by the country's richest banks, as if illustrating a thesis on the relations between Church, State, and High Finance. Or in the same way Brazilian conversation can veer from the eternal verities of Thomas Aquinas to the eternal real estate deals, and back again.)

Caminha was a good reporter; he describes the Indians' looks and behaviour, their food and houses, the brand-new wild life. He grows almost lyrical, as all the early voyagers did, over these first few idyllic honeymoon days,—in the amazing century when countries and continents intermarried and new countries were conceived. In his unscientific way, he was also the first of a long line of naturalists and ethnologists, some of the world's greatest, that has since been fascinated by South America and Brazil.

The Indians were friendly and docile, too docile for their own good, as was to be proved. Presents were exchanged, one of which was grimly prophetic: they gave the Portuguese head-dresses of their exquisite featherwork, and in return the Portuguese gave them one of the red woolen stocking caps worn by laborers. They attended the Easter Mass and mimicked the white men, kneeling, crossing themselves, and singing a hymn of their own. Afterwards, the Portuguese hung "tin crucifixes" that they had thriftily "saved from another voyage," around their necks.

The Portuguese were mercifully lacking in the bloodthirsty missionary zeal of the Spaniards. However, perhaps because he felt it was expected of him, or had some dim inklings of Manifest Destiny, Caminha wrote: "Our Lord gave them fine bodies and good faces, as to good men, and He who brought us here I believe did not do so without purpose." There is even a hint of envy, perhaps the earliest trace of the romantic, Noble-Savage, *Indianismo* that later colored the Brazilian imagination so strongly. The Indians were "clean and fat and beautiful," and they appeared to be healthier and stronger than the Portuguese themselves. As for the women: "she was so well-built and so rounded and her lack of shame was so charming, that many women of our land seeing her attractions, would be ashamed that theirs were not like hers." The Portuguese had always been romantically drawn to women of darker races; they had long taken Moorish wives and Negro concubines (there were already [. . .] Negro slaves in Portugal). In

Brazil it was only natural for them to become eager miscegenationists almost immediately.

Caminha concludes by saying that they had seen no gold, nor silver, nor any metal at all, but "the interior appears very large. Its waters are quite endless. So pleasing is it that if one cares to cultivate it, everything will grow." *Se plantando, dar.* This phrase is now a familiar saying, but it has changed its meaning, from a promise to a reproach to someone who is neglecting obvious opportunities. Surely that simple reversal of meaning reveals a great deal about the long history of the undeveloped resources and possibilities of Brazil since the year 1500.

Cabral left behind two convicts, who were last seen bewailing their fate while the Indians tried to console them. The condemned men were supposed to learn the Indians' language and to convert them to the True Faith. This was the usual Portuguese practice and no one knows how many hundreds of these wretched men were dropped along the coast. Most vanished forever, but here and there one survived and became a "great chief," took many Indian wives and produced many children. The *caboclo* (half-Indian, half-Portuguese) daughters would be ready to marry the next generation of Portuguese adventurers that arrived, and in this way a solid foundation was laid for a mixed, and easily mixable, race. Early Brazilian history has several half-legendary convict-heroes. In fact, its personalities are an oddly assorted crew: condemned convicts, devout Jesuit missionaries (Loyola was just starting his great work), and Portuguese noblemen, usually younger sons, who became the *capitães-mores,* the "great captains."

But no gold had been found; there were no cities to ransack such as the Spaniards had found on the western coasts of the continent, and for a quarter of a century more Brazil was left almost untouched.

Two things that everyone knows about Brazil are that it is the same size as the United States (now that Alaska is a state), and that the seasons there are the reverse of ours. It is big, stretching from north of the Equator to south of the Tropic of Capricorn, and west to the foothills of the Andes, an area of 3.3 million square miles. And while it is perfectly true that livestock (including dogs and cats) imported from northern countries have a hard time of it the first few years, and swelters through the Brazilian summers (January through March) in "winter" coats,—to say that the seasons are reversed is too strong. The Equator is not that much like the bottom frame of a mirror. Caminha thought the climate "equable," and although he really didn't know, he was more or less right.

Brazil is tropical and sub-tropical, with few extremes of temperature. The Amazon is roughly parallel to the Equator, yet, surpringly, the average temperature at Santarém, a third of the way up the river, is only seventy-eight degrees. In the cooler south, frosts occur only rarely as far north as São Paulo. If one can generalize at all about such a vast country, the average North American would be apt to say it is all just a little too hot. Never as hot as New York City in a prolonged heat wave, or as cold as a winter in Washington, D.C.—altogether a bit lacking in variety. On the other hand, the rainfall varies entirely too much,—over eighty inches a year in the Amazon basin, and in the northeast in some places it can scarcely be measured in inches at all. The State of Ceará is so dry and the sunshine so monotonous that when the sky is overcast the Cearenses greet each other hopefully with "What a beautiful day!"

The warm climate is still blamed by many historians, including Toynbee, and by the Brazilians themselves fairly continuously, for the country's lack of development and almost everything else wrong with it. It is held responsible for the "laziness" they regard as the greatest national defect (although on occasion it can be considered as a virtue, too). According to the usual theory, man needs alternating seasons and the stimulation of cold weather to keep him energetic and "progressing" properly. But this may not be true at all. "Laziness" may well be due more to bad health, poor food, and boredom, than to climate. Man is the most adaptable of animals. As we learn more about tropical diseases, nutrition, and psychology, and if the lot of the poor Brazilian is ever improved so that he is healthier and has more to work for in life, the old-fashioned, moralistic idea of "laziness" may disappear for good—and the Brazilians have one less item burdening their consciences.

Most of the [. . .] square miles are a vast, rolling plateau, with only one wave of mountain ranges that runs north and south, fairly close to the coast. The mountains are nowhere over 10,000 feet high, the highest near Rio de Janeiro. In the north they flatten out towards the Amazon, leaving more of the coastal plain for sugar-raising; in the south they flatten out into the Uruguay and Plata rivers, leaving plains for cattle-raising. But for most of the coast the line of mountains between the coastal plains and the higher, cooler interior has been the greatest of all hindrancess to the growth of Brazil. It forms a natural barrier that for four hundred years has kept all the cities and most of the population, as if encamped before a fortress, along the eastern edge of the country.

There is another big geographical handicap. There are great and navigable rivers, but they have never served to open up the country or help its economy to any great extent. Brazilians speak enviously of the Mississippi; if only they'd had a Mississippi things would be very different. It is probably true. Large freighters can go 2,300 miles up the Amazon, a river that makes the Mississippi look almost narrow, but that leads to no important cities or industrial centers. The second-largest river, the São Francisco, flows north, almost through the middle of the country. It, too, is navigable, but before it reaches the sea it is interrupted by the Falls of Paulo Affonso, and like the Amazon, it reaches no important cities, and serves for even less trade. Railroads have been built very slowly and for short stretches, serving one or two cities only. For centuries trade and communications were carried on entirely by coastal shipping, or mule trains over incredibly bad roads or trails. The air age is changing this state of affairs, and at the same time, or slightly later, trunk roads are at last beginning to connect the cities and towns from north to south, and from east to what few settlements there are in the west.

Brazil is still more than half-covered with forests. It contains, at a rough guess, more than fifty thousand vegetable species, and no one knows how many of these are potentially valuable to man. As well as all the fruits, native and early imported (like the banana), there are trees yielding: rubber, cacão, Brazil nuts, balsams, resins, fibres, cellulose, and tannin; and from the palm-trees alone, oils and waxes, as well as dates, coconuts, and palmito. There are many valuable and beautiful woods: teak, mahoganies, Jacarandas, satin-woods, and cedar—some woods so hard they can only be cut with special machinery.

As far as mineral resources go, the surface has barely been scratched. There is not much coal, and what there is is of poor quality—a fact that held back the railroads, and until recently, the growth of iron and steel industries. But—to quote from the staggering lists given in *The New World Guides*—there are: bauxite, bismuth, barium, asbestos, chromite, copper, gold, iron (15 million tons, approximately 25 per cent of the world supply), also "graphite, gypsum, kaolin, lead, limestone, manganese, marble, nickle, diamonds, zinc, radium, euxenite, mica, rock crystals, and tungsten."

There is a national oil industry, Petrobras, getting under way, and the source of great dissension. But expert geologists, Brazilian and foreign, believe that there are probably no very large deposits of petroleum in Brazil.

But all this Ali Baba's treasure was hidden from the 16th-century explorers, in the future as well as underground. They kept on risking ships and lives for what Lévi-Strauss calls "derisory" articles: pepper and other spices; & from Brazil only wood and curiosities: dye-wood, animals, birds, skins, and a few Indians, too.

•

Chapter II

kaolin, lead, limestone, manganese, marble, nickle, diamonds [and
many other semi-precious stones] zinc, radium, euxenite, mica, rock
crystals, and tungsten."

There is a national oil industry, Petrobras, getting under way,
and the source of great dissension. But expert geologists, Brazilian
and foreign, believe that there are probably no very large deposit/s
of petroleum in Brazil

But all this Ali Baba's treasure was hidden from the 16th
century explorers, in the future as well as underground. They kept on
risking ships and lives for what Levi-Strauss calls "derisory" articles:
pepper and other spices; from Brazil only wood and curiosities:
dyewood, animals, birds, skins, and a few Indians, too.

I give up here —

have to add more geography

later, probably —

Then things began to change. The trip around the Cape of Good Hope was no longer profitable; Portugal discovered that "for every grain of pepper she gave a drop of blood," and there were rumors of gold in Brazil. Around 1530, Portuguese fleets began coming regularly to patrol the coast, and to fight off the French and the Dutch, who also had designs on Brazil. A royal agent arrived and serious colonization began. The first town to be laid out was São Vicente, now an apartment-house-lined suburb of the port of Santos; the second Olinda, far to the north, now a suburb of Recife. (*O! Linda!*, that is "beautiful," because of its white, palm-studded beaches.) The captaincies were granted, each about 150 miles along the coast and stretching inland indefintely until they met the equally indefinite lands of Spain. (Surely the biggest examples of "strip farming" on record.) São Salvador da Bahia de Todos os Santos, otherwise Bahia, became the capital, and it was in the region around Bahia that sugar was introduced and the plantation system first grew up. Negro slaves started arriving from Africa as early as 1535. As Lévi-Strauss says: "the world, gorged with gold, began to hunger after sugar; and sugar took a lot of slaves." The Indians were too primitive; they knew only what now would be called an absolutely "permissive" life, in the shade of the forests; set to work, and in the sun, they simply died off.

In this first century, the French settled in and around what is now Rio, and were twice driven off. The second time the beginnings of the present city were laid out and given the name São Sebastião do Rio de Janeiro, in honor of the saint on whose day the victory was won, in the month of January—although the "river" was non-existent. These first Brazilian coastal towns often have the simplified names that sailors would have given them: River, Bay (Bahia), Reef (Recife, whose inhabitants still call it "The" Reef), Fortress (Fortaleza), etc.

The next 250 years repeat the usual history of colonial rule, or mis-rule, in the 17th and 18th centuries. It resembles the history of the American colonies under the English, translated to a tropical setting, and a Catholic, slave-holding society, thinly scattered along a much longer strip of coast. While deriving great wealth from Brazil, the Portuguese crown monopolized Brazilian trade completely, and did its best to prevent the development of any independent industries. There were unjust taxes and restrictions: the inevitable salt-tax, and high duties on all imported goods, and yet everything *had* to be imported from the mother-country since no manufactures were allowed except the simplest home industries. A particular grievance was textiles: except for the roughest stuffs, worn by the slaves, no cloth could be woven. No printing presses were allowed, so there were no journals or newspapers, and very few books. Gold was discovered, at last, but goldsmiths were forbidden to work it. Over and over we read of the smiths' forges being destroyed, but the treasure still in the sacristies of the old Brazilian churches proves that this restriction must often have been evaded.

The Jesuits, who came in great numbers during the first hundred years, tried to protect the Indians from slavery in the captaincies, They gathered them into large societies, called "reductions," each around a church, converted them, and taught them,—in other words, "civilised" them. Undoubtedly they did save thousands from slavery or slaughter, but the Indians died off, anyway, from small-pox, measles, and inanition, and their culture, primitive but unique, and their skills and arts died with them, or blended gradually into that of Portugese and African newcomers.

The first event that could be considered "national," implying a sense of identity and a small amount of cooperation between the northern settlements, at least, was the final driving out of the Dutch. For twenty years they had controlled the northern coast, and at the same time they had conquered the Portugese African colony of Angola, since they, too, needed Negro slaves and in the 17th and 18th centuries eastern Africa and sugar-raising northern Brazil were complementary. The Dutch had taken over the port of Recife as their capital, re-named it Mauritzstad, for the governor, Count Mauritz of Nassau-Siegen, and built it up "in the fashion of Holland," according to a city-plan, from 150 houses to about 2,000. Dutch forts can still be seen on the lower Amazon, and high, stepped, Dutch roofs in Recife. But they were finally driven out for good in 1654, a triumph for the Catholic Church and for Brazil. (Some of these Mauritzstad-ers eventually settled in New Amsterdam, i.e., New York City.)

After almost a century of rumors and occasional lucky finds, gold and silver and precious stones were at last discovered in quantity in what is now the State of Minas Gerais (General Mines). It was there that the first real expansion and development of the interior of Brazil took place, and almost entirely owing to the efforts of the famous *bandeirantes*. They came from around São Paulo, descendants of the Portuguese and the Indian girls, and they were energetic, cruel, and rapacious. They travelled in armed bands, "*bandeiras*," along with their wives, children, cattle, and Indian slaves. They made long treks and savage raids, for gold and for more slaves, for trading—even attacking and destroying the Jesuit "reductions," and carrying off their own blood-brothers into slavery. They penetrated far into the present States of Minas Gerais, Goiás, and Mato Grosso (the still almost "far-west" city of Cuiabá was originally one of their trading posts), and the discovery of the more glamorous parts of Brazil's mineral wealth was almost entirely due to them.

A small but brilliant constellation of mining towns grew up after the *bandeirantes.* "Mining town" suggests something quite different, however, from these miniature cities,—wealthy, isolated, small out-posts of 18th-century culture, and filled with late, beautiful examples of baroque architecture. Vila Rica (now Ouro Prêto, or "black gold," named for a dark, reddish gold) was the capital, and there were many more: Mariana, São João del Rey, Morro Velho, Queluz, to name a few. Diamantina, now almost unknown outside Brazil, was famous all over Europe as the diamond center of the world, until the discovery of the Kimberley lodes in Africa in 1870. During the century of the mining boom, a million slaves are supposed to have gone into this region alone, and the wealth rivalled that of the bigger, older, sugar capital of Bahia in the north.

But it was in this group of small, flourishing city-towns that the most important event of the 18th century took place, an event that should be of particular interest to Americans. It was an abortive and tragic attempt at independence from Portugal, called by the odd name of the "Inconfidencia Mineira," meaning, more or less, the Minas Conspiracy. The standards of culture and education in these towns were probably higher than in any other part of Brazil at the time, and besides miners—rather mine-owners—there were lawyers and army officers and teachers. A group of six of these young men were all poets and thought of themselves as a "school," not only that, but in those barren highlands, glittering with ores, they thought of themselves as Arcadians, took pastoral pen-names, and actually wrote pastoral poems—and epics and satires as well. It seems as though artificiality could not go much further—however, there were real talents among them, and they also were interested in politics, and particularly the recent successful American War of Independence. They were joined by other intellectuals and army officers, and their leader was a young lieutenant, Joaquim José da Silva Xavier. He occasionally practised dentistry and so was known as "Toothpuller," Tiradentes. He carried the American Declaration of Independence about with him in his pocket and liked to read it out loud. The group corresponded with Thomas Jefferson and finally one of them was sent to meet him in France, where he was minister plenipotentiary. Jefferson, on a trip for his health, met him cautiously in the Roman ampitheatre at Nîmes. Samuel Putnam, in his book about Brazilian literature, MARVELOUS JOURNEY, says: "this event, although most North Americans have never heard of it, has since become for Brazilians one of the strongest bonds between their democracy and our own."

Asked his advice about how to foment a revolution and found a republic, Jefferson, apparently, as a diplomat, could promise nothing more than his moral support. The envoy who met him died on the way back to Brazil, but the conspiracy in Minas went ahead and grew over-bold. It was found out, and all the *"Inconfidentes"* were drastically punished. One committed suicide, most were sent into exile in Angola, and Tiradentes himself was brutally executed, being hung, drawn and quartered. His house was destroyed and the ground where it stood was sprinkled with salt, in the good old medieval way.

The little "School of Minas," if it can really be called a school, was wiped out, and not only was the first Brazilian movement for independence destroyed but also the first real attempt at a literary movement in the country. The brave but impractical "Arcadian" poets of '89 could not arouse their country or do battle like our hard-headed small farmers of '76. But Tiradentes has remained the greatest national hero of Brazil; "Toothpuller Day" is a holiday; almost every town in Brazil has its Tiradentes square or street; and rebellion against Portugal had begun, although independence was not to come for thirty-three more years and then not in the form of a revolution at all.

Chapter 3

The history of South America in the 19th century resembles Shakespeare's battle scenes: shouts and trumpets; small armies on-stage, small armies off-stage; Bolívar here, Bolívar there; bloodshed, death-scenes, and long pauses in the action for fine speeches. But Brazil differed from the rest of the continent in two ways. First, while all the other countries rebelled against Spanish rule and finally broke up, into nine republics, Brazil managed to remain politically united. It had its minor civil wars, and secessions, some lasting several years, but it always pulled itself together again. And second, it had no real revolution or war of independence. It was ruled by the House of Braganza right down until 1889, and it still has a Braganza Pretender to the throne,—rather, with typical tropical proliferation of species, it has two Pretenders, first cousins.

The long period of relative stability enjoyed by Brazil in the 19th century gave it great advantages: a strong feeling of national unity and almost a century of history in which it still takes pride. But the pride is tinged with *saudades*, nostalgia, sometimes even despair. Brazilians feel that the national honor, international reputation, foreign credit—even the size and prestige of their Navy—have never again stood so high.

Modern Brazilian history begins with Napoleon. Everyone knows that he created an Empire and crowned himself Emperor. But it is not so well known that as a sort of by-product of the Napoleonic Empire the Empire of Brazil was also created, and lasted much longer than Napoleon's— sixty-seven years, to be exact. Not to be compared to the Roman Empire, to be sure, but remarkably long to have held out in the 19th century with revolutions crashing like thunderstorms in all the neighboring countries, and the forces of liberalism, equalitarianism, and republicanism growing stronger and more articulate all the time.

Many of the new countries of the West felt that the old monarchical system might still be the best way of stabilizing their governments. Argentina shopped around unsuccesfully for years for a suitable European prince, and the experiment was tried in Mexico and failed dismally, with

Maximilian. Even the United States had its small movement to make Washington the founder of a dynasty. But in the paradoxical way things often seem to happen in Brazil, what brought the country eventual political independence from Portugal was the arrival of the Portuguese royal family.

In 1807 Napoleon was trying to force Portugal to join his blockade against England and the Napoleonic armies were closing in on Lisbon. Maria I, the Queen, had long been insane, and her son, Dom João, was Regent. Portugal had been almost a protectorate of England for a hundred years. Caught, as the historian C. H. Haring puts it, "between the military imperialism of Napoleon and the economic imperialism of Great Britain," Dom João, never decisive at best, shilly-shallied. At the last possible moment he settled for Great Britain, and Britain decided for safety's sake to move the whole royal family and court to Brazil.

It was one of the strangest hegiras in history. In a state of near panic, the mad Queen, Dom João, his estranged wife (who was a little mad, too), their children, and the entire Portuguese court,—some fifteen thousand people—were squeezed aboard forty-two or -three merchant vessels. Under British escort they took off for Brazil, the unknown, romantic colony where all their wealth—and all their sugar—came from. The voyage was a nightmare of storms, sea-sickness, short rations, and stinking water. The courtiers behaved so badly that a royal command was issued that "only nautical subjects" were to be discussed. Meanwhile, Pedro, the nine-year-old heir-apparent, discoursed learnedly with his tutors on the *Aeneid* (according to the tutors' reports) and compared his father's plight to that of Aeneas. However, as Octavio Tarquinio de Souza, the best Brazilian historian of the Empire period, says: "Dom João saved the dynasty, and took with him intact the greatest treasures of the kingdom, including art, jewels, and books [sixty thousand of them, the nucleus of the present National Library] to the lands where he would found a great empire."

After fifty-two hideous days they reached Bahia, but it was not considered safe enough for them, so they went on to Rio. They were received with mad rejoicing. Only poor distracted Queen Maria, seeing Negros prancing around her sedan-chair, thought that she was in Hell and screamed that the devils were after her. Almost immediately Dom João issued his first Royal Letter, declaring the ports of Brazil open to "all friendly nations" (meaning England, mostly); he also won more popularity by allowing printing-presses, newspapers, goldsmiths, and many small industries to be set up. Brazil felt itself changed from a much-abused colony to an independent power, almost over-night.

Rio was a hot, squalid, waterfront city of about twenty thousand inhabitants, without sewage or water-supply. The royal family, oddly enough, settled down and began to like their new home and its easy-going ways. But the court in general hated everything and were hated in return by the Brazilians—a reaction that was to have serious political consequences. There were no carriages; the food was bad; they were afraid of the thunderstorms that bounced from peak to peak around the bay (the way they still do), afraid of the Negro slaves, afraid of the tropical diseases,—and it is true that they died off like flies during the first few years.

But the thirteen-year stay of the court changed Rio into a capital city and changed the state of affairs in much of Brazil. The administration of justice was somewhat improved; taxes lowered; the first bank founded; the naval academy and schools of medicine and surgery were established, as well as a library and the Botanical Gardens (still famous). The Regent was fond of music and the theatre. He brought an orchestra with him; he also became an addict of Negro music and entertainments. In 1815 Portugal was rid of the French, and in 1816 he invited a French Commission, architects, musicians, painters, and sculptors, to visit Brazil. He started a royal palace on the outskirts of the city. The mad Queen died, and the Regent became Dom João VI of Portugal and I of Brazil.

But by 1820 the liberal forces in Portugal made it necessary for Dom João to return, if he wanted to save his throne. Again he shilly-shallied, apparently partly because he could not face that ocean voyage a second time. But again under British auspices and promptings, he finally announced one constitution for Portugal, another one for Brazil, and sailed away. Before he left he wrote a letter to Dom Pedro, weeping as he wrote, in which he prophesied the secession of Brazil from Portugal and advised his son to take the crown for himself. He also cleaned out the treasury and took with him all the jewels he could collect,—and about three thousand Portuguese. This departure established a sort of precedent, unfortunately, for later abdications or "renunciations" (under the Republic), which are always discussed in terms of João I's sad career. Not all of them have filled their pockets as liberally as he did, and they have left for very different reasons, but the peculiarly Brazilian institution of leaving-the-country-in-order-to-govern-it-better had been established.

Dom Pedro had been badly brought up; he had led the luxurious but slovenly life of the small upper-class of Brazilians of his day; he had been friends with slaves and stable boys, and a notorious womanizer from the age of thirteen or so. He is, nevertheless, a fascinating character: brilliant, in spite of his faulty education, energetic, spoiled, dissipated, neurotic—and suffering from occasional epileptic fits. [Maria Graham, the Scottish woman who stayed in Rio in the 1820s and was even tutor to Dom Pedro's children for a brief period, has left a good account of his personality and the life of the court and city.] He was fundamentally kind-hearted (he was devoted to all his children and provided for them well, legitimate and illegitmate alike) and he wanted to be a good ruler, but the "court" still meant the hated Portuguese to many of the Brazilians. Dom Pedro still favored them, and things started to go badly for him almost immediately. Brazil wanted a king, but not too much of a king; and Dom Pedro was autocratic.

Orders started coming from Portugal; some of the hated taxes and restrictions were restored. While he was away in São Paulo an order came for him to return to Portugal immediately, to finish his education. It was handed to him as he sat on his horse on the banks of a little stream, the Ipiranga. Dom Pedro read it, waved his sabre in the air, and shouted "Independence or death!" This is the famous *grito*, or cry, of Ipiranga, and the day on which Dom Pedro gave it, September 7th, is the Brazilian 4th of July. The first lines of the Brazilian national anthem—even more complicated and difficult than "The Star-Spangled Banner"—describe this scene. The simple word *grito* is a by-word and has as many overtones for a Brazilian as, say, "cherry-tree" has for an American.

Dom Pedro was proclaimed Emperor of an independent Brazil, but his reign lasted only nine years. He considered himself a liberal, and a very advanced one, and the constitution that he granted in 1824 lasted until the end of the Empire in Brazil. But there were constant revolts, foreign soldiers made trouble, regional differences and needs were not attended to, and his private life became too scandalous for even the tolerant Brazilians. His notorious mistress, Domitila, whom he created the Marqueza de Santos, meddled in state affairs, and he was blamed for the death of his first wife, Leopoldina, whom the people loved. After the death of his father he became heir to the throne of Portugal, but his younger brother was already there and trying to take power. Rebellion broke out all over Brazil; his personal army deserted him, and then he, too, left the country, to begin, in Europe, the "War of the Brothers." Daumier left cartoons of them, two mean figures having a tug-of-war over a crown. This was the way things looked to Europeans, but Dom Pedro I had really been a much higher-minded ruler than that, greatly superior to his father, and honestly well-intentioned. Brazil has always proved hard to rule. And the ruler he now left behind was only five years old.

Except that he was equally energetic, Dom Pedro II was almost exactly the opposite of his mercurial, dissipated father. He had been carefully, even over-carefully, educated by a beloved governess and series of tutors and priests. He was serious, hard-working, cultivated, an amazing linguist; he wrote quite presentable poetry on all the important occasions of his life; and for forty-nine years he did his very best to govern his country. The nine years of his Regency were filled with bitter quarrels, and finally the two parties, Liberals and Conservatives, agreed that only the figure of the young Emperor could unify the troubled country. This was explained to Dom Pedro, aged fourteen, who replied in another famous historical phrase: *Quero agora.* "I want it now." He was crowned when he was fifteen, wearing the ugly, diamond-studded crown now in the Petrópolis Museum, and over his green velvet robes a yellow cape made from the breasts of toucans, a symbol of the Indian heritage of his country.

Dom Pedro was not a genius; but he was a very different type to appear in the Braganza line, and in most things, much in advance of his countrymen. He was an imposing Emperor: six feet four inches tall, plus his habitual top-hat; with blue eyes inherited from his German mother and a large bushy beard that early turned snow-white. He himself felt that he was better fitted for an intellectual life than a political one, but he did his duty. He ruled under the constitution his father had granted the country in 1824: the government was monarchial, constitutional, and representative; the laws were made by two houses, Senate and House of Deputies; Catholicism was the state religion but religious freedom was guaranteed, as well as freedom of speech and of the press.

He selected his own council of state and his cabinet; his chief strength was his "moderating power," under which he could dismiss almost anyone he wanted to, prorogue Parliament, and dissolve the Deputies if he thought the state of the country warranted it. These privileges, or some of them, had been added by the *Ato Adicional* of 1834, for the constitution had started out being over-optimistic about the political maturity of the country. According to his more liberal-minded ministers, he was apt to over-use his "moderating" power and change the government too often. According to Dom Pedro himself, he was the most republican man in Brazil and would have preferred to be president rather than Emperor (second to being an intellectual, of course). As he grew older he grew more patient, but also more liberal. He never took political revenge; he did appoint men for their good qualities, no matter what their loyalties were, and Brazil has never had men of such high calibre in public office since. However, he seriously underestimated—and given his background, how could he help it?—the growing commercial and business interests of his country (and of the 19th-century world), and he always favored the old land-owning aristocracy. Towards the end of his reign many liberals, who admired him personally, for political reasons came out against him as a "tyrant" and a representative of a decayed monarchy.

When he had ruled for more than thirty years he at last permitted himself to go abroad, to Europe, then to the United States, and then longer trips to Europe, Egypt, and the Holy Land. He always travelled incognito, as "Dom Pedro de Alcantara," and his democratic ways, gift for languages, good-humor, and boundless energy made him "the most popular crowned head in Europe." He sought out literary leaders wherever he went, and talked to them in their own languages. Victor Hugo called him "a grandson of Marcus Aurelius." He was fascinated by comparative religions (and thus shocked his more devout subjects) and always made a point of visiting synagogues and reading aloud in Hebrew.

In 1876 he paid a long visit to the United States, something he had long wanted to do, and the occasion of the Philadelphia Exhibition, celebrating one hundred years of American Independence, seemed like a good time. His one regret was never to have met Lincoln, whom he deeply admired (as do Brazilians to this day; "Lincoln" is a favorite name for boys), and he tried to meet Harriet Beecher Stowe. He had corresponded with the Boston Transcendentalists and the Abolitionists (his correspondence is staggering), and translated some of their writings. One was a poem by Whittier called "The Cry of a Lost Soul"—not an anti-slavery poem, as might be expected, but a poem about an Amazonian bird, and Dom Pedro sent the poet a case of these birds, stuffed (at least not alive, like the macaws of earlier centuries). But it has Abolitionist overtones, perhaps, and Dom Pedro may have felt it expressed his own hopes for freeing the slaves. The bird

"Lifts to the starry calm of heaven his eyes;
And lo! rebuking all earth's ominous cries,
The Cross [Southern Cross, naturally] of pardon lights the tropic skies!"

Longfellow gave a historical dinner-party for the royal visitor, and Dom Pedro attempted to give a Brazilian *abraço* ("hug") to the shy, Quaker Whittier, and at the end of the highly successful evening, succeeded. Longfellow called him a "modern Haroun-al-Raschid wandering about to see the great world as a simple traveller, not as a king. He is a hearty, genial, noble person, very liberal in his views." He visited Yale, Harvard, and Vassar, among other educational institutions, and seems to have met almost everyone of importance in the country. One exhausted Brazilian protégé called him "a library on top of a locomotive."

At the Philadelphia Exhibition he met Alexander Graham Bell and was one of the very first to order telephones; he had them installed in all his palaces in Brazil. He also took back several of the newly-invented sewing-machines to the ladies of his court. It was a triumphal tour of over ten thousand miles.

There is a photograph of the royal party taken on their visit to Niagara Falls. There is something sad, almost tragic about this little foreign-looking group, dominated by the towering old Emperor, all dressed in the ugly, conventional clothes of the period, paying the conventional visit to the conventional "sights" and having their picture taken—something ~~sugges-tive~~ of the state of Brazil at the time, and its faults and virtues. The ill-digested but eagerly grasped-at foreign influences, the attempt to adapt the inappropriate (even to clothing), and the neglect or ignorance of re-sources at home. Dom Pedro was the "owner," so to speak, of waterfalls three or four times greater and more magnificent than Niagara, but inac-cessible, and with all his curiosity and travelling, he never laid eyes on them. (To this day, upper-class Brazilians are amazingly unfamiliar with their own country, even its geography.)

During Dom Pedro's long reign Brazil's material expansion really began. In 1850 a Commercial Code was issued that has remained in force, with additions, to this day. More banks were established and foreign capital, still mostly British, began to come in. The first railroad started off towards Petrópolis, the Emperor's favorite place of residence, in 1854—only fif-teen kilometres of it to begin with; and gas-lights were put in the streets of Rio. Other short railroads were built, but transportation was, and contin-ues to be, one of the biggest problems of Brazil. Progress was slow partly because of Dom Pedro's life-long preference for the landed aristocracy, who were usually conservative and indifferent to "progress" and looked down on the new class of merchants and bankers. The towns were still mostly inhabited by artisans and Portuguese merchants, and the aristoc-racy lived on their estates and much preferred to go to Paris, when they could. Dom Pedro created many titles, mostly Barons, but with one big exception, they were all landed proprietors who had grown rich on sugar or coffee—for by now coffee was the leading crop and Brazil was provid-ing the world with it. The exception was the Baron de Mauá, later Vis-conde de Mauá, the J. P. Morgan of Brazil. Some of his many activities are reflected in his extraordinary coat of arms that shows a steamship, a loco-motive and four lampposts (like the ones he had installed in Rio).

Visconde de Mauá was an associate of the Rothschilds and part-owner of banks in London, New York, Uruguay, and Argentina. He was the figure that marks the change from the purely agricultural economy of the plan-tation world to the world of modern, expanding capitalism.

However, when ennobled, he, too, took an Indian name, as did almost all the others; it was the period of *Indianismo*; it was also considered stylish to have an Indian (a chief, preferably) among one's ancestors. The Counts of Itaboraí, Tamandaré, Barons Maracajú, Paranaguá—it is as if the United States had had Count Massachusetts or Baron Ohio.

There had been two foreign wars, the first undertaken to get rid of the brutal Rosas regime in Argentina, in 1851–52. The second was Brazil's one real war—against Paraguay,—and it lasted five years, from 1865 to 1870, and is still regarded by Brazilians with aversion, almost shame. Its beginnings were complicated, having to do with Brazilian citizens in Paraguay, and it was urged on the nation by the always more war-like south. Argentina, Uruguay, and Brazil were allies; Paraguay was completely ruined by the war, with one man left to every fifteen women in the population, and the war-debt incurred by Brazil hung over Dom Pedro for the rest of his rule. The war also ruined Visconde de Mauá, and one of the harshest criticisms heard of Dom Pedro is that he could have saved Mauá with a government loan, but didn't.

The biggest problem of Dom Pedro's reign, and probably of his life, as well, was slavery. So closely was it bound up with the Empire and the Emperor that the end of the Empire and the death of Dom Pedro both followed soon after the emancipation. He was against slavery; he felt it to be a shameful blot on his beautiful, beloved country (he had liberated all his inherited slaves as early as 1840). But he also thought that emancipation had to come gradually, in order not to upset the country's economy, dependent almost entirely, in the early years of his reign, on slave-labor. As a result of a bargain of Dom Pedro I with the English, the slave trade was prohibited in 1831, but thousands of slaves continued to be smuggled into the country every year, and this was a constant source of trouble with the English, who searched Brazilian vessels at sea and on occasion even blockaded Brazilian ports or landed marines on Brazilian soil.

Steps towards complete emancipation were taken, usually agitated for by the Liberals and then actually taken when a Conservative government again came into power. The law of the *Ventre Livre* provided that all children of slaves born after 1871 were free, and all slaves still belonging to the crown or to the states were free. The next step, in 1887, was that all slaves were free upon reaching the age of sixty. São Paulo freed all slaves within the city, various states began freeing theirs, and the army began to refuse to pursue run-away slaves. The institution of slavery was obviously doomed, but the landed proprietors in general did nothing to provide for their futures without slave-labor. There had been sporadic attempts to encourage immigration. Germans and Swiss had settled north of Rio, and later many Italians came to work on the huge São Paulo coffee *fazendas*. But, as Haring says, it was hard to get workers to come to a country "where agricultural labor was equated with human slavery."

In 1887 Dom Pedro again went to Europe, leaving Princess Isabel as Regent. He was sick, diabetic, and looked far older than his age. Isabel had always been an Abolitionist, and now, partly by her own wish and partly under pressure from the more liberal Abolitionists, she signed the emancipation proclamation, May 13th, 1888—another national holiday. Actually, out of about 4 million Negroes, only 700,000 still remained to be freed. There was a week of wild celebration. The Emperor lay very sick in Milan. When the news was brought to him he said it was the greatest happiness of his life, and wept, murmuring, "What great people! What great people!"

However, the rich planters had been ruined overnight, and 300 million dollars' worth of property was wiped out. Naturally, many of the land-owners immediately turned against the monarchy and joined the growing republican movement. It was led by Benjamin Constant (de Botelho de Magalhães), who was inspired by the dry doctrines of Auguste Comte, for the Positivist movement had taken a strong hold on intellectual Brazilians. (One Positivist church still survives in Rio; and one of their slogans, "Order and Progress," is on the green-and-gold flag, along with the stars of the Southern Cross.)

The end came very suddenly and was a complete surprise to most of the nation. Benjamin Constant engineered a small army revolt and involved two generals (one of whom had been for the Emperor), and on November 15th, 1889, the Republic was proclaimed. The Emperor left, on a dark and rainy night, with all his family, a few friends, and his doctor. He was offered a large pension, but impeccable and dignifed to the end, he refused it. His Empress died, probably of a broken heart, soon after, and he himself lived on, mostly in France, for two years philosophically studying, as always: Tupi, Hebrew, Arabic, and Sanskrit. He was never heard to say a bitter word against his political enemies.

In many ways Dom Pedro failed to accomplish much. The country was still almost empty, almost illiterate, and divided between the very rich and the miserably poor. In spite of his respect for education there were still no universities and the enrollments in schools of higher education were very small and the teaching inferior. His personal example of dignity, probity, and self-sacrifice could influence very few—given the conditions of the country, how could it?—but the calibre of the statesmen in the first years of the Republic was still much higher than it was to be ever since. However, Brazil had changed from an 18th-century, monarchial, slave-holding, primitive agricultural country to a republic, growing prosperous from its coffee trade, with equal rights, aware of the outside world (which was also more aware of it). Dom Pedro had achieved a very small part of his dreams for Brazil—but if there had been more monarchs like him, history would certainly make more edifying reading.

Chapter 4
The Three Capitals

Bahia, or Salvador, was the first capital of Brazil, appropriately enough since it was in the State of Bahia that the country had its beginnings. Cabral first landed on the coast there, and Caminha's first letter describes it. The year after Cabral's voyage another was made, with Amerigo Vespucci as navigator. This time the "bay," Bahia, was discovered, and the name *São Salvador da Bahia de Todos os Santos* (Saint Saviour of the Bay of All Saints) given to it. In the following year, Vespucci led the first expedition into the interior of the country, starting from Bahia. In 1534 the first captaincy was established, a small group of thatched huts inside a stockade. This was very soon attacked and destroyed by Indians, who also ate some of the unhappy adventurers.

The first Governor-General of Brazil, Tomé de Souza, arrived in 1549, with four hundred soldiers and six hundred convicts, and orders from the King to establish a "large and strong settlement," to serve as capital of the new country. He brought with him a map of the new city, complete with walls and bastions, churches and public buildings. According to the Portuguese tradition, it was to be built on the heights overlooking the sea, more like a fort than a town, for the sake of defense. According to the stories, the Governer-General helped in the construction with his own hands. Besides the 1,000 men, the first inhabitants were principally "pacified" Indians, and the huge family and following of the most famous of the legendary convict-chiefs, "Caramuru," who had been in Brazil since 1510, and who had married an Indian princess, the beautious "Paraguaçu."

The town grew so quickly that it overflowed the walls and descended to the beaches, dividing into the "higher" and "lower" towns, as it still is today. Cable-cars and elevators now connect the two towns; the chief elevator, that has become almost a symbol of Bahia, is the Lacerda, 234 feet high,—first built in 1875.

Bahianas are extremely proud of their city; they call it "the good place." The Cariocas, referring to the large numbers of Bahianas who come south to Rio every year, add to this ironically, "Yes . . . Bahia's the good place—it there, and me here!"

For travellers approaching by sea, it is usually their first Brazilian city, and the huge port, with its picturesque water-front life, heat, pungent smells, and large Negro population, makes a first and permanent impression as being "typically Brazilian." With its ancient forts on the ocean, its magnificent baroque architecture (supposedly three hundred churches), crowds of all colors, frequent religious processions, surviving folk-costumes, street vendors, open-air markets and restaurants, displays of folk-art—it is more what one expects Brazil to be like than any other city. Protected by the viceroys, and fabulously rich during the period of the sugar boom, it was also the biggest port of entrance for the Negro slaves, from Guinea, Mozambique, and Angola. Although from many African nations, at all levels of culture, many of these Negroes were Mohammedans, and well-educated; some are even supposed to have taught their owners how to read and write. They were skilled in iron-working, cattle-raising,—and cooking. They brought with them many arts, handcrafts, music; the cultivation of the banana and the palm.

The fact that the capital was transferred to Rio de Janeiro in 1763 is one of the reasons why Bahia has preserved its colonial character more than other old Brazilian cities. When it ceased to be the capital, although always remaining important until São Paulo took over, as the coffee capital, its building on a large scale more or less stopped. So that by the time "progress" or the modern building movement hit Bahia, its old buildings were regarded as sacred; they were protected by centuries of traditions, and spared destruction. In Rio or São Paulo, with their uninterrupted growth, there wasn't time for the colonial buildings to grow to honored old age. Every decade saw new construction, buildings torn down, and streets and avenues put through,—the ugly price of progress. Today, although Bahia continues to grow and build and modernise, the old city remains almost unchanged and dominates the newer sections.

Instead of being a relic, carefully preserved (or peacefully preserved as much as possible) by the Patrimônio Histórico e Artistico, like Ouro Prêto, Bahia is still a living city. Its folk-art and folk-traditions are not just survivals but are still being kept up and constantly adapted to the present.

There are six major churches and six convents, all architectural monuments . . .

Bahia's cooking is particularly famous, using *dende* palm oil, ginger, little dried shrimps, coconut milk, and dozens of exotic ingredients. The costume of the Bahianas, the mulatto women, is reminscent of that of Martinique, of French Empire styles. It consists of a full, printed skirt, a loose white chemise (usually homespun cotton), trimmed with handmade lace, a turban, earrings, necklaces, and the *balangandã*, a collection of large-size magic charms, fruits, crosses, etc., worn, tinkling and clanging, at the waist. In the old days the *balangandãs* were sometimes made of gold, and the wealth of the slave's owner was shown by the jewelry she wore. Bahianas, with their portable food-stands and little charcoal braziers, are familiar figures in São Paulo and Rio as well as in Bahia. They sell sweet, heavy cakes of manioc or tapioca, mysterious sweets wrapped in corn husks, broiled corn on the cob, and other specialties of the north. Their costume is considered as "typically Brazilian" (although it really isn't), and in beauty contests or costume balls, whenever a Brazilian wants to appear "in character" she dresses à la Bahiana.

Bahia has a constant succession of *festas* and pilgrimages. Famous all over Brazil is the *festa* of the *Senhor do Bonfim* (Lord of the Good Death), the patron of the city, the Salvador or Saviour Himself. The little 18th-century church is the object of a great pilgrimage every year, just after Epiphany. Not only the Negro population or the poor people trek to the Bonfim; statesmen, politicians, generals, millionaires, all can be seen regularly in the processions, carrying lighted candles in their hands. (The other great objects of pilgrimages annually are the Basilica of Nazareth in Belém, and the biggest of all, the Sanctuary of Our Lady Aparecida in São Paulo— Nossa Senhora Aparecida being the patron saint of Brazil.)

With its large Negro and colored population, Bahia is also the center of *candomblé* and *macumba* (voodoo, or vo-dung, religions) that highly-developed, intensely emotional mixture of African cults and Catholicism. From Bahia come the great "Babylons" or "Holy fathers," of these cults, leaders of their "churches" in Recife or Rio.

In Bahia, too, is practised the art of the *capoeira*, a form of combined wrestling and jujitsu, using the feet, lightning quick, graceful,—another importation from Africa.

Rio has its unsurpassed natural beauty, Recife its Flemish traditons, and São Paulo stands for progress,—but Bahia is above all the romantic city.

Bahia was built at the King's command, to be a capital, but the origins of Rio de Janeiro were more like those of Boston, say, a century later. It was established around 1555 on the Bay of Guanabara by a group of French Calvinists, without as much as a by-your-leave to the Portuguese. The colony called itself, ambitiously, "Antarctic France"; their leader was Nicolas Durand de Villegaignon (Villegaignon Island still marks the place of settlement) and they dreamed of establishing in the New World a "Utopia" according to Thomas More.

To expel the French, who were allied with the Indians, the Governor-

General of Bahia sent his nephew, Estácio de Sá, to the south. In the battle that gave the Portuguese victory over the French, Estácio, "a boy of gentle presence," was killed by an arrow in the face, but he became the lay-patron of the city he had founded on "Dog Face Hill," at the foot of the Sugar Loaf. For reasons of defense, the town moved across the bay to the Morro do Castelo (Fortress Hill), and it was there that the old colonial city grew up. Although still outlined by the oldest of Rio's churches, the Charity hospital, the Arsenal, etc.—the *morro*, or hill, itself was removed during the first Centenary of Independence, 1922—one of those amazing land-moving and scene-shifting operations that are so characteristic of the city and so surprising to visitors. "What has happened to Rio?" the Brazilian Carioca who has been away for two or three years always asks sadly— one who had been away for twelve years had to buy the latest map of the city before he could find his way around in his home town again.

The topography of Rio is fantastically beautiful, but sadly unsuited to any geometric mathematical-minded city-planning. The city has spread out and penetrated like the fingers of a hand between the towering peaks of granite and the steep hills, which were left uninhabited until the fairly recent (about twenty years or so) growth of the notorious *favelas*, or slums. Although poor people had always lived on the *morros* it is only during the last twenty years or so that they have become covered with shacks, mostly inhabited by immigrants from the north and northeast. It is estimated that one million of Rio's three million inhabitants now live in these slums, creating the worst of the city's many problems. Although life in the *favelas* would seem to offer nothing at all, except superior views and breezes, to the poor who come to them, nevertheless—as soon as a housing project removes a thousand or so people to better quarters, the same number stream into the city and fill up the old ones. Such are the attractions of city-life, even at its worst, as compared with the same poverty, plus boredom and isolation, of life in small towns in the interior. In the city there are the lights, there is radio and television (it is surprising how many aerials for both appear above these shacks), the *futebol*, the lotteries, the constant excitement and a sense of participation, even if on the lowest level, in the life of a great city, to offset the misery, the standing in line for water, & the frequent visits of the police.

Rio is a city of surprises. Right at the end of its Fifth Avenue, Avenida do Barão de Rio Branco, looms up a gigantic ocean liner. A dead-end street turns into an endless flight of steep steps. Since because of its peculiar physiognomy there is, or was usually, only one way to get to any one place, tunnels have been put through in all directions, or deep cuts right through the granite mountains. Upper-class dwellers in upper floors of apartment houses often look straight into *favelas* only a few yards away and are awakened by roosters crowing, at the level of the 10th floor, or babies not their own crying. One story, told as true, illustrates the intimacy of this chaotic mixture. A couple returning to their 8th-floor apartment at night heard a terrific bumping and crashing going on inside and thought "Burglars!" But when the door was opened a panic-stricken horse was found inside. So close are the protrusions of rock and earth to the buildings that he had managed to fall from his minute pasture on one straight onto their terrace—and it is perfectly possible.

Between the exuberant outcroppings of rocks and mountains on one hand, and the marshes and mangrove-swamps on the other, Rio developed as a huge city, but an isolated one, and its problems of transportation have always been very difficult. There is one highway leading from it into the interior; the main streets and avenues either wind between the mountains or are built on filled-in land along the bay. Almost all the old squares and plazas were originally lagoons or mangrove-swamps. The city could not expand along the coast because the marshes were uninhabitable because of the malarial mosquito. Now, however, modern sanitation has changed all this and enormous suburbs have spread out over the former swamps.

When the Portuguese court arrived in 1808, the capital was still only a dirty colonial village. The new arrivals quickly solved the housing-problem in a summary way: the King's quarter-masters requisitioned all the best houses for the members of the court. A bailiff merely painted on the door the letters P and R (Prince Royal). The Cariocas translated the letters in their own way as *Ponha-se na Rua*—"Get out in the street,"—and that was that.

The city made rapid progress under the Empire, but the biggest period of growth came after the consolidation of the Republic. In the euphoric days before the First World War it took on its present appearance. The mayors of that period destroyed many ancient alley-ways and streets (and unfortunately along with them many priceless fountains and old buildings), flattened out hills, filled in stretches of the bay, and opened up the avenues. They built the long line of quais and handsome warehouses where the black stevedores work in their ragged shorts and straw hats. The Copacabana section grew from almost deserted beaches to be the over-populated, apartment-house crowded "south zone." The cable cars to the top of the Sugar Loaf date from this period, as does the little funicular railway that ascends the Corcovado (hunchback) mountain. The 100-foot-tall figure of Christ the Redeemer was placed on top of Corcovado in 1931.

What will become of Rio now that the capital has been changed to Brasília? Opinions vary. The pessimists prophecy poverty and decay; at best Rio will turn into an immense Ouro Prêto, living on the memories of the past. At the other extreme, the optimists believe that the city, rid of the excess population it has attracted as the capital of the country, will actually improve. Without the thousands of government workers, bureaucrats, and people from the "provinces," they say that Rio will begin to function better than it does at present. Its position as the best-loved of Brazilian cities, the cultural capital of the country, the natural gaiety of the Cariocas, Carnival, the beaches—all its charms and advantages remain unchanged in spite of dire financial straits, lack of water, and all the rest of it. Rio gives no signs of realizing that it is no longer the capital. Although the capital has been in Brasília for almost two years, the greater part of the government remains still in Rio, and it is far easier to find a *Deputado*, or a Judge of the Supreme Court, in Rio than in his official place of residence.

Today, Brasília is looked on with great disfavour by many people, and not without some very good reasons. However, long before President Kubitschek began the construction of the new capital, the change from Rio to the Central Plateau had been a Brazilian dream, a sort of exodus for the land of Canaan, promised since colonial days, that would solve all the country's problems as if by magic. A capital in the interior would be a romantic repetition of the marches of the *bandeirantes* through the wildernesses, bringing civilization to the remotest areas and even as far as the western frontier. It was the myth of the city of gold, with the possibilites of providing wealth and opportunity for all.

José Bonifácio, the adviser to Pedro I (patriarch of independence), also dreamed of this capital in the hinterland; he may even be responsible for the name of "Brasília." In the middle of the 19th century, the Brazilian historian Varnhagen argued for a capital which would be at the meeting point of the principal drainage systems of Brazil—from the Amazon, the Paraná, and the São Francisco Rivers:—more or less the actual location of Brasília. And the first constitution under the Republic, influenced by the Positivists, included the marking out of a quadrilateral in the geographical heart of Brazil, where the future Federal District was to be situated. After the Vargas dictatorship ended in 1945, the new constitution insisted on a new capital in Goiás, and ordered a commission to prepare for the change. Every political candidate looking for popularity, every opportunistic journalist, spoke against the "crabs" who wanted to cling to the coastal regions and ignore the fertile interior. "The march to the west" had always been a Brazilian national aspiration.

So that when the Kubitschek government wanted to distinguish its term in office with some sensational and never-to-be-forgotten public work, the idea of turning the old dream of Brasília into a reality immediately occurred to them. Kubitschek, optimistic, energetic, and ebullient, refused to see any difficulties, or, later, to recognize the serious economic crisis and the spiral of inflation the country was entering. There was a great deal of opposition to it, and still is.

But it got built, even at the cost of over a billion dollars and the destruction of the national budget, at the expense of everything else. It also became a symbol to the Brazilian people and such a strong one that even politicians opposed to it (as the next candidate, Quadros, was known to be) did not dare speak of abandoning the whole project and returning the government to Rio. The government was installed on the 21st of April, 1960, and the government functionaries were all required to move there— or at least as many of them as there were buildings enough ready for. It has been hard to get a quorum in the Senate; the course of justice has become slowed almost to a standstill. The controversy still rages. It is only fair, of course, to try to distinguish between the really tragic drawbacks of the move, and those that are merely temporary discomforts, such as attended the building of Washington, D.C.

Even events leading up to the renunciation of Jânio Quadros as president have been blamed on Brasília.

In Rio, the Cariocas (and all Brazilians are potential Cariocas) conceal their jealousy, if they feel any, and laugh at the tribulations of Brasília. The fact is that no one is really yet accustomed to the idea of the new capital. The government that is there feels itself more like a "government in exile" than anything else. Rio continues to be the heart and soul of the country. São Paulo only recently overtook it in economic power and in population, and in Rio they still keep saying that good "Paulistas" when they die, come to Rio.

Chapter 5
Animal, Vegetable, and Mineral

While Brazil remains in many ways an agricultural country—agriculture produces almost 30 per cent of the national income and employs more than half of the working population—revenue from industry is beginning to overtake that from agriculture. In 1960 Brazil produced more than 134,000 vehicles with parts made almost entirely within the country. Steel production is increasing, and Brazil is now turning out more than 2 million net tons a year, compared with 350,000 net tons in the immediate postwar period. Even appliances are beginning to be produced in volume.

Remarkable as this achievement is, it does not necessarily mean that Brazil will soon become an industrial colossus. The country has ample resources—its hydroelectric potential alone is the world's greatest: 80 million kilowatts. But Brazilians, it is said, "collect the fruit without planting the tree." They have a national penchant for skimming off quick profits instead of laying the foundation for solid future earnings. The economic history of Brazil could almost be told in its long succession of spectacular booms. Brazil's economy was dominated by sugar, gold, and coffee in succession, with brief interludes devoted to other products. But the country is today trying to diversify, rather than depend on single crops or industries.

One of Brazil's earliest occupations was cattle raising, and it was necessarily an imported one. The Portuguese discoverers had been surprised to find that the Indians had no domestic animals, or at least no useful domestic animals. The Indians had only dogs, monkeys, and birds.

One of the first, and very difficult, undertakings of the Portuguese was to bring to Brazil all the domesticated animals they were accustomed to at home. In the middle of the 16th century cattle were brought to Bahia from Portugal and the Cape Verde Islands. They were the forebears of the cattle of the plains of the northeast.

Cattle were introduced in the south as early as 1532. The settlers who followed the *bandeirantes* took with them cows, horses, pigs, and goats. Later they drove the descendants of these animals through the one natural passage which penetrates the coastal mountain range and into the open stretch west of São Paulo. Horses and cows were allowed to range freely. As in the early days in the west of the United States, rustling and the roundup of wild herds—for the most part strays from the Jesuit villages— were important aspects of the life and legend of the region.

Although from the beginning sugar was the principal product in the northeast, cattle were a stimulus to colonization and the opening of new lands. In search of pastures for their herds, cattlemen pushed deep into the northeastern interior. Cattle raising changed from a simple adjunct of the great plantations to an independent activity. From it came the so-called "leather culture" that developed in this whole vast region of Brazil during the first centuries of the country's history. The horse, upon which cattle raising depended, today inseparable from the gaucho of the Brazilian pampas and the *vaqueiro* of the northeast, became acclimated throughout the country. Today Brazil has more than 8 million horses.

In the northeast most of the cattle are descendants of the original herds. They are small and give little milk, but are tough and resistant. Over the years, the government and progressive cattle raisers have improved the stock throughout the country by crossing it with the zebu, or Brahman, introduced from India. This animal is well-adapted to the harsh northern conditions of heat, drought, and meager pasturage, and it thrives where the finest European stock dies off or quickly sickens and degenerates. Zebus, with their high shoulder humps, high-domed skulls, and long, drooping ears, have become common in most of Brazil, adding an exotic yet somehow not incongruous note to the landscape.

At the turn of the 20th century, zebus were imported into the huge section of fine cattleland in Minas Gerais called the "Minas Triangle," which is now the center of the cattle industry. They became acclimated so successfully that zebu-owning became a passion with cattle raisers; prices soared, zebu buying and selling became a form of gambling, and there was wild speculation. In the 1920s the fever reached such a pitch that a single good bull brought as much as $7,500, compared to an average price of $250 for bulls of European breed.

Outside the beef-raising Triangle, the cattle of Minas Gerais are dairy cattle, and their products, including the white Minas cheese (no longer seen on every table at least once a day), are sold everywhere. Beef cattle need huge tracts of land, and with the rapid and progressive industrialization of the central-southern part of the country the cattle are being shifted to the wilder regions of Goiás and the Pantanal in Mato Grosso, which offer favorable conditions and are also near the biggest consumer of beef, the State of São Paulo.

In Pará, especially on the island of Marajó, the Indian water buffalo has been introduced and seems completely at home. The wilderness and abundant rivers and swamps of the huge island provide the kind of semi-aquatic life this semidomesticated beast prefers, while ordinary cattle, even the zebu, do not thrive there.

In a country with few refrigerators, the industry of making *charque*, a dried, salted meat which does not spoil easily and which is usually cooked with the staple black beans and rice, is very important. The industry started in the northeast and was taken by immigrants to Rio Grande do Sul. Although outranked in total number of cattle by Minas Gerais, this state now raises the country's finest beef and is a center of the meat-packing industry. With 72.8 million head, Brazil is second only to the U.S. in number of beef cattle, but not in beef production, primarily because of poor disease control, inadequate transport and refrigeration facilities, and antiquated methods.

The largest herds of sheep—Brazil has some 22 million head—are also in Rio Grande do Sul, and crude wool is beginning to rank as an important export. With cotton, a major export for years, these herds also provide some material for the textile industry, which has grown enormously in the last decade.

The country's immense coastline and teeming rivers should make fishing and processing fish much more important industries than they are. But commercial exploitation has just begun, and fish still represent one of the greatest undeveloped resources of the country. In the States of Pará and Amazonas there is, for example, the *pirarucu*, the "fresh-water codfish," weighing up to five hundred pounds.

The commercial catch in the Amazon runs to only 90,000 tons a year, largely because fishing techniques used in the river are still primitive, as are those of many of the coastal fishermen. The beautiful, traditional *jangadas* of the northeast are merely rafts made of balsa trunks lashed together. They have one sail, and every object aboard must be tied fast to the deck. The fishermen venture on the high seas aboard the *jangadas*, but the hauls of fish they bring back are usually so small that it has been said that the real place for the picturesque *jangada* is the folklore museum.

Some modernization has been taking place in the fishing industry. Several Japanese firms have formed motorized fleets in the south, specializing in tuna and whale. A whale-processing plant has been built at Cabo Frio, a coast town east of Rio. Whales are abundant, and whale meat is being urged on a somewhat reluctant public in the coastal markets as the cheapest form of meat. Lobster fishing has also been increasing, chiefly in Pernambuco and Ceará. Canning factories are being built along the coast.

Coffee has been subject to as many ups and downs as any other Brazilian resource, but it has certainly not been troubled by underexploitation. For many years it has been Brazil's best-known product; coffee has been the greatest item of export and the biggest source of income. Brazil produced almost 4 billion pounds in 1960. It supplied the world with nearly half its coffee, earning the country 56 per cent of its total foreign-trade income.

Brazilian coffee had modest origins. Early in the 18th century, a Brazilian stole shoots from French Guiana, where the French had started coffee plantations. The trees were first cultivated in the State of Pará. Later, seeds and shoots were distributed throughout the country. Cultivation remained small-scale until the 19th century, when coffee had its first great phase in Rio de Janeiro and Minas. The cultivation of coffee in these states, particularly in Rio de Janeiro, depended directly on slave labor, and coffee profits made the fortunes of the Rio de Janeiro barons. With the abolition of slavery in 1888 the barons went bankrupt.

São Paulo did not have as much slave labor and was far-sighted enough to encourage immigration. In the crucial years before and after abolition, immigrants—principally from Portugal and Italy—came in great numbers. In addition to this labor supply, São Paulo had its marvelous *terra roxa* ("purple earth"), which according to the Paulistas, God created especially for the raising of coffee. Also coffee, which already had been named "the vampire," since within a few years it exhausted the soil, had declined in the State of Rio. In the year of abolition, for example, the States of Rio and Minas produced twice as much coffee as São Paulo; ten years later São Paulo was producing much more than both states together. Nevertheless, even with improved methods of cultivation, the *terra roxa* of São Paulo in turn began to be exhausted. Coffee continued its march to the south and to the west; in the late 1920s tracts of the precious dark red soil were found in the wild country of northwestern Paraná. Like a green army, the coffee trees of the planters triumphantly took over, pushing back the virgin forest and driving the wild animals farther into the interior. In the shade of the coffee trees new towns were born. A typical example is Londrina, a modern and prosperous city located where only a few decades ago stood the untouched forest. At present the coffee trees are penetrating into the State of Mato Grosso.

•

As the mainstay of the Brazilian economy, coffee has suffered various crises, during which the entire national life has been threatened. The appearance of Africa among the coffee producers created one of the most serious
of these crises in the 1950s. Although still the coffee leader of the world,
Brazil has had to face previously unknown competition, and the competition is constantly becoming more acute. Brazil cannot today sell all its
coffee; in 1960 it had an accumulated stockpile of more than 5 billion
pounds.

Repeated crises in the coffee market are having the effect of arousing
the country to the necessity of agricultural diversification; Brazil is attempting to expand exports of other products like sugar, tobacco, and
fruit. The coffee problem has also stimulated the growth of industrialization, chiefly in São Paulo, Brazil's most prosperous state. It had undergone a tremendous boom since World War II. There was no heavy-machinery
industry before the war; today there are more than forty-five major plants
in São Paulo. In 1959 alone, the state manufactured more than 15,000
machine tools. It produces 53 per cent of the country's paper, 54 per cent
of its textiles, and 58 per cent of its chemicals, and it is a major bulwark of
the foreign market, exporting more than 1.6 million tons of manufactured goods a year. With the nearby State of Guanabara, São Paulo contributes almost half of Brazil's domestic income.

At the center of this industrial complex lies the city of São Paulo itself.
Only 80 years ago, it was a quiet town of 25,000 people. Today it covers
535 square miles and, with a population of 4.8 million, is the eighth largest metropolis in the world. Its traffic problem is even worse than that of
New York, and it has a bustling, cosmopolitan atmosphere.

Unlike the prosperous south, the states of the northeast remain almost
wholly agricultural. There sugar, which had its earlier heyday of monoculture before being dethroned by coffee, is still the basis of the economy—
although cotton and cacâo are grown in large quantities. Sugar developed
even as Brazil itself developed; it could almost be said that the first Portuguese arrived with shoots of sugar cane under their arms. The rich northeastern sugar plantations of Pernambuco and Bahia were major factors in
luring the Dutch to invade in the 17th century. Most of the profitable
sugar growing is now done in the south, but in Pernambuco, Alagoas, and
Paraíba, the cane fields still stretch to the horizon. Great refineries, which
are beginning to take the place of the primitive old ones, are improving
the product. But the methods of cultivation are extremely primitive, almost
semifeudal; and the sugar workers are among the poorest and most long-
suffering of Brazilian peoples. There is today a strong movement among

enlightened Brazilians for reform of the agrarian situation throughout the northeast. It is indeed a highly explosive area, ripe for Communist exploitation.

One product of the sugar cane is *aguardente*, generally called *cachaça* or *pinga*. A clear, fiery, powerful drink made since colonial times, it is known as "the brandy of the poor." *Cachaça* is now being exported. There is no Brazilian product surrounded by so much folklore as *cachaça*; a whole cycle of songs celebrates it. The names by which it is called, mostly affectionate nicknames—"the grandmother," "the little blonde," "the thread of gold"—show the esteem in which *cachaça* is regarded. When a man takes a drink at the nearest corner bar, he always spits out a little of the first mouthful onto the floor, as an offering to whichever saint he believes to be the donor of the liquor.

Rubber, too, once played a major economic role. The source of great but brief wealth, Amazon rubber suffered a blow in 1910 when the plantations in Malaya and the Dutch East Indies began to outproduce and undersell it in the world market. The towns that had flourished in the valley of the Amazon were rapidly transformed into dead or dying communities. The city of Manaus, situated near the meeting point of the Amazon and the Rio Negro, was the rubber capital of the world until the collapse of the market. Rich and luxurious, with a huge opera house, it imported troops of singers and dancers. Large ships made it a regular port of call. To the east of Manaus, Henry Ford established experimental plantations, Fordlândia and Belterra, in the late 1920s and early 1930s, but, finding the project unprofitable, abandoned it. Today owned by the government, the project still produces a small amount of rubber.

During World War II, when Japan seized the plantations of Malaya and the Dutch East Indies, there was a brief resuscitation in Amazonian rubber. But Brazil today imports some $40 million worth of Asian rubber each year. The Amazon, deprived of the market for its principal wealth, has also been attempting diversification in recent years. The area now produces substantial quantities of Brazil nuts, jute, lumber, sugar cane, and vegetable oils as well as manganese.

Like other Brazilian resources, lumber has had its brief fling, but it, too, has yet to reach its potential. In the Amazon basin alone, there are at least 5 trillion cubic feet of timber, and there are vast forests of prime woods in the south. One of the most attractive features of the national landscape is commonest in the States of Paraná and Santa Catarina—the groves of araucarias, the Brazilian pine tree. They are very tall trees with straight trunks and arched, bare branches terminating in characteristic cup-shaped bunches of needles. Besides being beautiful, the araucaria is extremely useful; its wood constitutes the principal wealth of the region in which it grows. So sought after was this wood that the government was forced to pass a law in 1942 prohibiting excessive cutting and providing for replanting.

With more than 600 known varieties, Brazil has more palm trees than any other country in the world. They are rich sources of fiber, oils, and fuel. From the leaves of the carnauba, an elegant, tall palm that flourishes only in northeast Brazil, comes a sticky deposit rather like beeswax which, when gathered, powdered, and melted by a difficult and primitive process, produces the famous carnauba wax. It was used in the manufacture of phonograph records, polishes, and varnishes. The carnauba is one of the principal economic supports of the States of Ceará, Piauí, and Maranhão, and the people of the dry *sertão* say that is the compensation given them by God for the scourge of drought—since when there is rain the palm produces no wax.

Tobacco is raised in most of Brazil, and has been for centuries an important trade merchandise for the slave dealers. It had developed into an industry in Bahia, whose cigars are famous and good enough to be compared with those of Cuba. Bahia cigarettes are also widely distributed, but the greatest number of cigarette factories is in the State of Rio Grande do Sul.

The European grape, introduced by Italian immigrants, grows very well in Rio Grande do Sul. The wine industry has developed rapidly and today Brazilians are proud of some of their wines, champagnes, and cognacs. In 1960 nearly 8 million gallons were exported to France. Also important to Rio Grande do Sul is wheat, although far from enough is produced to make Brazil self-sufficient. The country usually manages to produce enough corn, beans, and rice for domestic consumption.

Only recently has there been much interest in making use of Brazilian fruit for exportation or canning. Oranges are now exported on a large scale. Bananas, of which Brazil is the world's largest grower, are principally grown in São Paulo. The cashew fruit of the northeast provides the valuable cashew nut, and the fruit is processed in the form of syrups and pastes. And then there is the guava. Guava paste, accompanied by cheese, is a standard dessert all over Latin America.

Brazil's greatest mineral resource is iron. There are practically inexhaustible veins in the country, located mainly in the State of Minas. It is estimated that there are 65 billion tons of iron ore in Brazil, 35 per cent of the world's total reserve. The lack of high-quality coking coal has until recently prevented the development of steel mills commensurate in number with the quantity of ore. However, the coal of Santa Catarina, although of an inferior quality, has been energetically exploited, and the result has been the great steel mills of Volta Redonda, whose construction began in 1942 with U.S. aid. Brazil's iron and steel industry is now the largest industry in Latin America, and exploitation of the ore has barely begun.

The same is true of other mineral reserves. There are deposits of just about every known mineral, including precious and semiprecious stones, scattered throughout the country, some in vast quantities. Only with denser population in these areas and more specialized techniques will Brazil be able to profit from these hidden riches. In Espírito Santo and other areas the government is at present exploring layers of monazite sands rich in radioactive ores.

A matter of considerable controversy in Brazil is the extent of petroleum reserves. Some geologists have suggested that the vast sedimentary basins of the Amazon and Paraná, encompassing nearly 2 million square miles, contain extensive reserves. But so far only traces of oil have been found. Due to a fear of foreign exploitation, oil exploration and heavy oil production were restricted in 1953 to a single government monopoly, Petrobrás. Despite valiant wildcatting at a cost of some $50 million a year, Brazil produces only some 30 per cent of its own crude requirements, most of it from the wells in Bahia. And even if there are extensive reserves in the upper Amazon valley, geologists believe that they lie under rock and would present difficult and expensive problems. Transport would not be a problem, because of the nearness of the navigable Amazon. Throughout most of the country, however, transport is one of the basic problems which Brazil must solve before it can begin real exploitation of its truly magnificent resources. Today, Brazil has nearly 24,000 miles of railroads, but most of them are short-haul, east-west lines which penetrate inland only a short distance from the coast. Many of them are of different gauges, and there are few north-south connections in any event. The highway network still under construction will of course help to solve this problem.

Chapter 6
Unself-conscious Arts

The Brazilian of the interior owns almost nothing and has little cash income. He is not a "consumer"; he still makes most of the things he wears and uses. He lives close to the life of the Indian and the primitive African. These are some of the reasons why, once away from the coastal cities, the arts and handcrafts flourish in Brazil as they haven't in the United States since colonial days. Since the man of the interior also has no entertainment (or hadn't until the radio, now man's alter ego in Brazil as everywhere else), he still makes his own: songs; ballads; dances; ancient, sometimes very elaborate, folk-plays and rituals; according to the seasons and the saints' days. He weaves wool and cotton home-spun, plaits straw and wicker, makes pottery, carves. The richness and variety of these native arts owes much to the fact that they, too, like the people, are racially mixed. Portugese and Moorish, African and Indian,—and now in southern Brazil sometimes German, Italian, and Japanese, as well.

A curious fact about Brazilian folk-pottery is that, although familiar to the Portuguese for centuries, the potter's wheel is not used. This is supposed to be because the present-day potters in Brazil learned their art from the Indians rather than from Portuguese tradition. Even without the wheel, the Indians for a thousand years or so have made—and are making—bowls and urns, sometimes of enormous size: huge pots for fermenting liquor, or funerary urns big enough to hold the body of an adult, sitting in foetal position. These pots are built up by the "rope" method, long thin ropes of clay superimposed, round and round, until the required height and shape are reached, then the ridges smoothed down. The backlands potters (women, as with the Indians) make pots of great elegance in this primitive way, decorate them with black, white, and earth colors, and polish them with the rinds of fruit.

Besides dishes & jugs for practical purposes made by women, men sometimes make clay figures, an art derived from Africa. Sometimes colored and glazed, sometimes clay-color, these little statues or whole groups of them depict all the types and activities of their society: the "cowboys," soldiers, priests, hunters, a wedding, a funeral, a jaguar-hunt, a team of oxen, etc. Women potters occasionally make figures, and at Ipu, in Ceará, they are known for their miniature pots and pans, dishes and furniture and animals—toys for children, sometimes surprisingly like the toys the Greek and Roman potters made for children and that survive in the museums. From Bahia State come sitting-hens, turkeys, snakes, whole trees full of birds—brightly colored and gay. Pots for the baby copy exactly in clay the usual enamel model, those glazed inside costing a few pennies more than the unglazed ones.

Another art has developed in the zones the sociologists call the "leather-culture" (pastoral): a great variety of articles made from calf-skin. The most esteemed, however, are those of deer-skin—and deer are plentiful in the scrub-forests of the northeast. The cowboy's leather costume is made to protect him from the thorns and sharp-edged leaves of the *caatinga*, the scrub-forest, and its varieties of low-growing cacti and thorny trees. It is like medieval armor, made in leather: leggings, serving the same purpose as an American cowboy's "chaps," but tight-fitting and extending over the top of the foot, like spats; an apron, a "chest-protector," and over all the leather "doublet," with long sleeves meeting the leather gloves or mitts. On his head the cowboy wears a leather hat, with a strap under the chin. All these garments are fancifully decorated: embroidered, inlaid in different colored leather, stamped. Their saddles are equally objects of art, and their long, quilted capes, and decorated whips with fine lashes (made from bulls' pizzles).

Besides the art of pottery, the women of the north and northeast have inherited the art of working in straw from their Indian grandmothers: mats, bags, baskets, hats. In one part of Ceará they make straw hats similar to the "Panamas" of Panama and Chile in their softness and fineness. Baskets, fish-traps, coarse and fine sieves, mats woven to be used as ceilings below the naked rafters. In Pará State, influenced by Portuguese workers in wicker, there is a home industry of furniture-making in reeds, rushes, wickers, etc. Travellers on the Amazon are startled to be begged to buy large wicker rocking-chairs, perched across the sterns of tiny canoes.

The most famous straw-work, however, are the hammocks woven of cord or thread made from several varieties of palm. They are soft and supple, straw-colored, as fine as silk. They are not used for sleeping in, but hung for siestas on the shady porches. For sleeping, hammocks of woven cotton are used, but coarser ones in bright plaids (the Portuguese, like the Scotch, are devoted to plaids), unsystematic plaids or all-white—the more valuable kind. The foot-wide borders of these hammocks (called "varandas") are an art in themselves—special patterns, in "knotted lace" with long fringes. In the big ranch houses of the *sertãos* the "hammock chests" are an indication of the owner's wealth, big chests of cedar or other fragrant woods where dozens of the valuable snow-white hammocks are packed away with sprigs of marjoram between them.

One *casa grande* in the State of Ceará had 120 hammocks in its chests, for 120 guests. This was on the *fazenda* called "California," built in 1850 and hopefully named "California" for the California gold rush. This *fazenda* was founded in 1850, without a name. A friend of the owner inquired, "How's so-&-so with his California?" (referring to the American gold rush of '49) and so it was named "California." Besides the hammocks for 120 guests who might want to spend the night, there were special "priests' hammocks," for their periodical visits. The lace "varandas" of these showed crosses, crossed lances (emblems of the Passion), and bunches of grapes and ears of wheat (emblems of the Eucharist).

Another art inherited from the Indian is the *cúia*, or decorated gourd, enamelled black, used as dippers and for bathing. The enamel is a secret, handed down from generation to generation. The decorations are often very beautiful, incised in the gourd and left in natural color, or brightly painted: flowers, fruits, flags, and such sentiments as: *Souvenir, Independence or Death!, Mother Love,* or *Happy Birthday.*

From the Portuguese and also the Moors, the Brazilian women have inherited the art of lace-making, exquisitely fine lace that taxes the eyes and the patience: a hand's-breadth is often more than a day's work. Lace made from thread of banana-leaf fibres instead of commercial thread is particularly rare and valuable. The weavers of Mato Grosso also use this delicate fibre, an art learned from the Paraguayan Indians. Drawn-work, crocheted and knitted lace, embroideries—where the patterns have not been coarsened or "modernized"—are also very beautiful. The most famous lace-makers are from the town of Aracati in Ceará State, but the laces of the State of Santa Catarina, made by descendants of immigrants from the Azores are also famous. There is a whole group of folk-songs devoted to the lace-makers; some of them have to do with the saga of the notorious northeast bandit Lampião (killed in 1938). Strange to say, the war-song of Lampião's bandits was "The Lace Maker": "Oh, lace-maker! / Oh woman making lace! / Teach me how to make lace / And I'll teach you how to love . . ."

In the gold-mining regions, Minas Gerais, Goiás, Bahia, the goldsmith's art developed, with much skilled workmanship, often showing Moorish influence in its filigrees and arabesques. The stones set in these pieces are usually rough diamonds, or the many Brazilian semi-precious stones: aquamarines, topazes, amethysts, and tourmalines. A great deal of work is done in Bahia with gold and silver, ivory and coral, often in the form of amulets, lucky charms. The *figa*, or "fig," in English, is seen everywhere in Brazil: tiny ones hung around babies' necks, along with the medal of a saint, and big ones, of wood, hung on the walls. This immemorial image of a clenched fist with the thumb protruding between the first two fingers is seen everywhere in Brazil. (Shakespeare speaks of it, but it antedates Shakespeare by many centuries.) Also from Bahia are the *balangandás*, jingling bunches of charms formerly worn by slave women, at their waists, and now collectors' items. The charms are several inches long: pomegranites, cashew-fruits, musical instruments, phallic symbols, objects of *macumba* rites. From Goiás come rosaries of gold beads, with the "Our Fathers" of coral or baroque pearls.

In the region of Cariri, until recently the "wild west" of Brazil, land of bandits and religious fanatics, local workmen specialize in making knives and daggers. To this day they made silver daggers to be worn in high boots, and daggers with handles of ivory, enamel or gold filagree. So "wild" is Cariri even now, that during a friendly *futebol* ("soccer") game between the teams of two rival towns, above the applause and shouts could be heard the cries of a man selling locally made knives from a basket on his back, like popcorn or Orange *Croosh*: "Get your little daggers for after the game!"

The art of the saint-makers is traditional, passed on from father to son. Every little household chapel, or "oratorio," has its wooden images carved by the local saint-maker. Formerly, these saints were sometimes made with the bodies hollowed out, in order to hide gold and diamonds from the government inspectors, and the expression "a hollow saint" is still used to mean a hypocritical person. Figures of saints, made in the days of Aleijadinho, are still being made in the interior. Recently, however, the priests, unfortunately especially foreign priests, not appreciating the primitive in art, and wanting to get money for their churches, have been exchanging these often very remarkable wood carvings for the sentimental contemporary statues of tinted plaster, factory-produced, and sad to say the rural congregations' tastes are deteriorating as well.

Because of this, many of the good "saint-makers" have now turned to making "miracles" instead, ex-votos, to be offered as payment for promises fulfilled by miracle-working saints at the most popular shrines (Our Lady of Nazareth in Belém, St. Francis of Canindé in Ceará, Good Jesus of Lapa on the banks of the Rio São Francisco, Our Lord of the Good Death in Bahia, Our Lady of Penha in Rio, Our Lady of Aparecida in São Paulo). Each of the churches, usually raised by the Church to the dignity of basilica, has its special rooms for displaying ex-votos, veritable museums of popular art: legs, arms, hearts, heads, ears & eyes, and inner organs, in wood or wax, each attesting to a miraculous cure. Along with them are paintings: fishing-ships, *jangadas*, saved from storms, hunters from wild beasts or deadly snakes, souls from swarms of devils.

In the field of sculpture, however, the greatest folk-achievement was the figureheads used on the cargo boats on the Rio São Francisco—a custom rapidly dying out. Some of these figureheads are very fine, several feet tall, towering at the bow of the boat, and carved in a style reminiscent of Romanesque sculpture in its strength and simplicity. Animals, women, characters from Afro-Brazilian folk-lore—but principally "the Great Worm," the most dreadful of the spirits that live in the river.

One speciality that industrialization has not yet touched is the art of carpentry—inherited from the Portuguese ship-builders—particularly the manufacture of [. . .] for flour mills, cotton seed and cheese presses, and other domestic industries. They are complicated pieces, nuts and screws, rollers and scrapers and all worked in hard-wood, and in some cases, such as machinery for making manioc flour or wine or paste from the cashew-fruit, no metal can be used at all. The huge screws, more than six feet high, are carved in spirals, in "bow-wood," as hard as iron; the enormous wheels and travelling beams are made of whole tree-trunks, without a single nail or screw of metal, held together by a complex system of wooden pegs and joints. The carpenter's only tools are the axe, saw, adze, chisel, and his two hands.

Like other primitive peoples, Brazilians of the interior prize their folk-poets, whom they call "singers." They are often wanderers, playing the violin or guitar, and their verses are improvisations, sung to their own accompaniment but in strict, ancient forms and meters. They appear at rural *festas* and engage each other in interminable duels of verse, sometimes going on for several days, with the "singers" only stopping to eat and drink. The competitors try to outlast each other in ideas, rhymes, and good-temper. It is an art that could only develop in a Latin tongue like Portuguese, full of rhymes and assonance. The loser of the duel is the one whose rhymes finally fail him, and, exhausted, he yields the victory with a set of verses paying homage to the superior powers of his rival.

These singers are privileged people in the little communities of the *sertão*. They also have very high opinions of themselves and of their "memories," the word used to describe "poetic talent."

> "There's no man like the King,
> No woman like the Queen,
> No Saint like God Almighty,
> And no memory like mine . . ."

one of them sings.

Before the advent of the radio and television, which now compete with them but so far have not entirely silenced them, these singers were the real newspapers of the backlands; even today they continue to produce detailed and dramatic verse-accounts of the more sensational news. A few days after President Getúlio Vargas's suicide, a "Brazilian Writer" (as he signed himself) of Recife produced a ballad-pamphlet called "Getúlio in Heaven," that still sells in the weekly outdoor markets all over Brazil. The recent renunciation of President Quadros has already been put into verses, and the flight of Gagarin, and the biggest and latest aeroplane disaster. Usually the "writers" (who can't write; someone else takes down the verses for them) sing and declaim their compositions and then sell them in pamphlet form to the by-standers. The covers of some of these pamphlets are themselves works of art; although the text is badly printed, on poor paper, full of misprints and misspellings, the outside sheet is ornamented with crude but impressive wood-cuts.

Christmas (sometimes called "The Birth") and New Year's, or the Good-Year, are celebrated all over Brazil with *festas* that vary according to local traditions and the racial group predominating in the region. In the north and northeast, with ancient traditions of the "pastoral," the favorite celebration is the *Bumba-meu-boi* ("Beat my ox"). A little group of men (as in the classical theatre, women never take part in these performances) act out a story whose hero is the ox, who dances, sings, grows sick, dies, and then comes to life again to general rejoicing and more songs and dances. The bull, with his two dancers inside, is followed by other characters: Matthew, the cowboy, the horse, the donkey, the priest (who comes to give the last rites to the dying ox), the doctor (with an enormous clyster syringe, like a character in Molière), the clown, and the chorus of [...]. The music and action are interspersed with songs, and there is always a great deal of ad-libbing in the dialogues, whose wit and appositeness can make the reputation of a Matthew or a clown.

In the coastal regions, where Portuguese influence is stronger, they dance "Fandango" or "Cheganças" ("arrivals"): in a ship built on the site of the *festa*, they present the dramatic story of the ship *Catarineta*, based on an old Portuguese tale in verse that dates from the time of the discovery of Brazil. And where Negroes predominate, the play is a "Congo," also a dramatized tale: at the court of a king of the Congo, rivals betray the kingdom to the white invaders. The crown prince discovers the plot and is killed; then follows a battle, sometimes ending in tragedy and sometimes with the victory of King Congo. All the characters are richly dressed, with velvet capes, satin breeches, and golden crowns. The ambassador of the whites is always an imposing Negro dressed like an English Admiral, with a plumed hat—like Lord Nelson.

But everywhere, from the north to the south of Brazil, in the interior and in the cities, the play of the Shepherds appears, the group of shepherds in search of the Christ Child, singing and dancing in his honor. All these primitive plays are traditional, the words handed down from generation to generation, the dialogues, even the clown's jokes, as well as the songs.

However, all these folk festivals, and there are many others, including a variety of "rodeo" in the northeast, pale beside the great Brazilian passion, the Carnival.

Carnival reached Brazil by way of the old Portuguese *Entrudo*, a rude form of Carnival on Shrove Tuesday, in which masks figured, and "perfume lemons" (balls of colored wax filled with perfumed water) were thrown, but most of the rough fun consisted in throwing basins of cold water and paper sacks of flour.

In Brazil, in the cities (and Carnival is essentially an urban celebration), the *Entrudo* was gradually transformed into a mass-masquerade, an enormous public ball with general dancing in the streets and organized parades of dancers as well. (Not including the hundreds of private balls being given at the same time.) The paraders belong to special groups, the "ranchos" (meaning "districts," of the town) and the "Samba Schools," each group wearing its special costume, elaborate and often costly. The festivities go on for the three nights, all night long, preceding Ash Wednesday; and everything else comes to a complete stop: stores, banks, all work. The sambas of the year are constantly in the air; the streets are filled with slowly-moving samba-ing crowds, the air filled with confetti and streamers and the odor of the "perfume shooters"—flasks of compressed scented ether, that shoot a fine spray and not only perfume the air but give the person who gets hit a momentary thrill of icy coldness. Women samba with babies solemnly rising and falling rhythmically in their arms. It is a happy, good-humored crowd, one of the greatest shows in the world. It was, that is, because it is sad to say, but true, that Carnival, in the big cities, is rapidly being spoiled—by radio, mostly, and also by commercialism and a false idea of what appeals to the "tourist." Hollywood movies have had their bad effects, too—a few years ago the favorite Carnival costume was taken from a film that had recently been very popular, and hundreds, or thousands, of Davids and Bathshebas samba-ed in inappropriate and ludicrous getups.

But radio and loudspeakers have done the most damage. Perhaps something can be done to save Carnival. Its essence has always been in its spontaneity and the fact that all the songs, music, and dances came directly from the people themselves. When commercial song-writers start composing songs for it, and when these songs are broadcast long before the day, the freshness has gone. Also, when a crowd of thousands samba-ing along, singing their own favorite in unison, is confronted with the same samba or another one blaring over their heads at every corner from loudspeakers, in a different tempo & even interrupted by advertising—they give up singing and dancing, and shuffle along like sheep. Photographers have also been allowed to interfere with the street dancers, interrupting the prize-winning performances to get "good shots." In Rio during the past two Carnivals the crowds finally whistled and booed some particularly obnoxious photographers out of the streets.

But in Recife, for example, the festival still has an authentic folk-lore flavor. The ordinary man goes out to play, or "to break," as he calls having fun; if he can afford it, he dresses as a "Prince," a rooster, Indian, devil, or skeleton (very popular). If he hasn't any money, he improvises a costume, for example, a "woods beast"—simply a cape covered with leaves, like feathers, supposed to look like the primitive Indians. Or he shaves a strip of hair down the crown of his head, paints it red, and arranges it to look as if he has a tommy-hawk sticking in his skull. Or shaves all his head and paints it blue or green. With a parasol he sets out to dance the "frevo," wild and acrobatic, danced half-crouching. If all else fails, he can go in rags and paint, simply as a "dirty one."

Besides the radio and Hollywood, much of the fun has been spoiled by the government forbidding political caricatures, or making sport of the Church—some of the cleverest costumes used to be inspired by these old reliable objects of satire.

Rio de Janeiro has its own original institution, the Samba Schools. They are not exactly schools,—clubs, rather, where the members meet during the last months of the year to learn the songs and dances for the coming Carnival. Much time and money are devoted to these schools, whose members are almost entirely poor Negroes from the *favelas*. The songs are real folk-poetry and music: the themes are love (most important), "social criticism" of the government, the cost of living, politics,—even *futebol*. A general theme is given all the "Schools" for each Carnival, such as "The Discovery," or—a few years ago—"The Discovery of Gold." In one school, the women members danced with huge imitation gold nuggets sparkling on top of their heads. A favorite costume seems to be vaguely Louis XV, and no expense is spared. Where else in the world could one see three hundred Negroes in blue and white and silver Louis XV costumes, with white curled wigs and plumed hats, dancing down the middle of the main street at 4 AM? After them come the women, swaying and singing as they dance—hung with ropes of silver glass beads—and tiny white lights concealed in all the costumes—courtly, ravishing, gracious, to mad music on strange instruments—a fairyland for a night.

Chapter 7

In the field of contemporary arts, Brazil is certainly best known for its architecture. Not one of the cities along the coast, from Recife to Porto Alegre, is without its cluster, big or small, but ever-growing, of white "sky-scrapers." (A "sky-scraper" in Brazil is not necessarily very high; ten or twelve stories raises a building so far above the earlier two-, three-, or four-floored buildings that it qualifies for the title.) And each city also has its large apartment houses, private houses, housing-projects, hospitals, and schools, all built in the contemporary idiom. Many of these are excellent, and well-known, even if only through the architectural reviews, to architects the world over. The majority, as everywhere and in all periods, will probably rank only as mediocre attempts to be "in style." Nevertheless, it is perfectly true that there is probably more good contemporary architecture in Brazil today than in any other of the world's under-developed but rapidly growing countries.

This important artistic achievement, Brazil's greatest, is almost entirely due to a group of imaginative, energetic, sophisticated, and daring architects, most of them still quite young. But Brazilians in general, educated ones, that is, are more architecture-conscious than other peoples. Everyone seems to have strong opinions about modern architecture, pro or con (mostly pro), and to be able to speak with assurance of *brise-soleils* ("break-suns," or shutters; the French term is usually used) or *pilotis* (the pillars raising a building one story off the ground),—the two outstanding features of modern Brazilian building. Brazil is also one of the few countries where contemporary architecture is encouraged,—favored, even,— by the government. While Washington, for example, was sticking safely to the Graeco-Roman for a new Supreme Court building, Brazil was putting up what is still considered one of the best examples of modern architecture, the Ministry of Education in Rio de Janeiro. Competitions are required by law for public buildings, and the prizes usually go to the most advanced entries.

We have already spoken of Oscar Niemeyer and Lucio Costa in connection with Brasília, but a few other equally important architects should be mentioned. Jorge M. Moreira is perhaps the most "European," known for his delicate sense of proportion and suitability, his refinement of detail, and careful attention to finish (which unfortunately cannot be said of all Brazilian work). He is the architect of the huge University City going up outside Rio, now long delayed for lack of government funds. Those buildings already completed are admirable, and this enormous work will undoubtedly be Moreira's masterpiece. Affonso Reidy has always been interested in the sociological side of architecture; among his other such designs is the large working-class development of Pedregulho, with its own school and playgrounds, fitted to the contours of a high hill in the suburbs of Rio. He is also the architect of the new Museum of Modern Art. Sérgio Bernardes is perhaps the most imaginative of all; his style changes from building to building; he loves the spectacular, new materials, "tricks," and, at their best, his buildings—or bridges or pavilions,—have an unmistakable gaiety and bravura.

There are, of course, others; and all the better-known architects have apprentices working with them, young men from Europe, the United States, Japan, even refugees from Communist China. The architects, as a group, seem to be the freest, happiest, and least provincial people in the country; they never lack for commissions, and in spite of all the ups and downs of government and real estate, their art flourishes.

They have disadvantages, of course. Because of the backwardness of Brazil's steel industry, steel-girder construction is rarely used; even the highest buildings are of reinforced concrete. Until quite recently there was very little standardization of parts, which made construction expensive and slow. Such parts as are standardized, roofing materials, ceramics, etc., are often not quite standardized enough—the quality is uneven, or the colors or finishes are not permanent. This combined with economic problems is the real explanation of what Henry-Russell Hitchcock called Brazil's "fantastic disregard for upkeep."

But building in Brazil has many advantages that foreigners are not apt to realize and that may partly account for its fine tradition of solid, beautiful buildings over the centuries. Things are simplified in many ways: there are no earthquakes or hurricanes; there need be no heating, no screens, not much insulation. Many old houses still have no glass in their windows, just shutters to be barred at night. And though we think of the tropics as constantly swarming with insects, it is possible, in most of Brazil, to sit in the evenings the year round with open windows. Seasonal swarms of moths or termites, wandering fire-flies, bother no one, and a burning spiral joss-stick (called SLEEP WELL) keeps away mosquitoes . . .

The architect is spared our impedimenta of cellars, complicated window-frames and heating systems. He also has a much freer building code and can put up buildings that in stricter countries would be considered dangerous, or not allowed because of zoning laws. On the other hand, endless wild real-estate speculation hampers him, particularly in the cities, where building lots are too expensive for even the wealthy to have "yards," and town houses are crowded together, cutting off each other's views and breezes.

Copacabana Beach is the outstanding example of this unrestricted land speculation. A solid frieze of apartment-houses now cuts off every breath of air from the ocean so that only the privileged few along the front can keep cool; the rest of the huge suburb, really a city in itself, swelters between the wall of buildings on one side and the mountains on the other—and this disastrous lack of planning is being repeated all over Brazil.

Along with the architects, special mention should be made of the landscape-gardener and botanist Roberto Burle Marx. Like too many Brazilian specialists, he is better known outside his own country than in it; many people consider him the greatest landscape-gardener since André Le Nôtre. Until Burle Marx, the average public (or large private) garden in the tropics, or sub-tropics, was an inappropriate, sun-yellowed imitation of the Tuileries. He has changed this by introducing, for the first time, the wealth of native plants and trees in all their exotic colors, shapes, and textures; pools, cascades or falling sheets of water; and real rocks, instead of insipid or melodramatic statuary. For oil-rich Caracas, he is making a public garden bigger than Central Park in New York; and he is also working on public projects in Brazil on a smaller scale. One of his innovations is the use of two varieties of grass for lawns, two shades of green in geometric designs. Brazil's mosaic sidewalks are famous, particularly those of Copacabana Beach, laid out in black and white waves parallel to the ocean waves. This pattern was copied from the mosaics of Lisbon which commemorate the great earthquake of 1755 and its subsequent tidal wave. In one new garden Burle Marx has repeated this same wave pattern in lighter and darker grasses, a beautiful way of using one of the world's simplest decorative materials.

Although Brazil did not evolve a distinctive building style (as New England did, for example), its tradition was ancient and honorable and is still alive. One looks out of a sky-scraper apartment-house and sees a family at work building its own house, of mud-and-twigs or mud-and-rubble, with a thatch of straw or grass, according to a model thousands of years old, old long before Brazil was discovered. These huts and houses, little stores and bars, identical all over the country, could not be simpler or poorer, and yet with their white-wash (or pink or blue wash), their heavy shutters and half-doors, their effect is very pleasing. Along the Amazon the houses are more apt to be woven of palm leaves, Indian style, and resemble beautiful basket work. Even the *favelas* have a melancholy and horrible beauty. Built of old boards, tin cans, bamboo, sacks, any material that comes to hand, they are light and graceful, piled against the hill sides like birds' nests, painted in faded colors, and festooned with steps, ladders, potted plants, and the inevitable bird-cages.

The big old *fazenda* houses grew directly from the classical mud-and-twig huts, merely larger-scale, with thicker walls to keep out the heat and the same thatch roofs, later tile. They are not elegant; there are no halls and the rooms open one into another. There are the dark interior bedrooms where the young virgins of the family led their dreary lives. There is also a chapel and frequently a bedroom and sacristy for a resident padre. And always a room for guests, to one side of the porch, perhaps with the lock on the outside,—for although hospitality was obligatory, it was just as well to be cautious. The town houses are the same, only narrower and higher. But the plain facades, stone trims, and long concave sloping roofs (an Oriental effect, derived from Portuguese Macao) are appealing, and also the (again from Macao) ornamented ridge tiles and drain pipes carried out like trumpets above the narrow sidewalks.

By the 16th century Portugal had been de-forested and was a stone building country, and apparently it didn't occur to early arrivals in Brazil to use wood. The churches were like the houses, and at first carved stone was imported for their facades; later good native stone-cutting emerged. The smallest, earliest churches have paved squares in front for occasions when the congregation was too big to get into the church itself; sometimes these became roofed porches. The Brazilian Jesuit style flowered in the 17th and 18th centuries, and hundreds of beautiful, modest or magnificent, churches were built: Belém, Recife, Fortaleza, Bahia, Rio, São Paulo, and, slightly later, in the last fling of the Jesuit style, the churches of Minas Gerais. There are thirteen in Ouro Prêto alone and all the half-deserted towns of Minas attest to the former wealth and devoutness of the Mineiros.

Unlike the baroque or churrigueresque of Spanish America, the buildings are fundamentally simple and solid, even severe, and over-laid with decoration that grows thicker through the 18th century, with more twisted volutes, more delicate bell towers, and more fanciful windows. The slaves built churches of their own and since the Rosary was always an object of their special devotion the church of "Our Lady of the Rosary" is the high church—often the largest and most magnificent of all,—an odd side-light on the institution of slavery in Brazil.

Most of the art and architecture of this period is as anonymous as that of the middle ages, but two master-sculptors, both mulattoes, are known by name. Master Valentim da Fonseca studied in Europe, and when he returned he was employed by the Viceroy in Rio. He helped lay out the old *Passeio Público* (now adjoining a section of the city called, for obvious reasons, *Cinelândia*). Most of his work has vanished and the park is sadly diminished, but the pair of wonderful bronze alligators still there are by "Mestre Valentim." The other sculptor is known, even outside Brazil, as Aleijadinho, "The Little Cripple," Antônio Francisco Lisboa (1730–1814), the son of an architect and a Negro woman. It is believed that he was a leper, at least he lost the use of his hands; but he continued to work with tools strapped to his wrists. At the same time the Inconfidentes were dreaming of independence and producing their imitative Arcadian poetry in Ouro Prêto, Aleijadinho was producing his much greater and more original, although also belated, art. Designs for churches, wood-carving, stone-carving,—so many works are attributed to Aleijadinho that one becomes sceptical,—nevertheless, his distinctive style can be traced all through Minas. His favorite material was the gray-green soapstone of the region, soft to cut but turning harder with exposure. (It is still much used for pots and pans. According to the Mineiros, nothing is as good as a soapstone pot for cooking the daily rice.) His last and most famous work is at Congonhas do Campo, the Twelve Prophets in front of the church of Bom Jesus de Matosinhos. Crude, but powerful and dramatic, they gesticulate against the white church with its bright blue doors, and against the sweep of bare ore-filled hills.

As in Portugal, the *azulejos*, blue and white tiles, played a great part in the decoration of churches, and sometimes in the houses of the rich. Not always confined to blue and white, sometimes in browns, yellows, and pinks, whole house-fronts were covered with them, particularly in the northern towns. This material has been revised in contemporary Brazilian architecture, and although it is not always used very tastefully, it is one solution for the serious problem of weathering in a tropical climate.

Brazil's appreciation of its architectural heritage came late. Many churches were lost, beginning with those abandoned after the raids of the *bandeirantes*, and again after the expulsion of the Jesuits. Later, churches were sometimes deliberately torn down for their materials or to make way for wider streets. 1936 when the "modern" building boom began, was a year of drastic demolition, but it was also the year in which SPHAN was set up, the *Serviço do Patrimônio Histórico e Artístico Nacional*, to try to save as many as possible of the historical buildings of Brazil. This service has been directed by one man ever since, Dr. Rodrigo Melo Franco de Andrade, and his modesty and scholarship, and his absolute devotion to an almost hopeless task, have been courageous and admirable. There is little money available for such projects, and the people are indifferent, ignorant, and, as everywhere, resentful of interference with property. It is only too natural for the inhabitants of a remote village to prefer a new filling station to an 18th-century fountain.

There was one good architect in the French Commission invited to Brazil by João I, Grandjean de Montigny, the first professor of architecture at the Imperial Academy. Most of his buildings, in French neo-classical style, have been destroyed, but his influence can be seen in many 19th-century buildings. The large dignified early 19th-century French-style houses have sunk through the *pension* level to that of slums; picturesque and wretched, sheltering innumerable families, they are known as "pigs' heads,"—living quarters one step higher than the shacks of the *favelas*.

From de Montigny's delicately-balanced and well-proportioned style, Brazil went almost directly into the hideous neo-baroque public-building style so common everywhere in the world that it goes almost unnoticed. Art Nouveau also hit Brazil, but a rather glancing blow. And then around the early part of the 20th century the very rich started leaving their *fazendas* and building themselves town houses to please their always independent fancies, from Norman Chateau to Gothic Cathedral to Turkish Bath, often adorned with copies of Roman copies of Greek statues. One famous dark and crenellated Gothic mansion in Rio is fondly known as "the rotten tooth." It is to be hoped that some of these interesting monstrosities will be allowed to survive and not all quite cleared away in the eagerness for "Order and Progress."

Until the present century there is not much to be said about painting in Brazil. Mauritzstad had its Frans Post, who did fresh and still familiar-looking landscapes while in Brazil, then spent long years in Europe painting imitations of them. With the French Comissions the illustrators of *genre* scenes began to arrive: Debret, Rugendas, Ribeirolles, later Ender, who have given us volumes of fascinating detailed studies of slaves, costumes, street scenes, and buildings of the 19th century. Some of the church-painting that has survived is a fairly high quality, but of interest only to the specialist. But 19th-century easel painting is a dreary waste of realistic-romantic *bandei-*

rantes, slave-girls, court functions, and landscapes that look more like France or England than Brazil. It is not until the appearance of painters such as Emiliano di Cavalcanti and Candido Portinari that Brazilian painting can be said to have any life of its own.

On first arriving in Brazil, a stranger—if he is at all familiar with them—is struck by how true to Brazilian scenery are Portinari's early pictures: the round, almost conical green hills, the Negro women carrying white bundles on their heads, like ants with their eggs, the children playing *futebol,* the dry, broken graveyards—even details like kites, balloons, and the way the ever-present umbrella is worn hanging from the back of the collar—all are in Portinari's early work.

At present the abstract movement is triumphant, along with a depressingly out-of-date importation called "Concretismo." (This has also been taken up by some of the younger poets, who produce poems reminiscent of Eugene Jolas and *transition* magazine of the '20s in Paris. The Japanese, notably Manabu Mabe, have made contributions to the abstract movement, but more in their traditional calligraphic style than in that of "action" painters of the west.) The best Brazilian work at the moment seems to be in black-and-white. There are at least half a dozen good engravers, wood-cutters, and lithographers; Feyga Ostrawer, Roberto Delamonica, Edith Berhing, Anna Lyticia; typographers and painters like Aloisio Magalhães.

The São Paulo Biennial, started in 1951 by Francisco Matarazzo, has become an institution like the Biennial of Venice. Although one may have one's doubts about the desirability of bringing together over four thousand works of art at one time, it has undoubtedly greatly stimulated Brazilian painting with its many prizes, travelling scholarships, and opportunities for those who have to stay at home to see at first hand, for the first time, what is being done in the rest of the world. There is a real painting "boom" in Brazil at present; prices are soaring, collectors collecting, and new galleries are opening up every few weeks, it seems, in all the larger cities.

Brazilian "formal" or "sophisticated" music—it is hard to know exactly what term to use—is a complex subject in spite of its comparatively small body of work. There are Indian, African (and several different African), and Portuguese influences at work directly, and indirectly in the amazing variety of the folk-music. The music-loving Braganzas had their court composers and performers; the Jesuits their sacred operas and processional music from which many of the still-living folk-forms were derived. Quite recently a large body of late-baroque church-music has been discovered in Minas and is being transcribed and recorded, and undoubtedly much more material remains to be discovered and will help to fill in the long silences in Brazilian musical history.

The one big name in 19th-century music is Carlos Gomes, who was befriended all his life by Dom Pedro II. Unfortunately, his European training is now thought to have spoiled whatever native gifts he had. His most famous opera, *The Guarani,* based on the highly romantic novel by José de Alencar about a noble Guarani Indian, had a considerable success in 1870, although it has since been cruelly called "Meyerbeer's best work." The ballroom of the great semi-abandoned Manaos Opera House is decorated with scenes from *The Guarani,* and *bife-stek Carlos Gomes* still figures on the menus of Manaos restaurants.

The best contemporary composer is Heitor Villa-Lobos (1887–1959). He was melodic, prolific, and fluent, if not over-fluent, and made full use of the richness of Brazilian sources (Portuguese, African, Indian, and popular music); his *Bachianas* and *Ciclo Brasileiro* are well-known outside Brazil. Villa-Lobos also put together a musical textbook for use in schools (using as examples old songs and singing games), the *Guia Practica,* which is considered a model of what such books should be.

The "poet" is a special figure in Brazil, not at all like the unkown, unread figure of the same name in the United States. There has long been a tradition in Latin countries, old world and new, of poets in the Ministries of Foreign Affairs, vice-consuls, consuls, or ambassadors. In Brazil the word "poet" is actually a term of endearment. A man will fondly address a friend who may be an engineer or a politician as "my poet." Perhaps this is a relic of the days when all educated men wrote poetry; certainly writing poetry is still commoner here than with us. But in spite of this fondness for the *idea* of the poet as a man of special charm and privilege, unless employed in Foreign Affairs, he has, professionally, an even harder time of it than in the United States. Writing is very poorly paid and there are none of the fellowships and prizes, and a mere handful, compared to the thousands, of academic jobs that make life possible for both poets and prose writers in the United States. The writer has to be a doctor, lawyer, engineer, or professional journalist; journalism takes the place that teaching does in the United States, and with often just as deadening effect. There is a lack of good magazines and reviews. Every newspaper has its literary page, weekly, sometimes even daily, and it is there that one has to search for the good new poem, the original short story or article, half-lost among the endless warmed-over discussions of Baudelaire or Valéry, of

Thomas Aquinas or G. K. Chesterton, and translations of Graham Greene or Mauriac.

The Portuguese language itself is a barrier between Brazilian writers and the public they deserve. For most Americans who study Spanish rarely study Portuguese. More translation can remedy this situation for prose, but poetry is fairly impervious to translations and it is a pity that we remain almost totally ignorant of such fine contemporary poets as Manuel Bandeira (the father-figure of Brazilian poetry), Carlos Drummond de Andrade, Cecilia Meireles, Jorge de Lima, Vinicius de Moraes (who wrote the libretto for the opera that was made into the succesful movie *BLACK ORPHEUS*), João Cabral de Melo Neto—probably the best of the generation after Bandeira, who has written poems of great feeling about the *"flagellados"* ("beaten ones") of the north-east.

In Brazil someone who has been brought up a Catholic, in the usual way, left the church, and then returned to it again, is called a "convert." In somewhat the same sense of conversion, Brazil is now re-discovering the values of its earlier provincial, romantic, and humorous literature, just as we have been re-assessing our Hawthornes and Twains, although on nothing like our stupendous and costly scale. Even allowing for the inevitable differences, almost all Brazilian literature is sympathetic to us: one colonial understands another. With all its naïveté, religiosity (sermons and more sermons), and sentimentality,—it has many of the characteristics of the literature of our own first three hundred years. And as American literature has been divided into "paleface" and "redskin," so can Brazilian be divided roughly, in the same way, into that of the city and that of the country, those who looked to Europe, tradition, and "correctness," and those who were drawn to the wilderness, the Indian, the regional, and felt that only new forms could be used for the experience of a new country. Sometimes, as our own literature, the two strains are oddly woven together.

The poets of the "Inconfidentes" sang of cupids and swans and such un-Brazilian fauna. Yet here are a few lines from the best of them, Thomas Antônio Gonzaga, that Manuel Bandeira quotes in his *Anthology of Brazilian Poets of the Romantic Phase*. Gonzaga is addressing his great love, Marília de Dirceu:

> "You shall not see the skillful Negro
> Separate the heavy emery from the course sand,
> And the nuggets of gold already shining
> In the bottom of the *bateia*.

You shall not see the virgin forest destroyed,
 Nor the burning of the still green underbrush
To fertilize the ground with ashes,
   Nor the seeds being sown in the furrows.

You shall not see them rolling the black packets
Of dry leaves of fragrant tobacco,
Nor pressing out the sweet juice of the cane
   Between the cog-wheels . . ."

This is a rare moment of realism and accuracy, as evocative of rural Brazil today as when it was written. A *bateia* is the wooden bowl used for panning gold. It is still used, as is the destructive system of slash-and-burn farming. Tobacco, *fumo*, is still sold in long black ropes in the markets, and sugar cane juice, rather like a watery, grassy, molasses, is still a popular drink.

The two outstanding characteristics of the Brazilian romantic poets are their *saudades* and their anti-slavery sentiments. The fact that they were all sent to Coimbra to be educated probably has something to do with the former. They missed the easy, indulged life of young Brazilian gentlemen and suffered from homesickness as acutely as Brazilian students seem to do now at Boston "Tech" or the Sorbonne or Heidelberg. Gonçalves Dias (1823–1864), one of the greatest of the romantics, is responsible for the "Exiles Song," the "My Country 'Tis of Thee" of Brazil.

"My country has palm-trees
   Where the *sabiá* sings.
The birds don't warble here
   The way they do there . . ."

And Casimiro de Abreu (1839–1860) repeats:

"If I must die in the flower of my youth,
   My God, let it not be now!
I want to hear the *sabiá* sing
   In the evening, in the orange tree! . . ." etc.

The *sabiá*, a rather fat, brown thrush, is, precisely, to Brazilian poetry what the nightingale is to English poetry. Carlos Gomes uses its song in the interlude of his opera *THE SLAVE*; Brazilian literature is full of *sabiás*.

Castro Alves (1847–1871) was the most famous Abolitionist poet. His long dramatic poem, "THE SLAVE SHIP," was given in a form of group-

recitation last year, in Rio and São Paulo, and stood the test very successfully; even lines such as:

> "Exists a people whose banner serves
> To hide such infamy and cowardice! . . .
> My God, My God, what a flag is this . . . ?"

have recovered significance and dignity, a hundred years later.

Brazil's "*modernismo*" movement began with the now-famous "Week of
Modern Art" in the Municipal Theatre of São Paulo, in 1922. Beginning
with the influence of the Dadaists and Surrealists, it, too, soon divided
between the European-minded and the Indigenous-minded. There was
even a small movement within it that called itself *Cannibals* in their desire
to be native Brazilians and nothing else, and issued the "Anthropophagite
Manifesto." The name of Mário de Andrade cannot be omitted—starting
as a poet of the "modernismos" he became one of the greatest forces in
the Brazilian artistic renaissance. In music, folk art, poetry, and prose—
almost everything in contemporary Brazilian artistic life owes a great debt
to Mário de Andrade, and although he died in 1945 his name is mentioned constantly.

The two greatest personalities in Brazilian literature are prose writers,
and both are fortunately available, at least in part, in English. The first,
Joaquim Maria Machado de Assis (1839–1908), is the greatest writer the
South American continent has produced; some critics think the greatest
of both American continents, ranking him with our own Henry James.
Child of a poor Negro house painter and a Portuguese woman, born in
Rio on one of the *morros*, or hills now covered by the *favelas*, he worked as
typographer and journalist, married a middle-class Portuguese woman,
and published book after book of poems, stories, and novels. He grew famous, was highly respected and respectable, and in 1896 founded the
Brazilian Academy of Letters, whose president he was until he died. He is
a deeply pessimistic, sceptical, reserved writer; there is little of the Latin
rhetoric and nothing of its romaticism about his style. His best works are
Posthumous Memoirs of Brás Cubas (published in English under the title of
The Diary of a Small Winner), *Dom Casmurro*, *Quincas Borba*, and some of the
tales. Although the period is always the late Empire, and the setting Rio de
Janeiro, Machado de Assis's world is universal and his characters are real—
as Tolstoy's St. Petersburg is universal and Natasha not just a Russian girl.

The other great prose-writer, Euclides da Cunha (1866–1909), is the
author of one of the world's strangest books, *Os Sertões* (published in En-

glish as *Rebellion in the Backlands*). Da Cunha was a military engineer; his book is an account of a military expedition made in 1896 against a religious fanatic, Antônio Conselheiro, "The Counselor," who had fortified himself and all his followers in the little town of Canudos, far in the interior of the State of Bahia. They managed to hold out there for a year against repeated attacks by Brazilian regiments. The book is partly accounts of futile military manoeuvres, dry reports of suffering and atrocities (which remind one of Hemingway's famous retreat), and partly a long geographical rhapsody. The whole first half, although not a novel, does for the backlands what James Joyce's *Ulysses* does for the city of Dublin. Anyone who wants to get the feel of Brazilian life and landscape at their grandiose and disparate best and worst should read *Rebellion in the Backlands*. It is reminiscent of one of the Brazilian churches—solidly, almost crudely planned, but covered with a profusion of rich ornamentation and extraneous life, even to the point of being repellent.

It is perfectly true that in Brazil culture and the arts are more respected than in our own industrialized and middle-class country. Perhaps this is due not so much to European tradition as Brazilians like to think, as it is to the fact that, as in government, Brazil is one big family. In spite of examples of the democracy of the arts,—Aleijadinho, Machado de Assis, Mário de Andrade, and Portinari—most writers and artists come from the small educated, inter-related upper-class; in various degrees they are all cousins, and a mutual admiration society is apt to result. As in government, feuds become family quarrels; first names are used—even in serious critical articles; everything is taken too personally, and the atmosphere is curiously "feminine."

Although in this way they are spared the abrupt and cruel fluctuations of reputation that our artists suffer from, they nevertheless pay for the lack of serious criticism and competition. One sometimes feels that a 20th-century Brazilian Samuel Johnson, with all his dogmatism, might do wonders for Brazilian arts,—but maybe that is as bad as saying that Latin American countries *need* dictators.

There are two sayings, Anglo-Saxon and Brazilian, that sound a little alike but have very different meanings. They illustrate very well our different points of view on the career of the artist. We say, puritanically: "He has made his bed and must lie in it." Brazilians say, soothingly: *Cria fama e deita-te na cama.* "Create a reputation and stay in bed." Too many genuine talents seem to take to their beds too early,—or to their hammocks. (A favorite way for Brazilian writers to have their pictures taken is pleasantly supine, in a fringed hammock.)

Chapter 8
Groups and Individuals

There is one anecdote Brazilians never tire of telling to illustrate their attitude towards race-relations. When some of the ladies at Pedro II's court refused to dance with the famous Negro engineer André Rebouças, Princess Isabel herself crossed the room and asked him to dance with her. It is a nice story, and true; and it is also true that Pedro II employed several Negroes and mulattoes in high positions and that the devoted Rebouças followed him into exile and eventually died in poverty. Unfortunately this story does not necessarily prove racial tolerance; Princess Isabel was a true princess and had been well brought-up,—*bem educada*, as they say.

There is a better story. In 1950 Katherine Dunham was turned away from one of the big hotels in São Paulo with the excuse that there were no vacant rooms. Overnight this became a national scandal, and within days a law was passed against any discrimination whatsoever in the future. The fact that such a law had never even been thought of up until then tells almost all one needs to know about Brazil's attitude towards the Negro. (The hotel was supposed to have acted as it did out of deference to the prejudices of its North American clientele.)

Brazilians are proud of their fine record in race-relations. Rather, their attitude can be best described by saying that the upper-class Brazilian is usually proud of his racial tolerance, while the lower-class Brazilian is not aware of his; he just practises it. The occasional anti-Negro, or *racista* (and this applies equally well to the occasional anti-semite), usually proves to be one of two types: the unthinking member of "society" who has got into anti-Negro or anti-Jewish "society" in his travels, and has lost his native Brazilian tolerance, or sadder still—the European emigrant who comes to Brazil having suffered in his own country because of his race or poverty, and (probably unaccustomed to Negroes, anyway) despises and is rude to them.

The old upper-class looks down on the new middle-class, because of its vulgarity or bad manners, much more than on the Negroes or mulattoes. Part of this is nostalgia for the days when there was no middle-class, part economic pressure, and part old-fashioned snobbishness. One often feels sorry for the small but growing middle-class; surely old-fashioned Brazil should have more patience with it. The still-simple class-divisions and types seem 19th century,—almost Dickensian, if a writer so remote from everything Brazilian can be mentioned in connection with Brazil.

A young Jewish businessman, intelligent, but not well-read or well-travelled, was astounded when, planning his first trip to the United States, he was warned about "restricted" hotels. The idea of being discriminated against had never occurred to him. Also,—and this illustrates one of Brazil's great weaknesses, its provincialism, built up over long centuries of remoteness from Europe—(it took [. . .] days in a sailing vessel to get to Europe from Brazil, as compared with [. . .] days from North America)—this same young Jew was equally astounded to be told that the sufferings of the Jews under Hitler had anything to do with *him*, he had never realized there was such a thing as racial solidarity.

It is true that the Negro or mulatto is a "second-class citizen" rarely in important positions or even good jobs, and almost always poor. But since most of the population is in exactly the same situation and suffers the same deprivations, his sufferings do not mark him out as very different from anyone else. Negroes want to be "light," *claro*, have "good" (straight) hair, and "good" (not flat) noses. They are sometimes treated with the condescending, indulgent humor found in the southern U.S.—& there are hundreds of Negro myths—but again it is not so very different from the way lower-class whites are treated. They have equal opportunity and education, as far as it goes, which is usually not very far as yet; and in the arts. Aleijadinho, Machado de Assis, Mário de Andrade—all were mulattoes. After Machado de Assis's death a friend called on his widow. The Senhora Machado de Assis glanced at her husband's photograph on the table and made her only recorded comment on the fact that she, a white woman, had married a mulatto. "What a pity he was so dark," she said.

The widespread poverty, backwardness, ignorance, and suffering in Brazil are tragic; for millions, life is hungry and dirty, short and cruel. And yet—to a South African or a North American or anyone who has lived in a colonial country,—to be able to hear a black cook call her small, elderly, white mistress *minha negrinha* (my little nigger) as a term of affection, comes as a revelation,—a breath of fresh air at last.

It was not planned; it just happened. But Brazil now realizes that her racial situation is one of her greatest assets. Racial mixtures can be seen all over the country. In the north, in the Amazon region, Portuguese and Indian have produced the *caboclo*, small, well-built, straight noses, bright eyes—a very attractive physical type. The northeast, after generations of poor diet, has produced the *cabeça-chata*, or "flat-head," who is also apt to be small, somewhat rickety, with thin arms and legs and a large head, but quick, and certainly prolific. In the south under better living conditions and with little or no Negro admixture, the type is more Portuguese, sometimes with German blood, bigger, fairer, with clear skin, calmer—but pugnacious, even inclined to violence. It is in and around the big cities of Rio and São Paulo that one gets every racial type mixed together, types that have lost their racial clarity along with their former agricultural skills and beautiful backlands manners. A man in Goiás will know the name and habits of every beast and bird around him; but the people of regions that have fallen into agricultural decay are sickly-looking bad farmers, to whom every insect is only a *bicho*, or every tree is the "five-leaf," and all are subject to destruction. The importance of nutrition in Brazil is shown by the fact that the richer and older the family, the taller and bigger-boned they are apt to be. Sometimes their servants from the "north" or the "interior" appear almost like dwarfs beside them.

The Portuguese have naturally been the largest group of immigrants, and they still come in at the rate of 15,000 a year. They are mostly laborers and farmers, servants or gardeners. Also, certain ancient city trades are theirs: old-newspaper-and-bottle-dealing and knife grinding. In the cities, a great deal of freight is pushed about on hand-carts, and this too is the prerogative of the Portuguese. The actual official name for these hand-cart men is "Donkies without Tails." Their usual costume is wooden clogs, extra wide trousers, undershirts, and large floppy berets, and their faces are handsome, simple and stolid, compared to the often ugly, but subtle and mobile faces of Brazilians of several generations' standing. In endless jokes the Portuguese appears as absurdly literal-minded and naive. In the 19th- and early 20th-century Brazilian theatre, he was always represented as a loudly-dressed bumpkin, given to big gold watches and heavy watch chains. In Portugal on the stage at the same time, the Brazilian was always represented as a loudly-dressed bumpkin, given to big gold watches, etc., etc.

After the abolition of slavery, European immigrants started to arrive in large numbers, going mostly to the States of São Paulo, Paraná, Santa Catarina, and Rio Grande do Sul. Germans, Italians, and after 1908, Japanese all poured in. There are whole towns and villages of Germans in the south of Brazil. At present there are probably about half a million Japanese in the country, who are contributing enormously to the improvement of agriculture, particularly to fruit-growing, in the southern states. São Paulo has Japanese grocery stores, bookshops and even Geisha girls. The 6 million Italians have adapted themselves best of all, probably because the climate and working conditions are not unlike those of Italy, and Portuguese is easy for them to learn.

The founder and hero of the Indian Protection Service was General Cândido Mariano Rondon (1865–1958). He came from Cuiabá, capital of the State of Mato Grosso, and was himself part Indian. In 1907 as a young captain, he was given the task of building a telgraph network to link Mato Grosso with Amazonas and with the outside world. This meant exploring thousands of square miles of wilderness for the first time. Rondon's story is full of heroism and self-sacrifice. He believed that the Indians should and could be "pacified," as opposed to one popular opinion of the day which was all for exterminating them. The motto he gave the Indian Service was "let yourself be killed if necesaary, but never kill," and many of his lieutenants, soldiers, and workers did just that. He tried never to interfere with the Indians' way of life. There are still shameful stories of land-greedy men who cheat or murder the Indians, and sad "publicity stunts" involving them, but Rondon set a high standard of behaviour towards primitive men. The territory of Rondônia (larger than the whole of France) is named for him.

Just before the First World War Theodore Roosevelt went on a hunting and exploring expedition with Rondon. (He found, sad to relate, that there was just as good game in South America as any ever shot in Africa.) He pays high tribute to Rondon in his book "Through the Brazilian Wilderness," which probably brought Brazil to the attention of the average American for the first time since Dom Pedro II's visit to the Philadelphia Centennial Exposition. Rondon discovered fifteen major rivers, one named for Roosevelt, built over fifteen thousand miles of telegraph lines, and discovered many previously unknown tribes of Indians.

But the Indians continue to be a problem. Tribes that have never seen "civilization" are still turning up, while those that have seen it are gradually dying off in disease and degradation. Sometimes the problem is a dangerous one. As this was written, the body of a young English explorer was found, pierced by seven arrows of the Caiapós'. The isolated rubber-collector or cattle-raiser of Mato Grosso or Pará, living in the atomic age, still has more to fear from arrows or blow-pipes than from bombs.

One night on board a ship going down the muddy Amazon a young woman doctor was telling stories. She had been fifteen years with the S.E.S.P., the Serviço Especial de Saúde Pública, founded jointly by the

United States and Brazil in 1942, and soon to be taken over completely by Brazil. She was twenty-three years old when she entered the S.E.S.P.; she had gone up to Santarém, then another hundred miles or so by launch, and landed with her instruments and a few books at a small village on the Rio Tapajós. The first night a group of wild, ragged men asked her to make out the death certificate of a fellow-villager whose body had just been found in the river: death by drowning. She asked to be left alone with the body and found that, although it had been in the water for some time, the man had died of a stab in the back. Quite alone, at night, knowing that the murderer or murderers must be in the threatening group of men, she had refused to sign the death warrant and ordered someone to go for the nearest police representative—half a day's trip by motor boat,—she loved her work. She thought that the Indian Protection and the S.E.S.P. were the two best-run services in Brazil.

Small, fat, animated, dark, probably with Indian blood, she was a "modern" Brazilian woman. There are not many like this Amazonian doctor, but there are a few and the numbers are increasing.

Brazil is a man's country. The double standard could scarcely be more so; little boys are spoilt, according to Anglo-Saxon notion; everything in the home revolves around the head of the house or the son of the family, often referred to simply as "the man." The male, o macho, is the all-important, all-admired, principal. Women are: "the mother of my children," "the bearer of my name," and "religion is for Women."

But nothing is that simple. Even if poor women trail behind the men, carrying the baby in their arms and the water-jug on their heads, even if the Women's Pages of the papers are of an unbelievable vapidity, and even if men stay in one room at parties talking of politics & real estate and women stay in another babbling about servants and babies, things have changed a great deal since the first Portuguese carried off the Indian girls. In the old days women were scarce and were kept in harem-like seclusion, peering out at the city streets through muxarabis, or in the dark inner rooms of the old farm houses. For three hundred years they were rarely taught to read or write, and they were married off as young as twelve to neighbours, cousins, even to uncles. All the early travellers' accounts speak of the timidity of Brazilian women and how rarely they were seen by male guests. They grew white and fat in the darkened rooms, rarely walking, swaying in hammocks, or sitting cross-legged on pillows, while their husbands, according to most accounts, made merry in the slave quarters. After several generations of that sort of life, often the men had not much enterprise, and the wife would, in reality, run the sugar- or coffee-plantation, sitting on her pillows, being fanned, sewing, but issuing a stream of orders all day long.

It is only in the last hundred years that women have been educated in Brazil, and now lower-class girls even more than boys are lucky if they get a year or two of school. Upper-class girls go to convent schools, some good, some bad. But one cannot help but feel that the nuns have too often encouraged complacency and snobbery, not *noblesse oblige*. In spite of general kindliness, too many upper-class women still treat their servants or social inferiors in the old 18th-century way and let their children grow up doing the same thing.

Since women were illiterate there were naturally no women writers. We can learn the woman's side of 19th-century life from visitors like Maria Graham or the letters of the many foreign governesses. Some of the talent wasted can be guessed at. *The Diary of "Helena Morley"* (Alice Brant) is an authentic diary kept in Diamantina in the '80s by a young girl, certainly a novelist *manquée*. Women are now prominent in Brazilian letters. Cecilia Meireles is one of Brazil's best poets. Clarice Lispector is a short-story writer and novelist of considerable originality; and there are many others. The best known of all is Rachel de Queiroz, who at the age of eighteen wrote a short, brilliant novel about Ceará, *The '15*, the year of a particularly dreadful drought. She came to Rio, wrote plays and novels, and for many years has had a page in *O Cruzeiro*, the biggest weekly, in which she is consistently and courageously on the right side of political and social causes. During the Vargas dictatorship, when many intellectuals were arrested or exiled, she spent six months in jail, incommunicado. In 1961 President Quadros invited her to be Minister of Education, and later an ambassador. Although she refused both positions, this was the first time in Brazil a woman had been so honored.

Women were admitted to universities in [...]. There are now women in the government, congresswomen, lawyers, doctors, psychoanalysts, and engineers. The head of the Museum of Modern Art in Rio, Carmen Portinho, is an engineer, and the graceful viaduct of Canoas near Rio is the work of another woman engineer, Bertha Leitchic. We have seen how active women are in the arts. The pianist Guiomar Novaes has long been world-famous.

Special credit should be given to hundreds of anonymous Brazilian *normalistas*,—the young girls who start out every year as school-teachers, often in remote villages, in one-roomed school-houses, under heart breaking conditions.

But marriage at seventeen or eighteen and the grim race of procreation are the lot of even the rich and educated. Women themselves are against introducing divorce. Security for herself and her children is the most important thing in life.

Although women got the vote in Brazil in 1934, they still do not have full legal rights. They usually think as their husbands do and accept their husbands' infidelity as a matter of course. Some will even insist that they are happier than American women,—but that is usually after a visit to the United States, where they have seen how American women "do their own work," take care of their own children, or support themselves, and appear rushed and harassed.

Besides careers for women, another new development in Brazil is sports. Only thirty years ago, *futebol* ("soccer") was a strictly amateur affair, played for fun by the upper-class. Now like baseball in the United States, it is a big business, with high salaries, the buying and selling of players, and popular national heroes. Every newspaper devotes at least a page to it everyday. In 1958 Brazil was soccer champion of the world. (It is interesting to note that each player on the European tour was alloted thirty pounds of black beans.) The players are all shades, from white to jet black, graceful, nervous and incredibly quick. For years they lacked team play or cooperation.

[Popular heroes—"The Black Diamond," "Pelé," story from Carolina Jesus here. In 1958 the basketball champions of the year. Maria Ester. Bruno Hermanny.]

In the country on Sundays, the population of every small village will be out watching the local *futebol* teams. The big pale-green fields will be edged with people in their Sunday best, carrying babies, carrying umbrellas against the sun. The *Kibon* ("Eskimo Pie") man with his yellow wagon, a spun-sugar wagon (home-made, mounted on a bicycle); buzzards and delicate tissue paper kites hang overhead, and the players in their brilliantly striped jerseys and brief shorts are running, running.

It is also a common sight to see the local washerwoman's line hung with the jerseys of one team, sweaters striped like wasps, a cheerful display, sometimes against the background of a city dump, with buzzards and paper kites hovering above.

Chapter 9
The Republic

The Empire and the Emperor, Pedro II, were synonymous. The chief cause of the fall of the monarchy was undoubtedly the fear of what would happen when Princess Isabel inherited the throne. The Brazilians were suspicious of her husband, the French prince, Count D'Eu (grandson of King Louis Philippe); he was a "foreigner." Even Princess Isabel's great gesture, the emancipation of the slaves, couldn't calm the increasing anxiety about the "French" rule they were sure would follow the death of the sick and prematurely aged Emperor. This is the explanation of how an empire that had lasted for sixty-five years could fall without protest and without struggle.

But the Republic began as an improvised collaboration of ill-assorted elements: the Positivist "clique," the military group led by Marshal Deodoro, and the great landowners who had been ruined by abolition. (The great number of "Barons" and other titles that appear look strange among the prominent names of the young Republic.) It was a chance collaboration, bound to break up, and it did almost immediately.

The Positivists were the first to disassociate themselves from the new government. "This is not the Republic of our dreams!" they complained. But they left their slogan, "Order and Progress," on the new flag, and other features of the new regime were influenced by Positivist thought. General Deodoro was the next to go. In spite of having proclaimed the new Republic, he was reluctant to give up his position as an old Imperial General; he disagreed with his former accomplices, fought with the already strong opposition movement in the parliament. He attempted a military coup (or *golpe*, as Brazilians call it), dissolved the Assembly, and ended by "renouncing"—the first presidential "renunciation." The Vice President, Marshal Floriano Peixoto, nicknamed "The Iron Marshal" because of his ruthlessness, took over.

His term as president was marked by civil wars and rebellions, two of them very important: the rising of the "Federalists" in Rio Grande do Sul (always the hotbed of rebellion) and the revolt of the Royal Navy, that had never accepted the overthrow of the monarchy and was also jealous of the pre-eminence of the Army in the new government. The "Iron Marshal" stood almost alone but, with the people on his side, emerged victorious from these struggles. The Navy finally joined forces with the south, rebellious admirals with gauchos. In the last bloody battle there, the head of the Navy, Admiral Saldanha da Gama, was killed. Strange to say, Saldanha da Gama is now venerated as the model naval officer—the Brazilian Naval Academy is named for him.

The next president was a civilian from São Paulo, Prudente de Morais, who tried to restore order to the country, divided and exhausted by the struggles of the "Florianistas." It was also a difficult period. There were no longer riots in the cities nor declarations from the discontented military, but a new phenomenon: religious war in its most brutal form. A strange backlands leader, a sort of rustic saint, appeared, and attracted an immense following of religious fanatics in the arid plains of the northeast. This was Antônio Maciel, called "The Counselor" by his disciples. At first his movement had a religious cast: prayers, penances, forgiveness of sins, and mass pilgrimages of the ever-growing group through the vast wastes of the *caatinga*, or scrub-forest lands. Then the Counselor announced his new dogma: the Republic was the rule of the Anti-Christ, and they should fight for the return of the "King"—in other words, Dom Pedro II. A long, tragic struggle began. At the beginning it was thought that a mere police-operation, with small numbers of men, could put an end to the movement. But the Counselor's fanatic followers put up such amazing resistance that the operation assumed almost the proportions of civil war. More and more troops were decimated by the *jagunços* (a name orignally meaning "ruffian," but later used for the inhabitants of the backlands in general), entrenched in their stronghold of Canudos, in the harshest region of the interior of Bahia. Many soldiers and officers were killed—even one general. Alarmed, the government organized a full-scale expedition of war, and Canudos was finally utterly destroyed, with its defenders; there were almost no survivors. Today, a great dam across the Vaza-Barris River has flooded the old bloody battlefield of Canudos. The only remaining monument to the siege is Euclides da Cunha's famous book, *Rebellion in the Backlands*, (one of the [earlier] masterpieces of Brazilian literature), that had its simple beginnings in his reports as a war correspondent.

The next president, Campos Sales, undertook to straighten out the country's chaotic financial situation. Under the first two presidents and during the civil war, the country had entered a period of great disorder. The people complained and made bitter jokes, but tightened their belts. They called President Sales "President Selos" (President Stamps) because of the high taxes (and all the stamps the taxes entailed). However, order was restored, money was stabilized, and a period of prosperity began. This period marked the beginning of the remarkable progress of São Paulo, helped by the wave of European immigration that it had encouraged since the beginning of the century.

But the young Republic had still to produce a body of states-men; and in the mixed group of men, idealistic or resentful, that had provoked Dom Pedro's downfall, there were many quarrels and resignations. So it was natural that when order was restored and the country began to prosper, the men of the old Imperial regime, more gifted and better prepared for the task, came back into power. The newspapers ironically called this new ruling class "the government of the Counselors," since many of them actually had been Counselors under the Empire. The first was the new president, another Paulista, former Counselor Rodrigues Alves, who did much to beautify the city of Rio and improve its sanitation.

Another Counselor, while a famous Republican, was a figure of great importance for half century: Rui Barbosa (1849–1923), one of the great figures in Brazilian history. He had many talents: a powerful orator, a jurist of the highest calibre, a writer of pure and classical Portuguese. He devoted all his talents to the service of democratic government, and he was famous for his refusal to admit anything approaching the dictatorial, and for his defense of the under-dog. Small and thin, with a weak, nasal voice, nevertheless, he was a formidable opponent, equally respected by popular leaders and famous generals. Too many politicians feared to compete with him, or perhaps they feared his intransigence. The whole nation mourned his death. And until today, in political arguments, the man who manages to quote Rui Barbosa to support his opinions is the one who has the last word.

Another figure who emerged during the Empire and then became a tutelary angel of the Repubic was José Maria da Silva Paranhos—Baron of Rio Branco. With the proclamation of the Republic, he went abroad in a minor diplomatic position. There he stayed, until the government called him back to lend his services as technician and scholar in order to settle the long-disputed question of the Argentine boundary. Rio Branco, a great student of history, argued the case so well that he convinced the arbiter (the American President Grover Cleveland) that Brazil was in the right, and the settlement was favorable to Brazil. In honor of President Cleveland, a vast tract of the recovered territory was named *Clevelândia*, the name it bears today.

Other questions of disputed boundaries were given to Rio Branco and also settled with profit and honor for Brazil. The Alves government made him Minister of Foreign Affairs, and succeeding presidents, of no matter what party, kept the irreplaceable Baron in Itamaraty (the Department of

State). When he died, in 1912, his funeral was the greatest the country had ever seen. Every city in Brazil has one of its principal streets named for him (the Fifth Avenue of Rio is the "Avenida Barão do Rio Branco"); one of the "territories" (not yet a state) is named Rio Branco; and even a huge province of Uruguay is named Rio Branco, in honor of the man who settled its frontier.

Another great man of the Empire who also served the Republic, especially in diplomacy, was Joaquim Nabuco, famous as an Abolitionist, later Ambassador to the United States for many years.

With the return of the "Counselors" Brazil entered on a period of great progress; with the slogan of "Civilize Rio" the old city of Dom João VI began to open up avenues and install port facilities. With the help of a team of young technicians, especially the engineer Pereira Passos and the doctor Oswaldo Cruz, the city began to rid itself of its colonial atmosphere. Yellow fever, which had reached Brazil around 1850, had long been the scourge of the city; the Cariocas called it "the patriot" because it seemed to have a preference for foreigners. But it was now eliminated once and for all by a campaign for better sanitation. Compulsory vaccination against small-pox was introduced and even led to riots and bloodshed in the streets. The poor and ignorant were afraid of inoculation, and the remnants of the Positivist intellectuals sided with the masses, saying that compulsory vaccination was an "attack on the physical integrity of the citizen."

This period was the golden age of republicanism in Brazil. The country prospered, the money was sound, and coffee held sway. The presidents abandoned all the parliamentary tradition of the Empire and relied on the so-called "policy of governors" that transformed the Congress into a subsidiary of the Executive power. Under this regime, the big states dominated the smaller states, and two states dominated all the rest: São Paulo and Minas Gerais. The presidency long alternated between men from these two states. Since São Paulo was famous for coffee and Minas Gerais for its dairy products, this political arrangement was popularly called "coffee and milk," *café com leite*, the usual Brazilian breakfast.

It was not until the last period of the First World War, with the wave of social agitation it produced, that Brazil began to become "socially conscious." Reforms were demanded, particularly election reforms, since universal suffrage and with it true democracy were in reality just words.

The troubles began in the barracks; led by a few more ambitious or more politically advanced generals, the young officers became aroused. 1922 was the first centenary of Independence, celebrated with great public festivities, and on the 5th of July of that year the famous death march of the

"18 of Copacabana" took place, the first serious episode in the rebellion. Two years later, also on the 5th of July, revolution broke out in São Paulo. The rebels' chief complaints were that the Republic was becoming bureaucratic; that it still had not got rid of the corrupt politicians who had overthrown the Empire; and that political power was still in the hands of the old bosses in the interior, without taking into account the growing strength of the cities. This was the time of the first labor-agitations in Brazil and the formation of the first groups of the far left, the anarchists. The president was Artur Bernardes from Minas Gerais, rigid and narrow-minded; he demanded that Congress declare a state of siege for his entire term in office. And out of this "second 5th of July" of 1924 grew the movement of rebellion that in 1930 was to upset the "old Republic." The rebellious troops, driven back to Rio Grande do Sul, began one of the most singular movements in the history of Brazilian revolutions: the march of the "Prestes Column."

About 2,000 men, civilians, and soldiers, had refused to surrender to the government when the generals did. They were led by a group of young officers who have all left their marks on modern Brazilian history, but the most important for the moment, since he later bacame leader of the Brazilian Communists, is Luiz Carlos Prestes. They left Rio Grande do Sul, hid out in the forests of the State of Santa Catarina, and reached Mato Grosso. Then, like the 17th-century *bandeirantes*, the column made its way through the interior of Brazil, most of it as yet not even mapped. Prestes led them through the wild northeast, from Piauí to Bahia. It was not an army of aggression; they only defended themselves when attacked. They respected the people they came in contact with, and requisitioned no more than they needed, food and horses, giving receipts for everything they took, to be paid on "the victory of the Revolution." In general, the population received them with sympathy, or at least did not oppose them. Prestes became a legendary figure, and the newspapers gave him the sobriquet of "Knight of Hope." Finally, after almost two years of marching through the hinterlands of Brazil and covering 25,000 kilometres, the column split in two, one part finding political asylum in Bolivia, and the other in Argentina.

All the leaders of the column were to return as victors in 1930. All except Prestes, who during his exile stumbled on Marxism, became a member of the Communist Party, and went to Russia. He appears again as the leader of the pro-Communist movement of 1935, which provided the pretext for setting up the Vargas dictatorship.

In 1930 the president was Washington Luiz, from São Paulo. But instead of keeping to the "coffee and milk" understanding, and letting "milk," or a president from Minas Gerais, follow him, he succeeded in getting another Paulista elected as his successor. The powerful State of Minas naturally resented this tipping of the scales in favor of the rival state and aligned itself with the ever-present rebellious military elements. They won the support of the governor of Rio Grande do Sul, Getúlio Vargas,—a politician until then almost unknown to the rest of the country—and revolted against President Luiz. The "old Republic" had reached the end of its days, and the saying was, it was "ripe to fall." One by one, the state governors were put out by the insurrectionists. The exiled officers became the leaders of the movement, and at first it appeared that the governor of Minas would be able to seize power—the plan all along. But they hadn't counted on the political talents, opportunism, and qualities of leadership of the gaucho Vargas, who very quickly broke with all his early fellow-revolutionaries and became the President of the Provisional Government.

The Vargas dictatorship had arrived. Immediate elections were promised, but Vargas kept putting them off. São Paulo (the richest state in Brazil) was powerless, as well as humiliated by the conquerors, who handed it over to the mercies of the "officers" of the revolution. In 1932, under the awkward slogan of "Constitutionalization," São Paulo got ready to fight. There was talk of secession. The Paulistas took up arms as one man, but the rest of the country did not follow them, & Vargas, now running the army, crushed the "Constitutionalistas."

In the meantime he was having trouble maintaining his dictatorship, and in 1934 he had to permit elections for a new Congress. This Congress voted for a new and very liberal constitution, incorporating most of the [. . .] of the revolutionaries of '22, '24, and '30: secret ballot, female suffrage, and the representation of all classes. This same Congress then appointed Vargas president of the "New Republic," for a term of four years. The liberals & the revolutionary officers had triumphed; everything seemed for the best in the best possible of worlds. But Vargas, the "*caudilho*" of the frontier, did not care for the restrictions the new constitution placed on him and began to show his hand. The Communists promoted a united front movement of all the leftists, under the name of "Alliance of Liberation," and led by Prestes, who had returned from Russia, they succeded in stirring up revolution in Rio and in the northeast. Vargas quickly crushed this revolt, too, this time with great severity.

It was the time of fascist power: Hitler in Germany, Mussolini in Italy, Franco in Spain, and Salazar in Portugal. Vargas allied himself with Brazil's fascist party, the "Integralistas." Protected by the "state of war" he had decreed in order to combat the leftists, he secretly ordered his advisers to draw up a fascist-style constitution (copied, it was said, from that of Poland); he sent advance emissaries to all the states to guarantee the support of the governors, and he sent to jail, *en masse*, as political prisoners, all intellectuals and politicians who carried any weight with the public. On the 10th of November, 1937, in a surprise move, he surrounded the two houses of Congress with troops, closed them, and put his secret constitution into effect. (The people quickly called it the "Polish" one.) Under the name of the "New State," fascism began in Brazil.

The idea of dictatorship was intolerable to the majority of Brazilians; nevertheless, it is true that in spite of the abuses of power, it never took on (at least, not openly) the worst aspects of European fascism. As one commentator said, it was fascism "Brazilian-style," i.e., "fascism with sugar." No public executions, no shootings, no concentration camps. After the first few months most of the political prisoners were released; only a few leaders, condemned by the inquisitorial "Security Tribunal" remained in jail. Other leaders went into exile. The "Integralistas" themselves, who had been ridiculed by Vargas and robbed of all power, revolted; this revolt was also brutally put down.

At the start of World War II Vargas did not conceal his sympathies for the Axis powers, and the first Nazi victories lent support to his attitude. But public opinion, even gagged as it was by the dictatorship, made the most of every opportunity of showing its partiality for the Allies. President Roosevelt, for his part, did all he could to bring Brazil over to the side of the Allies, particularly after Pearl Harbor. Brazil ceded military bases to the Americans; the air-lift was established between Natal and Dakar, by means of which large numbers of American troops and quantities of supplies crossed the ocean. Finally, after the sinking of Brazilian ships by German submarines, campaigns in the newspapers, and demonstrations in the streets, Vargas was forced to declare war against the Axis powers. A contingent of Brazilian soldiers was sent to fight in Italy and suffered losses. At the end of the war in 1945, Brazil, in spite of Vargas and the dictatorship, was proud to be among the victorious Allies.

It was scarcely possible to maintain the "New State," typically fascist, even if moderate, after the enthusiasm Brazil had shown for the Allies and her own returning soldiers. The United States put discreet pressure on Vargas to permit free elections. The press, with one accord, disobeyed the government censorship, and Vargas was never able to impose it again. Finally, in October 1945, the highest-ranking military officer, realizing that the dictatorship was tottering, ordered Vargas out, and he was sent into exile, not abroad, but to his far-off *fazenda*, in Rio Grande do Sul.

Elections were held. The opposition candidate was the Brigadier General Eduardo Gomes, the only survivor of the national heroes, the "18 of Copacabana" of 1922. But even if Vargas was out, the political machine of the dictatorship was still functioning, and the same leaders who had supported the "New State" were still in power. They succeeded in electing their candidate, General Eurico Dutra, Vargas's ex–Minister of War, who had been called the "Constable of the New State."

Surprisingly enough, once in power Dutra showed respect for the constitution, (a liberal constitution was again in effect) and no tendency to seek personal power or permit military excessess. But he was a friend, an ally, of the deposed dictator. The political rights of Vargas had not been revoked; the necessary electoral reforms did not take place. So that, at the end of Dutra's five years in office, "Getúlio" ran again. He took advantage of the emotional paternalism the enormous propaganda machine of the "New State" had been preaching to the people for eight years—and that the Dutra government had not unmasked. And in 1951 Vargas, in a landslide victory, was again in power, this time as lawfully elected president.

But times had changed. Dutra had governed honestly and respected the law. The group that came back into power with Vargas was eager for power, fame, and money. The presidency was surrounded by a morass of corruption. The opposition fought bitterly and violently against Vargas and "Getúlismo." Carlos Lacerda, editor of the opposition newspaper, "Tribuna da Imprensa," was his most outspoken opponent and exposed graft and chicanery in government circles, and in Vargas's own family. (Vargas himself was believed to be honest, but deluded, and increasingly helpless.) Members of Vargas's bodyguard plotted to assasinate Lacerda. The attempt failed; Lacerda escaped with a bullet in the foot, but a young Air Force Major, who was with Lacerda to protect him from just such an attack, was killed. This political assassination produced a national scandal. Lacerda publicly accused the president of having instigated the crime. (It was later proved, however, that Vargas was ignorant of the whole thing.) The Air Force was determined to find out who was responsible for the death of their comrade; a group of them captured the culprit in the Presidential Palace itself. High-ranking members of the armed forces then demanded the president's renunciation, in a dramatic scene early in the morning of August 24th, 1954. Vargas apparently agreed; still in pajamas and dressing gown, he retired to his bedroom—and shot himself through the heart.

Happily, with the amazing Brazilian talent for resolving the worst crises peacefully, the country was not thrown into chaos by the president's suicide. The Vice-President, Café Filho (Coffee, Jr.), took power exactly as if the position had become vacant in a more normal way. (The current joke, of course, was: "What does the butler say when he knocks on the president's door in the morning?" "Time for coffee.") At the end of his term there were new elections. The candidate of the old "Getúlista" group was Juscelino Kubitschek, from Minas Gerais; the opposition was a general, Juarez Távora, one of the "young officers" of '30, who had later turned against Vargas. However, the Vargas machine was still powerful, in spite of the suicide,—or perhaps because of it. (Vargas had been a father-figure to the masses of the poor, particularly in the cities. His funeral in Rio, rather, the procession carrying his coffin through the streets to the airport to be taken back to Rio Grande do Sul, was a frightening and touching display of mass-hysteria.) Kubitschek won by a narrow margin; and since the soldiers and civilians who were for Távora began to question the legality of the election, the "Getulista" generals, with all the means of power at their command, gave *"golpe preventivo,"* declared the country in a state of siege for days and ensured the inauguration of Kubitschek.

Once in power, Kubitschek proved to be without rancor; he was hyperactive, optimistic, and ambitious. He undertook his great work, the building of the new capital, Brasília. He encouraged industrialization and began the construction of great dams in order to increase the country's supply of electrical power. But his government, more than any other, was favorable to corruption and graft. All the wealth of the country remained in the hands of a few powerful political and economic groups. Inflation, which had begun to grow in the days of Vargas, now increased at a nightmare rate. The cost of living increased every day; the false prosperity of Kubitschek's much-vaunted "development" finally was exposed.

There were elections. The official candidate was one of the generals of the *"golpe preventivo"* that had helped ensure Kubitschek's taking power, Henrique Lott. The other candidate was the ex-Governor of the State of São Paulo, Jânio Quadros, a young politician (a few months younger than President Kennedy) whose career had been meteoric. From history teacher, he had gone up all the steps of the political ladder—from alderman to presidential candidate—never having finished one term in office. (In Brazil a man cannot run for one office while holding another, so Quadros resigned regularly from each of his offices.)

Quadros was elected by a tremendous majority, the biggest election ever held in Brazil. The people wanted a change, wanted law, wanted austerity, even—to escape from the spiralling inflation and the long years of the Vargas regime and its successor. There was an atmosphere of hope and pride. In the first seven months of his presidency, Quadros appeared to be fulfilling his electoral promises, and already the country felt the effects of his administration.

Known as a difficult and temperamental man, he had already "renounced" once during his candidacy but had become reconciled to the parties backing him.

Brazil was hopeful when Quadros entered office in 1961, and at first all went well. As he had in São Paulo, Quadros ordered investigations into graft, fired superfluous government employees, and began reform and development programs. Congressional leaders became disturbed, however, when Quadros began sounding them out about the possibility of his being granted additional powers. Late in August, Lacerda made the sensational revelation that he had been asked to join a Quadros plot to close down Congress entirely.

On the morning of August 25, Quadros readied a resignation letter that, like the one supposed to have been left by Vargas seven years earlier, claimed devotion to Brazil and hinted at threats from mysterious foreign powers. Debate still rages over whether Quadros actually meant to resign or whether he was merely making a dramatic play for more power. In any case, the resignation was submitted and accepted by Congress. The country was stunned by the news that the president had "renounced" and on the following day he was on his way to England.

The Vice-President was João ("Jango") Goulart, a protégé of Vargas since the days of Vargas's exile in the south and head of the labor "syndicates" since the days of Vargas. He was in China at the time of Quadros's defection and suspected by the military heads of being red. They vetoed his return to take over the presidency, and for a week things were at a standstill: would Goulart be president, or wouldn't he? Rio Grande do Sul, as always, was the war-like state (and its governor was Goulart's brother-in-law), for its "native son." It prepared for civil war under the slogans of "Legality," and "upholding the constitution." The army officers in the north obviously did not want civil war, but they were afraid of Goulart's leftist politics. Finally, the crisis was again solved by the "spirit of compromise" (the very expression, like "land of unfulfilled promise," is almost a red flag to a Brazilian at present). The Congress voted a change to "*parlamentarismo*," that is, Goulart would be allowed to take office as president, but his powers would be curbed by having a prime minister—a system copied more or less after that of West Germany. The new cabinet was chosen. (It was immediately called the "bifocal government.") The country returned to a Parliament, the system responsible for the greatness of the Empire, some say, and, say others, responsible for its fall.

It is still too early to foresee the results of the change.

Chapter 10

The United States and Brazil have many things in common besides both being in the Western Hemisphere and sharing the name of Amerigo Vespucci. It is time we got to know and appreciate each other better; time that the United States gave more to Brazil than loans and those less attractive features of our culture that are thought to be "Americanizing" the world. The United States and Brazil have more in common than coffee and Coca-Cola, although we now have a great deal of both of those.

We are both big countries and very much aware of our size. Perhaps number, gigantism, the "biggest" this or that, mean too much to us. Culturally, too, although we have such different traditions, there are similarities. Both the U.S. and Brazil remained rather cautiously imitative for two hundred years or more, and both have suffered from (let us face it) inferiority-feelings at different periods in our histories. But we laugh at the same jokes, enjoy the same movies, and have almost the same legends of the "frontier," Indian chiefs, gold-rushes, pioneers, hunters, and savage beasts. Americans and Brazilians are equally quick to sympathy, on the side of the under-dog, hospitable, and kind; both have a sense of national destiny, of great things ahead, and the word "democracy" can still move us deeply.

By a combination of good luck and good mangagement, the U.S. has solved many of the administrative and economic problems of capitalistic democracy earlier than Brazil has. But we should not let that blind us to the many valuable things in the Brazilian "way of life." Brazil is coping with her Indian problem at least as well as, if not better than, we are ours. And certainly the social and racial problems left over from the days of slavery are being solved more gracefully, and with less suffering, in Brazil than in any other part of the world today. We may never be able to solve our race problem in the Brazilian way, but at least we should be able to think about it calmly.

In personal relations, their less guilt-ridden moral code and their franker attitude towards sex and marriage seem more adult than ours, and preventive of the miseries of prolonged adolescence and over-romanticism. The Brazilian lack of aggressiveness, willingness to compromise, live and let live, love and let love, and their acute sense of the ridiculous in public and private pretentiousness, are all qualities that we could use more of. Their enjoyment of life has not yet been spoiled by the craze for making money; they have not yet added up the hard sum of so much money, so much pay. Although this may come as the inevitable price of further industrialization, perhaps the Brazilians will somehow be able to make it less harsh and driving than we have done.

There are no earthquakes in Brazil, and no hurricanes. There is plenty of space. There is no death penalty. Brazil has no real enemies, has had no real war for almost a hundred years, and never has had a war of conquest. Brazil has no atomic bombs, and so far has never expressed any desire for them. Although the army has helped put an occasional president in or out of power, there has never been a military dictatorship, nor does the military show signs of craving one,—this was clearly demonstrated once more in the last governmental crisis.

Perhaps because of the lack of a middle-class, because the country has been divided between the very few rich and the many poor for so long, it is more democratic, in the popular sense of the word, than many other countries. There is little or no awareness of the insidious degrees of class feeling humanity is capable of. It is perfectly true that an enterprising young man or woman, in the arts or the professions, can pass from one extreme of society to the other without self-consciousness or condescension on the part of any one. Also, although there are proud old aristocratic families, they have never been of such great wealth and grandeur over long periods of time that they can consider themselves natural autocrats. No one is *that* rich in Brazil. There have been too many political ups and downs; too many families were ruined by the emancipation. There are no vast fortunes, no industries that circle the globe, no "oil for the lamps of China."

The *"Integralistas,"* Brazil's one proto-fascist party, existed only briefly twenty years ago. There are communists and nationalists [. . .].

There have been short-lived slogans like "The petroleum is ours" (*o Petroleo é nosso*)—even if there is not believed to be much petroleum in the country. The anti-American nationalist is almost always one of two types. Like the few "*racistas*" or anti-semites in Brazil, the first comes usually from the class of the "nouveau riche" and is very rarely a native Brazilian but a recent or first-generation immigrant. (Most of the new fortunes in the country have been made by immigrants.) His business has been granted privileges and strong government protection. Naturally he is afraid of foreign competion, particularly American large-scale competition and particularly if his own product is inferior or producing unfairly big profits. The other type of anti-American nationalist is, as is usual everywhere, the man who feels he must blame all his troubles on others: Jews, Negroes, or another nation. In political office such men can stir up anti-American feeling among the poor and ignorant. But since to most of the very poor and ignorant in Brazil, America means almost nothing, a land as remote as Atlantis, the blame is more apt to be put on a local politician. And it should be remembered that in both World Wars the Brazilian government was on the side of the Allies.

It is hard, almost impossible for the very rich to understand the poor,—something that Americans, with all their good intentions, often don't seem to realize. National poverty can produce the same symptoms and reactions everywhere, China or Brazil. Anything a foreigner questions in Brazil, from inefficiency to dirt, from unpainted public buildings to city-manners, from bad transportation to infant mortality—before blaming it on climate, laziness, or national character in general, he should first ask himself "Can this be traced back to simple poverty?" Nine times out of ten it can.

And yet it is not just money that Brazil needs,—far from it. As Eugênio Gudin, Brazil's most highly respected economist, and Finance Minister under President Dutra, said recently in a fine article in *O Globo*, Rio's widely circulated afternoon paper:

> "The principal cause of Brazil's economic underdevelopment resides in the great scarcity, on all levels, of men prepared for the task of increasing national productivity, from engineers, *entrepreneurs*, and administrators of high calibre, to skilled workmen . . . Our chief goal, therefore, should be the formation of nuclei of educated men . . .
>
> "For this we need . . . to import hundreds of technicians and teachers, and to send thousands of students to foreign countries, not only in the fields of the sciences but also in the various branches of engineering and industrial techniques . . ."

[Gudin] blames the present inflation and sad state of affairs in great part on the building of Brasília and the wild government waste & spending of the Kubitschek era. The United States helped build Brasília, just as we helped [*text breaks off*]

Large loans to an extravagant corrupt Federal government for vague areas of activity do no good. The only practical way to help Brazil is by helping the "educated nuclei," and the industries and developments that will actually increase the country's income.

There is no problem in Brazil that good government, good administration, could not resolve. This fact alone makes Brazil unique among the nations of the world. Under a good government, industrial and material progress would undoubtedly take place at a tremendous rate—all the essentials are there.

But before we condemn Brazil for not having achieved good government as yet—we should distinguish between "progress," "culture," and "civilization," all very different things. The idea of "civilization" has never been especially connected with that of good government. If one had to choose: Is "bad" government so much worse than "good" government that leads to large-scale wars? Is an occasional assassination (although Brazil has actually had very few of them), or an almost-bloodless revolution, any worse than the death of thousands of innocent soldiers? Brazil has a considerable body of both sophisticated and still-living folk-culture. It has many qualities of character and society that go only with high civilization. While I am not making any exaggerated cultural or social claims for Brazil—still, the Greeks got along with bad governments, and so did the Italians of the Renaissance—and no one thinks much the worse of them for it today.

Obviously barring some world-wide disaster, Brazil is going to push and be pushed into industrialization. For the time being however, it is still one country where human-man, poor as he may be, is still more important than producing-man or consuming-man or political-man.

Everyone who visits Brazil agrees that ordinary, average Brazilians are a wonderful people: cheerful, sweet-tempered, witty, and patient—incredibly patient. To see them standing in line for hours, literally for hours, in lines folded back on themselves two or three times the length of a city block,—only to get aboard a broken-down, recklessly-driven bus and return to their tiny suburban houses, where, these days, as like as not, the street has not been repaired, nor the garbage collected, and there may even be no water—is to wonder at their patience. It seems that there should be a revolution every month or so. They have never had the government they deserve, and one wonders how long it will be before they get it.

ESSAYS, REVIEWS, AND TRIBUTES

English Lang: 1975   X // one - & - one unrelated

IF YOU WANT TO WRITE <u>WELL</u> ALWAYS AVOID THESE WORDS:

potential

structure

life-style   Fewer apples — *explain*

birth-experience, life-experience - <s>any</s> kind of -experience. (It could be "experience of)

creative, and even more, creativity

negation   Conceptualization

selectivity — sensitivity - most ivity-words.

gut reaction   gut feeling   gut anything, except the word gut alone or cat gut, etc -

more importantly) mostly
) BOTH WRONG!   output input
hopefully   )

aspect

area

kind of, sort of,   a certain, some
                     (occasionally, 11 not often!)

like instea<s>d/</s> of as   or as if

relationship -

meaningful   life-style

basic   negation

specifics   negative -

commitment   (He answered in the negative
communicate   (He said no.
relate (to)

cope - as an intransitive verb

"to have sex"

gotten - (I have gotten) - got is much better

charisma   euphemisms like "going to the bathroom"
thrust   ask David for the list ?! (for next year)
stance   Remember "It's correct"! - WHY? (One reason I can think of.)
           "a negation of it" —

As We Like It

Miss Moore and the Delight of Imitation

As far as I know, Miss Marianne Moore is The World's Greatest Living Observer. The English language is fortunate in occasionally falling heir to such feats of description, say, as this, of lightning:

> Flashes lacing two clouds above or the cloud and the earth started upon the eyes in live veins of rincing or riddling liquid white, inched and jagged as if it were the shivering of a bright riband string which had once been kept bound round a blade and danced back into its pleatings.

Or this:

> Drops of rain hanging on nails etc. seen with only the lower rim lighted like nails (of fingers).

But they are prose and by Hopkins, and he is dead. Of course Hopkins occasionally did introduce instances of equally startling accuracy into his poetry with such lines as,

> When drop-of-blood-and-foam-dapple
> Bloom lights the orchard apple . . .

Or, to quote something approaching nearer Miss Moore's special provinces, the

> Star-eyed strawberry breasted
> Throstle . . .

and the famous

> rose-moles all in stipple upon trout . . .

But Miss Moore has bettered these over and over again, and keeps right on doing it.

> The firs stand in a procession, each with an
> emerald turkey-foot at the top . . .

>   the blades of the oars
> moving together like the feet of water-spiders . . .

>   The East with its
>   snails, its emotional
>   shorthand . . .

> Peter, her immortal cat, with his

>   small tufts of fronds
>   or katydid legs above each eye.

> and

> the shadbones regularly set about his mouth, to droop or rise in
> unison like the porcupine's quills . . .

> The swan

>   with flamingo-colored, maple
>   leaflike feet.

> and the lizard,

>   stiff,
>   and somewhat heavy, like fresh putty on the hand.

These things make even our greatest poet, when he attempts something like them, appear full of preconceived notions and over-sentimental. A wounded deer has been abandoned by his "velvet friends." And Shakespeare is supposed to have been familiar with deer.

> The wretched animal heav'd forth such groans
> That their discharge did stretch his leathern coat
> Almost to bursting, and the big round tears

> Cours'd one another down his innocent nose
> In piteous chase . . .
>
> *As You Like It*

I do not understand the nature of the satisfaction a completely accurate description or imitation of anything at all can give, but apparently in order to produce it the description or imitation must be brief, or compact, and have at least the effect of being spontaneous. Even the best *trompe-l'oeil* paintings lack it, but I have experienced it in listening to the noise made by a four year old child who could imitate exactly the sound of the water running out of his bath. Long, fine, thorough passages of descriptive prose fail to produce it, but sometimes animal or bird masks at the Museums of Natural History give one (as the dances that once went with them might have been able to do) the same immediacy of identification one feels on reading about Miss Moore's

> Small dog, going over the lawn, nipping the linen and saying that
> you have a badger

or the butterfly that

> flies off
> diminishing like wreckage on the sea,
> rising and falling easily.

Does it come simply from her gift of being able to give herself up entirely to the object under contemplation, to feel in all sincerity how it is to be *it*? From whatever this pleasure may be derived, it is certainly one of the greatest the work of Miss Moore gives us.

Sometimes in her poetry such instances "go on" so that there seems almost to be a compulsion to this kind of imitation. The poems seem to say, "These things exist to be loved and honored and we *must*," and perhaps the sense of duty shows through a little plainly.

> Did he not moralize this spectacle?
> O yes, into a thousand similes.
>
> *As You Like It*

And although the tone is frequently light or ironic the total effect is of such a ritualistic solemnity that I feel in reading her one should constantly bear in mind the secondary and frequently sombre meaning of the title of her first book: *Observations.*

Miss Moore and Edgar Allan Poe

In the poem "Elephants," after five stanzas of beautiful description of the elephant and his mahout, Miss Moore suddenly breaks off and remarks in rhetorical disgust,

> As if, as if, it is all ifs; we are at
> much unease

thereby giving dramatic expression to one of the problems of descriptive poetry, although actually she has only used "as if" once, so far. It is annoying to have to keep saying that things are like other things, even though there seems to be no help for it. But it may be noticed that although full of similes, and such brilliant ones that she should never feel the necessity of complaining, she uses metaphor rather sparingly and obliquely. In Poe's "Philosophy of Composition" he points out that it is not until the last two stanzas of "The Raven" that he permits himself the use of any metaphorical expression:

> Take thy beak from out *my heart*, and take thy form from off my door!

and

> And my soul *from out that shadow* that lies floating on the floor.

and then says that such expressions "dispose the mind to seek a moral in all that has been previously narrated." He has already stressed the importance of avoiding "the excess of the suggested meaning," and said that metaphor is a device that must be very carefully employed. Miss Moore does employ it carefully and it is one of the qualities that gives her poetry its steady aura of both reserve and having possibly more meanings, in reserve. Another result is that the metaphor, when used, carries a long way, reverberating like her "pulsation of lighthouse and noise of bell-buoys. . . ."

Miss Moore has said in conversation that she has been influenced by Poe's prose, and although it should not be pushed too far, an interesting study could be made of several points of comparison. Miss Moore and Poe are our two most original writers and one feels that Miss Moore would cheerfully subscribe to Poe's remark on Originality: "The extent to which this has been neglected in versification is one of the most unaccountable things in the world," and his painful edict that "In general, to be found, it must be elaborately sought, and although a positive merit of the highest class, demands in its attainment less of invention than negation," and also that it is greatly assisted by "an extension of the application of the principles of rhyme and alliteration."

In fact, although it might have surprised him, one might almost say that in some respects Miss Moore is Poe's Ideal Poet, the one he was unable to be himself.

Poe in his prose and Miss Moore in her verse strike a tone of complete truth-telling that is compelling and rare,—Miss Moore's being so strong as to lend veracity to her slightest comment, inducing such confidence that for years I even believed her when she said,

> Dürer would have seen a reason for living
>   in a town like this, with eight stranded whales
> to look at; with the sweet sea air coming into your house.

I can imagine her writing Poe's "Chessplayer" in verse, and I can imagine Poe writing parts of "The Hero," with its melancholy, repeated *o*'s, and

> Where the ground is sour; where there are
> weeds of beanstalk height,
> snakes' hypodermic teeth, or
> the wind brings the "scarebabe voice"
> from the neglected yew set with
> the semi-precious cat's eyes of the owl.

They both take delight in their wide reading and in sharing it, and both are capable of making something unexpected and amusing out of the footnote, that usually unsmiling paragraph.

And both are virtuosi, Miss Moore, of course, to a much higher degree. I do not want to go into problems of versification and shall simply say that the more one reads Miss Moore the more one is inclined to give up such problems and merely exclaim, "How does she do it!" She is able to develop some completely "natural" idea with so many graces and effects of hesitation and changes of mood and pace that one is reminded of what little one knows of the peculiarities of Oriental music. This constant high level of technical skill must cost her incredible effort, although one is rarely aware of it; but what may be an effort for her would for most poets be an impossibility.

Sometimes I have thought that her individual verse forms, or "mannerisms" as they might be called, may have developed as much from a sense of modesty as from the demands of artistic expression; that actually she may be somewhat embarrassed by her own precocity and sensibilities and that her varied verse forms and rhyme schemes and syllabic logarithms are all a form of apology, are saying, "It really isn't as easy for me as I'm afraid you may think it is." The precocious child is often embarrassed by his own understanding and is capable of going to great lengths to act his part as a child properly; one feels that Miss Moore sometimes has to make things difficult for herself as a sort of *noblesse oblige*, or self-imposed taxation to keep everything "fair" in the world of poetry.

Miss Moore and Zoography

This same willingness to do things in such a way as not to show off, not to be superior, is shown in Miss Moore's amazingly uncondescending feeling for animals. A great deal has been said in the last twenty years about how authors should not condescend to their working class or peasant characters, and the difficulties standing in the way of honesty in such a relationship have been explained and explained. Surely it is also very hard to write about animals without "pastoralizing" them, as William Empson might say, or drawing false analogies.

> Come, shall we go and kill us venison?
> And yet it irks me the poor dappled fools,
> Being native burghers of this desert city,
> Should, in their own confines, with forked heads
> Have their round haunches gor'd.
>
> *As You Like It*

It was perhaps consoling and popular to think that the animals were just like the citizenry, but how untrue, and one feels Miss Moore would feel, how selfish. There are morals a'plenty in animal life, but they have to be studied out by devotedly and minutely observing the animal, not by regarding the deer as a man imprisoned in a "leathern coat."

Her unromantic, life-like, somehow *democratic*, presentations of animals come close to their treatment in Chinese art, and I believe she feels that the Chinese have understood animals better than any other people.

Such are Miss Moore's gifts of portraying animal physiology and psychology that her unicorn is as real as their dragons:

> this animal of that one horn
> throwing itself upon which head foremost from a cliff
> it walks away unharmed,

proficient in this feat, which like Herodotus,
I have not seen except in pictures.

With all its inseparable combinations of the formally fabulous with the factual, and the artificial with the perfectly natural, her animal poetry seduces one to dream of some realm of reciprocity, a true *lingua unicornis*.

1948

Annie Allen

by Gwendolyn Brooks

Like Miss Brooks' first book of verse, this explores the life of the Northern urban Negro. The material is the same, the scene has not changed; but here Miss Brooks has turned from her earlier poetic realism to a strain of lyric emotion. She has turned, too, to elaboration and experimentation in language which, although not always successful, shows her desire not only to break out of set patterns but to make the tone of her work as variegated as possible. The story of Annie Allen becomes a kind of kaleidoscopic dream; and the wildly colored images and symbols shake into a design both stirring and moving, as the lyrics of which it is composed draw to their end. The poet's feeling for form is basic and remarkable. If her sonnets are dramatically projected, they are also classically firm. This underlying firmness, this sense of form, holds the book together despite its moments of extravagance.

1950

XAIPE: 71 Poems

by E. E. Cummings

The famous man of little-letters, e. e. cummings, presents here his first book of poems since 1 × 1 appeared in 1944. It is appropriate that the book should appear in the spring, since spring is Mr. Cummings' favorite season, speaking to him of flowers, rain, new moons, love and joy. Most of the seventy-one poems take up these themes, but there is the usual scattering of involuted and sometimes rather unpleasant epigrams, and this time a few sympathetic and touching portraits as well. Often Mr. Cummings' approach to poetry reminds one of a smart-alec Greenwich Village child saying to his friends: "Look! I've just made up a new game. Let's all write poems. There! I've won!" And in front of the wood-and-coal man's basement shop, on the wall of the Chinese laundry, along the curbs of the dingy but flourishing park, appear poems and ideograph-poems in hyacinth-colored chalks. The obscene and epigrammatic ones have most of this happy hoodlum quality; in the others he is still playing his game and winning it, but it has been refined into a game resembling a one-man Japanese poetry competition, using the same symbols over and over again, formally, but delicately, freshly and firmly, as no one else can.

In this collection there is a poem in memory of the critic Peter Monroe Jack, a particularly fine one in memory of Ford Madox Ford, one on a wood-and-coal man, and one on "chas sing," a laundryman. One can still enjoy Cummings' inexhaustible pleasure in double o's, parentheses and question marks, but when *honi soit qui mal y pense* becomes "honey swo R ky mollypants" one feels that something should be done about it. Yet at his best he remains one of our greatest lyricists.

1950

Love from Emily

Emily Dickinson's Letters to Doctor and Mrs. Josiah Gilbert Holland. Edited by their granddaughter, Theodora Van Wagenen Ward (Harvard University Press; $4).

In a sense, all of Emily Dickinson's letters are "love-letters." To her, little besides love, human and divine, was worth writing about, and often the two seemed to fuse. That abundance of detail—descriptions of daily life, clothes, food, travels, etc.—that is found in what are usually considered "good letters" plays very little part in hers. Instead, there is a constant insistence on the strength of her affections, an almost childish daring and repetitiveness about them that must sometimes have been very hard to take. Is it a tribute to her choice of friends, and to the friends themselves, that they *could* take it and frequently appreciate her as a poet as well? Or is it occasionally only a tribute to the bad taste and extreme sentimentality of the times?

At any rate, a letter containing such, to us at present, embarrassing remarks as, "I'd love to be a bird or a bee, that whether hum or sing, still might be near you," is rescued in the nick of time by a sentence like, "If it wasn't for broad daylight, and cooking-stoves, and roosters, I'm afraid you would have occasion to smile at my letters often, but so sure as 'this mortal' essays immortality, a crow from a neighboring farmyard dissipates the illusion, and I am here again." In modern correspondence expressions of feeling have gone underground: but if we are sometimes embarrassed by Emily Dickinson's letters we are spared the contemporary letter-writer's cynicism and "humor."

This beautifully edited collection of ninety-three letters written to Doctor and Mrs. Holland covers the last thirty-three years of Emily Dickinson's life. Dr. Holland had begun his career as a rather reluctant country doctor, and he went on to become a wealthy citizen, a popular lecturer, the editor of the *Springfield Republican*, and finally the founder and editor of *Scribner's Monthly*.

It is curious to think of the Dickinson family reading the *Springfield Republican* as religiously as they must have from the many glancing references to it; but except for generalizations usually turned into metaphors, current events rarely appear in these letters of gratitude and devotion. As in her poetry, Emily Dickinson is interested in Geography (in which "Heaven" seems to be one of the most familiar places) and the Seasons, and in her own combinations of both. "It is also November. The moons are more laconic and the sun-downs sterner, and Gibraltar lights make the village foreign. November always seemed to me the Norway of the year." "February passed like a skate. . . . My flowers are near and foreign, and I have but to cross the floor to stand in the Spice Isles." And in the concluding letters, when Mrs. Holland is visiting in Florida, Emily Dickinson speaks of it as if it were Heaven, with which she is familiar, as well as an earthly state of which she is very ignorant.

The use of homely images, and their solidity, remind one over and over of George Herbert, and as the letters grow more terse and epigrammatic, one is reminded not only of Herbert's poetry but of whole sections of his "Outlandish Proverbs." And one is grateful for the sketchiness: it is nice for a change to know a poet who never felt the need for apologies and essays, long paragraphs, or even for long sentences. Yet these letters have structure and strength. It is the sketchiness of the water-spider, tenaciously holding to its upstream position by means of the faintest ripples, while making one aware of the current of death and the darkness below.

The careful study of Emily Dickinson's changing handwriting, appended to this volume, bears out this image pictorially. Among other illustrations there is a charming photograph of Lavinia Dickinson, laughing, and holding one of her innumerable cats that seem to have been a trial to her adored sister. Twenty-nine of the letters are included in the most recent edition of *Letters of Emily Dickinson*, edited by Mabel Loomis Todd, with an introduction by Mark Van Doren (World; $3.75). Mrs. Holland died believing that all the others had been lost, but some sixty more have now been found and further ones may yet come to light.

1951

The Riddle of Emily Dickinson

By Rebecca Patterson (434 pp.; Boston: Houghton Mifflin Company; $4.50).

Why is is that so many books of literary detective-work, even when they are better authenticated, better written, and more useful in their conclusions than Mrs. Patterson's, seem finally just unpleasant? And why—but perhaps it is rather exactly because: in order to reach a single reason for anything as singular and yet manifold as literary creation, it is necessary to limit to the point of mutilation the human personality's capacity for growth and redirection. It could not very well be a pleasant process to observe.

For four hundred pages Mrs. Patterson tracks down the until now unknown person (she believes it to have been a person, not persons) for whom Emily Dickinson is supposed to have cherished a hopeless passion and to whom she is supposed to have written every one of her love poems. This person Mrs. Patterson proves, to her own satisfaction at least, to have been another woman, a Mrs. Kate Anthon (to use her second married name), a school friend of Emily Dickinson's sister-in-law, Susan Dickinson. She came to visit Susan Dickinson, next door to Emily Dickinson, in Amherst in 1859; she was then a young widow who preferred to go by her maiden name of Kate Scott. The two young women met and fell in love; about a year later Kate Scott broke it off in some way, and Emily Dickinson had been christened and launched on her life of increasing sorrow and seclusion. It was all as simple as that.

That her thesis is partially true might have occurred to any reader of Emily Dickinson's poetry—occurred on one page to be contradicted on the next, that is—but even so, why is it necessary for us to learn every detail of Kate Scott's subsequent life for fifty-seven years after she dealt Emily Dickinson this supposedly deadly blow? It is interesting enough to read: she was an attractive, generous woman who travelled a great deal, a devoted wife as well as an effusively affectionate friend—but none of this seems to have much to do with "the riddle of Emily Dickinson." Perhaps Mrs. Patterson is trying at such length to establish the fact that Mrs. Anthon was capable of the relationship Mrs. Patterson thinks she was—which again doesn't seem to prove much, considering the lengths of the lives of both women, the enormous emotional vitality both obviously had, and the number and variety of people in Kate Scott's life, and even, although of course to a much lesser degree, in Emily Dickinson's.

According to the book-jacket, Mrs. Patterson has long been an admirer of Emily Dickinson's poetry. In the avidity of her search for "proof," this fact seems to have been lost sight of, as well as a few more: the possibility of a poet's writing from other sources than autobiographical ones, the perfectly real enjoyment in living expressed in many of the poems, the satisfaction that Emily Dickinson must have felt in her work, no matter what, and, quite simply, the more demonstrative manners of another period. When the poems are quoted they are used or mis-used merely as bits of "evidence," and poor Mrs. Anthon's exuberant underlinings in the books of poetry she carried about with her are subjected to the same treatment.

These four hundred pages are still many sizes too small for Emily Dickinson's work. Whether one likes her poetry or not, whether it wrings one's heart or sets one's teeth on edge, nevertheless it exists, and in a world far removed from the defenseless people and events described in this infuriating book. Or, as a poetic friend of mine better summarized it:

> "Kate Scott!
> Great Scot!"

1951

What the Young Man Said
to the Psalmist

Pantomime, A Journal of Rehearsals. By Wallace Fowlie (Henry Regnery; $3.50).

Mr. Fowlie is an unabashed New Englander, and, to him, "things are not what they seem." "Art is long," though, at least French literature is, and there is something very disarming about the picture of a serious little Boston, or Brookline, boy becoming so infatuated with a foreign language and culture that when he read Baudelaire's *Le Balcon* it "flooded me with the desire to come to these poems with more experience than I had."

Chapter III of his autobiographical book, *Pantomime*, begins with these sentences: "I must have been about fifteen years old when I rode on a swan boat for the first time. That ride marked my initial distinct awareness of Boston as a city." He then describes a swan boat ride: the boats themselves, that "originated from Boston's early enthusiasm for *Lohengrin*," and the city, revolving about him "in a cyclical panorama." These few pages give an almost too neat sample of the quality of Mr. Fowlie's book. He says of himself: "Any happiness I have ever had . . . has been learned and rehearsed studiously, prepared and meditated on . . . a performance of a part fairly well insured against failure." It is as if he had waited until the fairly advanced age of fifteen, waited until he had formed the association with Wagner and grown familiar with Boston's buildings and statues, before he was ready to embark.

Tremont Temple and its Baptist sermons, Symphony Hall, the Harvard Glee Club, the Museum of Fine Arts—all these were part of my own childhood background, and as I read his book I could not help making comparisons between Mr. Fowlie's early impressions and my own. My own first ride on a swan boat occurred at the age of three and is chiefly memorable for the fact that one of the live swans paddling around us bit my mother's finger when she offered it a peanut. I remember the hole in the black kid glove and a drop of blood. I do not want to set myself up as a model of facing the sterner realities of swan boat rides in order to discredit Mr.

Fowlie's idealization,—but there is remarkably little of blood, sweat, or tears in Mr. Fowlie's book.

It would be unfair to infer any lack of conflict in Mr. Fowlie himself; he is human and it must be there. However it is fair to criticize that lack as the chief literary fault of the book. These twelve episodic, carefully edited chapters from the life of a scholar and teacher are interesting and often amusing, but one wants more of the facts. The curious thing about it is that the one fact responsible for the lack of conflict is at the same time the most interesting fact of all.

Most children are fascinated by a foreign language; many make up a shared or solitary gibberish, or even pig-latin will serve to give them a sense of privacy and power. But Mr. Fowlie, as later for the swan boat ride, waited patiently for his own language to appear, and he was amply rewarded. In the seventh grade he began studying French, and immediately he became an enchanted boy. The accent, the grammar, the literature— everything about the French language was magical to him, and like Aladdin's lamp, or the string that leads the hero through the maze, it solved his problems. It provided him with constant interest and, later on, work, and as a highly formalized exercise it offered him the "mask" he had been seeking without knowing it to put him at his ease in the world. Apparently it got him safely through the rigours of adolescence as well, although he presents these in all their solemnity.

The most entertaining sections of the book are those dealing with his early years of mastering French: Paul Claudel mystifying an audience at the Copley Plaza, his first Parisian *pension*, ("Mangez-vous les haricots à Chicago?") the scenes with his diction teacher, Mlle. Fayolle-Faylis. He is capable of seeing a joke on himself, as for example in the account of his sedate evening "on the town" in Paris with a more worldly friend. His unnecessary asthma cure, and his life-long passion for the movies are equally real.

It is in these more casual episodes that the charm of the book lies, and in them Mr. Fowlie is more spontaneous than he gives himself credit for. The story of his work on Ernest Psichari, and his interviews with figures of French literature are laborious in contrast. And he has chosen to interpret his various experiences by means of a mystique of clowns and angels, as the spectator and/or actor, that I find hard to follow. But he has attempted to present or suggest some troublesome frames of mind, and being, as I said, a good New Englander, to give the psalmist an honest answer, even in *arrière pensée*.

1952

The Manipulation of Mirrors

Selected Writings of Jules Laforgue. Edited and translated by William Jay Smith (Grove; $4).

In this book, William Jay Smith, poet and translator of Valéry Larbaud, gives us a judicious sampling of almost everything Jules Laforgue wrote in his tragically short life: a generous number of poems, two of the *Moralités légendaires*, travel pieces and letters, and excerpts from hard to find or hitherto unpublished "Landscapes and Impressions" and criticism. At the end there is a biographical sketch of Laforgue and a bibliography. Mr. Smith's introductions to each section are informal but informative; his translations, on the whole, are models of accuracy. The book is obviously a labor of love, and for the reader without French it should make an excellent introduction to Laforgue. The prose reads easily; the poems—but that, of course, is a different matter and perhaps it would be better for both reviewer and the reader new to Laforgue to begin with the prose.

The stories "date" more than the other prose, but they are still good and still amusing. In *Hamlet, or the Consequences of Filial Piety* (1886) Laforgue achieves what Warren Ramsey in his *Jules Laforgue and the Ironic Inheritance*, calls his "ironic equilibrium." It is a sort of acrobat's small landing-stage from which he surveys the scene of past flights of fancy and plans more daring ones—which, alas, he did not live to make. Hamlet says: "To be—well, to be if one must." He complains: "There are no longer any fine young ladies; they have all taken up nursing." After the debacle in the graveyard he tells himself, "Ah, how I must work this winter with all this new material!" It is all still recognizable and topical. The earlier story, *The Miracle of the Roses*, is much slighter, and mainly illustrates the poet's obsession with death; it prefigures *Zuleika Dobson* and Firbank. Also—an old argument about translating—should the translator, when possible, limit his choice of words and phrases to the period of the text? I found expressions like "a real son-of-a-bitch," "a hopeless ham," "corny," and "well-heeled," grating badly on my ear.

In the travel pieces, *Berlin, the City, and the Court*, Laforgue (who was reader to the Empress Augusta for five years) presents German royalty, militarism, and taste in a set of beautiful neat miniatures, always ironic, naturally. Then comes an article written to introduce a show of French impressionists to Berlin. The banker, Charles Ephrussi, one of the first to encourage the impressionists and collect their paintings, was Laforgue's friend, and Laforgue knew and understood his contemporary painters better than poets frequently do. (It was Ephrussi who obtained the post of reader for him.) If, as Mr. Smith remarks, Laforgue had odd ideas about the evolution of the eye, never mind—there was nothing the matter with his own. His poetry is filled with the same visual excitement as the impressionists', and the eight and a half pages of *Landscapes and Impressions* often sound the way the impressionists look. But these pages also throw light on the poetry. I wanted to quote "Noon":

One half the earth is lit by the sun, the other half black and spotted with fire, gas, resin, or candle flame. . . . In one place people are fighting, there are massacres; in another, there is an execution, in another a robbery . . . below men are sleeping, dying . . . the black ribbons of funeral processions winding toward the yew trees . . . endless. And with all this on its back, how can the enormous earth go on hurtling through eternal space with the terrible rapidity of a lightning flash?

This reminds us again that no poet has been so constantly aware of the whole solar system: burning, whirling, immense. Laforgue's "ironic equilibrium" is like a seesaw; the solar system weights one end and our tiny planet, laden with his clowns, casinos, and pianos, lit by "fire, gas, resin, or candle flame," the other. He never lets us forget outer space; it is the margin of his staccato lines.

The section of Literary Criticism consists of jottings on Baudelaire, Rimbaud, and Corbière. Of Baudelaire: "He was the *first* to write about himself in a moderate, confessional manner and to leave off the inspired manner." Add to this his remark in a letter to his sister: "I find it stupid to speak in a booming voice and adopt a platform manner," and obvious as it may seem, now, one has marked the shift in feeling that did more than anything else to transform English poetry after 1908.

The letters are so good that I would like to see Mr. Smith translate a whole book of them sometime. But why does he say, "Few young poets have at any time written with such candor and gaiety"? It seems to me a good many have. (But then, I have just been reading Coleridge's youthful letters, full of candor and gaiety, too, and he, by himself, may seem like quite a few.) At the age of twenty-one, Laforgue, poor and alone in Paris, writes to his favorite sister: "My depression began to constitute a sort of artistic joy." And, "Life is gross, that's true—but for heaven's sake, when it comes to poetry, let us be elegant as the sweet william. . . ." Shortly after his marriage he writes: "We have a good fire, a lovely lamp, some good tea in the tea set the Empress had [?] given me." Then, "You haven't heard anything for a long while about my literary affairs. . . . you can be sure . . . that I have the right to be proud of myself; there is no literary man of my generation who is promised such a future. . . . Alas, how I long to get well. . . ." A month later he was dead of tuberculosis, at the age of twenty-seven. Because Laforgue is so quiet, so disciplined, so "ironic," always, it is worse than Keats, almost—and yet one who accomplished so much, who did it so superlatively well, and to whom all modern poets owe such a debt, scarcely needs our pity.

To go back to the poetry. By now everyone knows how to review a book of translated poetry. First, one says it's impossible. Second, one implies that the translator is an ignoramus, or if that's going too far, that he has missed the plays on words; and then one carps about the inevitable mistakes. The first objection is still true: it is impossible to translate poetry, or perhaps only one aspect can be translated at a time, and each poem needs several translations. But Mr. Smith has made an exceptionally good try and I think his faithfulness to the French will impress most reviewers. But the quickness, the surprise, the new sub-acid flavor, have disappeared. Mr. Smith is too intelligent not to know this; he says:

> Translating poetry is like converging on a flame with a series of mirrors, mirrors of technique and understanding, until the flame is reflected in upon itself in a wholly new and foreign element. Such an operation is rarely, if ever, successful: the manipulation of the mirrors depends to such an extent on the sensibility and skill of the translator.

Besides being a pretty image, this is a true one, as anyone who has ever tried translating poetry will know. But surely, besides sensibility and skill, it depends (about 50 per cent, I'd say) on luck: the possibilities of the second language's vocabulary. Without luck the worst happens, the flame goes out, and we shouldn't blame Mr. Smith when it does.

> *Lune, ô dilettante Lune,*
> *A tous les climats commune,*

Tu vis hier le Missouri,
Et les remparts de Paris,

Les fiords bleus de la Norwège,
Les pôles, les mers, que sais-je?

"Moon, oh dilettante Moon,
With all the climates in common,

You saw the Missouri yesterday,
And the ramparts of Paris,

The blue fjords of Norway,
The poles, the oceans, and what else?"

But if anyone thinks he could do better he should sit down and try. Some of the poems, those with longer lines and those in free verse, are more successful.

It is a pity the poems have not been printed bi-lingually, or at least with a facsimile or two in the poet's curious, "artistic," but legible hand-writing. The four sketches from the notebooks are worth seeing, but Laforgue seems to have been so much of a piece (or is this a delusion we have about certain poets? It seems true of Hopkins, too): letters, poems, life—even to his appearance, that surely there should be a picture of that reserved, composed young face under its top hat? And even if this is not a critical study, shouldn't Verlaine's influence at least be mentioned? And—this has nothing to do with Mr. Smith's work, of course—the 1956 abstract water-color on the jacket doesn't go at all with Laforgue's sketches of 1885 inside.

Mr. Smith also says:

Laforgue was one of the few poets who could write convincing poetry around the tremendous discoveries of his age. . . . Laforgue was in so many respects in advance of his time that it is not surprising to find him writing poems one would not have thought possible until the present day.

I am not sure who that "one" is—but isn't this putting the cart before the horse? Do our three or four great poets who were born around the time of Laforgue's death, seventy years ago now, and who derive the most from him in one way or another, give us much more of what we are appalled to recognize as "our" time than he did? The truth may be, I think, that poeti-cally we are now away behind it.

This book should be most useful to: 1. very young, almost embryonic, poets and critics; 2. the more knowing reader whose languages don't include French or who is lazy about reading it; 3. anyone at all curious about the difficult work of translation. These should read it and then, if they are also interested to the slightest degree in poetry, they should sup-ply themselves with a French grammar and dictionary and the two vol-umes of the poems, published by *Mercure de France*, or even with the small volume in the *Poètes d'aujourd'hui* series, which skimps the poetry but is a fascinating little book, with pictures, and then, well—perhaps sign up at the nearest Berlitz School.

1956

Introduction to *The Diary of "Helena Morley"*

Minha Vida de Menina: *The Book and Its Author*

When I first came to Brazil, in 1952, I asked my Brazilian friends which Brazilian books I should begin reading. After naming some of Machado de Assis's novels or short stories, or Euclides da Cunha's *Os Sertões*, they frequently recommended this little book. Two or three even said it was the best thing that had appeared in Brazilian letters since Machado de Assis, and then they were apt to launch into animated exchanges of their favorite stories from it.

In English the title means "My Life as a Little Girl," or "Young Girl," and that is exactly what the book is about, but it is not reminiscences; it is a diary, the diary actually kept by a girl between the ages of twelve and fifteen, in the far-off town of Diamantina, in 1893–1895. It was first published in 1942 in an edition of 2,000 copies, chiefly with the idea of amusing the author's family and friends, and it was never advertised. But its reputation spread in literary circles in Rio de Janeiro and there was a demand for it, so in 1944 a second edition was brought out, then two more, in 1948 and 1952, making 10,000 copies in all. George Bernanos, who was living in the country as an exile when it first appeared, discovered it and gave away a good many copies to friends, a fact to which the author and her husband modestly attribute much of its success. He wrote the author a letter which has been used, in part, on the jackets of later editions. Copies of *Minha Vida de Menina* are now presented every year as prize-books to students of the Convent of the Sacred Heart in Rio.

The more I read the book the better I liked it. The scenes and events it described were odd, remote, and long ago, and yet fresh, sad, funny, and eternally true. The longer I stayed on in Brazil the more Brazilian the book seemed, yet much of it could have happened in any small provincial town or village, and at almost any period of history—at least before the arrival of the automobile and the moving-picture theatre. Certain pages reminded me of more famous and "literary" ones: Nausicaa doing her laundry on the beach, possibly with the help of *her* freed slaves; bits from Chaucer; Wordsworth's poetical children and country people, or Dorothy Wordsworth's wandering beggars. Occasionally entries referring to slavery seemed like notes for an unwritten, Brazilian, feminine version of Tom Sawyer and Nigger Jim. But this was a real, day-by-day diary, kept by a real girl, and anything resembling it that I could think of had been observed or made up, and written down, by adults. (An exception is Anne Frank's diary; but its forced maturity and closed atmosphere are tragically different from the authentic child-likeness, the classical sunlight and simplicity of this one.) I am not sure now whether someone suggested my translating it or I thought of it myself, but when I was about half-way through the book I decided to try.

I learned that "Helena Morley" was still very much alive; that the name was the pseudonym of Senhora Augusto Mario Caldeira Brant and that she was living in Rio, well known and much loved in Rio society. Her husband was then, although almost eighty years old, acting as president of the Bank of Brazil for the second time. The poet Manuel Bandeira, an old friend of the family, kindly gave me an introduction. Armed with a friend, Lota de Macedo Soares, to serve as interpreter because my spoken Portuguese was very limited, I went to call.

Senhora Brant, or Dona Alice as I shall call her in the Brazilian way ("Helena" and "Morley" are both names from her English father's family), now lives in a large, stuccoed, tile-roofed house, on the street that borders the "Lagôa," or lagoon. It is a fashionable place to live. The house is set in a yard with flowerbeds, coconut palms, eight fruit-trees and a servants' house and vegetable garden at the back. A stuccoed fence and wooden gates protect it from the street. A large Cadillac is sometimes parked in the driveway, and its mulatto chauffeur wears a white yachting cap: Cadillac, chauffeur, and white cap are all contemporary Rio fashion. Nearby rise the extravagant Rio mountains and across the lagoon towers the one called the "Gavea," or crow's-nest, because its shape reminded the sixteenth-century Portuguese explorers of the lookout platforms on their little vessels.

On our first visit we were ushered into a large living-room, parlor, rather, with its silk and lace curtains closely drawn, luxuriously furnished: vases, bronzes, and clocks on small tables, rugs, a chandelier, chairs and sofas covered in gold-colored satin. This room is divided from the hall and another living-room opposite by a fence and gate-way of wrought iron, painted white. One of Dona Alice's daughters, Dona Sarita, appeared and started talking to my friend. Although they had not met before, very shortly they were identifying and placing each other's relatives, something that seems to happen in Brazil as quickly as it does in the south of the United States, when Dona Alice herself came in.

She is a large woman, very tall for a Brazilian, looking younger than seventy-six, her hair not yet entirely white, with a handsome, lively, high-cheekboned face lit up by two small but exceedingly bright and gay reddish-brown eyes. Her half-English blood shows, perhaps, in the unusual fairness of her skin, the fairness that made her liable to the freckles she used to complain of in her diary. She began talking, laughing and talking, immediately, and in no time at all we were telling each other stories and Dona Alice was leaning forward to pat our knees with the greatest ease and intimacy. (This warmth and ease in meeting strangers is a Brazilian characteristic especially charming to Nordic visitors.) At the first interview a great deal of the conversation was lost to me. However, I did gather that Dona Alice was proud of the book she had unwittingly written more than sixty years before, pleased at the thought of its being put into English, and still somewhat puzzled by its success in Brazil and the fact that George Bernanos, French people, and more recently, Americans, had seemed to like it, too. I could also recognize her re-telling of some of the anecdotes in the very words of the diary, or in more detail, and with a great deal of hilarity.

Presently Dr. Brant came home from the Bank of Brazil, a small, modest-appearing man of brilliant intelligence, who also looks much younger than his age. He is proud of his wife and it was he who had undertaken to put together all the old scraps and notebooks and prepare them for publication. He has been a lawyer, a journalist, and was five times elected to the National Congress; under the Vargas dictatorship he was exiled, and spent five years in France and England. He reads English; that day, I remember, he told me he was reading Boswell's Journals. In answer to my question he said no, that Dona Alice had never written anything since her early diaries, nothing, that was, but "letters, letters, letters!"

I don't believe we accepted the invitation to stay to dinner on this first call, but we did on our second, even though we had taken along two friends, admirers of the book, to meet Dona Alice. Dona Sarita, another daughter, a son-in-law, a grandson of sixteen or so, a nephew—the number of people at the long table seemed to be constantly expanding and contracting. Dona Alice, very much a matriarch, sat at the head, Dr. Augusto Mario beside her at her left. She told stories, ladled soup, told stories, carved, told stories and served the multiple Brazilian desserts, occasionally interrupting herself to scold the maid, or the nephew, who used up a whole cake of soap, or so she said, every time he took a bath, in a sort of head-tone of mock-rage that disturbed no one in the slightest.

On one of our visits we were taken upstairs in Dona Alice's own elevator, to a panelled library and shown various copies of the book, the original of the letter from Bernanos, and some old photographs. By then it had been settled that I was to do the translation and I had hoped they might have some photographs of Diamantina and the people in the diary. They did have a few, but in poor condition. One was of Dona Alice's old home in the Old Cavalhada: plastered stone, two-storied, severe, with a double door opening onto a wide stoop. I said that I would like to get a copy of it for the book, but Dona Alice and Dona Sarita said Oh no, not *that* house, suggesting that I use a picture of Dona Alice's present house on the Lagôa in Rio. I'm not sure that my arguments for using the old photographs of Diamantina ever quite convinced them.

Diamantina is in the state of Minas Gerais (General Mines) and *mineiros*, miners, as the people who come from there are called, have the reputation for being shrewd and thrifty. There is a saying that the *mineiro* eats out of an open drawer, ready to close it quickly if unexpected company shows up. Dona Alice's hospitality belied this legend, but once when Lota de Macedo Soares went to see her she found Dona Alice seated in the upstairs hall darning linen, and was rather taken aback to be asked severely if she didn't employ her time on such chores when she was at home.

The diaries, I found, had been cut short where they now end by Dr. Brant because the next year marks his own appearance in them, and his acceptance as a suitor. I feel it is a pity he so firmly omits every incident of their courtship. By the time she was seventeen, "Helena" had already received five proposals of marriage from "foreign" miners living in Diamantina. Her girl cousins and friends had been reduced to hinting to her that if she didn't want any of her suitors perhaps she would let *them* have them. She had indeed become what she admits to yearning to be in her diary: "the leading girl of Diamantina." In true Brazilian fashion she chose a Brazilian and a cousin and at eighteen married Dr. Augusto Mario, whose family had been prominent in Diamantina since the eighteenth century. I am sure she has never for a moment regretted turning down those other offers, and that this is one of those rare stories that combine worldly success and a happy ending.

One story she told us, not in the book, was about the first time she received a serious compliment from one of the rejected suitors and at last became convinced that she was pretty, really pretty. She said that she had sat up in bed studying her face, or what she could see of it by the light of a candle, in a broken piece of looking-glass, all night long.

Dr. Brant has provided the following information about "Helena Morley's" English background:

"The family name is really Dayrell. Dona Alice's grandfather, Dr. John Dayrell, studied medicine in London. He married a Miss Alice Mortimer, the daughter of an Irish Protestant, Henry Mortimer, who was, or had been, a government official in Barbados, where he also had a sugar-cane plantation producing sugar and rum. His children were educated in London, and it was there that Alice Mortimer met and married Dr. John Dayrell.

"Dr. Dayrell left England between 1840 and 1850 to serve as physician to a gold mining concern at Morro Velho [Old Hill] belonging to the famous English São João del Rey Mining Company. A short while later there was a flood in the mine, and work came to a halt. The other officials went back to England, but Dr. Dayrell, who had a 'weak chest,' remained in Brazil and went to live in Diamantina, a town 5,000 feet high and famous for its fine climate.

"In Diamantina he established himself as a doctor, acquired a *fazenda* [farm or country-seat] near town, and practised medicine for about 40 years. He and his wife were the only Protestants in the town. He had eight children, two born in England and the rest in Diamantina."

Richard Burton, in *Explorations of the Highlands of the Brazil* (Tinsley Brothers, London, 1869), speaks of meeting Dr. Dayrell in 1867, and also Felisberto Dayrell, the real name of "Helena Morley's" father, who was even then at work mining diamonds, as he is later, throughout the pages of his daughter's diary.

Diamantina

Like most children, Helena Morley seems to have taken her surroundings and the scenery of the region where she lived very much for granted. There are few direct references to them in *Minha Vida de Menina*. She does speak of the streams where she and her sister and brothers take baths, or catch the most fish, of places where there are wildflowers and fruits, or where she can set her bird-traps. And she says a good many times that she likes "the country better than the city," the "city" being, of course, the tiny provincial town of Diamantina. But whatever love of nature she has seems part utilitarian and part, the greater part, sheer joy at not being in school.

However, what impresses the occasional traveller who visits Diamantina these days first of all is its wild and extraordinary setting. Diamantina, the highest town in Brazil, is about 200 miles northeast of Belo Horizonte, the modern capital of Minas Gerais, a state bigger than Texas. At the time of the diary the railway had not yet been put through; now, sixty years later, trains still run but are already outmoded for passengers, and a once-a-day plane makes the trip from the capital in a little less than an hour.

I went there in May, when the worst of the rains are over but roads are supposedly not yet too dusty. After leaving Belo Horizonte the plane flies higher and higher, the land below grows rockier and rockier, wilder and more desolate; not a sign of life is to be seen. A high sea of waves and crests of steely gray rock, eroded and fragmented, appears; the rolling land between is covered with greenish grass, but barely covered. There are unexpected streams among the rocks; slender waterfalls fall into small black pools or the streams fan out glittering over beds of white sand. Never a village nor a house; only hundreds of the pock marks, or large pits, of old gold and diamond mines, showing red and white.

The plane comes down on a bare, slightly swelling field. There is nothing to be seen but a long red dust-cloud settling behind it, an open shed with names and comic heads splashed on it in black paint, and a wretched little house with a baby and a few hens against a ragged washing strung on a barbed-wire fence. But the air is crisp and delicious and the horizon is rimmed all around with clear-etched peaks of rock. The three or four passengers descend, immediately feeling that they are *up* and exclaiming about the change in temperature. There is no sign of Diamantina. The highest peak of rock, to the northeast, is the mountain of Itambé, sharp and deceptively near.

A lone taxi drives to town. A church tower suddenly appears between the brown-green waves of grass and the wilder, broken waves of gigantic rocks; then other church towers, and then almost the whole of the red-tiled cluster of roofs comes into sight at once. The town climbs one steep hill, extends sidewise over a lower one and down the other side. The highway enters from above along the line of the railway, passing under the striped arm of a police "barrier."

There are sixteen churches, most of them diminutive, no more than chapels; the Cathedral is new and very ugly. The famous churches of the gold-mining town of Ouro Prêto are small, too, but with their baroque façades trimmed with green soapstone, their heavy curves and swirls and twin mustard-pot towers, they are opulent and sophisticated, while the little churches of Diamantina are shabby, silent, and wistful. For one thing, although they are built of stone, plastered and painted white, the window and door frames are of wood, in dark blues, reds, or greens, or combinations of all three colors. Ornamentation is skimpy or nonexistent, and belfries or clock-towers are square. The comparative poverty of the town is shown in the way, once the walls were up, the rest of the façade and the tower were simply constructed of boards and painted white to match the stone. Because of the steepness of the streets there is often a flight of stone steps at an angle across the front and off one side, and some churches are still fenced in by high old blue or red picket fences, giving them a diffident, countrified appearance.

The Church of the Rosário that figures prominently in Helena's diary, standing next door to her grandmother's house as it does, is still the most impressive. It is the Negroes' church, built by slaves in the middle of the eighteenth century; inside are three black saints: St. Benedict, St. Iphigenia, and St. Somebody; his name was unidentifiable. There are three crystal chandeliers, a great deal of red dust and faded blue paint, and a slightly rickety blue gallery for the black choir. The church has settled and everything is now askew. As in many old Brazilian churches, the ceilings are made of narrow boards, so that the scenes from the Life of the Virgin painted on them, copied from heaven knows what hand-me-down sources, are scored through by black lines. These ceilings have a sad appeal, like letters written in old copy-book handwriting on lined paper.

In front of this church there is a big tree of the *ficus* family. Looking up into its branches one is surprised to see a large black beam stuck in them, crosswise, then a rusty lantern and other indistinguishable rusty odds and ends that have no business being thirty feet up off the ground, in a tree. This is one of the town's modest "sights," and proves to be what is left of an enormous crucifix that once stood where the tree now stands. The air-borne seed started growing out from the side of the cross, grew upwards and downwards and took root, and now has taken over, broken up, and lifted the whole cross in the air: ladder, lantern, pliers, hammer and all.

These crosses are a common feature of the countryside around Diamantina, sometimes with all their accoutrements, sometimes bare or simply with stiff wooden streamers arranged over the arms and a flat tin rooster on top. The bird called *João de Barro*, John of the Mud, or Clay, builds his beehive-shaped adobe nests on the arms, and the hammock bird slings his woven ones underneath. One cross, on the high ridge of rock opposite the town, now burns brightly at night with hundreds of electric light bulbs. At Sopa (soup), where Helena's father went "to open a mine," there is a fine one, with a white skull and cross-bones on the black wood, silvered Roman centurions' helmets, and a flat rose-red "seamless garment" like a pattern for a child's dress. It stands near a small church known as the "Chinese Church" because the eaves of the roof and tower are turned upwards in Oriental style, a common feature of Brazilian colonial architecture, traced directly to the Portuguese colony of Macão. One becomes accustomed to it in Rio de Janeiro, but here far off in a desolate countryside it is strange to come across this church like a baby pagoda, and a crucifix almost as tall, loaded with its grim set of Christian iconography-toys.

The interiors of Helena's various churches are disappointing, cramped and musty, the Portuguese-style wedding-cake altars crowded with old artificial flowers and incongruously dressed, bewigged saints. The confessionals, however, are sometimes quaint and pretty: upright boards about five feet high; the priest sits on one side on a chair, the penitent kneels on the other; but the boards are gilded and painted in pastel blues and pinks, the upper part pierced with holes like a colander, or with long slits that make them vaguely resemble Biblical musical instruments, possibly some sort of organ. And the "masts" Helena speaks of as being set up on certain holy days lie in the sacristies or along the side aisles of their churches the rest of the year, big as telephone poles, painted in winding blue and white stripes.

I came upon the Church of the Amparo, that figures in the diary, unexpectedly, as it was getting dark. Its trim is dark peacock blue; on top a rusty rooster perches on a rusty globe; there is a minute balcony on either side of a large, faded coat of arms cut out of tin above the door, and over it a three-dimensional Dove of the Holy Spirit, dimly illuminated, nesting behind a quatrefoil window. Seen suddenly blocking the end of an alleyway, this church is stricken but dignified, like a person coming towards one whom one expects to beg, who doesn't beg after all.

Some of the church clocks by which Helena told the time have been removed. At about seven o'clock the light leaves the town rapidly and the surrounding sea of rocks, and the peak of Itambé, turn red. A few church-bells ring and then a great noise comes from the loud-speaker over the Cathedral door and reverberates all over town. *Ave Maria, gratia plena*; the town vibrates with it and the light bulbs on the high cross opposite snap into activity. It is the hour of the rosary, Helena's *terço*, which caused her so much "suffering" at family prayers and which is now broadcast every evening during the month of May. On Sundays the same loud-speaker is used to draw people to mass; at five o'clock it was blaring out *The Stars and Stripes Forever*.

In spite of these innovations and the Betty Grable film showing at the one cinema, the town has changed very little since the youthful Helena lived there and raced up and down its steep streets. Most of the streets have no sidewalks, some have narrow ones, two feet or so wide, long slabs of greenish stone raised a little above the cobblestones, the *pé de muleque*, or "ragamuffin's foot,"—that is, the confection we call peanut brittle, which it is supposed to resemble. Down the middle of the street runs another strip of long stones, set flush, much easier to walk on than the sidewalks that every so often stop altogether, or break up into steps. These footpaths are called *capistranas*, after a mayor of Ouro Prêto, who introduced them there.

The houses are thick-walled and solid, in the middle of the town of two or even three stories, but as one gets away from the Cathedral they become smaller and lower and the tile roofs turn to thatched ones. The taller houses have balconies, formerly often completely covered in by the lattice-work cages, called *muxarabis* (from the Arabian *muxara*, a shelter), showing the influence of the Moors on the architecture and way of life of Portugal. From them the women could watch what went on in the streets, in an Oriental seclusion. On either side of the windows giving onto these balconies are little lanterns, globes of colored or milk glass, *luminárias.* (The word has been extended to mean a kind of small cream-filled tart, highly thought of by our diarist.) The same kind of globe, without lights, decorates the railings, and sometimes Tecoma vines or grape-vines are trained along the ironwork.

The window frames are curved at the top, with double sashes of a dozen small panes each. Here the trimming becomes confusing, since some of the wooden frames are marbleized or painted to imitate stone, and some of the stone ones are painted to imitate grained wood. A good many of the windows still have stencils on the lower panes, a form of folk-art that also served to protect the privacy of rooms right on the street. A paper stencil in a formalized leaf-and-flower or other design is held against the glass and patted with a rag dipped in white paint. The effect is very decorative, like frost on the window panes in northern climates, only geometrical. The wide overhang of the eaves contributes to the town's surprisingly Oriental air, and this overhang is filled in solid with molding and is a favorite place for colored stripes and other ornamentation. The houses are in admirably bold or pretty colors. I particularly liked a crushed-strawberry pink one, with a double staircase of blue, and window frames and under-eaves marbleized in the same blue. There are mustard-colored houses with bright yellow and dark green shutters, white with dark blue and peach, mauve with dark blue and yellow. So that passers-by will not be drenched in the rainy season, the mouths of the rain-pipes are carried out two feet or more, across the sidewalks, and the funnels flare like trumpets. It is as if a band had suddenly stopped playing. Sometimes they have tin petals or feathers down them and around the mouth, and this decoration is repeated in tiles set edgewise up the ridges of the roofs, dragon-like and very "Chinese."

The grandmother's house still stands, to the right of the Rosário Church, but the Teatro Isabel, formerly on the other side, has been torn down and in its place is a large baby-pink jail from whose barred windows a drunken prisoner yelled at me incomprehensibly. The house is low, its stoop just a few inches off the ground, a deceptively small-looking house with a sweeping, concave old tile roof. The woman who lives there now knew *Minha Vida de Menina* and its author and kindly showed me through. The old rooms for slaves, extending along the street by the church, are let out. Inside there is room after room, high, square, sadly neglected, almost devoid of furniture. The walls are a yard thick, wooden shutters can be closed and barred on the inside; the ceilings are of boards or woven rushes painted white, the two common Brazilian types. After a good many of these high dark rooms we reached the kitchen, where a girl was cooking over an open fire. Stoves here consist of a long iron plate with four pot-holes in it, laid on the edges of a stone trough full of embers. A wood called *candeia* is commonly used. It has a peculiar sweetish smell, sickening until one gets used to it; at the dinner-hour this sweetish stench hovers bluely over Brazilian towns and villages.

Behind the house the grandmother's former garden covers about five acres, sloping down to a brook and a jungle of banana trees. There are huge *jaboticaba* trees, the same ones that Helena used to climb into for refuge. There are a few beds of lettuce and cabbages, and a grove of coffee trees, but everything is overgrown and gone to seed and it is hard to imagine how it must have looked in the old days, tended by the grandmother's ex-slaves. A big sociable pig stood up on his hind legs in his pen, to watch us.

One of the handsomest buildings is Helena's "Normal School," now the Grupo Escolar, and located in the middle of the town; big, white, rectangular, with bright blue doors and window-frames. Juscelino Kubitschek, the present president of Brazil and a former governor of Minas, was born in Diamantina. He had visited recently and a great canvas banner bearing his smiling face almost concealed the front of the building. There are also a Kubitschek Street and a Kubitschek Place with his head in bronze in it, less than life-size, as if done by the Amazonian head-shrinkers.

The market is a large wooden shed, with blue and red arches, and a sparse forest of thin, gnawed hitching-posts around it. The drovers are still there, with loads of hides and corn, but because of trains, better roads, and trucks, trade has dwindled to next to nothing since Helena's day. Near the Cathedral one is warned from the street or alley where the "bad girls" live. They are extremely juvenile mulattoes, sitting on their doorsteps with their feet stuck out on the cobblestones, gossiping and sucking sugar-cane in the sunshine. The live-forevers that Helena used to pick are still very much in evidence, in fact they are one of the town's few industries besides diamond-mining. They are a tiny yellow-white straw flower, less than half an inch in diameter, on a long fine shiny brown stalk. Tied up in bunches, the bundle of stems bigger than two hands can hold, they lie drying in rows on the streets all around the Cathedral, and freight-cars full of flowers are sent off every year, on their way to Japan. They are used, I was told, for "fireworks," or "ammunition," but I suspect that, dyed and glued, they merely reappear in the backgrounds of Japanese trays, plaques, etc. Brazilian-made fireworks play an important role in Diamantina, as they do in all provincial Brazilian towns, and are used in staggering quantities for religious holidays. I was shown a warehouse packed to the ceiling with firecrackers, catherine-wheels and Roman candles; the supply looked much larger than that of food-stuffs on hand at the same wholesaler's.

Diamonds and gold, but chiefly diamonds, still obsess the economy. The hotel manager (a new hotel, designed by Oscar Niemeyer, was finished in 1956), using almost the very words that Helena used in 1893, complained that he had to fly in vegetables from Belo Horizonte. "Here no one's interested in anything but gold and diamonds," he said. "They say they can't grow vegetables in this soil, but it isn't true. They think of nothing but diamonds, diamonds, diamonds." It is strange to see, on the side of a miserable little house, a blue and white enamelled sign announcing that here is a diamond dealer. I looked inside one of these houses and could see nothing but overhead a lurid plaster statue of St. George killing the dragon, with a small red electric light bulb glowing in front of it, and under it, on the table, a bunch of live-forevers and a fine pair of scales in a glass case. The scales are covered up at night, like the innumerable caged birds hanging everywhere. Curiously shaped stones, lumps of ores, clusters and chunks of rock crystal and quartzes are everywhere, too, used as door-stops and sideboard decorations. In the cold clear air, the town itself, with its neatness, rockiness, and fine glitter, seems almost on the point of precipitation and crystallization.

In the recently opened museum there are the usual polychrome saints and angels, sedan chairs and marriage beds, and then suddenly and horribly an alcove hung with the souvenirs of slavery: rusty chains, hand-cuffs, and leg- and neck-irons draped on the wall; pointed iron prods originally fastened to poles; and worse things. Driving about the region, the sites of the old slave encampments are pointed out. Trees, and a very fine short grass, supposedly from Africa, distinguish them, and they are usually beside a stream and near the pits of old mines. But now there is only the small Negro and mulatto population to show for all the million or more slaves who came here in the eighteenth and early nineteenth centuries.

I made an excursion to Boa Vista, where Helena's father mined. The mines are abandoned now, although they were worked on a large scale by foreign companies up until a few years ago. There is nothing to be seen but an immense excavation exposing soils of different colors (each with a different name; Burton's book gives an excellent account of them and the different methods of mining), and endless iron pipes. Boa Vista is slightly higher than Diamantina; although it is six or seven miles away one can see a church-tower. The road there is dirt, narrow, winding, and eventually the taxi scrapes over outcroppings of naked rock and splashes through streams. Battalions of grotesque rocks charge across the fields, or stand like architecture, pierced by Gothic-ruin windows. Large slabs balance on top of moldering turrets, with vines, bushes, and even stunted palm-trees on their tops. Helena Morley was not a fanciful child but I wondered at her riding on her borrowed horse, before sun-up, along this nightmare road, hurrying to get back to Diamantina in time for school.

I took with me a life-long friend of Helena's future husband, Dr. Brant, Senhor Antonio Cicero de Menezes, former local director of the Post Office service, now eighty years old, a very distinguished-looking man with a white Vandyke beard and moustaches, like an older, frailer Joseph Conrad. We came back through the hamlet of twenty or so houses that is Palha (straw) today and Seu Antonio Cicero said, in Helena's very phrase, "Now let us descend and suck fruit." So we sat in the tiny general store, surrounded by household and mining necessities: iron kettles and frying pans, salt beef and soap, and sucked a good many slightly sour oranges. A little boy brought them in a gold-panning bowl and Seu Antonio Cicero prepared them for me with his pocket-knife faster than I could suck. The storekeeper showed me a store room full of these wooden bowls, cowhides and tarry lumps of brown sugar and sieves for panning diamonds, piled on the floor, and boxes and boxes of dusty rock crystals, bound, he said, for the United States, for industrial purposes.

Near there we stopped again to watch a group of men looking for diamonds in a stream beside the road. The head of the group had four men, black and white, working for him; he gave me his name and asked me to print it; here it is: Manoel Benicio de Loyola, "diamond-hunter of Curralinho." They were shovelling in the shallow, sparkling water, damming it up, releasing it, and arranging piles of gravel on the bank. One of them took up a small quantity of gravel in the wide round sieve and held it just beneath the surface of the water, swirling it skilfully around and around. In a few minutes he lifted it out; the gravel was distributed evenly over the sieve in one thin layer. With the gesture of a quick-fingered housewife turning out a cake, he turned the whole thing upside down on the ground, intact. Senhor Benicio de Loyola then put on his horn-rimmed glasses, lowered himself to his knees in the wet mud, and stared, passing a long wooden knife over the gravel from side to side. In a second he waved his hand, got up and put his glasses back in his pocket, and his assistant got ready to turn out another big gravel pancake, while he and Seu Antonio Cicero talked about a large blue diamond someone had found somewhere a day or two before.

This is the simplest of all forms of diamond "mining." It goes on all around Diamantina constantly, and enough diamonds are found in this way to provide a meagre living for some thousands of people. One sees them, sometimes all alone, sometimes in groups of three or four, standing in every stream. Sometimes they are holding a sieve just under the water, looking for diamonds, sometimes they are sloshing their wooden bowls from side to side in the air, looking for gold. The bent heads and concentration of these figures, in that vast, rock-studded, crucifix-stuck space, give a touch of dementia to the landscape.

I also made an excursion to Biribiri (accented on the second and last "i"s), an enchanting spot, where Helena used to dance, and leap through St. John's Day bonfires. The factory, for weaving cotton, is still there, but nothing could look less like industrialization. One descends to a fair-sized river and the landscape is green and lush; there are many trees, and fruit trees around the blue- or white-washed stone houses along the one unpaved street. In the middle is the church, better kept up than any of the others I saw, trim, almost dainty. Indeed, it looks like an old-fashioned chocolate box. A blue picket fence encloses the flourishing flower-garden and over the door, below the twin towers, is a large rounded pink Sacred Heart with a crown of realistic ten-inch thorns, green wooden palm branches and blue wooden ribbons. Close around the church stand a dozen real palms, Royal palms, enormously tall and slender, their shining heads waving in the late afternoon sun.

"Helena Morley"

In one of his letters to Robert Bridges, Hopkins says that he has bought some books, among them Dana's *Two Years Before the Mast*, "a thoroughly good one and all true, but bristling with technicality—seamanship—which I most carefully go over and even enjoy but cannot understand; there are other things, though, as a flogging, which is terrible and instructive *and it happened*—ah, that is the charm and the main point." And that, I think, is "the charm and the main point" of *Minha Vida de Menina*. Its "technicalities," diamond digging, say, scarcely "bristle," and its three years in Diamantina are relatively tame and unfocussed, although there are incidents of comparable but casual, small-town cruelty. But—*it really happened*; everything did take place, day by day, minute by minute, once and only once, just the way Helena says it did. There really was a grandmother, Dona Teodora, a stout, charitable old lady who walked with a cane and managed her family and her freed slaves with an iron will. There really was a Siá Ritinha who stole her neighbors' chickens, but not Helena's mother's chickens; a Father Neves; a spinster English Aunt Madge, bravely keeping up her standards and eking out a living by teaching small obstreperous Negroes, in a town financially ruined by the emancipation of the slaves and the opening of the Kimberley diamond mines.

Some of the people in the diary are still alive, and the successors of those who are dead and gone seem to be cut very much from the same cloth. Little uniformed girls, with perhaps shorter skirts, carrying satchels of books, press their noses against the dining-room windows of the new hotel and are overcome by fits of giggling at seeing the foreigner eat her lunch—on their way to the school run by the Sisters of Charity, the same school that Helena ran away from. The boys still give them the same nick-names. (They call a freckled child of my acquaintance *Flocos*, "Flakes," but that is a new word in Brazil and Helena was spared it.) Mota's store, where she bought her boots, is now Mota's Son's store. There is still a garrison of soldiers, now outside the town; there is a seminary, and young priests walk in the streets and people talk to them through the latticed windows.

When the diary happened, Helena was tall and thin and freckled and always, always hungry. She worries about her height, her thinness, her freckles and her appetite. She is not a very good scholar and fails in her first year at Normal School. Her studies can always be interrupted by her brother, her many cousins, or even the lack of a candle. (The diary was mostly written by candlelight.) She is greedy; sometimes she is unfair to her long-suffering sister, Luizinha, but feels properly guilty afterwards, rationalize as she may. She is obviously something of a show-off and saucy to her teachers; but she is outspoken and good-natured and gay, and wherever she is her friends may be getting into mischief but they are hav-ing a good time; and she has many friends, old and young, black and white. She is willing to tell stories on herself, although sometimes she tries to ease her conscience, that has "a nail in it." She thinks about clothes a great deal, but, under the circumstances—she has only two or three dresses and two pairs of boots—who wouldn't?

She may grow tedious on the subject of stealing fruit, but it is, after all, the original sin, and remember St. Augustine on the subject of the pear tree. On the other hand, she seems to take the Anglo-Saxon sin of sins, "cheating," rather lightly. If she is not always quite admirable, she is always completely herself; hypocrisy appears for a moment and then vanishes like the dew. Her method of composition seems influenced by the La Fon-taine she hates to study; she winds up her stories with a neat moral that doesn't apply too exactly; sometimes, for variety's sake, she starts off with the moral instead. She has a sense of the right quotation, or detail, the gag-line, and where to stop. The characters are skilfully differentiated: the quiet, humorous father, the devout, doting, slightly foolish mother, the rigid Uncle Conrado. Occasionally she has "runs" on one subject; per-haps "papa" had admired a particular page and so she wrote a sequel to it or remembered a similar story.

In matters of religion, Helena seems to have been somewhat of an eighteenth-century rationalist. She steps easily in and out of superstition, reason, belief and disbelief, without much adolescent worrying. She would never for a moment doubt, one feels, that the church is "a good thing." With all its holidays, processions, mast-raisings, and fireworks, its christenings, first communions and funerals, it is the fountain-head of the town's social life. Her father remains in the background, smiling but tolerant, while her mother pleads with him to go to church and constantly prays for all the family. Like him, Helena is at first skeptical of a schoolmate who dies and acquires a reputation for working miracles; then she veers towards her mother's party. Her religion, like her feeling for nature, is on the practical side.

She lives in a world of bitter poverty and isolation. A trip to the capital, Rio de Janeiro, where a few boys go to study, takes ten days: eight on mule-back to Sabará, and from there two days by very slow train to Rio. Supplies are brought to town by the drovers, on long lines of mules or horses. One of the greatest problems is what to do with the freed slaves who have stayed on. Reading this diary, one sometimes gets the impression that the greater part of the town, black and white, "rich" and poor, when it hasn't found a diamond lately, gets along by making sweets and pastries, brooms and cigarettes and selling them to each other. Or the freed slaves are kept busy manufacturing them in the kitchen and peddling them in the streets, and the lady of the house collects the profits— or buys, in her parlor, the products of her kitchen.

Now that I can join in my friends' exchanges of anecdotes from the book, and have seen Diamantina, I think that one of my own favorite entries is Helena's soliloquy on November 5th, 1893, on the meaning of Time (her style improves in the later years):

"The rooster's crow never gives the right time and nobody believes it. When a rooster crows at nine o'clock they say that a girl is running away from home to get married. I'm always hearing the rooster crow at nine o'clock, but it's very rarely that a girl runs away from home.

"Once upon a time I used to believe that roosters told the time, because in Boa Vista when you ask a miner the time he looks at the sun and tells you. If you go and look at the clock, he's right. So I used to think that the sun kept time during the day and the rooster at night. Now I realize that this was a mistake. . . .

"In Cavalhada only the men have watches. Those who live in the middle of the town don't feel the lack of them because almost all the churches have clocks in their towers. But when papa isn't home the mistakes we make about the hours are really funny. . . . The rooster is mama's watch, which doesn't run very well. It's already fooled us several times." She goes on to tell about "mama's" waking her and Luizinha up to go to four o'clock

Mass, because the rooster has already crowed twice. They drink their coffee and start out. "I kept looking at the moon and the stars and saying to mama, 'This time the Senhora's going to see whether the rooster can tell time or not.' The street was deserted. The two of us walked holding onto mama's arms. When we passed by the barracks the soldier on duty looked at mama and asked, 'What's the Senhora doing in the street with these little girls at this hour?' Mama said, 'We're going to Mass at the Cathedral.' The soldier said, 'Mass at midnight? It isn't Christmas eve. What's this all about?'

"I was afraid of the soldier. Mama said, 'Midnight? I thought it was four o'clock. Thank you very much for the information.'

"We went home and lay down in our clothes. But even so we missed Mass. When we got to church later Father Neves was already in the Hail Marys."

I like to think of the two tall, thin little girls hanging onto their mother's arms, the three figures stumbling up the steep streets of the rocky, lightless little town beneath the cold bright moon and stars; and I can hear the surprised young soldier's voice, mama's polite reply, and then three pairs of footsteps scuttling home again over the cobblestones.

Food

The staple diet of Brazil consists of dried black beans and rice, with whatever meat, beef or pork, salted or fresh, can be afforded or obtained. And black beans, instead of the "bread" of other countries, seem to be equated with life itself. An example of this: when the Brazilian football team went to play in the Olympic Games recently, thirty-three pounds of black beans were taken along for each man. And recently in Rio the court ordered a taxi-driver to pay alimony to his wife and children in the form of twenty-two pounds of rice and twenty-two pounds of black beans monthly.

They are boiled separately and seasoned with salt and pepper, garlic, and lard. The common vegetables, such as pumpkin, okra, *couve* (a kind of cabbage), are usually made into stews with small quantities of meat or chicken. As in other Catholic countries, salt codfish is a common dish. But black beans and rice form the basis of the main meal, the heavy lunch, usually served early, between eleven and half-past twelve. At the time of the diary lunch was even earlier, at half-past ten or eleven, and dinner was eaten at three or four o'clock. This explains why everyone is always ready to eat again in the evenings.

A dish of roasted manioc flour is always served with the beans and rice, indeed it is what the unqualified word "flour" signifies. It is sprinkled over the food, to thicken the sauce, and perhaps to add a little textural interest to the monotonous diet, since its nutritional value is almost nothing. It is also used in making various cakes and pastries. There is an impressive variety of these in Brazil, using manioc and cornmeal as well as wheat flours, coconut, brown sugar, etc., each with its own name, frequently religious in origin and varying from region to region. Helena mentions a dozen or more and there are whole books on the subject. Desserts are often *pudims*, usually, or unusually, heavy, and a great variety of fruit pastes, guava, quince, banana, etc., served with a small piece of hard white cheese. On a good Brazilian table, desserts appear, or always used to, several at a time. Cinnamon is the universal spice. Most Brazilians have very sweet tooths.

Breakfast is simply coffee, black or with boiled milk, and a piece of bread, although Helena varies hers strangely with cucumbers. Coffee is served after the other meals, at intervals in the day, and inevitably to callers at any time, in the form of *cafezinhos*, "little coffees," black, boiling hot, and with the tiny cup half-filled with sugar. (The sugar is only partially refined so it takes quite a lot to sweeten a cup.) It is made by stirring the very finely ground coffee into boiling water, then pouring it through a coffee bag. These brown-stained bags and their high wooden stands are a symbol of Brazil, like black beans, and they are seen everywhere, even in miniature, as toys. There are laws to ensure that the coffee served in the innumerable cafés is unadulterated and of the required strength. (In an American movie being shown in Rio a character was told that he'd feel better after he had "a good breakfast, porridge and bacon and eggs and coffee," and this speech was rendered by the Portuguese sub-title, "Come and take coffee.")

A glance at the photographs will perhaps explain what may seem like Helena's over-emphasis on fruit, or unnatural craving for it. Through June, July, and August, the long dry winters in that stony region, when everything is covered with red dust, with a constant shortage of fresh vegetables and the only drinking water running in open gutters as it was at that time, "sucking oranges" must have been the best way to quench one's thirst, and stealing fruit an almost irresistible impulse.

Money

Dr. Brant has given me the following information about the value of money at the time the diary was kept.

The *mil reis* (a thousand *reis*, the plural of *real*, or "royal") was worth twenty cents of U.S. money. (As a banker, Dr. Brant points out that the dollar has since been devalued, so that a *mil reis* would be worth ten cents of today's money. But as Helena says, we are speaking of "bygone days" and it seems simpler to keep it at the earlier evaluation.) Five *mil reis* would therefore be a dollar, 100 *reis* two pennies, and so on. Dr. Brant gives a list of approximate prices of goods and labor at the time:

A pound of meat: 10¢
A pound of sugar: 3¢
A dozen eggs: 4¢
A quart of milk: 4¢
A pound of butter: 12¢
A pair of shoes: $3.00
A good horse: $20.00
Average rent for a good house: $8.00 a month
A cook: $2.00 a month
Wages of Negroes employed in mining: 40¢ a day (paid to the whites who rented them out. In the town, or in agriculture, Negro wages were less.)

Arinda receives about $100 for the diamond she finds, page 6, Helena makes $6.00 by selling her mother's gold brooch without a diamond in it, page 172 ff.; and the grandmother sends home a present of $10.00 to her daughter, on page 48, etc.

Acknowledgments

I am indebted to many friends and acquaintances for the help they have given me, both as sources of information about Diamantina and its life and vocabulary, and with the actual work of translation. Thanks are due:

In Diamantina, to Antonio Cicero de Menezes and his granddaughter; to Armando Assis, manager of the Hotel de Tourismo; and to many other inhabitants who showed me the way or went with me, invited me into their houses, and patiently repeated and spelled out the names of things.

To Vera Pacheco Jordão, who went with me to Diamantina and came to my assistance when my Portuguese failed me; to Manuel Bandeira; to Dora Romariz; to Otto Schwartz; and to Mary Stearns Morse, who typed the difficult manuscript.

To Rodrigo Melo Franco de Andrade, head of the Patrimonio Artistico of the Brazilian Department of Education, who took an interest in the book and who got out the Department's collection of photographs of Diamantina for me to choose from.

To my friend Pearl Kazin, who, in New York, received the manuscript and gave me invaluable help with it.

To my friend Lota de Macedo Soares, who reluctantly but conscientiously went over every word of the translation with me, not once, but several times.

To Dr. Augusto Mario Caldeira Brant, who also went over every word of the translation, and without whose remarkable memory for the customs and idioms of Diamantina in the '90's a great deal of detail might have been lost. I am grateful to him for many suggestions, and many of the footnotes are his.

But most thanks of all are, of course, due to Dona Alice herself for her wonderful gift: the book that has kept her childhood for us, as fresh as paint. Long may she live to re-tell the stories of "Helena Morley" to her grandchildren and great-grandchildren.

Sítio da Alcobacinha
Petrópolis
September 1956

A New Capital, Aldous Huxley,
and Some Indians

When Aldous Huxley and his wife visited Brasil recently, the Cultural Division of Itamarati, the Brasilian Department of Foreign Affairs, arranged for them to make a trip to Brasília, the new capital of the country, with an additional trip farther into the interior to see the Uialapiti Indians. The Department of Foreign Affairs is always referred to as Itamariti because it is housed in the former home of the Barons of Itamariti in Rio de Janeiro, a handsome, solid residençe, really a palace on a small scale. Behind its high walls, surrounded by magnificent Imperial Palms, are a garden and a formal pool complete with swans, where diplomatic dinner-parties are held.

The Brasilian nobility created by the first and second Emperors were fiercely nationalistic and proud of their semi-civilized country, and for their titles they invariably chose Indian place-names, such as Itaboraí, Tamandaré, or Itamarati. One could graph modern Brasilian history very patly on the three points connected by the Huxley trip: by way of Itamarati to the safe, democratic insipidity of the name "Brasília," and then beyond, to the dwindling tribes along the Xingu River, Indian again, for here as in the United States, many geographical names have held to their originals, or approximations of them.

Ten people went on the trip: Huxley and his Italian wife; two men from Itamarati, one the head of the Cultural Division, José Meira Penna; Antônio Callado, editor-in-chief of the biggest Rio morning paper, and his English wife; a Polish-Brasilian girl who practices architecture in Rio; a young Englishman from the British Embassy; a girl who had been acting as the Huxleys' interpreter in Rio; and myself, the only American. They were all to fly to Brasília from the state of Minas Gerais where the Huxleys had been taken to see a colonial town or two, and I was to meet them there for lunch, on a Saturday at the big new Oscar Niemeyer hotel.

Brasília is about six hundred miles northwest of Rio, in the state of Goiás; at present the railroad nearest to it ends at Annapolis, a small town eighty-five miles away. It takes three days, and trains on both regular gauge and narrow gauge tracks, to reach Annapolis from Rio; from there trucks and jeeps can go on to Brasília. So far only two trainloads of material for the new capital have managed to make the trip that way; all the rest—the staggering quantities of cement, bricks, steel, glass and wood necessary to start building a modern city—have gone by road, by bad roads— everything, that is, that has not been flown in by plane. Since gasoline is the biggest item of importation in Brasil, accounting for some 24 per cent of its dollar expenditure, this attempt to build a city before building a railroad to its site is one of the most serious criticisms of President Juscelino Kubitschek's new capital.

The change of capital was written into the Brasilian Constitution as far back as 1891, and it had been talked of as early as 1820. Among the reasons originally given for the change one was that Rio de Janeiro, being on the coast, was open to attack from the sea; a capital farther to the west would open up the vast uninhabited stretches of the interior to permanent settlers as no pioneering had (or has) been able to do. The first reason, of course, disappeared with the coming of the air age, but the second is still the chief argument of the pro-Brasília group. There are others, some rather similar to those for the establishment of Washington: legislation, the pro-Brasílias say, will be carried on more efficiently and fairly away from the pressures of the rival cities of Rio and São Paulo; and if the capital is simply the seat of government, senators and deputies will go there to conduct the nation's business and then return to their own states, rather than be seduced by the attractions of Rio, living there for years at a time and seeing their constituents rarely, if at all, as many of them do now. Also, Rio is badly overcrowded, constantly short of water, and its slums are mushrooming as more and more miserable immigrants trek in from the poorer or drought-stricken areas in search of work. Many of these, the argument goes, will now be drawn to Brasília; and it is true that some thousands of them have already gone there.

While everyone in Brasil who has ever thought about it at all agrees that the interior of the country has to be opened up somehow or other, and the sooner the better, those opposed to Brasília feel that it might be done to begin with more modestly and economically, and by means more in keeping with Brasil's present desperate financial state. Brasil needs schools, roads, and railroads, above all; then medical care, improved methods of agriculture, and dams and electric power, particularly in the drought-ridden northeast. These things, they feel, should be tackled more energetically and systematically, if necessarily slowly, before undertaking to build a luxury capital, an extravagant show-place, three hours by plane from·the fringe of cities along the sea-board. The founding of small towns and villages in the interior, and help with their industries and agriculture— especially by means of railroads and better roads, since at present 50 per cent of all produce spoils before it even reaches the markets—this, the anti-Brasílias say, is what would really open up the interior, and not a new capital. And why build a new capital, they ask, when, even if it may need a thorough overhauling at the moment, they already have one of the most beautiful capitals in the world, complete with government buildings? They think it will be years before the foreign embassies build there, although they have all bought land as a matter of course or of policy, and even longer before the senators and deputies can be persuaded to stay in Brasília for any length of time.

Whoever may be right time will tell, but Brasília is President Kubitschek's dream. He announced that eventually someone would have to keep the promise made the country in the Constitution in 1891, and he is going to keep it now. His five-year term has two more years to run; on April twenty-first, 1960, the government is supposed to make the great move.

I arrived there alone on a Friday afternoon clutching a piece of paper bearing the name of the man, a relative of someone important, who was supposed to meet me but never did. The first thing that greeted my eyes as I got off the plane was a three-throned shoe-shine stand against the wall of the small airport building. At the moment I was not in need of a shoe-shine but all departing passengers certainly were. To be sure, it was the tail-end of the dry season, but in the later summer of 1958 one's first and last impression of Brasília was of miles and miles and miles of blowing red dust.

Inside, the airport is a fair sample of the workaday atmosphere of the greater part of Brasília so far—rather like that of a small bus-station in the United States, a far-west bus station. Men in jeans, wide-brimmed felt hats and high boots, mill about drinking coffee and beer and eating stale pastries. (Women are still scarce in Brasília and I had been the only one on the plane.) There is a small general-store section of battered cans of milk, sardines, and hearts of palm, ropes of dry red sausage, bottles of *cachaça*, sunglasses, headache remedies, and yesterday's newspapers. On the wall is a line of little silk banners bearing the magic word BRASÍLIA, and also for sale are plastic plaques embossed in gold with the same word and, in profile, the head from which all this has sprung: Juscelino Kubitschek de Oliveira, in a blur of gold.

The four or five men, looking like engineers—one had a big T-square under his arm—who had arrived with me all got into jeeps and were driven off in clouds of dust. Finally I gave up waiting for my mentor and took the cream-colored Volkswagen Microbus lettered "Brasília Palace Hotel" and was driven off, too, the only passenger. It is over twelve miles from the airport to the hotel; it was a warm, clear day and we drove very fast over the bumpy dirt road.

The site of Brasília is an empty, barren, slightly rolling plateau, four thousand feet above sea-level. The place had been described to me, but I was not prepared for quite such dreariness and desolation: compared with almost any other inhabitable part of this fantastically beautiful country it seems really remarkably unattractive and unpromising. There are no mountains nor even real hills, no rivers, at least not in evidence (there is a small one some miles away and two small streams), no trees of any size, no feeling of height, nor grandeur, nor security, nor fertility, nor even just picturesqueness; not one of the qualities one thinks of as capable of giving a city charm or character. It reminded me, and other members of the party later said it reminded them, of the depressing landscape around Madrid. The two gifts Mother Nature seems to have bestowed on Brasília so far are sky and space, and when one imagines these endless swelling plains covered over with modern white government buildings, monuments, skyscrapers, shops, and apartment houses, the way they are eventually supposed to be, the only natural beauty left it is the sky. Of course there is now to be an artificial lake; there is even a yacht club marked on the map of the city; and friends who have been there in the rainy season say that it is very beautiful to see the rain-storms coming across the plains, from miles away. But for anyone accustomed to the hyper-glamorous beauty of Rio de Janeiro, where miles of white beaches, or even a view of the bay at the end of a city street, can make up for most of the city's shortcomings, Brasília seems like a sad come-down.

There are a few clumps of palms here and there, but in general the vegetation consists of sparse, scrubby trees, mostly a variety known as "apricot," which bears small wild fruits, no relation, however, to the true apricot. As far off the road as the eye can see these trees and the coarse grass are coated with the red dust constantly stirred up by passing trucks. Growing out of almost every thin trunk, half-way up, hideous and bigger than a man's head, is a white ants', or termites' nest. When I asked my driver, a depressed, dust-covered young man, about them he said dryly that termites build half-way up the trees to be that much nearer the fruit. Miles apart, a few clusters of roofs can be seen, colonies of the construction workers and other new inhabitants. By far the biggest of these is the "Nucleus of Pioneers," or "Flagbearers," to translate its romantic name literally, commonly called simply the Free City. This was officially opened in February 1957, with four hundred people, and now has, incredibly and encouragingly, forty-five thousand. "All built of wood," said the driver, and we heard that phrase many times because in a Latin country of stone, marble, tiles, and plaster, a whole city deliberately built of wood is a curiosity. "And it certainly is free," he added, and that was his last remark until we reached the hotel.

Oscar Niemeyer, world-famous architect, has been a friend of President Kubitschek ever since building a house for him, the first modern house in Belo Horizonte, when Kubitschek was mayor of that city. Later, when Kubitschek was governor of the state of Minas Gerais, he commissioned Niemeyer to build the resort of Pampulha, just outside Belo Horizonte, which is the state's capital. Now Niemeyer is responsible for all public buildings to be built in Brasília. In 1956 a competition was held for a "pilot-plan" for the new city of five hundred thousand people. It was any architect's dream come true, and dozens of plans were submitted, some extremely elaborate and detailed, down to suburbs and agricultural belts. Lucio Costa, Brasil's leading older architect and a friend and sponsor of Niemeyer since his student days, felt that at that early stage nothing very detailed should be attempted. He submitted only five or six little sketches, drawn rapidly, apparently, on small sheets of an inferior grade of paper. But his pilot-plan was immediately recognized as a brilliant little *tour de force*, and it was unanimously awarded the first prize, equal to about fourteen thousand dollars.

Following it, the city is laid out in the form of an aeroplane, or is it a bird, heading east, with a body seven or eight miles long. The wings, seven and a half miles across, will be the residential districts; the shopping center is at the tail; the body contains banks and office-buildings; along about the thorax come the foreign ministries, and the head is the "Esplanade of the Three Powers": Judiciary, Administrative, and Executive—this last being, on paper, Niemeyer's most spectacular and ambitious project to date. Set apart from the aeroplane or bird, to the east of its head, are the Brasília Palace Hotel and the Palácio da Alvorada (or "Palace of the Dawn"), the presidential residence, the only two large buildings completed at present; indeed, except for one small church and the foundations or skeletons of five blocks of apartment houses, they are almost the only permanent buildings to be seen.

For a recent number of *Modulo*, the Brasilian architectural magazine, Niemeyer wrote an article called "Testimony," lofty in tone but uneasy as to logic, about his work for Brasília. Politically he is a communist and in his "testimony" he takes himself to task for his past errors and promises to do better in the future, in the best communist manner. He says he still believes "that until there is a just distribution of wealth—which can reach all sectors of the population—the basic objective of architecture, that is, its social foundation, will be sacrificed, and the role of architect will be relegated to waiting upon the whims of the wealthy classes." He confesses to having done this in the past, to having thought of architecture as a "game" and even having deliberately built houses with eccentricities and extravagances for their rich owners "to talk about." But from now on, he says, things will be different; he intends that his works for Brasília shall all be "useful and permanent and capable of evoking a little beauty and emotion."

It might strike a critical visitor as ironical that for over two years thousands of workers have been left to build wooden houses or shacks and shift for themselves, while the first two buildings to be completed should both be called "Palace." However, to be fair, besides the Free City, attempts are being made to provide decent housing for workers and white-collar workers. Two blocks of five hundred houses each, "row" houses, designed by Niemeyer, have already been built by the *Fundação da Casa Popular*, and five "superblocks" of apartments are now going up, financed by five of the Brasilian *institutos*, a form of syndicate peculiar to Brasil, handling pensions, hospitalization, or loans, or functioning, as in this case, as banks.

At the end of four years, when enough housing will have been completed, the Free City is supposed to be razed; in fact, by then, one branch of the artificial lake is supposed to be rippling above its streets. Those most violently opposed to Brasília cynically predict that the Free City will never be razed; that it will remain and probably grow, the slums of the future city, like the wild and uncontrollable growth of shacks that now surrounds Rio de Janeiro.

(Also to be fair it should be explained that although the word "palace" for a president's residence may sound strange to American ears, in Latin countries the word does not have the overtones of royalty it has for us. It can mean merely "mansion," and *palacete*, "small palace," is often used for any large house.)

Surely it is to Kubitschek's credit that he has probably the most sophisticated taste in architecture of any head of any government. Educated Brasilians are apt to feel that although their country is in a bad transitional period, backwards in many respects, and may not have made much of a stir in the other arts, it has reason to be proud of its contemporary architecture. The outstandingly beautiful Ministry of Education building in Rio was begun in 1937, the very first and still one of the very few government buildings to be commissioned in modern international style. (Chandigarh was not begun until almost fifteen years later.) After all, Kubitschek could have chosen to build an Old Colonial capital, or a Greek-and-Roman, or even one in a particularly monstrous Swiss-chalet style that has sometimes been thought appropriate for Brasil. But as far as his choice of style goes the only objections I have heard of have been from the Army, which does not feel that an airy, glassy, or floating edifice will represent its view of things. But perhaps all generals secretly yearn for crenellations and drawbridges.

•

A friend of mine, a Rio interior decorator who had just finished doing up the new hotel, had made reservations for me by two-way radio. The Brasília Palace Hotel is in one block, a hundred and thirty-five rooms, one room thick and three stories high; only a small central section rests on the ground, the rest of the building on either side being supported by concrete pillars covered with black-anodized aluminum. At night these pillars almost disappear and the hotel appears to float like a luxury-liner, an effect that seems to be dear to Niemeyer's heart these days.

The entrance, reminding me vaguely of a New York subway entrance, is down a flight of steps into a sunken lobby; over it, at ground level, is a large, pleasant lounge, full of Saarinen chairs and marble-topped coffee-tables. The three floors of rooms face east to the Palace of the Dawn; three corridors run the full length of the west side of the building. There is one public staircase, about four feet wide, and two small elevators (one was not working when we were there), each holding at the most six people, so that there will certainly be serious traffic problems when the hotel is filled with its quota of three hundred guests. The entire west wall is made of large blocks of cement, five inches or so thick, and regularly set into each block are rows of little round glasses—real drinking glasses, the bell boys like to inform one—their circle-ridged bottoms sealing the wall on the outside. They let in the light in thousands of spots on the walls and gray carpeting of the corridors, an effect that is extremely pretty but unfortunately, from the moment the sun starts down the western sky until early next morning, fiendishly hot. Also, I wondered how could the insides of all those little glasses ever be cleaned? Already the more casual type of guest had begun to leave cigarette butts and other odds and ends in those within reach. Between each floor a row of blocks has been left without the glasses; the holes open into an airspace above the halls, where small screened openings alternate with light fixtures along the ceilings. This is supposed to provide ventilation, but not a breath of air came from the vents, and at night, when I walked the corridor to my room at the very end, before reaching its white formica doorway I would be dizzy from the heat. The bathroom ceilings are pierced with holes into this common airspace, too, with the unhappy result that one clearly hears the man next door taking his bath, limb by limb. The rooms, however, are large and cool, and except for the dressing-tables, well furnished. In the dressing-table mirrors a woman of barely average height (myself) sees only her chin.

Between the hotel block and the dining-room wing is a small space about as big as a tennis court and here grass had been planted and was being watered. Otherwise, in front and in back of the hotel, and for the half-mile tract between it and the presidential palace, the red dust blew unchecked. (A week or so after this, when President Gronchi of Italy visited Brasília, a thin layer of cement was poured over the area in front of the Palace.) Dust seeped into the hotel, tingeing the carpets and one's clothing and the gray marble floor of the lounge was powdered with it. I watched a workman trying to clean this floor with an electric polishing machine. After producing a few big spirals edged with banks of red dust, he gave up the attempt.

This particular floor comes to an end in a free-form curve four feet higher than the floor of the dining-room, into which the lounge opens. Plants and cacti hide coyly beneath the overhang, invisible from the lounge. The one occasion on our trip when I saw Aldous Huxley openly irritated was when, just after he arrived the next day, he started walking down the lounge, against the light, and almost fell over this drop. He showed distinct signs of anger, for him, and remarked that the handrail had been in use for some thousands of years and it seemed "a shame to abandon such a useful invention."

In front of the dining-room is the biggest swimming-pool I have ever seen: oval, lined with blue tiles, as yet waterless. The Presidential pool, at the far side of the Palace, is bigger than the standard Olympic pool, and this is a much bigger one than that. Permanent quarters for the hotel employees have not yet been built. Beyond the pool is a wooden paling, and inside it a collection of wooden shacks. Maids, bell boys, and chefs in their white hats, skirt the blue tile abyss and vanish into this shabby compound, and the dining-room looks out on it.

Concealed behind a curving black wall on the dining-room level are a bar and cocktail lounge, and also there was the source of some annoyance to the Huxley party—a loud, Brasilian equivalent of Muzak, which was turned on for two hours at lunch and dinner. The food was not bad, considering that all supplies have to be brought by truck or by plane from at least as far away as Annapolis; there were almost no vegetables, but always airlifted pineapples or papayas to provide us with vitamins, as well as the mushy Delicious apple, as ubiquitous here as in the United States.

That Friday night two far-off couples and I dined all alone in the big dining-room, the canned music struck up with the canned consommé, and the extra waiters looked on. After dinner two younger couples appeared in the lounge, with a baby in a basket and another small child to each couple. One mother in plaid slacks ran races with her little boy; the other joggled her baby's basket with her foot and read a detective story.

This peaceful family life, without the fathers, went on all the next morning. Around noon, when I was expecting my own party to arrive, several cars drove up rapidly from the direction of the airport and at least forty fashionably dressed men and women poured noisily down the steps into the subterranean lobby. They had come by special plane from São Paulo to attend a banquet and a ball that President Kubitschek was giving for them at the hotel that evening. The almost deserted, oddly domestic lounge suddenly swarmed with bejeweled women in sack dresses and men in pin-stripe suits. Parties like this, I was told, take place every week-end; in an air-age version of the hospitable old Brasilian custom of "showing the house to the visitors," Kubitschek invites groups from Rio, São Paulo, Porto Alegre, and other cities. Once, even, a whole convent of young girls came by special plane to look things over at the President's invitation. Tales of these week-end parties, of course, only increase the indignation of those opposed to Brasília on economic grounds—besides the expenses of entertainment, they say, just that much more gasoline is being used, in addition to the thousands of gallons burnt up by the trucks and planes bringing in building materials.

Five or ten minutes later the Huxleys and their party did arrive: very quiet, carrying books and cameras, and, slightly travel-worn, but looking alert and curious compared to the giddier set still swarming around the room-clerks. Laura Huxley and Maya Osser, the Polish-Brasilian architect, are old friends of mine, and I knew most of the others slightly or had met them.

Huxley is, of course, tall, pale, and thin, but he undoubtedly looks even taller, paler, and thinner than usual in Brasil, where most men, at least by Anglo-Saxon standards, are short and dark. Also, while the Brasilians were thinking of the season still as "winter" and in spite of the temperature were wearing dark suits and ties, Huxley always wore beige or light gray suits, or a white sports jacket, and he favored an extremely long, pale, satin necktie with Persian horsemen on it. His long hair, combed straight back, is a uniform gray-brown, his features large but well-modelled; he has beautiful teeth. Laura Huxley is about twenty years younger than her husband, small, trim, and blonde, with a rather large head and enormous gray-green eyes set far apart, in a remarkable Campigli-like style of Italian good looks. She is polite and friendly and animated, in French, Italian, or English, as the need arises. She shares Huxley's passionate interest in medicines, mescalin, and subliminal advertising, but on a more personal and practical level; in fact she adores to doctor people and occasionally handed out her various special pills to one or the other of us. With Huxley, it is hard to tell how much he is seeing, and since he usually talks very little, what he is thinking. By long self-discipline an original cool, English detachment seems to have been overlaid with an Oriental, or simply mystical, non-attachment. There is a slight cast to his bad eye, and this characteristic, which I always find oddly attractive, in Huxley's case adds even more to his veiled and other-worldly gaze. When examining something close to, a photograph or a painting, he sometimes takes out a small horn-rimmed magnifying glass, or, for distant objects, a miniature telescope, and he often sits resting his good eye by cupping his hand over it. He is unfailingly patient, never seems to tire (whenever anyone grew apprehensive about this his wife assured us that he never *does* tire), and smiling sweetly, displays occasional mild outbursts of interest. But he gives the impression of being inwardly absorbed in a meditation of his own, far removed from the possibly frivolous scenes of man's efforts that the Brasilian and Department of Foreign Affairs was proffering, and we all, to degrees that varied with our temperaments, behaved with him slightly like nervous hostesses.

After lunch and a two hours' rest we were taken off on a brief tour of the sights of Brasília, starting with the Palace of the Dawn. Kubitschek, meanwhile, had arrived for the party by his private Viscount. He sent over the old Lincoln convertible he keeps in Brasília, for the guests of honor. The Callados went with them; the rest of us climbed into the cream-colored Microbus and tagged along behind. Around the Palace is a barbed-wire fence and at the gate are a sentry box and two soldiers in tin helmets with tommy-guns under their arms. The Presidential car swept through the open gate but the sentries, not having been notified about the other car, refused to let us in and shut the gate under the bus's nose. The driver tried to explain but the young soldier said "No, no!" firmly and finally rather crossly, hugging his gun. The young Englishman hopped down from the bus and exclaimed "This is outrageous!" in the traditional English manner. Then someone drove back to the hotel, brought back the password, or at least permission for us to enter, and we were admitted after all, to catch up with the others.

The Palace of the Dawn is a large, rectangular, greenish (because Ray-Ban) glass box, framed lengthwise by swooping, off-white, pillars, ten on the far side in an unbroken series, and eight on the front, allowing a space for the entrance. From the outside it is certainly one of the most beautiful of all Oscar Niemeyer's buildings. The pillars, in particular, are an architectural triumph: it is, after all, no mean feat to invent a new "order." If one imagines a chain of huge white kites, poised upside down, then grasped by giant hands and squeezed in on the four sides until they are elegantly attenuated, one can picture them fairly accurately. They are covered with slabs of a crystalline Brasilian marble, and their bases, that is, the heads of the upside-down kites, theoretically narrow to point zero, and actually the part resting on the ground is only about six inches wide. In his *Modulo* article Niemeyer says that by means of these delicate dimensions he hoped to give the Palace "lightness and dignity—as if it had just landed gently on the earth." And in this he has succeeded completely, even if the other-planet atmosphere of all Brasília just now comes to his assistance—the incongruous soldiers, the strange, clumsy hotel, the hit-or-miss shacks and palm-trees, might all have "just landed," too—the effect of the Palace is completely original and yet immediately acceptable as a masterpiece of lightness and grace.

These pillars fascinated us all; they were patted and photographed and discussed for some time, Huxley and others even climbing down from the long porches to look at them from underneath. (They have quickly become a symbol for Brasília, appearing over and over in magazines and newspapers, as well as on the little silk banners, the hotel writing-paper and black imitation-leather zipper bags given to the guests.)

On either side of the entrance are square shallow pools of the same marble as the pillars; one contains a bronze statue of two female figures pierced with holes, by the Brasilian sculptor, Ceschiatti, the other a thin slab, like a sign-post, bearing an inscription in bronze. Also in front of the Palace we were shown a magnolia tree, about a yard high, that had been planted by Secretary Dulles just a few days before. (About a week later President Gronchi planted an Italian cypress in Brasília. There had been plans for Imperial palms grouped near the Palace but lately the variety of palm has been changed to the regional *buriti*, not so tall nor so elegant, but a very presentable tree, nevertheless.) The porch or gallery of the Palace extends beyond it on the left side, then curls around on itself and upwards in a small, exuberant, if snail-like chapel—a sort of airy, Latin, wave-of-the-hand concluding gesture to the static dance of the linked pillars. At least that is the idea; the chapel struck most of us as out of scale, perhaps a shade too small for the pillars. Its snail-with-a-sail facade is topped by a slender brass cross that looks exactly right, but the small window cut through the marble below it, a square hole opening onto space, seems a bit theatrical, even if it is strongly reminiscent of the small windows of the early mission churches in Brasil.

Once inside the Palace, I am sorry to say, the effect of coolness and airy grace vanishes. The decorating was done by Niemeyer and his daughter; the colors are frequently harsh and the furniture seems meagre and badly arranged—but surely many additions and changes will be made. We stepped in onto hot turkey-red carpets, extra-thick ("Nylon foam?" someone tentatively asked the secretary who was showing us around), laid down between walls of mirror and glittering gold tile. A rail-less, red-carpeted ramp (we were told that Secretary Dulles had almost fallen off that) goes up to the right, to the *Salão Nobre*. Here are a grand piano and a few groups of sofas, and upholstered and brass-and-leather chairs, some of which, at first glance, looked like the Mies van der Rohe Barcelona chair but which, as one discovers on trying them, are a smaller and not too comfortable copy of it.

Perhaps it should be said that Brasil, like Italy, Spain, or Portugal, has never had our northern ideas of comfort in the home. Until recently all beds were very hard, sometimes even of leather or cane, because hard beds are cooler in a hot climate; floors were of stone or tile or bare jacaranda planks; and chairs and sofas, when copied from foreign designs, often used woven cane instead of stuffed upholstery. The thick walls, extremely high ceilings, and small shuttered windows of colonial days were cool and appropriate; the "modern" interior, with its frequently soft and low furniture, light colors, and great areas of glass, has really not been completely adapted (as yet) to the Brasilian climate.

Perhaps we were too harsh in our criticisms as we trooped from room to room; I think that only Huxley failed to comment on the heat and glare. Across either end of the glass box that makes up the Palace is a long room, each with chairs and long table. One is the formal dining room, the other the Dispatch Room. Both are curtained only at the sides, that is, the ends of the box, and the afternoon sun pours into them through the glass front of the building; the wood of the tables was already crackling. The inner walls are panelled with large squares of deeply corrugated jacaranda, Brasil's handsomest wood. On the upper, shaded parts of the walls the effect is very beautiful, almost like tortoise-shell, but lower down, where the sun strikes, it, too, looks dried and lusterless. Perspiring and occasionally dropping onto the nearest chairs, we rudely asked our guide about air-conditioning, but he replied that it wasn't necessary.

A floating staircase goes straight from the *Salão Nobre* and is also carpeted in thick turkey-red. Upstairs, the halls are panelled in delicate tan "Ivory Wood," or satin wood. We saw only one bedroom, looking like any twin-bedded, chintz-hung guest room, but its adjoining bath was truly magnificent in chromium and thick gray marble, with a square sunken bath sloping from the ends to the middle, like a sagging double bed. Under the bedroom windows, overlooking the swimming-pool, runs a shaded balcony of highly polished slabs of rich green marble, a beautiful material but surely out of keeping with the building's light structure and the over-delicate panelling just inside.

At present the Palace walls are almost bare; downstairs are two tapestries and a few small paintings by Emilio Di Cavalcanti. This austerity and lack of ornament reminded Huxley of a very different tour he had once made through Buckingham Palace, where every inch of wall space is covered with paintings, and every table loaded with photographs commemorating incidents in the lives of the royal family. We gathered around him in the heat of the upstairs hall while he talked for quite a while, and very entertainingly, about George V's bedroom arrangements.

Outside, workmen were laying turquoise blue tiles in the cavernous swimming-pool while three or four soldiers with their tommy-guns peered over at them—out of curiosity, boredom, or perhaps it was their duty. In the middle of the pool is a high, jagged imitation rock or island, the top of which is supposed to be planted with a garden—at an acute angle. However, I was later told that Niemeyer is not pleased with this "modern" but curiously Gothic-revival detail and may change it.

To the right are the servants' quarters, a long, sunken wing with just a flat roof and a line of narrow windows showing above ground, connected with the Palace by a subterranean passage. This seems an extremely feeble, not to say depressing, solution to the problem of where to put the forty or so servants needed for the Palace. The crystal box is not for them, but there is certainly space enough in all directions, and apparently money enough, to have them at least housed on the surface, like their employers. In the old days, slaves were often kept in the dank basements of Rio houses; even now, the rooms and bathrooms provided for servants in up-to-date and luxurious Copacabana apartment houses shock the sensibilities of foreign residents—but surely in Brasília, sometimes referred to as "the most modern city in the world," Niemeyer, of all architects, should not have found it necessary to put them underground.

As we were leaving the Palace I realized that its more disappointing features had reminded me, in some way, of the house Niemeyer built for himself in 1954, on a hillside just outside Rio, and when I got back home I looked up what Henry Russell-Hitchcock had had to say about that in his book *Latin American Architecture*. Confirming my own amateur suspicions, I found this: "The pavillion contains only the main living areas and the kitchen. All other facilities are hidden away below the terrace with no relationship at all to the pavillion on top. Only, perhaps, its own designer and his family would find this an altogether comfortable residence . . ." Niemeyer's house, of course, is not at all like the Palace of the Dawn in Brasília, having been designed "in response to the landscape" in an interlocking set of curves, "in a harmony between the boldly rounded outline of the hills and the sinuous curves of his plan." Niemeyer's response to the flat empty spaces of Brasília has been this transparent, gracefully supported, but essentially severe, box; but in both cases his solution of practical problems seems to have been the same: put them underneath, or underground, like a lazy housewife shoving household gear out of sight under a deceptively well-made bed.

Off to the south east of the Palace, a small white triangle in the distance, is the "Hermitage of Saint John Bosco" a faithful copy in white marble of an Indian teepee—American Indian, that is, with the open tri-angular doorway but with a cross on top in place of criss-crossed tent-poles. One of the booklets about Brasília explains the presence of this rather surprising chapel: "In the book *Biographical Memories*, Vol XVI pages 385 and 395, can be found the tale of Saint John Bosco's prophecy. It tells there that Dom Bosco, on the thirtieth of August, 1883, had a dream-vision. We give the quotation in respect to Brasília.

" 'Between the fifteenth and twentieth parallels, in the place where a lake was formed, will be born a great civilization and this will happen in the third generation. Here will be the promised land.'

"We are in the third generation exactly. The great civilization under construction (and which is Brasília) is located between the fifteenth and the twentieth parallels. The lake will be formed by the streams Torto and Gama.

"Thus the prophetic dream of Dom Bosco will be fulfilled."

Laura Huxley was familiar with the life of this Italian saint, the founder of the Silesian order (which does much work in Brasil), and was eager to start off on a walk to see the "hermitage." However, it was pointed out that actually the chapel was about a mile away, and at that moment the light was beginning to change to a clear uniform pink, the beginning of the sudden sub-tropical sunset. As we left, a group of small soldiers, members of the Brasília *Guarda Especial*, marched solemnly past changing guard, pounding with their heavy boots; in their unstarched green uniforms, they always look like wilted string beans.

In the hotel lounge before starting out, Maya, the Polish girl, had run into another Polish former-refugee, Countess Tarnowska, who had invited us all to come to the Santos Dumont Hotel in the Free City for a drink before dinner. Some time before Countess Tarnowska had opened a movie house in Annapolis and shortly after the founding of Brasília she opened another one in the Free City. There were then three hundred people in the town and her cinema was in a wooden barn; now she has the largest building there, of corrugated iron, seating three hundred people, and there is even a rival movie house. She is young and handsome; in excellent English she told us blithely, "We love it here! Of course there are lots of fires. The bank next door burned down yesterday. We were frightened for the cinema a bit, but everything turned out all right. Too bad you missed the excitement!" Dressed in blue jeans, with a straw hat tightly bound down with a white scarf that swathed her neck, she and her beautiful dark-eyed daughter, also in jeans and khaki shirt, had resembled two heroines of an old western, a sepia western, since they were both covered with the usual dust.

We now drove towards the city, over the head of the bird, where the Esplanade of the Three Powers will be. At present it is a confusing, noisy scene of earthwork, trucks and bulldozers, with work going on day and night. Someone behind me was trying to explain the lay-out of the Esplanade. "You see, it's a triangular rectangle," he kept saying. The Englishman was trying to find the land acquired by his country for its future Embassy and when a vague area of the scrubby, termite-infested land was pointed out to him he said, "Oh! I'm so disappointed!" in such a crestfallen way that everyone laughed.

We passed the "superblocks" of apartments being built by the *institutos*; skeletons of steel and cement, it was hard to tell much about them except that they are very high and very close together, and again, with infinite space in all directions, it is hard to understand why they should be placed together at all, and with courtyards and area-ways not much larger than those in Rio—explicable because there actually is very little building space left, and real-estate values are higher than in New York.

The streets of Brasília have been planned to do away with traffic lights completely by means of over- and under-passes. Since the present capital is famous for the terrifying speed of its traffic, light-jumping, mad busdrivers, and high accident rate, this is one innovation that has been welcomed by all.

It was growing dark when we reached the Free City, but it was not too dark to see it: almost that old, familiar, Metro-Goldwyn-Mayer frontier town, but real, and greatly enlarged. The wide dirt streets are without sidewalks— "Imagine what it's like when it rains!" we told each other—and the wooden houses, with peaked roofs and occasional false fronts, are set close together, all shapes, sizes, and colors. We passed the corrugated iron cinema, and a big red barn with IGREJA PRESBYTERIANA in white letters across the gable. The traffic is mostly trucks, of all makes and ages, and jeeps, jeeps, jeeps, American, English, and Brasilian-made, with a few old cars and even a few men on horseback, all churning up thick clouds of dust.

The Hotel Santos Dumont is a low building, indistinguishable from the rest except for its sign and a few metal porch chairs placed on a narrow strip of cement flush with the street. Once inside, however, we seemed to have been bodily transported to a new little *boîte* or espresso bar in Greenwich Village—new because all the colors were bright and fresh, almost the only fresh colors I saw in the whole of Brasília. It was a rectangular room about thirty feet long, with a varnished bamboo bar and two boys in mess jackets; the table cloths were scarlet, there were black "drugstore" chairs, and bright yellow and green frills around the windows. Music was playing; I looked and saw Villa Lobos, Stravinsky, and Bartók records lying on the victrola. All this had been lugged in six hundred miles or more by truck. The Santos Dumont was modestly doing its best to be chic and cheerful and I think all our hearts warmed towards it.

Tables were pushed together and Countess Tarnowska, now clean and polished in an India print dress and bandanna, called for whiskey sours. But our temperate little party, perhaps slightly over-awed by Huxley (he had spoken once or twice about the unnecessary drinking and smoking that go on in the United States), refused alcohol for the most part and drank orange juice, which was mysteriously available. Countess Tarnowska, the daughter, and a heavy, blond Polish gentleman who was staying at the hotel, too, had just returned from a three-weeks' hunting trip, farther to the west, and she began telling us about it. They had had bad luck; they had been after *onça*, the Brasilian jaguar, but hadn't found any, and instead they had shot a great many of what she referred to with flashing eyes as "stags." It had been the daughter's first hunting trip and, said her mother proudly, "She shot twelve alligators." From hunting Tarnowska went on to speak of murderous propensities she had observed in Brasil in general and in Brasília in particular. "They like killing," she assured Huxley, with beautiful vivacity, and told an anecdote about a recent gratuitous shooting. At my end of the table the Huxleys, Maya, the Englishman and myself all being rather strongly anti-shooting, man or beast (and my own experience of Brasilians being that they are the least bloodthirsty of peoples) the conversation began to fall a little flat, and Huxley, who had said almost nothing so far, shaded his eyes with his hand and seemed lost in meditation over his mysterious orange juice.

She then told a story of her movie house that illustrated the national character a bit better. The forty-five thousand citizens of the Free City mostly come from the interior, the "north" or the "south"—and it is hard to realize the weight of the vast unknown, or half-known, that these ordinary terms of direction can still carry in Brasil—simple, old-fashioned, country people, a type called *condangos*. One of the films shown recently had been "And God Created Woman." The audience, many more men than women, had watched quietly, thinking heaven knows what, until the story reached the disrobing scene. Brigitte Bardot had undone one button when the movie suddenly stopped and the lights went up. The man in the projection booth, who had obviously watched it through before, said, "Will all the *senhoras* and *senhoritas* please leave, and wait outside." And leave they did, without demur, and stood outside in the dusty street in a little crowd. The theatre was darkened and the men watched the love scene that followed. Again the film stopped, the lights went on, and the ladies were invited back in, to see the rest of the show coeducationally.

We asked what was playing that night, with some idea of going to see it. It was a travelling show of skits, singing and dancing, and Countess Tarnowska, who had watched a rehearsal, did not recommend it.

We left the hotel and took a walk down the main street. Almost every building has its own electric generator (using more precious gasoline every minute), so there is a background music of pulsing and chugging and the lights vary from building to building, yellow, blueish, or grayish, with here and there the deep yellow of kerosene lamps or the blue-white glare of gasoline pressure lanterns. We strolled along observing barber shops and *pharmácias* (both doing rush business), grocery stores, dry good stores, and shoe-shine and shoe-repair shops—boot, rather, since all the male population of Brasília wears high boots, usually of a variety with an accordion-like section of imitation ripples above the ankle. Boarding houses, dormitories and restaurants; banks and airline offices, given a spurious city-look with ripped wall-board and a potted palm. Some furniture stores with new furniture but most crammed with second-hand Brasilian Grand Rapids, always included the lean *armoires* of closetless countries. The Butcher Shop of the Good Jesus, the suspended meat an iridescent violet under the light of hissing gasoline lamps. (And where had *it* come from?) Then small glass-fronted shops, exactly like other such shops all over Brasil: shoddy shirts and blouses and pink and blue undergarments, plastic bags and belts, and hung up in front, rows of umbrellas, black for men and brightly colored for women—because in Brasil everyone, no matter how poor, with the possible exception of the Indians we were going to see, owns an umbrella. Also baby dresses, booties and bibs, and even christening robes in glistening little piles like marshmallow sauce, because also no matter how poor, Brasilians will spend money on finery for their babies. A popular song, sung in English, blared out from a shop selling radios and victrolas.

As we went along we bought packages of cigarettes, boxes of matches, and *Salva Vidas*, Life Savers, to take to the Indians the next day. Antônio Callado, more experienced with the Indians than the rest of us, went into a shop full of boots, felt hats, machetes and guns, and came back with fish-hooks and nylon fish lines. The radio at the Indian post we were going to had been broken for over a month and there was no way of letting them know we were coming, so he also laid in a supply of sausage in case their food supply should be low.

Several of us met in a narrow bar at right angles to the streets, painted a dark sea-green. In it, alluring as a mermaid in her cave, stood a plump, sulky, pretty young woman with bleached hair and a very *décolleté* black sweater. Two small, pink-cheeked children, a boy and a girl, obviously hers, on the counter, staring at the one customer, a man drinking beer. Laura

Huxley decided to get a photograph of the children with her Polaroid Land camera, using the headlights of the Volkswagen bus for light, and they posed, shy and blinking. From time to time the girl's husband stuck his head through a flowered curtain at the back of the bar, keeping his eye on us. The girl's parents had been Lebanese immigrants; she spoke a little French. We asked her how she liked living in Brasília, or in the Free City, and she replied promptly: "*Je le déteste!*—But my husband likes it all right." They were from São Paulo and she missed the city; she was of a new, sophisticated city class, without the formal, old-fashioned manners of the *condangos*. When we left she stood languidly holding the drying photograph, almost forgetting to call "Thank you" after us. Brigitte Bardot would not have surprised *her*.

Then back the fifteen miles to the hotel (and distances seem even farther than they are, perhaps because there are so few landmarks), for a dinner that ended after eleven o'clock. News that Huxley was at the hotel had spread among the party-guests from São Paulo; before dinner the taller man from Itamarati had been taken for Huxley and another woman of the group for Mrs. Huxley, and both asked for autographs. When the mistakes were corrected, Huxley and Laura obligingly signed their names on dinner menus (*Bife Stroganoff*). Huxley didn't mind not being recognized; at dinner he told a little story of another recent experience of mistaken identity. Before starting out for Brasil he had visited his dentist in Beverly Hills, and as he walked out of the elevator he met a woman about to get in. She looked up at him and stepped back in astonishment, then inquired, "Pardon me, but aren't you Theda Bara's husband?"

After midnight, kept awake by strains of dance-music from the hotel dining-room, where the President's party was in progress, I lay in bed studying the illuminated green-blue aquarium of the Palace of the Dawn, off in the distance. It is a pity, I decided, that the kite-like pillars are not spot-lit at night. As it is, their effectiveness is lost after dark because they show up only as formless shadows on the lighted glass box. But undoubtedly they eventually will be.

The next day, Sunday, was the day for the Indians. At six-thirty we met outside the hotel in the damp, chilly dawn; the Volkswagen bus was supposed to be there, but, with the confusion probably incidental to founding a new city, it kept us waiting for almost an hour, and to keep warm we took brisk walks around the cement parking space. The stork-like Huxley legs went around it faster than anyone else's without any effort, and watching those giant steps our clammy little group, laden down with books, baskets, and sun hats, murmured to each other in Portuguese that he looked "young for his age." We were a rather highbrow set. On our way to see the most primitive people left in the world, except for the African pygmies, we had, among us: Martin Buber's "The Eclipse of God," Huxley's "The Doors of Perception" and "Heaven and Hell," in Portuguese, and "Grey Eminence" in English. Also being taken along to fill in the time on the trip were a thick French book titled simply "Plato" and a pocket edition of "The Mill on the Floss."

Finally the bus arrived and we retraced the long red road to the airport. A few birds were singing, but not many, and the termites were hard at work in their unsightly red nests. Red ostrich plumes of dust rose here and there, trucks moving along with their loads of cement, girders, or fill, and the nagging sound of bull-dozers came from the direction of the Esplanade of the Three Powers.

At eight we took off in a Brazilian Air Force DC-3. It was a pleasant plane, if one can use the word for a plane, new, bare of all the usual paddings and curtains, but with blue plush seats, the backs of which could be folded over. It was meant for twenty-four passengers, and although several unknown men had now joined the party there were still so many extra seats that we could turn down the backs of alternate ones and put our feet up, the way we used to do on trains as children.

The continent rolled out underneath us to the west, a full-scale, dun-colored, bas-relief map. Trees grow along the wrinkles; the smaller streams are opaque olive-green. Occasionally higher ground breaks out into crumbling, fortress-like rocks, possibly the formations, Callado told us, that had given rise to the legend of the lost city that Colonel Fawcett searched for; we were flying over Fawcett territory. After a while we saw one large blue river, the Araguaia, flowing north, as all the rivers do, to join the Amazon, over a thousand miles away. Callado, dressed today in khaki drill, went down the aisle giving us each an anti-malaria pill from an enormous bottle: "Mostly for the psychological effect," he said, "although we may meet some malarial mosquitoes." Until it grew warmer the Air Force men kept on their stylish reefers of gray-blue wool with long-peaked caps to match. They were friendly and hospitable and began feeding us immediately: sandwiches, then gumdrops and jelly beans, and then paper cups of sweet black coffee, at least three times, but this is *de rigueur* on any Brasilian plane, sometimes even on Brasilian buses. Later the plane filled with the smell of oranges as a helpful aviator sliced off the peels of a whole tray for us.

We dipped into our various books and swapped them across the aisle; we changed places to talk to each other, like a dance. The young interpreter ate a large chocolate bar and devoted herself to a magazine called *Lady* (pronounced "Lah-dee"). She handed it across to show Huxley.

There was a full page photograph of him at a recent press conference in Rio, shading his eyes and looking very sad. His wife was indignant about the expression: "Oh, why do they always take him looking like that! He really doesn't look like that at all!" I was bothered more by the huge caption: THE OLD HUXLEY SAYS—something about world peace. Although Huxley does not know Portuguese, he does know Spanish and I was afraid he might recognize the similar word for "old." I had a brief argument with myself as to whether I should try to explain or not, then decided to hold my tongue. In this case I felt the word was meant affectionately, or "old" only in the sense of Huxley's having been famous for many years. (For two weeks Huxley had been making a deep impression in Rio; the bookshops were filled with his books, in five languages, and he had received nothing but unqualified praise and consideration from the press.)

One of the men who had joined us was an exuberant type, who couldn't sit still but kept prancing up and down the aisle with a leather gaucho hat tied under his chin. Another was old and tiny, large-eared and mournful-eyed. He, I discovered, was the man who had been supposed to meet me at the airport two days before; at that very moment, he confessed, he was supposed to be meeting a party arriving from Rio, but on the spur of the moment had decided to come along with us instead. He carried a clip-board with "Aldous Huxley" printed in capitals across the top sheet. He presented this and asked if Huxley would write a message on it—his impressions of Brasília, anything at all—for a collection of such messages from all visiting celebrities he was making, to be put in a future Brasília museum. Huxley took out his pen and set to work, and after tearing up two or three sheets of paper he produced a few phrases about the interesting experience of flying from the past (the colonial towns in Minas) to the future, the brand-new city of Brasília. Two days later this appeared in the Rio papers as a telegram Huxley had sent to President Kubitschek, giving a rather odd impression of the Huxley telegram style.

We were now flying more north than west and the scenery below had gradually changed. We flew over the River of the Dead, and then the River of the Souls. There were areas of what Callado called the "cauliflower forests." From above, jungle trees do look like massed cauliflower, or even more, broccoli, although here not as thick nor as vivid a green as in the Amazon region. At last someone exclaimed "Look! An Indian village!" and sure enough, there in a clearing beside a muddy little river were five round roofs of palm thatch and two or three stick-like boats pulled up on the bank. Beyond them was an air-strip, an inch or two of faded red tape dropped into the jungle. It was the post of Xavantina, named for the Xavante Indians (*x* is pronounced *sh*), formerly fierce warriors, the Indians who are familiar from photographs posing on one leg, and wearing their hair in long bobs. However, we were going on farther, to the Uialapiti at Captain Vasconcelos Post, on a small tributary of the Xingu River.

Callado, who was responsible for this part of the Huxley tour, now began to have a slight attack of nerves. He began to tell us not to expect too much of the Indians we were about to see; after all, they are at a Post, they are a mixed lot, sometimes as many as five tribes will be visiting there together, and those who live there permanently are somewhat "uninteresting," he put it, not like those who live completely isolated in their own villages. Some of them sometimes wear a shirt or a pair of trousers (but the only possible reason for wearing clothes that they can understand is that they keep off the mosquitoes), and one man had actually been taken on a trip to Rio, to see the Carnival.

At last another air strip appeared, and another clearing on another small river, this time with clear water and the thatched roofs were oval. We circled over *buriti* palms and one tall purple *îpé* in full flower, without a single leaf—one of the loveliest of Brasilian flowering trees. As we dropped down we could see Indians coming out of the houses and running along a rough road from the village to meet us, and when we stepped from the plane five or six men were already there and women with babies were bringing up the rear. They were very glad to see us, beaming with smiles, reaching eagerly for our hands, right or left, and squeezing them; two or three of the men said "Good-day, good-day" in Portuguese. More and more kept coming running, squeezing our hands or shaking them limply, smiling with delightfully open and cheerful expressions, showing square, widely spaced teeth.

The Uialapiti are short but well-built, the men almost plump, with smooth muscles, broad shoulders, and smooth broad chests. They are naked except for shell necklaces and strings of beads or shells around the hips; the women wear a symbolic *cache sexe* of palm leaf folded into a little rectangle about an inch and half long, secured by a fine string woven from the same palm. This almost invisible article of dress is important; sometimes they stop and turn their backs to adjust the string. Their hair is very thick and surprisingly fine and glossy; the women wear it long, with bangs; the men in inverted bowl haircuts. They have almost no hair on their bodies; the occasional hair is pulled out. Most of the men had locks of hair or the whole crown of the head smeared with a bright red, sticky paint they make from the *urucum* tree, the only dye, and color, they possess; some of them were powdered with it, ears, necks, or chests, hot red. Their skin is fine and soft, a deep dusky color. Some of the children, girls, had two parallel black lines drawn down the outside of their legs, and one young girl had a bright red forehead, suggestive of a bad headache. Both men and women carry the babies, and besides their own shell beads most of them wear strings of blue and white glass ones. A baby girl, about ten months old, looked fetching in nothing but six strands of big Woolworth pearls. They are sweet-smelling and clean (they go swimming several times a day)—excepting that the children had filthy, muddy faces. However, that didn't stop the Air Force men from plucking the babies (including the pearl-clad one) from the parents' arms and carrying them off. There was an agreeable Old-Home-Week atmosphere. Callado and the pilots knew most of the men; some of them spoke a little Portuguese, and a simple, repetitious conversation started that kept going without ceasing all during our visit. Huxley was introduced as a "great captain," *um grande capitão*, and allowed himself to be admiringly handled.

It was dusty and very hot; we walked through the cleared path to a big hard-beaten space where four houses stood. A large black sow with baby pigs rushed off when she saw us, and there were many skinny dogs. More Indians kept coming to meet us and stare and hold our hands in their hard hot ones, and sometimes to pat us discreetly to make out whether we were men or women, since the women of the party were in slacks. All the Indians were quite naked except one old man who had on an Army shirt and two young women who wore red and white flowered cotton dresses. One of these, fourteen or fifteen years old, was far advanced in pregnancy, and the other, older one, was a dwarf or hunchback, a queer, sad little figure whom we kept seeing bustling about the village all during our visit, as if she worked more than the others, or wanted to give the impression that she was as active as anyone else.

Suddenly a white man appeared, middle-aged, thin, a week's growth of black beard on his pale face, wearing pants and shirt but in his bare feet. It was the man in charge of the Captain Vasconcelos Post, Claudio Villas Boas, one of three brothers who have all worked for the Indian Protection Service for many years. Because of the broken radio he couldn't have known we were coming until he heard the sound of the plane, but he showed not a trace of surprise until his eyes happened to light on Huxley. Huxley and Laura were introduced. In Portuguese, in a weak voice, Villas Boas exclaimed, "Not the *Huxley? Contraponto?*" and for a moment he actually seemed about to faint. He took Huxley's hand and talked away to him in Portuguese, with his eyes filled with tears. At this moment another clothed white man in his bare feet appeared from nowhere, a tall, handsome, baby-faced boy with a bushy black beard. He, too, exclaimed, but in the accents of upper-class England, "Huxley! I certainly never expected *this!*" He turned out to be a Cambridge graduate student, a historian, who had been at the post for a month. He was working on a thesis on the effects of contact between two different cultures, and also writing a book. "Or I'd better be," he said, "since I've already sold it."

With Villas Boas leading we all trooped into the shadowy interior of one of the houses; this one joined another smaller one with walls half-way up and a large table, and a third hut attached to it that served as a sort of kitchen. Huxley got into one of the hammocks and lay back (it became him very well); Villas Boas squatted Indian-style beside him, and with two or three people all helping to interpret, he began talking to Huxley in a rusty, agitated voice as if he had been wanting to talk to him for years. We gathered round to listen and it was a strained, moving little scene: the great shadowy hut, the oddly-assorted, oddly-dressed white people, the ring of naked, smiling Indians, and Huxley, swaying slightly back and forth, his long legs trailing on the ground, passive and attentive. Villas Boas told him that he had read all his books that had been translated into Portuguese, how much they had meant to him, going on to speak of Huxley's grandfather's books, too. Then he told about his years in the Indian service, how hard it is to help the Indians, a losing battle against disease and corruption; how even with the help of Army doctors he lives in dread of infections brought in from outside, the one case of measles, for example, that can wipe out whole villages. The Indians own no land; there are no reservations for them to retreat to if the lands where they live should ever be sold. Even if that will probably not happen for a long time, the land is subject to speculation, and the founding of Brasília has brought the possibility nearer by six hundred miles. In the whole Xingu region he thinks there are now only about thirty-five hundred of them left.

Laura Huxley had wandered outside and was setting up shop with the Polaroid camera; these Indians knew all about cameras and were happy to pose, in rows, with their arms about each other's necks. Those inside pressed up against us, not exactly begging, but certainly eager for the presents they knew we'd have, and half-embarrassed, we handed out our miserable cigarettes, matches, and Life Savers. One woman kept pinching me gently asking *Caramelo? Chocolate? Caramelo?* and I was sorry I hadn't known of this preference in sweets. The hammocks were filling up; the man with the volume labelled *Plato* reclined in one, a pilot was playing with a baby in another, and the gaucho-hat man was in another with another baby, who now wore the hat. I got into a hammock, too, and looked up. The high shadowy roofs are beautifully made, palm leaves folded over horizontal branches, in overlapping layers, and the big dome is braced towards the top with a framework of unpeeled branches. Pigeons roosted there, cooing, and a pair of parakeets. A gorgeous blue and yellow macaw sat on the dining-hut wall eyeing us and talking away in *Nu-aruak*, presumably—the language group to which the Uialapiti belong. Several *mutum*, a kind of turkey, black and shiny, with crests like ball-edged combs and patches of pale green on either side of their chic little heads, strolled about clucking under our legs. The gloom, the gentle voices, the pats and smiles and swaying hammocks, were restful and dreamlike, down-to-earth, even nostalgically back-to-earth, after the three hours in the plane.

I could hear an Indian questioning the Air Force man in the nearest hammock. He asked Huxley's name, which woman was his, and how many children they had. The man answered the questions; the Indian studied Huxley, smiling, asked them all over again, and received the same answers. (Their conversation, I was told, moves rather like a glacier. A simple story can go on for hours, even for days.) As any one who has ever seen photographs of Huxley on his book-jackets knows, he is a very handsome, aristocratic-looking man, but the Indian's final opinion, given in a tactfully lowered voice, was "Homely . . . homely . . ." And under the circumstances Huxley did appear, not homely, but exceedingly long, white, refined, and misplaced.

After a while we went outside and down to the river, where some of us went for a swim, the Indians sociably joining in. Usually the villages are as far as a mile inland from the rivers, to get away from the mosquitoes, and the whole village files through the jungle every morning, or morning and evening, to go swimming.

One young Indian was a visitor from the Caiapos, a tribe that has been in contact with white men for only two years. (New tribes are still being met, while there are some who have been known for two hundred years.) The visitor appeared in pants and a shirt, his hair flowing down his back and tied with a white hair-ribbon, and in his lower lip a smooth oval plate of wood, four inches across, the under side dyed red. He was a cheerful, talkative boy ("Nice, but rather foolish," Callado said); when asked to pose for a photograph he politely removed his clothes. In swimming with us, doing a kind of breast-stroke, he threw water into his mouth with the wooden plate and drank like a duck. The English boy called him "Ronny," which was fairly close to his vowel-filled Indian name.

Because it was the end of the dry season the little river was only waist deep, but the bottom was clean and sandy, and there were green hummocks, vines, and clumps of delicate palms, all rather like the wood-engravings in old books of exploration. "Ronny's" boat was on the bank, filled with bundles of palm thatch ready to take back to his own village. It had been simply made, by slitting the bark of a tree length-wise and prying it off in one piece with wedges; the bark shell is then pried open with sticks, the ends bent upwards, it is left to dry out, and with very little trouble, you have a very nice light canoe. We dawdled about on the bank, taking more photographs. The Indians loved the Polaroid pictures (in fact a Polaroid camera and a large supply of film should see one through the jungle), almost tearing them apart to see the results; Huxley's pocket was adroitly picked of some unsuccessful ones that Laura had stored in it. A mass of pale yellow Sulphur butterflies settled, quivering, in the wet mud at the river's edge, like the start of a yacht race; a few magnificent ones of a variety unknown to me among them, the closed wings exactly mimicking a big silver-gray dead leaf and when open flashing two bars of pure, startling rose-red velvet. Huxley took great pleasure in these butterflies, leaning far over from his great height to examine them close to with his magnifying glass.

Then we were called to lunch: the sausage we had brought, a pot of brown beans, and two platters of under-cooked rice. (The usual food is manioc; the rice had been a recent present.) "Ronny" put on trousers and helped wait on us, filling tin mugs with water, ladling out the runny beans, and flapping his lip-plate up and down in a friendly way. The blue and yellow macaw was prevented from jumping onto the table and the Indians stood close, watching every bite and smiling hard whenever one caught their eyes. I was wearing small gold earrings and every once in a while the lobe of my ear would be gently pinched. After the beans and rice came more little coffees; we lit cigarettes for the Indians, they painstakingly lit cigarettes for us, and langour settled over us all.

After half an hour's siesta we were invited to see a wrestling match put on for our benefit. Two of the sleekest young men began, with the rest of the population sitting in the strips of shade along the houses to watch. The men crouch almost on all fours, grasp each other's hands in a hard shake, and then grab for the backs of each other's necks and hold on, still bent over and giving loud, hooting grunts—the only sounds we heard them make that could be called "savage." The object of the match is to throw the opponent over and pin his shoulders to the ground, but as soon as one man senses he is the stronger he rarely forces it to a conclusion. He simply lets go, they stand up, smile, and walk off abruptly, in different directions. The quick, red-bedaubed, naked men, stamping and hooting in the urine-scented dust, resemble fighting-cocks more than anything else.

Then we paid a call at the largest of the houses, thirty-five or forty feet long, dark and sooty. Men were swaying in their hammocks, women messed about with manioc and clay pots on the floor. The men asked for more cigarettes and to please them I lit a cigarette apiece for them with my lighter. The one old man grinned mischievously and I saw, tucked away in the hammock between his tough black feet, four whole packages of cigarettes he had already collected, and several little blue boxes of *Fiat Lux* matches. Across one end of the house was a man-high fence of twigs and palm-leaves. The Cambridge student told us that behind it, in the dark, a young girl was undergoing her puberty initiation. "You can look through the fence; this isn't the really secret part," he said. Peering into the gloom we could make out a lean-to, perhaps two feet wide at the base, against the far wall. In it, silent and invisible, the girl is supposed to stay for three months, six months in some tribes, only coming out at night to get a little fresh air. When the initiation is over, they are very weak and many shades lighter than their normal color. The dwarf in the scarlet dress scuttled in with a pan of water and another of rice and set them down, in silence. Hanging in the rafters over our heads was an enormous polished black calabash and someone asked the Cambridge man what it was doing there. "Oh, they just happened to like it," he informed us, and added innocently, "They're human beings too, you know."

In this region the nights get quite cold. The naked Indians keep warm by building small fires right under their hammocks and, too, the resulting smoke drives away the malarial mosquitoes. One woman was holding a very sick baby, the only sick, and thin, Indian we saw; all its small bones showed and its cough sounded like bronchitis. I believe we all felt the same horror and urge to do something, without being able to do anything at all. The adult Indians were all quite young, the man in the army shirt was the only one with gray hair and without teeth. They are short-lived and have few children, and also high infant mortality keeps the families down to one or two children a couple. I noticed several little vials of the kind used for injections scattered about, and every round dusky behind bore a vaccination mark (their rounded behinds and childishly smooth legs, in both sexes, are remarkably pretty).

Half a mile from the village they cultivate a manioc patch, their only attempt at agriculture, and manioc, soaked and scraped, was drying on frames outside the houses in white, sour-smelling cakes. Manioc and fish are the staple diet; they have no salt and rarely eat meat. A small wild fruit, strong and oily, called *pequis*, is thought to contribute something essential to the diet, but no one seems to know exactly what. Callado asked in vain for one dish for us, a kind of thin pancake of toasted manioc rolled up with fish and red pepper inside—their only food, he said, that is palatable to a white man. But that week there was to be a big funeral feast lasting several days, and they were smoking whatever fish they caught to save up for the occasion. The death, that of a head man in another village, had occurred some time ago, but the festivities had to wait until the supply of fish on hand warranted them.

We were also sorry not to see them fish with bow and arrow; they were extremely skillful at hitting the moving fish in the moving water, making allowances for refraction; they rarely miss. The children play with care-

lessly made bows and arrows, and their arrows are tipped with small cala-
bashes pierced with holes, so that they make a long screaming noise in
flight. The Uialapiti make no pottery nor baskets. For centuries one tribe
has made one article, pots, bows and arrows, baskets, shell collars, etc.,
and exchanged it for the speciality of another tribe. They do no work at
all, as we consider work; in fact as the Portuguese found out very early in
the history of Brasil, if put at any kind of steady labor they promptly sicken
and die. They are gentle with each other and with their children; so much
so that when, at the edge of the river, a mother began scrubbing a little
boy's face, and he began to scream in a perfectly normal way, the unexpected, unique sound startled us all. They never strike or punish the children; in fact they have no conception of punishment. If an Indian murders
another, everyone is very sorry; the murderer is very sorry, too, and perhaps gives presents to the widow, but nothing further is done about it. All
property is in common and the Indian Protection Service itself follows the
tactful policy of at least not appearing to keep anything locked up; they
do, naturally, but the Indian is allowed to rummage through much of the
Service's belongings.

Our pilots wanted to get back to Brasília before dark if possible, the
landing field there not being well lighted, so about four o'clock we reluctantly gathered ourselves together and walked back to the plane. When we
got there, someone was missing; the young interpreter had disappeared
with the Cambridge boy. So we sat down in the shadow of a wing and
waited, we and all the village that could squeeze into the shade with us,
making conversation as best we could. The man in the gaucho hat had an
accumulation of bows and arrows and two spears. By now we were thirsty
and tired; we looked the other way as he still pranced energetically about
in a war-dance of his own invention. Our pilot appeared, naked to the waist,
very pleased with himself, with a small green parrot on his shoulder; he
had given his shirt for it. A little girl with black lines down her legs leaned
on my knees and the man who so admired my earrings leaned on my
shoulder and asked my name for the tenth time, while a brighter-looking
friend repeated it correctly. "Laura" was easy for them; "Aldous" gave trouble, and they gave us their own names over and over, pointing, cooing like
doves. The earring-fancier examined my wristwatch and then asked once
more if I were single. He pointed to his chest and said he was a widower,
then talked away in Nu-aruak to the brighter friend, who started to laugh.
He had asked if I would stay behind and be his wife. This produced a great
deal of tribal merriment, and although I was vain of having been singled
out, I was afraid he merely did not want to be the Indian who threw away
the pearl, richer than all his tribe.

Besides his miniature magnifying glass and telescope, Huxley had a pair of queer black plastic spectacles, with innumerable fine holes, like sieves, where the lenses would normally be. These, he told us, were an ancient invention of the Chinese, useful for both near-sighted and far-sighted eyes. Laura remarked that she also found them very useful for going to sleep, and when we finally got on the plane she put them on and promptly did so. The rest of us snoozed, too, drank tepid water, and finished up the curling sandwiches; we all seemed a little depleted and remote. We tried to settle down to "Grey Eminence," "The Eclipse of God," and "Lah-dee," but without much success. I remember discussing "The Mill on the Floss" in a dream-like way, and then having a conversation with Huxley about Ezra Pound and T. S. Eliot, or rather, his reminiscing about them, gently as always. He then spoke about Utopia, the subject of his next novel. His is set on an island, I think in the Indian Ocean, in a mingling of the best of both eastern and western cultures. It is a society "where men are able to realize their potentialities as they have never been able to in any past or present civilization." It seemed quite natural to be hearing about it five thousand feet up in the air, deserting one of the most primitive societies left on earth, rushing towards still another attempt at "the most modern city in the world."

Shortly after dark we were home, home to Brasília, that is. Our Microbus failed to meet us and we were driven back to the hotel in a brand new bright yellow truck, with benches in back. It was suddenly very cold; the Southern Cross was brilliant; the driver got lost and we wound up back at the Palace of the Dawn again.

Clean, quiet, asking each other for *Cafiaspirinas*, some with freshly shampooed damp heads, we assembled for another late dinner, while the canned music struck up especially for us. The table wobbled—they all did—and the elderly Italian waiter rushed up to put a wad of paper under a leg, exclaiming disgustedly "*Tutti moderni! Tutti moderni!*" then talked feelingly in Italian with the Huxleys on this subject.

During dinner Callado told us, in his pleasant way and beautiful English, more about the Indian Service and the three Villas Boas brothers. From a middle class São Paulo family, with only elementary educations and very much against their parents' wishes, all three grew up with the same passion for the Indians and have given their lives to them. The Indians seem to inspire a deep affection in almost anyone who has to work with them; we had all noticed how gentle and friendly the Air Force men had been. Or, it may be partly due to the childlike charm of the Indians themselves and partly almost to the old Portuguese colonising gift; they were (and are) almost completely without racial or color prejudices and treated whatever strange races they ran across with the same amused, affectionate familiarity that they had for each other. Callado also spoke of the founder of the Indian Service, the famous part-Indian General Rondon (who as Captain Rondon, once took Theodore Roosevelt hunting in Brasil); he had died a few months before. Huxley was very much taken with Rondon's motto for the Service: "Let yourself be killed if necessary, but never kill."

The next morning we left bright and early again for the cluttered little airport. Three society women from São Paulo, left over from the President's party, were there, telling each other ecstatically how much they liked Brasília. The Huxleys were leaving first, for São Paulo; the rest of us were returning by another plane to Rio. Some of us were carrying the slightly funereal black bags presented by the hotel. The Huxleys had one, and several air-line bags as well, and Huxley said that that was really the way contemporary man should travel, just a collection of such bags on a string over his shoulder. The head of the Cultural Division of Itamarati was doing his best to draw some final, enlightening, summarizing statement about Brasília from Huxley before he left, but he was not having much luck. Huxley would only commit himself to saying that he'd like to come back in ten years' time. I felt, however, that in ten years or in twenty, it would be all the same: Brasília, the Uialapiti, the continent of South America itself, would be being viewed *sub specie aeternitatis.*

A day or so later, in his newspaper the *Correio da Manha,* Antônio Callado printed an account of the trip called "A Sage among the Savages." Of Brasília he said parenthetically: "It is a city of consumers, set down in a desert where not even a cabbage plant can be seen. For a long time to come, its red dust will absorb, like blotting paper, the energies of the country . . . Doesn't a city begin with railroads and agriculture? Brasília is living like Berlin at the time of the Russian invasion. On one hand there are palaces, on the other the slums of the Free City; on one Old Fashioneds in the hotel bar, on the other *cachaça* in the real 'saloons' of that fantastic slum. One notices there a Teutonic preoccupation with problems that have not yet arisen. For example: the airport is miles from everything in order to prevent future congestion, when there could easily be a temporary airport near the hotel . . ."

Another English author, more outspoken than Huxley, wrote: "I have a strong idea that no man can ordain that on such a spot shall be built a great and thriving city. No man can so ordain even though he leave behind him . . . a prestige sufficient to bind his successors to his wishes.

"There is much desolate land within the country, but I think that none is so desolate in its state of nature as three-fourths of the ground on which is supposed to stand the city. . . . There is a map accurately laid down, and taking that map with him on his journeys a man may lose himself in the streets . . . as one does in the deserts of the Holy Land. In the first place, no one knows where the places are, or is sure of their existence, and then between their presumed localities the land is wild, trackless, unbridged, uninhabited, and desolate.

"For myself, I do not believe in cities made after this fashion. Commerce, I think, must elect the site of all large congregations of mankind. In some mysterious way she ascertains what she wants, and having acquired that, draws men in thousands around her properties."

Those are a few of Anthony Trollope's gentler comments on the city of Washington in 1861. The United States of the nineteenth century and the Brasil of the twentieth are not, perhaps, really very comparable; however, Trollope, and his mother, and all the many other prophets of failure were wrong about Washington, and it behooves Americans to be particularly careful in predictions about Brasília. But the tone of Callado's remarks seems to echo the feelings of all intelligent Brasilians I know on the subject. Rather desperately and resignedly, they are hoping for the best. Perhaps we should also all spare a little hope for the Indians.

1958

"I Was But Just Awake"

Come Hither: A Collection of Rhymes and Poems for the Young of All Ages. Made by Walter de la Mare (Knopf; $7.50).

Although much of the poetry I happen to admire is not to be found in it, I still think this is the best anthology I know of. First published in 1923, it waited for thirty-four years to be reissued in this new edition, prepared by Walter de la Mare shortly before his death. There are now 483 poems (besides many more in the notes) and the notes have been expanded from 171 to 294 pages. It is a marvellous book for children, but not at all a "children's book"; de la Mare maintains a little of his air of mystery even as to whom his readers are to be. It *looks* like a nice old-fashioned book: big and solid, opaque paper and large type, unlike those scholarly or contemporary anthologies with thin pages that stick together, pairs of dates after every poem, and meager biographical notes in fine, fine type. Auden has said that he learned more from it "than I have from most books of overt criticism." I don't believe in forcing poetry on anyone, even a child, but if one knows a child at all interested in the subject, this is the perfect birthday book. One can't expect a little Auden every time, but at least, as he also said about the possible effects on children of reading de la Mare's own verse, "he will not have a tin ear." It is a fine book to memorize from; and I think that the custom of having children recite to company rather than entertain them with discourse is one that could be revived for the benefit and pleasure of all.

The introduction is a de la Mare-ish allegorical account of how he discovered poetry as a boy,—or perhaps it is not allegorical but the literal truth. This is the one part of the book that might seem a bit dated to an adult reader; but by means of dream-like landscapes, old ladies in lost farmhouses, mysterious tower rooms crammed with old trunks and books, in his own way de la Mare is explaining how the anthology was made up, and also letting fall some wise thoughts on the writing of verse in general.

In the tower room the boy finds books filled with copied-out poems and sets to work re-copying them for himself. "I had never sat in so enormous a silence; the scratching of my pen its only tongue. . . . I chose what I liked best . . . such as carried away the imagination; either into the past or into another mind, or into the all-but-forgotten; at times as if into another world."

The old lady says to him: "Remember you are as old as the hills which neither spend nor waste time, but dwell in it for ages, as if it were light or sunshine."

Later on in the notes he tells the story of the mediaeval traveller who made a complete circuit of the world without knowing it, and came back to where he'd started from. To illustrate this story the book begins and ends with the same poem: *This is the Key of the Kingdom*: a gentle hint to turn back and read it through again. He also points out that "many of the customs, beliefs, lore they [ballads] refer to may be found scattered up and down throughout the world." Since his vision of both time and poetry seems to be cyclical, he is implying, I think, by the story of the copying, that simple repetition of poetry, copying or memorizing, is a good way of learning to understand it, possibly a good way of learning to write it. Isn't the best we can do, he seems to be saying, in the way of originality, but a copying and re-copying, with some slight variations of our own?

The book proper consists of songs and ballads, folk-poetry, and frankly romantic poems, all chosen for melodiousness as well as romance. There is nothing "intellectual", "metaphysical", or even "difficult", as de la Mare says when he gives *Sabrina fair* . . . leaving out the passages most clotted with classical reference. Of Shakespeare, for example, there are only songs; of George Herbert, *Easter, Virtue*, and *Love* (the one that meant so much to Simone Weil). Donne and Hopkins are mentioned only in the notes; of Donne he says (and this explains many of the selections or omissions): "It is a poetry that awaits the mind as the body grows older, and when we ourselves have learned the experience of life with which it is concerned. Not that the simplest poetry will then lose any of its grace and truth and beauty—far rather it shines the more clearly, since age needs it the more." Blake, Shakespeare, and Shelley have the most poems; Coleridge, Keats, and Christina Rossetti come next. But it is not an anthology to be judged by names or allotments, and there are many more anonymous and single poems than anything else. The sections have titles like *Morning and May, Dance, Music, and Bells*, and *Far*, to name but three of the sixteen. But there are also sections on war and death; and under *War* I was very glad to see *Mine eyes have seen the glory of the coming of the Lord*, which de la Mare calls "magnificent". (I have always wished it could be the national anthem.) There is a late 17th century poem by William Cleland, *Hallo My Fancy*, that might almost be describing the anthology itself.

> In melancholic fancy,
> Out of myself,
> In the vulcan dancy,
> All the world surveying,
> Nowhere staying . . .

De la Mare has some practical things to say about meters (which he used so beautifully himself), and even suggests how to read certain of the poems; but he never speaks directly of any of the usual concerns of the critics; for one, let's say, "imagery". Instead, the old woman of the introduction tells the boy: "learn the common names of everything you see . . . and especially those that please you most to remember: then give them names also of your own making and choosing—if you can." And wouldn't that be imagery? He loves "little articles", home-made objects whose value increases with age, Robinson Crusoe's lists of his belongings, homely employments, charms and herbs. As a result he naturally chose for his book many of what Randall Jarrell once called "thing-y" poems, and never the pompous, abstract, or formal.

After the poems come the notes, and the book is well worth buying for them alone. It is a Luna Park of stray and straying information. He quotes journals, letters, samplers, gravestones, and his friends; then throws in a few recipes. He discusses the calendar, that "anomalous litter of relics". He is against rigid rules of spelling, and cruelty to animals and children. Would you like to know the name of Noah's dog? Or the derivation of "cat's-cradle"? Or read the world's earliest poem? They are all here, and de la Mare's transparent delight in what he is telling provokes immediate replies, which is probably just what he intended. One wants to interrupt: "Speaking of birds, Mr. de la Mare,—did you ever run across that pretty notion of Sir John Narborough's, when he spent the winter of 1670 on the bleak coast of Patagonia, that the inquisitive penguins were like 'little children standing up in white aprons'?" Since this is not in the book, I'm afraid he couldn't have.

At my house as I write there is a four-month-old baby who has just discovered his voice; not his crying voice, but his speaking, singing, or poetry-voice, and he devotes stretches of the day to trying it out. He can produce long trills, loud or soft, and repeated bird-like cries, obviously with pleasure. There is also a little black girl of three who vigorously pedals a tricycle around and around in perfect time to an old Portuguese children's song. *Tere—sínha de Je—sús* she goes, in mixolydian (I think), telling another story about the same Teresa as Crashaw's (who is not in *this* book). And in the kitchen her mother sings one of this year's crop of sambas, "home-made" annually in endless variety by the poor Negroes of the slums, full of topical facts and preposterous fancies: *Come away with me on my little Lambretta,* she sings.

Besides the hundreds of better-known and loved poems he chose, surely it is of this kind of random poetry that Walter de la Mare can make child readers, or us, aware; the kind to which he lent his fine ear with such loving attention. As the boy in the tower room copies his poems, "an indescribable despair and anxiety—almost terror even—seized upon me at the rushing thought of my own *ignorance*; of how little I knew, of how unimportant I was . . ." Then daylight comes, he puts down his pen and goes to the window: "I was but just awake: so too was the world itself, and ever is." And in reading this book we can often recapture what children and other races perhaps still share: de la Mare's lyrical confidence.

1958

Blurb for *Life Studies*

by Robert Lowell

As a child, I used to look at my grandfather's Bible under a powerful reading-glass. The letters assembled beneath the lens were suddenly like a Lowell poem, as big as life and as alive, and rainbow-edged. It seemed to illuminate as it magnified; it could also be used as a burning-glass.

This new book begins on Robert Lowell's now-familiar trumpet-notes (see "Inauguration Day"), then with the autobiographical group the tone changes. In these poems, heartbreaking, shocking, grotesque and gentle, the unhesitant attack, the imagery and construction, are as brilliant as ever, but the mood is nostalgic and the meter is refined. A poem like "My Last Afternoon with Uncle Devereux Winslow," or "Skunk Hour," can tell us as much about the state of society as a volume of Henry James at his best.

Whenever I read a poem by Robert Lowell I have a chilling sensation of here-and-now, of exact contemporaneity: more aware of those "ironies of American History," grimmer about them, and yet hopeful. If more people read poetry, if it were more exportable and translatable, surely his poems would go far towards changing, or at least unsettling, minds made up against us. Somehow or other, by fair means or foul, and in the middle of our worst century so far, we have produced a magnificent poet.

1959

"Writing poetry is an unnatural act . . ."

Writing poetry is an unnatural act. It takes great skill to make it seem natural. Most of the poet's energies are really directed towards this goal: to convince himself (perhaps, with luck, eventually some readers) that what he's up to and what he's saying is really an inevitable, *only* natural way of behaving under the circumstances.

Coleridge, in *Biographia Literaria,* in his discussion of Wordsworth, has a famous sentence. It says: "the characteristic fault of our elder poets is the reverse of that which distinguishes too many of our recent versifiers; the one conveying the most fantastic thoughts in the most correct and natural language, the other in the most fantastic language conveying the most trivial thoughts." He then goes on to quote some of George Herbert:

VIRTUE
"Sweet day, so cool, so calm, so bright,
    The bridal of the earth and sky:
    The dew must weep thy fall tonight;
        For thou must die!"

LOVE UNKNOWN

that begins

"Dear friend, sit down, the tale is long and sad:
And in my faintings, I presume, your love
Will more comply than help. A Lord I had . . ."

Another Herbert: LOVE

"Love bade me welcome, but my soul drew back,
    Guiltie of dust and sinne."

and ends:

> " 'You must sit down,' sayes Love, 'and taste my meat.'
>   So I did sit and eat."

This, I later discovered in *Waiting for God*, was Simone Weil's favorite; she translated it and knew it by heart.

The three qualities I admire in the poetry I like best are: *Accuracy, Spontaneity, Mystery*. My three "favorite" poets—not the best poets, whom we all admire, but favorite in the sense of one's "best friends," etc. are Herbert, Hopkins, and Baudelaire.

THE CHURCHE-FLOORE
> "Hither sometimes Sinne steals, and stains
> The marbles neat and curious veins: . . .
> Sometimes Death, puffing at the doore,
> Blows all the dust about the floore . . ."

His magnificent poem, THE SACRIFICE

> "Arise, arise, they come. Look how they runne!
> Alas! What haste they make to be undone!
> How with their lanterns they do seek the sunne!
>   Was ever grief like mine!"

He has spontaneity, mystery, and accuracy, in that order?

Hopkins, WRECK OF THE DEUTSCHLAND

> "Ah, touched in your bower of bone
>   Are you! turned for an exquisite smart,
> Have you! make words break from here all alone,
>   Do you!—"

THE GRANDEUR OF GOD "it will flame out like *shining from shook foil* . . ."

> "I am all at once what Christ is, / since he was what I am, and
> This Jack, joke, poor potsherd, patch, matchwood, immortal diamond,
> Is immortal diamond."

Auden's   B [Baudelaire] here—

> "Altogether elsewhere, vast
>   herds of reindeer move across

> miles—miles of golden moss
> silently and very fast."

It's accurate, like something seen in a documentary movie. It is spontaneous, natural sounding—helped considerably by the break between adjective and noun in the first two lines. And it is mysterious.

The first lines of D. Thomas's "Refusal to Mourn":

> "Never,

Miss Moore's—["Plagued by the Nightingale":]

Frost's—

[Wordsworth, Shakespeare's "Prithee undo this button"—everyone is moved to tears by it; it certainly is the height of spontaneity, and yet it is so mysterious they are still arguing as to whether it's his own button or his daughter's button . . .]

Burns:—lacks mystery, maybe—but—weaker in the mystery—

"No matter what theories one may have, I doubt that they are in one's mind at the moment of writing a poem or that there is even a physical possibility that they could be. Theories can only be based on interpretations of other people's poems, or one's own in retrospect, or wishful thinking."

I'm not a critic. Critics can't rest easy until they have put poets in descending orders of merit; they change the lists every night before they go to bed. The poet doesn't have to be consistent.

Marianne Moore, MARRIAGE, that begins:

> "This institution,
> perhaps one should say enterprise . . ."

NEW YORK
> "the savage's romance,
> accreted where we need the space for commerce—
> the center of the wholesale fur trade . . ."

accuracy: from A GRAVE

> "The firs stand in procession, each with an emerald
> turkey-foot at the top . . ."
> skeleton

FROST: the ghost that "carried itself like a pile of dishes."

ending of "Stopping by Woods on a Snowy Evening"

Auden here—

a single word does it all

ROBERT LOWELL:

> "Remember, seamen, Salem fishermen
> Once hung their nimble fleets on the Great Banks."

hung suggests the immensity, the depths of the cold stormy water and the tininess, the activity of the small "nimble" ships—and yet it's the simplest sort of natural verb to use—

> THE DEAD IN EUROPE
> "After the planes unloaded, we fell down
> Buried together, unmarried men and women . . ."

> "O Mary, marry earth, sea, air and fire;
> Our sacred earth in our day is our curse."

DYLAN THOMAS:

> "Pale rain over the dwindling harbour
> And over the sea wet church the size of a snail
> With its horns through mist and the castle
> Brown as owls . . ."

> A REFUSAL TO MOURN
> "Never until the mankind making
> Bird beast and flower
> Fathering and all humbling darkness
> Tells with silence the last light breaking
> And the still hour
> Is come of the sea tumbling in harness . . ."

Baudelaire: "Les soirs illumines par l'ardeur du charbon . . ." where *charbon* is the telling word—surprising, accurate, *dating* the poem, yet making it real, yet making it mysterious—

Spontaneity—Marianne's "Marriage," "N.Y."—

Herbert's EASTER

> "Rise, heart; the Lord is risen."

Hopkins' "Glory be to God for dappled things"—

My maternal grandmother had a glass eye. It fascinated me as a child, and the idea of it has fascinated me all my life. She was religious, in the Puritanical Protestant sense and didn't believe in looking into mirrors very much. Quite often the glass eye looked heavenward, or off at an angle, while the real eye looked at you.

> "Him whose happie birth
> Taught me to live here so, that still one eye
> Should aim and shoot at that which is on high."

Off and on I have written out a poem called "Grandmother's Glass Eye" which should be about the problem of writing poetry. The situation of my grandmother strikes me as rather like the situation of the poet: the difficulty of combining the real with the decidedly un-real; the natural with the unnatural; the curious effect a poem produces of being as normal as *sight* and yet as synthetic, as artificial, as a *glass eye*.

(call the piece "Grandmother's Glass Eye"???)

spontaneity occurs in a good *attack*, a rapid line, *tight* rhythm—

Brazilian Poetry: I am reading B.P. I began naturally with the living poets & I intended to work backwards into Brazilian and Portuguese poetry. I've found many good things, but I feel that I don't know the language well enough, or the body of poets. To say anything about it at present would be an impertinence.

late 1950s–early 1960s

Some Notes on Robert Lowell

Robert Lowell, born in 1917, is the Prodigal Son of the "Pilgrim Fathers," the Concord Transcendentalists, and the nineteenth-century industrialists. He is considered by nearly all of the good critics, American or English, as the greatest poet of the generation following that of Pound, Cummings, Marianne Moore, Wallace Stevens, etc. In the years 1940–1950, his work was for Americans a surprise almost as great as that, some years later and in a totally different way, of Dylan Thomas for the English.

T. S. Eliot predicted that, with the battle won for "free verse" and demotic language in poetry, there would be a return to formal meter and stanza, even "intricated," and to strict rhyme. The poems of Robert Lowell seem to have come to fulfill that prophecy, and sooner than was expected. His first book, *Land of Unlikeness*, was published in 1944, in an edition limited to 150 copies. His first trade book was *Lord Weary's Castle*, 1946, which made him famous and for which he received, among other honors, the Pulitzer Prize for poetry. Some years later there appeared *The Mills of the Kavanaughs*, and more recently *Life Studies*. Since the publication of *Life Studies*, Lowell has devoted some of his time to translation; in 1961, we had his translation of Racine's *Phaedra*. A book of shorter translations, from Baudelaire, Rilke, Montale, Pasternak, etc., appeared recently under the title *Imitations*. Lowell deliberately chose this word to describe his technique in translation; the poems are far from being literal translations; they constitute, in reality, new poems, in the already famous Lowell style. And as such they are praised by those who admire that style and criticized by those who prefer the more common form of word-for-word translation.

Lowell is of course a famous New England name. There is a city called Lowell that evolved around the Lowell mills of cotton textiles in the early nineteenth century. Robert Lowell is related to the famous nineteenth-century poet James Russell Lowell (who for many years was Ambassador to England) and also to the celebrated poet of "free verse," Amy Lowell. He was born and raised in Boston, with the privileges but also the burdens accompanying that powerful local name. As expected, he went to Harvard, but he couldn't adapt, and two years later transferred to Kenyon College, in Ohio, where he had as his "mentor" the southern Agrarian poet and "New Critic," John Crowe Ransom.

At the beginning of the war, Lowell made a first attempt to enlist in the navy (his father had been a naval officer), but he was rejected for reasons of health. During the course of the war, however, he changed his mind about things and, when he was finally drafted for military service, he refused to serve. The United States had hundreds of conscientious objectors working in hospitals and special camps, but since Lowell had failed to register as a "pacifist," he was sent to jail as a common criminal. Before that, he had already shocked his family and the city of his birth, by turning against New England Calvinism, even to the point of becoming a convert to Catholicism. I believe that at this time—like Eliot, Auden and others—he is a practicing Anglican. His poetry is profoundly religious and rich in biblical and ecclesiastical images, primarily so in his first two books. His religious interpretation of the world is in the tradition of his New England "ancestors": the Mathers, Jonathan Edwards, Thoreau (who also went to jail), Hawthorne, etc. and the Brook Farm group.

It cannot be denied that, to the uninitiated reader, his poetry is difficult. Yet (in contrast, I think, to some of the more popular poems of Dylan Thomas), Lowell's poetry, always totally honest with the reader, is invariably written in perfectly logical syntax and meaning. One's initial difficulty, at times, lies in knowing what the poem's subject actually is. Many of his poems are dramatic, spoken by different characters; on this score, he has been frequently compared to Browning. But, once one knows the scene and the character, the poem itself, despite its being subtle, involved, and full of linguistic associations—an astonishing mixture of demotic and formal language—is always lucid.

In the strange title of his second book, *Lord Weary's Castle*, there is already embedded in part an explanation of Lowell's poetry. It comes from the old ballad about a poor stonemason named "Lambkin" who built a castle for one Lord Weary, but who was deprived of his just payment. In this legend Lowell sees a parable for the modern world—the "castle"—the crushing superstructure of our civilization. Randall Jarrell, in *Poetry and the Age*, describes *Lord Weary's Castle*: "The poems understand the world as a sort of conflict of opposites. In this struggle one opposite is that cake of custom in which all of us lie embedded . . . the inertia of the stubborn self . . . the obstinate persistence in evil that is damnation . . . imperialism, militarism, capitalism, Calvinism . . . the 'proper Bostonians,' the rich. . . . But struggling within this . . . is everything that is free or open, that . . . willingness that is itself salvation . . . the Grace that has replaced the Law, of the perfect liberator whom the poet calls Christ."

The poems in this book and in *The Mills of the Kavanaughs* are almost all in rigorous stanzaic form with the frequent enjambment that has become Lowell's characteristic mark. This technique gives these poems of profound religious belief and anguish, which were written during the war, their affect of urgency, panic almost.

In *Life Studies*, published in 1959, the heavy-beat rhythms and trumpet sounds are modified, modulated. The lines still rhyme, but irregularly so, and their extension depends more on phrasing that is natural or breathlike than on strophic forms. These poems are almost always elegiac and autobiographical, on everything that is his, family, father and mother, wife (he is married to Elizabeth Hardwick, the renowned literary critic and novelist) and only child. Lowell's language is as grand, as moving, as brutal, at times, as formerly—but the poems are full of "humor," of compassion, and of a simple affection for persons and places.

I have heard Brazilians affirm that the American writer Dreiser, for example, is a better writer than Henry James! And I believe that the same type of Brazilian reader might well make the same mistake about Lowell's poems by deciding that Robert Frost or Carl Sandburg or even our rather pathetic "beat poets" come closer to the idea than he does to what should be the true "American" poet. To those readers I can only say this: the idea they have of American literature (and, incidentally, of America itself) is wrong. Our great, though difficult, artist-craftsmen—including, among others, James and Lowell—are the finest representatives of American literature.

Simply because the course of the language of poetry in English diverged so much from the same course in the Latin languages, Lowell will probably appear to the Brazilians to be more exotic stylistically than he really is. The battle to write poetry that is "at least as well written as prose," as Pound used to say, and in spoken language, had almost been won by 1920. It must be difficult for Brazilian readers to realize that in this domain (I refer only to demotic language versus "poetic" language), English poetry is many decades ahead of poetry in the Latin languages. Lowell represents a sharp change in direction, even, if you wish, a turning backwards. Like Dryden, he once again made poetry hard, difficult, soaring, and masculine. In reality, the arts, it is clear, cannot be compared, but, by means that are very different from those employed by our "action painters," Lowell expresses, with the same energy and beauty, the problems that any citizen of the United States who is over forty, has already faced and continues to face: the Depression, the War (or Wars), the Affluent Society, the ethics of foreign relations, the Bomb.

I am certain that the reader who manages to understand even a small portion of Robert Lowell's poems—and they have no snares—will come to a better understanding, in the same measure, of the contemporary American land from which he comes.

1962

A Sentimental Tribute

When it means a book, I love the word Reader; it has only pleasant associations for me. I learned to read out of a reader, a small brown book still in my possession, rather worn and dirty, with some of the pictures colored in in crayon and my name appearing a good many times, in embryonic handwriting. My reader, like this selection of Miss Moore's writings, is a mixture of prose and poetry. I seem to know it by heart, and I know some of Miss Moore's poems by heart. The likenesses end there. No, not at all: a few of Aesop's Fables appear in both books and both give "The Goose that Laid the Golden Egg" (except that in Miss Moore's translation of La Fontaine's version of the story, the goose is a hen). I find the presence of this small, pure, literary stream or rivulet both touching and miraculous: rising somewhere in the sixth century before Christ, running through millenniums of Ancient History and Middle Ages, flowing faster to refresh the jaded court of Louis XIV, sending off, here and there, little branches as far as country-school "primers,"—and then reappearing, "to sparkle out among the fern" in the work of our most sophisticated, most childlike, and dearest poet. "For men may come and men may go, / But I go on for ever."

Miss Moore has proved her fondness for La Fontaine; probably she and Aesop would have got along well, too. All three derive much profit and pleasure from the folk-ways of birds and animals; they have little of the professional writer about them (I don't know much about Aesop but I doubt that he had); their imaginations are strongly original but decorous and uninsistent, and they do relish a good moral. I am speaking here of the translator-and-essayist-Miss Moore; the poet-Miss Moore has all the same characteristics but is an infinitely more complicated personality, mysterious but frank, generous but strict, intimidating but lovable. Probably everyone who knows anything at all about American poetry has some sort of mental picture of Miss Moore; probably thousands have seen her. We have been lucky that in her later years she has been so generous and courageous about travelling all over the country to give readings and lectures. She has become almost a familiar figure, and this is one of the happier wonders of the literary age. I first met Miss Moore by appointment, in 1934, in the New York Public Library. I had actually picked out a tall, eagle-nosed, be-turbaned lady, distinguished-looking but proud and forbidding, as a possible Miss Moore, when to my great relief the real one spoke up. One can't imagine a college student of literature making such a mistake these days.

A reader, says the dictionary, is to teach one how to read. It seems doubtful that anyone needs or wants to be taught to read Miss Moore at this date. However, in case any readers (in the "dear reader" sense) are unfamiliar with her work and this book is their introduction to it, I shall make a few suggestions as to how to read it. First, read the Foreword carefully. Then skip to the back and read the Interview with the Paris Review. Then concentrate for a long time—a week or so—on the twenty-three marvelous earlier poems. After that I think I'd read the prose pieces in chronological order (the dates are given at the back of the book); and by then one should be advanced enough to study the La Fontaine translations, or to take a holiday with the Carnegie Hall and Yul Brynner poems.

The Foreword is full of wonderful things, and it explains a lot, too, for those who want explanations. The best way to take it (and to take all of Miss Moore's writing, poetry and prose) is as she herself takes the statements of ex-President Eisenhower (see page xvi)—*at her word*. "More than once after a reading," she says, "I have been asked with circumspectly hesitant delicacy, 'Your . . . poem, *Marriage*; would you care to . . . make a statement about it?' *Gladly*." (My italics.) It is the word *gladly* that is typical of Miss Moore: the obliging promptitude, the willingness to respond to all normal interest and requests, the democratic refusal to consider herself a privileged being, a White Goddess, to drape herself in chiffon and assume a deep, dark voice. Her sense of the age, her real sense of style (in clothes, I should add, as well as words), have kept her reassuringly 19th-century, yet, at the age of seventy-four, still the most modern of moderns.

"Appoggiaturas," she says, "—a charmed subject. A study of trills can be absorbing to the exclusion of everything else." One hesitates. Is that going too far? But then one remembers that *gladly*. She believes that what the poet and scientist have in common is their willingness "to waste effort." Let us be poets over and above the call of duty. Give more than is required; throw in trills and appoggiaturas for the joy of it. Both in writing her own poetry and in judging that of others, her guiding principles are seen to have been passion, accuracy, and pleasure. Under each of these headings, of course, one could set down sub-headings, sometimes contradictory ones. For example: how does Miss Moore reconcile pleasure with the fatigue and drudgery that must go into writing? I once saw in her apartment two bushel baskets, the kind apples come in, full of rejected versions of a rather short review. I thought it was one of her very best reviews, but it is not in this collection. Does that mean that after two bushel-baskets-full of work it did not come up to her standards?

She admits the hard work: "I never knew anyone who had a passion for words who had as much difficulty in saying things as I do and I know I'm trying." In spite of her wish to be clear and simple, this last phrase brings up the question that always baffles us with great artists of Miss Moore's kind: the supremely original, nevertheless unpretentious, small-scale ones: Klee, Bissier, or Webern, for example. Just how deep does their self-consciousness go? I certainly can not measure it, and there is always the perfectly agreeable possibility that I am being teased a little on purpose. Lately I have heard one or two poets and critics sound upset because they don't think that the poem about Yul Brynner is as good as, say, *The Pangolin*. How solemn can one get? Surely by now Miss Moore is entitled to write any old way, any new way, she wants to.

It is nice to think that the correspondence with the Ford Company will outlast the Ford. Imagine an examination for future English scholars, based on the First Ford Epistle: "I have seen and admired Thunderbird as a Ford designation. It would be hard to match; but let me, the coming week, talk with my brother who would bring ardor and imagination to bear on the quest."

1. Give the derivation of the word Thunderbird.
2. Describe how the custom developed, in the mid-twentieth century, of asking famous poets to christen the *automobile*.

Miss Moore says of animals and athletes: "they look their best when caring least." She says, "I had no ambition to be a writer" and I believe her implicitly. This is her greatest secret and her greatest lesson for us now, when ambition comes first, publicity-seeking second, and writing third. Think of Miss Moore's years at the Branch Public Library; go to the tortoise, thou hare!

Another lesson we can learn from Miss Moore—if I may relish a moral or two myself—is in how to lead the city-life. Besieged by "culture," bewildered as to what we should like and shouldn't like, timid TV watchers or brave non-TV watchers, spending so much time and energy in criticising and comparing likes and dislikes—Miss Moore shows us how it is possible to preserve one's own pure taste and go one's own sweet way. We carp and are niggardly, but she can find a moment of lucidity in Eisenhower, and admire the Duke of Windsor's prose.

She says she didn't use to care for the word "poetry" and refused to use it for her "observations," but that now she minds it less. She does not say why, but I believe that one reason why she minds it less is that she herself has done so much to elevate the associations with the word "poetry" since those 1920's when she began to publish. She once told me (I hope I have the story right) that in the days of the suffragette parades she climbed to the top of a mail box during a demonstration. Whatever Miss Moore contributed to the cause of Votes for Women, how much more recklessly, bravely, and generously has she contributed to—let us use the word—poetry.

I should like to add a few complaints about this Viking Reader, complaints that really amount to why isn't there more of it? I like the series of Viking Portables (some of which are called Readers, as well) much better. They are chunky books, semi-limp (I think it is called), pleasant to hold or carry or read in bed, the same size as my old original reader, only thicker (perhaps I think all readers should be that size), and they run to 600 or 700 pages. Think how much Miss Moore would go into one of them. And the price is (or was; maybe it has gone up) $2.00, instead of $6.95. I know I shall never understand publishers—but why shouldn't Miss Moore be given in full, and why shouldn't she be Portable too? Where, oh where are: *The Hero, The Jerboa, The Plumet Basilisk, the Frigate Pelican, Peter,* the gorgeously beautiful *An Octopus?*

And also I don't like a bright orange jacket for someone whose great-great-grandfather came from Merrian Square, Dublin.

1962

Flannery O'Connor: 1925–1964

I never met Flannery O'Connor, but we had been exchanging occasional letters for the last eight years or so. She invited me to visit her at "Andalusia" in Milledgeville, and how deeply I regret now that I never did. The closest I got to it was once when a freighter I was traveling on to South America put into Savannah for overnight. Wandering through those dusty, fusty little squares, I suddenly realized I was in Flannery O'Connor country and thought perhaps I could get to see her. I put in a telephone call from the booth in the lobby of the largest hotel; I remember that while I waited I studied a display of pecans and of boxes of "Miss Sadie's Bourbon Balls" on the candy and cigar counter just outside the booth. Quite soon a very collected, very southern voice answered and immediately invited me to "come on over." Alas, the bus connections didn't work out so that I could get back to my freighter in time to sail.

Later she sent me some colored snapshots of herself, some with her peacocks, some of her alone, always on crutches. In these amateur snapshots she looks, in spite of the crutches, younger than her age and very much alive. From Brazil I sent her a cross in a bottle, like a ship in a bottle, crudely carved, with all the instruments of the Passion, the ladder, pliers, dice, etc., in wood, paper, and tinfoil, with the little rooster at the top of the cross. I thought it was the kind of innocent religious grotesquery she might like, and I think she did, because she wrote:

> If I were mobile and limber and rich I would come to Brazil at once after one look at this bottle. Did you observe that the rooster has an eyebrow? I particularly like him and the altar cloth a little dirty from the fingers of whoever cut it out. . . . I am altogether taken with it. It's what I'm born to appreciate.

I feel great remorse now that I hadn't written to her for many months, that I had allowed this friendship to dwindle just when she must have been aware she was dying. Something about her intimidated me a bit: perhaps natural awe before her toughness and courage; perhaps, although death is certain for all, hers seemed a little more certain than usual. She made no show of *not* living in a metropolis, or of being a believer,—she lived with Christian stoicism and wonderful wit and humor that put most of us to shame.

I am very glad to hear that another collection of her stories is to be published soon. I am sure her few books will live on and on in American literature. They are narrow, possibly, but they are clear, hard, vivid, and full of bits of description, phrases, and odd insights that contain more real poetry than a dozen books of poems. Critics who accuse her of exaggeration are quite wrong, I think. I lived in Florida for several years next to a flourishing "Church of God" (both white and black congregation), where every Wednesday night Sister Mary and her husband "spoke in tongues." After those Wednesday nights, nothing Flannery O'Connor ever wrote could seem at all exaggerated to me.

1964

On the Railroad Named Delight

In the Western Hemisphere a 400th anniversary for a city is a rare event, and so Rio de Janeiro is celebrating its quatercentenary in 1965 off and on all year.

It began at New Year's midnight, or even a few hours before. There had been a superb parade of bands and dancers down the Avenida Getúlia Vargas in the center of the city before—at the stroke of 12 (Rio time)—Pope Paul VI touched a button in the Vatican and illuminated, with a new set of floodlamps, the figure of Christ the Redeemer that overlooks the city from atop Corcovado Mountain. Air Force planes flew overhead, dropping "silver rain" of bits of foil painted with the name of the State Bank.

That was also the night of Yemanjá, Goddess of the Sea, and her worshipers crowded Copacabana and the other beaches. Cabalistic-patterned trenches had been dug at high-water line and thousands of white candles set in them. The sand was strewn with white flowers, mostly lilies, and quantities of "white" alcohol, called *cachaça*, were drunk. Lines of girls and women, all in white, holding hands, and men in white, singly, waded into the surf singing hymns to Yemanjá and throwing their sheaves of flowers out as far as they could.

All together, the city's activities were a completely Cariocan—that is to say, a Rio de Janeiran—mixture: Latin and African, Catholic and pagan; mildly military, with a touch of progress; a bit disorganized, but with a great deal of unexpected beauty.

Now the year's biggest festival—Carnival, the four days preceding Ash Wednesday—has come and gone. As always, the first night, Saturday, was devoted to fancy-dress balls, with the most ostentatious being held at the Municipal Theater. These balls are really costume competitions. No expense is spared, and the winners are invariably dressed in the height of extravagant bad taste.

On Sunday night came the parades of dancers—first, the *frêvos*, in a wild, crouching dance from the north, then the dozens of samba "schools," each with hundreds of members in green and pink, silver and blue, red and white. In the tradition of Carnival, the parades lasted all night (and it should be remembered that this is the rainy season in Rio), with the best schools saved to the last, bravely dancing down the avenue at sunrise.

Tuesday night brought the *ranchos*, huge allegorical floats, many of them mechanized with revolving wheels, opening flowers and giants with rolling eyes. This year, in honor of the quatercentenary, many depicted real or imaginary scenes from Rio's history.

Through all this no work was done. Public buildings, banks and shops all were closed. Though it is now the fashion for the wealthier and more sophisticated to leave Rio during Carnival, the streets were packed each night. By day, the population recuperated at home. Yet there was remarkably little drunkenness or disorder. This year, the traditional perfume throwers, flasks that shoot a fine jet of scented ether, giving a smart shock and a sensation of icy cold on the skin, were officially banned as dangerous. They had been banned before—with equally little effect.

Visitors to Rio de Janeiro usually exclaim: "What a beautiful city." But sooner or later, the more thoughtful are likely to say: "No, it's not a beautiful city; it's just the world's most beautiful setting for a city."

Guanabara Bay is one of the largest landlocked harbors in the world, and many travelers say it is the most beautiful. Sharp granite peaks rise around it almost directly from the water in a series of fantastic shapes that suggested rather simple names to the Portuguese mariners who first came here: Sugar Loaf, Crow's-nest, Rudder, Two Brothers, Hunchback (or Corcovado).

Because the mountains are so close to the ocean the moisture in the sea winds condenses quickly and clouds float unusually low about them. This makes for considerable humidity; fussy people complain that their silver tarnishes quickly and their shoes mildew in the closets. But the dampness also gives a softness to the atmosphere that is one of Rio's charms. Although distant objects are clear they are bathed in a pink or bluish light—dreamy and delicate.

The granite peaks still bear all manner of tropical vegetation. Lianas hang from them, and wild palms wave on their tops—between and over city blocks—with a romantic effect unlike that of any other city.

Beautiful as it is, this setting does not lend itself to city planning. For 400 years, the city has probed slowly between the peaks in every direction—until it has grown like a lopsided starfish.

•

As in most capital cities (of which Rio was one until the capital was moved to the newly constructed Brasília in 1960), most of the population seems to come from somewhere else. The very poorest Brazilians—those from the north and northeast—have arrived in increasing numbers for 20 years or more. Now they come packed in old buses or in trucks filled with benches called *arraras* ("macaw perches").

Some find work; some are unemployed. Some move on. But very, very few go home, because city life—wretched as it may be—is still more diverting and satisfying than life in the dead little towns or villages they come from.

These people swell the sad and notorious Rio *favelas* (slums). More ambitious and prosperous people, bright young men seeking university degrees, young bureaucrats and politicians also flock to Rio. Many of the "real" Cariocas themselves are Cariocas from only one or two generations back—when the family left the old *fazenda* (or estate) and moved to the city for good.

Even if São Paulo is now a much bigger and richer city, many intellectuals prefer to live in Rio. It is still at least the intellectual capital of the country. In its extremes of wealth and poverty, it mirrors the inflation brought on by former President Juscelino Kubitschek's breakneck drive for industrialization, and by the graft that flourished under both him and his successor, João Goulart. It is a city that reflects the uncertainties of the entire nation since an army coup last March and April ousted Goulart and installed Marshal Humberto Castelo Branco as President. Finally, after 400 years, it is a city that has grown shabby.

There has been a "Paint Rio" campaign, with photographs in the newspapers of the presidents of paint companies handing gallons of free paint to the mother superiors of orphan asylums. House cleaning is needed badly; even the reputedly glamorous section of Copacabana is full of stained and peeling 10-story apartment houses.

Some parts of the city have new street signs, also badly needed. These light at night, helpfully, because Rio is a very dim city these days, but they bear advertisements as well as street names, and are criticized for being commercial and in bad taste.

In contrast to the general decrepitude, there is the brand-new Flamengo Park, with a new beach, gardens, an outdoor bandstand and dance floor, a marionette theater and rides for children. It is by far the city's best birthday present to its citizens, and although it is only about three-quarters finished, the citizens are embracing it by tens of thousands.

Flamengo Park is narrow, but almost 4 miles long, reaching from the edge of the commercial section of the city southwest along Guanabara Bay. It now looks like a green tropical atoll just risen from the water, but it is really the result of three years' hard work on an unpromising, hideous stretch of mud, dust, pipes and highways long known as "the fill." It is the one esthetic contribution of Gov. Carlos Lacerda's administration of the city and its suburbs.

Most of the beaches have been refurbished a little. Copacabana has just had its lifeguard "posts" taken down—as suddenly as landmarks vanish in New York. For years, Cariocans have said: "I live between *posto* three and *posto* four," or: "Meet me at *posto* six," and it will seem strange not to have these points of reference any more.

Because of the quatercentenary, hotels have been booked solid by out-of-town Brazilians and tourists. Elderly American ladies in print dresses and sunglasses walk the mosaic sidewalks determinedly, looking for something to do. The trouble is, there isn't anything to do or not much. Rio is not really ready for large-scale *tourismo*. The bon mot of the moment is to refer to the 4th *Centenário* as the 4th *Sem Ter Nada*. Spoken fast, they sound much alike, but the second phrase means "without a thing." Meanwhile, two or three luxury liners arrive every week with more tourists.

A sight-seeing boat has been launched, something Rio has long needed, since its greatest attraction is still that fabulous bay and its islands. Eight gondolas are being built for the Lagoon, a large, enclosed body of water south of the city. According to the papers, these are "copied exactly from a bronze model Governor Lacerda brought from Italy," and will have "red velvet awnings." Provision has been made for outboard motors, too, in case it gets too hot for rowing. Two new cable cars are about to start making the trip to the top of the Sugar Loaf and back. Again according to the papers, the "visibility" will be better from these than from the old ones. This is hard to believe: How could that panorama be improved?

Although the pace of city life increases constantly, there is still time to stand and stare in Rio. Men linger in groups in downtown cafés or at newsstands to discuss the latest political moves or look at the passing girls. Visitors are always surprised at how many men who would be—in Henry James's word—"downtown" in New York are on the beaches at 10 o'clock on weekday mornings. This does not mean that Cariocans do not work hard when they work. They just go about it differently.

There is, in fact, much moonlighting. With the present inflation, it is hard to see how workers or the middle class could make ends meet if it were not that everyone down to the humblest nursemaid and lottery-ticket seller did not have some little "business" going on on the side.

There was some talk of having Carnival for a whole week, in honor of the quatercentenary, instead of just the usual four days, but even Rio finally quailed at the thought and the idea was dropped. But Carnival sambas were in the air for weeks in advance; each night, groups went singing and dancing through the streets with their drums, rehearsing. Traffic would stop, or edge around them, and little boys tag along. No Cariocan can resist that rhythm: The cook sambas in the kitchen, and the guests in the *sala* move to it unconsciously (the word is *rebolar*) as they go on with the conversation.

The sambas, *marchas* and other Carnival songs are the living poetry of poor Cariocans. (The words "rich" and "poor" are still in use here, out of style as they are in the affluent parts of the world.) Their songs have always been made from whatever happened to be on their minds: obsessions, fads, fancies and grievances; love, poverty, drink and politics; their love for Rio, but also Rio's three perennial problems: water, light, and transportation. As an old samba says:

> Rio de Janeiro,
> My joy and my delight!
> By day I have no water,
> By night I have no light.

One of this year's sambas gives the honest reaction of the masses to last spring's "revolution":

> Kick him out of office!
> He's a greedy boy!
> I've nothing to investigate,
> What I want is joy!
> Justice has arrived!
> "Pull" won't work again!
> Some have fled to Uruguay;
> Some have fled to Spain!

And here is this year's version of the annual complaint about the Central Railroad, the line that carries thousands from the huge working-class suburbs north of the city in to work. It is addressed to President Castelo Branco:

> Marshál, Illustrious Marshál,
> Consider the problem
> Of the suburbs on the Centrál!
> I'm sorry for poor Juvenal,
> Hanging in the old Central
> All year long . . .
> He works in Leblon
> And lives in Delight,*
> And gets to work mornings
> Late at night.
> Marshál!

Because of its difficult, if lively, topography, the traffic problems of Rio are even more of a nightmare than those of other big cities. Governor Lacerda appointed a tough air force man, Colonel Fontenelle, to see if he could solve them. First, to everyone's confusion and rage, he changed the direction of almost all the one-way streets: then he attacked double, triple and, some swear, quadruple parking. His system is simple: The police go around letting the air out of the tires of illegally parked cars.

It must be said that this measure, considered much too "hard" by the easy-going Cariocans, has partly succeeded. Anyway, bus travel in the city has been speeded up. This year at least three sambas refer to Colonel Fontenelle's campaign (with appropriate noises). The odd thing is that these sambas were composed, and are mostly sung (and hissed), by those who have never owned cars in their lives and never expect to.

The words of sambas are nothing without the music, and some of the longest-lived and musically most beautiful have the most hackneyed lyrics. Love—light love and serious love—infidelity, prostitution, police raids and line-ups (the subject of a very pretty one this year), moonlight, beaches, kisses, heartbreak, and love again:

> Come, my mulatta,
> Take me back.
> You're the joker
> In my pack,
> The prune in my pudding,
> Pepper in my pie,
> My package of peanuts,
> The moon in my sky.

*At opposite ends of the city.

How much longer the samba can hold out against commercialism, television and radio is impossible to say; there are already signs of deterioration. Especially deadly is the new practice of broadcasting sambas over loudspeakers during Carnival itself, so that the people don't, or can't, sing them the way they used to.

Ironically, what may prove to be the real kiss of death to the spontaneity of the samba is that the young rich, after years of devotion to North American jazz, have discovered it. A few years ago only the very few Brazilians, mostly intellectuals, who cared for their own folk-culture took the samba seriously, or went to the rehearsals of the big schools up on the *morros*, the hills. This year, crowds of young people went, one of the symptoms, possibly, of a new social awareness since the "revolution." And some of this year's crop of songs show a self-consciousness, even a self-pity, that is far removed from the old samba spirit.

Poets are also taking up popular songs, inspired perhaps by Vinicius de Moraes, who wrote the libretto of the movie "Black Orpheus." He has lately been appearing at a nightclub, Zumzumzum (Rumor), singing his own songs. A young imitator of Yevtushenko, from the south of Brazil, declaimed his poetry to a packed house in Rio, wearing red sweater, white trousers and no socks, with his hair in his eyes. His book is called "The Betrayed Generation." In fact, a conviction, more or less clearly defined, and more or less justifiable, of "betrayal" seems to be the attitude of both rich and poor, while for the younger rich, a slight subversiveness is considered chic. The Little Castle is a new night club out on Ipanema Beach, and its rich young clientele are often called the "Castelinho Communists"—or parlor pinks.

The most popular show for many weeks has been "Opinion," named for the samba "Opinion," by Zé Kéti, a Negro song writer from the *favelas*. The cast consists of Nara Leão, one of the first girl singers of "good family" ever to appear in Rio, who represents the repentant uppercrust; Zé Kéti himself, who represents the *favelas*; and a young Negro from the north, João Batista do Vale, representing the alienated worker who comes to the big city. The three meet, tell their stories, sing, wander about, sit on crates, etc., to the accompaniment of drums, a flute and a guitar. Joan Baez and Pete Seeger are popular now, and so some rather irrelevant North American spirituals and chain-gang songs are included. The death sentence of Tiradentes, "Toothpuller," the national hero who was condemned for rebellion against Portugal in 1792, is read aloud. There are jokes like: "Red? That color's out of style now."

What is depressing about "Opinion" to North Americans in the audience is not its vague "message" (considered daringly left in Rio) or its amateurishness (that is rather endearing). It is the sudden, sad, uncanny feeling of *déjà vu*: it is all so reminiscent of college plays in the early thirties with Kentucky miners, clenched fists and awkward stances.

Other plays go on as usual. Arthur Miller's "All My Sons" is one, and "How to Succeed in Business Without Really Trying" has been running a long time. There is Goldoni's "Mirandolina," and, more typically, plays like "The Moral of Adultery," "Let's Fall in Love in Cabo Frio" and "The Nuder the Better." In general, the theater in Rio is far behind the other arts, and acting is in a sort of historical "pocket," miraculously preserved from about 1910.

The question always in the air is: When are elections to be held? At first they were to be this year; now they have been postponed until 1966, and no one knows the date, or year, for sure. Carlos Lacerda is the only Presidential candidate so far. Ex-President Kubitschek is in self-imposed exile—mostly in Paris—with his political rights taken away for 10 years.

If his followers could find a way of getting around that, he would probably be only too glad to run again. Although his enemies blame the worst of the inflation on Kubitschek's industrial-progress-at-any-cost policy, and his building of Brasília, and believe his Government to have been hopelessly graft ridden, nevertheless they agree he did get things done. And his many partisans, particularly those who grew rich during his term, are eager to get him back.

Pro-Kubitschek propaganda has reached a height of absurdity. Poor, poor Kubitschek, it goes, he lives in a small apartment in Paris, *he drives his own car*, and—worst deprivation of all to the family-minded Brazilians—he hasn't seen his latest grandchild yet. His enemies have given this movement the very Cariocan name of "Operation *Coitadinho*," a splendid example of the diminutive of *coitado*, "poor little one," one of the most frequent exclamations on the lips of the soft-hearted, but ironical, Brazilians.

Many people were disappointed when President Castelo Branco announced that he would not run for a full term. They had hoped he would, or at least felt it was too early for him to make such a decision. He has almost no demagogic appeal for the masses, and he has not attempted to cultivate it. He is a sad man, still mourning his wife, who died the year before he became President, and he works hard at the almost impossible job he was reluctant to accept.

He has always been respected; now there seems to be a growing admiration and fondness for him. His unfailing dignity, refusal to play politics or make promises and fine speeches, his preference for appealing to law in emergencies, rather than to emotions—all are something new in Brazil, and a welcome relief after the hysterical atmosphere of the past few years.

The press is free, if wildly inaccurate and frequently libelous, and political arrests, which flourished after last spring's coup, have almost ceased. Talk about police and army brutality and torture has died down, and one can only hope that what Brazilians felt was a national disgrace has been really cracked down on, hard, at last.

Inflation produces an atmosphere unlike any other. It is felt even in the way money is handled: tired old bills wadded into big balls. Bus conductors neither give nor expect exact change any more; there is no change. Shopkeepers give the customer's child a piece of candy, instead. Taxi fares have gone up so many times that the meters are several adjustments behind. At the moment, the fare is twice what the meter says, in the day-time. After dark, it is more or less what the driver says.

In Rio, the inflation has almost lost its power to shock; at least, people no longer talk about it constantly the way they did a year or so ago. The minimum wage has gone up and up, but never quite enough. The poor take the inflation more stoically than any other class, since they have never had any savings to lose, anyway. Some of the rich are undoubtedly getting richer. It is the very small middle class that feels the pinch the most. All eyes are fixed on the movements of the dollar, as on a sort of North Star, and the mood might be described as numb, but slightly more hopeful than it was.

For the first time, the Brazilian Government is adhering to a scheme of economic planning; there has been a renewed flow of foreign capital and the pace of inflation has certainly slowed. The prices of gasoline and bread are way up, because the Government has taken away their former impossibly high subsidies. Fighting inflation has to be done slowly and cautiously in Brazil. Because of the ignorance and the high illiteracy rate—and the long-standing skepticism as well—no strong measure against inflation can be explained to the people. The Government does not dare stop public-works projects, even though they are draining the Treasury; that would be considered too "hard." Wages and prices will go on rising yet a while, although they are supposed to level off this year.

But in spite of the shabbiness, the shortages, the sudden disconcerting changes for the worse in standard products and the inflation, life in Rio has compensations. Carnival is gone, but next will come St. John's Day, the second-best holiday of the year; then St. Peter's Day. For highbrows, a large exhibition of contemporary French painting will arrive in July, in honor of the quatercentenary, and later Spain is sending a ballet and an opera by de Falla. There is also to be a series of concerts of the compositions of Father José Mauricio, the 18th-century Rio de Janeiran priest-composer.

Far more enduring and important than these small treats, in what is now essentially a provincial city, is another compensation for those who have to put up with the difficulties of life in Rio. One example will make it plain. Recently a large advertisement showed a young Negro cook, overcome by her pleasure in having a new gas stove, leaning across it toward her white mistress, who leaned over from her side of the stove as they kissed each other on the cheek.

Granted that the situation is not utopian, socially speaking, and that the advertisement is silly—but could it have appeared on billboards, or in the newspapers, in Atlanta, Ga., or even in New York? In Rio, it went absolutely unremarked on, one way or the other.

1965

Gallery Note for Wesley Wehr

I have seen Mr. Wehr open his battered brief-case (with the broken zipper) at a table in a crowded, steamy coffee-shop, and deal out his latest paintings, carefully encased in plastic until they are framed, like a set of magic playing cards. The people at his table would fall silent and stare at these small, beautiful pictures, far off into space and coolness: the coldness of the Pacific Northwest coast in the winter, its different coldness in the summer. So much space, so much air, such distances and loneliness, on those flat little cards. One could almost make out the moon behind the clouds, but not quite; the snow had worn off the low hills almost showing last year's withered grasses; the white line of surf was visible but quiet, almost a mile away. Then Mr. Wehr would whisk all that space, silence, peace, and privacy back into his brief-case again. He once remarked that he would like to be able to carry a whole exhibition in his pockets.

It is a great relief to see a small work of art these days. The Chinese unrolled their precious scroll-paintings to show their friends, bit by bit; the Persians passed their miniatures about from hand to hand; many of Klee's or Bissier's paintings are hand-size. Why shouldn't we, so generally addicted to the gigantic, at last have some small works of art, some short poems, short pieces of music (Mr. Wehr was originally a composer, and I think I detect the influence of Webern on his painting), some intimate, low-voiced, and delicate things in our mostly huge and roaring, glaring world? But in spite of their size, no one could say that these pictures are "small-scale."

Mr. Wehr works at night, I was told, with his waxes and pigments, while his cat rolls crayons about on the floor. But the observation of nature is always accurate; the beaches, the moonlight nights, look just like this. Some pictures may remind one of agates, the form called "[illegible]"; Mr. Wehr is also a collector of agates, of all kinds of stones, pebbles, semi-precious jewels, fossilized clams with opals adhering to them, bits of amber, shells, examples of hand-writing, illegible signatures—those small things that are occasionally capable of overwhelming with a chilling sensation of time and space.

He once told me that Rothko had been an influence on him, to which I replied, "Yes, but Rothko in a whisper." Who does not feel a sense of release, of calm and quiet, in looking at these little pieces of our vast and ancient world that one can actually hold in the palm of one's hand?

1967

An Inadequate Tribute

Randall Jarrell was difficult, touchy, and oversensitive to criticism. He was also a marvelous conversationalist, brilliantly funny, a fine poet, and the best and most generous critic of poetry I have known. I am proud to remember that, although we could rarely meet, we remained friends for twenty years. Sometimes we quarreled, silently, in infrequent letters, but each time we met we would tell each other that it had meant nothing at all; we really were in agreement about everything that mattered.

He always seemed more alive than other people, as if constantly tuned up to the concert pitch that most people, including poets, can maintain only for short and fortunate stretches.

I like to think of him as I saw him once after we had gone swimming together on Cape Cod; wearing only bathing trunks and a very queer straw cap with a big visor, seated on the crest of a high sand dune, writing in a notebook. It was a bright and dazzling day. Randall looked small and rather delicate, but bright and dazzling, too. I felt quite sure that whatever he was writing would be bound to share the characteristics of the day and of the small man writing away so busily in the middle of it all.

1967

Introduction to *An Anthology of Twentieth-Century Brazilian Poetry*

edited by Elizabeth Bishop and Emanuel Brasil

Poets and poetry are highly thought of in Brazil. Among men, the name of "poet" is sometimes used as a compliment or term of affection, even if the person referred to is a businessman or politician, not a poet at all. One of the most famous twentieth-century Brazilian poets, Manuel Bandeira, was presented with a permanent parking space in front of his apartment house in Rio de Janeiro, with an enamelled sign POETA—although he never owned a car and didn't know how to drive. When he was quite old, Bandeira taught for a few years at the University of Brazil, reaching retirement age long before he had taught the number of years necessary for a pension. Nevertheless, the Chamber of Deputies, to great applause, unanimously voted to grant him a full pension.

Almost anyone—(any man, that is, for until very recently poetry has been exclusively a masculine art in Brazil)—with literary interests has published at least one book of poems, "anyone" including doctors, lawyers, engineers, and followers of other arts. Jorge de Lima was a painter and a well-known Rio doctor as well as a poet. Candido Portinari, the painter best known outside Brazil, wrote autobiographical poems and published a book of them shortly before he died. The doings and sayings of popular poets like Carlos Drummond de Andrade and Vinicius de Moraes are constantly and affectionately reported in the newspapers. In the United States only a Pound or a Ginsberg receives as much attention from the press, but for different reasons and in different tones. Poets who produce volumes after long intervals of silence are called "Leap Year Poets," *Bissextos*; Bandeira edited an anthology of contemporary "Leap Year" poets, showing that although their output may be small, they are esteemed and not forgotten.

It does not follow, of course, that the poetry in the many small volumes is necessarily great or even good, or that poetry is any more welcomed by publishers or sells any better in Brazil than in the United States. Editions are very small, of three hundred copies, for example; books are paperbound, as in France, and so cost comparatively little; and the poet earns very little from them. It may seem to the American visitor that the educated people whom he meets in Brazil read more poetry and *know* more poetry (often by heart) than people in the same walks of life at home. But it should be remembered that the educated elite is still a very small class, living almost entirely in five or six of the larger coastal cities, and that in a country of widespread illiteracy (forty per cent the figure usually given), the potential book-reading, book-buying public is limited. Partly because of poor communications, literary groups in these larger cities are more isolated from each other than they are in the United States—where so much has been made of the "isolation of the artist." And if anything, Brazilian poets have a harder time making a living than do poets in the United States. There are few reviews and magazines, and these pay next to nothing. The fellowships, awards, readings, and "poet-in-residence" academic posts that help along poetic careers in North America are almost non-existent there.

Poets work in the civil service: Carlos Drummond de Andrade, usually considered the greatest living Brazilian poet, had worked for the Ministry of Education for more than thirty years when he retired in 1966. A few teach, and more go into journalism, sometimes writing columns for newspapers or picture magazines. Since his retirement, Drummond de Andrade has had a regular column of news comment and trivia in a leading Rio paper; occasionally he uses it to publish a new poem. But no matter how he earns his living, there is respect for the poet, his work, and his opinions, and for the more worldly and better connected there is opportunity in the long Latin tradition of appointing poets to diplomatic posts, even as ambassadors. Like Claudel and St.-John Perse in France, Gabriela Mistral and Neruda in Chile, Vinicius de Moraes and João Cabral de Melo Neto, among others in Brazil, have held diplomatic posts. Vinicius de Moraes (commonly known as just "Vinicius"), famous for his film-script for *Black Orpheus* and more recently for his popular songs, performs in night-clubs, produces musical shows in Brazil and other countries, and makes recordings in Europe—all ways of augmenting his income.

This anthology, consisting of selections from the work of fourteen poets of the modern generation and of the post-war generation of 1945, is a modest attempt to present to the American reader examples of the poetry written in Brazil during this century. Inevitably, it is more representative of the editors' personal tastes than all-inclusive. With a population of some ninety million, Brazil is by far the largest Portuguese-speaking country in the world, but Portuguese is a relatively unknown language in the United States. It is understandably hard to find good American poets willing to undertake translation, much of which necessarily has to be done from literal prose translations of the Brazilian poems. The editors feel that the translators have done extremely well, keeping close to the texts and yet managing to produce "poems" preserving many of the characteristics of the originals.

Grammatically, Portuguese is a difficult language. Even well-educated Brazilians worry about writing it, and will ask friends to check their manuscripts for grammatical errors. Brazilians do not speak the way they write; the written language is more formal and somewhat cumbersome. In fact, Portuguese is an older language than Spanish, and still retains in its structure Latin forms dating from the Roman Republic. The tendency in this century has been to get away from the old, correct written style, in both prose and poetry, and to write demotic Portuguese. But this has not been completely realized, and Portuguese is still rarely written as it is spoken. A few novelists come close, in passages of conversation, and some columnists and younger poets use slang, *gíria*, almost unintelligible and changing constantly. One of the goals of the famous "Modern Art Week" in São Paulo in 1922 was to abandon the dead literary language of the nineteenth century and to write poetry in the spoken language. Much poetry of the '20s attempted this, using slang, abbreviations, ellipses, and apostrophes to indicate letters or syllables left out in ordinary, rapid speech. Very much the same thing had happened in English poetry about a decade earlier. Perhaps it is a recurring phenomenon, desire, or ideal in modern literature. This style in poetry later declined with "the generation of '45," and poetry of the '40s, '50s, and '60s, visually at least, is more conventional than those first, early attempts at modernism.

Like other Latin languages, Portuguese has a high number of perfect rhymes and frequent, inescapable assonances. The ease of rhyming in these languages has been envied, sometimes eyed with suspicion, by poets writing in the more obdurate English. But facile rhyme and inevitable assonance can become liabilities, handicaps to originality. With time familiar sets of rhymes grow tiresome, and free verse must have come as a great relief. Almost all the poems in this volume are in free verse or unrhymed metrical verse, but since assonance is innate, many contemporary poets make deliberate use of it to give effects of near-rhyme, casually or in regular patterns. Brazilian poetry, even free verse, can rarely avoid melodiousness, even when the sense might seem to want to do so.

The rules of versification in traditional Portuguese verse are like those of French verse: short and long syllables determine the number of feet in a line, not stress, as in English; and no irregularities in meter are permitted. When contemporary Brazilian poets write in traditional forms (as does Vinicius de Moraes in most of his *Sonnets*) they obey these rules of versification. Punctuation in modern Brazilian poetry is often puzzling. Apparently, the poets are influenced by, or perhaps simply copy, French usage: no punctuation at all except one stop at the end of the poem; sets of dashes where

English poetry might use commas or semi-colons; dashes instead of quotation marks, and so on. In fact, anyone reading Brazilian Portuguese, prose or verse, soon becomes aware of its unperturbed inconsistency in both punctuation and spelling; points of style that have become fixed in English have not yet jelled in Brazil. It resembles our own language in its freer, earlier days. In these translations, the original punctuation has been retained when possible, and only tampered with when it, or the lack of it, might confuse the English-reading reader.

Brazilian poetry cannot be considered truly Brazilian—that is, independent of that of Portugal—until after the Proclamation of Independence in 1822. Its development is more or less predictable, in that its movements parallel those of western Europe, especially France, with a time-lag of ten, twenty, or more years. As in American writing, this time-lag has decreased over the years, growing always shorter, until at present sometimes Brazilian poetry actually seems more advanced than that of the countries it formerly derived from. As in American poetry, there are exceptions to this, apparent regressions in the modernist movement, but none happens to come within the period covered by this volume. There is no space in this brief introduction to give a history of Brazilian poetry over the last hundred fifty years. We shall merely give the highlights, naming a few outstanding poets and their books and briefly outlining the movements that make up the Brazilian heritage of the fourteen poets represented.

The nineteenth century was, as elsewhere, the romantic century, and Brazilian Romanticism is considered to have started with the publication of a book of poems by Gonçalves Magalhães (1811–1882), called, romantically indeed, *Poetic Sighs and Longings*. The four outstanding romantic poets, however, were: Gonçalves Dias (1823–1864); Álvares de Azevedo (1831–1852); Casimiro de Abreu (1837–1860); and Castro Alves (1847–1871). All four used genuinely Brazilian themes, Gonçalves Dias* romanticising the Brazilian Indian for the first time, and Castro Alves, in his melodramatic poem "The Slave Ship," being the first poet to protest against the horrors of the

---

*Perhaps Gonçalves Dias was partly responsible for the awakening of interest in the Brazilian Indian, the "noble savage," in the middle of the nineteenth century. Almost every one of the barons created by Dom Pedro II, the last Emperor, took an Indian name and Indian names are still in common use. There is also the opera *Guarany* by Carlos Gomes, to bear evidence to this continuing fashion for all things Indian. "The Slave Ship," having been considered bad art by the more sophisticated for decades, has, of late, made something of a comeback, owing partly to new humanitarian, anti-racist feelings, and partly to a brilliant young group of reciters of verse, the Jongleurs of São Paulo, who have included it in their repertory with great success.

slave trade. They and the other poets of the movement were much influenced, by way of France and Portugal, by the English romantics. *Saudade*, the characteristic Brazilian longing or nostalgia, and plain homesickness appear obsessively in their poems—perhaps because most of these young poets, "of good family," made the long ocean voyage to study at the University of Coimbra in Portugal, for Brazil had no universities until the late nineteenth century. Several of them died very young, as did Keats and Shelley, usually of tuberculosis. Gonçalves Dias drowned, shipwrecked on his native shore, while returning from Portugal.

The romantic period gave way to a period of realism, called the Parnassian movement (from around 1870 to 1890) and a brief period of Symbolism (1890–1900). The so-called "realists" were strongly influenced by the French Parnassian school of Gauthier, Banville, Lesconte de L'Isle, and Heredia. The most famous poet of this school was Olavo Bilac (1865–1918), three of whose books are *Poesias* (1888), *Poesias Infantis* (1904), and *Tarde* (1919). The Symbolist movement produced one important figure, the black poet Cruz e Souza (1861–1918). German and English romantic poetry were known to the Brazilians, but French literature and philosophy were, and have remained, until very recently, the strongest influences in Brazilian literature and thought. They are still perhaps of primary importance, but English and, even more, American prose and poetry are now rapidly becoming better known. English is now becoming the most important and fashionable foreign language.

From the turn of the century until 1922, Brazilian poetry went through a period of eclecticism, with no one style predominating, reflecting in general the intense nationalism prevalent at the time. In 1912 Oswald de Andrade, later considered the most radical poet of the 1922 movement, returned from Europe with a copy of Marinetti's *Futurist Manifesto*. About that time he created a sensation by publishing a poem without rhyme or meter, entitled "Last Ride of a Tubercular through the City by Streetcar." The subject-matter and tone of poetry were changing, and in 1917, when Manuel Bandeira published his first book *Ash of the Hours*, the critic João Ribeiro announced that Olavo Bilac, admired for so long, was "now out of date."

The year 1922 marked the centennial of Brazilian independence. A group of writers and artists, most of whom had lived in Europe, decided to celebrate by holding a festival at which they would present the avant-garde theories they had enthusiastically adopted in Paris and Italy to their artistically backward compatriots. "Modern Art Week" took place in the Municipal Theatre of São Paulo on the 13th, the 15th, and the 17th of February. It has become as much a landmark in Brazilian culture as the New York Armory Show of 1913 is in the culture of the United States.

The night of the 15th was the most dramatic of the three. The poet Menotti del Pichia made a speech presenting the aims of the new artistic movements, summarizing them with these words: "We want light, air, ventilators, airplanes, workers' demands, idealism, motors, factory smokestacks, blood, speed, dream, in our Art. And may the chugging of an automobile, on the track of two lines of verse, frighten away from poetry the last Homeric god who went on sleeping and dreaming of the flutes of Arcadian shepherds and the divine breasts of Helen, an anachronism in the era of the jazz band and the movie." Poets and prose writers then read excerpts from their works. The audience took offense, and there followed an uproar of booing, whistling, and shouted insults. Mário de Andrade read from his book *Hallucinated City*, and later he confessed in a long essay regarding Modern Art Week that he did not know how he had had the courage to face such an audience.

Mário de Andrade (1893–1945), a mulatto from São Paulo, was one of the most important figures in contemporary Brazilian art and literature. A critic, poet, and novelist, he was also one of the very first intellectuals to discover and to become seriously interested in the great untapped resources of Brazilian folklore and popular music. It is hard to think of any form of contemporary artistic activity in Brazil that does not owe a debt to him. In the year of the twenty-fifth anniversary of his death, 1970, every newspaper and review printed critical studies, biographical essays, and tributes to him, and loving memoirs were written about him as teacher and friend. The vitality of his personality and the wide range of his interests have been of the utmost importance in helping create a richer artistic self-consciousness in Brazil.

The Modernist poetic movement repudiated French and Portuguese influences, and, as in other countries, it rejected the ideas of the Romantics, Parnassians, and Symbolists. It believed in using the material of everyday life, and attempted a complete honesty, bringing the anguish and conflicts of the period into poetry for the first time. The Modernist group originally included, among other poets, Manuel Bandeira, Mário de Andrade, and Oswald de Andrade. There were also the painters Anita Malfatti and Di Cavalcanti; the sculptor Victor Brecheret, and the composer Villa-Lobos. Only Villa-Lobos is well-known outside Brazil, but the others all took part in the artistic transition from the outworn forms of the nineteenth century to the forms of the present.

In 1924, in Paris, Oswald de Andrade published an important book of poems called *Brazilwood*. With extreme economy of means, in simple language, he treated Brazilian themes, customs, superstitions, and family life directly, and for the first time in Brazilian poetry humorously. These qualities have marked Brazilian poetry ever since; they represent the real achievement of Modern Art Week and *modernismo*. A word of tribute should also be given to the French poet Blaise Cendrars, who lived in Brazil for several years. His free style, brilliant imagery, and fresh, ironic treatment of the modern world were all important influences on the poets of the Modernist movement.

Manuel Bandeira, Mário de Andrade, and Carlos Drummond de Andrade have been mentioned; other poets in the Modernist movement are included in this anthology. Carlos Drummond de Andrade is regarded as the most important—and is probably the most popular—poet of the contemporary period. Vinicius de Moraes is also extremely popular, especially with the younger generation, some of whom are ignorant of his early and more serious work, but adore him for his "Bossa Nova" songs (a style now considered out-of-date), and his present constant outpouring of gentle, romantic songs and music, almost invariably about love.

The most recent date marking a shift in poetic styles in Brazil is 1945, the year of the dropping of the first atomic bomb—about which every Brazilian poet seems to have written at least one poem—and the end of World War II. Brazil itself was just coming to the end of a dictatorship that had lasted for fifteen years and was passing through a phase of redemocratization. It was the year of the death of Mário de Andrade, and a new generation of poets was appearing on the scene, the Neo-Modernists, or the generation of '45. As early as 1929 the writer Luis Martins had remarked: "Modernism suffered from the demoralizing influence of its adherents. As in the time of Parnassianism everyone wrote sonnets, in the time of Modernism everyone began to write nonsense in free verse." The generation of '45 was against the exaggerated use of the free verse that had dominated poetry for more than twenty years; they wanted more concision and less sentimentality (always a danger in Brazilian verse) as well as a more accurate use of words.

João Cabral de Melo Neto, born in 1920, came of age in this generation; today he is considered one of the major poetic voices in Latin America. His first book *Stone of Sleep* (1942) showed the characteristics of his mature style: striking visual imagery and an insistent use of concrete, tactile nouns. He is "difficult"; but at the present time his work displays the highest development and the greatest coherency of style of any Brazilian poet.

The younger poets, many, diverse, and talented, including the Concretionists and others whose work takes the form of song lyrics—and Brazil has produced in recent years some of the best popular songs ever written—are not in this anthology. The editors hope to introduce them in a second volume, in order to give the American reader a more complete picture of the variety, profundity, and originality of Brazilian poetry today.

The Editors

1972

A Brief Reminiscence
and a Brief Tribute

I had hoped that this photograph, so unflattering to almost everyone in it, would never be seen again. The occasion was a party for Edith and Osbert Sitwell, given by LIFE Magazine, at the Gotham Bookmart. I hadn't wanted to attend, but Marianne Moore was firm about it. "We must be *polite* to the Sitwells," she said, and so I went. There were a great many people there. The photographers, as is their custom, were *not* polite. There were difficulties in separating the poets from the non-poets (some of whom wanted to be in the picture, too) and in herding the poets into the back room to be photographed. (In the fray, a few got left out.) Poets tripped over trailing wires and jostled each other to get in the front row, or in the back row, depending. They were arranged, hectored, and re-arranged. Miss Moore's hat was considered to be too big: she refused to remove it. Auden was one of the few who seemed to be enjoying himself. He got into the picture by climbing on a ladder, where he sat making loud, cheerful comments over our heads.

The picture was taken with a sort of semi-circular swoop of the camera, with two hesitations and clicks. The poets at the clicks (I was one) came out looking rather odd. (Seeing the picture in LIFE, one of my best friends told me I looked like a salt-cellar with the top screwed on the wrong way.) I was wearing a small velvet cap and after the party Miss Moore said regretfully, "I wish *I'd* worn a *minimal* hat like that."

I met Auden only a few times, and although I wanted to, I was a little afraid of talking to him. I regret this now very much. I find it sad that the young students and poets I have met in the past four years usually seem to know only a few of his anthology pieces, rarely read him at all, and apparently never for pleasure. One reason for this may be that Auden, the most brilliant of imitators himself, has been, or was, so much imitated that his style, his details and vocabulary, the whole atmosphere of his poetry, seems over-familiar, old hat. But when I was in college, and all through the thirties and forties, I and all my friends who were interested in poetry read him constantly. We hurried to see his latest poem or book, and either wrote as much like him as possible, or tried hard not to. His then leftist politics, his ominous landscape, his intimations of betrayed loves, war on its way, disasters and death, matched exactly the mood of our late-depression and post-depression youth. We admired his apparent toughness, his sexual courage—actually more honest than Ginsberg's, say, is now, while still giving expression to technically dazzling poetry. Even the most hermetic early poems gave us the feeling that here was someone who *knew*—about psychology, geology, birds, love, the evils of capitalism—what have you? They colored our air and made us feel tough, ready, and in the know, too.

I almost always agree with Auden critically, except when he gets bogged down in his categories (and except that I haven't yet been able to read Tolkien), and I admire almost all his poems except the later preachy ones. I'd like to quote some characteristic lines:

> Doom is darker and deeper than any sea-dingle.

*

> Easily my dear, you move, easily your head,
> And easily as through the leaves of a photograph album
>   I'm led
> Through the night's delights and the day's impressions,
> Past the tall tenements and the trees in the wood,
> Though sombre the sixteen skies of Europe
>   And the Danube flood.

*

> We made all possible preparations,
> Drew up a list of firms,
> Constantly revised our calculations
> And allotted the farms . . .

*

> For to be held for friend
> By an undeveloped mind
> To be joke for children is
> Death's happiness
>
> Whose anecdotes betray
> His favorite color as blue
> Colour of distant bells
> And boys' overalls.

*

Now the leaves are falling fast,
Nurse's flowers will not last;
Nurses to the graves are gone,
And the prams go rolling on.

*

From SPAIN, 1937

Many have heard it on the remote peninsulas,
On sleepy plains, in the aberrant fisherman's islands,
    In the corrupt heart of the city;
Have heard and migrated like gulls or the seeds
    of a flower.

They clung like burrs to the long expresses that lurch
Through the unjust lands, through the night, through
    the alpine tunnel;
        They floated over the oceans;
They walked the passes; they came to present their lives.

*

From REFUGEE BLUES

Saw a poodle in a jacket fastened with a pin,
Saw a door opened and a cat let in;
But they weren't German Jews, my dear, they weren't
    German Jews.

Went down to the harbour and stood upon the quay,
Saw the fish swimming as if they were free:
Only ten feet away, my dear, only ten feet away.

Walked through a wood, saw the birds in the trees;
They had no politicians and sang at their ease:
They weren't the human race, my dear, they weren't the
    human race.

These verses and many, many more of Auden's have been part of my
mind for years—I could say, part of my life.

1974

TRANSLATIONS

From *The Diary of "Helena Morley"*

. . . Thank God Carnival is over. I can't say that it was very pleasant, because grandma beat me, something she never does.

It's my fate that everyone who loves me makes my life miserable. The only people who have any authority over my cousins are their fathers. Oh! If only it were like that with me! My father is the person who annoys me least of all. If it hadn't been for grandma's and Aunt Madge's interfering I'd have gone to the masquerade ball at the theatre. Since the age of seven I've dreamed of being twelve so that I could go to the ball. And now I'm almost thirteen and I'm beaten for not going!

Aunt Quequeta was the one who made me want to go to the ball, telling me about what they used to do in her day. A friend of hers put on a masquerade costume, disguised her voice, and flirted with her father all evening until he fell madly in love with her and the next day instead of coming in to lunch he kept walking around in the garden with his head hanging down, thinking of the masked woman. Another friend of hers let her husband go to the ball first and she went later, masked, flirted with him, and he fell madly in love with her, to such a degree that he kept sighing the whole evening.

My aunts still have the hoop skirts they used to wear. How I wish they still wore them! They don't wear anything like that now, but I'd like to go like that even so.

It was my cousin Glorinha who gave me such a swelled head that I thought I could go. I asked mama and she said, "If your grandmother will let you I'll let you." I asked grandma, "Grandma, mama will let me go. Will you let me go to the ball with Glorinha?" she said, "I certainly will not!" I stamped my foot hard and I ran and threw myself on her bed, angry. She came in and took off her slipper and hit me twice, saying, "That'll give you something to cry about!" I thrashed my legs around but I didn't get up.

But it was worth it because today I got the material for a dress and a silver two milreis piece.

•

. . . Knowing that I and my sister have that failing of laughing at everything, how did papa have the courage to send a guest to our house the way he did? You can't imagine what our life has been like with this man in the house! Papa has been in Parauna for a week. He went to see a mine that a Frenchman wants to buy and asked papa if he'd go to see if it's worth it. There papa's the guest of this man he sent us. But you wouldn't believe it if I told you what his visit has been like.

We have a little Negro girl, Cesarina, very funny, who makes us laugh all the time at the things she says and does. On the day this man arrived something happened to us that couldn't possibly happen in any other house; there were only two tallow candles in the house. When mama discovered it there weren't any stores open. But these candles aren't any good; they don't last at all. One was used up before I'd even finished my lessons. Mama had the other one put in the guest room. In our house we only use kerosene in the kitchen and even the kitchen lamp was dry. When my candle came to an end I still had lessons to do, there was nothing else to do but send Cesarina to the guest room, to see if he'd gone to sleep. If he had, she was supposed to steal the candle without waking him up! She went and came back laughing so hard at finding the man still awake that she could only speak to us by making signs.

She held her hands up in the air and made spectacles with her fingers, meaning that the man had his eyes open. She made this sign and all the time she was having such a fit of the giggles that she couldn't speak.

We are idiots about laughing. We began that night and even now we can't look at our guest without a fit of giggling. We just have to see the man and then we remember Cesarina's spectacles and simply burst. Mama, *coitada*, doesn't know what excuse to give the man. She's said everything except that she has two lunatics in the house.

And I think that these attacks of laughing that we've had are due to our having as a guest a man who's never seen us before, and his being silent, without saying a word, in the house and at the table. Now mama's forbidden us to come to the table, but even in the kitchen we shake with laughter to see the man and mama sitting there in silence! I don't know what she'll tell papa. He's been here three days and it already seems like a week. I envy people who don't have giggling spells the way I have.

At the saddest moments, sometimes, when we shouldn't have had cheerful faces, we've laughed. . . .

When papa got back he asked mama if we had treated the guest in our house well, and said, "He and his family couldn't have done more for me at their house; they almost overwhelmed me with attention. His daughters are homely and not very attractive. I thought he'd come back enchanted with my girls, but when he got back he was silent and didn't say a thing. I couldn't keep from asking him if he'd seen my daughters and he told me, 'I never saw their faces; they laughed from the minute I got there until I left.'"

. . . Today we went to Jogo da Bola Street for lunch. There were two guests there, friends of the family. The man is called Anselmo Coelho. He's good-looking and very nice, married to a terribly homely woman, who speaks through her nose, called Toninha. I asked my cousins why such a handsome man had married such an ugly woman, and they said that he was the widower of a very pretty wife, and, living in Itaipava, he met this teacher, and because she wouldn't be any expense to him, he married her.

At the table I noticed how little feeling the man had for his wife, and I felt sorry for her, *coitada!* After lunch we stayed at the table and he got the conversation onto his first wife. He praised her brains, her beauty, and her sympathy so much that I kept looking at the poor creature and feeling sorry for her. He said, "But she was so jealous that she made me suffer. When I miss her I always try to remember how jealous she was. If I had to go out alone on business, before I got to the door she'd fall down in a faint." He told all this and then added, "I even miss the faints."

After a while he looked at his watch and said, "It's time. I have to go." He got up to go and that fool of a homely wife ran and held onto his arm, trying to imitate the other wife. He kept going out, saying, "Stop it, Toninha. Stop this nonsense!" And the woman kept clinging to his arm and he kept on going. We stayed at the table pretending not to notice in order not to embarrass him. Suddenly we heard a noise, the sound of a body falling on the doorstep. We all ran and there was the poor homely woman stretched out on the ground, with a horrible face, and her husband prodding her with his foot and saying, "Get up, fool! Stop acting! Get up! Don't disgrace me!" He said this still prodding his wife with his foot, without leaning over. Naninha said, "*Coitada!* She's had an attack!" He said, "She wants to do what I said the other one did. But you can leave her here, it isn't anything. She'll get up in a little while." And off he went.

We waited a little for her to open her eyes. When she didn't open them, we carried her, two with her arms, two with her legs, almost dragging her, and put her on the bed and ran outside to laugh.

Aunt Agostinha said to us, "Now you see, while you're girls, that men don't care for silly women. He treats her well, but you see what she did today."

. . . Today I'm tired because it's one of the days when I have the most work. But shouldn't I tell what happened to me yesterday, here in my dear diary? I imagine that today all Diamantina hasn't any other subject of conversation: "Did you see Helena and Luizinha dancing all night long last night, with their aunt lying in her coffin?" I'm only sorry that they won't say it to me personally, because I could explain. But what bad luck we have! Aunt Neném spent the whole month dying and then had to draw her last breath yesterday.

I know very well that Aunt Neném is my father's oldest sister and that he esteems her highly. But I confess that I can't cry for the death of an English aunt whom I didn't know. She's been sick for many years at the fazenda and none of her nephews or nieces knew her. When my father learned that she was very low he went there, a week ago. We'd already been invited to Leontina's wedding here. It was the first dance I'd ever been to. My rose-colored dress was the first pretty dress I'd ever had. How could I miss all that?

Then, I don't know how, the news spread through town. Papa only wrote to mama, who was all ready to go to the wedding, too, and didn't go; but she herself thought it was a shame that we couldn't go, after getting the news at the last minute. She planned it with us: "You go with your cousins and I won't tell anyone about Neném's death today. I'll keep the news until tomorrow." But I'm so unlucky that I'd barely put my foot in the door of the bride's house when I received condolences. It seemed like spite. But I lied bravely, with a blank face. "Condolences for what?" "The death of your aunt." "Who said that? It isn't true. My father's at the fazenda and he hasn't sent word to mama." But they wouldn't leave me alone until they convinced themselves that I was more interested in amusing myself than in weeping for the death of an unknown aunt.

Oh! What a wonderful night! In spite of everybody's eagerness to spoil my fun, they didn't succeed. It was the first time I'd gone to a dance. How wonderful dancing is! And how quickly I learned all the steps! If I hadn't gone to the wedding yesterday I could never have been consoled for having missed it. There's a party like that so seldom! And then I think nobody's going to remember the lack of feeling we showed for very long. It would have been better if Aunt Neném had died after the wedding and we could have shown more feeling. But it wasn't God's will. What could we do?

. . . *Superstition in Diamantina.* Since I was little, I've suffered from all sorts of superstitions. If there were thirteen people at the table, I was always the one who had to leave. Combing one's hair at night, under any circumstances, sends one's mother straight to hell. Sweeping the house at night upsets one's life. Breaking a mirror is bad luck. Rubbing one foot against the other, walking backwards, and other things I don't remember now, are all unlucky. They can explain why some of them do harm, but not others. Such as, for example, if a visitor stays too long, stand the broom behind the door, or throw salt in the fire, and she'll go away. I believe that salt in the fire works if the visitor hears it crackle, because she knows what it means.

The funny thing is that everybody knows that superstition is a sin, but they prefer to confess it rather than do something that somebody says brings bad luck.

Once I asked grandma, "The Senhora doesn't like to sin, and how is it that you know superstition is a sin and yet have so many superstitions?" She answered, "There are things that are born in us, daughter. Nobody can see proofs, the way I have—such as thirteen people at the table and within a year one of them dying, or a mirror that fell and broke in Henrique's house and he had such bad luck afterward—without being afraid. The priests all say it's a sin, but I don't doubt that they believe in it, too. It's something we're born knowing, the people's voice is the voice of God." I said, "I know for my part that I'm not going to believe these things, grandma. If it's a sin it's because God thinks it's absurd." And she said, "Yes, my child, I don't say that you should believe in a lot of them, I think that's nonsense. But some are true and you oughtn't to ignore them. Like thirteen people at the table, and a broken mirror, you can't make light of them."

I'm almost fourteen years old and already I think more than all the rest of the family. I think I began to draw conclusions from the age of ten years, or less. And I swear I never saw anybody from mama's family think about things. They hear something and believe it: and that's for the rest of their lives.

They're all happy like that!

. . . I'm going to unburden myself here of the disappointment, the rage and the sorrow, that I suffered yesterday at my cousin Zinha's wedding. She's my rich uncle's daughter, and the wedding was an important occasion.

My uncle ordered dress-lengths of silk from Rio de Janeiro for his girls. All my other cousins were making themselves silk dresses, too. Mama bought two lengths of fine pink wool for me and Luizinha. Aunt Madge took mine to make and Luizinha's went to another dressmaker.

Aunt Madge came back from Rio recently and since then I haven't had any peace. I have to carry a parasol so I won't get sunburned, because the girls in Rio don't have freckles. I have to wear my hair loose because the girls in Rio wear their hair loose. The same nagging all the time; the girls in Rio dress this way, the girls in Rio wear their hair that way. I

didn't mind if the dress was made like those the girls in Rio wear. I just
wanted it to be pink.

Aunt Madge took the material and never asked me to try it on. I went
to her house every day as usual, and saw nothing of the dress. Once I got
up my courage and asked for it. She said, "Don't worry. You're going to
the wedding looking prettier than all the others."

The wedding was day before yesterday. I and Luizinha went to Dudu's
house to have our hair arranged, and we left delighted, with hairdos that
made us look like young ladies. Luizinha dressed up in her dress and we
went to Aunt Madge's; my dress was nowhere to be seen. Aunt Madge said,
"There's no hurry, child. It's early yet." And taking a comb, she said, "Sit
here. You're a little girl, why do you want to wear your hair like a young
lady?" She wet my hair, pulled out the curls, and let it fall down on my shoulders. Then she went and brought in the dress; a simple dress of navy blue
wool with just a row of buttonholes down the back, bound with red ribbon.

Today I think it's a pretty dress; but at the moment I had one of my attacks of rage and I couldn't hold back my tears. Unable to say a word, I kissed
my aunt's hands and ran out in the street. Luizinha followed me, in silence.
I went up Burgalhau Street, into the Cavalhada Nova, and into Direita Street,
running all the way, and blind with rage. I couldn't see a thing. Grandma's
been at Uncle Geraldo's for several days, waiting for the wedding. I went into
her room and fell on her bed in such a storm of tears it frightened her. But
all she said was, "My God! What's happened!" Luizinha came in and grandma
asked, "What's the matter?" Luizinha said, "It's because she was longing for
a pink dress and Aunt Madge dressed her like that."

When I break down, it's always with grandma. I feel she's the only one
who understands me. Then grandma began with her usual remarks: "Another of Madge's and my trials with this girl! She doesn't understand that
we're only trying to do what's right for her. She wants always to be just like
all the plain girls!" Then I raised my head sobbing, and said, "I'm the most
miserable, the skinniest, the stupidest of them all, grandma, and I always
have to be inferior in everything. I'm so envious of Luizinha because Aunt
Madge doesn't like her!" Grandma said, "Stop crying over nothing, silly
child. Some day you'll see that your godmother, who's so good to you, and
I were right. Go wash your face and let's go to the parlor. They're all there
already." Then I showed her my hair and said, "Do I have to go into the
parlor with my hair like a lunatic from the asylum, grandma?" She said, "It's
pretty, child." I said, "Grandma, the Senhora just doesn't know what I'm
going through. I was looking forward to my pink dress with such pleasure,
and today, to dress like a widow, and to see all the rest of them in pink and
pale blue and everything? No, grandma, it was too cruel of Aunt Madge. I
don't want her to take any more interest in me, grandma. This is the end!"

•

. . . If there were diviners of dreams today, the way there were in the time of Joseph of Egypt, what a fine thing it would be! I can never get that story of the seven fat cows and seven lean cows, that meant seven years of plenty and seven years of famine, out of my head.

I suffer a great deal from dreams and one of the worst I had when I was little was the disillusionment I suffered when I died and went to heaven. How horrible heaven was that night! I remember until today the dismal life I led in heaven until I woke up. It was an enormous yard, clean and bare, filled with old women in cloaks, with shawls on their heads, holding their hands up in prayer, not paying any attention to each other. No São Pedro, no angels, nothing. When they were tired of kneeling they walked around in that enormous yard with their heads bent, still praying. When I woke up and saw I wasn't in heaven, what a relief!

Dreaming that I'm at Mass at the Cathedral in the middle of the crowd in my underwear is something horrible that's always happening to me. Lots of times I've dreamed I was at school in my bare feet, without knowing where to hide them. It's a constant martyrdom. But I've had marvelous dreams, too. I can't count the times I've flown, without wings, to Boa Vista or over the houses of the city. It's delightful! Or I was in a marvelous palace, like the little girl and the dwarfs. And I've dreamed of being in a field of peanuts, and I kept pulling up the plants and finding silver coins at the roots.

But last night's dream was horrible. I dreamed I'd turned into a monkey, and in spite of my grief I could have resigned myself to being a monkey if I hadn't had a tail, but my tail was enormous!

. . . Grandma's been sick a week today and everyone in the house is in a state of the greatest anxiety, because they say that if she shows improvement today by tomorrow she'll be saved.

I don't know why God let me know grandma! I might have been so happy, because my parents are both strong and healthy, if I'd never known her. If only she'd died when I was little the way the other one did!

I'm in agony today! Esmeralda came to help us and taught us some prayers that God can't possibly not listen to. We're all praying with such faith! We've done almost nothing else all day today. There wasn't even anyone to receive the callers.

I spent the day in anguish, seeing grandma in that condition, with nobody able to help her. The doctor comes and prescribes things, and goes away, and then she gets worried about herself!

What mama says is always right. Sometimes I thought it was absurd when she said that life is made up of suffering. Now I see she was right. Life really is made up of suffering. These days since grandma's been sick I've forgotten all the joy I ever had and suffering is all I can think about. And since they said that tomorrow would be the crisis, I've been in such agony that all I can do is stay on my knees with the others, praying. When they get tired I take a walk around the garden, come back through the kitchen, the parlor, and go to every corner of the house, trying to find some peace, but I can't. And if I go in grandma's room, it's worse torture.

Why does God punish us all this way? We never hurt anyone. I wait for the day He'll remember and release grandma and us from this suffering.

. . . Grandma died!

Oh dear grandma, why has God taken you away and left me all alone in the world, missing you so much! Yes, my dear little grandmother, I'm all alone, because weren't you the only person who's ever understood me up until now? Shall I ever find anyone else in this life who'll tell me I'm intelligent and pretty and good? Who'll ever remember to give me material for a pretty new dress, so I won't feel I'm beneath my cousins? Who'll argue with mama and always try to defend me and find good qualities in me, when everyone else only finds faults?

Why did you love me so much? Me, the most mischievous of the grandchildren, and the noisiest, and the one who gave you the most trouble? I remember now with remorse the struggle you had to get me in from play every evening and onto my knees, when it was time for the rosary. But here in secret I confess now that it was an hour of sacrifice you made me undergo. Even the rage I felt, when after saying the whole rosary and all the mysteries, my aunts and that hypocrite of a Chiquinha used to remember all our dead relatives and we had to say one more Our Father or Hail Mary for the soul of each and every one! I used to think that my prayers might even be sending souls back to hell, because I was always praying under protest. No one else could have made me do it. But I know, grandma, in spite of everything I did, you felt how fond I was of you and you saw the suffering written on my face when I saw you so sick. And I used to see how happy it made you when I came from school and ran to tell you my marks. Now that I'm unburdening myself here I remember all your tenderness, all your kindness. The thought of the day I compared you to Our Lady comes back to me.

On the anniversary of the Proclamation of the Republic two officials came to grandma's to ask my aunts for two little girls, to make up the twenty to represent the States. They needed two more for the States of Piauí and Rio Grande do Norte. The girls were to walk in line, dressed in white, with red liberty bonnets on their heads and wide ribbons across their chests with the names of the States on them in gold letters. I followed all my cousins' preparations with great interest because it seemed to me it was an extremely important occasion. But I got sadder and sadder all the time because they hadn't even considered me.

The day of the celebration came and my aunts put my cousins up on the table so they could work over them better, arrange the dresses and the bonnets and tie the ribbons. They were both very proud, with everyone admiring them, and they were gloating because I was jealous. Somebody said, "How pretty they look!" Somebody else said, "Aren't they sweet!" I looked and listened in silence until I felt a lump in my throat and I ran out and threw myself face down on the grass behind the church. I was crying and sobbing when I felt your cane tap my shoulder. I turned over, frightened, because I was so well-hidden and hadn't expected anyone there. It was you, grandma! You'd been watching me and reading my soul, and you understood what I felt and had followed there in my steps. You'd walked there with the greatest difficulty, holding onto your cane with one hand and the walls with the other. I remember until now the kind words you said to me that day: "Get up, silly! You came here to cry because you're jealous of those homely little girls, didn't you?" I didn't have time to answer, and besides, I already felt comforted, and you went on: "I don't know why a girl as intelligent as you are doesn't understand some things. Don't you see that this holiday is for idiots, and that a girl like you, pretty, intelligent, and of English descent, couldn't take part in it? It's silly to celebrate the Proclamation of the Republic. The Republic is something for common people. It doesn't concern nice people. They know your father's a monarchist, that he isn't one of the turncoats, and he wouldn't let his daughter go out in the streets to play the fool in an idiotic celebration like that. Let the rest of them do it. Don't be jealous, because you're better than any of them."

Oh grandma, you can't imagine what your words meant to me! You made me get up, took me around by the back door without anyone's seeing us to wash my face, and you made me laugh and waited until I looked cheerful again, so no one would notice I'd been crying.

That was the day, grandma, I remember I compared you to Our Lady and I thought to myself, "She's so good and so holy that she can even guess what I suffer, to comfort me." But now who will ever comfort me? I have my mother and father, my sister and brothers, but none of them can be to me what you were. Why? Because you were more intelligent? Or because you loved me even better than my own parents?

. . . Today, Sunday, it's raining in Boa Vista, and I am thinking notalgically of my First Communion. When all the little girls had studied the catechism a year, Father Neves told us that we were ready for our First Communion, which would take place in a month.

I was in raptures at this news and I told mama to begin to get everything ready immediately: the long white dress, the veil, the wreath and the decorated wax candle.

On the evening of the great day, Father Neves brought all the pupils together in the church, and he went behind the grating of the screen to hear our confessions. The little girls knelt outside, confessing and then going away. My turn came and I knelt down with my list of sins all memorized: Gluttony, Envy, Luxury (the desire for pretty dresses), stealing fruit from my grandmother, gossiping. I told everything and made my act of contrition, but I left the confessional with a small nail in my conscience.

There were lots of ex-slaves at grandma's who told nursery tales, tales of the spirits of the other world and the sins that had carried them off to purgatory and hell. If one stole an egg, for example, then the egg would turn into a hen, and one would have to spend as many years in purgatory as the hen had feathers. They also believed that it was an unpardonable sin to think that a priest was homely.

I listened to everything attentively and I couldn't have stolen an egg under any circumstances. But the sin of finding a priest homely haunted me all year long. Every time Father Neves came into church I thought to myself, "Am I really committing a sin? I do think he's so homely!" I kept trying to put this wicked thought out of my head but it kept coming back again, and even at the end of the catechism class it hadn't left me.

When I went to confess that day, I reasoned, "No, I haven't committed a sin because I've never told anyone I think Father Neves is homely. It's better not to think about it any more."

I left the confessional very penitent but not quite as peaceful and relieved as one should be. I made a retreat all that day with as much contrition as a seven-year-old girl is capable of.

On the next day, the great day, mama woke me up early and helped me get dressed, giving me some last bits of advice on how to make a good communion. When I got to church I found all my playmates already in their places, just waiting for me for the priest to begin the sermon.

To give this sermon, Father Neves had asked an Italian priest, rather fat and red, who knew how to shout and make a big impression on little girls. The priest began:

"My children, this day is the happiest and most important of your lives. You are going to receive the body, blood and soul of Jesus into your hearts. It is an amazing grace, my dears, that God grants you! But to receive it you must be prepared, and contrite, and you mustn't have concealed any sin whatsoever in the confessional. To hide a sin and then to receive communion is an abomination! I know of many horrible cases, but I am going to tell you just one as an example.

"Once a group of little girls were making their First Communion just the way you are making it today. They received the host and went solemnly back to their places, and at that very moment one of them fell down and died. The priest said to the little girl's mother, 'God has taken her to Glory!' And all the others were envious of their playmate who had died in the grace of God. And then, what do you suppose they saw? The devil dragging the body of the miserable little girl behind the altar. Do you know why? Because she had concealed a sin in the confessional."

When I heard this I amazed everyone by bursting out howling. Father Neves ran to find out what was wrong. I said, "I concealed a sin in the confessional." Father Neves tried to comfort me very gently, "Don't be so upset, daughter; come and tell the sin and God will forgive you and you can take communion." I told him, "I want to tell the sin to the other priest, not to you, Senhor." He took hold of my hands, still very gently, and said, "You can't do that, little one; you confessed to me so you have to tell me the sin. Don't be afraid; the priest is here to listen to everything. Come on. I'll look the other way; you can tell me and go away in just a minute."

He took me to a corner of the sacristy and was very nice and insisted that I confess. Sobbing and horrified at what I was going to say I hung my head and whispered, "I confess to having thought that a priest was very homely." Father Neves said, "That isn't a sin, my child. What's wrong with thinking that a priest is homely?" I took courage and said, "But the priest is you, Father!"

Father Neves let go of my hands and got up, exclaiming, "I really *am* homely! And what of it? I can't stand such silly little girls! Here I spend the whole year struggling to get them ready for communion, and at the end they come to me to confess that I'm homely. It's too much!"

1957

Stories by Clarice Lispector

The Smallest Woman in the World

In the depths of Equatorial Africa the French explorer Marcel Pretre, hunter and man of the world, came across a tribe of surprisingly small pygmies. Therefore he was even more surprised when he was informed that a still smaller people existed, beyond forests and distances. So he plunged further on.

In the Eastern Congo, near Lake Kivu, he really did discover the smallest pygmies in the world. And—like a box within a box within a box—obedient, perhaps, to the necessity nature sometimes feels of outdoing herself—among the smallest pygmies in the world there was the smallest of the smallest pygmies in the world.

Among mosquitoes and lukewarm trees, among leaves of the most rich and lazy green, Marcel Pretre found himself facing a woman seventeen and three-quarter inches high, full-grown, black, silent—"Black as a monkey," he informed the press—who lived in a treetop with her little spouse. In the tepid miasma of the jungle, that swells the fruits so early and gives them an almost intolerable sweetness, she was pregnant.

So there she stood, the smallest woman in the world. For an instant, in the buzzing heat, it seemed as if the Frenchman had unexpectedly reached his final destination. Probably only because he was not insane, his soul neither wavered nor broke its bounds. Feeling an immediate necessity for order and for giving names to what exists, he called her Little Flower. And in order to be able to classify her among the recognizable realities, he immediately began to collect facts about her.

Her race will soon be exterminated. Few examples are left of this species, which, if it were not for the sly dangers of Africa, might have multiplied. Besides disease, the deadly effluvium of the water, insufficient food, and ranging beasts, the great threat to the Likoualas are the savage Bahundes, a threat that surrounds them in the silent air, like the dawn of battle. The Bahundes hunt them with nets, like monkeys. And eat them. Like that: they catch them in nets and *eat* them. The tiny race, retreating, always retreating, has finished hiding away in the heart of Africa, where the lucky explorer discovered it. For strategic defense, they live in the highest trees. The women descend to grind and cook corn and to gather greens; the men, to hunt. When a child is born, it is left free almost immediately. It is true that, what with the beasts, the child frequently cannot enjoy this freedom for very long. But then it is true that it cannot be lamented that for such a short life there had been any long, hard work. And even the language that the child learns is short and simple, merely the essentials. The Likoualas use few names; they name things by gestures and animal noises. As for things of the spirit, they have a drum. While they dance to the sound of the drum, a little male stands guard against the Bahundes, who come from no one knows where.

That was the way, then, that the explorer discovered, standing at his very feet, the smallest existing human thing. His heart beat, because no emerald in the world is so rare. The teachings of the wise men of India are not so rare. The richest man in the world has never set eyes on such strange grace. Right there was a woman that the greed of the most exquisite dream could never have imagined. It was then that the explorer said timidly, and with a delicacy of feeling of which his wife would never have thought him capable: "You are Little Flower."

At that moment, Little Flower scratched herself where no one scratches. The explorer—as if he were receiving the highest prize for chastity to which an idealistic man dares aspire—the explorer, experienced as he was, looked the other way.

A photograph of Little Flower was published in the colored supplements of the Sunday papers, life-size. She was wrapped in a cloth, her belly already very big. The flat nose, the black face, the splay feet. She looked like a dog.

On that Sunday, in an apartment, a woman seeing the picture of Little Flower in the paper didn't want to look a second time because "It gives me the creeps."

In another apartment, a lady felt such perverse tenderness for the smallest of the African women that—an ounce of prevention being worth a pound of cure—Little Flower could never be left alone to the tenderness of that lady. Who knows to what murkiness of love tenderness can lead? The woman was upset all day, almost as if she were missing something. Besides, it was spring and there was a dangerous leniency in the air.

In another house, a little girl of five, seeing the picture and hearing the comments, was extremely surprised. In a houseful of adults, this little girl had been the smallest human being up until now. And, if this was the source of all caresses, it was also the source of the first fear of the tyranny of love. The existence of Little Flower made the little girl feel—with a deep uneasiness that only years and years later, and for very different reasons, would turn into thought—made her feel, in her first wisdom, that "sorrow is endless."

In another house, in the consecration of spring, a girl about to be married felt an ecstasy of piety: "Mama, look at her little picture, poor little thing! Just look how sad she is!"

"But," said the mother, hard and defeated and proud, "it's the sadness of an animal. It isn't human sadness."

"Oh! Mama!" said the girl, discouraged.

In another house, a clever little boy had a clever idea: "Mummy, if I could put this little woman from Africa in little Paul's bed when he's asleep? When he woke up wouldn't he be frightened? Wouldn't he howl? When he saw her sitting on his bed? And then we'd play with her! She would be our toy!"

His mother was setting her hair in front of the bathroom mirror at the moment, and she remembered what a cook had told her about life in an orphanage. The orphans had no dolls, and, with terrible maternity already throbbing in their hearts, the little girls had hidden the death of one of the children from the nun. They kept the body in a cupboard and when the nun went out they played with the dead child, giving her baths and things to eat, punishing her only to be able to kiss and console her. In the bathroom, the mother remembered this, and let fall her thoughtful hands, full of curlers. She considered the cruel necessity of loving. And she considered the malignity of our desire for happiness. She considered how ferociously we need to play. How many times we will kill for love. Then she looked at her clever child as if she were looking at a dangerous stranger. And she had a horror of her own soul that, more than her body, had engendered that being, adept at life and happiness. She looked at him attentively and with uncomfortable pride, that child who had already lost two front teeth, evolution evolving itself, teeth falling out to give place to those that could bite better. "I'm going to buy him a new suit," she decided, looking at him, absorbed. Obstinately, she adorned her gap-toothed son with fine clothes; obstinately, she wanted him very clean, as if his cleanliness could emphasize a soothing superficiality, obstinately perfecting the polite side of beauty. Obstinately drawing away from, and drawing him away from, something that ought to be "black as a monkey." Then, looking in the bathroom mirror, the mother gave a deliberately refined and social smile, placing a distance of insuperable millenniums between the abstract lines of her features and the crude face of Little Flower. But, with years of practice, she knew that this was going to be a Sunday on which she would have to hide from herself anxiety, dreams, and lost millenniums.

In another house, they gave themselves up to the enthralling task of measuring the seventeen and three-quarter inches of Little Flower against the wall. And, really, it was a delightful surprise: she was even smaller than the sharpest imagination could have pictured. In the heart of each member of the family was born, nostalgic, the desire to have that tiny and indomitable thing for itself, that thing spared having been eaten, that permanent source of charity. The avid family soul wanted to devote itself. To tell the truth, who hasn't wanted to own a human being just for himself? Which, it is true, wouldn't always be convenient; there are times at which one doesn't want to have feelings.

"I bet if she lived here it would end in a fight," said the father, sitting in the armchair and definitely turning the page of the newspaper. "In this house everything ends in a fight."

"Oh, you, José—always a pessimist," said the mother.

"But, mama, have you thought of the size her baby's going to be?" said the oldest little girl, aged thirteen, eagerly.

The father stirred uneasily behind his paper.

"It should be the smallest black baby in the world," the mother answered, melting with pleasure. "Imagine her serving our table, with her big little belly!"

"That's enough!" growled father.

"But you have to admit," said the mother, unexpectedly offended, "that it is something very rare. You're the insensitive one."

And the rare thing itself?

In the meanwhile, in Africa, the rare thing herself, in her heart—and who knows if the heart wasn't black, too, since once nature has erred she can no longer be trusted—the rare thing herself had something even rarer in her heart, like the secret of her own secret: a minimal child. Methodically, the explorer studied the little belly of the smallest mature human being. It was at this moment that the explorer, for the first time since he had known her, instead of feeling curiosity, or exaltation, or victory, or the scientific spirit, felt sick.

The smallest woman in the world was laughing.

She was laughing, warm, warm—Little Flower was enjoying life. The rare thing herself was experiencing the ineffable sensation of not having been eaten yet. Not having been eaten yet was something that at any other time would have given her the agile impulse to jump from branch to branch. But, in this moment of tranquility, amid the thick leaves of the Eastern Congo, she was not putting this impulse into action—it was entirely concentrated in the smallness of the rare thing itself. So she was laughing. It was a laugh such as only one who does not speak laughs. It was a laugh that the explorer, constrained, couldn't classify. And she kept on enjoying her own soft laugh, she who wasn't being devoured. Not to be devoured is the most perfect feeling. Not to be devoured is the secret goal of a whole life. While she was not being eaten, her bestial laughter was as delicate as joy is delicate. The explorer was baffled.

In the second place, if the rare thing herself was laughing, it was because, within her smallness, a great darkness had begun to move.

The rare thing herself felt in her breast a warmth that might be called love. She loved that sallow explorer. If she could have talked and had told him that she loved him, he would have been puffed up with vanity. Vanity that would have collapsed when she added that she also loved the explorer's ring very much, and the explorer's boots. And when that collapse had taken place, Little Flower would not have understood why. Because her love for the explorer—one might even say "profound love," since, having no other resources, she was reduced to profundity—her profound love for the explorer would not have been at all diminished by the fact that she also loved his boots. There is an old misunderstanding about the word love, and, if many children are born from this misunderstanding, many others have lost the unique chance of being born, only because of a susceptibility that demands that it be me! me! that is loved, and not my money. But in the humidity of the forest these cruel refinements do not exist, and love is not to be eaten, love is to find a boot pretty, love is to like the strange color of a man who isn't black, love is to laugh for love of a shiny ring. Little Flower blinked with love, and laughed warmly, small, gravid, warm.

The explorer tried to smile back, without knowing exactly to what abyss his smile responded, and then he was embarrassed as only a very big man can be embarrassed. He pretended to adjust his explorer's hat better; he colored, prudishly. He turned a lovely color, a greenish-pink, like a lime at sunrise. He was undoubtedly sour.

Perhaps adjusting the symbolic helmet helped the explorer to get control of himself, severely recapture the discipline of his work, and go on with his note-taking. He had learned how to understand some of the tribe's few articulate words, and to interpret their signs. By now, he could ask questions.

Little Flower answered "Yes." That it was very nice to have a tree of her own to live in. Because—she didn't say this but her eyes became so dark that they said it—because it is good to own, good to own, good to own. The explorer winked several times.

Marcel Pretre had some difficult moments with himself. But at least he kept busy taking notes. Those who didn't take notes had to manage as best they could.

"Well," suddenly declared one old lady, folding up the newspaper decisively, "well, as I always say: God knows what He's doing."

A Hen

She was a Sunday hen. She was still alive only because it was not yet 9.00 o'clock.

She seemed calm. Since Saturday she had cowered in a corner of the kitchen. She didn't look at anyone, no one looked at her. Even when they had selected her, fingering her intimately and indifferently, they couldn't have said whether she was fat or thin. No one would ever have guessed that she had a desire.

So it was a surprise when she opened her little wings, puffed out her breast, and, after two or three tries, reached the wall of the terrace. For an instant she vacillated—long enough for the cook to scream—and then she was on the neighbor's terrace, and from there, by means of another awkward flight, she reached a tile roof. There she remained like a misplaced weather vane, hesitating, first on one foot, then the other. The family was urgently called and, in consternation, saw their lunch standing beside a chimney. The father of the family, reminding himself of the double obligation of eating and of occasionally taking exercise, happily got into his bathing trunks and resolved to follow the itinerary of the hen. By cautious jumps he reached the roof, and the hen, trembling and hesitating, quickly picked another direction. The pursuit became more intense. From roof to roof, more than a block of the street was traversed. Unprepared for a more savage struggle for life, the hen had to decide for herself which routes to take, without any help from her race. In the young man, however, the sleeping hunter woke up. Lowly as was the prey, he gave a hunting cry.

Alone in the world, without father or mother, she ran, out of breath, concentrated, mute. Sometimes in her flight she would stand at bay on the edge of a roof, gasping; while the young man leaped over others with difficulty, she had a moment in which to collect herself. Then she looked so free.

Stupid, timid, and free. Not victorious, the way a rooster in flight would have looked. What was there in her entrails that made a being of her? The hen is a being. It's true, she couldn't be counted on for anything. She herself couldn't count on herself—the way a rooster believes in his comb. Her only advantage was that there are so many hens that if one died another would appear at the same moment, exactly like her, as if it were the same hen.

Finally, at one of the moments when she stopped to enjoy her escape, the young man caught her. Amid feathers and cries, she was taken prisoner. Then she was carried in triumph, by one wing, across the roofs and deposited on the kitchen floor with a certain violence. Still dazed, she shook herself a little, cackling hoarsely and uncertainly.

It was then that it happened. Completely overwhelmed, the hen laid an egg. Surprised, exhausted. Perhaps it was premature. But immediately afterward, as if she had been born for maternity, she looked like an old, habitual mother. She sat down on the egg and remained that way, breathing, buttoning and unbuttoning her eyes. Her heart, so small on a plate, made the feathers rise and fall, and filled that which would never be more than an egg with warmth. Only the little girl was near-by and witnessed everything, terrified. As soon as she could tear herself away, she got up off the floor and shrieked: "Mama! Mama! Don't kill the hen any more! She laid an egg! She likes us!"

Everyone ran to the kitchen again and, silent, stood in a circle around the new mother. Warming her child, she was neither gentle nor harsh, neither happy nor sad; she was nothing; she was a hen. Which suggests no special sentiment. The father, the mother, and the daughter looked at her for some time, without any thought whatever to speak of. No one had ever patted the head of a hen. Finally, with a certain brusqueness, the father decided: "If you have this hen killed, I'll never eat chicken again in my life!"

"Me too!" the little girl vowed ardently.

The mother shrugged, tired.

Unconscious of the life that had been granted her, the hen began to live with the family. The little girl, coming home from school, threw down her school-bag and ran to the kitchen without stopping. Once in a while the father would still remember: "And to think I made her run in that state!" The hen became the queen of the house. Everyone knew it except the hen. She lived between the kitchen and the kitchen terrace, making use of her two capacities: apathy and fear.

But when everyone in the house was quiet and seemed to have forgotten her, she plucked up a little of the courage left over from her great escape and perambulated the tile floor, her body moving behind her head, deliberate as in a field, while the little head betrayed her: moving, rapid and vibrant, with the ancient and by now mechanical terror of her species.

Occasionally, and always more rarely, the hen resembled the one that had once stood plain against the air on the edge of the roof, ready to make an announcement. At such moments she filled her lungs with the impure air of the kitchen and, if females had been able to sing, she would not have sung, but she would have been much more contented. Though not even at these moments did the expression of her empty head change. In flight, at rest, giving birth, or pecking corn—it was the head of a hen, the same that was designed at the beginning of the centuries.

Until one day they killed her and ate her and the years went by.

Marmosets

The first time we had a marmoset was just before New Year's. We were without water and without a maid, people were lining up to buy meat, the hot weather had suddenly begun—when, dumfounded, I saw the present enter the house, already eating a banana, examining everything with great rapidity, and with a long tail. It looked like a monkey not yet grown; its potentialities were tremendous. It climbed up the drying clothes to the clothesline, where it swore like a sailor, and the banana-peelings fell where they would. I was exhausted already. Every time I forgot and absentmindedly went out on the back terrace, I gave a start: there was that happy man. My younger son knew, before I did, that I would get rid of this gorilla: "If I promise that sometime the monkey will get sick and die, will you let him stay? Or if you knew that sometime he'd fall out the window, somehow, and die down there?" My feelings would glance aside. The filthiness and blithe unconsciousness of the little monkey made me responsible for his fate, since he himself would not take any blame. A friend understood how bitterly I had resigned myself, what dark deeds were being nourished beneath my dreaminess, and rudely saved me: a delighted gang of little boys appeared from the hill and carried off the laughing man. The new year was devitalized but at least monkey-less.

A year later, at a time of happiness, suddenly there in Copacabana I saw the small crowd. I thought of my children, the joys they gave me, free, unconnected with the worries they also gave me, free, and I thought of a chain of joy: "Will the person receiving this pass it along to someone else," one to another, like a spark along a train of powder. Then and there I bought the one who would be called Lisette.

She could almost fit in one hand. She was wearing a skirt, and earrings, necklace, and bracelet of glass beads. The air of an immigrant just disembarking in her native costume. Like an immigrant's, too, her round eyes.

This one was a woman in miniature. She lived with us three days. She had such delicate bones. She was of such a sweetness. More than her eyes, her look was rounded. With every movement, the earrings shook; the skirt was always neat, the red necklace glinted. She slept a lot, but, as to eating, she was discreet and languid. Her rare caress was only a light bite that left no mark.

On the third day we were out on the back terrace admiring Lisette and the way she was ours. "A little too gentle," I thought, missing the gorilla. And suddenly my heart said harshly: "But this isn't sweetness. This is death." The dryness of the message left me calm. I said to the children: "Lisette is dying." Looking at her, I realized the stage of love we had already reached.

I rolled her up in a napkin and went with the children to the nearest first-aid station, where the doctor couldn't attend to her because he was performing an emergency operation on a dog. Another taxi—"Lisette thinks she's out for a drive, mama"—another hospital. There they gave her oxygen.

And with the breath of life, a Lisette we hadn't known was revealed. The eyes less round, more secretive, more laughing, and in the prognathous and ordinary face a certain ironic haughtiness. A little more oxygen and she wanted to speak so badly she couldn't bear being a monkey; she was, and she would have had much to tell. More oxygen, and then an injection of salt solution; she reacted to the prick with an angry slap, her bracelet glittering. The male nurse smiled: "Lisette! Gently, my dear!"

The diagnosis: she wouldn't live unless there was oxygen at hand, and even then it was unlikely. "Don't buy monkeys in the street," he scolded me; "sometimes they're already sick." No, one must buy dependable monkeys, and know where they came from, to ensure at least five years of love, and know what they had or hadn't done, like getting married. I discussed it with the children a minute. Then I said to the nurse: "You seem to like Lisette very much. So if you let her stay a few days, near the oxygen, you can have her." He was thinking. "Lisette is pretty!" I implored.

"She's beautiful!" he agreed, thoughtfully. Then he sighed and said, "If I cure Lisette, she's yours." We went away with our empty napkin.

The next day they telephoned, and I informed the children that Lisette had died. The younger one asked me, "Do you think she died wearing her earrings?" I said yes. A week later the older one told me, "You look so much like Lisette!"

I replied, "I like you, too."

CORRESPONDENCE WITH ANNE STEVENSON, 1963–1965

Caixa Postal 279, Petrópolis
Estado do Rio de Janeiro, Brasil
January 22nd, 1963

Dear Mrs. Stevenson:

I have just received a letter from Marianne Moore in which she says that you would like some information about me for the "Twayne Publishers Author Series . . ." I can't seem to remember what this is, although I probably should know—will you tell me something about it? She quotes you to the effect that I "despise professionalized criticism". But I don't think I do, and I wonder where that idea came from? (Unless "professionalized" means something very bad!) Anyway—if I can be of any help, I'll be glad to. Sometimes letters take a long time; sometimes only four or five days—

Sincerely yours,

Elizabeth Bishop

Caixa Postal 279, Petrópolis
Estado do Rio de Janeiro, Brasil
March 18th, 1963

Dear Mrs. Elvin:

After reassuring you about the comparative speed of the mails here, of course I happenned to be away "in the interior" as they say—on the coast, actually—for a long stay over Carnival, where I can get no mail. I shall get off just a note to you today to tell you I did get your letter, and a second installment will be along this week.

Thank you for sending me the Twayne's U S Author Series rules & regulations. I am enlightened, but not very much! I wonder who is the editor of the contemporary poets, what other poets are being written, up, etc? Do you think that Mrs. Bowman would be good enough to send me one or two of the books already published? Please don't think I am interfering or am going to be difficult—but I am naturally curious.

I'd like to read your analyses of my poems very much. Are you intending to publish something in a magazine, perhaps, before the book appears?

In any case—I have another book ready—20–25 poems, some of which you may have seen in magazines—and I think you should have a copy of this as soon as possible. The title is QUESTIONS OF TRAVEL, from one of the poems, and if all goes well Farrar, Straus & Cudahy shd. be publishing it this year. I'll write and have them send you a copy—unless I can find a complete MMS here this week. I think if you write to Farrar, Straus, & Cudahy they will surely send you a free copy of THE DIARY OF HELENA MORLEY (*Minha Vida de Menina*), the Brazilian book I translated a few years ago. (I'll write my agent* about the poems and mention this, too) The English title was against my wishes—very poor, I think; the best review I saw was Pritchett's in The New Statesman & Nation. My introduction might be of some interest to you, as a critic—the diary perhaps only as the mother of a daughter!

The biographical note in Who's Who is correct—or was, the last time I saw it. I never lived in Worcester, however—I left before I was a year old and spent only a few months there when I was 6–7, with my father's parents. The rest of my childhood I spent with my mother's parents in Nova Scotia—mostly long summers, although I started school there—and with a devoted aunt, in or near Boston, until I went away to school at 16. I also went to summer camp on Cape Cod for 6 summers. I've never lived in Newfoundland—I took a walking trip there one summer when I was at Vassar. Since Vassar I've lived in New York, Paris, Key West, Mexico, etc.—mostly New York, and Key West until about 1948.—Then since late 1951 Brazil—with several trips back, of course, one of 8 months or so. I was very much amused by the clipping from the Worcester paper . . . (I've also read 2 or 3 times that I was born in Maine, or lived there—I can't imagine where that came from. I've stayed various times on Deer Isle (or is it Island?) visited Robert Lowell in Castine, etc.—that's all.) I have two published autobiographical stories, GWENDOLYN, & IN THE VILLAGE. This last is in the recent New Yorker anthology—and sticks to the facts—compresses the time a bit. Robert Lowell compressed it even more, recently, into a very short poem that was in Kenyon Review, called "The Scream". I could give you a great deal more information if you want it!—However, for your purposes it may not be necessary. I am 3/4ths Canadian, and one 4th New Englander—I had ancestors on both sides in the Revolutionary war. My maternal grandparents were, some of them, Tories, who left upper N. Y. State and were given land grants in Nova Scotia by George III. One of my great grandfathers was

*Brandt & Brandt—the MMS is with them

an owner-captain of a ship—bark, I think—and was lost at sea off Sable Island in a famous storm when 40 or so ships went down. (I have also been to Sable Island, via the Canadian Lighthouse Service) That line of my family seems to have been fond of wandering like myself—two, perhaps three, of the sea-captain's sons, my great uncles, were Baptist missionaries in India.

You are right about my admiring Klee very much—but as it happens, THE MONUMENT was written more under the influence of a set of frottages by Max Ernst I used to own, called Histoire Naturel. I am passionately (I think I might say) fond of painting; in fact I'd much rather talk about painting than poetry, as a rule. I am equally fond of music—although I am rather behind with that, living in Brazil. Next time round I'd like to be a painter—or a composer—or a doctor—I seriously considered studying medicine for several years and still wish I had. I am also very much interested in architecture and helped translate a huge tome on contemporary Brazilian architecture a few years ago.

I want to get this in the mail so I must get to Petropolis quickly—I live about 8 miles outside the town, although at present I divide my time about equally between here and Rio—50 miles away. While I am here this week I'll write you another note—I'll answer your questions about whens and wheres—although I don't believe there are any rules about the *place*—poems—after, during, or before—And I'll certainly try to get off the other book to you in MMS—or see that you get a copy—

I do want to see your analyses—but I believe that everyone has the right to interpret exactly as they see fit, of course, so as I said, please do not think I shall be "interfering." My only request of that sort may be quite unecessary—It is just that I am rather weary of always being compared to, or coupled with, Marianne—and I think she is utterly weary of it, too! We have been very good friends for thirty years now—but except for 1 or 2 early poems of mine and perhaps some early preferences in subject matter, neither she nor I can see why reviewers always drag her in with me. For one thing—I've always been an umpty-umpty poet with a traditional "ear." Perhaps it is just another proof that ~~critics and~~ reviewers really very rarely pay much attention to what they're reading *& just repeat each other*—

I hope your little girl is better and I am extremely sorry to hear of the death of your mother. I believe you teach, don't you? I wonder what and where? I'll write again in a few days—

Sincerely yours,

Elizabeth Bishop

Please forgive this bad typing—the machine I keep here is very different from that in Rio & it takes me a few days to get used to it—

Caixa Postal 279, Petrópolis
Estado do Rio de Janeiro, Brasil
March 20th (?), 1963

Dear Mrs. Elvin:

I mailed a very hurried letter to you two days ago and now I'll try to answer your other questions. I am also writing the agent today—Carl Brandt, 101 Park Avenue, to see if he can have a copy of the MMS of the new book, almost complete, sent to you—and I'll mention that DIARY of Helena Morley as well.

There isn't any particular logic to when and where the poems were written. The first 5 in the book I gather you have were written in N.Y, in 1934–5. Large Bad Picture was written ~~a good many years~~ later, in Key West. (Memory poems are apt to pop up from time to time no matter where one happens to be, I find. —I mean childhood-memory poems.) Man-Moth is another very early one, and Country to the City, the Miracle sestina, Love Lies Sleeping, later N.Y. ones, after my first winter in Paris, I think. The Weed I wrote on Cape Cod (It seems so obviously derived, to me, that I'm sure you've spotted it by now!) Paris 7 Am I did write in Paris, Quai D'Orleans, too but the second stay there—in between comes Florida—and Cirque d'Hiver was written during a later stay on Cape Cod. You ask about the title—well, the Cirque d'Hiver did ~~use~~ have a team of little trained ponies wearing ostrich plumes, etc.—but I think the title referred to the mood more than anything else. (Again, I think you'll probably spot the derivation of this poem, although I believe it was unconscious.) All the others in the first book are from Key West—except Anaphora—the first stanza came to me in Puebla when the cathedral bells clanged just a few yards away from my pillow, or so it seemed—and a year or two later I finished it in Key West. So you see there is no system to them at all.

A Cold Spring is not in chronological order. There is some more Key West in it, two trips to Nova Scotia, a little New York, and at the end, the first year in Brazil. The poem about Miss Moore was written instead of an "essay" for a ~~commemorative~~ birthday number of Quarterly Review.

The book you will receive has necessarily a lot of Brazil in it—But the one Amazon poem—(unless I finish another one in time to get in it, too) was written <u>before</u> I made a trip on the Amazon. There are also several memory poems in it.

Varick Street—I had a garret on King Street in NY for a good many years—the buildings are now torn down—between 6th Avenue and Varick Street, & in warm weather it was very noisy. I use dream-material whenever I am lucky enough to have any and this particular poem is almost all dream—just rearranging a bit—so was Rain Towards Morning—and most of the 1st stanza of Anaphora—The last four lines of the 1st stanza of At the Fishhouses—

"~~He has scraped the scales~~"* etc where also a donnee, as James would say, in a dream. But all this is nothing at all out of the ordinary, I'm sure.

I studied music—piano and counterpoint—for some years and have a clavichord here, although I'm afraid I don't play it much. It is hard to hear good music in Brazil,† except recordings—and *they* are hard to get in—but I do listen to the hi fi a lot. (Roosters, I remember, I got rather stuck with, and a recording of Kirkpatrick—I took a few lessons with him long ago—of Scarlatti got me going again in a particular rhythm.) I do like Webern—from the album I have—perhaps because he is small-scale and reminds me of Klee‡ (I believe they were friends). I don't care much for grand, all-out efforts—but on the other hand, I sometimes *do* . . . I admire Robert Lowell's poetry very much and much of Lord Weary's Castle couldn't be more all-out . . .

He and I have been very good friends since 1946, I think it was—and Jarrell is another friend, although of course I rarely see him. The Lowells were here visiting me last summer. I suppose that he & I both like the SEA a lot, which sounds rather silly—but we always seem to be going swimming together when we meet! But I have lived so much out of New York that I have never had much "literary" life, just occasional stretches of it. Edmund Wilson helped me once a great deal by publishing Roosters in a Literary Supplement to The Nation he was getting out. Jarrell has also always been very kind, critically—in general I feel I have been extremely lucky that way—

Calder is a friend *(not close)* who gets to Brazil every once in a while, and Loren MacIver, the American painter is an old friend, too—from about 1938—*Fizdole & Gold, the pianists, are old friends*—Calder is someone else who although so unlike Dewey impresses one by the old-fashioned uncompromising New England *honesty* of his character—and sweetness, like Dewey.

Of course I read all Miss Moore's generation from about 1928 on and undoubtedly learned enormously from them. I think of Marianne, Cummings (we shared the same maid in N.Y. for several years), Dr. Williams, Crane, Frost, as Heroes . . . I wrote a poem about Pound (it is in the last Partisan Review anthology) that expresses my feelings about him fairly well, I think. Strange to say, it was put to music by Ned Rorem and, I hear, was sung a few days ago in Carnegie Hall by Jennie Tourel. (She'd already sung it here & there before—but really, I think she must be about 80 now . . . ?) I hope I get the recording safely.

I have always wanted—like many other poets, I think—to write some really "popular" songs, not "art" songs. One thing I like very much in Brazil

---

* *"There are sequins"*
† *I find it hard—maybe there is some I don't know of*
‡ *I'm also extremely fond of Schwitters—have one here that has to be watched for termites and mildew constantly*

is the popular music—the yearly sambas are, or were (too much U S influence now, I'm afraid), often superb spontaneous folk-music, and I want very
much to write a piece about them—the collecting is very difficult here, however. There is also a living tradition, in the interior, of the ballads—news
events, old tales, etc.—not such good poetry as the sambas but rather wonderful all the same— Besides the DIARY I translated, and work on the book
about contemporary architecture, I have done, recently, some translations
of Brazilian poetry. (I'll let you know when they're published—some are to
be in POETRY, I think.) But I really don't care much for doing it, or believe
in it, and my translations are rather literal—unlike Lowell's—so I only do
poems that seem to go into English without much loss—very limiting,
naturally.

Another friend who influenced me—<u>not</u> with his books but with his
character—was John Dewey, whom I knew well and was very fond of. He
and Marianne are the most truly *naturally* "democratic" people I've known,
I think.—He had almost the best manners I have ever encountered, always
had *time*, took an interest in everything,—no detail, no weed or stone or
cat or old woman was unimportant to him.

Now if you have any more questions please let me know. In about 3 weeks
I am going on a trip, "to the interior", really, this time, and will be out of
touch with mail for two or three weeks, probably. Perhaps I should add one
thought—perhaps it is just because I went to Europe earlier than most of
my "contemporary" poets—and I am a few years older than some of them—
but it is odd how I often feel myself to be a late-late Post World War I
generation-member, rather than a member of the Post World War II generation. Perhaps the Key West years also had something to do with it.—
(Until her death Pauline Hemingway was one of my best friends there,
etc.) But I also feel that Cal (Lowell) and I in our very different ways are
both descendents from the Transcendentalists—but you may not agree.

Again please excuse my bad typing—I'm not very good at best, but this
keyboard with all its Çç and a §§ out of place doesn't help—

I hope your little girl's rash is all cured by now—

Sincerely yours,
    Elizabeth Bishop

                                            44 Porter Street
                                            Watertown, Mass.
                                            March 28, 1963

Dear Miss Bishop,
    I am delighted with both your letters—really, I can't tell you *how* de-

lighted. I was in real trepidation after I sent off my letter to you in, was it February? Thought I had asked silly questions, or questions which you couldn't or wouldn't answer. I am amused that you call me a "critic" (one up from a reviewer?) for I am a raw amateur, preferring teaching or mothering or writing poems myself to this awful task of trying to say badly what someone else has said well. However I was pleased, when we arrived back from an early spring visit to Vermont last week, to find the streets full of children, clothes hanging out on the lines (Watertown being Watertown "awful but cheerful") spring arrived and your letter in our mailbox. I'll try to answer it point by point, as you did mine, and then go on to your second letter which arrived today.

I will write Miss Bowman today and ask her to send you (and me) some of the books which have been written already. I know a kind and well-meaning professor in Ann Arbor (I don't mean those adjectives to sound derogatory) who has written a book on Wilbur and is working on one on Lowell. The Wilbur book is finished, I think. Otherwise, I don't know who Miss Bowman has found to embellish her list of famous authors writing famouser ones. Don Hall says she is a "nut". I suppose that means she is somewhat scatterbrained and doesn't herself know what she wants. I have not heard from her since I left Ann Arbor (I did a MA degree there last year) so this is another reason for me to write to her.

Although I have no plans to publish something in a magazine, I do want to talk over my impression of your poems with Robert Lowell. He is lecturing at Harvard this semester; I went with some friends of mine to a poetry workshop he conducts at the Loeb theatre a week ago and arranged to show him what I had written. Then I came home and decided that everything had to be *re*-written, and I haven't yet had the courage to go see him. I am such a ponderous worker, you will have to forgive me. But I would rather wait years than produce something half-baked. I plan to finish a twelve to fifteen page plan of action, so to speak, which I will send to you and to him.

Yes, I should very much like to have your new book, and I am exceedingly grateful to you for having written to your agent. I shall write to him too so that he will know that I am real. I am of course most anxious to read it, and the *Diary of Helena Morley*. I'll look up Pritchett's review and also your two published stories when I next get to Widner. (I must confess that library stacks rather terrify me—I put off going to them in the same way I put off going to the supermarket) I am grateful, too, for the information you give me about your childhood and background. Can you perhaps tell me a little about your parents. Did you know them at all? What sort of people where they? was your father a businessman of some sort? Don't answer if you don't want to, naturally. I like your seafaring ancestors.

I am glad to know that you are fond (passionately) of painting. And of music and architecture. I'd suspected this, and its good to have your confirmation. One of the points I am making about your poetry is that is is visual but not what I call Impersonal. That is, your sense of personality of places and people, is suggested in visual terms. There is an interaction between the animate and inanimate world which suggest that you distinguish between them in order to show how they are alike. Everything you describe seems, too, as Philip Booth put it in one review, "to build toward a metaphorical whole." But your metaphors, while exact as paintings on one hand, are open, really, on the other. That is what I like best about poems like The Imaginary Iceberg, The Bight, The Fish, even Cirque d'Hiver. It seems to me that, while your subjects are not what you call "all out" ones, they echo with a sort of alloutness which makes them, unu[su]ally, big poems and not trivial ones. If a poet is supposed to comment upon his age (is that Spender?) you do, surely, if obliquely, even in so light a poem as The Gentlemen of Shalott (I taught that to my senior high school class this fall and they loved it—we were "studying" Tennyson). As certainly it is not imposing high sounding interpretations on your Cirque d'Hiver, Over 20000 etc (a reference to concordance of the Bible?) and Man-Moth to suggest [that] they have something "strongly worded" to say about contemporary life.

Well, this is very difficult. I think I had better send you a more organized essay next week sometime. I hope to catch you before you depart for the interior. One thing more about the poems, though. I agree that you and Marianne Moore should not be "dragged in" with each other; you write very differently, I think. If I mention Marianne Moore it will be as a friend of yours, not as an "influence." That odious word!

Your second letter is as full of wonderful and necessary information as your first. I know that *where* you wrote poems is not all that relevant to *how* they arrived, yet what you say is interesting; I wonder if people don't like to be told that sort of thing. Thanks also for the dream background of Varick Street, Rain Towards Morning, the last stanza of Anaphora (this last puzzles me). Of what significance [is] the title—it means a repetitive phrase at the beginning or end of successive verse in my dictionary, but does your poem repeat any phrases? Oh yes, and I wanted to ask you about your use of "syllabics." The Roosters *looks* as if it were written by counting syllables, but I don't think it is. The rhythm seems to me more subtle . . . as you suggest, heard, not counted.

I am interested to hear that you were a friend of John Dewey. My father is a philosopher—C.L. Stevenson, he wrote a book on Ethics called Ethics and Language and is to give the Alfred North Whitehead lectures here in May—who has the same quality of humility and honesty . . . no Transcendentalist, however. You ask about me. Yes, I am doing some part time teaching at the Cambridge School this year, but I am not going to continue after the summer. Mark (Elvin) is my second husband; (Caroline is my daughter by a first disastrous marriage) we were married only last November, having known each other only a month or so. He is an Englishman, historian, sinologist, linguist, brilliant and sensitive but not very well. His eye for painting and for contemporary music (he also is fond of Webern) is much better than mine, and he tells wonderful stories from Chinese, Japanese, Indian, Summerian mythology to Caroline. She adores him. I studied the cello when I was at college as an undergraduate at Michigan and I still play in string quartets when I have time. Both my sisters are violinists and my father is a fine pianist. Caroline is affectionate, beautiful, passionate and vain. I have some fears regarding her future, but many of these are motherly imaginations I think. That will give you some idea of who I am. I suppose I really think of myself as a poet. I send you these because they seem to me to "follow" you to a certain extent. I read your poems for the first time only last winter. Thank you so much again, for your patience and help.

> Caixa Postal 279, Petrópolis
> Estado do Rio de Janeiro, Brasil
> August 24th, 1963
> (in Rio)

Dear Mrs. Elvin:

Thank you for your note of August 14th—I'm in Rio at present it just reached me here yesterday. I'm sorry your first letter got lost—I believe I did warn you! I'm glad you got the DIARY and I have also written Brandt & Brandt to send you copies of the poems they have on hand—I am not sure how many, but they're most of the next book. (If one called EXCHANGING HATS appears, please omit.) Since the last book is 8(?) years old, I think you should see some later poems.

You have been having a wonderful summer, I see, and you've been to all the places in the U S A I've never been to (except New Orleans; I have been there). And camping—heavens!

I wonder how Phyllis Armstrong is—and she's still at the Library, I gather. I was fond of her, and she's been a most admirable secretary to all the poets who ever worked there. But I think you should realize that we were never "close" at all; that she knew me very slightly and during probably the lowest nine or ten moths of my life, long ago in 1949–50. I did not enjoy Washington, nor the Library,—and I am afraid Phyllis may have given you a false impression of me as a figure of gloom and reclusion. If you have the opportunity, it would be much better to talk to some of my friends and colleagues—Randall Jarrell, Robert Lowell, say—or May Swenson, Howard Moss, or the painter, Loren MacIver. These are all old friends and would have more accurate ideas of me—

Here is a snapshot of Robert Lowell and me taken when he visited me here last year—

I do not mind criticism of my *work*. ~~But~~ That stay in Washington still remains a nightmare to me and my life there mercifully totally unlike most of the rest of it!

I am looking forward to seeing your chapters in September.

Sincerely yours,

Elizabeth Bishop

Caixa Postal 279, Petrópolis
Estado do Rio de Janeiro, Brasil
October 2nd, 1963

Dear Miss Elvin:

Thank you for your letters. I am actually staying in the country this week so I received them first-hand and quickly. I like what you say in the September 24th one, 2nd paragraph, about the poems. But oh dear—"the moon finds everything amusing"—how on earth did that get in there? That's a mistake—it's from something I never finished, scarcely wrote, I think. Will you please throw it out, and also one called "Exchanging Hats" if it has turned up again? I'm not sure what you did get. I have about eighteen poems towards a book, but I am not satisfied with them and hope to add a few more.

Since I work so slowly myself, how could I possibly object to anyone's working slowly? Please don't worry about it.

About Phyllis Armstrong—yes, I was a bit nervous. As I said, I liked her and I think she liked me. But at that time—1949–50—I felt that she understood very little about poetry, couldn't tell good from bad, didn't seem to get "the principle of thing" at all—and misunderstood, or misinterpreted, her varying poets as well, probably. She undoubtedly has learned, or had to learn, a lot since then, poor girl! And it was a bad year for me.

Now letter 2—the "Chronology"—I'll just go straight through it making a few corrections and answering your questions as they come along.

My father was a contractor, oldest son of J. W. Bishop (who came from Prince Edward Island, so I'm ¾ths Canadian). 50 years and more ago the Bishop firm was very well known—they built public buildings, college buildings, theatres, etc., not houses. (Many in Boston, including the Public Library, the Museum of Fine Arts, etc.) My father died when I was 8 months old.

I lived some with my maternal grandparents in a *very* small village called Great Village, in Nova Scotia, and started school, just "Primer Class", there. I lived one winter with my paternal grandparents in Worcester. Then I lived with an aunt, married but childless, in and around Boston for several years, until I went away to school. I used to go back to Great Village summers and other times, and also went to a summer camp at Wellfleet (no longer in existence) for six summers where I became passionately fond of sailing. I had very bad health as a child and my schooling was irregular until I got to Walnut Hill—that's why I was a year or two older than average in getting through college.

My mother's maiden name was BULMER (not Blumer, as you have it).

Yes, I began college thinking I'd "major" in music, then switched to literature. (Now I wish I'd "majored" in Greek & Latin.) I studied the clavichord briefly at the Schola Cantorum in Paris, and more briefly with Ralph Kirkpatrick. *I have a Dolmetsch clavichord here—*

I didn't go to Key West until 1937 or '38—just for a fishing trip. The next year I went back and lived there off and on for about nine years. The last year I kept a small garret—a real one—in Greenwich Village, too. I went to Yaddo once briefly in a summer (1947?) and later for longer—1950.

I don't remember how I used the Guggenheim now! Living expenses, probably—

I wish we could forget about the Brazil Book! It is so badly written and scarcely a sentence is as I originally had it; the first 3 chapters are closest to the original. But you left out the "Diary of Helena Morley", and I am not ashamed of that.

"In the Village" is accurate—just compressed a bit. *"Gwendolyn" is, too.*

By all means say I'm a friend of Marianne's! I met her in 1934 through the college Librarian, an old friend of hers, and it was one of the great pieces of good fortune in my life. Also mention Cal (Robert Lowell, that is) and Jarrell (although I haven't seen him for several years) (if you want to). Cal is one of my closest friends and I have the greatest admiration for his work.

I feel that the biographical facts aren't very important or interesting. And I have moved so much, mostly coastwise, that I can't keep the dates straight myself.

In the Pound poem, "Visits to St. Elizabeth's", the chracters are based on the other inmates of St. E's, the huge government insane asylum in Washington. During the day, Pound was in an open ward, and so one's visits to him were often interrupted. One boy used to show us his watch, another patted the floor, etc.—but naturally it's a mixture of fact and fancy. The poem appeared in Partisan Review, not Kenyon as you have it. That's not very important—but I have published quite a bit in Partisan, from away back, and the editors have always been friends, gave me another award, etc.—

You ask the name of the friend I took the Newfoundland walking trip with—we were not "literary" friends and I'm afraid we lost track of each other years ago, so I don't think it matters.

I began publishing either junior or senior year at college. First, I think, were a story and a poem, maybe two, in a magazine called THE MAGAZINE edited for a few years by Ivor Winters. Before that I *had* received honorable mention (for the same contributions, I think) in a contest for college writing held by HOUND & HORN. I worked on the college newspaper off and on, and I was editor of my class year-book (but that had *nothing* to do with writing). Mary McCarthy, Eleanor Clarke, Eleanor's sister Eunice, and I, and two or three others, started an anonymous and what we thought "advanced" literary magazine. It succeeded so well that we were asked to join our original enemy, the official college literary magazine. (But I was NOT a member of Mary McC's GROUP—the one her recent novel's about. She was a year ahead of me.) The story Robert Lowell referred to, I think (since he likes it) must be one called IN PRISON. It's in the first Partisan Review Anthology—but it was published after college. The first poem of mine they published, I think, was "Love Lies Sleeping." At least I remember getting a letter from Mary McC when I was in Paris, saying that PR was starting up again and would I send them a poem, and I think that's the one I sent—

During the war I worked briefly for the Navy, in the optical shop in the Key West Submarine Base—on binoculars. I was allergic to the acids used to clean the prisms so I had to stop, but I liked the work—and the "shop."

While in Mexico I knew Pablo Neruda and I now realize he had more influence on me than I knew at the time. I studied Spanish with a refugee, a friend of his, we read a great deal of poetry—Lorca, Neruda, and early Spanish poets, etc.

I think that answers both your letters. I am not worried about time, so please don't you be. I think you are probably right about my anthropomorphism—although people speak, or used to, against it, it seems to be a fairly constant ingredient in all kinds of poetry through the ages, in varying amounts—Yes, I'd like to see the Twayne Aiken very much—hope it arrives safely. I know what you mean about "mechanical" troubles—we have them here, & also light rationing, because of the drought—which means lighting candles or oil lamps for a while every evening. In the country it seem fairly natural, but in apartments, shops, restaurants, etc. in Rio, it is very strange—

Sincerely yours,
Elizabeth Bishop

P.S. I read this over and see that I have made my hiking-companion sound mysterious without meaning to. Her maiden name was Evelyn Huntington and she was a year or two ahead of me. I am sorry I have lost track of her and hope to see her again sometime because she was a very entertaining girl—and we had a very good time. She was a Public Health worker—If you want *names*, just ask—but I gather the biographical sketch is sketchy.— Others who were in on our anonymous college magazine were Frani Blough Muser (later an editor of *Modern Music* for many years)—and Margaret Miller, who was with the Museum of Modern Art in New York for 20 years, I think—We were all interested in "modern" art, music, and writing— sophomores and juniors at the time, I think.

I believe I mentioned that I think John Dewey also influenced me— NOT his writings, which I have scarcely read, but his personality. The *poem* "A Cold Spring" is dedicated to his youngest daughter, an old friend, although quite a bit older than I am. The *book* "A Cold Spring" is dedicated to Dr. Baumann, my doctor in New York for many years—also now the Lowells' doctor and doctor to many of my friends—a general practitioner.

44 Porter Street
Watertown, Mass.
October 28, 1963

Dear Miss Bishop,

I received your letter of October 2nd quite some time ago. I probably should have answered it right away to reassure you about the mails, but I wanted to send you something more than a reassurance. You are very generous about my ponderous progress, but I am less so and keep wishing I could work more swiftly. However, I think I have an outline at last that will work. Next week or at worst, the week after, I'll send you twenty or thirty pages of a first draft—really very rough, I'm afraid, but including some comments on THE FISH, THE MAP, THE IMAGINARY ICEBERG, CHEMIN DE FER, THE COLDER THE AIR, LOVE LIES SLEEPING, CAPE BRETON, AT THE FISHHOUSES, ROOSTERS OVER 2000 ILLUSTRATIONS ETC. and a number of other poems. This looks like a grab-bag, I'm sure, but I am at last satisfied that I have a skeleton of a book. I am most grateful for your corrections and amendments. These I will write up in as finished a form as I now can and send along—so as to be sure to get nothing terribly wrong. You are quite right—I must have omitted *Helena Morley* in the sketch I sent you. An oversight, I admire it very much, especially because you seem to have *translated* it, not reinterpreted it. I am very dubious about most translations, although I don't mind out and out imitations like Robert Lowell's. There seems to be no pretense of accuracy there. On the other hand, Ben Belitt's translations of Neruda that I have been reading this week seem to me unreliable. Germanic and squashed, entirely out of keeping with the Spanish. Unfortunately, my Spanish is such that I need a pony if I am to read with any speed at all. I am glad you told me that you liked him. (Neruda, not Belitt) Although I never feel the violence in your poems that I do in his, nor the sensuality, there is a real affinity. Especially in the sea poems and in the ones about animals.

I sent off the Aiken volume, glowing like a stop light, last week. I don't think it will tell you much about what I am doing, however. I am not an academic, neither do I think there is much point in encouraging the current mystique of author-worship by writing a lot about your life. One of my troubles in getting started with this book has been to decide what, exactly, is important in your poetry. The outline which follows may give you an idea of my conclusions. Perhaps you won't agree, but I think you may at least be interested. Of course, I'll be glad to revise and rethink. At any rate, I have taken a number of excursions—into Transcendentalism, into Imagism, into contemporary German Art—or contemporary in the 1930's and 40's—all with great benefit to *me*, returning from circuitous voyages much enriched. My husband, who is a sinologist but who also has an incredible knowledge of philosophy and art, suggested that Wittgenstein as well as Klee and Ernst, was concerned at one point in his career, with the nature of seeing. In his notebooks he writes, "All that we see could also be otherwise; all that we can describe at all could also be otherwise." This seems to descend from Hegel—a fact that has escaped most positivist philosophers today—whose distinction between Actuality and Reality is like that of the Transcendentalists and indeed of many mystics. This kind of insight may lie behind "surrealistic["] poems like the MONUMENT, even more, behind the kind of inversion of realities implied in THE MAP and in the last two or three stanzas of LOVE LIES SLEEPING. Perhaps this is of more interest to me than any one else, however. My father—who studied with Dewey once—is fairly well known as a follower of Wittgenstein, and is fairly hated by the theoretical poets who misinterpret what he is doing. So you see how untranscendental my own background has been.

But let me sketch my outline for you. I won't fill in with details just now, but leave them for the next installment.

Chapter I. THE TRAVELLER A simple, rather austere account of life and travels, friends, too, like Marianne Moore and Robert Lowell who have affected your writing. Since so many poems are concerned with travel and the coast, I'll illustrate from them from time to time. Also, mention your two childhood stories. Other sources of poetry, dreams, pictures, and a feeling for natural, unsophisticated people (*Jeronimo's House, Cootchie,* even *Helena Morley*) will work into the introductory chapter too, so that a reader who doesn't know you at all will get a notion of what to expect, at least.

Chapter II. THE ARTIST   I'm not altogether sure about the title of this one. I think you're an "artist" more than you are a "writer"—that is, you are preoccupied with form. What you have to say is very much the way you say it, in the stories as well as the poems. In this you are like Webern who defined life, I think, as a search for form "To life, that is to defend a form." Also like Wittgenstein who was unable to make a system of his philosophy because he was unable not to think clearly. In this chapter, I'll mention your liking for Klee and Ernst—artists very different in temperament but who worked in the same atmosphere in Germany and must have had an effect on you. In temperament you are probably more like Klee than the flamboyant Ernst, but *Man Moth* and the *Monument* and some of your sleeping (or not sleeping) poems are very Ernstish. I think both Klee and Ernst used hallucinatory and dream material as much as they could, and I'll mention this. However, I think it is important to understand that they, and you too, I believe, regard dream experience as part of the continuum of experience in general. That is, there is no split personality, but rather a sensitivity that extends equally into the subconscious and the conscious world. That was one of the discoveries of the surrealists and symbolists too. Or perhaps I'm wrong? What do you think?

Chapter III. AFFINITIES   This chapter will follow through your suggestion that you are a "descendant" of the Transcendentalists. Thoreau, I think, more than Emerson and some of the others. For the more intellectual transcendentalists, Nature was what Emerson called "a dream and a shade[,]" a veil in which God was immanent. They presumed that a moral order was present in the Universe, and that man interpreted that order through his observations of Nature, and, like Wordsworth, regained knowledge of immortality and eternity. It's hard for anyone now to regard things in so simple a manner. However, once the metaphysics fades, what remains is an amazing sense of nature itself, animals as animals, plants as plants;—Thoreau's views all along. There is a poem about the sea which I will quote, in which Thoreau says he would rather "stroll upon the beach" picking up pebbles and talking to shipwrecked sailors than plunge into the depth of the sea where there are fewer pearls. I'll quote this in connection with *The Imaginary Iceberg*. I think too, that it is no longer possible to anticipate great ends for mankind. *Cirque d'Hiver*, "Well, we have come this far." And the "half is enough" of *The Gentlemen of Shallot*, are hardly transcendentalist views.

I think Emily Dickinson moves away from transcendentalism in the direction of Thoreau. For her, there is a theological framework of course. Yet she opts for the real world when it appears to be at odds with Heaven. In that wonderful poem "I cannot [live] with you/ it would be life . . ." she labels paradise "sordid". And the poem, "Because I could not stop for death . . ." proceeds, in thought and image, your CHEMIN DE FER. I wonder if I am right in detecting a note of loss in many of your poems. Loss of the religion Emily Dickinson had. I take the whole of CHEMIN DE FER as a parable, a conceit, really, in which the pool and the old hermit can be understood as symbols of the church, and of Christ, possibly. I'm not sure it should be overlaiden with "meaning", but that is what I make of it. Then, your lyrics use half rhyme as E.D. did. And you personify, occasionally, as she does. "A warning to the *startled* grass/ That darkness is about to pass." Again, in your sestina *Miracle for Breakfast* I take it there is a reference to the Eucharist . . . often alluded to by Emily Dickinson. Your view is far more complex than hers, and I think that particular poem plays with vision as Ernst does, but is less bitter in its implications. There's a wonderful quotation from Hoffmansthal that I'll quote in connection with the sestina . . . describing the collapse of the visible world: "My mind compelled me to view all things with uncanny closeness; and just as I once saw a piece of skin from my little finger under a magnifying lens, and it looked like a landscape with mighty furors and caves, so it was now with people and what they said and did." This in connection with the breadcrumb that turns into a mansion. I love that poem.

I hesitate to mention, as a last *Affinity*, the Imagists because so many critics seem to have lined you up with them. There is, however, something to be said here. When a poet "paints pictures" or images he also, like the painter, *interprets*. That is, he chooses how to present something, and he presents it in a way that says something. What he says, of course, is open to interpretation of a secondary sort. I think you are right to think that the reader should make of your poems what he wants to. Nevertheless, the poet limits the canvas. William Carlos Williams limited his canvases. I know what his moral views of life are, even though he is true to his dictum, "no ideas but in things." The same with you. When the pelicans crash "unnecessarily" hard, it is you who see them, it is you who intrude the qualification. I don't think

this is wrong—on the contrary, it is necessary and it makes the poem resonant. But I think one should mention that imagism is not so far from the
stream of English Literature as some people suppose.

Chapter IV. PRECISION AND RESONANCE. I think I mentioned this pet
theory of mine to you before. The success of imagist poetry depends, I
think, on the tension maintained between the accurate descriptions and
their possible meanings. This goes with what I mentioned above concern-
ing interpretation. Mere accuracy is boring and flat, like a text book. (I'll
find more examples to illustrate) On the other hand, it is often more
annoying to read poetry which seeks resonance without precision. In the
light, Ezra Pound's whole career may be regarded as a search for resonance, sometimes achieved, as in the translations from the Chinese, sometimes failing miserably, as in the more obscure Cantos because the allusions
are not precise enough. Since I am anxious to get this to the mail, I'll leave
the illustrations from your poems and stories—IN THE VILLAGE is full of
resonance—for a later letter.

Chapter V. SOURCES OF RESONANCE. There are common sources of
resonance—i.e. metaphor, literary allusion, allusion to common social
phenomena and background. These are frequently found in your poems
and I'll give examples. But I think there are two or possibly three sources
of resonance that you have, in a sense, developed. The first I call the *ambiguity of appearances*. The crumb can be a mansion. The map can be more
real than the land; tapestry of landscape suddenly lifts and floats away
before the Christians. [. . .] with this visual ambiguity, is the possibility of
inversion—correction, almost, through inversion.

In LOVE LIES SLEEPING, for instance, the man who "sees" is the man who
sees the inverted city as correct. (Is this also a play on the theory of optics?)
And in *Insomnia*, the image of the moon in the mirror is truer, or appears
more true than the moon titself. I could find many more examples—from
the new poems, too.
  Another source of resonance is, I think, your use of personification.
However, I think there are a number of kinds of personification. Usually the
pathetic fallacy is a device—saying one thing by means of another—pure
metaphor. As in "the heavy surface of the sea,/ swelling slowly as if *considering* spilling over" or "The moon in the bureau mirror/looks out a million

miles." This is quite usual in poetry, and I don't think you overpersonify. There are times when the landscape does not seem to be really personified but vivified—or given a life of its own, as Neruda gives the sea life and animals and plants life. *Florida* begins with ordinary personification—the tanagers are "embarrassed" the birds "hysterical" but then the landscape begins to live. The turtles are not like men, but like themselves, the shells lie helplessly on the beach. Perhaps I exaggerate. Yet I get a similar sense of the life of the beast from the *Fish* and *The Armadillo*.

But this will need much more working out—and I'm not sure I need make such a distinction. Certainly it is true, though, that you switch characteristics of things back and forth. There is an official name—metonymy or synecdoche.

CHAPTER VI, the last chapter has no name as yet. I'll try to summarize what I have said and remark on "the poet's contribution to American literature." Because I do think there is such a contribution, I hope not to sound too asinine. I want to mention Helena Morley again, and your feeling for the truth of the child's world—an unsentimental one for you—as for anyone who knows children at all. (I really get rather sick of people who are unsympathetic with any child but the memory of themselves. Even mothers who can't be bothered to understand their own children, but who will reminisce about their own childhoods as if they grew up in the Golden Age.)

This is enough. I wonder if you can read it. I've written in a rush because [I'm going] out soon. And I don't think everything I've said can be reasonable. But let me know what you think.

Samambaia, December 30th, 1963
name of place, 8 miles outside P—
means "giant fern"—Petrópolis is always the mailing address
Dear Mrs. Elvin: (or may I call you Anne?)

I have two long letters to you here, one over a month old, and I've carried them (off for a week at Cabo Frio) up here to the country and tried re-writing them from time to time. I am sorry to be so slow—they are in answer to yours of October 28th. I thought it was a very good letter and I have been trying to do it justice. I also received the Aiken book safely and thank you very much. I am glad to have one on hand—but I am sorry now you went to the trouble of sending it because while it was on the way a whole set of the books appeared at the Jefferson Library in Copacabana right near where I live in Rio. I've looked them over and taken out *Edward Taylor* to read (a bit dull!) They seem quite scholarly; your letter seems very scholarly! Hegel, Wittgenstein, etc—I am delighted. I have always been weak at philosophy so I am impressed by your being able to connect me with such brains. Like M. Jourdain speaking prose—I must have been philosophizing without realizing it.

Also—please don't apologize for your typing or spelling—I'm not very strong in those subjects, either.

And thank you for the nice little Chinese drawing. In return I am sending you (I've had it ready to mail for weeks but held off in order to try to finish the letter) a *very crude* Brazilian wood-cut—one of those used on the outside of the little ballad booklets they still sell by the thousands here, particularly in the north. I suppose there are 1,000 years, technically, between your picture and mine. The poem inside mine, however,—*about a spectacular murder*—would be in a very strict old Portuguese form, almost like Camões. I hope you are happy to be going to England and when is it you go? Saturday I had the U S Cultural Attaché up here for the day and he brought along a young couple—Tom Skidmore—who is here learning Brazilian history in order to teach it at Harvard next year. Perhaps you know him?—an English wife.—I meant to ask him if he knew you, but somehow the chance escaped me. I've been up in the country for about ten days—and hope to stay over the week-end. This is where I really live, but have spent very little time here for three years now because—I may have said this before— the friend I live with here is working for Carlos Lacerda, the Governor of Guanabara State (where Rio is) and so we have to stay in the city. After looking over the Aiken book a few things have struck me—one is that for the chronology I think you could put in Lota's name—I owe her a great deal; the next book of poems will be dedicated to her, and we have been friends for 20 years or so. (We also own, and are still building, this house together.) Something like: "November 1951—went on a trip to S.A. with the money from Bryn Mawr. Stopped over in Rio to visit Maria Carlota de Macedo Soares, an old friend, got sick—and then stayed on"—and on— However you wish to phrase it.

This is not for your book, ~~especially~~—but the more I looked at those books the more I wondered how you can make one out of me!—just for your information. Lota is president of the group that is turning an enormous *fill* along the Rio harbor into a park—It is about three miles long, full of highways, beaches, playgrounds, etc. and a tremendous undertaking for this bankrupt city—and while Lacerda is still in office we'll be stuck in Rio, more or less. This park is very badly written up [in] Don Passos's last book—(I *don't* recommend it). I'll save the rest for the letter I hope to

finish and get off to you tomorrow. With all best wishes for the New Year—
and thank you very much for your letter and your card—

Faithfully yours
Elizabeth

Started then—now it's Rio, January 20th—St Sebastian's Day
Samambaia, January 8th, 1964

Dear Anne:

I hope you got my large registered envelope. The mails are quite crazy
these days—I have received magazines from September, and a big pink
letter addressed to "The Bishop of the Methodist Church of Brazil."

*

To go on with my reply. After studying the Aiken book, I think you might
also just as well say in the chronology: "1916. Mother became permanently
insane, after several breakdowns. She lived until 1934." I've never concealed this, although I don't like to make too much of it. But of course it
is an important fact, to me. I didn't see her again.

I live in a very "modern" house outside Petrópolis that Lota & I own
together—she had started it when I came here and we have been building
it ever since, although it has been more or less finished for about seven
years. It was awarded a prize by Gropius and has been in many shows,
magazines, and books. I'm saying this not to boast but because I am interested in architecture and, if I do say—I think it's a good house—not grand,
elegantly finished or anything like that—that would be difficult here, even
if we had the money. "L' Architecture d'Aujourdhui" for June–July, 1960,
pps. 60–61, has some fairly good photographs of it, although it was still
unfinished when they were taken. (In case you're interested!) I have foolishly not kept carbons of my letters to you and I'm afraid I may be repeating myself—but another thing I've done since living in Brazil was to work
on a big book called "Contemporary Brazilian Architecture", by Henrique
Mindlin. I translated some for the English edition and tried to improve
his introduction, rather unsuccessfully. I also did the book on Brazil for
the LIFE World Library Series, 1962 (or did I say *this* before?). I undertook
it for money and had a disagreeable time with the editors before it was
done. I have just refused to revise it for them for a new edition—the political chapter is out of date, mostly. I was very much distressed by it. The text
is more or less mine, but somehow is also full of their bad grammar, clichés, etc. I was not responsible for captions (mostly quite wrong!) or photographs, although I did fight to get better pictures in it, and got a few.
However—imagine a book about Brazil without one bird, beast, butterfly,

orchid, flowering-tree, etc. They also cut all those things out of my text, & the paragraphs about famous naturalists, etc. Recently, however, a few tourist friends coming here have told me how "useful" they had found this book (there is very little about Brazil in English), and so I look at it more calmly. But if you see it, please make allowances!

These things haven't much to do with poetry, of course. You also spoke of translations in your letter. Perhaps you saw the small group of translations in the November POETRY?—from a long poem by João Cabral de Melo Neto. I am also publishing soon two groups by Carlos Drummond de Andrade, one in POETRY and the other in THE NEW YORK REVIEW. I don't think much of poetry translations and rarely attempt them,—just when I see a poem by someone I like that I think will go into English with less loss than usual. That means it isn't necessarily one of the poet's best poems. My translations are almost as literal as I can make them,—these from Brazilian poets are in the original meters, as far as English meters can correspond to Portuguese—which uses a different system. I wouldn't attempt the kind of "imitation" Robert Lowell does, although he makes brilliant Lowell-poems that way, frequently. Ben Bellitt's translations (you mention them) are AWFUL—have you see his Rimbaud?—very sad, since he obviously works so hard at them.

Kenyon Review is publishing, Spring or Summer issue, three very short stories I translated from a Brazilian writer, Clarice Lispector. I hope that's all the translating I do for some time now.

The most satisfactory translations of poetry, I think, are those Penguin Poets, with a straight prose text at the bottom of the page—at least those in languages I know something of seem quite good. You once mentioned Evtushenko. He seems awfully brash to me.—(I can read just enough Russian to tell how they rhyme, usually.) Pasternak one feels sure is good—and I am surprised by how good Esenin seems—but it is all gamble and guess-work. I never have enjoyed Rimbaud as much as the summer I read him in Brittany, living all alone, and really knowing very little French then. (Although I still think he's superb, of course.)

You also mention Neruda again. As I probably said, my poem to Marianne Moore was based on a serious poem by him, one of his best. (Mine is not serious.) Since I was interested in surrealism long before I met him, I don't believe his poetry had much influence on mine. But I like some of it—up to and including the Macchu Pichu poem, more or less. His later poetry is mostly propaganda, and bad. He was my first experience of a full-scale communist poet, in fact my only experience of a good communist poet (there are plenty of bad ones, here and elsewhere—or Brecht, I suppose, is another good one)—sad man, aware, I felt sure, of having betrayed his talent. He said many things that made me feel this, and he would tell me NOT to read certain of his poems, political ones (I knew him during the war), because they weren't any good. I met Neruda quite by chance; I did NOT like his politics. I had introductions to ~~many~~ of the other party in Mexico and knew and liked Victor Serge, etc.—

I've never studied "Imagism" or "Transcendentalism" or any isms consciously. I just read all the poetry that came my way, old or new. At 15 I loved Whitman; at 16 someone gave me the book of Hopkins that had just been re-issued (I'd already learned the few bits of Hopkins that were in my Harriet Monroe Anthology by heart). I never really liked Emily Dickinson much, except a few nature poems, until that complete edition came out a few years ago and I read it all more carefully. I still hate the oh-the-pain-of-it-all poems, but I admire many others, and, mostly, phrases more than whole poems. I particularly admire her having dared to do it, all alone—a bit like Hopkins in that. (I have a poem abut them comparing them to two self-caged birds, but it's unfinished.) This is snobbery—but I don't like the humorless, Martha-Graham kind of person who does like Emily Dickinson . . .

In fact I think snobbery governs a great deal of my taste. I have been very lucky in having had, most of my life, some witty friends,—and I mean real wit, quickness, wild fancies, remarks that make one cry with laughing. (I seem to notice a tendency in literary people at present to think that any unkind or heavily ironical criticism is "wit," and any old "ambiguity" is now considered "wit," too, but that's not what I mean.) The aunt I liked best was a very funny woman: most of my close friends have been funny people; Lota de Macedo Soares is funny. Pauline Hemingway (the 2nd Mrs. H) a good friend until her death in 1951 was the wittiest person, man or woman, I've ever known. Marianne was very funny—Cummings, too, of course. Perhaps I need such people to cheer me up. They are usually stoical, unsentimental, and physically courageous. The *poor* Brazilians, the people's, sense of humor is really all that keeps this country bearable a lot of the time. They're not "courageous," however—far from it—but the constant political jokes, the words to the sambas, the nicknames etc. are brilliant and a consolation—unfortunately mostly untranslatable. Only their humor sometimes manages to sweeten this repugnant mess of greed & corruption.

I have a vague theory that one learns most—I have learned most from having someone suddenly make fun of something one has taken seriously up until then. I mean about life, the world, and so on. This is again a form of snobbery. I dislike extremely bookish people (I do happen to love some, but I think they'd be better off if they *weren't* so bookish), and I don't enjoy writers who talk literary anecdotes all the time or are preoccupied in putting other writers in the proper pecking order. Criticism is important, "weeding out has to be done," (R. Lowell), but *I* don't want to do it. I feel that art would probably struggle along without it in very much the same way, probably. I trust my own taste and usually don't want to explain it—at the same time I occasionally wish I could it explain it better.

You mention Ernst again. Oh dear—I wish I had never mentioned him at all, because I think he's usually a dreadful painter. I liked that *Histoire Naturelle* I mentioned, and his photo-collages still seem brilliant. Klee I like, of course, and Schwitters—but then—I like so much painting. Some Seurats, for example—one smallish quiet, gray & blue one of Honfluer, with posts sticking up out of the beach—at the Museum of Modern Art in N.Y.—I'd give anything to have painted that! I often think I have missed my vocation, and I do paint myself occasionally—not at all well. But I like music just as much, and that is what one misses most here. I believe I must have the "artistic temperament . . ."

Now I'll be confidential. The Pauline Hemingway mentioned above sent my first book to Ernest in Cuba. He wrote her he liked it, and, referring to "the Fish," I think, "I wish I knew as much about it as she does." Allowing for exaggeration to please his ex-wife—that remark has really meant more to me than any praise in the quarterlies. I knew that underneath Mr. H and I really are a lot alike. I like only his short stories and first two novels—something went tragically wrong with him after that—but he had the right idea about lots of things. (NOT about shooting animals. I used to like deep-sea fishing too, and still go out once in a while, but without much pleasure, & in my younger tougher days I liked bull-fights, but I don't think I could sit through one now.) H said, horribly, that critics in N. Y. were like "angle-worms in a bottle." Perhaps Gibbon put it better: "A cloud of critics, of compilers, of commentators, darkened the face of learning, and the decline of genius was soon followed by the corruption of taste."

I don't like arguments (too bad, since I now live where argument, mostly about politics, is the favorite occupation . . .)and I approve of D.H. Lawrence's saying he hated people discussing politics and the news they'd all read in the same newspapers. I admire both Hemingway & Lawrence—along with others—for living in the real world and knowing how to do things. I am a little vain of my own ability to do things, perhaps,—or perhaps I have just been lucky in my interests, experiences, and friends. (And perhaps on the other hand I have just dissipated my energies.) But I'm often thunder-struck by the helplessness, ignorance, ghastly taste, lack of worldly knowledge, and lack of observation of writers who are much more talented than I am. Lack of observation seems to me one of the cardinal sins, responsible for so much cruelty, ugliness, dullness, bad manners—and general unhappiness, too.

This may have little to do with the arts or with my own poetry—except that I may express some of these notions in my verse; I can't very well tell myself. What I mean is of course more than "observation" or knowing how to care for the baby, row a boat, or enter a drawing-room! (Some of the Marxian critics have expressed it, I think.) It is a living in reality that works both ways, the non-intellectual sources of wisdom and sympathy. (And of course both Hemingway and Lawrence were capable of horrible cruelties—why did I pick them?) A better example, and something I have read & read since I have been in Brazil, is Chekov. If only more artists could be that *good* as well as good artists. He makes most of them look like pigs—and yet he sacrificed nothing to his art, either. I feel I could die happy if I could write one story—or poem—about Brazil one third as good as "Peasants."

To take up your chapters.   I. Most of my poems I can still abide were written before I met Robert Lowell or had read his first book. However, since then he has influenced me a great deal, in many ways. He is one of the very few people I can talk to about writing freely & naturally, and he is wonderfully quick, intuitive, modest, and generous about it. With the exception of Marianne, however, almost all my friends up until Cal (Lowell), and since, have not been writers.

II   Yes, I agree with you. I think that's what I was trying to say in the speech above. There is no "split." Dreams, works of art (some), glimpses of the always-more-successful surrealism of everyday life, unexpected moments of empathy (is it?), catch a peripheral vision of whatever it is one can never really see full-face but that seems enormously important. I can't believe we are wholly irrational and I do admire Darwin! But reading Darwin, one admires the beautiful solid case being built up out of his endless heroic *observations*, almost unconscious or automatic—and then comes a sudden relaxation, a forgetful phrase, and one *feels* the strangeness of his undertaking, sees the lonely young man, his eyes fixed on facts and minute details, sinking or sliding giddily off into the unknown. What one seems to want in art, in experiencing it, is the same thing that is necessary for its creation, a self-forgetful, perfectly useless concentration. (In this sense it is always "escape," don't you think?)

III   I don't believe I've read Thoreau's poetry until quite recently, actually, just prose. I agree with what you say, however. At the same time I've always thought one of the most extraordinary insights into the "sea" is Rimbaud's *L'eternite*:

> "C'est la mer allée
> Avec le soleil."

This approximates what I think is called the "Anesthetic revelation," (William James?). Two of my favorite poets (not best poets) are Herbert (I've read him steadily almost all my life), and Baudelaire. I can't attempt to reconcile them—but you are obviously a very clever girl and perhaps you can!

You are probably right about a "sense of loss," and it is probably obvious where it comes from—it is not religious. I have never been religious in any formal way and I am not a believer. I dislike the didacticism, not to say condescension, of the practicing Christians I know (but maybe I've had bad luck). They usually seem more or less on the way to being fascists. But I am interested in *religions.* I enjoy reading, say, St. Theresa, very much, and Kierkegaard (whom I read in vast quantities long ago, before he was fashionable), Simone Weil, etc.—but as far as people go,—I prefer Chekov. I'm appalled by the Catholicism, or lack of it, in this Catholic country, while remaining very interested in the architecture it produced. (In the U S A, for example, it is barbarous & shameless that only now, last year, have the clergy taken the stand on race-relations that they should have taken several centuries ago.) Nevertheless, there have been *some* good Christians! Just the way here in the midst of massive inertia and almost total corruption you occasionally find a real expert at something-or-other, working away unknown, honest and devoted. (The greatest authority on butterflies here was a postman for years—and you can't get much lower, here—and was recognized & given medals, etc. in Europe before Brazil ever heard of him. But please don't get the idea I romanticize such people. They just do come along often enough, in Church or State, or the arts, to give one hope.)

You mention Williams. I may have been influenced by him. I've read him always, of course, and usually like his flatter impressionistic poems best, not when he's trying to be profound. (Of his late poems I do like *Asphodel.*) But that diffuseness is exhausting (like Pound's). Williams had that rather silly language theory—but it has just occurred to me (I've been listening to some contemporary music on the hi-fi) that *perhaps* he really made some sort of advance like that made by composers around 1900 or so, and that a new set of rules & regulations might appear, to go on from there, that could make his kind of poetry more interesting and satisfying—like "serialization" in music. This isn't exact at all—but I feel that both he & Pound, and their followers, would be vastly improved if one could lean on a sense of "system" in their work somewhere . . . (After an hour of W. I really want to go off and read Houseman, or a hymn by Cowper.—I'm full of hymns, by the way—after church—going in Nova Scotia, boarding-school, and singing in the college choir—and I often catch echoes from them in my own poems.)

Wallace Stevens was more of an influence, I think. At college I knew "Harmonium" almost by heart. ("Wading at Wellfleet" I believe is the only poem that shows this influence much.) But I got tired of him and now find him romantic and thin—but very cheering, because, in spite of his critical theories (very romantic), he did have such a wonderful time with all those odd words, and found a superior way of amusing himself. Cummings was often doing the same thing, don't you think?

Now I've lost track of your chapter. Well—I do usually prefer poetry with form to it. I was very much wrapped up in 16th & 17th century lyrics for years (still am, in a way). I spent days in the New York Public Library copying out the songs from masques, etc. (Now you can get them in books, but a great many you couldn't then—in the 30's.) I also wrote about a dozen strict imitations of Campian, Nashe, etc. while at college (one or two were in that "Trial Balances" book, I think). I do have a weakness for hymns, as I said—and Cowper's "Castaway," etc.

But I don't need to give you a list of my eclectic reading—

You must be right about the Eucharist in "A Miracle for Breakfast." I had never noticed it myself until a Brazilian, Catholic, of course, translated that poem into Portuguese a few months ago and said the same thing to me.

IV   I think that is a good point and, from what you say, I agree—

V   This seems to make very good sense, too. It is odd what you say about "optics" in "Love Lies Sleeping," because I was reading, or had just read, Newton's *"Optics"* about then. (Although again I wasn't aware of this until you pointed it out to me!) (I think the man at the end of the poem is dead.) At the risk of sounding Cocteau-like—I believe I told you that I did work in the Optical Shop in the Key West Submarine Base for a very short stretch during the war? Cleaning & adjusting binoculars, mostly. I'm sure I told you this—I liked it, but had to leave because I was allergic to the acids used for clean the prisms.

VI   That will be hard—my "contribution"! Because of my era, sex, situation, education, etc. I have written, so far, what I feel is a rather "precious" kind of poetry, although I am very much opposed to the precious. One wishes things were different, that one could begin all over again. One almost envies those Russian poets a bit—who feel they are so important, and perhaps are. At least the party seems afraid of them, whereas I doubt that any American poet (except poor wretched Pound) ever bothered our government much. But then I remember that in the late 16th century poetry that was even *published* was looked down on; the really good poetry was just handed around. So one probably shouldn't worry too much about one's position, and certainly never about being "contemporary."

My outlook is pessimistic. I think we are still barbarians, barbarians who commit a hundred indecencies and cruelties every day of our lives, as just possibly future ages may be able to see. But I think we should be gay in spite of it, sometimes even giddy,—to make life endurable and to keep ourselves "new, tender, quick."

It would take me months to answer your letter properly so I shall send this jumble along. Please ask any questions you want to. Just please don't quote me exactly, however, without telling me?—because I think I've put things rather badly. I needn't have bothered you, probably, with so many likes & dislikes. I wish you could take a trip down here—I'm sure we could cook up lots of interesting notions in a few days. *Please tell me when you go to England. With all best wishes for the New Year—which was still new when I began—

   Faithfully yours,
   Elizabeth

Postscript. I mentioned that the "surrealism of everyday life" was always more successful,—or more amazing—than any they can think up,—that is for those who have eyes to see. Yesterday I saw such a good example of what I meant by that and some of my other remarks that I must add it. I went to see O Processo—"The Trial"—which is absolutely *dreadful.* Have you seen it? I haven't read the book for ages—but in spite of the morbidity of Kafka, etc. I like to remember that when he read his stories out loud to his friends he used to have to stop because he got to laughing so. All the way through the film I kept thinking that any of Buster Keaton's films give one the sense of the tragedy of the human situation, the weirdness of it all, besides being *fun*—all the very things poor Orson Welles was trying desperately to illustrate by laying it on with a trowel. I don't like *heaviness*—in general, Germanic art. It seems often to amount to complete self-absorption—like Mann & Wagner. I think one can be cheerful AND profound!—*or, how to be grim without groaning*—

Hopkins's "terrible" sonnets are terrible—but he kept them short, and in form.

It may amount to a kind of "good manners," I'm not sure. The good artist assumes a certain amount of sensitivity in his audience and doesn't attempt to flay himself to get sympathy or understanding. (The same way I feel the "Christians" I know suffer from bad manners—they refuse to assume that other people can be good, too, and so constantly condescend without realizing it. And—now that I come to think of it—so do communists! I've had far-left acquaintances come here and point out the slums to me, ask if I'd seen them—after 12 years—how can I bear to live here, etc . . .)

* *Perhaps I'll see you there—*

44 Porter Street
Watertown, Mass.
January 29, 1964

Dear Elizabeth,

Yes, I did receive your New Year's woodblock. Mark and I like it extremely—such a decorous murder! I was glad to have your note with it
since I was beginning to fear that in spite of having registered my letter to
you, it had gone astray. Yours arrived with a snow storm about two weeks
ago. Then, yesterday, with a second snow storm (I'm beginning to think
there must be a connection) your seven page letter! Delighted that you
seem to understand and even to like what I still feel is an inchoate mess of
ideas. I agree with you in almost everything you say, which makes writing
this book a pleasure, and not the burden I first thought it would be. (Agree
with your views regarding gaiety and profundity emphatically. I think that
is why I liked your poems so much when I first read them. Especially as this
view is so unfashionable, or seemingly unfashionable among poets writing
today, poets of, alas, my generation who seem to be utterly lacking in perspective. And I feel as you do about writers and literary circles. When I was
at Michigan two years ago I knew a lot of literary people, liked them, but
felt they never came to terms with anything *except* writing. Terribly limited
as people, thought I never felt this about musicians, for instance, or physi-
cists. But then, very few of the musicians or scientists I know read poetry.
Very distressful.)

I did keep a carbon copy of my letter to you in October, and I am conscious of having broken my promise. I did mean to send you some parts of
my completed manuscript, but, as usual, I did not complete anything to my
satisfaction before November and then I had a miscarriage which sent me
into a spin of depression (one feels so aware of the fortuitousness of things,
like Greeks, at the mercy of fate) so that I could not write anything or read,
hardly. Then Christmas and all that Nonsense. The awful dilemma of bringing up a child in this contaminated world—well, I won't go on, but I'll ask
you to be patient. It's hard to extract poems from the context of what I'm
writing. I want to finish the three middle chapters—on the Artist, Precision
and Resonance (I've almost done that one and I like it.) and the problem
of ambiguity—before I begin on the first, which will be easier. I think, in
view of your remarks on "contribution" (and I want to avoid that word—
also to avoid words like "influence" and "isms" as much as possible. Much
better to stick to concrete examples) I'll try to mention your feelings about
the need for gay profundity. "Awful but cheerful," one of your best lines I
think. You say you think you are "snobbish" and that your poems are "precious". Well—yes, if you mean by snobbish opposed to the mediocrity which
is published and published and praised and praised everywhere these days,

and by "precious" a kind of dogged determination to express at least what you honestly feel about the world. Being you, you couldn't write like a peasant without being false. Art is always precious, in the other sense, in the sense that it is rare. As you say, circumstances being what they are, one can't pretend that one is natural and primitive—when at least in my case and in the case of everyone in the US, the cities are submerged in coils of super-highway and one plans to visit, by car or by air, places that should, in mood and temperament, be months away. Sorry. I am wandering from the point. (I think, who better to mention the predicament American poets are in, to contrast, as you suggest, to the Russians.)

Since writing that first letter, I have come to feel that my chapter on the artist should include this: that form is a tension in your work between what I should call New England or Yankee earthiness, humor, a reticence, even a penchant for the macabre and a more sophisticated European "modernist" attitude. Perhaps I don't make myself clear. But what you called Transcendentalism sometime back isn't Emerson & CO., but although the Concord people had many qualities of the New England character; what I think you meant, though, is that, in form and in content, your poetry is in some ways very Yankee. For instance, the number of poems about the sea. The way you know *coldness*, everything about it. You seem to take delight in superstition and eerie effects without believing—and yet you believe, too, like Hawthorne and Melville, although you have more humor. The story IN PRISON is Poe-like to me. Written in his style, anyhow. Do you see what I mean? I think there is more truth in this than in the Transcendentalist connection, especially since all of them except Thoreau were naïve optimists of a variety that doesn't grow today (except possibly in the Southern Churches! I once taught in Atlanta, Ga., and I never heard such nonsense as was preached to the respectable parents of my girls.) I have long wanted to write a story based on a sermon I once heard. "The Signposts of Sin." I never can get the right tone, though.)

I am very glad that you told me so much about your tastes in reading. Yes, Chekov is very fine. Mark gave me a paperback copy of the short stories by Isaac Babel for Christmas; and these are splendid, too. Like Chekov's, but tougher and stronger without sacrifice of nuance. Some of them horrible. You no doubt know these, but if you don't have them I'll send you a copy. Another present, the *Pillowbook of Sei Shonagon*, the diary of a 10th century Japanese court lady, translated with excellent commentary by Arthur Waley, might interest you too. A society so innocent, so literary and so immoral. I was reminded of *Helena Morley*, not because Sei Shonagon resembled her in any way but because the diary has the same duality of innocent self-revelation. She's awfully witty and a good poet too. I'll send you this if you don't have it. (I really *love* sending books to people who like them.

So you musn't feel embarrassed.) Another book Mark introduced me to this summer was R. H. Blyth's four volumes on Haiku. A bit repetitious, but excellent on the poetry. Out of the modern "genre" of critical writings. Do you know that? Mark, you see, is so remarkable because he has such a *huge* range of interests and knowledge, (but is not "bookish" in a prideful or harmful way) and is able to see our era as part of a historical spectrum. That's so easy to say, but he really does, so that no fashion sways him. He's difficult to live with sometimes because he is usually right! His criticism of my analytical thinking makes me furious. But I'm grateful, and this book will be good, if it is any good, because of him and you. We are reading J. R. R. Tolkien's "Fellowship of the Ring" to little Caroline Margaret in the evenings after supper. Mark and I both love it, but it's a little beyond Margaret. Do you know that? Epic in its proportions. The supreme fairy tale.

There are hundreds of things I could say about your letter, but I don't want to write too much today because I think you should get this soon. Suppose I stop now to get this in the mail. Later on, this week or next, I'll write again. I have a few questions about the newer poems. Oh, how I wish I could fly to Brazil, but I can't see how we could ever afford it. England I know well—I married, quite disastrously, in England just after I graduated from Michigan in 1954 and lived in London for 6 years. Margaret was born there. At that time I never would have had the sense to understand anything, however. I look forward to going back. Love Ireland and Scotland, but Cambridge is queer, though queerly tough.

Much love,

Rio, February 16th, 1964

Dear Anne:

It was a compliment to be the "class aesthete" . . . Two friends & I were cartooned, at Vassar, with the caption "The Higher Type." Thank you very much for offering to send me books, and I am going to accept the *Pillowbook of Sei Shonagon*, because I've heard so much about it. But if it is at all expensive *you must let me pay for it*. I have already given away here two copies of that edition of Isaac Babel you mention, so you see what I think of him. He is superb. That brief account of the Reds taking over an old monastery (my copy's up in the country so I can't give the title) is one of the most beautiful short pieces of reporting I know.—He's the other writer besides Chekov I wish some Brazilian genius would come along and write *like*—except that Brazil is closer to Chekov, a decidedly "feminine" country and Babel is a masculine writer. If one should make these distinctions—but compared to England, or Germany,—Brazil is ~~decidedly~~ "feminine."

I'd be grateful if you'd somehow make the point that my reasons for staying here so long are personal. I'd rather live in my own country if I could. But my feelings about both the USA and Brazil would look like seismographs during earthquakes, just during any week, no doubt. My last trip back was late 1961 and I was horrified by pre-Christmas New York—it had all grown so much worse. Now I am horrified by things here, as the situation deteriorates very fast. But no one outside the country can really understand what is going on so I won't [. . .]

Please forgive this long digression—I am really trying to cheer myself up—things are so bad here—by talking English. I have written several poems about Brazil recently—one you will see shortly in The New York Review, and another—a fausse naïve ballad, very long, in The New Yorker.

I am very sorry to hear about the miscarriage and I know they have very bad effects . . . When is it you are going to England? There is a slight chance that I may go there myself for a month or two, perhaps in April. I haven't been for so long it is hard to get going, but I'd like to make a tourist trip and see literary things I didn't see on my trips long ago. I once drove around most of Ireland and had a lovely time—probably before you were born! If I do get there I'll certainly try to meet you somewhere.

Some of Robert Lowell's poetry, the first two books, certainly, is very difficult—a few poems I never did understand until I'd asked him. But then they do make very good sense. He has written a few really lovely ones in the past year or two—lyrical, finished,—musical, too—two I think among his best poems. Randall, I think—well, I think that sentimentality is deliberate, you know—he is trying to restore *feeling*, perhaps—but I just don't think we can believe in it these days. I think he was influenced some years ago a bit too much by Corbière. Frost is a complicated case—a lot of what he wrote about was just homely to me, after my Nova Scotia days, but the kind of things I have tried to avoid sentimentalizing. I hate his philosophy, what I understand of it—I find it *mean*—while admiring his technique enormously. "Two Tramps at Mudtime" for example—what is it but a refusal to be charitable? (and he was hideously uncharitable, conversationally, at least.) Well—as Cal says frequently—"We're all flawed,"—and as far as poetry goes I think we have to be grateful for what we do get. They all rise above their flaws, on occasion.—I am interested in Berryman and wish he'd publish that long poem soon. I wish I knew something of Chinese poetry—a nice old ex-missionary teacher in Washington told me a lot about it the year I was there and enlightened me some—and I was properly impressed by the sophistication and elaboration, etc.

Shapiro, Winters, etc.—seem sad to me—the problem is how to be justly but *impersonally* bitter, isn't it.—(Even Marianne Moore's disappointments show through too much sometimes, I think—but then she is very Irishly cagey and manages by avoiding a great deal . . . She's a wonder!)

No—I just have a couple of small paper-backs on the haiku—and I don't know how good Donald Keene (?) is (they're up in the country, too.) I have never read Tolkien's work after one attempt several years ago—I didn't seem to have time, so I couldn't have liked it much! For children—well, I still think Beatrix Potter wrote a fine prose style . . . I admire Jemima Puddleduck, Tom Kitten, etc. very much, and have introduced the series (along with New England Fish Chowder) to many Brazilians. This is idle chat and I must get to work—I am glad you sound happily married—As a very stupid uncle of my friend Lota's used to say*—"I prefer my friends to be rich. I like rich happy friends better than poor unhappy friends."

Affectionately,
Elizabeth

44 Porter Street
Watertown, Mass.
March 6, 1964

Dear Elizabeth,

As you see, I am sending you a revised chronology which I hope you'll correct, amend, delete etc. as you see fit. As I work on the first chapter I find that I may need more factual information, and, if you don't mind, I'll ask a few questions before trying to answer your long letter properly. I don't think the little I write about biography needs to be too detailed, but on the other hand, it's best not to sound evasive, and worse, to make mistakes.

1. About your mother's family. Was your grandfather a sea captain like his ancestors? Did his whole family come from Nova Scotia . . . and were there two or three aunts? Perhaps it would be helpful to know the name of your aunt in Boston—the one you liked because she was amusing. Is there anything you remember particularly about people in your childhood? Who introduced you to music, to poetry . . . Teachers? One can tell a great deal about your childhood in Nova Scotia from the two New Yorker stories, and the "feel" of it is in poems like Cape Breton, but I would like to be a little more precise about people and exact places. ~~Sorry, but I must picture things to write about them.~~

2. You say you studied at the Schola Cantorum in Paris and later with Ralph Kirkpatrick. When was this?

as if he'd made a discovery

3. I wonder who you knew when you went to Paris in 1935 or so? There was so much "in the air there". One thinks of Gertrude Stein, Hemingway, D.H. Lawrence, the Surrealists, painters and poets like Andre Breton. A great period of blossoming forth in that curious euphoric between-war period. And then the people on the Partisan Review, so fervent and determined to be "liberal" without knowing the consequences. I was looking at some old issues of PR in the library the other day and was seized with an awful sense of the bravery and, really, the fruitlessness of it all. I think it must have been exciting at the time. Again, when did you meet Calder, Dewey, Loren McIvor, Randall Jarrell. You seem to have been very fortunate in your friends. I think you are quite right about your belonging to the post world war I generation. Or, at least, I think one must make a distinction between the "you then" and the "you in Brazil." That leads me to the poems.

4. What impresses me about the 1956 volume is a wonderful awareness of the ambiguity of things. "Faustina," for instance . . . the *impossibility* of knowing her thoughts, that they might be either. Or the end of "Roosters" in which the sun "climbs in" . . . "faithful as enemy *or* friend." This kind of uncertainty perhaps characteristic of the time as well of perhaps you. The new poems, except for *Questions of Travel* and *Brazil, January 1,* don't seem to spring from the same kind of uncertainty or urgency, but from a new climate and culture really. They have the same qualities of exact discription but the perspective is different. Even the poems about childhood—Sestina, and Cousin Arthur and Manners are "detached" (Is that what I mean?) from your old vision. They don't seem quite "it" . . . while the Brazilian poems have almost a settled quality. *Manuelzinho,* for instance, and curious mixture of superstition and mysticism and absurdity of *The Riverman.*

Understand I am not criticizing these new poems. I like many of them very much—and besides, as you see, I can't really say what I mean about them. Therefore I don't think I'll say as much about them as about the others. *The Fish, The Imaginary Iceberg, The Map, The Man Moth, Cootchie, Florida* these all seem to me masterpieces—better and better as I read them. But unless you think me terribly "dated" I would rather not deal with what probably should be called the "contemporary poetic scene". It's a dreary one, in general, I think, and I'm not sure that any of your poems have much to do with it.

I see that I have "gone all muzzy again," as Mark would put it. Well, maybe you can help me out. I do want to thank you for your long letter and to assure you that I will quote nothing without asking you. There is a passage that I would like to use, if I may, or if you approve. It concerns what you say about the "always-more-successful surrealism" of everyday life. As you have it, it is like this:

"There is no "split." Dreams, works of art, glimpses of the always-more-successful surrealism of everyday life, unexpected moments of empathy (is it?), catch a peripheral vision of whatever it is one can never really see full-face but that seems enormously important." And then what you say of Darwin who builds an "endless heroic case" of observations "and then comes to a sudden relaxation, a forgetful phrase, and one *feels* the strangeness of his undertaking, sees the lonely young man, his eyes fixed on facts and minute details, sinking or sliding giddily off into the unknown . . ."

It is that point where rationality and irrationally meet that that your poems "catch fire" for me. Their resonance, their *real* perceptions—not just the fine descriptions—comes from the central awareness . . . the hardest and most elusive thing in the world to catch.

Two weeks ago I ran away to Ann Arbor to visit my father . . . and to be by myself for a while. While I was there I did a sort of Victorian Table of Contents of this whole book . . . all the ideas written out in outline form with references to poems etc. . . . now I'm fitting what I have already written into my outline (and throwing reams away). So it looks as if there may be a book after all in spite of viruses, ear-aches, and headcolds which seem to afflict my family—even the cat has a cold! I haven't yet looked up the photography of your house—I will, I'm glad you told me about "L'Architecture d'Aujord'hui" I hope I have everything you suggested include incorporated into the chronology. No, I havn't seen "The Trial" and I won't after your description. And I've been re-reading Chekov. Yes, Yes, Yes. Have you written any stories about Brazil? Somehow I think you should . . . What is it that makes good prose but isn't poetry—or perhaps it is.

I'm "baby sitting" with a friend's little girl and my own—we take turns—and I wish you could see the raisins and graham crackers piling up around the typewriter. And milk spilling! I think the time for literature has come to an end. Again, thank you for your kindness and help and patience in reading my letters to you.

Answers to your questions of March 6th—[1964]

1. It was my greatgrandfather (maternal grandmother's father) who was a sea captain. William Hutchinson. He was lost at sea—all hands—in a famous storm off Sable Island when my grandmother was 9 years old. No—Cape Sable, I think—they're two different places, but Cape Sable would be on his way into the Bay of Fundy. Better not say. I made a trip to *Sable Island* (as I believe I've said) on a Canadian Lighthouse Service Boat, around 1949—

My maternal grandmother had four brothers; three were Baptist missionaries in India, the 4th a painter who spent most of his life in England, George Hutchinson. (Israel Zangwill's "Our Lady of the Snows" is supposed to be about him but I haven't read it.) One of the others was also President of Acadia College in N S, and another taught there, etc. The Hutchinsons seem to have had brains, talents, and were rather eccentric. As I think I said—one wrote bad novels, including the first novel in *Telegu*.

Great Uncle George went to sea at 14 or so (he is in "Large Bad Picture") except he never taught school; I don't know why I said that. For a few years. Even before then, he had started painting pictures of ships for the local ship-builders; Great Village was a ship-building place then, as many Nova Scotian villages were. But it came to an end around the turn of the century. Of the Bulmer side I don't know very much. As I said—there were Tories from N.Y. state, given farms in N S at the time of the Revolution, and more recent Scotch, Scotch-Irish, and English additions. My maternal grandmother's mother however was from England—London—which probably accounted for many anglicisms my grandma used, such as "hard as the knockers of Newgate." I have a lot of notes from ~~aunt~~ Aunt *Grace* about this side of the family—the ship my greatgrandmother arrived in, her fearful trip, etc.—but I don't believe they'd be of much interest to you, really.

On my mother's side I had three aunts: Maud, Grace, and Mary. You don't need to mention names, I think—I lived with Maud and was—and am—fondest of Grace. Mary is only 12 years older than I am—she is mentioned in both those stories. These last two are both living in Canada; Aunt Maud died about 1942—I'm not sure. She and her husband stayed near me for two or three winters, or parts of winters, in Key West. There was also a brother, Uncle Arthur—of the poem—Their father, my grandfather, was my favorite grandparent. He owned the local tannery, until local tanning vanished—the pits for it were still there, and part of the old shop, when I was small. Also small-scale farming, like everyone else, almost, in Great Village. He was a darling; sweet-tempered, devout, and good with children. ("Manners" is about him) He was a deacon of the Baptist church and when he passed the collection plate he would slip me one of those strong white peppermints that say (still, I think) CANADA on them.

Great Village is very small and well-preserved—the last time I saw it, at least—1951, like a small New England village, all white houses, elm trees, one large white church in the middle (designed I believe by great uncle George).* It is in the rich farming country around the head of the Bay of Funday: dark red soil, blue fir trees—bur birches, a pretty river running into the Bay through "salt marshes"—a few remains of the old Acadian dikes—it is Evangeline country—Cape Breton is quite different; sparsely populated, forested, full of lakes—supposed to be like Scotland, and more Gaelic is spoken there than anywhere else in the world. I spent a summer there—48, I think, when I wrote a few poems about it. My mother went off to teach school at 16 (the way most of the enterprising young people did) and her first school was in lower Cape Breton somewhere—and the pupils spoke nothing much but Gaelic so she had a hard time of it at that school, or maybe one nearer home—she was so homesick she was taken the family dog to cheer her up. I have written both a story and a poem about this episode but neither satisfy me yet.

I went very briefly to the real "country" school where we wrote on slates and had many classes in each room—not all in one, because G V had the country school, so it was fairly large. You took a bottle of water and a rag to clean your slate—the bad boys spat on theirs. A little Micmac Indian boy, Jimmy Crow, was in "primer class" with me; most of the rest had Scotch names and looked very Scotch. Muir MacLaughlin I made the childish mistake of calling "Manure"—When I found him running a local store on my last trip there he recognized me and reminded me of this. The teacher's name was Georgie Morash and I can see her clearly. She sang in the choir— as did my various relatives—and all those who sang in the choir I remember very well because I spent so many sermons studying them one by one. Miss Patriquin, (aunt of Gwendolyn "Applyard" whose name was really Gwendolyn Patriquin) taught the infant Sunday School class I attended. She later went mad and chased bad boys through the village with a carving knife. My aunt Mary and I actually attended school together at this stretch. She made me late and I howled in the cloakroom (I have always been over-punctual) until Miss Morash came and consoled me. Mary was very pretty and had many suitors. It was during the first World War—the village boys (a kilted regiment) would come to say goodbye and their clothes were wonderful, of course. Most of them were never seen again—almost every boy in that tiny place, from 18–22, was killed in one of the big battles—

*the Presbyterian church

Canadians first, of course—and the whole village was in mourning—but this was after I'd left. (Over 20 boys, I think) I had a dachshund, "Betsy"— given to my mother when I was born, and she sent her to G V to her mother—the only dog of that sort ever seen there, of course, and a village character. The "big boys" hung around on the bridge, and she was afraid of them—so in order to cross the village to meet my grandfather on his way back from the farm, etc.—she would make a long detour and actually cross the river at a wide shallow place, on stepping stones. One summer Sunday afternoon, all good Baptists in the church, the doors open, Dr. Francis, the minister, was on his knees praying, when a patter-patter was heard and Betsy trotted down the aisle past our pew. She was fond of Dr. Francis and went right up on the platform and jumped to lick his face. He opened his eyes and said "Why, hello Betsy" and then went on praying.

Mary played the piano, quite well—all the aunts played some—and I think that and the hymns were how I came to love music from the beginning. This whole period in my life was brief—but important, I know.* The village was 50 years or so backwards—we made yeast from the hopvine on the barn; had no plumbing, oil lamps etc. My grandmother was a famous butter-maker. Everything is quite changed now of course. But when I came to live first in Samambaia and we had oil lamps for two or three years, etc. a lot came back to me. I helped design our sitting room stove for example needed up there "winters" and without ever having done such things before I found myself baking bread, making marmalade, etc.—When the need arises apparently the old Nova Scotian domestic arts come back to me!

Like most poets, I have a very morbid total recall of certain periods and I could go on for hours—but I won't!

I know next to nothing about the Bishops, and have no idea when they "came over", rather I have forgotten. There were 3 brothers, one was a doctor in Plymouth, Mass., I *think*—the 2nd I'd don't know—the 3rd farmed in White Sands, Prince Edward Island. My grandfather B, according to the family story, ran away aged 12, with a box of carpenters' tools on his back, and went first to Providence. His was an Horatio Alger story. He married very well, and made a "million," etc. Sarah Foster, his wife, came from a very very old New England family, originally from Quincy—she came from Holden. I also have a batch of papers from that branch, about her ancestors in the Revolution on that side—but again they are really not very interesting. One man, I remember, was in and out of the army many times—the way they were—and was imprisoned in the notorious prison ship in New York harbor—and seems to have survived it because he was a *cook*.

*Aunt Maud had a very good alto and sang to me a lot, too

The Bishop grandparents came to visit in Canada several times, apparently—twice that I remember. Although my father had married a poor country girl the older generation were still enough alike, I think, so that they got along in spite of the money difference—it was the next generation that made me suffer acutely. The B's were very early motorists— once they actually drove to G V and their huge car and chauffer made a sensations—also the fact that they wired the local hotel for rooms & bath— when there wasn't a bath in the village. I was probably regarded as a small fairy princess, but I was too young to notice. It The thrill of riding with that grandpa on the dusty country roads—and the chauffeur, Rondal Rondald, of whom I became fond and who was very nice to me later on in Worcester. (*We* had only a buggy, of course, or two, rather, one with fringe, and a wagon, and in the winter a sleigh and a "pung.") The B's were horrified to see the only child of their eldest son running about the village in bare feet, eating at the table with the grown-ups and drinking *tea*, and so I was carried off (by train) to Worcester for the one awful winter that was almost the end of me. 1917–18.

I had already had bad bronchitis and probably attacks of asthma—in Worcester I got much worse and developed exzema that almost killed me.* One awful day I was sent home from "first grade" because of my sores—and I imagine my hopeless shyness has dated from then.—In May, 1918, I was taken to live with Aunt Maud; I couldn't walk and Ronald carried me up the stairs—my aunt burst into tears when she saw me. I had had nurses etc.—but that stretch is still too grim to think of, almost. My grandfather had gone to see my aunt M privately and made the arrangements—he said my grandmother didn't "know how to take care of her own children", most of them had died.—My aunt was paid to care for me—but she would have anyway, I imagine, if there'd been no money. She really devoted herself to me for years until I got better—she probably never slept for nights and nights, getting me injections of adrenaline, etc. etc.—

When I couldn't go to school in Worcester—well, I remember one evening I was sitting under the living room table building blocks and my Grandfather said as if to himself, "I wonder if some little girl would like to take piano lessons"—so Miss Darling came to teach me. I was too small, but loved it—and always took lessons, but never had a good teacher until I got to Walnut Hill.

I began writing poetry at about 8 and when I was 11 or so I remember Aunt Grace giving me some good advice about listening to criticism, not getting one's feelings hurt, etc. I went to school off and on, but remember

*And had the beginnings of St. Vitus Dance along with everything else—

chiefly lying in bed wheezing and reading—and my dear aunt Maud going out to buy me more books. When I was 13 I was well enough, summers, to go to camp, and it wasn't until then, briefly, and then at Walnut Hill, that I met girls who were as clever, or cleverer than I was, and made friends, and began to cheer up a bit.

The last time I was in Boston I went to see an elderly uncle by marriage (his 1st wife, my father's sister, died the year I was born) and he told me that he had tried to adopt me legally that year in Worcester because he felt so sorry for me—he had three children of his own. He also said "Your mother was the most beautiful skater I ever saw—I fell in love with her, too, when I saw her skate." These bits of information always surprise me very much, since I know so little—I have a lot of cousins here and there—The next to last Bishop, an aunt, died last year aged 86 or 87—I'm the last actually, of that short and undistinguished line. I never fought with what family I had, never had to "rebel", etc.—I was always on more or less visiting terms with them, and I feel that has had a profound and not altogether good effect on me—it produces passivity, detachment, etc—on the other hand making one's friends one's family, really. But from the age of 18 I have always been independent and gone where I wanted to. My relatives now, I think, chiefly wonder why I don't write best sellers and earn some money if I'm supposed to be so smart—the phrase is "Too smart for her own good," I believe . . .

2. I don't think my music studies are worth mentioning, really. I took clavichord lessons the first winter in Paris, and the next year I took some more with Kirkpatrick in New York—when I lived at the old Hotel Chelsea for a few months—but I never was any good at it, at all. I always dream of studying some more, also the piano again. The clavichord is here now, in its traveling case, because I've at last found someone in Rio who can tune it for me—but I was never a performer—I played piano in public a few times at college and lost my nerve forever. (Two very good old friends of Lota's and mine are Fizdale & Gold, the two-piano team—if you've ever heard them? They are *superb*. We visit them whenever we can—) So—just say I love music!

3. On my first stay in Paris (and the 2nd one, after about ten months) I knew very few people. I could have, if it hadn't been for this "shyness"—or whatever is the word now—whatever it is, it had made my life quite different from what perhaps it might have been—I had published a few poems. I remember Sylvia Beach invited me to a party—or parties—Spender was at one, Joyce at another—and I'd get to the door, lose my nerve and run

away. (I never did speak to Spender until last year in Brazil.) I had letters to people in London, *Life & Letters To-day*, etc. and the same thing happened—I took a taxi to the door and didn't dare go in. (I'm afraid you'll begin to think I am a hopeless idiot, after this True Confession, but there it is.) Also—I'm a dreadful linguist. I understand French perfectly, (and now Portuguese) and some Spanish, and read them all—but I hate to talk a foreign language—particularly French. (Do have your little girl learn a language or two well—to speak it—it will improve her social life all her life . . .) In Paris I did meet a lot of famous people, I suppose,—even Picasso for a moment—and many more to look at, a good many painters, etc.—but that doesn't mean I ever exchanged any words with them except "Enchantée." G. Stein and Alice B—I was invited to tea, with a friend— and the friend went without me, finally. What an idiot! (Since then—just a year or so ago—I've corresponded with Alice B who wanted to come to Brazil, of all places—I discouraged her firmly.) What was going on in Paris then was mostly surrealism, that I remember—André Breton & his gallery; I met Ernst, Giacometti, etc—but—I just looked at them. I spent a lot of time taking walks, also at the Deux Magots and the Flore—quite different then than now—

I have learned to disguise my *social* terrors quite a lot, and also—always— if I really like someone well enough I don't get them—Marianne, for example—the one "celebrity" I have ever deliberately tried to meet in my life.— and We got along immediately. I was never afraid for a moment of Neruda, or Cummings, or, Cal—Jarrell, etc.—And then I have improved— over the years—

I met Loren in 1939, I think, in N.Y.—I'd seen a few of her paintings and liked them. We became friends immediately and she & her husband, Lloyd Frankenberg, stayed with me for two winters in Key West. John Dewey bought a painting she did that first winter. He bought it in N.Y.—but he used to go to KW winters then, too,—I had stared at him and his daughter as I ate the 50¢ fish dinner in a little restaurant, but never met them (the daughter who has since been a friend for 24 years—to whom the poem Cold Spring is dedicated). When Loren came back to KW we all went to call.

I met Neruda quite by accident in a hotel in Merida—I had no idea who he was when he invited me to go off to Chichen Itza with him and his wife.

Randall was in NY the winter of 1946, I think it was—he invited me to dinner to meet Cal.

Calder is really Lota's friend. He's been in Brazil several times and I didn't really know him until here. I admire him very much—again with that odd in-between-generations feeling. As I said before—the simple fact that I did *my* traveling earlier than the poets who aren't so much younger than I am, after all, seems to have put me in a different category—and often I'm afraid I have felt old and sophisticated, and certainly more knowledgable about art, etc.—While they were teaching and marrying, I was out observing the world.—(Mrs. Tate once reminisced about a night in Paris that I'd already heard another version of from Pauline Hemingway, etc.—Very odd.)

5. I'm afraid I agree with you only too well.

I don't know whether this is due to Brazil, age or what.—However, I feel I could NOT have stayed on in N.Y. And I have been personally very happy here, except for this recurring sense of anxiety and loss. However, one always hopes and hopes.—Now I am hoping a trip will do wonders—and this year so far I have written a lot, for me. Good or bad I can't say.—(Cal likes the poem in the New York Review, I think, quite a bit—)

I should mention one teacher at Walnut Hill, probably—she later taught at Wellesley. Miss Prentiss—she was an excellent teacher of English *for that age* (hopelessly romantic!)—and we ~~went~~ *read some* Shakespeare with her, She helped me even more, probably, by lending me all her books I took a fancy to and admiring my early verse—too much, no doubt.

[There was also an excellent Latin teacher, Miss ? *The best teacher there, really*]

Miss Farwell, the assistant principal, was also very kind to me and had the excellent idea of taking me to some sort of psychiatrist in Boston,—Unfortunately, I clammed up and wouldn't talk at all. But she had the right idea—too bad it didn't work.

We were taken to Symphony Concerts, of course—also concerts at Wellesley—where, ~~with~~ through my piano teacher (how awful I've forgotten her name) I shook hands with Myra Hess (my teacher's old teacher—later *scorned* by Kirkpatrick) and Prokofiev.—P's wife sang ~~some~~ from "The Love of Three Oranges",* and that and his way of playing I remember as giving me a whole new idea of music.— Possibly the idea of "irony" in music was a revelation, because at that time I liked his piano pieces best (now they're not very interesting to me) of my simple repertoire—

I also saw one of the first Calder shows, at Pittsfield, around 1931—his very first mobiles, that had cranks, or little electric motors. We spoke of this show the last time he was here—last year—and it was funny how many of the pieces I could still remember, so it must have made a big impression—

Although I think I have a prize "unhappy childhood", almost good enough for the text-books—please don't think I dote on it.—Almost everyone has had, anyway—and since then I have been extremely lucky in many

*1929

ways. I never had any difficulty getting published—I have had all those helpful awards—I often think I have been praised beyond my due—

Under 3 you speak rather disparagingly of Partisan Review in the late 30's and 40's . . . well, at the time I was writing the poems I like best I was very ignorant politically and I sometimes wish I could recover the dreamy state of consciousness I ~~levd in~~ lived in then—it was better for my work, and I do the world no more good now by knowing a great deal more. I was "left" ~~just~~ because my friends were, mostly—although of course we all felt the effects of the depression profoundly, and ever since noticing the split in my own family and going through my Shelley period, around 16, I had thought of myself as a "socialist." (I was also a vegetarian until after college, I think!—and I revert to it every once in a while. I don't advocate it or even believe in it—but they drive the cattle to market here, and after each encounter with one of the cattle trains—you park the car and let the poor beasts pour around you—I give up meat again for a week or so.)

I was always anti-communist, I believe—after one or two John Reed Club affairs. I don't know whether this was due to my intelligence (No—not intelligence—just instinct and snobbery—) or what—but all the really "red" girls at college (one is taken off cruelly, but very comically in "The Group") I found too silly—and now they're the real rich conservatives, in general.

But—before the war—we knew much ~~much~~ less. The purges in the 30's were what opened most people's eyes, of course. Here now it is dreadful for me to see young men I know making the same mistake that US intellectuals were making around 1930. *How* they can is hard to see.—They seem totally unaware of recent history. But Brazil is unbelievably provincial, and also one of its greatest drawbacks to any kind of maturity, I'm afraid, is that it has never been through a war. However—nothing here is explainable in terms that apply in the U S.—But believe me—things are very bad ~~here~~ now, and I may *have* to leave. Or Lota and I may finally choose to—

Rio, March 23rd, 1964

Dear Anne:

I'll enclose the fragments of a letter I did write you over a month ago, just to show you I tried. Many things have kept me from answering properly; guests, partly, but mostly I think the political situation, that is keeping everyone on edge now and which, because of Lota's job and her close connections with the State government in Rio, I can't forget for a moment. I made tentative reservations to go to England by boat next month, just for a breathing spell,—but just today we have decided to go to Milan in May for the

Triennale May 20th we want to see—then I'll probably stay on and go to England for a month or six weeks alone. Perhaps I'll be able to see you there then? I think I'll be visiting friends in Sussex, but staying mostly in London—and perhaps go to Edinburgh, since I have never seen it & want to.

I'm sending back the Chronology pages and I hope you can read my corrections. You have it mostly right, however. Somewhere along the line I had an Amy Lowell Travelling Fellowship and now I have a Chapelbrook—have had it for over two years but haven't been able to make any use of it yet. I'm also a member of the Institute of Arts & Letters—but I'm not sure of the date. Although I'm always grateful for all the money I've received—considering how little I have accomplished—I feel that none of these names and awards really means too much—however they'll help fill your page . . . I've answered your questions, too, in a garrulous way—a lot of what I've said you don't need at all, but I'll let it go because perhaps anything that contributes an "atmosphere" will help you with the writing? I am appalled at how narrow, petty, gloomy, masochistic, even, this kind of condensation of my "life" sounds—but of course I'm sure you know there's more to life than an outline!—This is just the sketchiest of armatures, really, leaving out so many friends, people, places, events—false beginnings, retreats, mistakes, and so [on].

Yes, quote my remarks on Darwin if you like. I think I said to you, when you asked about Dr. Williams, that one of his poems I admire is "Asphodel, that greeny flower . . ."? Well, I re-read it the other day and was surprised to see he mentions Darwin, too—not in my sense at all, but he says, "But Darwin / opened our eyes / to the gardens of the world . . ." I really just got off on Darwin because of my readings about Brazil when I first came here; his first encounter with the "tropics" was on the outskirts of Rio and a lot he says in his letters home about the city and country is still true. Then I became very fond of his writing in general—his book on Coral Island is a *beauty*, if ever you have a long stretch to read in,—specialized but beautifully worked out. It seems to me that in the world of hate and horror we all inhabit that contemporary artists and writers, some of the "action painters" (although I like them, too), the "beats," the wildest musicians, etc.—have somehow missed the point—that the *real* expression of tragedy, or just horror and pathos, lies exactly in man's ability to construct, to use form. The exquisite form of a tubercular Mozart, say, is more profoundly moving than any wild electronic wail *& tells more about that famous "human condition"* . . . But this is an idea it has probably been beyond my gifts to express in poetry.

I hesitate to suggest any reading to you since I know you must be burdened with lots of things—and perhaps you'd rather not get into such subjects—but I think that Arnold Hauser's "The Philosophy of Art History" in the chapter called "Psychoanalysis & Art", makes a lot of good clear points about romanticism, neurosis, what's neurotic & what isn't in art, and so on,—and the relationship of an artist's life to his work.

I feel rather foolish using all these words in any connection with myself. Imagine how it must have *felt* to be Tennyson, to be a "bard"—It is hard to know how one *should* feel certainly, and for me the solution most of the time has been to forget all about it. That is not altogether right—on the other hand I dislike very much the romantic self-pity and sense of privilege I feel in some poet friends.

(Forgive this typing—I have three machines of different ages—but even the newest is already rusting in this climate. Then when I switch from one to the other I make more mistakes than usual, too)

I hope you are feeling better. I'm having copies made of a few snapshots to send you next week—mostly Samambaia (that's the name of the place in Petrópolis—means "giant fern". The actual name of the hillside we're on is Sitio da Alcobaçinha, "Little Alcobáça"—that's a favorite name here, not original with us—after Alcobaça in Portugal.)—I am very fond of cats, too (I'm going through your last paragraph) and have always had them, even if they do give me asthma—a bit—dogs do too much to attempt. I'll send a picture of Tobias if I can find the negative—he's thirteen now, very handsome—also a clever if not very "good" Siamese, and a Bebe Daniels–style angora who recently died and was buried under the orange tree. I have cats in the country and birds in the city—practical solutions being best. I had a toucan, Sammy, for six years—(but in the country)—and a wonderful funny bird I adored, with eyes like blue neon lights and that huge beak. I'm fond of pets, and babies up till three . . . I say this because we have just had a friend with two little daughters, 11 months and 3 years, here all week, and so I know how demanding child-care is, & all about colds and shots and earaches, etc. The little one slept in my room and what I really liked best about her was the way she was quite willing to stay awake for hours in the middle of the night, standing up and chattering away at me agreeably. That's [indecipherable] age. After three comes an age I don't like—then they improve.

I am sorry I've been so slow replying—I should acknowledge your letters even if I can't answer them right away, so you'll know whether I got them or not, at least. We have just had two hours warning— ~~th~~ there'll be no water for 48 hours. This kind of thing is very common—at one point recently we had no water, no light, and no gas. The light was off for two hours only, *every night*, and since we were lucky enough to have an electric skillet we managed; until the gas co. strike was over—most of the wretched city ate cold food. But we'll be going up to Petrópolis for a long Easter weekend, thank heavens. It is incredibly beautiful here—and so hopeless—

imagine the million or more favela (slum) dwellers here these two days—
no water—all those babies. But I shouldn't add to your own troubles—
  Affectionately Yours—Elizabeth

I should say—I am quite looking forward to your book, now!

                                    Rio de Janeiro, April 8th, 1964
Dear Anne:
    It would add interest, certainly, to your book if you could have a foot-
note saying I'd been shot in the Brazilian Revolution of April Fools' Day,
1964—but I wasn't. We had forty-eight rather bad hours and then it was
all over much sooner than anyone had expected. My friend Lota was naturally very much involved, she and one other woman the only ones in the
siege of the Governor's "palace"—and I could get news of what was going
on there only by short wave occasionally since the President held all radio,
T V etc here in the city.—It was a tremendous relief when we finally learned
he had run away and all was over—The celebration, in the pouring rain—
the whole "revolution" took place in the rain—was a weird wet sight, with
paper, confetti, streamers, flags, towels, everything, *sticking*—& dancing
in bathing trunks, raincoats, with umbrellas, etc—I'll spare you the politics of it all; however, what I see from U S papers is half-wrong, as always—
    I hope you got a mass of rather uninteresting personal stuff that was
mailed to you about two weeks ago now—the mails have naturally been
worse than ever. If not, I'll send you most of it over again.
    I am going away, probably about May 20th, and probably first to Italy
for three weeks, then to England for a couple of months—I hope. I want
to go someplace where I can speak the language, more or less, and where
I think they care very little about Brazil and its politics—I'd like to forget
them both for a little while. Politics are scarcely my element, and here
we've heard absolutely nothing else for months—
    I'll give you an address in England as soon as I know one—and per-
haps you'll do the same? If you write me here again before I leave, it might
be a good idea to register the letter—or maybe that's just a Brazilian superstition I've acquired.—With kindest regards—
    Affectionately yours,
    Elizabeth

*Petrópolis, Sunday, April 12th? I received your letter of April 4th when I got here
yesterday for the week-end—Thank you so much for your kind invitations in England and I'm sure I'll take you up on one of them, at least—But I'll wait until I get
back to Rio tomorrow to answer you because I have no typewriter here and my writing,*

I know, is awful—Lota & I are going to Italy   —so I probably won't get to London until about June 20—not a good time, I know. I'll be visiting friends at Bexley Hill (near Petworth Sussex) for a while. - // The "revolution" now has a military junta—a middle-class revolution—Castelo Branco (the president until next year's election) has a good reputation—moderate, "liberal" (for here), honest,—& ironical—not rhetorical, at least—the new vice p. an old crook, alas.—But desperate measures had to be taken—

I wonder if you ever saw Randall J's <u>second</u> review of my book? He said some very acute things, I think—about painting, etc.

Rio, May 5th, 1964

Dear Anne:

In the midst of travel preparations I can't remember whether I answered your letter of April 4th or not—I *think* I did. And thanked you for your kind invitations? My addresses will be simply:

May 13th to June 13th—C/O American Express, Milan.

June 13th, August 1st—   "   "   " , London. *(Haymarket)*

In Italy I'll be in Florence a week, Venice a bit longer, and start and wind up in Milan—so that's the best general address. I am not sure exactly when I'll be staying in London, it depends on the friends I'm visiting, etc. But you could drop me a note there with telephone numbers, perhaps, and I'll get in touch with you? I hope you have a nice sea voyage—I'm returning by boat but wish I were going by boat, too.

Yesterday I received a letter from my aunt Grace (Mrs. William Bowers)—enclosing the letter you wrote to the Great Village "Chamber of Commerce." I'm awfully sorry it turned out that way. I know you were just doing your job and naturally tried to "check up" on the informations I've been writing you. But Great Village is so small there isn't any such thing as a Chamber of Commerce there, and everyone knows everyone else, of course. Whoever got your letter just handed it over to my aunt. She is almost eighty years old now (although the rest of her letter was all about her first trout fishing of the season) and apparently she was baffled and a bit put out—She has never wanted to discuss the past with me at all, although she was more concerned with my mother than anyone else, and I think now, almost fifty years later, she has almost succeeded in burying it completely. She was the only daughter of that family who "went back home;"* she married a farmer, a widower with eight children, produced three more of her own, and for many years has lived on the largest farm in N.S. (They

---

Arthur never left

used to raise trotting horses, among other things.) By now she has many grandchildren and dozens of step-grandchildren—and so has a great deal of "life" to have buried the past under.

I know you should be able to confirm my statements somehow but I honestly can't think how.

I'll answer your questions myself—but again, it's just my word for it! Long ago I used to try to get details from Aunt Grace but I never succeeded.—She is an active, strong, humorous woman, my favorite relative as I've already said—and she believes in living in the present. I think, too, like most families, mine has no idea that I could possibly have done anything that the rest of the world would be interested in—at least they apparently haven't thought much of my life and works since I went away to school! Aunt Grace has given me some information about the Bulmer family, what little I do know—she and the aunt I lived with—

Well—I'll answer for the "Chamber of Commerce" (if you could see the "Village" I think you'd be amused.)—and I wish I could think of an outside source for you . . .

My great-grandfather's (One of them) name was Robert Hutchinson. He was part-owner and captain of a brig or barque (I'm not sure which) that sailed out of G V when it was a ship-building place—hasn't been since the beginning of the century, probably.

Aunt Grace is the only real "Bulmer" left, there.—There is a sister-in-law, and some distant cousins live around there—There were five children, in this order: Maud, Arthur, Gertrude, Grace, and Mary. Aunt Mary lives in Montreal (Mrs. J.K. Ross),—the others you know about.

It has always been said that what set off my mother's insanity was the shock of my father's death at such an early age, and when they'd only been married three years. (He was 39 *she was 29*). It is the only case of insanity in the family, as far as we know. She had undoubtedly (*I* think) shown symptoms of trouble before—perhaps traits that in our enlightened, etc. days might have been noticed and treated earlier. As it was, she did receive the very best treatment available at that time, I feel sure. She was in McLean's Sanitarium outside of Boston* (you must have heard of that)—once or maybe twice. Aunt Grace herself went with her, and also, I think, though I'm not positive, took her to doctors in N.Y.—At any rate, the Bishop family "spared no expense." Since Aunt Grace was so involved with it all she naturally does not like to remember it, I suppose. That generation took insanity very differently than we do now, you know. *My father did not beat her* or anything like that—really! I am telling you the facts as I have always been given to understand them, and a lot I remember pretty well. (Of course I may have

Newton?

distorted it, but as I'm sure you know, children do have a way of overhearing *everything*.) The tragic thing was that she returned to N S when she did, before the final breakdown. At that time, women became U S citizens when they married U S citizens,—so when she became a widow she lost her citizenship. Afterwards, the U S would not let her back in, sick, and that is why she had to be put in the hospital at Dartmouth, Nova Scotia (across the harbor from Halifax). My Bishop grandfather tried for a long time to get her back in the US. One always thinks that things might be better now, she might have been cured, etc.—Aunt Grace suffered most of all because of it, and being the kind of woman she is, her technique is to bury it, not speak of it, etc.

Well—there we are. Times have changed. I have several friends who are, have been, will be, etc. insane; (I visited Pound many times) they discuss it all very freely and I've visited asylums many times since. But in 1916 things were different. After a couple of years, unless you cured yourself, all hope was abandoned—

I think that greatgrandfather was the only real "sea-farer"—the only one I know of. As I said, my mother's father ran the tannery for many years. His people were farmers from "River Philip" (wherever that is!—I just remember hearing that). One of his cousins, very rustic, used to appear once or twice a year when I was small, with gifts of bear meat and venison, in sacks in the back of the buggy.

If I can think of anyone I know now in G V who might help you I'll let you know—but it's a long time ago. And they really wouldn't understand your reasons, you know—

Well—*adiozinho*, as we say here—

Affectionately yrs, *Elizabeth Bishop*

P S. I don't know much about my father except that his remaining sister, my last "Bishop" relative, who died last year, was devoted to him, and so had been all my mother's side of the family, too. He was apparently quiet and gentle; I have a letter or two he wrote to my Bulmer grandmother, very funny and affectionate. He was tall and good-looking (neither of which characteristics he handed on to me). He liked to stay at home and read. Most of his books unfortunately were sold before I grew up, but I have a half-dozen or so. This week I have been reading his very elegant edition of "Stones of Venice", with his bookplate, given him by two of his sisters for Christmas, 1898. What a madman! (Ruskin, I mean, not my pa—)

I don't think I thanked you enough, really, for your invitations in England. I'll get there around June 14th, I think, although my dates are a bit vague. I am hoping Lota can come with me but I'm afraid she'll be flying back from Milan then—she can't leave her park; no one does any work when she's not on hand. I have a sailing back for August 1st, my comings and goings in England depend somewhat on some old friends I'm visiting, and I also want to get to Scotland for ten days, possibly.

I made a long automobile trip in Ireland long ago and had such a nice time I don't think I want to go back unless I can drive around again that way. It seems to be much more popular for tourists than it was when I went. I saw just about all the coastline except for Wicklow, I think—spent a couple of weeks in Dublin, etc.—

About Brazilian politics—I see I've ignored your remarks without meaning to, and I shouldn't have because people rarely take that much real interest in Brazil . . . There seems to be a tendency in the U S to take Brazilian leaders at their word—and their word, or words, for the last thirty years or so, haven't been worth a penny. ENCOUNTER sent me a pamphlet by John Strachey about "Democracy"—platitudinous and simple as it is (meant for broadcasting, perhaps) he does make intelligent distinctions about "democracy"—how there is really so very little of it, and that little pretty much confined to the U S, Britain, and France (he says). The U S—from the press—seems to feel that the last two presidents here were really, underneath, democrats and liberals trying to help the poor masses, etc.— and *were* held back by greedy Senators and an entrenched rich greedy aristocracy. Well, they couldn't be more wrong—but I've rarely been able to tell any American this, and have almost given up trying. One was a psychotic who had a breakdown—& this last was a crook.—I said several years ago he was closer to Jimmy Hoffa than anyone else—and my American friends thought I had turned "reactionary". He has now, thank heavens, been kicked out—and has taken a huge fortune with him, and left the biggest property in *land* ever acquired in South America (~~this~~ acquired by crooked deals, while he preached "land reforms")—probably to join Peron and Franco in Spain. This is the 1st time anything *quite* so corrupt has happened in this now thoroughly corrupt country; the Brazilians feel ashamed, and are, in general, determined to clean things up, I think. WE (US) urge "democracy" and "anti-communism" on them for years; the minute they act on this we again turn on them and accuse them of "witch hunting"! What do we want, I wonder. April 2nd (the Day After) an important man at the US Embassy met Lota on the street and said "*We don't like your revolution!*" (She had been in the Governor's palace for 48 hours, in some real danger—while the maid and I stuck it out here at the apartment, worrying about her—)

I'm glad I wasn't along because I really think I would have slapped him. Now the Americans are all talking in a superior way about "McCarthyism"—which is absurd, no matter what injustices—and there are some, undoubtedly—are being committed. In the 1st place this is *real*—(I actually met several of those Chinese spies, years ago now—& wrote my friends, who thought I was being *funny*) and in the 2nd, there's no McCarthy at all. The new government is honest, at least—Castelo Branco pretty bright, one gathers—for a general, amazingly bright—his new cabinet good, on the whole, too. But the mess is too great, the financial situation too hopeless, for any one government to clean it up. And though the entrenched aristocracy is pretty much a legend by now—there *are* "conservatives" who won't give up anything at all. The worst weakness of the so-called "right" (the terms we use make no sense here) is, even when well-meaning, the gap between classes here—and the horrifying lack of *feeling*.

Brazilians are not civic-minded, that's all.—Rich, religious, well-educated old families, living blameless, charitable lives by their lights, commit hideous cruelties without realizing it—sometimes just a matter of intonation. They don't like animals, don't understand "pets." They'll have three gardeners—a Picasso on the wall—a library in four languages—and throw the garbage out in the street. (As Picasso might, too!—It's something to do with being Latin, I'm afraid—and so many of the things I like them for have the same roots, it's hard to disentangle) They are mixtures of 17th century Portugal, "Victorian"-style 19th century family-life and sentiment, and contemporary industrialized man—this last a very small admixture that doesn't affect the "masses" much at all—To expect them to act—overnight—or react, like the U S A, or an American of the same social or financial standing, is plain silly.—I never in my previous life dreamed for a minute that I'd be *glad* to have an army take over—but I have been, here,—twice now—

You see, unfortunately (I often think) I am very much involved in politics here because of Lota.—It is such a small society and her family has been prominent in diplomacy etc for generations. Carlos Lacerda (you must have read of him, by now) is an old old friend of hers, and quite a good friend of mine, too—old neighbors in the country—She is working here at his request, and I suppose we are *for* him (he's running for President, and I hope wins)—in spite of many reservations, and his obvious faults.—This is a part of life I never would have had much of an idea of if I had stayed in the U S and just paid my taxes and voted, and never had come within miles of any of the real leaders.

"Industrialization" is inevitably the future for all these backward countries, no doubt. Since it is a choice of evils, apparently, for Brazil (I had hoped they'd find another, neutral way out, but I don't think they're strong enough to)—I'd much prefer the American variety to the Russian—which is all Russia amounts to any more, isn't it?

Carlos has been invited to England—he was so rude to the French (& very witty, too) that England immediately invited him over. Now if he'd only study British Trade Unions—but he probably won't!

Rio, April 10th, 1965

Dear Anne:

I suddenly have realized that more than a month has gone by—almost six weeks—since I wrote you and that I haven't heard from you. I wonder if my letter could have got lost?—or perhaps yours back did? . . . The "revolution" did improve the mails at first, but lately we have been losing things again—one I know of, coming from England a few weeks back—maybe your letter was in the same batch (I think they disappear in batches, and occasionally re-appear in batches, weeks later). I am packing up to spend a week or ten days in Petrópolis this morning and started putting your BOOK in my bag, when I remembered that I hadn't heard from you at all, and I thought how awful it would be if you hadn't received my first letter about it . . . Heavens—so much has been happening here lately, I hadn't realized just how long it had been. I do hope you haven't been worried or thought—oh dear—I didn't LIKE the book!

This is just a note—I'll write from the country. I did write and acknowledge the book and said I'd be sending you a long letter soon—well, the soon is now six weeks—but I'll get it off from Petrópolis. Just now all I'll say is (and if you got my letter forgive me for more or less repeating myself)—I know how hard you had to struggle, so I think perhaps you'll be surprised when I say my first impression was one of remarkable *freshness* and *spontaneity*. Compared to the other Twayne books I've seen, it sounds fresh, young, sensitive,—not a bit like those tired academics parading all their tired little theories and clichés.—It also sounded as if (or I *think* it did) you had really enjoyed some of my work—and I hope you did, and are not forever incapacitated from liking it again, after all your work. I liked the quotations (I'll write more about Wittgenstein to you someday) and delighted you dedicated it to Mark. It you have already received a letter saying all these same things, forgive me—and if you haven't, forgive the Post Office—and forgive me for letting so much time go by before it dawned on me I hadn't heard from you.

My "long letter"—is just a sheet or two of small corrections, all in the biographical part—nothing to do with the other parts. I must have written you awfully hurried and confused letters, like this one. The corrections are all just facts,* nothing to do with your interpretations (very nice) or opinions, etc.—I thought I'd better get them straight, since yours is the first book to publish them, and probably the last—dates, names, etc.—So please don't worry. And as I said before—congratulations on a really difficult piece of work well done. There was so little to say about me—and you did find enough, and said it awfully well—more later . . . Now I hope

* *about myself*

you haven't been sick, or your family hasn't, and that's why I haven't heard—and where is your book of poems? I am eager to see that.

Much love,
Elizabeth

Did the permission get cleared up? I wrote HM [Houghton Mifflin], and the agent—long ago now. The agent was also furious with HM—"absurd" he said.

> Here for a few days only—
> Ouro Prêto, Minas Gerais
> May 20th, 1965

Dear Anne:

I hope you can forgive my long silence, and I do hope I haven't held up the book or given you a lot of trouble about it . . . I really don't know why I found such difficulty writing about it, except that I don't seem to like to talk about myself any more. I am afraid you will think these many little corrections both finicky and egotistical. But you are the first person who has ever written any of this down, and you may well be the only one to, and so I'd really like to get the facts right, this once. I'm sure you can understand that feeling? They aren't important to anyone but me, really.—I must have written to you hastily and incoherently and now I am putting you to a lot of work, and I am really sorry.

Perhaps I'll mail off just this first page today and re-write the other corrections—all Chapter 1*—and mail them from Rio. I see I started to do this for you in *March* . . . I have never stalled so before. I really am dreadfully sorry.

You know, I didn't receive your letter written from the hospital—and I am sure now that you didn't get at least one of mine. I have lost a lot of letters lately—Write only to the Petrópolis address (oh—I think you already do that)—because I suspect I lose even more of those sent to Rio. Now I see that a month ago you said you'd write after you got properly moved, and I do hope *that* didn't go astray. I hope your new house is working out nicely—how very exciting, and send me a snapshot of it! Lota and I were supposed to go to Italy on May 2nd—and had to change our plans because of her job. I had thought I might get back to England just about the time I did last year. Now we are planning to go to Italy in late September or the first of October—but I must say it seems a bit doubtful to me, she is so busy with this last stretch of park-building.

---

*(your "opinions"! naturally, are all your own!)

I am sorry to hear about the miscarriage—and I've always been told by my friends that they have an awfully depressing after-stage. I wonder when your child & husband take off on their summers, and if you are really all alone in Cambridge? Where is Mark going? And what are you writing? Yes—please don't get a dog until I know when I am coming back!—unless you are just too lonely, or need a watchdog badly—Surely I could stay at some inn or other—only they're apt to have dogs, too, in England. I am trying to persuade Lota—to come to England with me—telling her London is the best place to shop in the world, because that's what she likes to do best—but so far I haven't had much luck.

I have been working away seriously at Wittgenstein, some every morning, after coffee, in bed,—and it still comes and goes, but I have found some wonderful paragraphs. I think the quotation you use at the beginning is splendid.

I've read your book through three times now, I think.—And, I think I told you—and hope it finally reached you—that my first impression was one of real freshness, spontaneity—and feeling how wonderful it is to have even one reader as good as you. Do you suppose there are any others—or even a few half as perceptive? The other Twayne books are academic-sounding—"competent", all done in the latest approved clichés—yours is very different, thank heavens, I think it must have been horrible to do—my life is so uneventful and I have done so very little, really—but you managed it, somehow. Lota read it, and said right away "This sounds as if she really liked your poetry." And I hope you did at the time, and are not forever incapacitated from doing in the future. [. . .]on Monday. Please do forgive me, once more—I feel very guilty about this slowness. I hope you're all well and will please write me again very soon—

Love,
    Elizabeth

INTRODUCTION
P iii, 5 lines from the bottom. Shouldn't <u>or</u> be left out?
P v: My grammatical mistake, pure carelessness. PLEASE change to "interpret exactly as he sees fit." Horrors.

CHRONOLOGY
1934 went like this: Met MM. Mother died. Graduated. And leave out Mary—we had been friends for three years, but she graduated in 1933, and other friends were more important to me. I'm afraid I sound a bit too friendless in this part and in chapter one—I really wasn't!

•

1939,—again, the emphasis seems a bit wrong. I had friends in N Y and in Key West. Loren MacIver, the painter, and her husband, Lloyd Franken-berg, stayed with me in K W, and through Loren I met the Deweys. Leave out Mrs. Hemingway here—we were closer friends in the later '40s.

1951—Academy Award earlier—a year before Bryn Mawr, I think, or 1 in the spring, other in the fall.

1952. Lota's name is Maria Carlota Costelat de Macedo Soares, no accent marks. But you don't need all that, just Lota de Macedo Soares. You could say "stopped over to visit friends in Brazil" (I had others beside Lota—I met several Brazilians in N Y during the war) "Had a violent allergic reac-tion to cashew fruit and had to give up trip to the Straits of Magellan." That is what actually happened. I hate "ill" and think it sounds too myste-rious, or neurasthenic. (See Chap 1, p 16, for the same thing. Couldn't you say there that I had asthma and bronchitis? Except for asthma, a hereditary tendency, I am really *very* healthy, and I think it is better to come out and say what ails one rather than give the impression one is a hypochondriac, or perhaps a dope-fiend . . .)

1952—"short stay" in N Y, rather than a "visit". I still feel like a New Yorker. I kept my garret in N Y all the time I was in Florida, too—so I could get back whenever I wanted to. I would now if I could afford it—

1961—yr. I went to the Amazon 1st (I'm going again next month). But I have traveled some almost every year I've been there.

1962—Chapelbrook Fellowship

1964—Book on architecture comes 1st; I worked on it in 1956. I wish you'd skip the translations. They amount to next to nothing, no real work, and no real interest. Or just say I have translated some prose & some poetry, from the Portuguese. I can't be considered a cultural go-between, *nor do I want to be.* The fact that I live in Brazil seems almost entirely a matter of chance . . . *perhaps not, but that's the way it seems to _me_.*

QUESTIONS OF TRAVEL is coming out in October, with Farrar, Straus & Giroux. Houghton Mifflin is bringing out a re-print (paper back) of the 1st 2 books, about now. Chatto and Windus is also bringing out another collection this year or next.

I am working on a book of prose pieces about Brazil,—places, mostly, with a bit on baroque churches, popular music, one or two life-stories,—maybe. This will be done in about a year or 18 months. At present I am using the title BLACK BEANS AND DIAMONDS:

> Petrópolis, this time—but Rio is the best
> address these days—
> November 14th, 1965

Dearest Anne:

You have been hiding your light under a bushel—at least as far as I knew. I am very much impressed with your book and think some of it is wonderful, and all good, and that you have enormous talent. Although I'd like to have seen some of these before, I also think you're wise to spring the whole book on people like that because it does make much more of an effect. and also shows character, *patience*, etc.—& patience particularly seems to be a necessary ingredient in writing poetry . . .

I hope you haven't been expecting to hear from me long before—I did stay in Minas for over two months to buy a completely unnecessary house, but a beauty—but this is a secret for a while, please. I'll tell you all about it later. Lota kept forwarding batches of letters she thought were important, but she didn't send books or magazines, etc., and then at the end she kept a lot of letters because I meant to leave, couldn't get a plane for a week because of the weather, etc. Your books (I got 2) had been unwrapped, so I don't know when they were mailed to me. So I'm sorry if I have been indifferent or impolite—

I hadn't any idea you could write such good poetry and it is such a nice surprise—however, I would have thought you'd write careful & beautiful poems, if you did write them—I just never dreamed of the number or the really high quality. It has really cheered me up a great deal when I rather needed a little cheering, too. I like very much: To My Daughter in a Red

Coat, (the last three lines are lovely); Fairy Tale; The Traveller (almost best of all, I think—more later); Nightmare in North Carolina; and the title poem—and lots of others, too, but those are my favorites so far. Why haven't I seen them, I wonder—well—I get Poetry but don't always read it carefully I'm afraid—and I used to get Paris Review but finally let it stop— and the others you acknowledge I don't see—that's why.

The Fullbright Prof. of American Lit. in Rio this year was so much taken with "The Travellers" he wants to put it in an anthology he and Donald Justice (??—I think—someone fairly well-known) are doing. His name is Mark Strand—you'll probably be hearing from him. He borrowed my 2nd copy to study and might like more *poems*. Also—while I'm on this promotion paragraph—Ashley Brown, one of the founders, and an advising editor still, on SHENANDOAH, thinks he would like to see some chapters of your book on me and perhaps—if Twayne agrees—one could be used in that magazine. It's Ashley Brown, 921 Gregg St., Columbia, South Carolina, 29201—if you want to write him. I have just sent him your address, too, so probably you'll hear from him, if you'd rather wait. He was the Fullbright Prof. here last year and we saw a lot of him—very intelligent—I may have mentioned him—I went to Bahia and Ouro Prêto, etc. with him—an excellent traveler. That would be a good place to send some poems, too, I think—send them c/o him *Shenandoah & mention me*—but then it is better, I suppose, to tackle the more famous ones first—Partisan, N Y Review of Books, Kenyon, or Hudson, etc.—or the New Yorker. (As you know perfectly well.)

"Harvard" is another one I like very much, too. "Winter", too— particularly the first stanza, very beautiful, I think. I realize I know much more of you now, reading that little note at the end, than I ever did before. (And you know so many boring and unnecessary things about me!)

I brought some letters up with me to answer today but don't seem to have one from you among them—and I'm not at all sure I really answered your last, that I received in Ouro Prêto, or not. I'll see when I get back Tuesday. And I'll try to write again soon. Such a lot of things accumulated because I stayed away so long. I am going to Seattle in January, or the end of December, to be a poet-in-residence for two terms—I've been shilly-shallying about this for a long time but finally made up my mind to mostly because I need the money to remodel my house! (1720–30—) supposed to have a treasure buried in the walls—well, I'll write you about it and send you a picture, too.

This is just to thank you very much for your book and to tell you I really like it very much and am deeply impressed. The poems are all honest and careful and yet have great feeling, I think—I trust them completely! I'm just sorry they didn't make a prettier book for you. Well, mine, that you may have received by now, is a bit too pretty, I'm afraid. I don't really like the drawing of me on the back, either—but publishers always insist so on photographs, and if not a photograph of one smoking into one's type-writer, a collection of mis-leading blurbs—so I decided this was more im-personal, since it doesn't look much like me, and also would please a lot of Brazilian friends. I'm afraid you'll find the contents only too familiar, and also very thin—it should be twice the size.

It is so beautiful here I can't imagine why I want *another* house. (Well, to save it, for one thing—it's falling down)—I think Mark would find my view almost Chinese in the ancient way—cascade and waterfall to the right, cov-ered rocks, semi-tropical trees, and a lot of blue agapanthus lilies to the left—all seen through a very fine rain *today*.

Please write me when you can—to Rio. I have to go back to Ouro Prêto for a week or two before Christmas, to get the work started on the house,—but I'll be in Rio most of the time until I leave now. I hope you are all well—how's the daughter?

With much love,
Elizabeth

Sometime I want to go into more <u>details</u>—

APPENDIX: EARLY PROSE

On Being Alone

Perhaps there are ghosts at school, or wicked wolves in hiding on the ridge, or evil spirits that dwell in the depths of the furnace room and grope their sinister way up through the pipes and into our rooms. But we have never seen them. We have lived for two seasons untouched by the slightest hint of the supernatural; there are no haunted houses in the immediate vicinity, and no neglected grave yards—scarcely even a blighted tree, in this spring term, or a barren field to hold before us a symbol of terror and death. Why is it then, when there is nothing to fear, and we have surely outgrown the bogies of our younger days, that so many of us seem to dread being alone? We say to each other, "I hate Sundays; there are so many quiet hours," or "It must be wonderful to have a room-mate, someone to talk to in study hour." All this is rather strange. Why does being alone, when we have a hundred companions most of the time, present such a great trial, or why should we wish to keep the conversation going so endlessly? The fear of a "quiet hour" alone is greater than the fear of all those innumerable quiet hours alone that are ahead of all of us.

There is a peculiar quality about being alone, an atmosphere that no sounds or persons can ever give. It is as if being with people were the Earth of the mind, the land with its hills and valleys, scent and music: but in being alone, the mind finds its Sea, the wide, quiet plane with different lights in the sky and different, more secret sounds. But it appears that we are frightened by the first breaking of its waves at our feet, and now we will never go on voyages of discovery, never feel the free winds that have blown over water, and never find the islands of the Imagination, where live who knows what curious beasts and strange peoples? Being alone can be fun; alone the mind can do what it wants to without even the velvet leash of sleep. But we can never understand this while we stand on the shore with our backs to the water and cry after our companions. Perhaps we shall never know the companion in ourselves who is with us all our lives, the nearness of our minds at all times to the rare person whose heart quickens when a bird climbs high and alone in the clear air.

1929

A Mouse and Mice

About a week ago there came a certain evening with a particularly long and quiet twilight—a dove-colored twilight, filled with shadow and the smoke of burning leaves. It was the kind of weather to make you forget a great many of the important things such as dates and the winds of last March and the snows of next February. You seemed at home, more or less, in the interior of a large and mist-grey pearl, and knew no more than that. Little things might seem of greatest importance if you lived inside a pearl, and so they were that evening of strange moment in the obscurities of half-light and quietness. The leaves hung asleep upon the trees dreaming themselves through death; the clouds lay low on the hill-tops, even on the roof-tops; color had fled beyond the sky forever with the smoke of the leaves' scarlet burning. All the world said softly yet without speech,

> Fear no more the heat o' the sun,
> Nor the furious winter's rages. . . .

Where a treetop touched the sky I saw a bat flutter out and downwards in a darkly diabolic circle over my head, and a little network of icy chills spread down my back. I felt myself a foreigner in a strange land, whose people I had never seen and whose language was too delicate for my human ears. It was the expectant moment before something happens, and just then in the dead, brown leaves at my feet, there was a movement and a rustle. It was a little mouse, small and long-tailed as a fairy mouse, on his way home from what tiny errand with the cornstacks and fallen apples? He was dressed completely in modest grey and his ears were quite large and petal-shaped. I walked behind him through the leaves while he ran nervously on ahead, occasionally looking at me over his shoulder with shining little black eyes. He was so small and yet so artistically perfect, so absorbed in his minute autumn world and its traffic with him. I followed him until he disappeared under the side of a building, and then I walked off, thinking of mice and their unknown ways. I pictured them en famille—

eating supper in one of their narrow dining rooms between our own, from a red check tablecloth; and father mouse in a tasseled nightcap pulling off his cat-skin boots with a faint sigh and calling it a Day. . . .

There is something about such creatures both amusing and strangely touching. In a certain mood, represented in its atmosphere by that clouded autumn evening, they can seem to be significant and even ominous. A cold, bony finger has been laid for a second at our lips—we look over our shoulders and think we may have laughed because we did not know. Perhaps the mouse's eyes, holding two almost invisible candle flames, can see more than we can. Perhaps they see the bat overhead and the mystery he traces in the dusk, the dead leaves decaying to the earth under our feet, and more that we can not see on the clearest of summer mornings. We become for the moment apprehensive of ourself and mice and our evanescent journeys to and fro.

"Sunt lacrimae rerum et mentem mortalia tangunt."

Well, such little things may take the place of punctuation marks in the world. The bat may stand for no more than a dot over an i, or an apostrophe on the wing ' And here is a whole family of mice , , , , , , , , , , , , , , , , ,

1929

The Thumb

Stanley first took me to see Sabrina one afternoon for tea. She had one of those silk-hung apartments, with sunlight coming in at the windows through pale lime-colored curtains, and clear fragrant tea running out of a silver teapot all day long, more or less. By some chance, perhaps because it was an unnaturally hot day for May, we were the only people there. I could see at once that she was beautiful, and I could feel at once, too, that she had another gift besides beauty. A sort of magnetism, I suppose. Anyway, it was a gift that made people willing to sit and drink tea all of a May afternoon, just for the sake of being near her. I'd known people like that before—some of them not beautiful, either—who had the trick of making the atmosphere of a room faintly exciting—charged with a bit of lightning, waiting for a sudden electric storm. Sabrina always had it with her—that was the trouble—it was there even when you didn't want it to be. Well—

She was quite a small woman, very little and light. "Small bones," you would say; or "Light as a feather." In the first moment I realized vaguely that her face was extraordinarily beautiful, and that she wore a dress colored like dim gold—gold under water, maybe. Then, because it's a sort of game I play with new people, I began to look at her very slowly, bit by bit, saving her face till the last. It took me quite a while to manage the tea-drinking and to look slowly enough so as not to appear rude, but Stanley saved me from having to talk much, and I kept quiet. Her feet were small and slender and her legs, and the line of her thigh was thin, too. She was pleasing to watch as she talked to Stanley—full of little motions and quick, almost nervous, gestures. Her left hand lay along her knee, her fingers pressed against the soft gold cloth. The hand was palely gold-colored, too, with a narrow wrist and delicate fingers. A civilized hand, you would call it, interesting to watch or touch. After a while I began to study her face, and I found in it the same color and fineness I had seen in her hand—a rather sophisticated face, gay yet quiet. If you could think of a Madonna whose face was thinner about the cheek and chin, with a look of humor and something subtly emotional about it—well, that would be Sabrina. Her eyebrows were straight across and black, her eyes were grey, and so was her hair—really I suppose it was brown—dove-brown, if there is any such color.

I began to enjoy the afternoon immensely. It was a delightful room and I felt slightly exhilarated, as if I were intoxicated on tea. Stanley had promised me that Sabrina could do a lot for me if I became friendly with her, and I seemed to be succeeding pretty well. She knew just about everyone, and though fortunately unliterary herself she really had quite a little influence—friends among all sorts of artists and writers. I began to be dangerously elated and I talked and laughed and brought out all my best conversational tricks. I pictured many more such afternoons to myself, maybe just Sabrina and me alone. She was beautiful enough, certainly.

Just as I had reached this pitch Sabrina turned to face me moving her body and placed her right hand on the left arm of her chair. I was watching her face and for a minute I was just conscious of the pale shape of her hand extending below the gold cloth. Then she suddenly lifted her fingers with one of her quick movements, and I quite involuntarily looked down at her hand. I had already noticed her left one—this appeared just the same hand, small and fine. Why did I keep on looking? There was something queer about that hand—I couldn't tell right away what it was. There was no mark, no deformity. Good God!—the woman had a man's thumb! No, not a man's,—a brute's—a heavy, coarse thumb with a rough nail, square at the end, crooked and broken. The knuckle was large. It was a horrible thumb, a prize fighter's thumb, the thumb of some beast, some obscene creature knowing only filth and brutality. . . .

Well, I looked away very quickly and attempted to think of something light, something joking to say. But I was horrified. In the midst of that charming, sunny room, that friendly atmosphere, I was frightened. Something mysterious and loathsome had crept out of the night and seized me as I sat there drinking tea. Lord! and there I'd been—all ready to fall in love with the woman. I might even now; I still looked at her face and admired, although I could feel the perspiration of fear on my forehead. I tried not to look again, but I couldn't keep my eyes turned away from her hand, as it lay there innocently enough on the chair arm. Was it my imagination? I looked—and saw on the back of the thumb, where it lay in the sunlight, there was a growth of coarse, black hairs. . . .

Finally Stanley said that it was time for us to leave. I stood up and my knees felt as if I had been sick and in bed for a week. Sabrina was smiling and I knew I could not keep myself from smiling back, from responding to her beauty. For a second there seemed to me something corrupt about that beauty. What was that phrase? "Flowers of Evil"—yes. And yet when I

looked into her eyes I found my sinister thoughts denied and made ridiculous. "Will she shake hands?" I thought. "She didn't when we came,
maybe she won't now. I simply can't." But Sabrina smiled and held out to
Stanley her left hand, as a French woman does. It must have been her
custom because he took it naturally enough and I did as he had done,
bowed over her left hand, while her right hung at her side. She asked us
to come again and Stanley accepted for us while I stood with my eyes fixed
on her face, or Stanley's face, anywhere except down at her right side,
frantically longing to be gone.

However, I went back again, like a fool, led on by that woman's un-
imaginable beauty and personality—and the thumb, too, for all I know,
though I certainly tried to forget it. I felt that I had been wrong if I thought
there was anything unnatural about Sabrina. Surely she was no more than
she seemed—a charming, intelligent woman who had the misfortune of
one ugly thumb. We talked so well together; we were, or might have been,
so much at our ease. "Damn that thumb," I thought, "I'm going to see as
much of her as I can and maybe I'll forget it."

But it wouldn't work. Every time I saw her I felt more and more a peculiar shivering fascination that made me look down at her hand, to those
lovely fragile fingers and that horrible misshapen thing that was one of
them. Yet I couldn't blame her. She was the most natural thing in the world—
the trouble must be with myself. Some morbid streak in my imagination,
I supposed, something that took the slightest suggestion of horror and
magnified it until my whole mind was filled with awful thoughts and dark
shadows. "Now this time see that you don't get theatrical," I would say. Then
I would sit beside Sabrina, just she and I alone, and I would begin again
that struggle against the insidious spirit that seemed to overcome me when
I was with her. I thought of dreadful things—if she should be in an accident, if something should happen so that her thumb would have to be
taken off. I might have fallen in love with her—I surely would have, had not
all my emotions been so bewildered and fevered with horror. I had never
touched her in any way except always, at leaving, that slight pressure of
her left hand. My mind dwelt upon what it would be like to touch her—to
take that hideous hand and hide it in my own. I realized that all this was
bound to lead me into something wrong, but I couldn't seem to escape it.
I kept on going to see her, knowing every time that sooner or later I would
yield to my curious desire and touch that thumb—and I hardly cared what
might happen when I did.

She asked me to see her more and more often and at last I realized
that whatever was the meaning of my tangled emotions about her, she was
in love with me. I couldn't talk to her so easily after that and there used to
be long silent places in our conversations. She would sometimes look at

me with a sad, almost frightened look, and then I would swear at myself and wonder why in Heaven's name I didn't leave her as gracefully as I could and never come back. But there I would sit and brood, as if bound fast in some black prison, my eyes half turned away from her right hand which lay in the folds of her dress.

One afternoon in September I went to see Sabrina for the last time. She was in the same room where I had first seen her—the room hung with silk and lime-colored curtains, with a pale, soft sunshine coming in at the windows. She had on the same golden dress, and I'd truly never seen anyone look so beautiful as she did. She sat there, quiet and somehow arranged, with her hands in her lap. I was making desperate efforts to keep hold of myself, but every second I could feel a dark, choking rush of something—rage—madness—I don't know what, rushing up from those unholy wells I guessed were in my heart. I sat quite near her. I longed to ask her to forgive my silence, to explain the thing—I thought that then I might have sat beside her calmly and have forgotten the old fear. I had just about decided to, when she moved so that her right hand was in the light, right under my eyes. I felt myself staring, but I couldn't stop. Her thumb, that heavy, horrible thumb—it was a monstrosity. I put out my hand slowly and laid my fingers across the back of her hand. It was cool and soft—and then I felt that rough, swollen knuckle, those stiff, coarse hairs against my palm. I looked at Sabrina quickly and I found that she was looking at me with a peculiar tender look in her eyes and what I could only describe as a simper across her mouth. I have never felt the disgust, the profound fear and rage of that moment. She thought—well—she thought I was going to tell her I loved her.

I suppose that anyone except a fool, that is except myself, would have escaped forever from the dread and disgust of that moment. I suppose that anyone else who had seen that look in Sabrina's eyes and that emotion so unconcealed upon her face would have been—delighted. I don't know. I can't even find the right words for my own feelings or an apology for my actions. Perhaps it was because I suddenly felt tired, sick to death of the whole affair. I've argued it out over and over again and pictured the whole thing, but I can't make the ending any different. "Ridiculous," you say, "morbid." Anyway, I got up and left her without a word and I never went back.

1930

Then Came the Poor

Giving a glance around the room, father visibly and carefully braced himself with his left hand on the table, trembled his right hand holding the telephone, and thrust his face forward courageously. He would have paled if he could, but that was out of the question and he just grew a shade more self-consciously red.

Mother was torn between a desire to whimper and an admiration for and desire to imitate father's manly attitude.

"Keep quiet, Lil," he said over his shoulder in a whisper, "it's Jim."

I could hear my Uncle Jim's voice, roaring and excited, apparently saying the same thing over and over. My two brothers were each smoking a pipe and eyeing each other appraisingly. George, the eldest, carried it off better; he leaned against the mantle with the air of one who is about to say "Yes, sir, it's a very serious proposition . . ." My two sisters were being nonchalant and earnest in turn, Myrtle all dressed up in embroidered Chinese pajamas, the pinkness of her ankles showing that she'd just had a bath; and Alison in evening clothes, with her fur coat still around her. It was almost one o'clock—this would be the last message we'd get tonight. There'd been a telegram about an hour ago; I held it in my hand and read it over and over.

REDS WIN DAY SULLIVAN AND KROWSKI SHOT THREE THOUSAND HEADED EAST VACATE OR OFFER NO RESISTANCE ELIOT MAY HOLD YET GENERAL MACLAUGHLIN.

I wondered how the Western Union happened to be still working. The telephone company had stopped running two days ago and Uncle Jim was talking over our private wire from his house down at the Neck, about twelve miles away. Among the throaty telephone sounds there was one with a hiss to it, which I recognized as—*Nerissa*, the name of Uncle Jim's yacht.

"Yes, Jim, yes—we can make it. We'll be there. You've saved our lives. . . .

I say, you've saved our lives." Father hung up dramatically. I shut my eyes, knowing the My God that was coming. It would be such a poor substitute for the expression father needed, a wooden doll in the garments of Lady Macbeth. "Now I bet he wishes he'd saved it," I thought.

"My God," said father. (Better than I expected.) "It's all up. MacLaughlin got stabbed, Jim says; one of his own men and half of them gone Red. They're turning every minute. We've all got to get out, Lil. Clear out and get up to Canada if we can. Jim's got the *Nerissa* ready and we've got to get down there before it gets light. Let's see, that gives us about four and a half hours.

"My God, (father put his arm around mother) Jim says the Slaters are all murdered, Lil. They set fire to their house. Thank God we have the *Nerissa*."

My family all stood awkwardly, looking around as if for the best thing to carry off first, and with a shade of satisfaction because we had the *Nerissa*. I remembered that the crew had all deserted a couple of weeks ago, when the servants left, but then Uncle Jim was a fair navigator.

Mother shook off father's arm. "New England Ancestry" was suddenly written all over her. She made straight for the dining-room and the spoons. Myrtle began to cry but father stopped that. "You girls go and get dressed warmly," he said, "good substantial clothing. George and James, go down to the garage and drive the cars around front. I'll drive the Packard, you take the little Buick with the silverware, and you take the beach wagon. A lot of things will go in that."

The famous MacLaughlin couldn't have arranged better.

Father began piling things in the front hall. I'd often wondered what rescuing things from a fire would be like and now I was finding out in a much cooler, probably more leisurely way. I looked around for something to save and remembered the old banjo clock in the dining-room. Mother was tying up the green felt rolls of silver in a set, mechanical way, and didn't even look at me. I climbed up on a chair, lifted the clock off its hooks and carried it out to the hall to add it to father's mounting pile. Just as I got there it slipped and fell with an awful crash onto the marble floor. The case cracked, the glass broke, there were several snaps and whirrs from the inside, and it stopped going.

"Please be careful, dear," Mother's voice said the familiar phrase unconsciously, while the rapid laying out of silver never stopped. I checked an hysterical laugh, gave up all thought of doing anything to aid the exodus and walked in to the small Louis Quinze parlor off the hall.

It was very dark in there, just a long rectangle of light from the doorway to the wall on the other side, one gilt chair standing in it, the corner of a gilt table, the final flounce of a brocaded shining curtain. I stepped across this alleyway of glitter into the dark and sat down on a small satin sofa over in the corner. I heard two cars drive up and stop; I heard mother shout to father.

"George! the wall-safe in my room! My jewel box and papa's watch and Lizzie's miniature. Oh, and the children's pictures—"

"I've already got them, Lil. What about the chandelier? D'you suppose we could manage it? In the beach wagon . . ."

"What are you going to wear, Alison?" my sister shouted. "What about a ski-suit?"

My whole family might have been getting ready for some wonderful picnic or party. And yet they were scared. I wasn't scared, as I might have been about a picnic or party, but as I usually did, I decided to stay at home. I'd be damned if I'd go with them and the cousins on the old *Nerissa*. I wouldn't be brave and martyred and a gentleman till the last. Surely there was some place around the estate to hide out in; and anyway I wanted to see what they'd do to the place, the three thousand who were coming.

Well, I sat there for a long time and finally I had to go out because my brother George suddenly started walking around the house shouting my name. I went out into the hall grabbing a pair of little gilt statues, Adam and Eve, off a table as I went to serve as some sort of excuse for my disappearance. All the family was out there. Most of the pile of stuff had been stowed away in the cars except for some stray objects that were of an awkward size, or had been broken, or had turned out to be not very valuable after all. Mother's favorite white alabaster lamp lay broken in three pieces; two chairs stood in attitudes almost social and conversational, there was an awful mess of tramped-on table-linen, and strangest of all a dish of small red roses, tipped over, with the water spilling out in a long thin stream towards the broken lamp, and the green leaves lying flat to the floor as if exhausted.

We all looked at each other like a group of thieves or house-breakers. Father said "Are you all set, Lil?" and mother answered "Yes, let's get away, George. I'm getting nervous," and she began to cry.

I stared around at my brothers and sisters. Myrtle had actually put on the ski-suit—a bright red one. "Aren't you being a little ironic?" I asked her, and she glanced down at herself and frowned slightly, looking worried. Alison was draped in black, and wore a large black hat, that she rather fancied as making her look glamorous, I knew. George wore, yes actually, khaki shorts and heavy wool socks. "Good Lord," I thought, "nothing will persuade me to go with this party of sentimentalists."

"What about getting all the old port up?" asked father.

"Oh come on, father, the *Nerissa* isn't the Ark. Let's get going," George growled at him.

I found myself saying, as if in a dream, "I think I'll stay here."

My family's mouths fell open with one gesture, as automatic as so many steam-shovels. Then they all began to shout at me, and to tell each other that the fear and strain had gone to my head. I'd be shot, stabbed, crucified. . . . I should have been dragged along willy-nilly, another wealthy refugee, only just then, far off to the west came a tremendous explosion. The house shook. My family made for the door, George helping mother politely by the elbow. I noticed that father, who was wearing a golfing cap, picked up a derby from the table near the door and carried it off with him. It was still dark out, but the cars' lights were off. Father and mother and Myrtle piled into the already loaded Packard; James and Alison got into the Buick, (a large globe of the heavens and the handle of a vacuum cleaner stuck out of the rumble seat) and poor George drove off by himself in the beach wagon looking very Boy-Scoutish. I suppose each thought I was in another car.

I wandered around the house, turning on all the lights and putting up all the window-shades in each of the thirty-nine rooms. "Pardon me if my preparations are rather hasty," I addressed the approaching three thousand. In the drawing room, father had apparently tried to get the beautiful crystal chandelier off the ceiling. It lay all sprawled out on the floor like a monstrous frozen polyp and the whole surface of the floor glittered with iridescent particles. At the foot of the kitchen stairs I came upon grandpa's watch and Aunt Lizzie's miniature, both smashed. In the library a lot of books had been taken off their shelves and piled about on the floor. "A good chance to try out those 'Books I'd take to a desert island' lists" I thought. It was about four o'clock. I took a package of cigarettes and some matches out of a box in the library and went out, leaving the front door open.

Down in the meadows it gradually got to be daylight. I kept my back to the west and tried to concentrate on watching the sun come up. I didn't know exactly what I was going to do, but at least I was glad I'd stayed behind. All those things. . . . If they did get to Canada what on earth would they do with them? I felt helpless, but not much afraid. The house looked strange up there, all the lights in the top story shining out in the morning twilight. It looked not as if it were separate rooms, separately lighted, but just a sort of perforated shell, enclosing a star or a sun. It was off the highway—maybe the three thousand wouldn't get to it. But then father was well known, a Big Man, and they would probably want to ransack it— and kill me if they caught me? The sun came up and it got a little warmer. Finally I fell sound asleep.

When I woke up it must have been ten o'clock. Faint cheerings and shoutings were coming from the house. I peered up cautiously and to my surprise there were actually three men standing on the roof of our house, shouting a song for all they were worth. One of their army songs, I suppose; anyway it sounded like the crazy ending of a comic opera. All I could see was the roof tops, but I could hear an uproar of shouts and yells and singing with an occasional crash or thud. No shots, however.

I made my way around and up the hill to the stables without being seen and slipped in. I hunted around and sure enough there were some old pairs of overalls left by the stable-boys; a lot of old clothes in fact. I threw away my coat and pants and put on a pair—I looked messy enough, anyway, after sleeping in the grass down there.

"Well, they've found father's cellar, all right," I thought, listening.

A wild, magnificent lawn-party was going on. There seemed to be about fifty people: men, women, and children, all rushing around calling to each other, and engaged in preparing a kind of grand breakfast. They'd put all our tables together in a big horse-shoe under the trees, and covered them with our table-linen (stamped here and there with black footprints). There was a great fire of coals, and four men were cooking over it, coffee and bacon and eggs. Apparently they mistrusted our electric range. Women were running in and out of the house with bread, fruit, glasses, boxes of cigars, everything they could find that might be of use to a banquet. Corks were popping out of bottles, peaceful little explosions right and left, and a few men were already lying around drunk. I went up to the men who were doing the cooking.

"Some place, ain't it, buddy?" one of them said to me. "Been in the house yet?"

I said I hadn't, but I thought I'd take a look, and strolled in the front door. In the hall two women were fighting over the remains of a roasted chicken, both pulling. The marble floor was greasy and muddy; the red roses were ground to a pulp by now. People were coming and going in excited groups, pointing and grabbing and exclaiming, some of them dressed in fantastic costumes put together from the wardrobes of my departed family. It was an hilarious affair. I felt like the host of a house party whose guests had gone mad, which was, nevertheless, a great success.

From father's large bathroom came loud laughter, splashings and slappings. I looked in and discovered two naked men jumping in and out of the shower and bath, throwing powder and bathsalts at each other, spitting shining spouts of water out the window into the sunlight and onto their amused friends below.

In the drawing room there was an old lady sitting on the floor in a ring of dirty petticoats. She was carefully unhooking the cut glass pendants from the chandelier. One by one she held them up to the sunlight and admired the rainbows they made on the wall, then hung them on some part of her clothes or person. She was bedecked and a'dazzle from top to toe.

In mother's French bed, canopied with lime colored satin, someone had put two filthy babies to sleep. . . .

I went out again to join the breakfast party, toasting each other madly and throwing bottles over trees and chimneys. "What'll you have, kid?" they yelled at me. I saw a bottle of champagne. "Champagne," I said, pointing.

"Aw, champagne? That stuff's no good. Just like pop. . . . Have some real stuff, buddy. Have a man's drink. Have some whiskey."

After a while they began to make preparations for some sort of lot drawing. I couldn't make out quite what it was all about. Everyone wrote his or her name on a slip of paper and dropped it in our large silver coffee urn. Then one of them, a leader, got up, closed his eyes elaborately and drew some of the slips.

"William Brinker!"

A fat, tow-headed man, about forty, got up and essayed a bow, grinning. Everyone cheered, clapped him on the back, offered him a drink. He made his wife and four tow-headed children stand up, too, all smiling and bowing in a row.

"Minna Schlauss!"

Minna was young but enormous. So stormy was her black, wiry hair and general determinedly uncouth appearance that I thought at once of Beethoven. She had two ancient men in charge, her father and his brother they must have been, and her mother was the old lady whom I'd found decorating herself with crystals from the chandelier.

"Jacob Kaffir!"

And then an amazing little man stood up. He was exactly the color of a well used penny and he wore a small moustache and, of all things, a fez. He received his applause shyly, but with delight, and made a timid, sweeping bow.

Somebody remarked, "But he ain't got any children." . . .

Somebody else said, "What'll he do with all them rooms?"

It dawned on me what this mysterious drawing of lots meant. They were portioning out our house, and three families, probably more, were to live in it. (For half a second I imagined father and mother and my four brothers and sisters returning, with a sigh, from Canada and being met by William, Minna, and Jacob. . . .)

"Get somebody else, Jakie," they were saying, "A couple more single guys like you. That'll even it up all right."

I caught Jacob's eye and smiled as hard as I could, raising my forefinger like a man saying "One, next the wall," in a restaurant.

"Him!" Jacob shouted. "He live with me. O. K. to you?"

"You bet," I said. "Well it may be sort of fun for a while," I thought.

Apparently Jacob had the same idea. "We'll have fun, huh?" he said, waving an empty bottle at me, and he gave me a wink I could almost hear. "Seems like home already, don't it."

1933

From "Time's Andromedas"

Now Time's Andromeda on this rock rude . . .   —Gerard Manley Hopkins

One afternoon last fall I was studying very hard, bending over my book with my back to the light of the high double windows. Concentration was so difficult that I had dug myself a sort of little black cave into the subject I was reading, and there I burrowed and scratched, like the Count of Monte Cristo, expecting Heaven knows what sudden revelation. My own thoughts, conflicting with those of the book, were making such a wordy racket that I heard and saw nothing—until the page before my eyes blushed pink. I was startled, then realized that there must be a sunset at my back, and waited a minute trying to guess the color of it from the color of the little reflection. As I waited I heard a multitude of small sounds, and knew simultaneously that I had been hearing them all along,—sounds high in the air, of a faintly rhythmic irregularity, yet resembling the retreat of innumerable small waves, lake-waves, rustling on sand.

Of course it was the birds going South. They were very high up, a fairly large sort of bird, I couldn't tell what, but almost speck-like, paying no attention to even the highest trees or steeples. They spread across a wide swath of sky, each rather alone, and at first their wings seemed all to be beating perfectly together. But by watching one bird, then another, I saw that some flew a little slower than others, some were trying to get ahead and some flew at an individual rubato; each seemed a variation, and yet altogether my eyes were deceived into thinking them perfectly precise and regular. I watched closely the spaces between the birds. It was as if there were an invisible thread joining all the outside birds and within this fragile net-work they possessed the sky; it was down among them, of a paler color, moving with them. The interspaces moved in pulsation too, catching up and continuing the motion of the wings in wakes, carrying it on, as the rest in music does—not a blankness but a space as musical as all the sound.

The birds came in groups, each taking four or five minutes to fly over;

then a pause of two or three minutes and the next group appeared. I must have watched them for almost an hour before I realized that the same relationships of birds and spaces I had noticed in the small groups were true of the whole migration at once. The next morning when I got up and went to the window they were still going over, and all that day and part of the next whenever I remembered to listen or look up they were still there.

It came to me that the flying birds were setting up, far over my head, a sort of time-pattern, or rather patterns, all closely related, all minutely varied, and yet all together forming the *migration*, which probably in the date of its flight and its actual flying time was as mathematically regular as the planets. There was the individual rate of each bird, its rate in relation to all the other birds, the speed of the various groups, and then that mysterious swath they made through the sky, leaving it somehow emptied and stilled, slowly assuming its usual coloring and far-away look. Yet all this motion with its effect of precision, of *passing* the time along, as the clock passes it along from minute to minute, was to result in the end in a thing so inevitable, so absolute, as to mean nothing connected with the passage of time at all—a static fact of the world, the birds here or there, always; a fact that may hurry the seasons along for us, but as far as bird migration goes, stands still and infinite.

Gerard Manley Hopkins

Notes on Timing in His Poetry

It is perhaps fanciful to apply the expression *timing* to poetry—race horses, runners, are timed; there is such a thing as the timing of a crew of oarsmen, or a single tennis-stroke—it may be a term only suited to physical motions. But as poetry considered in a very simple way is motion too: the releasing, checking, timing, and repeating of the movement of the mind according to ordered systems, it seems fair enough to admit that in some way its discipline involves a method of timing, even comparable to that used for literal actions. For me at least, an idea of *timing* in poetry helps to explain many of those aspects of poetry which are so inadequately expressed by most critics: why poets differ so from each other; why using exactly the same meters and approximate vocabularies two poets produce such different effects; why some poetry seems at rest and other poetry in action. Particularly in referring to Father Hopkins, the most intricate of poets technically and most taxing emotionally, does some such simplified method of approach seem necessary.

The most general meaning of *timing* as applied to any particular physical activity is co-ordination: the correct manipulation of the time, the little duration each phase of the action must take in order that the whole may be perfect. And the time taken for each part of an action is decided both by the time of the whole, and of the parts before and after. (This sounds involved, but can be made quite clear, I think, by picturing for a minute a crew of men rowing a shell, and considering the enormous number of tiny individual motions going to each stroke, to each man, and the whole shell.) The whole series together sets up a *rhythm*, which in turn enables the series to occur over and over again—possibly with variations once it is established.

Just so in poetry: the syllables, the words, in their actual duration and their duration according to sense-value, set up among themselves a rhythm, which continues to flow over them. And if we find all these things harmonious, if they amalgamate in some strange manner, then the *timing* has been right. This does not mean that a monotonous, regularly beating meter means good timing—duration of sense and sound each play a part, I believe, nearly equal, and *sense* is the quality which permits mechanical irregularities while preserving the unique feeling of timeliness in the poem.

I suppose that the most characteristic feature of Hopkins' poetry is that a great part of it is in "sprung rhythm." Such a departure from the verse traditions of three hundred years must be indicative of a desire or necessity of expressing different sorts of rhythm, involving different sorts of timing from those we find in other poetry. I cannot go into a full explanation of "sprung rhythm" here—both because it is a complicated subject and because I don't know enough about it,—but enough must be said so that the importance of its *timing* and its resultant peculiarities may be illustrated. (For simple explanations of sprung rhythm see Hopkins' own Preface to his poems, and Chapter VI, *The Craftsman*, in his biography by G. F. Lahey, S.J.) The most obvious thing about it is that the stress is considered as always falling on the first syllable of the foot, and the foot may be monosyllabic or followed by one, two or three weak syllables—even a greater number for special effect. The rhythm is thus unified, but mixed, and flexible, something in the manner of the Greek "logaoedic." In ordinary running rhythm we are accustomed to the variation of reversed feet, dactylls, etc., which if repeated gives us the effect of counterpointing— the original rhythm running underneath the superimposed rhythm. In "sprung rhythm" the rhythm felt corresponds to that of the counterpointing in running rhythm—minus the original underlying rhythm. It must be added, too, that all feet are assumed to be of equal length or strength, and the inequalities common to English are naturally made up by pause or stressing, according to the sense, or indication.

From this much I think it is evident that verse based entirely upon sprung rhythm, or sprung and running rhythms mixed, will have a very different quality about its co-ordination—maintaining the rhythmic beat customary to poetry, with an enormous increase in the variations possible for setting it up. Take, for example, the first lines of Hopkins' well known sonnet "God's Grandeur," in ordinary running rhythm:

> "The world is charged with the grandeur of God.
> It will flame out like shining from shook foil;
> It gathers to a greatness like the ooze of oil
> Crushed. Why do men then now not reck his rod?"

and compare it with the last lines, in sprung rhythm, of the amazing "Windhover":

> "No wonder of it: sheer plod makes plough down sillion
>   Shine, and blue-bleak embers, ah my dear,
>   Fall, gall themselves, and gash gold-vermillion."

To show pictorially the versatility of feet in sprung rhythm, here is the scansion of the three lines:

$$u/{-}u\ u\ u/{-}/{-}u/{-}u/{-}u/$$
$$-u/{-}u/{-}u/{-}u/{-}/$$
$$-/{-}u\ u\ u/{-}/{-}u/{-}u/$$

   The difference in movement between the two quotations is plain to see; and yet I think the reader feels exactly as much unity in the rhythm of the latter, the same wholeness (even intensified) that he gets from the broken iambics of the more conventional sonnet. The action pulls more ways at once; new muscles are touched and twinged, and the interrelations of stressed and slack syllables knit the poem more closely since they refer us not alone to a general meter but to other particular feet. For example, the foot—u u u which occurs in the first and last lines quoted. The lines have said themselves exactly with that poise I label *timing*, and there has been more action compacted into the lines by reason of the use of sprung rhythm.

   One license allowed by sprung rhythm becomes, through Hopkins' use of it, almost an elucidation of timing and a proof of its existence and excellence. That is the possibility of *hangers* or *outriders*: unaccented syllables added to a foot and not counting in the scansion—placed in such a way that the ear recognizes them as such and admits them, so to speak, under the surface of the real meter. An example of this is found in the second line of the above quoted "Windhover."

> "I caught this morning morning's minion,
>   kingdom of daylight's dauphin, *dapple-dawn-
>   drawn-Falcon, in his* riding . . ."

Here the timing and tuning of sense and syllable is so accurate that it is reminiscent of the caprice of a perfectly trained acrobat: falling through the air gracefully to snatch his partner's ankles he can yet, within the fall, afford an extra turn and flourish, in safety, without spoiling the form of his flight.

   Hopkins' abundant use of alliteration, repetition, and inside rhymes are all characteristics which place firm seals upon his words, joining them, at the same time indicating the sound relationships in the same way that guide lines, or repeated forms might, in a drawing. Excess of these poetic tricks in ordinary meter produces often the rhythmical vulgarity of much of Swinburne; in Hopkins' their frequent combination with an intricate sprung rhythm keeps them subtle, in various lights and shades of rhythmical importance. Listen to the ending of "That Nature is a Heraclitean Fire."

> "In a flash, at a trumpet crash,
> I am all at once what Christ is, since he was what I am, and
> This Jack, joke, poor potsherd, patch, matchwood,
>   immortal diamond,"

The first aspect of *timing* I have been talking about might be defined paradoxically as the accuracy with which poetry keeps up with itself. There is perhaps yet another element helping to bring about this result of co-ordination, an element depending very much on the individual poet and working for the perfecting of the poem generally, not alone in respect to timing. Perhaps I should not attempt to bring it in here, only considering the sustained emotional height of most of Hopkins' poetry, and the depth of the emotional source from which it arises, I believe it is important to try to express, however inadequately, the connection between them. A poem is begun with a certain volume of emotion, intellectualized or not according to the poet, and as it is written out of this emotion, subtracted from it, the volume is reduced—as water drawn off from the bottom of a measure reduces the level of the water at the top. Now, I think, comes a strange and yet natural filling up of the original volume—with the emotion aroused by the lines or stanzas just completed. The whole process is a continual flowing fullness kept moving by its own weight, the combination of original emotion with the created, crystallized emotion,—described by Mr. T. S. Eliot as "that intense and transitory relief which comes at the moment of completion and is the chief reward of creative work." Because of this constant fullness each part serves as a check, a guide, and in a way a model, for each following part and the whole is weighed together. (This may explain why last lines in poetry are so often best lines; and why, often too, they seem so concocted and over-drawn for the rest of the poem—those were composed separately, without the natural weight of the creation of the rest of the poem behind them.)

One stanza from "The Wreck of the Deutschland" illustrates this perfectly, with its mounting grandeur and partly self-instigated growth of feeling:

> "I admire thee, master of the tides,
>   Of the Yore-flood, of the year's fall;
> The recurb and the recovery of the gulf's sides,
>   The girth of it and the wharf of it and the wall;

Stanching, quenching ocean of a motionable mind;
Ground of being, and granite of it: past all
      Grasp God, throned behind
Death with a sovereignty that heeds but hides, bodes but abides."

II

So far I have meant by *timing* some quality within the poem itself; now I wish to take the same expression and use it in a different way, for a different thing. A man stands in a shooting gallery with a gun at his shoulder aiming at a clay pigeon which moves across the backdrop at the end of the gallery. In order to hit it he must shoot not at it directly but a certain distance in front of it. Between his point of aim and the pigeon he must allow the necessary small fraction of space which the pigeon will cross in exactly the same amount of time as it will take the bullet to travel the length of the shooting gallery. If he does this accurately the clay pigeon falls, and his *timing* has been correct. In the same way the poet is set on bringing down onto the paper his poem, which occurs to him not as a sudden fixed apparition of a poem, but as a moving, changing idea or series of ideas. The poet must decide at what point in its movement he can best stop it, possibly at what point he can manage to stop it; i.e., it is another matter of timing. Perhaps, however, the image of the man in the shooting gallery is incorrect, since the mind of the poet does not stand still and aim at his shifting idea. The cleavage implied in the comparison is quite true, I think—anyone who has even tried to write a single poem because he felt he had one somewhere in his head will recognize its truth. The poem, unique and perfect, seems to be separate from the conscious mind, deliberately avoiding it, while the conscious mind takes difficult steps toward it. The process resembles somewhat the more familiar one of puzzling over a momentarily forgotten name or word which seems to be taking on an elusive brain-life of its own as we try to grasp it. Granted that the poet is capable of grasping his idea, the shooting image must be more complicated; the target is a moving target and the marksman is also moving. His own movement goes on; the target must be stopped at an unknown critical point, whenever his sense of timing dictates. I have heard that dropping shells from an aeroplane onto a speeding battleship below, in an uncertain sea, demands the most perfect and delicate sense of timing imaginable.

Hopkins, I believe, has chosen to stop his poems, set them to paper, at the point in their development where they are still incomplete, still close to the first kernel of truth or apprehension which gave rise to them. It is a common statement that he derives a great deal from the seventeenth century "Metaphysical" poets—his exceeding rapidity of idea, his intuition, and to a lesser degree, his conceits—and I think he has also a very close bond with the prose of the same period. The manner of timing so as to catch and preserve the movement of an idea, the point being to crystallize it early enough so that it still has movement—it is essentially the baroque manner of approach; and in an article on "The Baroque Style in Prose" by M. W. Croll* I have found some striking sentences which I think express the matter equally well as regards Hopkins. Speaking of the writers of baroque prose he says: "Their purpose was to portray, not a thought, but a mind thinking. . . . They knew that an idea separated from the act of experiencing it is not the same idea that we experienced. The ardor of its conception in the mind is a necessary part of its truth; and unless it can be conveyed to another mind in something of the form of its occurrence, either it has changed into some other idea or it has ceased to be an idea, to have any evidence whatever except a verbal one. . . . They . . . deliberately chose as the moment of expression that in which the idea first clearly objectifies itself in the mind, in which, therefore, each of its parts still preserves its own peculiar emphasis and an independent vigor of its own—in brief, the moment in which truth is still *imagined*."

I have already mentioned a few of the characteristics of Hopkins' use of sprung rhythm which give to his lines their special significance, and now I shall take up further characteristics from the point of view of what they contribute to the *movement* in his poetry, to the depiction of "a mind thinking." The scansion is again very important; in sprung rhythm, since the stress always falls on the first syllable of a foot and any weak syllables at the beginning of a line are considered part of the last foot of the line before, it is natural that the scansion is continuous, not line by line. This is what Hopkins calls "rove over" lines, and he says "the scanning runs on without break from the beginning, say, of a stanza to the end and all the stanza is one long strain, though written in lines asunder." In this manner the boundaries of the poem are set free, and the whole thing is loosened up; the motion is kept going without the more or less strong checks customary at the end of lines. Combined with the possibility of *outriders* that I have already spoken of the poem can be given a fluid, detailed surface, made hesitant, lightened, slurred, weighed or feathered as Hopkins chooses.

Along with the general device of the rove over line Hopkins is very fond of the odd and often irritating rhyme: "am and . . . diamond, England . . . mingle and," etc. These usually "come right" on being read aloud, and contribute in spite of, or because of, their awkwardness, to the

*Of Princeton University. Printed in *Studies in English Philology in Honor of Frederick Klaeber* (University of Minnesota, 1929).

general effect of intense, unpremeditated unrevised emotion. He occasionally uses quasi-apocope for the same excited effects:
From No. 41:

> "Huddle in a main, a chief
> Woe, world-sorrow; on an age-old anvil wince and sing—
> Then lull, then leave off. Fury had shieked "No *ling-*
> *ering!* Let me be fell: force I must be brief."

From number 44:

> "England, whose honour O all my heart woos, wife
> To my creating thought, would neither hear
> Me, were I pleading, plead nor do I: I *wear-*
> *y* of idle a being but by where wars are rife."

These may be serious faults making for the destruction of the more important rhythmic framework of the poem, but at the same time they do break down the margins of poetry, blur the edges with a kind of vibration and keep the atmosphere fresh and astir. The lines cannot sag for an instant; by these difficult devices his poetry comes up from the pages like sudden storms. A single short stanza can be as full of, aflame with, motion as one of Van Gogh's cedar trees.

At times the obscurity of his thought, the bulk of his poetic idea seems too heavy to be lifted and dispersed into flying members by his words; the words and the sense quarrel with each other and the stanzas seem to push against the reader, like coiled springs against the hand. It seems impossible to get the material into motion in its chaotic state. But as Mr. Croll says further on "baroque art always displays itself best when it works on heavy masses and resistant materials; and out of the struggle between a fixed pattern and an energetic forward movement arrives at those strong and expressive disproportions in which it delights." In all his form and detail, and above all in the moment he has selected for the transference of thought to paper, Hopkins is a baroque poet.

1934

The Last Animal

Roger sat looking out the parlor window of his father's house, at a rather dismal view of a small lawn, two small trees, and a fire hydrant, all trapped together in a heavy spring rain. There was never much to look at out the windows of the house because it was set, not as most houses are on a street where people are going by, a side street at least, but rather at an extra re-move from all traffic—within the boundaries of a college campus. His fa-ther was the professor of Zoology at Merton College, the only professor of the subject there, and Roger himself held the official position of Class Baby to the present senior class. He was rather old for a class baby, being eight which would have made him four when chosen for the office—and most of the Class Babies were chosen while still infants in arms. But Roger had not been a very handsome baby, in fact he was still a rather unappeal-ing child, and had it not been for the fact that four years ago there had been a sharp decrease in the birth rate among the professors' families, leaving him as the only available child, it is unlikely he would ever have been singled out at all.

Roger's uncomfortable position at the college was equalled, perhaps surpassed, by that of his father, Professor Rappaport. The college trustees had been trying, as he well knew, for some years to do away with the chair of Zoology completely and it was only the requirements of a bothersome legacy (which paid Professor Rappaport his meagre salary) that kept him there at all. Zoology, everyone agreed, was a dead science, and Merton aimed to be a college for practical vocational training. Zoology was no longer living, it was only a matter of interest to a few doddering professors or reactionaries (like Professor Rappaport) who could not face the facts of modern life and must win their only happiness by poking around in a passive and dusty past. Argue as he might, that no one could lay claims to a thorough education without a knowledge of Zoology, that no one could properly understand English without a knowledge of Zoological deriva-tions, that Zoology was a wealth of myth and fable—scarcely anyone would listen to him. The ground had been cut from under his feet bit by bit, both by the cruelty of his fellowmen and by the persistence of the objects of his study in vanishing—in dying off one after the other like so many Civil War veterans, and leaving him, so to speak, not an iota of a field. The lab. work had had to be done, for the last three years, on two crayfish only, and this year they had not survived the rashness of the five freshmen, taking Zoology as a "snap" course. He had had to let his lab. assistant go—there were no longer even any Infusoria. The laboratory was now being turned into a bowling alley. The brutal authorities were even threatening the Professor with confiscating the museum room; the Personnel Department would soon need more filing space—and really, they said, those six stuffed creatures of yours are shedding their hair frightfully. Only the buffalo has stood up at all well.

Roger Rappaport was rather old for his age, as children who are left to themselves are apt to be, and so he was thinking somewhat along these lines as he looked out through the pouring rain. He was waiting for his father to come home from the Monday afternoon Faculty Meeting, for although unpopular, Professor Rappaport was very proud of the collegiate tradition and made a great point of never omitting a detail of his professorial life, no matter what it cost him. Poor papa, thought Roger, he has such a bad time. Why it seems only yesterday that there was a fair number of animals around at the various institutions and papa's work was alive and exciting. And now everyone thinks there's nothing left of it except a lot of old pictures with names underneath.

He pushed his forehead bitterly against the window until the cold glass gave him a sharp pain between the eyes. Out on the lawn, just below the window, stood a life-size cast-iron deer, with its right hoof forward to tap the grass, and its nose raised proudly into the rain. In front of it was a little wooden block, like those on business men's desks, which said DEER. Roger could remember when the deer had come to take his stand on their lawn. It had been three years ago: some people excavating around Salem had struck with a pick into the head of this creature, just a foot or so below the surface of the ground. When they had dug out one antler they became tremendously excited, thinking, of course, that they had come across an ossified animal in fine condition, and they sent a long and frantic telegram to Professor Rappaport. He had started off early the next morning, too excited to eat any breakfast, carrying several little black leather instrument bags. It had been a heart-breaking affair when the deer, by undeniable proof, had turned out to be not stone, but iron. The Professor, however, had made the best of a bad bargain, and decided to purchase the deer, anyway, for the honor of his college, and it followed him home on the next freight train.

It had been Professor Rappaport's idea, too, to paint the deer in natural colors, and Roger had sat on the front steps most of each day for a week, while his father daubed away with brushes of assorted sizes, several reference books opened at the Colored Plate Section, lying around him on the lawn with stones on the pages to hold them down. The deer was done in two inch stripes of yellow and fawn, and the fawn stripes contained many white spots bordered with black rings. The eyes were dark with green spots, the antlers deep brown, and the scut was painted with phosphorescent paint, because according to the best authorities deer had followed each other by means of watching the tail of the deer ahead, *which shone in the dark.* Of course at the beginning of every college year, the deer was an object of considerable merriment on the part of the incoming Freshmen: they hung their caps on its antlers, and once, indeed, had dressed it in a complete suit of clothes and a pair of spectacles and labelled it: Old Rappy—but by November the novelty usually wore off. Anyway, the deer stood there firmly, as if to advertise the profession of the man who lived in the house behind him.

When Roger had been staring gloomily at the deer and the trees and the rain for some three-quarters of an hour he suddenly realized that in their place he was staring at a man walking by the path to the house. Not the Professor, but an old man, a country man dressed in a cap and dirty blue jeans and carrying a large-sized straw basket on his arm, with some sheets of newspaper stuck through the handle to keep the rain out. Roger was extremely excited, he had never seen the man before, and he had still the childish belief that things coming in baskets were probably presents for *him.* He rushed to the door and let the man in.

"Is this Mr. Rappaport's house?" the old man asked Roger, taking off his cap, but still holding on to the basket. Roger shut the front door quickly so that he had the man inside, at least.

"Yes," he said in his rather unpleasant way, "and I'm Mr. Rappaport's little boy. What do you want? What's in your basket?" He led the way into the parlor.

The old man said, "Well, perhaps you'll do. Your father's the man who knows about those animals, isn't he?"

Roger said he was, and that he, Roger, would most certainly do. The old man sat down, holding the basket on his knees.

"Well, I'll tell you my boy, I've got something here for your father. I've found,—by golly, I've found a *animal.*"

Roger gave an incredulous gasp. Once or twice when he was younger he had tried this same trick on his father, with poor effect. But the old man was pulling the newspapers away from the basket. "There you are," he muttered and reached in with both hands and dragged out what certainly did look like some sort of animal. Roger almost fainted away. The old man set the animal down on the floor and Roger made as if to snatch it, but he was pushed back onto his chair.

"Leave it alone. It don't run much. Now look at that. Ain't that the damndest thing you ever did see? It's a real honest-to-goodness animal, living and breathing."

The animal just sat there on the carpet, breathing, certainly, and rather fast at that. It was perhaps two feet long, rather stumpy and rounded, and all covered with a kind of straw-grey fur, very thick and fine. It had a pointed nose and whiskers and close round ears, and extremely large dark eyes that were full of tears. In fact, anyone who knew anything about animals might have felt it was rather pretty—until he looked closely at the tail, which was short and scaly and had a few long hairs on it. Roger didn't bother to think whether he really took to the animal: it became an object of divinity to him immediately, and he knelt beside it on the floor. He patted its round back gingerly and the animal shed one tear, which was at once replaced by another.

"Where did you find it? What kind do you suppose it is? Will it die?" Dying was the chief characteristic of all the animals Roger had known.

"Well, I was just starting to do my spring plowing and I ran the plow into a sort of little hole and there sat this thing, snug as you please, looking out at me. Must have been there all winter long. I haven't heard tell of a animal for a good many years now, so I thought I'd just bring it along to your pa to see what he made of it. Well now, if you'll just sort of keep your eye on it till your pa comes home, why I'll be getting along."

The old man got up and took his basket and left the room, but Roger, absorbed in the animal, didn't pay the slightest attention. He patted it and stroked it and spoke in its round ears and the animal lay perfectly quiet and occasionally shed tears on the carpet. It was rather sad to see Roger's gentleness and discretion with the creature. Born at an earlier day he would probably have made one of those people who cannot mingle comfortably with their own sort, but in the society of animals became at once charming and lovable. However, as things were, Roger, except for this short while, was destined to go through life never appearing at his best and always rather disliked.

Finally the animal's tears ceased and it even showed faint signs of pleasure in Roger's company. It arched its short neck to his hand, and switched its tail around on the floor. Roger vaguely remembered that to be the sign of gratitude on the part of some animal, but he could not think which one. He peered into the creature's eyes. Should he feed it? And what? Could it understand what he was saying? It seemed rather lifeless on the whole, but papa would be extremely pleased anyway. He waited patiently stroking the creature rhythmically, which was the manner, he had decided, it liked best.

Professor Rappaport had never had even a modest success in his life, and now of course, he had a triumph. He sent the old farmer who had brought the animal twenty-five dollars. In the backyard of the Professor's house were two little houses with wire pens attached to them where several years ago he had kept one or two other animals, and this one was promptly assigned the larger house. All the professors came to see it first, by invitation, then the student body was allowed to troop through the backyard and stare. Professor Rappaport, though not exactly popular, did come to be a campus character of some stature. He even gave a tea, the most important feature of which was a close view of the animal for all the guests, and a brief lecture on it by the Professor.

1934

Dimensions for a Novel

The lines are straight and swift between the stars.   —Wallace Stevens

Perhaps to give the above title to a paper is as ridiculous as it would be to make measurements for a suit of clothes and then grow the body to fit them. Bright ideas about *how* to do a thing are to be mistrusted, and the only bright idea which ever proves its worth is that of the thing itself. The discovery, or invention, whichever it may be, of a new method of doing something old is often made by defining the opposite of an old method, or the opposite of the sum of several old methods and calling it new. And the objective of this research or discovery is rather the new method, the new tool, than the new thing. In the come and go of art movements, movements in music, revolutions in literature, and "experiments" in everything, we often see this illustrated. The modern French composers who devised the ingenious and seemingly pregnant method of using two or three or more keys against each other, where one alone had been used before, are often very disappointing because despite the possibilities suggested by poly-modality and poly-tonality the themes in themselves are meagre and uninteresting.

It is a very common theory, and, I think, a true one that the substance of a piece of writing defines its form. By this I mean more than classification—essay, story, poem, etc.—the actual shape the writing takes within its particular *genre*. For example, say, *The Return of the Native* takes place within the limitations of a year and a day and follows a definite scheme of chorus, action, chorus, action, not because Hardy thought that was an interesting new way of writing a book (although he undoubtedly did), but something in the story itself suggested that form, made it the only possible one for the book. I remember reading quite a while ago an essay by Julian Huxley on "The Size of Living Things." I have forgotten the scientific reasons or speculations underlying it, but I can remember how strangely it struck me for the first time that although the size of living creatures varies from the germ to the elephant and each species shows variations in itself— yet there is really no danger that I shall ever get much beyond six feet, or stop growing at the size of seven. Even the lobster cannot shrink to crayfish size or ever exceed the capacity of the ordinary lobster pot. Whatever this mysterious regulating power may be, there is another power somehow corresponding to it, and as mysterious in its way, which I believe regulates, or should regulate, the forms of writing. Before a genuine change in form takes place, maybe quite a while before, the actual substance, the protoplasmic make-up of the writing must be changed. A novel can be forced into all sorts of forms (built up from manipulating *opposites* of preceding forms) just as I could, or the lobster, and yet they would improve it little more than I should be improved by being trained in an S, unless this first inner change had made the forms imperative.

I am saying all this because it will appear that I am attempting to be one of the inventors or discoverers, with a bright idea for doing something but no ideas as to the thing itself. It is presumptuous, but I must ask you to believe that at the back of my mind are the changing ideas which make me want to write on the dimensions for a novel as their result, rather than as an exercise in inventiveness.

I

Mr. T. S. Eliot in his essay "Tradition and Individual Talent" speaks in this way of the individual artist's duty to the past:

> The necessity that he shall conform, that he shall cohere, is not onesided; what happens when a new work of art is created is something that happens simultaneously to all the works of art which preceded it. The existing monuments form an ideal order among themselves, which is modified by the introduction of the new (the really new) work of art among them. The existing order is complete before the new work arrives; for order to persist after the supervention of novelty, the *whole* existing order must be, if ever so slightly, altered; and so the relations, proportions, values of each work of art toward the whole are readjusted; and this is conformity between the old and the new.

Mr. Eliot is of course speaking of the placing of works of art in their place in the line of tradition, but by changing the subject of the paragraph I find it puts into words, exactly, a certain aspect of the novel. Novels as we know them are still fairly linear; they go *along*, in some sort of army style; I can think of none to which the march figure could not be applied. We may have halts and retreats and flights in disorder—but that we are moving from one point (usually in time) to another is always certain. The author guides us along this line of march, marshals and directs.

This is Sunday. If I try to think of Friday I cannot recreate Friday pure and simple, exactly as it was. It has been changed for me by the intervening Saturday. A certain piece of work that on Friday I planned to have finished on Saturday I did not finish, so that now looking back from Sunday I discover a certain ironic tinge about Friday evening. Someone came to see me Friday afternoon whom I was delighted to see; but since that time many things have come back to mind and it is impossible to look at the visitor with the eyes of Friday. Saturday will always intervene, and Friday and Saturday will come between me and Thursday. A constant process of adjustment is going on about the past—every ingredient dropped into it from the present must affect the whole.

Now what Mr. Eliot says about the sequence of works of art seems to me to be equally true of the sequence of events or even of pages or paragraphs in a novel. I have mentioned what I call the "march" of the novel, implying movement and a linear sequence to the writing; but I know of no novel which deliberately makes use of this constant readjustment among the members of any sequence. (Perhaps characters occasionally think back over their relationships with one another and reinterpret actions or speeches, but I am speaking here of reinterpretation as an integral part of the whole book, not the proper working out of the story.) It seems almost too simple to say that in the existing novel the ending throws back no light on the beginning, but (excepting of course the rough example of the detective story!) I think it is true. Present events run both forwards and backwards, they cannot be contained in one day or one chapter. All the past forms, to use a musical expression, a frame of reference for the future, and the two combine to define and expand each other. ". . . for order to persist after the supervention of novelty, the *whole* existing order must be, if ever so slightly, altered; and so the relations, proportions, values . . . toward the whole are readjusted; and this is conformity between the old and the new."

In preparatory school we used to draw diagrams of the "development" of novels on the blackboard. We took for granted that the affairs of a book should grow out of one another; in fact all events which could be explained only by accident or coincidence were rather apologized for, as if they showed some fault in the author. Our diagrams usually rose and fell like so many waves: one alone, a bent line, or possibly a double wave, or, at their subtlest, two waves pursuing each other. This is simplification with a vengeance, of course, but nevertheless the fact that it could be done and would express for us a certain amount of truth about the novel explains somewhat what I have just been saying. I know of no novel which has ever, say, in giving a life history, managed to blur for the reader the childhood of the hero as it would be when he reaches fifty. Joyce's "moocow" is blurred, but blurred at the age at which he beheld it; when the reader reaches the end of the book he is still in possession of, as of a hard fact, Stephen's earliest days.

Some attempt has been made to get around this problem by the kind of novel (Proust's, for example) that picks one moment of observation and shows the whole past in the terminology of that particular moment when the writing is being done. This method achieves, perhaps, the "conformity between the old and the new," at least one instance of it, but since the conformity itself must be ever-changing, the truth of it, the thing I should like to get at, is the ever-changing expression for it. In conversation we notice how, often, the other person will repeat some word or phrase of ours, perhaps with quite a different meaning, and we in turn will pick up some adjective or adverb of theirs, or even some pun on their words—all unconsciously. This trick of echoes and re-echoes, references and cross-references produces again a kind of "conformity between the old and the new," and it illustrates fairly well both the situation possible to reveal in the novel and a method of approaching it. The thoughts and symbols which Mrs. Woolf produces over and over again in *The Waves* have an amazing sameness about them. A symbol might remain the same for a lifetime, but surely its implications shift from one thing to another, come and go, always within relation to that particular tone of the present which called it forth. We live in great whispering galleries, constantly vibrating and humming, or we walk through salons lined with mirrors where the reflections between the narrow walls are limitless, and each present moment reaches immediately and directly the past moments, changing them both. If I were to draw any more diagrams of the development of novels, the lines, although again greatly oversimplified, I am afraid would look something like a bramble bush.

II

To requote again: "The existing monuments [read moments] form an ideal order among themselves . . ." and, "The existing order is complete before the new work arrives . . ."

Almost, it seems to me, one is born with a perfect sense of generalities. At five years one looks around the dinner table at the cumulative family with as great a sense of recognition and understanding as ever comes later on. There is always an absolute pitch, a perfection to the understanding which may shift, branch out suddenly, or retreat, and yet can never be "improved on." The existing order is complete; every other is absorbed into it.

When you see someone for the first time, in the blank moment just before or during a hand-shake, this knowledge of them slips into the mind and no matter what you may learn of them later this is always the first fact about them: a knowledge of recognition which when compared to the things you may learn later is much the more amazing. The connection between this and my idea of the interplay of influence between present and past may seem at first a little obscure, but in reality the latter depends directly upon it. I can think of the existing moments which make up their "ideal order" as existing first of all as these moments of recognition. From a vacant pin-point of certainty start out these geometrically accurate lines, star-beams, pricking out the past, or present, or casting ahead into the future.

Cross-references, echoes, cycles, take on in their lowest forms the name of "superstitions," and an author who wrote a novel filled with such might be called either a primitive or, worse still, a mystic. But I have always felt a certain amount of respect for superstitions and coincidences; the fact that a friend's birthday falls on the same day as my own impresses me; always I am startled when something I have dreamed comes true, or someone I have been thinking of arrives on the scene. I have always looked askance at the theory of irreversibility. The point is: the moments I have spoken of occur so sharply, so minutely that one cannot say whether the recognition comes from the outside or the inside, whether the event or the thought strikes, and spreads its net over past and sometimes future events or thoughts. Over all the novels I can think of the author has waved a little wand of attention, he holds it in one position, whereas within the shiftings produced by the present over the past is this other shifting, rhythmical perhaps, of the moments themselves.

To do justice to one's sense of characters, events, thoughts, I think that not only should they be presented in such a way as to show perpetually changing integration of what has been written with what is being written, but also the *recognition* itself of what is being written must be kept fluid. These recognitions are the eyes of the novel, not placed on the face-side looking ahead, but rather as in certain insects, capable of seeing any side, whichever seems real at the moment.

III

A paper I wrote recently ended with these sentences:

Is it possible that there may be a sort of *experience-time*, or the time pattern in which realities reach us, quite different from the hour after hour, day after day kind? All books still seem bound to this much order, but I have a suspicion that it will go next and writers will discover new beauty in breaking up this most ancient of patterns and rearranging it. If you've seen boys dive after pennies you know how the coins sink shimmering to the bottom at unequal rates, and the diving boys sometimes pick them up halfway down, or even get there before the coins do. Why should the days behind me retreat systematically—Friday, Thursday, Wednesday, Tuesday—and not any other way? why not Wednesday, Friday, Tuesday, if they seem that way to me? And why should even Gertrude Stein say, "Now then to begin at the *beginning*..."?

We have all had the experience of apparently escaping the emotional results of an event, of feeling no joy or sorrow where joy or sorrow was to be expected, and then suddenly having the proper emotion appear several hours or even days later. The experience could not really have been counted chronologically as having taken place, surely, until this emotion belonging to it had been felt. The crises of our lives do not come, I think, accurately dated; they crop up unexpected and out of turn, and somehow or other arrange themselves according to a calendar we cannot control. If, for example, I have a "feeling" that something is going to happen, and it does, then the feeling proper to that experience has come too early—its proper place was afterwards. If I suffer a terrible loss and do not realize it till several years later among different surroundings, then the important fact is not the original loss so much as the circumstance of the new surroundings which succeeded in letting the loss through to my consciousness. It may seem that when a novelist talks *about* such things he is giving them the credit they deserve, but it seems to me that the fact of experience-time can be made of use possibly in its own order, in order to explain the endless hows and whys of incident and character more precisely than before. Again, I do not believe this in any way contradicts my belief in the expression of the constant re-adjustment of the actions within a novel—rather, it only helps to bear it out. Events arriving out of accepted order are nevertheless arriving in their own order, and the process will be just as true, no matter whether 2:4 :: 4:8, or 4:2 :: 8:4.

This is very plainly related to my original conviction that each successive part of a novel should somehow illuminate the preceding parts for us, that the whole should grow together. A belated emotion points back, of course, to whatever caused it, which was experienced in two different ways, each way exerting its own influence, the two seeking to eradicate or supplement each other.

IV

I have been speaking more or less of a new form and some reasons for its existence; now I should like to go on and speak of a particular reason why some modern novels seem unsatisfactory to me. One remove behind the truism that the substance of a piece of writing defines its form, comes a second truism: the author's frame of mind defines the substance. This is a very murky stretch of woods, impossible to get under cultivation in a paper of this length, but there is one small path following naturally from what I have been saying.

A frame of mind is shown in what I think of as "keeping up the front" of a novel—by which I mean not letting the reader see the under side of it. Gertrude Stein keeps up a magnificent front, as terrifying as a crusade of vacant-faced children. Hemingway attempts to do it by putting up a bluff. But some writers, such as Thomas Mann in *The Magic Mountain*, James Joyce in certain sections of *Ulysses*, and often Virginia Woolf, approach one in a series of outriders and sallies with constant returns to headquarters. For example, the chapter in *The Magic Mountain* called an "Excursus on the Sense of Time" is just such a retreat to headquarters. When the author says, "We have introduced these remarks here only because our young Hans Castorp had something like them in mind when, a few days later . . ." etc., it is as if he were confessing the problem to be a little too difficult. His ideas on *time* cannot be injected into the actual story—the two must be presented side by side and the reader must take one as a chaser, so to speak, for the other. In this book, as in *The Waves* (although it is doing Thomas Mann a great injustice to couple them), it seems often as if we were confronted with sections of a story combined with sections of an essay upon it; the reader must do the work, fuse one with the other. He is let in on the problem either in order that he may realize its difficulties, or as the only way of solving it. The question is still left open. What does Mrs. Woolf's talking *about* flux do if her characters remain as rocks? In some parts of *Ulysses* it seems as if Stephen-Joyce were rather experimenting in thought than expressing the thought through the medium of novel-experiment, although Joyce has probably gone further with this latter work than any other modern author. (Hemingway is so determined to avoid this particular pitfall that he goes to the other extreme. In limiting himself to what he can do in the story and in getting the proper distance between himself and the finished writing he rids himself of problem after problem. He lops them off, refusing to talk about them or to attempt to incorporate them into the substance of his work—until the work reminds us of a hero coming back complacently from the wars in a basket.)

It would seem to me that if a novel is to stand alone all philosophies, theories, etc., pertaining to the author should somehow work themselves out in the actions and the designs within the story. I do not like the habit of asking, "Now where does Mr. So&so tell us what he is trying to do?"—if Mr. So&so has said anything about his intentions after the preface, I think he has been too frank.

V

In a recent little book called *Acting*, by Richard Bolislavsky, rhythm is defined as "the orderly, measurable changes of all the different elements comprised in a work of art—provided that all those changes progressively stimulate the attention of the spectator and lead invariably to the final aim of the artist." This definition, plain enough when applied, say, to the music of Mozart may seem rather obscure when applied to the loose form of the novel. But just possibly everything I have been saying could be set down under the heading of *rhythm*. The "ideal order," the relation of present to past in the novel, naturally arises from "the orderly, measurable changes of all the different elements comprised." And my belief in the peculiar cross-hatchings of events and people also amounts to a feeling for rhythm. A superstition or coincidence, even, is "rhythmical" in that it achieves a motion between two things and a balancing of them. And what is "experience-time" but a more careful, exact method of looking at the materials to be used, and perhaps a means of marshalling them more rhythmically.

Possibly now I have staked claims, so to speak, on a novel-site, and laid out certain measurements which seem to me too important to be overlooked. A general idea of the novel constructed according to these measurements would appear to be something like this: First, a very few primary ideas or facts would suffice, and they could be told immediately. The interest would not lie in watching a "march" through a segment of time, but rather the complete absorption of each item, and the constant re-organization, the constantly maintained order of the whole mass. The process perhaps resembles more than anything the way in which a drop of mercury, a drop to begin with, joins smaller ones to it and grows larger, yet keeps its original form and quality. Coupled with this, would be the maintaining of the "front" of the novel, a stricter feeling that it is a detached form of art, not a conveyor of ideas except in its own structure. By this method, helped possibly by cross-references, re-iterations, and a device built on the idea of experience-time, perhaps the novel could show at work that "perfection of generalities" in its highest sense, a clearer sense of things and people.

1934

NOTES ON THE TEXTS

INDEX

Notes on the Texts

The following list indicates first publications and the location of unpublished Bishop manuscripts:

ABBREVIATIONS AND REFERENCES USED IN THE NOTES

CPr: Elizabeth Bishop, *Collected Prose*, edited with and introduction by Robert Giroux, Farrar, Straus and Giroux, 1984

Vassar: Vassar College Libraries for Special Collections

The Blue Pencil is the student literary magazine at the Walnut Hill School

Con Spirito was a Vassar undergraduate magazine founded and edited by Elizabeth Bishop, Eunice and Eleanor Clark, and Mary McCarthy; the publications were anonymous

STORIES AND MEMOIRS

Facsimile: IN THE VILLAGE & OTHER STORIES table of contents (n.d.; Vassar)

"The Baptism" (*Life and Letters To-day*, Spring 1937)

"The Sea and Its Shore" (*Life and Letters To-day*, Winter 1937)

"In Prison" (*Partisan Review*, March 1938)

"Gregorio Valdes, 1879–1939" (*Partisan Review*, Summer 1939)

"Mercedes Hospital" (1941; *CPr*)

"The Farmer's Children" (*Harper's Bazaar*, February 1948)

"The Housekeeper" (*The New Yorker*, September 11, 1948, under the name Sarah Foster)

"Gwendolyn" (*The New Yorker*, June 27, 1953)

"In the Village" (*The New Yorker*, December 19, 1953)

"Primer Class" (c. 1960; *CPr*)

"The Country Mouse" (1961; *CPr*)

"The U.S.A. School of Writing" (1966; *CPr*)

"A Trip to Vigia" (1967; *CPr*)

"Efforts of Affection: A Memoir of Marianne Moore" (c. 1969; *CPr*)

"To the Botequim & Back" (1970; *CPr*)

"Memories of Uncle Neddy" (*Southern Review*, Fall 1977)

BRAZIL

Facsimile: *Brazil* table of contents (Vassar)

(Time Incorporated, 1962; typescript: Vassar; Bishop's annotated copy: Houghton Library, Harvard)

ESSAYS, REVIEWS, AND TRIBUTES

Facsimile: IF YOU WANT TO WRITE *WELL* ALWAYS AVOID THESE WORDS (Vassar, 1975)

"As We Like It: Miss Moore and the Delight of Imitation" (*Quarterly Review of Literature*, Spring 1948)

Review of *Annie Allen* by Gwendolyn Brooks (*United States Quarterly Book Review*, March 1950)

Review of *XAIPE: 71 Poems* by E. E. Cummings (*United States Quarterly Book Review*, June 1950)

"Love from Emily" (*The New Republic*, August 27, 1951)

Review of *The Riddle of Emily Dickinson* (c. 1951; Vassar)

"What the Young Man Said to the Psalmist" (*Poetry*, January 1952)

"The Manipulation of Mirrors" (*The New Republic*, November 19, 1956)

Introduction to *The Diary of "Helena Morley"* (Farrar, Straus and Cudahy, 1957)

"A New Capital, Aldous Huxley, and Some Indians" (Vassar, 1958; *Yale Review*, July 2006)

"I Was But Just Awake" (*Poetry*, October 1958)

Robert Lowell's *Life Studies* (jacket copy, Farrar, Straus and Cudahy, 1959)

"Writing poetry is an unnatural act . . ." (late 1950s–early 1960s?; Vassar; *Edgar Allan Poe & The Juke-Box*, ed. Alice Quinn, Farrar, Straus and Giroux, 2006)

"Some Notes on Robert Lowell" (originally published as "Algumas Notas Sobre Robert Lowell," in Robert Lowell, *Quatro Poemas*, Série Cadernos Brasileiros, Rio de Janeiro, 1962; English translation by George Monteiro, *Elizabeth Bishop Bulletin*, Summer 1998)

"A Sentimental Tribute" (*Bryn Mawr Alumnae Bulletin*, Spring 1962)

"Flannery O'Connor: 1925–1964" (*The New York Review of Books*, October 8, 1964)

"On the Railroad Named Delight" (*The New York Times Magazine*, May 7, 1965)

Gallery Note for Wesley Wehr (March 1967; Vassar; Elizabeth Bishop, *Poems, Prose, Letters*, edited by Robert Giroux and Lloyd Schwartz, Library of America, 2008)

"An Inadequate Tribute" (*Randall Jarrell 1914–1965*, ed. Robert Lowell, Farrar, Straus and Giroux, 1967)

Introduction to *An Anthology of Twentieth-Century Brazilian Poetry* (Wesleyan University Press, 1972)

"A Brief Reminiscence and a Brief Tribute: W. H. Auden 1907–1973" (*Harvard Advocate*, vol. 108, 1974)

TRANSLATIONS

From *The Diary of "Helena Morley"* (*Harper's Bazaar*, December 1957)

Clarice Lispector, "The Smallest Woman in the World," "A Hen," "Marmosets" (*Kenyon Review*, Summer 1964)

CORRESPONDENCE

Elizabeth Bishop and Anne Stevenson (1963–1965; Modern Literature Collection/Manuscripts, Washington University)

APPENDIX: EARLY PROSE

"On Being Alone" (*The Blue Pencil*, June 1929)

"A Mouse and Mice" (*The Blue Pencil*, 1929)

"The Thumb" (*The Blue Pencil*, 1930)

"Then Came the Poor" (*Con Spirito*, February 1933)

From "Time's Andromedas" (*Vassar Journal of Undergraduate Studies*, 1933)

"Gerard Manley Hopkins" (*Vassar Review*, February 1934)

"The Last Animal" (*Vassar Review*, April 1934)

"Dimensions for a Novel" (*Vassar Journal of Undergraduate Studies*, May 1934)

Index